# *Exploring*
# PROVERBS
VOLUME TWO

## THE JOHN PHILLIPS COMMENTARY SERIES

*Exploring 1 & 2 Thessalonians*
*Exploring 1 Corinthians*
*Exploring 2 Corinthians*
*Exploring Acts*
*Exploring the Book of Daniel*
*Exploring Colossians & Philemon*
*Exploring Ecclesiastes*
*Exploring Ephesians & Philippians*
*Exploring the Epistle of James*
*Exploring the Epistle of Jude*
*Exploring the Epistles of John*
*Exploring the Epistles of Peter*
*Exploring the Future*
*Exploring Galatians*
*Exploring Genesis*
*Exploring the Gospel of John*
*Exploring the Gospel of Luke*
*Exploring the Gospel of Mark*
*Exploring the Gospel of Matthew*
*Exploring Hebrews*
*Exploring the Love Song of Solomon*
*Exploring the Minor Prophets*
*Exploring the New Testament Book by Book*
*Exploring the Old Testament Book by Book*
*Exploring the Pastoral Epistles*
*Exploring People of the New Testament*
*Exploring People of the Old Testament, vol. 1*
*Exploring People of the Old Testament, vol. 2*
*Exploring People of the Old Testament, vol. 3*
*Exploring Proverbs, vol. 1*
*Exploring Proverbs, vol. 2*
*Exploring Psalms, vol. 1*
*Exploring Psalms, vol. 2*
*Exploring Revelation*
*Exploring Romans*
*Exploring the Scriptures*

THE JOHN PHILLIPS COMMENTARY SERIES

# *Exploring* PROVERBS

VOLUME TWO

*An Expository Commentary*

JOHN PHILLIPS

Kregel Publications

Grand Rapids, MI 49501

*Exploring Proverbs, Volume Two: An Expository Commentary*



Published in 2002 by Kregel Publications, a division of Kregel, Inc., 2450 Oak Industrial Dr. NE, Grand Rapids, MI 49505.



Scripture quotations are from the King James Version of the Holy Bible.

ISBN 978-0-8254-3479-2

Printed in the United States of America

6 7 8 9 / 24 23 22

# CONTENTS OF VOLUME TWO

Proverbs 19:6–31:31

# DIRECTORY OF OUTLINES

# SUMMARY OUTLINE
# OF THE BOOK OF PROVERBS

*The outline is expanded throughout the body of the text.*

### Volume One

## Introduction (1:1-9)

## Observation (1:10–29:27)

### Part One: Moral Issues (1:10–9:18)

Section 1: The Way of Wickedness (1:10-19)

Section 2: The Way of Wisdom (1:20–9:18)

I. Wisdom's Plea (1:20-33)
II. Wisdom's Protection (2:1-22)
III. Wisdom's Path (3:1–5:23)
  A. It Is a Pleasant Path (3:1-22)
  B. It Is a Peaceful Path (3:23-26)
  C. It Is a Positive Path (3:27-35)
  D. It Is a Parental Path (4:1-9)
  E. It Is a Proper Path (4:10-19)
  F. It Is a Perfect Path (4:20–5:23)
    1. The Way of Virtue Pondered (4:20–5:2)
    2. The Way of Vice Pondered (5:3-23)
IV. Wisdom's Precepts (6:1-35)
  A. How They Goad Us (6:1-11)
  B. How They Guide Us (6:12-19)
  C. How They Guard Us (6:20-35)
V. Wisdom's Presence (7:1-27)
VI. Wisdom's Patience (8:1–9:18)
  A. Her Plea Is Public (8:1-9)
  B. Her Riches Are Real (8:10-21)
  C. Her Influence Is Infinite (8:22-31)
  D. Her Friends Are Fortunate (8:32-36)
  E. Her Blessings Are Boundless (9:1-6)
  F. Her Foes Are Fools (9:7-12)
  G. Her Paths Are Pure (9:13-18)

## Part Two: Miscellaneous Issues (10:1–19:5)

Section 1: The Lot of the Godly and the Ungodly Contrasted (10:1–15:33)

I. Blessings Gained or Lost (10:1-32)
II. Behavior Good and Bad (11:1–15:33)
  A. Values to Be Considered (11:1-31)
  B. Vignettes to Be Considered (12:1-28)
  C. Verities to Be Considered (13:1-25)
  D. Viewpoints to Be Considered (14:1-35)
  E. Virtues to Be Considered (15:1-33)

Section 2: The Life of the Godly and the Ungodly Compared (16:1–19:5)

I. The Right Focus in Life (16:1-33)
II. The Right Features in Life (17:1–19:5)
  A. How to Build Contentment (17:1-28)
  B. How to Build Character (18:1–19:5)

# Volume Two

## Part Three: Monarchial Issues (19:6–29:27)

Section 1: Proverbs of Solomon—Edited by Himself (19:6–24:34)

I. The Favor of the Throne (19:6-11)
II. The Fury of the Throne (19:12–20:7)
III. The Fear of the Throne (20:8-30)
IV. The Functions of the Throne (21:1–24:34)
  A. His Majesty's Intentions (21:1–22:10)
  B. His Majesty's Intimates (22:11-29)
  C. His Majesty's Interests (23:1–24:34)
    1. Words to His Subjects (23:1-14)
    2. Words to His Son (23:15–24:34)

Section 2: Proverbs of Solomon—Edited by Hezekiah (25:1–29:27)

I. The King and His Subjects (25:1–27:27)
  A. Those of Whom to Beware (25:1–26:28)
  B. Thoughts on How to Behave (27:1-27)
II. The King and His Sins (28:1–29:14)
III. The King and His Sons (29:15-27)

## Conclusion (30:1–31:31)

# OBSERVATION

Proverbs 1:10–29:27

## PART THREE:
## Monarchial Issues

Proverbs 19:6–29:27

# OBSERVATION (1:10–29:27)

## PART THREE: Monarchial Issues (19:6–29:27)

The psalmist declared, "My heart is inditing a good matter: I speak of the things which I have made touching the king: my tongue is the pen of a ready writer" (Psalm 45:1). Solomon might well have penned those words and put them at the beginning of Part Three of the book of Proverbs. Having already set before us a series of proverbs dealing with *moral* issues in Part One (1:10–9:18) and a series dealing with *miscellaneous* issues in Part Two (10:1–19:5), he began a series dealing by and large with *monarchial* issues (19:6–29:27). In Part Three Solomon talked mostly about the throne and the kind of behavior and judgment a nation has a right to expect from those who rule over it.

We can divide the proverbs in Part Three into two sections: the proverbs of Solomon edited by *himself* (19:6–24:34) and the proverbs of Solomon edited by *Hezekiah* (25:1–29:27).

# CHAPTER 1

Proverbs 19:6–20:30

Section 1: Proverbs of Solomon—Edited by Himself (19:6–24:34)

- I. The Favor of the Throne (19:6-11)
  - A. Currying Favor (19:6-7)
    - 1. Look Out for Princes (19:6)
    - 2. Look Out for Paupers (19:7)
  - B. Cultivating Fundamentals (19:8)
    - 1. Psychological Well-being (19:8a)
    - 2. Prospective Well-being (19:8b)
  - C. Condemning Falsehood (19:9)
  - D. Curbing Folly (19:10)
    - 1. What Is Seemly (19:10a)
    - 2. What Is Sovereign (19:10b)
  - E. Conveying Forgiveness (19:11)
- II. The Fury of the Throne (19:12–20:7)
  - A. Wrath Considered (19:12)
  - B. Woes Considered (19:13-14)
    - 1. The Calamity (19:13)
      - a. Of a Foolish Son (19:13a)
      - b. Of a Fretful Spouse (19:13b)
    - 2. The Contrast (19:14)
      - a. The Right Kind of Wealth (19:14a)
      - b. The Right Kind of Wife (19:14b)
  - C. Warnings Considered (19:15-25)
    - 1. Beware of Idleness (19:15)
    - 2. Beware of Indifference (19:16-18)
      - a. Regarding Piety (19:16)
      - b. Regarding Poverty (19:17)
      - c. Regarding Parenthood (19:18)

3. Beware of Intolerance (19:19-22)
    a. The Man with the Ungovernable Temper (19:19)
    b. The Man with the Unteachable Temperament (19:20-22)
        (1) Do Not Forsake Guidance (19:20)
        (2) Do Not Forsake God (19:21)
        (3) Do Not Forsake Goodness (19:22)
4. Beware of Independence (19:23)
5. Beware of Indolence (19:24)
6. Beware of Insolence (19:25)

D. Wasters Considered (19:26-27)
1. Shameful Conduct (19:26)
2. Shoddy Counselors (19:27)

E. Witnesses Considered (19:28-29)
1. The Testimony of the Scornful Witness (19:28)
2. The Troubles of the Scornful Witness (19:29)

F. Wine Considered (20:1)

G. Wisdom Considered (20:2-7)
1. Some Cautions (20:2-4)
    a. A Sure Way to Be Punished (20:2-3)
        (1) Infuriate the King (20:2)
        (2) Interfere in a Thing (20:3)
    b. A Sure Way to Be Poor (20:4)
2. Some Commendations (20:5-7)
    a. The Deep Man (20:5)
    b. The Dependable Man (20:6-7)
        (1) How Rare He Is (20:6)
        (2) How Rich He Is (20:7)

III. The Fear of the Throne (20:8-30)

A. The King's Power (20:8-9)
1. His Legislation (20:8)
2. His Limitation (20:9)

B. The King's Principles (20:10-18)
1. Doing Right, Not Wrong (20:10)
2. Discerning Right from Wrong (20:11-12)
    a. The Human Judge (20:11)
    b. The Higher Judge (20:12)

3. Defining Right and Wrong (20:13-18)
    a. The Sluggard (20:13)
    b. The Salesman (20:14)
    c. The Sage (20:15)
    d. The Simpleton (20:16)
    e. The Scoundrel (20:17)
    f. The Sovereign (20:18)

C. The King's Pronouncements (20:19-25)
  1. A Man and His Mouth (20:19-20)
      a. The Man with the Big Mouth (20:19)
      b. The Man with the Bad Mouth (20:20)
  2. A Man and His Money (20:21)
  3. A Man and His Motives (20:22-24)
      a. Seeking Revenge (20:22)
      b. Stolen Riches (20:23)
      c. Self-Reliance (20:24)
  4. A Man and His Morals (20:25)

D. The King's Policies (20:26-30)
  1. His Might (20:26-27)
      a. Displaying Practical Wisdom (20:26)
      b. Developing Pondered Wisdom (20:27)
  2. His Mercy (20:28)
  3. His Men (20:29)
      a. Those Who Administer (20:29a)
      b. Those Who Advise (20:29b)
  4. His Method (20:30)

## I. The Favor of the Throne (19:6-11)

### A. Currying Favor (19:6-7)

Solomon began by telling us to *look out for princes:* "Many will intreat the favour of the prince: and every man is a friend to him that giveth gifts" (Proverbs 19:6).

All rich and powerful men are surrounded by sycophants and scroungers—people who have ulterior motives and people who, obviously or covertly, have their hands out. The truly competent ruler knows how to handle such people. Let them beware. They may think they are using the king, but the king is using them.

Proverbs 19:6 reminds me of England's notorious Henry VIII. When he came to the throne, England had just emerged from the shattering civil war commonly called the War of the Roses. She was not yet a great power, but she rapidly became one because of the boldness of Henry VIII and the craftiness of Thomas Wolsey, a son of a butcher in Ipswich. Wolsey eventually gave England the balance of power in Europe, a position England held until the end of World War II.

Wolsey had entered Oxford at age eleven and graduated at age fifteen. His natural talents made him a promising candidate for the priesthood and in time he became chaplain to the archbishop of Canterbury. Consumed with ambition, Wolsey eyed the court and cultivated Henry's friendship while Henry was still heir to the throne. Although twenty years older than Henry, Wolsey adapted himself to his friend's style and tastes. Wolsey was clever, accommodating, and wholly unscrupulous. He could laugh and joke or be grave and serious, as the occasion demanded. He gained many honors and a tremendous hold over Henry's mind. Wolsey was on his way up.

He entered the king's privy council and took over most of the business of governing so that Henry could spend his time hunting, dancing, carousing, and banqueting. The king was delighted with this arrangement and the priest became the virtual ruler of the realm. Wolsey was rewarded for his efforts. He was named archbishop of York, a position in the British hierarchy second only to the archbishop of Canterbury. Wolsey became a cardinal (and desired to be the next pope). Then as lord chancellor, the cardinal sat in the highest seat of political power in England, where he had no master except the king.

Wealth, much of it diverted from the revenues of the church, flowed into Wolsey's coffers. He acquired prime property fifteen miles southwest of St. Paul's and there built Hampton Court, a magnificent example of Tudor architecture. He now lived in state in a home more sumptuous than any royal palace. Wolsey was not without his enemies, however, and to strengthen his hold on Henry, he deeded Hampton Court to the king. The cardinal also showed Henry a will in which the king was named as Wolsey's sole heir.

Wolsey arrayed himself in scarlet, velvet, and silk. His shoes were embroidered with gold and silver and were inlaid with pearls and precious stones. He had more than five hundred servants and retainers, including nine or ten lords. The two tallest and most handsome priests in the land carried two huge silver crosses ahead of Wolsey whenever he appeared in public.

But the day of reckoning was coming, for he was toying with a dangerous tyrant. Henry VIII had grown up. His pride, lust, towering ambition, imperious self-will, and intolerance had taken a firm grip on his heart. He was not a man to trifle with. Wolsey was on thin ice.

Henry, now tired of his wife Catherine of Aragon, wanted to marry Anne Boleyn and demanded that his cardinal arrange a divorce with the pope. The pope was in a quandary. His predecessor, Julius II, had declared Henry's marriage to Catherine to be lawful; if the pope reversed that decision, he would be challenging papal infallibility. Moreover he could not afford to offend Charles of Spain, who championed the cause of his aunt Catherine. On the other hand the pope could not afford to annoy Henry. The pope dithered and intrigued, and Wolsey did some double-dealing of his own. While assuring the impatient Henry that he was doing all he could, Wolsey played up to Charles of Spain, who promised to help Wolsey become the next pope if he threw difficulties in the way of the divorce.

The divorce was denied and Anne Boleyn blamed Wolsey. When the cardinal's duplicity was discovered, the furious Henry ordered the prelate to return the great seal and retire to Esher to await the king's pleasure. Wolsey was ruined. Henry had him arrested and summoned him to London where trial, tower, and ax awaited him. The once-powerful Wolsey was broken, depressed, and ill. He traveled as far as Leicester Abbey where he died. His last words have gone down in history: "Had I but served God as diligently as I have done the King, he would not have given me over in my gray hairs."[1] Look out for princes!

Solomon continued by telling us to *look out for paupers:* "All the brethren of the poor do hate him: how much more do his friends go far from him? he pursueth them with words, yet they are wanting to him" (Proverbs 19:7).

The poor man always needs something. He is always asking for help and those who are well-off get tired of his requests. They resent the demands made on their purses, yet their consciences make them feel uneasy when they give nothing or less than they could. No matter how much people of means give, it is never enough. The poor man and multitudes of his kind are still there—with their hands out. We have tried to solve the problem by shifting responsibility for the poor to the government, but still the poor remain poor.

In many lands poverty is regarded as part of the human lot—to be avoided if at all possible, to be relieved or ignored as the occasion may suggest. Although ranked alongside sickness, pestilence, earthquake, tempest, and death, poverty is not necessarily despised. It is simply an unhappy fact of life and the poor man is perhaps to be pitied. But in countries where making money is raised to the status of a moral duty, he tends to hang his head in shame or react in violence.

In Victorian England—the England of Disraeli, Dickens, and Engels—there arose a new phenomenon: the working class district where no man of means or position ever lived. The East End of London, for example, became known for its miles of shabby, squalid streets. It was no accident that Karl Marx derived part of his inspiration from that part of the British capital.

In the East End artisans rubbed shoulders with outcasts. They had one thing in common: they were poor. Many of them were pale, sickly, gin-sodden, and starved. Their clothes, once the pride of some darling of society or baron of industry, had been handed down through the various strata of respectability and had become so vile that they stank and left stains wherever their owners rested. The people of the East End were herded together in ugly, bug-infested tenements. Some slept in cheap lodging houses, or on the banks of the Thames, or under railway bridges. They were "the skeleton at the rich Victorian feast, the squalid writing on the whitened wall."

The condition of the poor was a menacing reminder to the rich, respectable, and religious of what unemployment, sickness, or moral carelessness could do. Seeing the circumstances of the poverty-stricken, the upper-middle and upper classes realized how important it was to own property. One observer described the scene where the lower classes of the East End lived:

> I recall the alleys which run into Oxford Street, stifling lanes encrusted with human exhalations; troops of pale children nestling on the muddy stairs; the seats on London Bridge where families, huddled together with dropping heads, shiver through the night; particularly the Haymarket and the Strand in the evening. Every hundred steps one jostles twenty harlots; some of them ask for a glass of wine; others say, "Sir,

> it is to pay my lodging." This is not debauchery which flaunts itself but destitution—and such destitution! The deplorable procession in the shade of the monumental streets is sickening; it seems to me a march of the dead. That is a plague-spot, the real plague-spot of English society. Once down in that mire there was no rising again. The sordid round of drink, debauchery, violence, punishment, incompetence and hideous destitution never ceased. The great social mill crushes and grinds here…the lowest human stratum.[2]

This was the London of Jack the Ripper, the London of William Booth and The Salvation Army.

The East End produced communism, a philosophy born of atheism and rage. But now communism itself stands bankrupt. It has its own legions of the poor. Obviously government cannot abolish poverty by legislation. Socialism, carried to its extremes, makes whole nations destitute.

Who then will help the poor? In Solomon's graphic picture even the relatives of the poor man run away from him and his friends distance themselves, even though he pursues them with pleas for help.

How we respond to the poor says a great deal about us and our status in the kingdom of God. Jesus felt the pinch of poverty. He joined the ranks of the poor. He loved them, taught them, and on two occasions fed them. He extended a helping hand to the poor and sought to lift them up. Finally He bequeathed them to us.

### B. Cultivating Fundamentals (19:8)

"He that getteth wisdom loveth his own soul: he that keepeth understanding shall find good." Solomon had the secret of getting wisdom: he implored God to give it to him.

Solomon used his gift of wisdom with stunning effect in the early days of his reign. People came from all over to sit in on his court cases. Even the queen of Sheba lauded his wisdom. She said: "It was a true report that I heard in mine own land of thy acts and of thy wisdom. Howbeit I believed not the words, until I came, and mine eyes had seen it: and, behold, the half was not told me: thy wisdom and prosperity exceedeth the fame which I heard" (1 Kings 10:6-7).

We can obtain wisdom the same way Solomon did. James, in what was probably the first book of the New Testament, wrote, "If any of you lack wisdom, let him ask of God, that giveth to all men liberally, and upbraideth not; and it shall be given him" (James 1:5). Somewhere in His Word, God addresses every problem we will face in life. We have one infallible source of wisdom: the Bible! It is worth more than all the books in all the libraries in all the world.

The Bible will not tell us how to split the atom or put a man on the moon; only knowledge is needed to accomplish such feats. When we need more than mere knowledge—that is, wisdom—we can turn to the Bible. It is a book of precepts, proverbs, parables, and principles. It is a book about people. If we give God a chance, He will direct us to wise words that adequately cover any situation.

It is foolish, however, to hope that when we just flip the pages of the Bible, some verse will magically catch our eye and give the guidance we need. We must read the Bible methodically, meditatively, and prayerfully. We must consider verses in their proper contexts, seek clear direction from God, and obey the heavenly vision when it comes. We must be like little Samuel, whom old Eli taught to say, "Speak, Lord; for thy servant heareth" (1 Samuel 3:9).

As we reach our teenage years, and even more so when we reach middle age, we are tempted to think that we can manage on our own. We rely on human wisdom. Supposing that we know all the answers, we get careless, and many of us make fools of ourselves at mid-life. Some are even shipwrecked during old age. Paul had a fear of finishing up as a castaway on one of the rubbish heaps of time; see 1 Corinthians 9:27. When Solomon wrote Proverbs 19:8, he was already well down the road to ruin. The light that was in him would soon turn to darkness (Luke 11:35)—and how great that darkness would be!

The key to a good ending in life is simply to keep on journeying with God day after day. Those who finish well keep on—no matter what, even when others are giving up. Keeping on was the genius of Columbus. Many mariners had sailed west, but none of them had remained on a westerly course so determinedly for so long. Joaquin Miller described his persistence:

> Behind him lay the gray Azores,
> Behind the Gates of Hercules;
> Before him not the ghost of shores,
> Before him only shoreless seas.
> The good mate said: "Now must we pray,
> For lo! the very stars are gone.
> Brave Admiral, speak, what shall I say?"
> "Why, say 'Sail on! sail on! and on!'"
> . . . . . . . . . . . . . . . . . .

They sailed and sailed, as winds might blow,
Until at last the blanched mate said:
"Why, now not even God would know
Should I and all my men fall dead.
These very winds forget their way,
For God from these dread seas is gone.
Now speak, brave Admiral, speak and say"—
He said: "Sail on! sail on! and on!"

Get wisdom! Keep understanding! Find good! Sail on! Finish well!

## C. Condemning Falsehood (19:9)

In Proverbs 19:5 the punishment for lying is *declared.* In 19:9, which is almost the same as 19:5, the punishment is *defined:* "A false witness shall not be unpunished, and he that speaketh lies shall perish." Since the king was brought into the picture in 19:6, the false witnessing and lying in 19:9 assume greater significance, for perjury is in view. Lying under oath is a serious, punishable offense.

Alexander the coppersmith was a false witness. We first meet him at the time of the riot against Paul in Ephesus. Paul had remained in that great pagan city for more than two years and God had blessed his ministry there. The church that the apostle founded in Ephesus became one of the landmarks of his missionary career. The impact of the gospel on the city was remarkable. Miracles were performed; evil spirits were exposed; evil books were destroyed in a bonfire. So many people were converted that the sales of images of the goddess Artemis (Diana) markedly declined; consequently one of the silversmiths, Demetrius, fomented a riot.

The whole city was thrown into confusion. The Jews were afraid that latent antisemitism, never far from the surface in a Roman town, would be ignited. There was also consternation in the Jewish quarter because the Jews feared that if the trouble spread to the Jewish colony, they would be blamed for the riot. The Jewish leaders put Alexander forward to speak on their behalf. Evidently he was a clever speaker, but on this occasion he was not able to influence the rioters. As soon as the mob realized that he was a Jew, they shouted him down (Acts 19:34).

Apparently the coppersmith professed Christianity, but by the time Paul wrote his first letter to Timothy, Alexander had apostatized completely. Paul had known all along that trouble would come to Ephesus (Acts 20:29-30). After his release from his first Roman imprisonment, he and Timothy may have visited the city to help the elders hold the line against error, and Alexander seems to have sided with the heretics. Paul later wrote that Alexander was among those who had "made shipwreck" of their faith. So he could "learn not to blaspheme," the apostle delivered Alexander to Satan (1 Timothy 1:19-20).

Doubtless when Alexander was still a professing believer, he made many eloquent speeches in support of the gospel. He had a captivating tongue, but after defecting he used it to blaspheme. Terrible were the things he said, fearful was his denial of the faith, and dreadful were his bitter words against the truth he had once affirmed.

Paul mentioned him one more time. The apostle felt it was necessary to warn young Timothy about Alexander, for the coppersmith had become a false witness. No one is more implacable than a complete renegade and no man among Paul's other enemies hated and hunted the apostle as Alexander did. When Paul was rearrested at the time of Nero's persecution of the church, Alexander seems to have run off to Rome to see if he could poison the minds of the emperor and the tribunal against the apostle. So Paul wrote: "Alexander the coppersmith did me much evil: the Lord reward him according to his works: Of whom be thou ware also; for he hath greatly withstood our words" (2 Timothy 4:14-15).

As a false witness Alexander became a tool of the devil. The lies he told about Paul were not circulated through ignorance. They were minted out of malice. Paul had handed Alexander over to Satan (1 Timothy 1:20), but the coppersmith had not learned his lesson. He only became worse. So we read in 2 Timothy 4:14 that the apostle finally handed him over to the Lord for judgment. As Solomon said, "A false witness shall not be unpunished, and he that speaketh lies shall perish."

Some people have tried to make excuses for Paul because he did not forgive Alexander, but no defense is necessary. The coppersmith was beyond forgiveness. Paul knew that Alexander had sinned willfully after receiving knowledge of the truth. For him there remained "no more sacrifice for sins, But a certain fearful looking for of judgment and fiery indignation, which shall devour the adversaries" (Hebrews 10:26-27). Truly, "it is a fearful thing to fall into the hands of the living God" (10:31). Those were the hands into which Paul delivered Alexander. The apostle knew perfectly well what he was doing.

## D. Curbing Folly (19:10)

"Delight [luxury] is not seemly for a fool; much less for a servant to have rule over princes." Many a fool has turned into a tyrant. Consider the case of "the hobgoblin chancellor." He is known to history as William de Longchamp—a fictitious name, some think, he invented to give himself the pretense of nobility. He was a hunchbacked dwarf noted for his unblinking stare. Longchamp's unusual appearance, it seems, was what first caught the eye of the man who was soon to become known as Richard the Lionheart.

A clever clerk in government service, Longchamp was a ferret. He was always poking his nose into state papers, always digging out odd bits of potentially useful information, and sometimes coming up with original ideas—all in a tireless pursuit of power. When Richard first spoke to him, he was ready with a suggestion: an idea for raising money for the crown. Richard took Longchamp in tow and made him chancellor of Poitou.

Then Richard became king. He made Longchamp chancellor of England and chief justice for southern England. Nobody could believe the news. Longchamp's new residence was the Tower of London and his job was to raise money for Richard. The king did not care how the money was raised, for his eye was on the East. He wanted to become the greatest of Crusaders with the largest, most ably led, and best-equipped army that had ever fought to free Jerusalem from the Saracen hordes.

Longchamp proceeded to make himself the most powerful and most hated man in England. Richard was preoccupied with fighting Saladin. *Let Longchamp rule,* the king thought, *as long as the money keeps rolling in.* So Longchamp put everything up for sale. He handed over houses and lands to the highest bidders and auctioned every post. Satisfied that the raising of money was in capable hands, Richard cared little what happened to his realm.

Soon Longchamp's unlimited power went to his head. He began to act as though he were the king. He arrayed himself in rich vestments and surrounded himself with all the trappings of royalty. He strutted and stormed and rode on a magnificent horse. He threw people out of office and installed relatives and lackeys. Everywhere Longchamp went, he was accompanied by a small army. When he arrived at a castle to begin his appraisals, he demanded the royal suite and rich banquets, and insisted on being waited on by sons of the nobility.

In the end the queen mother went off to find Richard to make him aware of what was happening. Reluctantly the king agreed to curb the power of this unscrupulous menial. But Longchamp hung onto his privileges and power until at last the wrathful people of England ran him out of the country.[3]

Solomon was right. It is not seemly for a fool to wallow in luxury or for a servant to have the rule that belongs to princes.

## E. Conveying Forgiveness (19:11)

"The discretion of a man deferreth his anger; and it is his glory to pass over a transgression." To pass over transgressions is the divine prerogative extolled in Samuel Davies' great worship hymn:

Great God of wonders! all Thy ways
Are matchless, God-like, and divine;
But the bright glories of Thy grace
Above thine other wonders shine.

Such deep transgressions to forgive!
Such guilty sinners thus to spare!
This is Thy grand prerogative,
And in this honor none shall share.

Our God makes it His business to defer His anger and pardon sin, as Jonah discovered. We read about his discoveries in the book of Jonah. Its four chapters divide the book into four simple parts: (1) a word *from* God; (2) a word *with* God; (3) a word *for* God; (4) a word *about* God.

After running away from God's call to preach a message of doom and gloom to Nineveh, Jonah received a second commission. He finally did what God told him to do. Jonah stalked into Assyrian Nineveh and cried, "Yet forty days, and Nineveh shall be overthrown" (Jonah 3:4). The Assyrians were famous not for tender mercy, but for fierce vengeance, so we can imagine that Jonah fully expected to be seized and flayed alive or impaled on a spike.

Although there was not one word of mercy or grace in the prophet's message, revival broke out in Nineveh. Tokens of repentance were displayed on every man and beast—from the monarch on his throne, to the beggar on the street, to the cattle in the stalls. And, of course, God stayed His hand.

But secretly, deep in his soul, Jonah wanted Nineveh to be overthrown. He hoped some flaw in the Assyrian repentance would cause God's judgment to fall. Jonah went to a spot overlooking the city and built a small shanty where he could wait out the forty days.

There God found him sulking. Wrapped in self-righteousness and resentment, Jonah was filled with bitterness over the fact that God had deferred His anger and passed over Nineveh's transgressions.

Jonah was like the elder brother in the Lord's parable of the prodigal son. As the prophet neared Nineveh and heard the music and dancing of a people spared by the great God of wonders, he became angry and would not go in. God Himself had to come out and reason with him (see Luke 15:25-32). Jonah was the Old Testament counterpart of the unmerciful servant to whom the king said, "O thou wicked servant, I forgave thee all that debt, because thou desiredst me: Shouldest not thou also have had compassion on thy fellowservant, even as I had pity on thee?" (Matthew 18:32-33)

Jonah prayed, "I knew that thou art a gracious God, and merciful, slow to anger, and of great kindness, and repentest thee of the evil" (Jonah 4:2). Although spoken in anger, these are the greatest words about God in the Old Testament and they have no equal in the New Testament until we hear "a greater than Jonas" praying for those who nailed Him to the tree: "Father, forgive them; for they know not what they do" (Luke 11:32; 23:34). Solomon said it is the glory of a *man* to pass over a transgression. How much greater is the glory when *God* passes over it!

## II. The Fury of the Throne (19:12–20:7)

### A. Wrath Considered (19:12)

"The king's wrath is as the roaring of a lion; but his favour is as dew upon the grass." Here Solomon gave us two pictures: one of terror and the other of tenderness. The pictures are contrasting, for the dew never comes when the weather is stormy, but the roaring of an angry lion can shake the earth.

This proverb can be illustrated by two contrasting incidents in a story told by Henry Rider Haggard. I grew up on a diet of his books. Years later when I emigrated from Britain to Canada and settled in British Columbia, I visited a community known as Crescent Spur, the site of a thriving logging operation. The small township was flanked by two mountain peaks, part of a range leading toward the Rockies. When I learned the names of the peaks—one was called mount Rider and the other, mount Haggard—I was unexpectedly reminded of one of my favorite novelists.

Sir Henry Rider Haggard spent much of his life in Africa during the early days of British colonization. He was keenly interested in the history of the continent and was especially fascinated by the warlike Zulu people and their kings: Chaka, Dingaan, Panda, and Cetewayo. In *Child of Storm*, the second book in a trilogy on the Zulus, Haggard told how Cetewayo wrested the throne from his brother Umbelazi, in spite of the fact that their father Panda threw his support behind his beloved Umbelazi.

During the war between Cetewayo and Umbelazi, the white hunter Allan Quatermain (Haggard's hero) was commissioned by Panda to lead one of his regiments. Quatermain's instructions were to throw the regiment into the battle only if it seemed that Umbelazi was in peril. The treachery of a wronged petty chieftain named Saduko gave rise to just such a situation, but the intervention of Quatermain's regiment proved to be only a delaying action, for Umbelazi lost the battle after all and perished shortly afterward. Quatermain—known to the Zulus as Macumazahn—was summoned to the victorious Cetewayo's court to account for his actions.

At this point in the story Haggard related an incident that illustrates Proverbs 19:12b: "[The king's] favour is as dew upon the grass." Quatermain is speaking:

> "*Siyakubona,* Macumazahn," [Cetewayo] said, stretching out his hand to me, which I took, though I could not find it in my heart to wish *him* "good-day."
>
> "I hear that you were leading the Amawombe, whom my father, the King, sent down to help Umbelazi, and I am very glad that you have escaped alive. Also my heart is proud of the fight that they made, for you know, Macumazahn, once, next to the King, I was general of that regiment, though afterwards we quarrelled. Still, I am pleased that they did so well, and I have given orders that every one of them who remains alive is to be spared, that they may be officers of a new Amawombe which I shall raise. Do you know, Macumazahn, that you have nearly wiped out three whole regiments of the *Usutu,* killing many more people than did all my brother's army, the *Isigqosa?* Oh, you are a great man. Had it not been for the loyalty"—this word was spoken with just a tinge of sarcasm—"of Saduko yonder, you would have won the day for Umbelazi. Well, now that this quarrel is finished, if you will stay with me I will make you general of a whole division of the King's army, since henceforth I shall have a voice in affairs."
>
> "You are mistaken, O son of Panda," I answered; "the

> splendour of the Amawombe's great stand against a multitude is on the name of Maputa, the King's councillor and the *induna* of the Black One (Chaka) who is gone. He lies yonder in his glory," and I pointed to Maputa's pierced body. "I did but fight as a soldier in his ranks."
>
> "Oh, yes, we know that, we know all that, Macumazahn; and Maputa was a clever monkey in his way, but we know also that you taught him how to jump. Well, he is dead, and nearly all the Amawombe are dead, and of my three regiments but a handful is left; the vultures have the rest of them. That is all finished and forgotten, Macumazahn, though by good fortune the spears went wide of you, who doubtless are a magician, since otherwise you and your servant and your horse would not have escaped with a few scratches when everyone else was killed."[4]

The king's favor was like dew on the grass. (Quatermain politely declined Cetewayo's offer to make him a general.)

The king questioned Quatermain about the death of Umbelazi. When Cetewayo heard the story, he mourned:

> O my brother Umbelazi, I mourn for you, my brother, for, after all, we played together when we were little and loved each other once, who in the end fought for a toy that is called a throne, since, as our father said, two bulls cannot live in the same yard, my brother. Well, you are gone and I remain, yet who knows but that at the last your lot may be happier than mine. You died of a broken heart, Umbelazi, but of what shall *I* die, I wonder?"[5]

Haggard went on to relate the incident that illustrates Proverbs 19:12a: "The king's wrath is as the roaring of a lion."

An old acquaintance of Quatermain showed up: a petty chieftain named Umbezi. Claiming that he had killed Umbelazi, Umbezi carried a gory spear in one hand and a head-plume of ostrich feathers in the other. "Give me audience of the son of the King!" he said. "I have a song to sing to the Prince. I have a tale to tell to the conqueror, Cetewayo." Quatermain observed the scene:

> I stared. I rubbed my eyes. It could not be—yes, it was—Umbezi, "Eater-up-of-Elephants," the father of Mameena. In a few seconds, without waiting for leave to approach, he had bounded through the line of dead princes, stopping to kick

one of them on the head and address his poor clay in some words of shameful insult, and was prancing about before Cetewayo, shouting his praises.

"Who is this *umfokazana* [low fellow]?" growled the Prince. "Bid him cease his noise and speak, lest he should be silent for ever."

"O Calf of the Black Cow, I am Umbezi, 'Eater-up-of-Elephants,' chief captain of Saduko the Cunning, he who won you the battle, father of Mameena the Beautiful, whom Saduko wed and whom the dead dog, Umbelazi, stole away from him."

"Ah!" said Cetewayo, screwing up his eyes in a fashion he had when he meant mischief, which among the Zulus caused him to be named the "Bull-who-shuts-his-eyes-to-toss," "and what have you to tell me, 'Eater-up-of-Elephants,' and father of Mameena, whom the dead dog, Umbelazi, took away from your master, Saduko the Cunning?"

"This, O Mighty One; this, O Shaker of the Earth, that well am I named 'Eater-up-of-Elephants,' who have eaten up *Indhlovuene-Sihlonti*—the Elephant himself."

Bombastic Umbezi continued his story. He said the mighty warrior Umbelazi had run away from him, fallen before him in hand-to-hand combat, and rolled into the river. "As he rolled," Umbezi said, "I snatched away his plume. See, is it not the plume of the dead dog Umbelazi?" Quatermain went on:

Cetewayo took the ornament and examined it, showing it to one or two of the captains near him, who nodded their heads gravely.

"Yes," he said, "this is the war plume of Umbelazi, beloved of the King, strong and shining pillar of the Great House; we know it well, that war plume at the sight of which many a knee has loosened. And so you killed him, 'Eater-up-of-Elephants,' father of Mameena, you who this morning were one of the meanest of his jackals. Now, what reward shall I give you for this mighty deed, O Umbezi?"

"A great reward, O Terrible One," began Umbezi, but in an awful voice Cetewayo bade him be silent.

"Yes," he said, "a great reward. Hearken, Jackal and Traitor. Your own words bear witness against you. You, *you* have dared to lift your hand against the blood-royal, and with your foul tongue to heap lies and insults upon the name of the mighty dead."

Now, understanding at last, Umbezi began to babble excuses, yes, and to declare that all his tale was false. His fat cheeks fell in, he sank to his knees.

But Cetewayo only spat towards the man, after his fashion when enraged, and looked round him till his eye fell upon Saduko.

"Saduko," he said, "take away this slayer of the Prince, who boasts that he is red with my own blood, and when he is dead cast him into the river from that rock on which he says he stabbed Panda's son."

Saduko looked round him wildly and hesitated.

"Take him away," thundered Cetewayo, "and return ere dark to make report to me."

Then, at a sign from the Prince, soldiers flung themselves upon the miserable Umbezi and dragged him thence, Saduko going with them; nor was the poor liar ever seen again.[6]

Truly the wrath of a king is like the roaring of a lion.

## B. Woes Considered (19:13-14)

### 1. The Calamity (19:13)

Here Solomon underlined the calamities of *a foolish son* and *a fretful spouse:* "A foolish son is the calamity of his father: and the contentions of a wife are a continual dropping." One suspects that Solomon wrote this proverb with a bitter heart, ever mindful of his own disordered household. Pity the man who has a fool for a son and a scold for a wife, the man whose house is kept in turmoil by one or the other.

We have all felt sorry for poor Joe Gargery, the kind and patient blacksmith in *Great Expectations* who was married to a shrew. Charles Dickens had barely dipped his pen in ink when he described the woman. He used Pip to tell the tale:

> My sister, Mrs. Joe Gargery, was more than twenty years older than I, and had established a great reputation with herself and the neighbours because she had brought me up "by hand." Having at that time to find out for myself what the expression meant, and knowing her to have a hard and heavy hand, and to be much in the habit of laying it upon her husband as well as upon me, I supposed that Joe Gargery and I were both brought up by hand.

She was not a good-looking woman, my sister; and I had a general impression that she must have made Joe Gargery marry her by hand. Joe was a fair man, with curls of flaxen hair on each side of his smooth face, and with eyes of such a very undecided blue that they seemed to have somehow got mixed with their own whites. He was a mild, good-natured, sweet-tempered, easy-going, foolish, dear fellow—a sort of Hercules in strength, and also in weakness.

My sister, Mrs. Joe, with black hair and eyes, had such a prevailing redness of skin, that I sometimes used to wonder whether it was possible she washed herself with a nutmeg-grater instead of soap. She was tall and bony, and almost always wore a coarse apron, fastened over her figure behind with two loops, and having a square impregnable bib in front, that was stuck full of pins and needles. She made it a powerful merit in herself, and a strong reproach against Joe, that she wore this apron so much. Though I really see no reason why she should have worn it at all; or why, if she did wear it at all, she should not have taken it off every day of her life.

Joe's forge adjoined our house, which was a wooden house, as many of the dwellings in our country were—most of them, at that time. When I ran home from the churchyard, the forge was shut up, and Joe was sitting alone in the kitchen. Joe and I being fellow-sufferers, and having confidences as such, Joe imparted a confidence to me, the moment I raised the latch of the door and peeped in at him opposite to it, sitting in the chimney corner.

"Mrs. Joe has been out a dozen times, looking for you, Pip. And she's out now, making it a baker's dozen."

"Is she?"

"Yes, Pip," said Joe; "and what's worse, she's got Tickler with her."

At this dismal intelligence, I twisted the only button on my waistcoat round and round, and looked in great depression at the fire. Tickler was a wax-ended piece of cane, worn smooth by collision with my tickled frame.

Presently the termagant came home and Pip continued the story:

"Where have you been, you young monkey?" said Mrs. Joe, stamping her foot. "Tell me directly what you've been doing to wear me away with fret and fright and worrit, or I'd have you out of that corner if you was fifty Pips, and he was five hundred Gargerys."

"I have only been to the churchyard," said I, from my stool, crying and rubbing myself.

"Churchyard!" repeated my sister. "If it warn't for me you'd have been to the churchyard long ago, and stayed there. Who brought you up by hand?"

"You did," said I.

"And why did I do it, I should like to know?" exclaimed my sister.

I whimpered, "I don't know."

"*I* don't!" said my sister. "I'd never do it again! I know that. I may truly say I've never had this apron of mine off, since born you were. It's bad enough to be a blacksmith's wife, (and him a Gargery), without being your mother."

Poor Joe knew all about the fretful spouse.

Readers are not surprised to find that Dickens later struck this woman dumb and still later got rid of her altogether. Eventually Joe married a decent wife—but not before he had another disappointment, for Pip proved to be a foolish son.

Pip came into some money, went away to London, and acquired an education. Before long he became ashamed of his roots, especially because he aspired to marry into society. When he received news that Joe was coming to see him, he said:

> I received this letter by post on Monday morning, and therefore its appointment was for next day. Let me confess exactly, with what feelings I looked forward to Joe's coming.
>
> Not with pleasure, though I was bound to him by so many ties; no, with considerable disturbance, some mortification, and a keen sense of incongruity. If I could have kept him away by paying money, I certainly would have paid money.

Joe arrived and Pip could hear his clumsy feet coming upstairs:

> I thought he never would have done wiping his feet, and that I must have gone out to lift him off the mat, but at last he came in.
>
> "Joe, how are you, Joe?"
>
> "Pip, how AIR you, Pip?"
>
> With his good honest face all glowing and shining, and his hat put down on the floor between us, he caught both my

hands and worked them straight up and down, as if I had been the last-patented Pump.

"I am glad to see you, Joe. Give me your hat."

But Joe, taking it up carefully with both hands, like a bird's-nest with eggs in it, wouldn't hear of parting with that piece of property, and persisted in standing talking over it in a most uncomfortable way.

"Which you have that growed," said Joe, "and that swelled, and that gentle-folked"; Joe considered a little before he discovered this word: "as to be sure you are a honour to your king and country."

"And you, Joe, look wonderfully well."

Joe was introduced to Pip's friend Herbert. Conversation was strained and when Herbert left, Joe spoke at once:

"Us two being now alone, Sir," began Joe.

"Joe," I interrupted, pettishly, "how can you call me Sir?"

Joe looked at me for a single instant with something faintly like reproach. Utterly preposterous as his cravat was, and as his collars were, I was conscious of a sort of dignity in the look.

"Us two being now alone," resumed Joe, "and me having the intentions and abilities to stay not many minutes more, I will now conclude—leastways begin—to mention what have led to my having had the present honour. For was it not," said Joe, with his old air of lucid exposition, "that my only wish were to be useful to you, I should not have had the honour of breaking wittles in the company and abode of gentlemen."

The blacksmith explained that he had only come to convey a message that he thought Pip would very much want to hear. He explained that he had wanted Biddy, his housekeeper, to write out the message in full:

"Biddy," pursued Joe, "when I got home and asked her fur to write the message to you, a little hung back. Biddy says, 'I know he will be very glad to have it by word of mouth: it is holiday-time, you want to see him, go!' I have now concluded, Sir," said Joe, rising from his chair, "and, Pip, I wish you ever well and ever prospering to a greater and greater height."

"But you are not going now, Joe?"

"Yes I am," said Joe.

"But you're coming back to dinner, Joe?"

> "No I am not," said Joe.
>
> Our eyes met, and all the "Sir" melted out of that manly heart as he gave me his hand.[7]

Dickens left us in no doubt as to which of the two was the real Christian and the true gentleman. Pip was the calamity of poor old Joe, who had been better than a father to him. However at the end of the story Dickens brought Pip to his senses and he learned the meaning of true values in life.

2. The Contrast (19:14)

Having shown us a home where a foolish son and a contentious wife live, Solomon let us peep inside the house next door. What a difference! There we see *the right kind of wife* and *the right kind of wealth*: "House and riches are the inheritance of fathers: and a prudent wife is from the Lord" (Proverbs 19:14).

Which address would we prefer to visit in the city of Proverbs in Poetry County in Old Testament Land: 14 Nineteenth Street or 13 Nineteenth Street? Surely we would line up to visit number 14, where there is an atmosphere of domestic harmony and security. The husband is a good provider and the wife is a prudent manager. The husband provides the house; the wife turns it into a home.

We could have found such a house in the Jewish quarter of Corinth in the days of the early church—the home of a godly Christian couple named Aquila and Priscilla, who had been driven out of Rome by an outbreak of antisemitism during the reign of Claudius. Paul found that house. And after the couple left Corinth, Apollos found their house in Ephesus.

Apollos was an Alexandrian Jew. The famous lighthouse and the equally famous library were as much a part of his cultural heritage as Jerusalem and the river Jordan. He studied Homer, Plato, and Philo along with Moses and Isaiah.

Apollos was eloquent and mighty in the Scriptures, but he was handicapped, for he had only progressed in the gospel as far as John the Baptist. What he knew, however, he preached with passion and power.

When Apollos came to Ephesus, Aquila and Priscilla attended the synagogue each sabbath and listened to him preaching about John—when he should have been preaching about Jesus. They invited Apollos to their home for supper. Then when the children were safely tucked in bed, Aquila and Priscilla talked to him about Jesus (Acts 18:24-28).

Imagine two tentmakers/carpet-weavers—their fingers calloused from working with stiff goat's hair and looms—teaching the polished Alexandrian Jew! What a picture! But Apollos sensed the solid reality of this couple and noticed their air of quiet assurance. Their humble home breathed peace, love, and joy in the Holy Ghost. Aquila and Priscilla spoke with authority and not as the scribes. To the end of his days Apollos never ceased to thank God for that home.

When Paul went to Corinth after his encounter with sneering intellectuals in Athens, he was bruised in spirit. But the moment he met Aquila and Priscilla, he knew that they were his own kind of people, and the godly couple took it for granted that Paul would stay with them while he evangelized Corinth (Acts 18:1-3).

Probably their home was not much of a place—four wooden walls with a roof of sailcloth put up by Aquila. Perhaps the house had partitions and a corner was curtained off for Paul.

All day long as Paul labored at one of Aquila's looms in the marketplace, he would be surrounded by a circle of men and women. While his work-worn fingers automatically busied themselves with the threads, and his feet worked the treadles below, his tongue would be equally active as he expounded to all who would listen the glorious gospel of Christ.

At the end of the day Paul would return to that little suburb of Heaven that Aquila and Priscilla called home. There the apostle would enjoy a good meal and an evening of prayer and Bible teaching. At 14 Nineteenth Street in the city of Proverbs, true riches could be found. Aquila—and Apollos and Paul—knew it was a house where lived a prudent wife. She was a gift from God to Aquila.

## C. Warnings Considered (19:15-25)

### 1. Beware of Idleness (19:15)

"Slothfulness casteth into a deep sleep; and an idle soul shall suffer hunger." The extreme sloth that Solomon so often decried was depicted by Jack London in his short story *In a Far Country*.

In London's tale Carter Weatherbee had given up his snug job of clerk in the big city and had hurried off to Edmonton. This trip was the first leg of a journey to the Klondike to search for gold. Percy Cuthfert too had felt the lure of the Mother Lode and had left his life of affluence, culture, and ease. He was seeking for adventure and romance. The pair joined a party of men teamed together in a trek toward the Mackenzie river and the beckoning North. The reality and roughness of the journey soon stripped away their dreams of quick and easy wealth. Wrote London:

> Day in and day out, they labored with the batteaus and canoes, fought mosquitoes and kindred pests, or sweated and swore at the portages. Severe toil like this lays a man naked to the very roots of his soul, and ere Lake Athabasca was lost in the south, each member of the party had hoisted his true colors.
>
> The two shirks and chronic grumblers were Carter Weatherbee and Percy Cuthfert. The whole party complained less of its aches and pains than did either of them. Not once did they volunteer for the thousand and one petty duties of the camp. A bucket of water to be brought, an extra armful of wood to be chopped, the dishes to be washed and wiped, a search to be made through the outfit for some suddenly indispensable article—and these two effete scions of civilization discovered sprains or blisters requiring instant attention. They were the first to turn in at night, with a score of tasks yet undone; the last to turn out in the morning, when the start should be in readiness before the breakfast was begun. They were the first to fall to at mealtime, the last to have a hand in the cooking; the first to dive for a slim delicacy, the last to discover they had added to their own another man's share. If they toiled at the oars, they slyly cut the water at each stroke and allowed the boat's momentum to float up the blade. They thought nobody noticed; but their comrades swore under their breaths and grew to hate them, while Jacques Baptiste sneered openly and damned them from morning till night. But he was no gentleman.
>
> At the Great Slave, Hudson Bay dogs were purchased, and the fleet sank to the guards with its added burden of dried fish and pemmican. Then canoe and batteau answered to the swift current of the Mackenzie, and they plunged into the Great Barren Ground. Every likely looking "feeder" was prospected, but the elusive "pay dirt" danced ever to the north.

The prospectors were still more than four hundred miles from the Yukon and another five hundred miles or so from Dawson. Some hard decisions had to be made, for winter was coming on. Ahead lay a thousand miles of the stiffest hardship man can conceive. The two chronic grumblers elected to stay where they were. There was food, water, a cabin, and plenty of timber for firewood. The rest of the party loaded up and pulled out, glad to leave the two lazy men behind. London continued:

> Things prospered in the little cabin at first. The rough badinage of their comrades had made Weatherbee and Cuthfert conscious of the mutual responsibility which had devolved upon them; besides, there was not so much work after all for two healthy men. And the removal of the cruel whiphand, or in other words, the bulldozing half-breed [Jacques Baptiste], had brought with it a joyous reaction. At first, each strove to outdo the other, and they performed petty tasks with an unction which would have opened the eyes of their comrades who were now wearing out bodies and souls on the Long Trail.
>
> All care was banished. The forest, which shouldered in upon them from three sides, was an inexhaustible woodyard. A few yards from their door slept the Porcupine [river], and a hole through its winter robe formed a bubbling spring of water, crystal clear and painfully cold. But they soon grew to find fault with even that. The hole would persist in freezing up, and thus gave them many a miserable hour of ice chopping. The unknown builders of the cabin had extended the side logs so as to support a cache at the rear. In this was stored the bulk of the party's provisions. Food there was, without stint, for three times the men who were fated to live upon it. But the most of it was the kind which built up brawn and sinew but did not tickle the palate. True, there was sugar in plenty for two ordinary men; but these two were little else than children. They early discovered the virtues of hot water judiciously saturated with sugar, and they prodigally swam their flapjacks and soaked their crusts in the rich, white syrup. Then coffee and tea, and especially the dried fruits, made disastrous inroads upon it. The first word they had was over the sugar question. And it is a really serious thing when two men, wholly dependent upon each other for company, begin to quarrel.

The two men had nothing in common, nothing to talk about, no mutual interests. London went on with the story:

> With little to do, time became an intolerable burden to them. This naturally made them still lazier. They sank into a

physical lethargy which there was no escaping, and which made them rebel at the performance of the smallest chore. One morning when it was his turn to cook the common breakfast, Weatherbee rolled out of his blankets, and to the snoring of his companion, lighted first the slush lamp and then the fire. The kettles were frozen hard, and there was no water in the cabin with which to wash. But he did not mind that. Waiting for it to thaw, he sliced the bacon and plunged into the hateful task of breadmaking. Cuthfert had been slyly watching through his half-closed lids. Consequently there was a scene, in which they fervently blessed each other, and agreed, henceforth, that each do his own cooking. A week later, Cuthfert neglected his morning ablutions, but none the less complacently ate the meal which he had cooked. Weatherbee grinned. After that the foolish custom of washing passed out of their lives.

As the sugar pile and other little luxuries dwindled, they began to be afraid they were not getting their proper shares, and in order that they might not be robbed, they fell to gorging themselves. The luxuries suffered in this gluttonous contest, as did also the men. In the absence of fresh vegetables and exercise, their blood became impoverished, and a loathsome, purplish rash crept over their bodies. Yet they refused to heed the warning. Next, their muscles and joints began to swell, the flesh turning black, while their mouths, gums and lips, took on the color of rich cream. Instead of being drawn together by their misery, each gloated over the other's symptoms as the scurvy took its course.

They lost all regard for personal appearance, and for that matter, common decency. The cabin became a pigpen, and never once were the beds made or fresh pine boughs laid underneath. Yet they could not keep to their blankets, as they would have wished; for the frost was inexorable, and the firebox consumed much fuel. The hair of their heads and faces grew long and shaggy, while their garments would have disgusted a ragpicker. But they did not care. They were sick, and there was no one to see; besides, it was very painful to move about.

To all this was added a new trouble—the Fear of the North. This Fear was the joint child of the Great Cold and the Great Silence, and was born in the darkness of December, when the sun dipped below the southern horizon for good.[8]

"Slothfulness casteth into a deep sleep," said Solomon. London could have added, as he did at the end of this story, that slothfulness ends in murder and death.

2. Beware of Indifference (19:16-18)

Solomon warned against indifference toward piety, poverty, and parenthood.

Proverbs 19:16 is a warning against *indifference regarding piety:* "He that keepeth the commandment keepeth his own soul; but he that despiseth his [God's] ways shall die." Solomon was stating the essence of Old Testament religion. The Lord told Moses to tell the children of Israel, "Ye shall therefore keep my statutes, and my judgments: which if a man *do,* he shall *live* in them: I am the Lord" (Leviticus 18:5, italics added). When Moses presented the law to Israel, the people promised: "All that the Lord hath spoken we will *do*" (Exodus 19:8, italics added). This foolish promise was based on their ignorance of the law and their ignorance of their own hearts.

The law, when it was fully given, embraced 613 specific commandments—a list of dos and don'ts that probed every nook and cranny of life. There were criminal laws and contractual laws; laws for rulers and laws for rituals; martial laws, marriage laws, and medical laws; laws concerning murder, malpractice, and manslaughter; social laws, sabbath laws, and sexual laws; laws concerning feast days and fast days; laws for the sanctuary and laws about the sacrifices; laws pertaining to false worship and laws about false witnesses; laws against prostitution and laws against perversion; laws about leprosy and laws about loan sharks; laws about diet and laws about dress. And over this great body of legislation brooded the death penalty.

The Decalogue summed up all the laws in five commandments dealing with man's duty to God and five commandments dealing with man's duty to man. The Lord Jesus reduced the legislation to two commandments: "Thou shalt love the Lord thy God with all thy heart, and with all thy soul, and with all thy mind, and with all thy strength....Thou shalt love thy neighbour as thyself" (Mark 12:30-31).

The essence of Old Testament religion was *doing,* but Calvary brought a change. Where the law says, "Do!" the Lord says, "Done!"

At the end of one of D. L. Moody's campaigns, a man came to him with a question. When others had gone forward, the man had hesitated. Now the last sermon had been preached, the last altar call had been given, the last song had been sung, and the last benediction had been breathed. The cleanup crew was already putting away the chairs.

"Mr. Moody," the man asked, "what must I do to be saved?"

"You're too late," Mr. Moody said.

"Too late? Surely I'm not too late."

"You're two thousand years too late," Mr. Moody replied. "If you wanted to *do* something to be saved, you should have been born two thousand years ago. Now all you have to do is 'believe on the Lord Jesus Christ and thou shalt be saved.'"

The Lord's ways were greatly simplified at Calvary. Now all His ways begin at the cross, and "he that despiseth his ways shall die." Jesus said, "I am the way, the truth, and the life: no man cometh unto the Father, but by me" (John 14:6). As the old hymn says:

> I must needs go home by the way of the cross,
> There's no other way but this;
> I shall ne'er get sight of the gates of light,
> If the way of the cross I miss.[9]

Moving on to Proverbs 19:17, we see a warning against *indifference regarding poverty:* "He that hath pity upon the poor lendeth unto the Lord; and that which he hath given will he pay him again." It is impossible to outgive God. We must be careful not to neglect giving to the poor. God's eye is ever on them, and on those who have "bread enough and to spare."

One day during His earthly ministry, the Lord Jesus "sat over against the treasury" (Mark 12:41). We can picture Him and His disciples watching the people come and go with their gifts. Edersheim described the scene:

> Weary with the contention, the Master had left those to whom He had spoken in the Porches, and, while the crowd wrangled about His Words or His Person, had ascended the flight of steps which led from "the Terrace" into the Temple-building. From these steps—whether those leading up to the "Beautiful Gate" or one of the wide gates—He could gain full view into "The Court of the Women," into which they opened. On these steps, or within the gate (for in no other place was it lawful), He sat Him down, watching the multitude. The time of Sacrifice was past, and those who still lingered had remained for private devotion, for private sacrifices, or to pay their vows and offerings. Although the topography of the Temple,

> especially of this part of it, is not without its difficulties, we know that under the colonnades, which surrounded "the Court of the Women," but still left in the middle room for more than 15,000 worshippers, provision was made for receiving religious and charitable contributions. All along these colonnades were the thirteen trumpet-shaped boxes *(Shopharoth);* somewhere here also we must locate two chambers: that of "the silent," for gifts to be distributed in secret to the children of the pious poor, and that where votive vessels were deposited. Perhaps there was here also a special chamber for offerings. These "trumpets" bore each inscriptions, marking the objects of contribution—whether to make up for past neglect, to pay for certain sacrifices, to provide incense, wood, or for other gifts.[10]

As we read between the lines of Scripture, we can imagine the people placing their offerings in the boxes for the Lord and/or the boxes for the poor. And we can hear the applause of the crowd as the rich men came and with fanfare and flourish tossed in handfuls of gold coins. Judas's eyes gleamed with greed, but the Lord was not impressed. He remained silent, watching and waiting.

"Ah! Here she comes," He said to Himself. He knew all about her. She was a desperately poor widow. All she had in the world were two small coins, the smallest in circulation. Only those two coins stood between her and hunger, but she had come with her mind made up: she was going to give half of all she had. The Lord could read her every thought. His eyes never left her.

She pulled out her purse and took out one of the two mites. She was about to drop it in a box marked for the Lord when she saw a box marked for the poor. She was familiar with the pinch of poverty. She knew what it is like to be poor, so she moved toward that box. But she paused again, remembering that if she gave her mite to help the poor, she would not have anything to give to the Lord. She loved the Lord and wanted to give something to Him. Her hand hovered first over one box and then over the other. Suddenly she plunged her hand back into her purse and took out the other mite. Quick as a flash she put one mite into the box for the Lord and the other into the box for the poor. Then she scurried away, hoping no one had seen how small her coins were. The Lord was absolutely delighted. "This poor widow hath cast in more than they all," He said (Luke 21:3).

I have often wondered what she found when she got home. Only a day or so before, Zacchaeus had been spectacularly saved and had promised the Lord that he would give half of his goods to the poor (Luke 19:1-10). I like to think that when this widow arrived home, she found Zacchaeus sitting on her doorstep, and that he was waiting to give her half of his goods. She had given to the poor. She had lent to the Lord and He always pays back such loans with interest. He adds interest beyond all our power to reckon.

The next warning of Solomon is against *indifference regarding parenthood:* "Chasten thy son while there is hope, and let not thy soul spare for his crying" (Proverbs 19:18). Someone has said that this proverb is "Solomon's cure" for the lawlessness in much of modern family life. We have traded Solomon's wisdom for mere psychology and we are much the worse for it.

Vance Havner introduced a message at the 1982 Moody Bible Institute Founder's Week Conference with a poem that sums up the folly of our refusal to listen to Solomon's advice regarding the whole question of child-raising. One of America's best-loved preachers, Havner was known for his keen insights and penetrating wit. Here is the poem:

Junior bit the meter man
Junior kicked the cook,
He's just *anti-social* now
According to the book.

Junior smashed the clock and lamp,
Junior hacked the tree;
*Destructive trends* are all explained
In chapters 2 and 3.

Junior threw his milk at Mom,
Junior screamed for more;
Notes on *self-assertiveness*
Are found in chapter 4.

Junior tossed his shoes and socks
Out into the rain;
*Aggression*! Well, that's normal
Disregard the stain.

Junior got in Grandpa's room
Tore up his fishing line;
That's to *gain attention*,
Chapters 8 and 9.

Grandpa seized a slipper,
Yanked Junior 'cross his knee;
For Grandpa hadn't read a book
Since 1893.

Grandpa knew all about "Solomon's cure" for bad behavior and was prompt in its practical application.

### 3. Beware of Intolerance (19:19-22)

#### a. The Man with the Ungovernable Temper (19:19)

"A man of great wrath shall suffer punishment: for if thou deliver him, yet thou must do it again." The person who cannot control his temper is always going to be in trouble. When he loses his temper, he loses control of himself. He says and does things he cannot take back. There is no telling what the consequences will be.

Adolf Hitler was an intolerant man who was given to rage. His speeches were outright temper tantrums, designed to intimidate his enemies and whip up the passions of the German people.

His fury was unleashed in more private settings as well, according to a prison psychologist who recorded stories he heard during personal conversations with several of the defendants at the Nuremberg trials of Nazi war criminals. He talked, for instance, with Joachim von Ribbentrop, Germany's strutting foreign minister, who claimed that he had "only done his duty in supporting Hitler" and that he had always warned the British and French about the führer. Von Ribbentrop said that Hitler had once screamed at him in 1940 and he could never contradict him after that. The psychologist also talked with Baldur von Schirach, a former Nazi youth leader. He said that in 1943 when he backed up his wife's question about the way the Jews were being treated, Hitler flew at him in such a rage that he thought he would be arrested then and there.[11]

Just before the seizure of Austria, Hitler summoned the Austrian chancellor to Berchtesgaden and raved at him and bullied him for hours on end. Then the führer handed him an ultimatum and frightened him into signing it.

When the German generals were terrified at the prospect of invading Czechoslovakia, they tried to stand up to Hitler. Alfred Jodl, chief of operations for the high command, noted in his diary that the tyrant became furious and raged against his generals for their spinelessness. Almost to a man, they cowered before him.

When the assassination attempt against him failed but rumors of a revolt in Berlin persisted, Hitler nearly went insane with rage. Foaming at the mouth, he leaped from his chair. "I'll put their wives and children into concentration camps," he raved. "I'll show them no mercy." Grabbing a telephone, he shrieked orders to the Gestapo in Berlin: everyone the SS suspected was to be shot at once.

And so it went on. In his last will and testament Hitler again became the angry young man he had been in the Vienna gutters. He cursed the Jews of the world. He expelled Hermann Göring and Heinrich Himmler from the Nazi party and raged against his generals one more time. He said: "Above all, I enjoin the government and the people to uphold the racial laws to the limit and to resist mercilessly the poisoner of the nations, international Jewry."

Those were his thoughts at 4:00 a.m., Sunday, April 29, 1945. He went to bed as dawn was breaking, and that afternoon he learned of the fate of Mussolini. At 2:30 a.m. on April 30 he emerged from his private quarters in the Berlin bunker and shook hands with his staff. Later that afternoon Hitler and Eva Braun said their last farewells and by 3:30 p.m. they were dead. Such was the end of a man of great wrath.

b. The Man with the Unteachable Temperament (19:20-22)

Urging us to be teachable, Solomon warned us *not to forsake guidance:* "Hear counsel, and receive instruction, that thou mayest be wise in thy latter end" (Proverbs 19:20). The illustration that instantly comes to mind is the case of Balaam.

Balaam was what the Bible calls a soothsayer and what we would call a psychic. He was in touch with an evil spirit who gave him a limited ability to prophesy. This soothsayer had a reputation in Mesopotamia for the pungency of his curses. Thus when Balak, king of Moab, found the all-victorious Hebrews on his doorstep, he thought of Balaam. It occurred to Balak that since he could not conquer the Israelites, who were on their triumphant march to Canaan, it might be a good idea to curse them. No one was better qualified to do the job than Balaam.

Soon ambassadors from the court of Balak appeared at Balaam's house. They brought a royal invitation to come to Moab. The king wanted Balaam to come armed with his most potent imprecations so that he could curse the Israelites. Eyeing the fat honorarium dangling before him, the soothsayer had no trouble making up his mind. He would go!

Then God stepped in and spoke to him. Balaam had never heard such a voice before. "Thou shalt not go with them," God said. "Thou shalt not curse the people: for they are blessed" (Numbers 22:12). That should have been the end of the matter, and so it was for the time being.

But before long the ambassadors returned, accompanied by ranking members of the Moabite nobility who offered even greater incentives and inducements. This time God said to the hireling preacher, whose gifts were for sale to the highest bidder, "Go with them; but yet the word which I shall say unto thee, that shalt thou do" (22:20). The Lord was warning Balaam that if he went, he would be sorry. God had not changed His mind about allowing someone to curse those He had blessed.

But the soothsayer was not receptive to guidance. He refused to listen to God. Persuading himself that he could outwit God, Balaam saddled his ass and went off with the ambassadors.

The next message came from Balaam's donkey! Alarmed at the sight of an angel, the animal balked and refused to go any farther, even though Balaam whipped it furiously. Finally, in one of the most extraordinary miracles in the Bible, the donkey spoke to the headstrong prophet. Then Balaam's eyes were opened and he too saw the angel. The angel of the Lord warned the prophet that he was on the wrong path and said, "Thy way is perverse before me" (22:32). Balaam could go if he insisted, but if he went, he would be in God's permissive will, contrary to His primary will. Balaam would be allowed to say only what God wanted said.

In Moab he tried four times to curse God's redeemed people. Each time the Lord took hold of his tongue—as He had taken hold of the donkey's tongue—and turned the attempted curse into a resounding blessing. If Balaam had paid any heed to the four amazing prophecies that came out of his mouth, he would have been a wiser man. He would have abandoned his traffic with demons and thrown in his lot with the people of God.

Instead, alarmed at the rising wrath of Balak and seeing his fat honorarium flying away, he put his crafty mind to work to figure out a way to replace the blessing of God with the anger of God. "My lord king," Balaam said in effect, "if you cannot curse God's people, corrupt them." Such was the doctrine of Balaam. It worked only too well (see Numbers 25).

Balaam was an evil man, but his experiences in Moab must have made some impression on his mind, for he cried, "Let me die the death of the righteous, and let my last end be like his!" (23:10) He failed to realize that if we want to die the death of the righteous, we have to live the life of the righteous. In order to live the life of the righteous we have to do what Balaam refused to do. We have to turn to the Lord, repent of our sin, give up our wicked ways, and throw in our lot with the people of God. As Solomon said, "Hear counsel, and receive instruction, that thou mayest be wise in thy latter end." We should not forsake his guidance, for sooner or later the time to die comes to us all. Balaam did not live the life of the righteous and he died under the avenging sword of Israel (Joshua 13:22).

Next Solomon warned us *not to forsake God:* "There are many devices in a man's heart; nevertheless the counsel of the Lord, that shall stand" (Proverbs 19:21). Balaam experienced the truth of this proverb and the principle behind it is illustrated everywhere in both sacred and secular history.

The word translated "devices" in Proverbs 19:21 means "schemes." Man's schemes come to nothing in the end. God always has the last word.

Consider, for example, God's counsel to make good to the nation of Israel all of the blessings He sovereignly bestowed on Abraham (Genesis 12:1-3; 15; 17). God has unconditionally promised to protect the Hebrew people, even when He is punishing them. He has signed a treaty with them, the terms of which depend on His faithfulness, not theirs. He has promised them a land that ultimately is to stretch from the Nile to the Euphrates. Over the years He has added many promises to the original treaty. The nation of Israel is to be a blessing to all mankind. The Lord Jesus is to sit on the throne of David, just as He now sits on the throne of His Father in Heaven. There is to be a thousand-year golden age during which time the Hebrew people and the nation of Israel will be the center of activity. If we read the Bible as literally and grammatically as we read any other book, these great truths become abundantly clear.

The fact that the nation of Israel has been reborn and many Jews from all parts of the world have gone back to their ancestral home is evidence enough that God will keep His word. Events are again beginning to move toward the final fulfillment of all God's "exceeding great and precious promises" to the nation of Israel. "The counsel of the Lord, that shall stand."

Of course many people deny the truth about the future of Israel. "There are many devices in a man's heart," Solomon said. An enormous propaganda offensive is being mounted against Israel by the Arab-Muslim bloc. This offensive is being financed by the virtually limitless resources of the Middle Eastern oil barons; "nevertheless the counsel of the Lord, that shall stand." The United

Nations has passed numerous resolutions condemning the beleaguered nation of Israel; "nevertheless the counsel of the Lord, that shall stand." The United States vacillates in its policy toward Israel, as do the European powers; "nevertheless the counsel of the Lord, that shall stand." Russia will one day back the Muslim world, unite the antisemitic nations, and launch a massive invasion of Israel; "nevertheless the counsel of the Lord, that shall stand." The antichrist will come and inaugurate policies aimed at the extermination of the Jews and the elimination of the nation of Israel. "Nevertheless the counsel of the Lord, that shall stand."

Much of the professing church has embraced covenant theology, a system of interpretation that equates the church with Israel. According to proponents of this theology, all the literal promises of God to Abraham, Isaac, Jacob, David, the prophets, and the nation of Israel must be "spiritualized." The curses are conveniently left for the Jews, but the blessings and promises are appropriated by the church. There is no future for the nation of Israel and no millennial reign of Christ. This doctrine may be popular, but popularity is no proof of a doctrine's truth. Covenant theology's interpretative "device" may appeal to some; "nevertheless the counsel of the Lord, that shall stand." The rebirth of the state of Israel and numerous other recent events of prophetic significance show that the dispensationalists were right all along.

Solomon also warned us *not to forsake goodness:* "The desire of a man is his kindness: and a poor man is better than a liar" (Proverbs 19:22). Two words are translated "man" in this proverb. The first, *'ādām,* means the ordinary man, the common man. The second, *'īsh,* means a man of higher rank. By linking the word translated "poor" with *'īsh,* Solomon reinforced his statement that an honest, hard-working, decent commoner is better than a lying sprig of the aristocracy. Although the poor man may lack the means to do as much as he would like to do, he excels the well-to-do liar.

One rich and influential liar was named Caiaphas. The high priest of Israel at the time of the trial and crucifixion of Christ, Caiaphas came from a serpent's brood and married the daughter of Annas. Dean F. W. Farrar wrote about the background of Annas:

> It is probable that he and his family had been originally summoned by Herod the Great from Alexandria, as supple supporters of a distasteful tyranny. The Jewish historian calls this Hanan the happiest man of his time, because he died at an advanced old age, and because both he and five of his sons in succession—not to mention his son-in-law—had enjoyed

> the shadow of the High Priesthood—so that, in fact, for nearly half a century he had practically wielded the sacerdotal power. But to be admired by such a renegade as Josephus is a questionable advantage. Annas and his sons were noted for their meanness and avarice. In spite of his prosperity he seems to have left behind him but an evil name, and we know enough of his character, even from the most unsuspected sources, to recognize in him nothing better than an astute, tyrannous, worldly Sadducee, unvenerable for all his seventy years, full of a serpentine malice and meanness which utterly belied the meaning of his name ("Merciful") and engaged at this very moment in a dark, disorderly conspiracy, for which even a worse man would have had cause to blush.[12]

Caiaphas was a worthy son-in-law for the malicious Annas. Made high priest by Valerius Gratus, Caiaphas had less force of character than Annas, but was equally crafty and unscrupulous. Caiaphas had no hesitation about giving Christ a mock trial and packing the witness stand with liars like himself. After the resurrection, in an attempt to counter the impact of the empty tomb, he bribed the soldiers who had been guarding it to lie about what had happened.

One poor man who was far better than well-to-do Caiaphas was Peter. Caiaphas thirsted for power, but Peter's desire was to be kind. On his way into the temple one day shortly after Pentecost, Peter and John saw a beggar sitting at the Gate Beautiful (probably the east gate distinguished by its covering of Corinthian bronze). When the beggar optimistically asked for alms, Peter said, "Silver and gold have I none; but such as I have give I thee: In the name of Jesus Christ of Nazareth rise up and walk" (Acts 3:6). Immediately the lame man was healed.

The crowds came running since the beggar, who had been a notable fixture at the gate, was now loudly proclaiming and proving his healing. It wasn't long before Peter seized Opportunity by the forelock and preached Christ to the crowd. And it wasn't long before he and John and the healed man were face to face with an indignant Caiaphas.

Solomon was right: "A poor man is better than a liar." In reality Peter had everything and Caiaphas had nothing.

4. Beware of Independence (19:23)

"The fear of the Lord tendeth to life: and he that hath it shall abide satisfied; he shall not be visited with evil." The *Jehovah*

("Lord") of the Old Testament, of course, is the *Jesus* of the New Testament. Non-Christians entertain a variety of thoughts and emotions about God: ignorance of God, denial of God, hatred of God, terror of God. Those who know God, on the other hand, entertain a healthy fear [reverence] of God—a fear conditioned by a warm love for Him.

Once "the fear of the Lord" is established in our hearts, everything "tendeth to life." We see reverence for the Lord resulting in new life in the case of Saul of Tarsus. He was on the Damascus road when he caught his first recorded glimpse of the Lord. Armed with authority from the high priest in Jerusalem, Saul was headed toward the Syrian capital to wreak havoc in the church in Damascus. Then the Lord appeared to him in a blaze of light that paled the sun. A voice rang out, "Saul, Saul, why persecutest thou me?" Blinded by "the brightness of his glory," the grand inquisitor fell to the ground. "Who art thou, Lord?" he asked. "I am Jesus," came the reply (Acts 9:4-5; Hebrews 1:3). From that day forward, Saul was never the same. The fear of the Lord entered his soul and he entered into *spiritual* life. Soon he abandoned his old name and became well known as the apostle Paul.

Paul had his second recorded glimpse of the Lord when he was stoned at Lystra (Acts 14:19-20). Later he told the Corinthians that he had been caught up into Heaven and had seen things untranslatable (2 Corinthians 12:1-5). He had entered into *resurrection* life. From then on, he lived on resurrection ground, triumphant over all the vicissitudes of time—no longer a constant visitor to Romans 7, but a permanent resident of Romans 8.

Paul wrote to the Ephesians that God "hath raised us up together, and made us sit together in heavenly places in Christ Jesus" (Ephesians 2:6). About the same time he wrote to the Philippians, "I count all things but loss...that I may know him, and the power of his resurrection" (Philippians 3:8-10). He also wrote to the Colossians, "Ye are...buried with him in baptism, wherein also ye are risen with him through the faith of the operation of God, who hath raised him from the dead" (Colossians 2:11-12). It is a high-water mark in our Christian lives when we who have spiritual life realize our identification with Christ and enter into resurrection life.

When Paul was in Rome and Nero was on the rampage, the apostle's doom was sure. It was only a matter of time before he would face the executioner's ax. Paul wrote:

> I am now ready to be offered, and the time of my departure is at hand. I have fought a good fight, I have finished my course,

> I have kept the faith: Henceforth there is laid up for me a crown of righteousness, which the Lord, the righteous judge, shall give me at that day (2 Timothy 4:6-8).

Paul was about to enter into the enjoyment of *eternal* life (Romans 6:23). As Proverbs 19:23 says, he who has life "shall abide satisfied; he shall not be visited with evil." Evil itself will be fended off. Hallelujah! What a Savior!

5. Beware of Indolence (19:24)

"A slothful man hideth his hand in his bosom, and will not so much as bring it to his mouth again." The word translated "bosom" here is rendered elsewhere as "dish" (2 Kings 21:13). The picture suggested is that of an oriental meal where the guests recline around a table and help themselves from a communal dish. Sometimes the host dips a piece of bread into the dish, scoops up an especially succulent tidbit, and hands it to a guest he wants to honor. Among the other guests is a man too lazy to take a morsel and carry it to his mouth. Instead he simply opens his mouth, implying that food should be placed there by his host. The picture, of course, is ludicrous. Its hyperbole depicts gross laziness. A person who refuses to do even the smallest, most necessary things for his comfort and well-being invites our scorn and revulsion.

Laziness is a bad habit and it worsens with time, but probably no one has ever seen such well-developed indolence as that lampooned by Solomon. I have never seen a man too lazy to feed himself, but I have seen other evidences of extreme slothfulness.

Some years ago when I was on a preaching tour in the West, I spent a week in the home of a church member whom I will not name. It was early spring and although the weather was still cold, the family did not seem to feel it. In fact they left the front door open most of the time. I stayed in my room and tried to keep warm by huddling in blankets while I sat at the desk.

The two sons shared an upstairs room. I passed their room a dozen times a day and noticed that their door was always tightly closed. One day I discovered why it was kept shut, for as I was walking by their room, the door happened to be wide open and the light was on. The room looked as though it had been bombed and I had little doubt that the boys were under strict orders to keep the door shut.

On the bunk beds were tangled heaps of sheets, blankets, and pillows. The bedspreads were on the floor. The shelves were covered with dust and every conceivable kind of junk—apple cores, orange peels, banana skins, and scraps of paper. Candle grease had run down the dresser. On top of the dresser were needles, knick-knacks, a couple of broken chessmen, an empty matchbox, and a grimy photograph or two. The floor was a disaster of smelly socks, dirty shoes, dirty underwear, crumpled shirts and sweaters, and discarded pants and jackets—all inextricably intermingled with broken hockey sticks, empty cartons, piles of newspapers, and dirty dishes. A guitar with two broken strings stood forlornly in one corner. A shotgun dangled precariously from a nail in the wall; a box of live cartridges had fallen down and its contents were scattered about. Over the scene brooded an odd odor of sweaty socks, musty underwear, decaying fruit, and unwashed humanity.

When I was safely ensconced in the none-too-clean room assigned to me, I was glad to hear the door down the hall bang. The bang was accompanied by a not-too-polite expression voiced by the boys' mother. I opened the window and, in an effort to get the lingering odor from my nostrils, breathed in the piercing Canadian air.

The laziness of those two boys is the kind of indolence Solomon was deploring. And since Solomon was writing under the direct inspiration and illumination of the Holy Spirit, we know that God condemns this kind of slothfulness.

### 6. Beware of Insolence (19:25)

"Smite a scorner, and the simple will beware: and reprove one that hath understanding, and he will understand knowledge." The principle here is that of making a public example of a particular person or a particular group of people in order to send a warning to others. An illustration of this principle is found in C. S. Forester's novel *Mr. Midshipman Hornblower.*

In the story Horatio Hornblower, barely more than a boy, had recently joined the *Justinian* as its lowliest midshipman. A January gale was blowing and although the warship was at anchor, its motion brought on an embarrassing bout of seasickness for the new recruit. He was surveyed with callous indifference and a generous measure of contempt by the men in the wardroom. He was lonely, shy, and desperately unhappy. The ship's captain, a sick and melancholy officer who took little interest in his men, interviewed Hornblower and dismissed him to his duties and the "tender mercies" of the wardroom.

Hornblower's life was made miserable by Midshipman Simpson,

a born bully whose temper was not improved by the fact that he had just failed an examination for a commission as lieutenant. Simpson took a dislike to young Hornblower and used every opportunity to put him down. The fact that Hornblower was a clever mathematician who excelled in navigation made matters worse. Since Simpson was big and strong, it would have done the undersized Hornblower no good to try to fight the bully. Eventually the wretched young man began to think of suicide. Death, he believed, would be better than the life he was forced to live.

One day Simpson and Hornblower were part of a press gang trying to fill out the ship's complement of men by raiding inns in nearby Spithead. The raiding party was comprised of men from various ships in port. Before going back to their ships, they stopped at an inn for a meal and later began a game of cards. Hornblower's retentive memory and natural cleverness with figures stood him in good stead. He was doing so well that Simpson, a constant loser, accused him of cheating. Hornblower recognized his chance; he instantly challenged the bully to a duel.

The duel brought up the question of weapons. The seventeen-year-old Hornblower confessed that he had no skill with a sword. "It had better be pistols," said his second. That idea was not much better, however, because Simpson was presumed to have some skill with pistols. Then Hornblower ventured the cold-blooded suggestion that made him famous throughout the squadron: "We could make the chances exactly even," he said. "Have two pistols, one loaded and the other empty. Simpson and I would take our choice, without knowing which was which. Then we stand within a yard of each other, and at the word, we fire."[13]

How the duel was fought and what the result was, is of course the subject of the rest of the chapter. The point is that Hornblower sent a message to the bully—and everyone else—that he was not to be picked on. He made a public example of Simpson. Smiting a scorner, said Solomon, will smarten everyone up.

## D. Wasters Considered (19:26-27)

Considering wasters, Solomon looked first at their *shameful conduct:* "He that wasteth his father, and chaseth away his mother, is a son that causeth shame, and bringeth reproach" (Proverbs 19:26).

Jeroboam, the first ruler of the northern kingdom of Israel, is an Old Testament illustration of a waster. He was given the chance of a lifetime: the opportunity to found a dynasty that could have lasted until the coming of Christ. Instead he plunged the ten tribes into gross idolatry and thereafter became known as "Jeroboam the son of Nebat, who made Israel to sin" (see 2 Kings 15:9, for example). He not only brought dishonor upon himself; he also brought shame upon his father.

Judas is a New Testament illustration of a waster. Two of the Lord's disciples were named Judas. One of them, carefully distinguished from the traitor, was the brother (or perhaps son) of James (Luke 6:16).[14] Judas is also called Thaddaeus and Lebbaeus Thaddaeus (Mark 3:18; Matthew 10:3). The name *Judas* must have been a heavy cross for him to bear because that name was forever disgraced by the other disciple who bore it: Judas Iscariot, the son of Simon Iscariot (see John 6:71 in the Revised Standard Version).

Judas Iscariot was a great waster, as Solomon would have put it. Jesus, a "greater than Solomon" (Matthew 12:42), called Judas "the son of perdition" (John 17:12). The word translated "perdition" *(apoleia)*, which can also be translated "destruction," literally means "to waste." In other words, Jesus called Judas "a son of waste." It was a waste of creative energy to make him. It was a waste of parental love and care to raise him. He wasted the opportunity that was his as a disciple. He wasted the precious blood of Christ that was shed for him.

We do not know how Judas behaved as a boy. We only know how he behaved as a man, but that is enough. From what he did to Jesus, we can infer that Judas treated his parents shabbily. He wasted his father (the word translated "wasteth" in Proverbs 19:26 means "preyeth upon"). We can well believe that Judas stole from his father and chased away his mother. In any case he brought eternal shame upon them, for every time his infamous name is mentioned, so is theirs; he was Judas *Iscariot.*

As Solomon continued his consideration of wasters, he looked next at *shoddy counselors:* "Cease, my son, to hear the instruction that causeth to err from the words of knowledge" (Proverbs 19:27). A bad teacher is worse than no teacher at all.

A preacher friend of mine told me about a bitter experience he had with "shoddy counselors." In his student days he was exploring the possibility of going to the mission field and he was told that he would have to enroll in one of his denomination's seminaries. The mission board recommended one with a notorious record of promulgating soul-damning liberal theology.

My friend went to that seminary. The subject of one of his first classes was the Gospel of John. The teacher opened the session by boldly announcing her utter rejection of the accepted view that the fourth Gospel was written by the disciple John. She said it had really been written for the followers of John so that at his death they would not fall apart. They had been worshiping the disciple, she claimed, and John—not Jesus—was the focus of the Gospel.

Noticing the astonished reaction of a number of her students, she continued, "When I was first told that the Bible contained errors, I wept for three days. I was the daughter of a conservative pastor. Now I have accepted the fact that there are errors in the Bible. It has been proven to me." Surveying the class she added, "Hang in there! It's not the end of the world to discover errors in the Bible. You'll get over it."

This teacher was an apostate and her ideas about the Gospel of John were nonsense. It is an undeniable fact that by the last quarter of the second century the fourth Gospel was accepted as authoritative and the Lord's disciple John was accepted as its writer. Apart from an offhand statement by Papias, the church fathers had no doubt as to who wrote the Gospel. Irenaeus, Clement of Alexandria, Tertullian, and Eusebius—all of whom had access to many works now lost to us—agreed that the apostle John wrote the Gospel that bears his name.

Modern scholars such as Meyer, Lange, Godet, Lightfoot, and Westcott support the conservative view, and the internal evidence of the book is impressive and convincing. The author was obviously a Jew, a native of Palestine, an eyewitness of the events he described, and an apostle—in short, the apostle John. It is criminal for a teacher to hand out rationalism to eager students who earnestly desire to be taught the Word of God and to be equipped for the ministry.

How did my friend respond? He protested and left the school. He was wise enough to heed Proverbs 19:27. Although his denomination called the school a theological *seminary,* he would call it a theological *cemetery.*

## E. Witnesses Considered (19:28-29)

Solomon pointed next to *the testimony of the scornful witness:* "An ungodly witness scorneth judgment: and the mouth of the wicked devoureth iniquity" (Proverbs 19:28). The expression translated "ungodly witness" can be rendered "a witness of Belial." A false witness does the work of the devil himself.

The false prophet of Revelation 13 will be an "ungodly witness." The soul-twin of the antichrist, the false prophet will have two horns, look like a lamb, and speak like a dragon. His words will be set on fire of Hell itself. Although he will seem harmless, he will exercise all the antichrist's power. The false prophet will work astonishing miracles and endow the image of the antichrist with life and speech—not through electronic wizardry but by a genuine Satanic miracle. The false prophet will persuade the world to worship the image of the antichrist and receive the beast's mark. The mark will be a badge of loyalty to the empire and proof of adherence to the new religion. Those who do not receive the mark will suffer persecution of such horrendous dimensions that it will make the Nazi holocaust seem like a Sunday school picnic.

The false prophet will be the ultimate "witness of Belial." The world has already known many false witnesses. Buddha was one, and so was Muhammad. Joseph Smith, Charles Russell, Madame Blavatsky, Mary Baker Eddy, Karl Marx, and Joseph Goebbels (Hitler's propaganda chief) were all false witnesses. But nobody will compare with this coming apostate Jewish orator whose golden tongue will set men's hearts ablaze.

Hitler had such a tongue. When he so desired, he could speak with a sweet voice, a soft voice, a low-keyed voice, a voice full of reasonableness, a caressing voice, or a spellbinding voice. Or, as when he was fully committed to take over Czechoslovakia, he could whip himself up into a fury. His voice would become a high-pitched scream and he would pour out diatribes of hate. People would be literally shaken with emotion; women would swoon and men would sob.

The false prophet will outdo Hitler and all the others who have gone before. The mass of people will respond to the false prophet's threats and promises. The eloquent oratory of this "witness of Belial" will be so utterly convincing that God will send an angel to warn men against believing the lies they are being told (Revelation 14:9-11). Another angel will preach the "everlasting gospel" in order to win people to God at the last moment before it is forever too late (14:6-7).

But the false prophet will receive his due, for *the troubles of the scornful witness* are inevitable. As Solomon said, "Judgments are prepared for scorners, and stripes for the back of fools" (Proverbs 19:29). Retribution is often received in this life, but sometimes punishment is delayed until the life to come.

Proverbs 19:29 is well illustrated by the life of H. G. Wells. This popular English author seemed to take perverse delight in poking fun at Christians and God. Wells was filled with a bitter, blasphemous hatred of God and an angry animosity toward the Bible. In 1934 at the age of 68 he wrote *Experiment in Autobiography.*

In this book (more than three hundred thousand words long) he expressed his hatred and anger and made some statements so foul as to be unrepeatable.

At the end of his autobiography Wells was still longing for "an escape from individual vexations and frustrations, from the petty overwhelming pains, anxieties and recriminations of the too acutely ego-centred life."[15] What an amazing confession! Every life outside of Christ is certainly an "acutely ego-centred life." That is what Christ came to deliver us from.

Shortly before he died, Wells wrote *Mind at the End of Its Tether.* A small book of fewer than forty pages, it is an agonizing scream of utter hopelessness and despair. It compares our world to "a convoy lost in darkness on an unknown rocky coast, with quarreling pirates in the chartroom and savages clambering up the sides of the ships to plunder and do evil as the whim may take them."[16] As the apostle Paul said centuries ago, a man without God is a man without hope (Ephesians 2:12).

One night during World War II when London was being bombed, Elizabeth Bowen found Wells visibly shaking with fright. "It's not the bombs," he told her. "It's the dark. I've been afraid of the dark all my life." H. G. Wells has now gone out into what the Bible calls "the blackness of darkness for ever" (Jude 13). Rightfully afraid of the dark, he was a fool not to come to the Light.

After his death he was cremated. His two sons took his ashes to the Isle of Wight and cast them into the sea. If Wells thought that this last act of defiance would help him, he was sadly mistaken, as the Bible at which he scoffed would have told him (Revelation 20:13).

Said Solomon, "Judgments are prepared for scorners, and stripes for the back of fools." He was far wiser than H. G. Wells, who turned out to be the fool of whom the psalmist wrote (Psalm 14:1).

## F. Wine Considered (20:1)

"Wine is a mocker, strong drink is raging: and whosoever is deceived thereby is not wise." Here Solomon began a series of warnings against strong drink. Wise people, he said, will not be deceived by it. Other proverbs in the series state that wine leads to poverty (21:17; 23:21); it produces sorrow, strife, needless wounds, gossip, and red eyes (23:29-30); however desirable it may seem, it is a deceiver and harms all who drink it (23:31-32); it fills a person's thoughts with lust and leads to adultery (23:33); and, finally, it is addictive (23:35).

Addiction to strong drink was the undoing of Alexander the

Great. He conquered the world before he was forty, then died prematurely because he could not conquer his desire for alcohol. Today eleven million Americans are hooked on alcohol and seventy-six million have alcoholics in their families. Studies show that 10 to 15 percent of all Americans over sixty are alcoholics.[17] What incredible folly it is to take that first drink.

Suppose we go to the airport to board a plane and as we present our tickets at the gate, we are told that one seat in every eighteen will fall through the floor before the flight is over. Startled, we ask which seats will fall. The attendant says, "We don't know, but probably more of them are on the left side of the plane." What person in his right mind would board such a plane? When someone takes his first drink, he is like a person who would board that plane. To embark on such a course is to risk becoming a confirmed drunkard before the journey of life is over.

Throughout the Scriptures drunkenness is treated as a sin. The first recorded drunkard in Scripture was Noah (Genesis 9:20-27). Reading on, we learn that Lot was forever disgraced while he was drunk (Genesis 19:30-36). Nabal added drunkenness to his other unlovely traits (1 Samuel 25:36). Attempting to cover his own guilt, David added to it by trying to get Uriah drunk (2 Samuel 11:13).

In the 1960s the American Medical Association declared alcoholism, a polite euphemism for drunkenness, to be a disease. Men may classify drunkenness as a sickness, but the Holy Spirit classifies drunkenness as an excommunicating sin of the flesh (1 Corinthians 5:11; Galatians 5:21). People are not normally culpable for sickness, but God holds them culpable for drunkenness.

A tendency to become an alcoholic may indeed be inherited, since the sins of the fathers are often visited on the children (Exodus 20:5). This possibility, however, merely strengthens the case for total abstinence.

If alcoholism is a disease, why does the government allow brewers to spend enormous sums of money to promote the products that spread the disease? The industry lobbies vigorously against the various "sin taxes" placed on their destructive products. Brewers invest vast sums of money to improve their image and persuade people to buy their brands of poison. According to one official statement, brewers and beer distributors spend up to twenty million dollars a year just to market their products on college campuses—thus encouraging drinking and "contributing to poor grades, excessive vandalism, many injuries, and not so infrequently, death."[18]

Not all doctors concur with the AMA. Some bluntly label alcoholism as "learned behavior" and "a style of life." Many ordinary people would agree. They view drunkards as nuisances or as little better than criminals. Most people whose loved ones have been killed by intoxicated drivers would not consider alcoholism a disease. In one year alone (1990) alcoholism cost Americans 136 billion dollars and more than sixty-five thousand lives; twenty-two thousand of these deaths occurred on the highways.[19]

Scripture says, "Wine is a mocker, strong drink is raging: and whosoever is deceived thereby is not wise." We would be much wiser to accept God's evaluation of alcohol than man's. To write drunkenness off as a disease is a modern deception.

## G. Wisdom Considered (20:2-7)

### 1. Some Cautions (20:2-4)

#### a. A Sure Way to Be Punished (20:2-3)

One sure way to be punished, cautioned Solomon, is to *infuriate the king:* "The fear of a king is as the roaring of a lion: whoso provoketh him to anger sinneth against his own soul" (Proverbs 20:2).

Although Sir Thomas More was a Roman Catholic and vigorously opposed England's independence from Rome, he demonstrated courage and conviction in daring to stand up against the roaring rage of Henry VIII.

More's intelligence and attractive manners early gained him a place on the staff of John Morton, who was archbishop of Canterbury, lord chancellor of England, and friend of Henry VII. Morton sent his protégé to Oxford, where he came under the spell of such men as Erasmus. After Oxford, More studied law and later became one of England's leading lawyers. Then as a member of Parliament he opposed the financial demands of Henry VII and fell into disfavor.

In 1509 eighteen-year-old Henry VIII came to the throne. He fancied himself a scholar and, seeking to surround himself with men of learning, cultivated the friendship of Thomas More. The two were often seen strolling arm in arm about the palace grounds.

Honors came swiftly to More. He was made a privy councilor in 1514, he was knighted in 1521, and he became the first layman to occupy the powerful seat of lord chancellor of England in 1529. In this position he sought to reform the monasteries, uphold the church of Rome, and curb "heresy." More was noted for his diligence and honesty. He looked forward to a time when war would be outlawed, when there would be no class distinctions, and when all men would be free. Soon, however, he had forebodings about the headstrong king. More knew that to provoke Henry VIII was "a sin unto death."

The king soon discovered that More was even more inflexible than his predecessor, Cardinal Wolsey, on the matter of the king's decision to divorce Catherine and marry Anne Boleyn. When Henry persisted, More resigned his post. Then the king obtained from the pliable Parliament the Act of Supremacy, whereby he overthrew the power of the papacy in England. More opposed the king and refused to acknowledge him as head of the Church of England. Enraged, Henry had More committed to the Tower of London. Steadfastly refusing to yield, he was accused of high treason and beheaded. Solomon was right: one sure way to be punished is to infuriate the king. Few men have the courage to face the king's wrath.

Another sure way to be punished is to *interfere in a thing:* "It is an honour for a man to cease from strife: but every fool will be meddling" (Proverbs 20:3). In other words, it takes two to make a fight.

Abraham was determined to "cease from strife." Consider the time when he and his nephew Lot had so much cattle that strife broke out between their herdsmen, who squabbled over the available pastureland. The arguing was especially reprehensible because "the Canaanite and the Perizzite dwelled then in the land" (Genesis 13:7). For believers to quarrel is bad enough, but to fight in front of the unsaved is even worse.

Abraham acted quickly, stating, "We be brethren" (13:8) He knew that the things that bind us are more important than the things that divide us. He suggested that he and Lot part company—a solution that Lot would have done well to reject. Abraham also made his nephew an exceedingly generous offer. "You choose the land you want," he said in effect. "I'll take what is left." Since God had deeded all the land to Abraham, this offer was a remarkable surrender of his own rights.

Had Lot been honorable, he would have refused to take advantage of his godly uncle. Had Lot been spiritual, he would have refused to walk away from the fellowship of a man who was "the friend of God"—just for the sake of financial gain. Moreover, had Lot asked the Lord what to do, he would never have chosen the Jordan valley with its proximity to the foul, doomed city of Sodom. But Lot did choose that valley—to his ultimate spiritual undoing. His name has been handed down to posterity stained with dishonor, whereas Abraham's name has come to us ablaze with glory and honor. As Solomon said, "It is an honor for a man to cease from strife."

The rest of the verse—"every fool will be meddling"—tells us to mind our own business. This proverb is reminiscent of the story Uncle Remus told about Brer Rabbit, Brer Fox, and the Tar-Baby. Unable to catch Brer Rabbit, Brer Fox decided to capitalize on Brer Rabbit's inability to avoid involving himself in things that didn't concern him. The fox made what he called a Tar-Baby—a creation that looked like a baby but was covered with tar. Said Uncle Remus:

> He tuck dish yer Tar-Baby en he sot 'er in de big road, en den he lay off in de bushes fer to see what de news wuz gwineter be. En he didn't hatter wait long, nudder, kaze bimeby here come Brer Rabbit pacin' down de road—lippity-clippity, clippity-lippity—dez ez sassy ez a jay-bird. Brer Fox, he lay low. Brer Rabbit come prancin' 'long twel he spy de Tar-Baby, en den he fotch up on his behime legs like he wus 'stonished. De Tar-Baby, she sot dar, she did, en Brer Fox, he lay low.
>
> "Mawnin'!" sez Brer Rabbit, sezee—"nice wedder dis mawnin'," sezee.
>
> Tar-Baby ain't sayin' nothin', en Brer Fox, he lay low.
>
> "How duz yo' sym'tums seem ter segashuate?" sez Brer Rabbit, sezee.
>
> Brer Fox, he wink his eye slow, en lay low, en de Tar-Baby, she ain't sayin' nothin'.
>
> "How you come on, den? Is you deaf?" sez Brer Rabbit, sezee, "Kaze if you is, I kin holler louder," sezee.
>
> Tar-Baby stay still, en Brer Fox, he lay low.
>
> "Youer stuck up, dat's w'at you is," sez Brer Rabbit, sezee, "en I'm gwineter kyore you, dat's w'at I'm a gwineter do," sezee.
>
> Brer Fox, he sorter chuckle in his stummick, he did, but Tar-Baby ain't sayin' nothin'.
>
> "I'm gwineter larn you howter talk ter 'specttubble fokes ef hit's de las' ack," sez Brer Rabbit, sezee. "Ef you don't take off dat hat en tell me howdy, I'm gwineter bus' you wide open," sezee.
>
> Tar-Baby stay still, en Brer Fox, he lay low.
>
> Brer Rabbit keep on axin' 'im, en de Tar-Baby, she keep on sayin' nothin', twel present'y Brer Rabbit draw back wid his fis', he did, en blip he tuck 'er side er de head....His fis' stuck, en he can't pull loose. De tar hilt 'im. But Tar-Baby, she stay still, en Brer Fox, he lay low.

"Ef you don't lemme loose, I'll knock you agin," sez Brer Rabbit, sezee, en wid dat he fotch 'er a wipe wid de udder han', en dat stuck. Tar-Baby, she ain't sayin' nothin', and Brer Fox, he lay low.

"Tu'n me loose, 'fo I kick de natal stuffin' outen you," sez Brer Rabbit, sezee, but de Tar-Baby, she ain't sayin' nothin'. She des hilt on, en den Brer Rabbit lose de use er his feet in de same way. Brer Fox, he lay low. Den Brer Rabbit squall out dat ef de Tar-Baby don't tu'n 'im loose he butt 'er cranksided. En den he butted, en his head got stuck. Den Brer Fox, he sa'ntered fort', lookin' des ez innocent ez one er yo' mammy's mockin'-birds.

"Howdy, Brer Rabbit," sez Brer Fox, sezee. "You look sorter stuck up dis mawnin'," sezee, en den he rolled on de groun', en laughed en laughed twel he couldn't laugh no mo'. "I speck you'll take dinner wid me dis time, Brer Rabbit."

The little boy listening to the story asked, "Did the fox eat the rabbit?"

Uncle Remus replied, "Dat's all de fur de tale goes."[20]

We can be sure that Solomon would have been delighted with the yarns about Brer Rabbit.

### b. A Sure Way to Be Poor (20:4)

"The sluggard will not plow by reason of the cold; therefore shall he beg in harvest, and have nothing." This proverb underlines the old law of sowing and reaping. Solomon was exposing once again the folly of laziness. He could see no excuse for the sluggard's behavior.

Nonproductive members of society are always a problem. Their chronic poverty makes them a continual burden on the productive members of society who are taxed to provide social aid. Nobody begrudges the help the welfare system gives to those who are old, sick, or disabled. Able-bodied people who *will* not work are the problem. The task of the philanthropist is to determine who deserves help.

In the big cities beggars are everywhere, confronting people on the sidewalks, in their cars, and on the subway. Houses of worship are visited by an almost endless stream of drifters who come looking for handouts. Inner-city churches have been stung so often that many of them have established policies and procedures for screening requests for help. Professional beggars have well-rehearsed routines, most of which have long since worn thin with pastors. Often hardened panhandlers will not go near the Red Cross, The Salvation Army, the city mission, or other charities and agencies that have the resources and experience to help needy people; these beggars know only too well that the staffs of these organizations quickly weed out phonies.

Even in the affluent United States the number of homeless people is estimated to run anywhere from three hundred thousand to nearly two million.[21] One-third of the homeless are said to be mentally ill and there is no doubt that many of them genuinely need help. They would work if they could. But what about the shiftless crowd who are too lazy to work? The big cities are getting fed up with people who are content to move from place to place looking for charity. In 1988 the mayor of New York City, Ed Koch, actually urged people to help banish the panhandlers by refusing to give them anything. "Give to established charities," he said. What was his rationale? "Many people who panhandle just don't want to work."[22] Solomon came to the same conclusion three thousand years ago.

2. Some Commendations (20:5-7)

a. The Deep Man (20:5)

"Counsel in the heart of man is like deep water; but a man of understanding will draw it out." We sometimes describe people as "deep" or "shallow." The deep man is thoughtful, wise, and usually silent. Still waters, we say, run deep. Just as the deep waters of a well have to be drawn out, the deep man is often reserved. His acquaintances have to get to know him and learn how to draw out his thoughts. The thoughtless man, on the other hand, chatters like a brook that babbles to this pebble or that rolling stone. Both the brook and the shallow man can be heard from a distance.

At the beginning of John's Gospel we meet two contrasting people who need the counsel of Jesus. One is a man; the other is a woman. One is a Jew; the other is a Samaritan. One is the picture of moral rectitude; the other has had five husbands. One is a high-caste Hebrew; the other is an outcast half-breed. One comes to Jesus by night; the other comes at noon. One deliberately seeks out Jesus; the other stumbles across Him unexpectedly. One comes with profound questions; the other has all the answers. One becomes a secret disciple; the other brings many others to Christ. One begins the conversation courteously, calling Jesus a rabbi; the other begins the conversation contemptuously, calling Jesus a "Jew." Part of the genius of the gospel is that people at opposite ends of the social, racial, religious, economic, moral, cultural, and intellectual poles can be made one in Christ.

I am referring, of course, to Nicodemus and the woman at the well. They were utterly different, but they had one thing in common: they both were able to draw out of the Lord Jesus that which they needed most. Nicodemus had a mental need; the woman at the well had a moral need. Jesus answered both their needs by revealing their much deeper spiritual needs.

Nicodemus with his mental need began by saying, "We know" (John 3:2). The woman with her moral need responded to Jesus by wistfully saying, "I know" (4:25). The Lord answered Nicodemus by referring him to his Bible—to divine revelation (3:14). The Lord ended the conversation with the woman by referring her to Himself—to divine revelation. "I...am he," He said (4:26). Nicodemus went home, eventually to take his stand for Christ in the Sanhedrin. The woman went home to take her stand for Christ in Samaria.

Jesus was only too willing to be drawn out. He still is. No matter what our needs are, we will find in Him what Nicodemus found: how to be born again. We will find in Him what the woman at the well found: a well of water springing up into everlasting life. Jesus talked to Nicodemus about the wind and to the woman about the well, and He will talk to us about our greatest needs. The counsel of His heart is like deep water. If we are people of understanding, we can draw it out.

### b. The Dependable Man (20:6-7)

"Most men will proclaim every one his own goodness: but a faithful man who can find?" (Proverbs 20:6) Speaking of the dependable man, Solomon was saying in effect, *"How rare he is!"*

The Bible is full of examples of people who proclaimed their own goodness. Cain proclaimed his own goodness by founding a new religion—and a terrible religion of hate and murder it turned out to be (Genesis 4:1-16). Job proclaimed his own goodness in three chapters (Job 29–31) by using the personal pronouns *I, me,* and *my* 195 times in 96 verses. The Pharisee of Luke 18:11 "prayed...with himself"! Saul of Tarsus imagined himself to be a very fine fellow, the man most likely to succeed, the Sanhedrin's man of the year, "an Hebrew of the Hebrews" (Philippians 3:5).

This syndrome can afflict even the most godly. Consider the case of Elijah. What a mighty man he was! A mountain of a man, he towered head and shoulders above prophets, priests, and kings. He was a veritable Melchizedek, introduced without father or mother or beginning or ending of days (Hebrews 7:3). We have no knowledge of Elijah's background, but his name tells us all we need to know; it means "My God is Jehovah." We think of Elijah and we think of God! Alexander Whyte wrote, "He was a Mount-Sinai of a man, with a heart like a thunderstorm."[23]

When we think of Elijah, we see him standing before wicked King Ahab and bluntly proclaiming a drought on Israel until further notice because of Ahab's and Jezebel's sins. We see Elijah calling down fire from heaven, slaying the false prophets of Baal, and then summoning a storm to end more than three years of drought. We see Elijah standing before God as the wind rends the mountains, the earthquake shakes the earth, and the fire plays around the Horeb heights. We see Elijah choosing Elisha to be his apprentice. We see Elijah denouncing Ahab for the murder of Naboth and foretelling the deaths of Ahab and Jezebel. We see Elijah calling down fire from heaven to consume company after company of soldiers sent to arrest him. When we think of Elijah, we see him being taken home to glory in a chariot of fire.

We never think that such a man could ever have stooped to proclaim his own goodness. Yet that is just what he did after the Carmel conflict when depression set in and he fled from Jezebel to the shades of Sinai. There he was confronted with a question: "What doest thou here, Elijah?" (1 Kings 19:9) What a question for God to ask! Read it again and again, each time putting the emphasis on a different word. Then listen to Elijah's dismal reply: "I have been very jealous for the Lord God of hosts: for the children of Israel have forsaken thy covenant, thrown down thine altars, and slain thy prophets with the sword; and I, even I only, am left; and they seek my life, to take it away" (19:10). And as though once were not enough, he repeated all that a few minutes later (19:14). The Lord's answer was in effect a resounding "Nonsense!" His actual words were a blunt statement that He knew seven thousand people who had not bowed the knee to Baal (19:18).

Giving Elijah the name and address of one of these faithful men, the Lord said, "Elisha the son of Shaphat of Abel-meholah shalt thou anoint to be prophet in thy room" (1 Kings 19:16). A man like Elijah is rare, but God always knows where to find one when He needs one.

Solomon had more to say about the dependable man: "The just man walketh in his integrity: his children are blessed after him" (Proverbs 20:7). His true source of wealth is his children, who follow in their father's footsteps. *How rich he is!*

Amram walked in his integrity, and although he and Jochebed lived in a slave hut on the banks of the Nile in the Goshen ghetto, their children were blessed. We know very little about this godly couple, except that their faith overcame their fear and they defied the decree of the Egyptian tyrant mandating that they murder their son Moses. The name *Jochebed* meant "God my glory," and Jochebed moved like the shekinah glory-cloud around that prison compound and turned her hovel into a suburb of Heaven. The name *Amram* signified "a high people." So with a father to carry their thoughts on high and a mother to bring Heaven's glory down to earth, it is no wonder that the children of that remarkable home were a Moses, an Aaron, and a Miriam.

The first thing we read about Amram is that he was a Levite: "And there went a man of the house of Levi, and took to wife a daughter of Levi" (Exodus 2:1). It was not revealed until later, but there was something special about the tribe of Levi. The Levites were to be the priestly tribe, the tribe set apart for God. The tribe was to own no separate territory because it was to have its inheritance in God. The name *Levi* communicated the idea of being "attached" to someone, and the tribe was to be attached to God. Amram did not take that attachment lightly. Not wanting to be unequally yoked, he married a woman who had the same attachment he had. Amram walked in his integrity as a Levite, and his children were blessed.

We are told little else about Amram, but much else about his offspring. Moses became a mighty prophet; Aaron became a ministering priest; Miriam became a melodious partner. The three children of Amram took the lead in bringing God's people from the house of bondage to the boundaries of the promised land. Moses taught the children of Israel how to be saved (Exodus 12:13). Aaron taught them how to be sure (Leviticus 16). Miriam taught them how to be satisfied (Exodus 15:20-21). Well done, Amram and Jochebed! We wish you had written a book to tell us how you raised such an extraordinary family.

## III. The Fear of the Throne (20:8-30)

### A. The King's Power (20:8-9)

#### 1. His Legislation (20:8)

"A king that sitteth in the throne of judgment scattereth away all evil with his eyes." It takes nothing more than a look from a strong king to make evil men quail.

Doubtless Solomon had learned the power of a look. When a prisoner was brought before him, the king could just sit and stare right through the accused. Convinced that Solomon's eyes could read the hidden secrets of his soul, many a man had given himself away.

"Peter went out, and wept bitterly" when the Lord Jesus "turned, and looked upon [him]" (Luke 22:62,61). The sound of the cock heralding the dawn had not broken Peter—he had forgotten what Jesus had said. It was the look that made him realize he had failed the Lord. Instantly the oaths and curses died on his lips and horror seized his soul—all because of a look.

The believer at the judgment seat of Christ and the unbeliever at the great white throne will both quail before the look of the King. Every sin not under Christ's blood will be exposed to view. How ashamed we will be! How terrified, how self-accused, how self-condemned the Christ-rejecting unbeliever will be! There will be no escaping, no hiding from that look.

In *Oliver Twist* the memory of Nancy's eyes drove her murderer, Bill Sikes, half insane with terror. Charles Dickens described the dreadful deed that led to the look:

> The housebreaker freed one arm, and grasped his pistol. The certainty of immediate detection if he fired, flashed across his mind even in the midst of his fury; and he beat it twice with all the force he could summon, upon the upturned face that almost touched his own.
>
> She staggered and fell: nearly blinded with the blood that rained down from a deep gash in her forehead; but raising herself, with difficulty, on her knees, drew from her bosom a white handkerchief—Rose Maylie's own—and holding it up, in her folded hands, as high towards Heaven as her feeble strength would allow, breathed one prayer for mercy to her Maker.
>
> It was a ghastly figure to look upon. The murderer staggering backward to the wall, and shutting out the sight with his hand, seized a heavy club and struck her down.
>
> Of all bad deeds that, under cover of the darkness, had been committed within wide London's bounds since night hung over it, that was the worst. Of all the horrors that rose with an ill scent upon the morning air, that was the foulest and most cruel.
>
> The sun—the bright sun, that brings back, not light alone, but new life, and hope, and freshness to man—burst upon the

> crowded city in clear and radiant glory. Through costly-coloured glass and paper-mended window, through cathedral dome and rotten crevice, it shed its equal ray. It lighted up the room where the murdered woman lay. It did. He tried to shut it out, but it would stream in. If the sight had been a ghastly one in the dull morning, what was it, now, in all that brilliant light!
>
> He had not moved; he had been afraid to stir. There had been a moan and motion of the hand; and, with terror added to rage, he had struck and struck again. Once he threw a rug over it; but it was worse to fancy the eyes, and imagine them moving towards him, than to see them glaring upward, as if watching the reflection of the pool of gore that quivered and danced in the sunlight on the ceiling. He had plucked it off again. And there was the body—mere flesh and blood, no more—but such flesh, and so much blood!"

Sikes fled the scene, but he was pursued. Wrote Dickens:

> [After nightfall] he went on doggedly; but as he left the town behind him, and plunged into the solitude and darkness of the road, he felt a dread and awe creeping upon him which shook him to the core. Every object before him, substance or shadow, still or moving, took the semblance of some fearful thing; but these fears were nothing compared to the sense that haunted him of that morning's ghastly figure following at his heels. He could trace its shadow in the gloom, supply the smallest item of the outline, and note how stiff and solemn it seemed to stalk along. He could hear its garments rustling in the leaves, and every breath of wind came laden with that last low cry. If he stopped, it did the same. If he ran, it followed—not running too: that would have been a relief: but like a corpse endowed with the mere machinery of life, and borne on one slow melancholy wind that never rose or fell.
>
> At times, he turned, with desperate determination, resolved to beat this phantom off, though it should look him dead; but the hair rose on his head, and his blood stood still, for it had turned with him and was behind him then. He had kept it before him that morning, but it was behind him now—always. He leaned his back against a bank, and felt that it stood above him, visibly out against the cold night-sky. He threw himself upon the road—on his back upon the road. At his head it stood, silent, erect, and still—a living grave-stone, with its epitaph in blood.

> Let no man talk of murderers escaping justice, and hint that Providence must sleep. There were twenty score of violent deaths in one long minute of that agony of fear.
>
> There was a shed in a field he passed, that offered shelter for the night. Before the door, were three tall poplar trees, which made it very dark within; and the wind moaned through them with a dismal wail. He *could not* walk on, till daylight came again; and here he stretched himself close to the wall—to undergo a new torture.
>
> For now, a vision came before him, as constant and more terrible than that from which he had escaped. Those widely staring eyes, so lustreless and so glassy, that he had better borne to see them than think upon them, appeared in the midst of the darkness: light in themselves, but giving light to nothing. There were but two, but they were everywhere. If he shut out the sight, there came the room with every well-known object—some, indeed, that he would have forgotten, if he had gone over its contents from memory—each in its accustomed place. The body was in *its* place, and its eyes were as he saw them when he stole away. He got up, and rushed into the field without. The figure was behind him. He re-entered the shed, and shrunk down once more. The eyes were there, before he had laid himself along.
>
> And here he remained, in such terror as none but he can know, trembling in every limb, and the cold sweat starting from every pore, when suddenly there arose upon the night-wind the noise of distant shouting, and the roar of voices mingled in alarm and wonder. Any sound of men in that lonely place, even though it conveyed a real cause of alarm, was something to him. He regained his strength and energy at the prospect of personal danger; and springing to his feet, rushed into the open air.

In the end Sikes tried to hide in the noisome den where he was known, but the law and the mob found out where he was. In a last desperate attempt to escape, he grabbed a rope and climbed to the roof. While the crowd urged the police to go up after him, the murderer tied one end of the rope around a chimney stack and fashioned the other end into a running noose to put around himself. He figured he could let himself down nearly to the ground, but that was not to be. Dickens continued:

> At the very instant when he brought the loop over his head

> previous to slipping it beneath his arm-pits...at that very instant the murderer looking behind him on the roof, threw his arms above his head, and uttered a yell of terror.
>
> "The eyes again!" he cried in an unearthly screech.
>
> Staggering as if struck by lightning, he lost his balance and tumbled over the parapet. The noose was on his neck. It ran up with his weight, tight as a bowstring, and swift as the arrow it speeds. He fell for five-and-thirty feet. There was a sudden jerk, a terrific convulsion of the limbs; and there he hung, with the open knife clenched in his stiffening hand.[24]

Two haunting eyes—that was all it took to bring judgment to Bill Sikes. A look was enough. Often a look from Solomon on his throne was enough to scatter evil. One day a look from the Lord upon His throne will be enough to silence all sinners (Romans 3:19; Revelation 20:11-15).

2. His Limitation (20:9)

Although an earthly monarch is powerful, there are some things not even a king can do. "Who can say, I have made my heart clean, I am pure from my sin?"

Solomon knew only too well that he could not say he had made himself pure. He could sit in judgment on others, but he could not acquit himself. He was guilty of many sins. Yes, he could plead that polygamy was an accepted lifestyle under the Mosaic law, but how could he justify a *thousand* wives and concubines? Lust had mastered him long ago. He couldn't keep his eyes or his hands off an attractive woman. He had legalized his lust, but lust it remained—unbridled, unblushing, and unblessed.

We are all in the same boat. Our transgressions may not be the same as Solomon's, but like Job we have often cried: "Who can bring a clean thing out of an unclean? not one" (Job 14:4). The whole Bible takes a stand against our sin.

After God had taken Job in hand, he admitted, "Behold, I am vile" (Job 40:4). A short while later he said, "I abhor myself, and repent in dust and ashes" (42:6).

After Nathan confronted David, the guilty king confessed, "I have sinned against the Lord" (2 Samuel 12:13). In one of his penitential Psalms, David wrote: "I acknowledge my transgressions: and my sin is ever before me....Behold, I was shapen in iniquity; and in sin did my mother conceive me" (Psalm 51:3-5).

When Ezra discovered that the repatriated Jews—including the

Levites and the priests—were going back to the sins that had brought on the Babylonian captivity, he prayed, "O my God, I am ashamed and blush to lift up my face to thee, my God: for our iniquities are increased over our head, and our trespass is grown up unto the heavens" (Ezra 9:6).

When Isaiah began to prophesy, he poured out one woe after another on the people (Isaiah 5:8,11,18,20-22). But as soon as he saw the holiness of God, he cried out, "Woe is *me!* for I am undone; because I am a man of unclean lips, and I dwell in the midst of a people of unclean lips" (Isaiah 6:5, italics added). Obviously he was comparing his uncleanness to that of a leper.

When Daniel saw the Lord in all His awesome splendor, he wrote, "There remained no strength in me: for my comeliness was turned in me into corruption, and I retained no strength" (Daniel 10:8).

When the Lord told Peter to "launch out into the deep, and let down [his] nets," he immediately protested, "We have toiled all the night, and have taken nothing." Then, condescendingly, he added, "Nevertheless at thy word I will let down the net." When Peter did as he was told and caught an extraordinary number of fish, he was confident that he could pull in the net, but it broke. Undaunted, he beckoned to his partners. Together they managed to bring the great catch on board and Peter, still self-confident, believed that his troubles were over. But then the ships began to sink and Peter broke down. "He fell down at Jesus' knees, saying, Depart from me; for I am a sinful man, O Lord" (Luke 5:1-8).

When John, who had so often leaned on Jesus' breast, saw the glory of the risen Lord, he said, "When I saw him, I fell at his feet as dead" (Revelation 1:17).

Even the great apostle Paul could see, as he put it, "sin…working death in me…that sin by the commandment might become exceeding sinful" (Romans 7:13). Later he confessed himself to be the chief of sinners (1 Timothy 1:15).

"Who can say, I have made my heart clean…?" No one! But anyone can say that Christ has made it clean (1 John 1:8-9). We can thank God for His cleansing.

## B. The King's Principles (20:10-18)

### 1. Doing Right, Not Wrong (20:10)

"Divers weights, and divers measures, both of them are alike abomination to the Lord." God hates all double-dealing, but this proverb refers specifically to the practice of keeping two sets of books: one set for the auditor, tax inspector, and general public; and a second secret set showing the real position of the company. This illustration of fraud comes from the world of commerce, but "sharp" practices can surface anywhere when people enter into agreements, transactions, and common enterprises.

In his book *Death Sails With Magellan* Charles Ford developed the theory that the Portuguese navigator Ferdinand Magellan had a secret scheme in mind when he started out on his historic voyage. This scheme certainly was not the plan he presented when he sought financing from the king of Spain for an expedition to the rich Spice Islands. That plan was to find the islands by sailing westward, without trespassing on the hemisphere that the pope had assigned to Portugal.[25] According to Ford, Magellan really intended to sail eastward directly to the islands, thus defying the pope, Spain, Portugal, and everyone else.

Magellan set sail with five small patched-up caravels manned by a motley assortment of Spanish and Portuguese sailors. Heading southward, he hugged the west coast of Africa as long as he could. He managed to carry out his secret scheme until the squadron was becalmed off the coast of Sierra Leone. The disgruntled crew forced his hand, so he took the fleet westward across the Atlantic to the east coast of South America. Almost at the extreme southern reach of that continent the ships passed through what became known as the straits of Magellan and entered the Pacific ocean in 1520. Death, disease, and disaster pursued them.

The two heroes of Ford's story are Sebastian del Cano and Gonzalo. Del Cano, a hidalgo of Guetaria, was a true mariner with a sound knowledge of navigation. Gonzalo, a sailor from the fishing village of Vigo, Spain, was del Cano's friend and understudy. Del Cano realized that something was terribly wrong with Magellan's navigation and he confided some of his conclusions to his young friend.

One day toward the end of January 1521 Magellan asked the pilots of the caravels how they had determined the position of the expedition. They replied that as usual they had plotted the direction and speed of the vessels from one noon observation of the sun to the next, the line of travel being marked on charts or globes. So that possible errors might be averaged, the pilots had from time to time, as was their custom, exchanged their findings of latitude and longitude. Magellan told them their conclusions were wrong. The fleet, he said, had moved so far from the Pole Star that its pull on their compass needles had lessened. Indeed, he continued, the compass had swung two points more to the west than it should have, so their plotted positions were inaccurate; all their charts would have to be corrected accordingly.

Del Cano, who was not deceived, showed Gonzalo the expedition's true position. Del Cano had traced the route with a red line on his globe. He said:

> Do you see, Gonzalo, how our red line has already moved over those places where we thought there were islands? Magellan has a globe like this and he can see what we see. That is why he tells this fable about the Pole Star. He would have the pilots falsify their charts so that it would seem that we do not go as far to the west as is true. He wants no man to know where he takes this fleet. But you and I, Gonzalo, shall prick off the true route on my globe. Let the pilots be fooled by Magellan, we shall tell only what is the truth.[26]

Whether or not Ford's assessment of Magellan is true is for historians to decide. We do know that after the death of Magellan, del Cano successfully completed the circumnavigation of the globe and brought the two surviving caravels, laden with riches, safely back to Spain.

If Ford's story is true, it is an excellent illustration of Proverbs 20:10. Magellan used the navigational equivalents of "divers weights" and "divers measures" to deceive his captains and falsify records. The wily, unscrupulous, and ruthless Magellan came to a bad end. He was killed in a fight with the natives of Mactan island on April 27, 1521. And the celebrated straits of Magellan were not such a remarkable discovery after all. Had Magellan continued south a little longer, he could have sailed around the actual southern tip of Latin America without enduring the terrible winds, tides, and currents the expedition encountered in the implacable straits.

### 2. Discerning Right from Wrong (20:11-12)

#### a. The Human Judge (20:11)

"Even a child is known by his doings, whether his work be pure, and whether it be right." It doesn't take long to discern what the inner character of a person is. Even children reveal what they are like by the things they do and say.

Consider the case of Alexander, who was "known by his doings" long before "the Great" was appended to his name. Several pages of *The Lives of the Noble Grecians and Romans* are devoted to the future conqueror's childhood and youth. Plutarch wrote:

> His temperance, as to the pleasures of the body, was apparent in him in his very childhood, as he was with much difficulty incited to them, and always used them with great moderation; though in other things he was extremely eager and vehement, and in his love of glory, and the pursuit of it, he showed a solidity of high spirit and magnanimity far above his age. For he neither sought nor valued it upon every occasion, as his father Philip did (who affected to show his eloquence almost to a degree of pedantry, and took care to have the victories of his racing chariots at the Olympic games engraven on his coin), but when he was asked by some about him, whether he would run a race in the Olympic games, as he was very swift-footed, he answered, he would, if he might have kings to run with him....
>
> While he was yet very young, he entertained the ambassadors from the King of Persia, in the absence of his father, and entering much into conversation with them, gained so much upon them by his affability, and the questions he asked them, which were far from being childish or trifling (for he inquired of them the length of the ways, the nature of the road into inner Asia, the character of their king, how he carried himself to his enemies, and what forces he was able to bring into the field), that they were struck with admiration of him, and looked upon the ability so much famed of Philip to be nothing in comparison with the forwardness and high purpose that appeared thus early in his son....
>
> Philonicus the Thessalian brought the horse Bucephalus to Philip, offering to sell him for thirteen talents; but when they went into the field to try him, they found him so very vicious and unmanageable, that he reared up when they endeavoured to mount him, and would not so much as endure the voice of any of Philip's attendants. Upon which, as they were leading him away as wholly useless and intractable, Alexander, who stood by, said, "What an excellent horse do they lose for want of address and boldness to manage him!" Philip at first took no notice of what he said; but when he heard him repeat the same thing several times, and saw he was much vexed to see the horse sent away, "Do you reproach," said he to him, "those who are older than yourself, as if you knew more, and were

> better able to manage him than they?" "I could manage this horse," replied he, "better than others do." "And if you do not," said Philip, "what will you forfeit for your rashness?" "I will pay," answered Alexander, "the whole price of the horse." At this the whole company fell a-laughing; and as soon as the wager was settled amongst them, he immediately ran to the horse, and taking hold of the bridle, turned him directly towards the sun, having, it seems, observed that he was disturbed at and afraid of the motion of his own shadow; then letting him go forward a little, still keeping the reins in his hands, and stroking him gently when he found him begin to grow eager and fiery, he let fall his upper garment softly, and with one nimble leap securely mounted him, and when he was seated, by little and little drew in the bridle, and curbed him without either striking or spurring him. Presently, when he found him free from all rebelliousness, and only impatient for the course, he let him go at full speed, inciting him now with a commanding voice, and urging him also with his heel. Philip and his friends looked on at first in silence and anxiety for the result, till seeing him turn at the end of his career, and come back rejoicing and triumphing for what he had performed, they all burst out into acclamations of applause; and his father shedding tears, it is said, for joy, kissed him as he came down from his horse, and in his transport said, "O my son, look thee out a kingdom equal to and worthy of thyself, for Macedonia is too little for thee."[27]

"Even a child is known by his doings," said Solomon. Today we would add, "As the twig is bent, so grows the tree."

b. The Higher Judge (20:12)

If *we* can draw proper inferences from available data—from what we hear and see—how much more can God, for "the hearing ear, and the seeing eye, the Lord hath made even both of them."

The mechanism of an ear is marvelous. From the auricle, which acts as a sound-gathering device, a one-inch canal runs down to the eardrum. In this canal there are a large number of hairs and some four hundred wax glands that trap dust, insects, and other irritants and help guard against infection.

The eardrum, a thin tissue slightly more than a quarter of an inch across, separates the outer ear from the middle ear (the tympanic cavity), where the complicated process of hearing really begins.

Sound waves strike against the tissue like a drumstick beats against a drum in a band. Even faint vibrations set up by a mere whisper can push the eardrum inward. The movement is infinitesimal, maybe about a billionth of a centimeter, but it triggers an awesome sequence of events.

The middle ear resembles a six-sided box about the size of a bean. Three small bones—the anvil, the hammer, and the stirrup (or stapes)—are hinged together in the middle ear to pick up the tiny vibrations on the drum and amplify them twenty-two times. These vibrations are then passed on to the inner ear by way of an oval window attached to the stirrup.

In the complex inner ear the actual miracle of hearing takes place. The inner ear, which is well protected inside the skull, has so many intricate chambers and passageways that it is called a labyrinth. It is filled with fluid and has three connected parts: the vestibule, the semicircular canals, and the cochlea. The vestibule is the central part of the inner ear. Above and behind it are the three semicircular canals that give us our sense of balance. The cochlea, which looks like a snail shell, contains the sense organ for hearing—"the organ of Corti." The cochlea is studded with thousands of microscopic, hair-like nerve cells, each tuned to a particular vibration.

Suppose middle C has been picked up by the oval window leading to the inner ear. The cochlea's middle C hair cell vibrates, waving in the lymph fluid like seaweed in a tidal current. This activity produces a tiny electrical response that feeds into the auditory nerve. Having only the diameter of a lead pencil, the auditory nerve contains more than thirty thousand circuits. Thus the vibration of the hair cell stimulates the nerves attached to it, and the nerve in turn sends a message to the brain. As the cochleae in both ears feed in thousands of electrical messages, the brain unscrambles the data and converts it into meaningful sound. We do not know how the hearing mechanism of the body makes a distinction between sounds of different pitch. Surely the God who created the ear is a God of wonders.

The eye is even more marvelous than the ear. No bigger than a ping-pong ball, the eye contains tens of millions of electrical connections. It can handle a million and a half simultaneous messages.

The seeing process begins when rays of light fall on the dime-sized cornea, which bends them into orderly patterns. The pupil is an adjustable window that expands and contracts according to the amount of light that strikes the cornea. The lens, a small envelope of fluid about the size of a vitamin pill, is surrounded by strong muscles that adjust the eye for near or distant vision.

Lining the rear two-thirds of the eye is the retina. Although it covers less than a square inch, the retina contains 137 million light-sensitive receptor cells, including 130 million rods for black-and-white vision and several million cones for color vision. The rods, scattered all over the retina, react to even the smallest ray of light. Light reaching the rods bleaches rhodopsin, a colored pigment in the rods. This bleaching action generates an electrical response (a few millionths of a volt) that in turn is fed into the straw-sized optic nerve and carried to the brain. The entire complex electrochemical process takes about .002 of a second. Even more intricate is the process whereby the cones sort out color. The theory is that the cones have red, green, and blue bleachable pigments and that these colors are blended to make all the other hues.

Stereoscopic vision, the ability to judge depth, is achieved when the optic nerves from the two eyes fuse at the optic chiasma near the brain.

On a clear night the eye can detect light from a match several miles away. It can detect light from stars that are millions of light-years away. Unaided it can see an object as small as the point of a pin. With instruments it can see red blood cells so small that the head of a pin would be an ample arena for sixty thousand of them.

The evolutionist would have us believe that all these engineering and biochemical marvels just happened. Solomon knew better. He knew that the Lord made the eye and the ear.

We shouldn't need to be reminded that the God who made the ear is able to hear what we say and that the God who made the eye is able to see what we do. What we say and what we do cannot be hidden from our higher Judge.

### 3. Defining Right and Wrong (20:13-18)

As he was defining right and wrong, Solomon once more pointed out the error of *the sluggard:* "Love not sleep, lest thou come to poverty; open thine eyes, and thou shalt be satisfied with bread" (Proverbs 20:13). The sluggard needs to learn that money doesn't grow on trees. If we want to make adequate provision for ourselves and our families, we have to get up in the morning and go to work.

Henry Ford did not know the meaning of laziness. His father saw to it that, apart from school hours, young Henry was kept busy on their small farm in Michigan. "I have followed many a weary mile behind a plow and I know all the drudgery of it," he said.[28]

At age sixteen he left the farm and worked at two jobs. Back to the farm at age nineteen, he tried to build a tractor. Later he joined the Edison Company and became the firm's chief engineer, even though he had little formal education. Most of what he knew he had taught himself.

In the back of his house in Detroit was a brick shed where he spent every spare minute trying to make a car. Always tinkering with odds and ends, he finally came up with a veritable "Tin Lizzie" in 1896. It had four bicycle wheels and a bicycle saddle for a seat. His car had two speeds—ten or twenty miles per hour—but no reverse gear and no brakes. Having made his first car, Ford at once began to design and build a better car.

The Edison Company told him to make up his mind: work for them or work for himself. He raised some capital and went to work for himself. He invented the Model T and the assembly line. Louis Untermeyer said, "He made cars fast, and he made cars cheap.... He raised wages and reduced prices." Ford sold fifteen million Model T cars and changed the way people lived.

His profits were enormous and other people profited as well. One cautious schoolteacher, for example, was persuaded to invest a hundred dollars (half her life savings) in Ford's fledgling company. By the time she was bought out by the corporation in 1919, her investment had brought her $355,000.

Next came the Model A, a sleeker and more efficient car that was still attractively priced. A month after the new model was introduced, the plant was manufacturing six thousand cars a day. During Ford's lifetime, his company produced more than thirty million engine-propelled vehicles, most of them at the rate of one per minute. Ford achieved virtual miracles of production. A load of iron arriving at the docks near the River Rouge factory would be smelted, made into steel, converted into parts, assembled, shipped, and sold in four days!

Henry Ford was a man after Solomon's own heart. He opened his eyes in the morning and plunged at once into another day of work. He lived a full, satisfying life. By 1940 it was no longer possible even to guess his total wealth; he had the Midas touch for turning pig iron into gold. Solomon would have enjoyed telling Ford's story to every sluggard he knew!

The next proverb shows that *the salesman,* as well as the buyer, needs to be able to distinguish between right and wrong: "It is naught, it is naught, saith the buyer: but when he is gone his way, then he boasteth" (Proverbs 20:14). Solomon of course was thinking of an oriental market where bartering, bluffing, and bullying are part of every transaction. The seller starts by inflating the value of the article. The buyer starts by depreciating its value (the expression translated "It is naught" can also be rendered "It is very bad"). The haggling can be fierce, but when agreement is reached, both the seller and the buyer are convinced that they have made a good bargain.

This proverb is illustrated in Dorothy Sayers' mystery *Gaudy Night.* The story revolves around Harriet Vane, who had returned for her "gaudy" (class reunion) at her old college in Oxford and was trying to track down the author of a series of poison-pen letters. Her friend Lord Peter Wimsey occasionally offered his help and at the same time tried his best to win Harriet's hand in marriage.

For some time Harriet had admired a set of antique ivory chessmen displayed in the window of a shop in town. They were far too expensive for her, but when she at last gave the wealthy and aristocratic Lord Peter permission to give her a personal gift, she suggested that he purchase the chessmen.

The couple arrived at the shop and saw that the set was still in the window. There was some stiff bargaining ahead, so Harriet reined in her eagerness before entering the store with Lord Peter. Sayers described the ensuing confrontation:

> The proprietor...recognizing after a preliminary skirmish of superlatives that he had to do with an obstinate, experienced and well-informed customer, settled down with something like enthusiasm to a prolonged siege of the position. It had not previously occurred to Harriet that anybody could spend an hour and forty minutes in buying a set of chessmen. Every separate carved ball in every one of thirty-two pieces had to be separately and minutely examined with finger-tips and the naked eye and a watchmaker's lens for signs of damage, repair, substitution or faulty workmanship; and only after...a long discussion about trade conditions in China, the state of the antique market generally and the effect of the American slump on prices, was any figure mentioned at all; and when it was mentioned, it was instantly challenged, and a further discussion followed, during which all the pieces were scrutinized again. This ended at length in Peter's agreeing to purchase the set at the price named...provided the board was included.... The dealer rather reluctantly agreed, after having it firmly pointed out to him that the board was sixteenth-century Spanish—clean out of the period—and that it was

> therefore almost a condescension on the purchaser's part to accept it as a gift.[29]

The shopkeeper, satisfied with his profit, went off to wrap the chessmen. And Lord Peter remarked to Harriet that the chessman were truly ancient and worth a great deal more than the amount the proprietor had named. That kind of bargaining is not so common in our day, but Solomon would have known all about it.

Proverbs 20:15 defines the right kind of wealth: "There is gold, and a multitude of rubies: but the lips of knowledge are a precious jewel." The riches of *the sage* are better than "the treasures in Egypt" (Hebrews 11:26). Riches without knowledge soon vanish.

Egypt's valley of the kings was discovered by Theodore Davis in 1906. From 1907 to 1912 Lord Carnarvon and Egyptologist Howard Carter dug in the area with small success. During World War I excavation activities were suspended, but from 1919 to 1921 Carter resumed digging and systematically prospected the valley of the kings. Carnarvon, who was Carter's sponsor, became discouraged with the lack of results and considered calling the whole project off, but exploration continued, and on the morning of November 4, 1922, Carter made one of the greatest finds in archaeological history. He stumbled on the tomb of youthful King Tutankhamen.

On November 25 Carter cleared the staircase and opened the famous door that gave access to a tunnel that led to a second door. On November 26 Carter opened this second door. He took elaborate precautions to offset the poisonous effects of bad air and then with the help of the feeble light of his candle he peered into a room that was later called the antechamber. Carnarvon anxiously asked his colleague if he could see anything and with great excitement Carter replied, "Yes, wonderful things."[30] And so he did, for in the antechamber lay an extraordinary quantity of objects—so many that it took a year of patient labor to properly unearth, catalog, photograph, describe, and pack them.

On February 17, 1923, the door between the antechamber and the burial chamber was opened, revealing beautifully decorated shrines that dazzled from the brilliance of their gold. The immense yellow quartzite sarcophagus was not opened until October 10, 1925.[31] Carter wrote about that day:

> The tackle for raising the lid was in position. I gave the word. Amid intense silence the huge slab, broken in two, weighing over a ton and a quarter, rose from its bed. The light shone

> into the sarcophagus. A sight met our eyes that at first puzzled us. It was a little disappointing. The contents were completely covered by fine linen shrouds. The lid being suspended in mid-air, we rolled back those covering shrouds, one by one, and as the last was removed a gasp of wonderment escaped our lips, so gorgeous was the sight that met our eyes: a golden effigy of the young boy king, of most magnificent workmanship, filled the whole of the interior of the sarcophagus. This was the lid of a wonderful anthropoid coffin, some 7 feet in length, resting upon a low bier in the form of a lion, and no doubt the outermost coffin of a series of coffins, nested one within the other, enclosing the mortal remains of the king.

Carter continued:

> Enclasping the body of this magnificent monument are two winged goddesses, Isis and Neith, wrought in rich gold-work upon gesso, as brilliant as the day the coffin was made. To it an additional charm was added, by the fact that, while this decoration was rendered in fine low bas-relief, the head and hands of the king were in the round, in massive gold of finest sculpture, surpassing anything we could have imagined. The hands, crossed over the breast, held the royal emblems—the Crook and the Flail—encrusted with deep blue faience. The face and features were wonderfully wrought in sheet-gold. The eyes were of aragonite and obsidian, the eyebrows and eyelids inlaid with lapis lazuli glass. There was a touch of realism, for while the rest of this anthropoid coffin, covered with feathered ornament, was of brilliant gold, that of the bare face and hands seemed different, the gold of the flesh being of different alloy, thus conveying an impression of the greyness of death.[32]

When the lid of the first coffin was raised, a second coffin was revealed, fitting perfectly into the first. Within the second coffin was a third one, wrapped in a red linen shroud. This innermost coffin was made of solid gold and weighed more than a ton. When it was opened on October 28, 1925, the gold death mask was revealed. The mummy wore between the layers of its wrappings more than a hundred gold ornaments. The most prodigious treasure any archaeologist could dream of finding was brought to light in this one small room.

Beyond the burial chamber was the treasury, which also abounded in riches. It was a kind of museum of the arts and crafts of Egypt. An annex too was filled to the ceiling with all kinds of objects.

All this vast treasure was lavished on the burial of an unimportant boy king who came to the throne at the age of nine and died before he was twenty.

Oh, yes, "there is gold"! Solomon had his share of it and so did Joseph. The "treasures in Egypt" were put at his disposal when the pharaoh appointed him grand vizier. But Joseph had something worth much more than these fabled riches. He had wisdom—"The lips of knowledge are a precious jewel." Joseph's knowledge of God was a far greater treasure than all of Egypt's wealth. Joseph's "lips of knowledge" were what attracted the pharaoh to him in the first place and it was because of them that all the riches of Egypt were placed under his control.

In contrast to the sage is *the simpleton.* Proverbs 20:16 refers to him when it states, "Take his garment that is surety for a stranger: and take a pledge of him for a strange woman." The simpleton does not understand that to serve as security for someone he doesn't know is a good way to lose his shirt, as we would say.

Notice that the proverb mentions a pledge made for a *foreign* woman. Solomon had become a veritable fool in his marital affairs, marrying foreign women in order to cement alliances with neighboring pagan powers. He was writing out of bitter experience to help us define right and wrong.

The best illustration of Proverbs 20:16 is found in the history of the founding father of the royal tribe of Judah, the tribe to which Solomon belonged. About the time Judah played his despicable role in the selling of Joseph, he married a Canaanite woman. Such a marriage was a sin against the covenant. Three sons were born of this union and the first two were so evil that they died summarily under the judgment hand of God.

When God slew the first son, he left a widow, Tamar, but no children. The second son married Tamar in accordance with the law, but he behaved so despicably toward her that God slew him as well. According to the law Tamar, now widowed for the second time and still childless, should have been married to Judah's third son. But by this time Judah had become superstitious and he refused to allow this third wedding to proceed.

When it became obvious to Tamar that she was being abandoned to a childless widowhood, she planned to trap her father-in-law. Knowing Judah's low morals, she dressed like a harlot, covered her face with a veil, and sat in a place where Judah was sure to pass. Her strategy worked, for he propositioned her.

"What wilt thou give me...?" she asked.

"I will send thee a kid from the flock," Judah promised.

"Wilt thou give me a pledge, till thou send it?" Tamar demanded.

"What pledge shall I give thee?" he asked.

"Thy signet, and thy bracelets, and thy staff that is in thine hand," she replied (Genesis 38:16-18).

The inevitable followed. When Judah sent a friend with the kid to redeem the pledge, the harlot had vanished and the neighbors denied any knowledge of such a woman. Three months later news leaked out that Tamar was pregnant. Judah was enraged. "Bring her forth, and let her be burnt," he exclaimed (38:24). This penalty under the code of Hammurabi was in force throughout Canaan at this time. Tamar was dragged to the execution site, but before the harsh and unjust sentence was consummated, she demanded a hearing. She had entrusted to a friend the articles that Judah had given as a pledge. At Tamar's word, the friend produced the signet, the bracelets, and the staff. Judah, confronted by the evidence, was forced to confess: "She hath been more righteous than I" (38:26).

Although perhaps not an exact parallel of the proverb, the story of Judah and Tamar illustrates how our pledges as well as our sins come home to roost.

As Solomon continued to define right and wrong, he wrote about *the scoundrel* who practices deceit: "Bread of deceit is sweet to a man; but afterwards his mouth shall be filled with gravel" (Proverbs 20:17). The expression "filled with gravel" implies the most complete disappointment.

The outstanding Biblical example of a scoundrel is Judas Iscariot. Was ever another man born of a woman given a greater chance in life? Only he among the disciples was a Judean like Jesus. Judas could have done the work for which Paul, as "one born out of due time," was later anointed (1 Corinthians 15:8). Judas's name might have been engraved for all eternity on one of the foundation stones of the celestial city (Revelation 21:14-20). Instead his name has gone down in history as synonymous with deceit, treachery, infamy, and shame.

The "bread of deceit" was sweet to Judas. We do not know how long he had been swindling the apostolic band by helping himself to the contents of the bag, but we do know that he was a thief and that he invested his ill-gotten gains in property. We also know that he made a pretense of being concerned about the plight of the poor. Imagining himself to be clever and the disciples to be gullible, he thought he was getting away with his thievery. He shrugged off the veiled warnings of Jesus.

In the upper room the Lord again sounded a warning, but by then Judas, who was completely disillusioned with Jesus, had made his pact with the devil. His wretched purse, full of silver, was hidden in his robe.

"One of you shall betray me," Jesus said, dropping the bombshell.

"Is it I?" Peter demanded.

"Is it I?" exclaimed Thomas and John and Matthew.

"Is it I?" echoed Judas, reaching out for another morsel of roast lamb.

"Lord, who is it?" John asked.

"He it is, to whom I shall give a sop, when I have dipped it," Jesus replied (John 13:21-26; Matthew 26:22).

Evidently Jesus, following the custom of hosts in the Middle East, scooped up some meat and sauce in a piece of thin pocket bread and handed it to Judas. The wretched man took that special fragment from the hand that would soon be pierced. The scoundrel put the food into his mouth and, as Solomon would have phrased it, his mouth was "filled with gravel." Hastily Judas left the table and fled into the dark—and into despair, death, and eternal doom.

The next proverb states, "Every purpose is established by counsel: and with good advice make war" (Proverbs 20:18). It is particularly important for *the sovereign* to be able to determine what is right.

In his book *Finished,* the third volume in his series on the Zulus, Sir Henry Rider Haggard told how Cetewayo, the Zulu king, took counsel as to whether or not he should wage war on the English. He sought advice from Allan Quatermain, who had a reputation for integrity. Quatermain, whose native name *Macumazahn* meant "one who keeps his eyes open," told the story:

> "Macumazahn," he said, "the Great Queen's man who has come to Natal (Sir Bartle Frere) threatens me with war because two evil-doing women were taken on the Natal side of the Tugela and brought back to Zululand and killed by Mehlokazulu, being the wives of his father, Sirayo, which was done without my knowledge. Also two white men were driven away from an island in the Tugela River by some of my soldiers."
>
> "Is that all, O King?" I asked.
>
> "No. The Queen's man says I kill my people without trial, which is a lie told him by the missionaries, and that girls have been killed also who refused to marry those to whom they were

given and ran away with other men. Also that wizards are smelt out and slain, which happens but rarely now; all of this contrary to the promises I made to Sompseu when he came to recognize me as king upon my father's death, and some other such small matters."

"What is demanded if you would avoid war, O King?"

"Nothing less than this, Macumazahn: That the Zulu army should be abolished and the soldiers allowed to marry whom and when they please, because, says the Queen's man, he fears lest it should be used to attack the English, as though I who love the English, as those have done who went before me, desire to lay a finger on them. Also that another Queen's man should be sent to dwell here in my country, to be the eyes and ears of the English Government and have power with me in the land; yea, and more demands which would destroy the Zulus as a people and make me, their king, but a petty kraal-head."

"And what will the King answer?" I asked.

"I know not what to answer. The fine of two thousand cattle I will pay for the killing of the women. If it may be, I wish no quarrel with the English, though gladly enough I would have fought the Dutch had not Sompseu stretched out his arm over their land. But how can I disband the army and make an end of the regiments that have conquered in so many wars? Macumazahn, I tell you that if I did this, in a moon I should be dead....Therefore to-day I stand like a man between two falling cliffs. If I run towards the English the Zulu cliff falls upon me. If I run towards my own people, the English cliff falls upon me, and in either case I am crushed and no more seen. Tell me then, Macumazahn, you whose heart is honest, what must I do?"

So he spoke, wringing his hands, with tears starting to his eyes, and upon my word, although I never liked Cetewayo as I had liked his father, Panda, perhaps because I loved his brother, Umbelazi, whom he killed, and had known him do many cruel deeds, my heart bled for him.

"I cannot tell you, King," I answered, thinking that I must say something, "but I pray you do not make war against the Queen, for she is the most mighty One in the whole earth, and though her foot, of which you see but the little toe here in Africa, seems small to you, yet if she is angered, it will stamp the Zulus flat, so that they cease to be."

Later Cetewayo convened the great council of the nation to hear the opinions of the other chiefs. Each took a stand: some were for peace; others were for war. Old Sigananda reviewed the history of the Zulus from the days of Chaka; the aged chief concluded:

> I have noted, O King and Councillors, that whenever the black vulture of the Zulus was content to attack birds of his own feather, he has conquered. But when he has met the grey eagles of the white men, which come from over the sea, he has been conquered, and my heart tells me that as it was in the past, so it shall be in the future. Chaka was a friend of the English, so was Panda, and so has Cetewayo been until this hour. I say, therefore, let not the King tear the hand which fed him because it seems weak, lest it should grow strong and clutch him by the throat and choke him.

Undabuko, Dabulamanzi, and Magwenga—the king's brothers—favored war. Umahu, the king's uncle, counseled peace and advised Cetewayo to "bend like a reed before the storm, so that after the storm had swept by, he might stand up straight again." Some of the chiefs agreed with Umahu, but others wanted war. The prime minister, Umnyamana, "declared fiercely that if the Zulu buffalo hid itself in the swamp like a timid calf when the white bull challenged it on the hills, the spirits of Chaka and all his forefathers would thrust its head into the mud and choke it."

Again the king turned to Quatermain. Asked how many soldiers the white Queen (Victoria) could summon, Quatermain answered:

> I do not know for certain. But if the Zulus can muster fifty thousand spears, the Queen, if there be need, can send against them ten times fifty thousand, and if she grows angry, another ten times fifty, every one armed with a rifle that will fire five bullets a minute, and to accompany the soldiers, hundreds of cannon whereof a single shot would give Ulundi to the flames. Out of the sea they will come, shipload after shipload, white men from where the sun sets and black men from where the sun rises, so many that Zululand would not hold them.

And so the haggling continued. In the end the decision was left with Zikali, an aged witch doctor who nursed a secret but insatiable hatred of the Zulus in general and the Chaka dynasty in particular.

He performed some ritual magic in the course of which he materialized a famous small assegai that Chaka had used as the scepter of his power in days gone by. This spear, falling from the sky, pierced Cetewayo's knee, which bled. In Haggard's story this incident was the final weight that tipped the scales:

> "Your word, King," said Zikali. "Is it for peace or war?"
> Cetewayo looked at the assegai, looked at the blood trickling from his knee, looked at the faces of the councillors.
> "Blood calls for blood," he moaned. "My word is—*War!*"[33]

Solomon would have approved of much of Cetewayo's decision-making process. Yet the Zulu sovereign was foolish indeed to allow the counsel and magic of an old witch doctor to carry so much weight. In the end the Zulus were laid low before the imperial power of Britain.

## C. The King's Pronouncements (20:19-25)

### 1. A Man and His Mouth (20:19-20)

Solomon spoke of *the man with the big mouth:* "He that goeth about as a talebearer revealeth secrets: therefore meddle not with him that flattereth with his lips" (Proverbs 20:19). Often a talebearer is also a flatterer. The classic Biblical example of the flattering talebearer is Doeg the Edomite, who told tales to King Saul about Ahimelech, the high priest who had given aid to David (1 Samuel 21–22).

Some say that Joseph was a talebearer (Genesis 37:2), but such an accusation slanders his character. He was his father's accredited agent, not a spy. Joseph had nothing to gain and much to lose by telling his father the truth about his brothers' behavior.

An example of a woman with a big mouth is found in another scene from *Gaudy Night* by Dorothy Sayers. The setting of this portion of the story is the Senior Common Room at Shrewsbury College, an imaginary women's college connected with Oxford University. The poison-pen letters had raised tensions among the school's personnel.

Most of the staff had returned after vacation, but Mrs. Goodwin, a widow with a ten-year-old son who had the measles, had taken a few days off to care for her sick child. Mrs. Goodwin, the dean's secretary, aroused the scorn of Miss Hillyard, an acid-tongued, man-hating history teacher.

When the dean complained about the inconvenience of commencing a new term without a secretary, Miss Hillyard poured out her venom against Mrs. Goodwin. "I don't see what else you can expect, if you give jobs to widows with children," she sneered. When Miss Lydgate, an English tutor, tried to defend Mrs. Goodwin, Miss Hillyard silenced her with a caustic comment. Warming to her theme, she said, "If the domestic responsibility is to take precedence of the public responsibility, then the work should be handed over to someone else." Miss Hillyard lost her patience completely when the dean argued that Mrs. Goodwin was an excellent secretary. The conversation degenerated into a tirade by Miss Hillyard against every one of the spinster dons who had "an inferiority complex about married women and children." She added a wholly gratuitous slur: "*Last* time [Mrs. Goodwin] was away, we had no trouble from anonymous letters."[34]

*Gaudy Night,* of course, is only a story. But the incident is remarkably true to life. There is nothing worse than the person with a big mouth unless it is *the man with the bad mouth,* for Proverbs 20:20 tells us, "Whoso curseth his father or his mother, his lamp shall be put out in obscure darkness." Solomon was referring not only to premature death, but also to death without posterity, a fate worse than death among the Hebrews.

God insists in His Word that children obey their parents and honor them. This principle applies whether the parents are good, bad, or somewhere in-between. The problem of unworthy parents has to be left with God; He has His own ways of dealing with such imponderables. The fifth commandment requires us to honor our fathers and our mothers.

Some scholars have divided the Decalogue of Exodus 20 into two unequal groups: four commandments regarding man's duty to God; and six commandments regarding man's duty to man. This four-and-six division provides for the fifth commandment to be included in the latter group. More correctly the Decalogue should be divided into two equal parts. The fifth commandment rightly belongs with the first four, which deal with man's duty to God. This five-and-five division is evident in the text, for the expression "the Lord thy God" occurs in each of the first five commandments and thus links them together. The reason the fifth commandment rightly belongs with the first four is that a child's parents stand in the place of God to him until he reaches the age of understanding and responsibility.

A young person may earn God's disapproval by *disobeying* his parents or *deceiving* his parents or *disliking* his parents, but woe betide the child who *defames* his parents. Cursing one's father or mother reveals a condition of heart and mind that is ripe for judgment. The Holy Spirit's warning in Proverbs 20:20 is solemn and sobering.

The sin of cursing one's parents was so rare under Israel's stern patriarchal system that it is hard to find even the ghost of an illustration in the Bible. It would perhaps not be so hard to find illustrations in our own day when defiance of authority and blatant disobedience of parents is common (Romans 1:30). Such behavior is a mark of the endtimes (2 Timothy 3:1-2).

Although the Bible does not actually say that Absalom cursed David, he came as close to the sin of cursing his father as he dared. When Shimei cursed David, the brokenhearted king spoke of Shimei's curses and Absalom's rebellion as being of equal weight and significance (2 Samuel 16:5-13). Having shown utter contempt for his father by what he did to David's concubines (16:21-22), Absalom died on a tree, cursed of God (Galatians 3:13). He was buried in a pit over which the people "laid a very great heap of stones" as a mark of abhorrence (2 Samuel 18:9-17).

Absalom's lamp was "put out in obscure darkness," for although he had three sons and a daughter (2 Samuel 14:27), it seems that his sons died prematurely. The historian wrote: "Now Absalom in his lifetime had taken and reared up for himself a pillar, which is in the king's dale: for he said, I have no son to keep my name in remembrance: and he called the pillar after his own name: and it is called unto this day Absalom's place" (18:18). Solomon may have had the sad history of Absalom in mind when he penned Proverbs 20:20.

2. A Man and His Money (20:21)

"An inheritance may be gotten hastily at the beginning; but the end thereof shall not be blessed." The classic Biblical example of this proverb is the parable of the prodigal son.

Some time ago when I went to a small town in Ohio to speak at a church, the pastor drove me past a run-down building. "The man who owns that building won a seven-million-dollar sweepstake several years ago," he said. "It ruined him. He and his wife are divorced. His children will not speak to each other. He literally wasted the money. He made hopeless investments and lost every penny of it. He is worse off now than he was before he fell heir to it."

Since we live in an age when wealth is worshiped, enticements to acquire riches quickly are tempting. The average householder is inundated by mail that offers the (remote) possibility of getting rich overnight if he responds to a sweepstakes offer. There are state lotteries, school raffles, church bingo parties, legalized gambling, and the stock market. Temptations abound, but we must remember that the sudden acquisition of wealth tends to demoralize character; Proverbs 20:21 is based on this principle and the same principle explains why any form of gambling is sinful.

Commenting on the mentality of the compulsive gambler, one observer said: "All compulsive gamblers share a common failing—they must lose. They never quit while they're ahead."

Speculating on the stock market can be risky business too. On Tuesday, October 20, 1987, the *New York Times* headline read: "Stocks plunge 508 points, a drop of 22.6%; 604 million volume nearly doubles record." *Time* magazine reported that this crash was "a collapse on a scale never seen before—no, not even in 1929."[35] On Monday prices had plummeted, "swiftly wiping out an entire year's spectacular gains." By the time the closing bell rang at 4:00 p.m. at the New York Stock Exchange, that October 19 had become known as Black Monday. "Some $500 billion in paper value, a sum equal to the entire gross national product of France, vanished into thin air." In London, Tokyo, Paris, Toronto—all over the world—panic spread. The week was written up as the worst in financial history.

According to analysts the Dow Jones Average, one of the market's price indexes, had been inflated. The market was trading at 2700 when, economists say, it should have been trading at 2000 at the most. Frank Korth said, "We were 700 points ahead on sheer greed." People were betting that the Dow would go as high as 3000. One overseas observer said that even though the market was overspeculated, investors were promising themselves that they would get out promptly at the first tremor. But they didn't have the chance, for the collapse was too sudden, and they called the day "meltdown Monday."

One couple, who had three-quarters of their assets in the stock market, lost more than two hundred thousand dollars in a matter of minutes. "We're praying a lot, but it's not working," said the wife.

An Iowa farmer, who had been hit by hard times, gloated: "It was good the way those rich people were getting hurt—just as us poor guys have been." He was not so jocular when grain, cattle, and hog prices followed a corresponding downward trend.

In evaluating what happened in 1987, one analyst spoke of stock market prices taking off, beginning in August 1982, on a five-year climb. The value of shares on the New York Stock Exchange nearly tripled, rising from $1.1 trillion to $2.8 trillion. One out of every three adult Americans climbed on the bandwagon. Millions of others were carried along, like it or not, through pension funds, savings funds, insurance policies.

Win or lose, participation in any kind of get-rich-quick scheme erodes character, for all such schemes lack the blessing of God. "An inheritance," wrote Solomon, "may be gotten hastily at the beginning; but the end thereof shall not be blessed." The Bible ethic is a work ethic.

3. A Man and His Motives (20:22-24)

In Proverbs 20:22 Solomon made a pronouncement about *seeking revenge:* "Say not thou, I will recompense evil; but wait on the Lord, and he shall save thee."

The Old Testament ethic expressed in the Mosaic law was plain and clear: "eye for eye, tooth for tooth" (Exodus 21:24). Whatever people did to you, you did to them. If a man committed murder, the punishment was death. A man who committed accidental manslaughter had to flee at once to a city of refuge, for the avenger of blood would be hard on his heels.

Solomon lived in an age when it was appropriate to write imprecatory psalms, read curses, and demand one's pound of flesh. Even so, examples of forgiveness could be found. Under the severest provocation David forgave Saul, Shimei, and Absalom. It seems that the only person David could never forgive was himself.

Solomon knew also of Moses and his almost endless patience with the backsliding, backbiting children of Israel. And who could forget Joseph and his majestic, magnanimous forgiveness of his brothers?

Today we have an example of forgiveness that Solomon never had. He outshines all the others as a candle pales before the full flood of the dawn. We know of One "who, when he was reviled, reviled not again" (1 Peter 2:23).

Eager to usher in Armageddon, twelve legions of angels, with swords drawn, strained over the battlement of Heaven when Jesus was battered, bruised, spat upon, mocked, crowned with thorns, scourged to the bone, and nailed to a tree. But what did He do? All power was His. Those iron bolts of Rome could have become thunderbolts in His hand. He could have stamped the high hills of

Judah flat and turned the waters of the seven seas to blood. But what did He do? He said, "Father, forgive them; for they know not what they do" (Luke 23:34).

"Wait on the Lord, and he shall save thee" wrote Solomon, but those words did not seem true on that terrible morning when Jesus died. His enemies mocked, "He saved others; himself he cannot save" (Mark 15:31). Then darkness came and His agonizing cry, ringing out from the depths of that mysterious midday-midnight, was answered by total silence.

Solomon's words did not seem true when Joseph, Nicodemus, and a handful of weeping women washed Christ's blood-stained remains and wrapped them for the entombment. Those words did not seem true when for three days and three nights the world went nonchalantly on its wicked way, heedless that its mighty Maker lay, a lifeless corpse, in a manmade cave near a skull-shaped hill. But then came Sunday—the first day of the week, the dawn of a new day, a new dispensation! Solomon's words *were* true. Jesus proved for all mankind for the rest of time that the Lord will save!

In Proverbs 20:23 Solomon made a pronouncement about *stolen riches:* "Divers weights are an abomination unto the Lord; and a false balance is not good." About a dozen verses back, the Holy Spirit had inspired him to say the same thing (20:10). Because the human heart is deceitful above all things (Jeremiah 17:9), this kind of instruction cannot be repeated too often.

Using the expression "is not good," Solomon stated the truth negatively. If he had phrased the same thought positively, he would have used the expression "is very evil." Solomon was repeating the idea conveyed by the term translated "abomination," a strong word meaning "loathsome." That is the word the Holy Spirit writes across all crooked business deals and He reinforces His repugnance of all such practices by repetition. It is as though the Holy Spirit is saying, "It is loathsome; it is loathsome!"

A person who will make a crooked business deal is crooked all the way through. No matter how fine his Sunday clothes are, or how beautifully he sings in the choir, or how diligently he teaches a Sunday school class, or how unctuously he ushers his neighbors to their seats, he is still a crook. As the nursery rhyme says:

> There was a crooked man
> Who walked a crooked mile.
> He found a crooked sixpence
> Upon a crooked stile.
> He bought a crooked cat,

Which caught a crooked mouse,
And they all lived together
In a little crooked house.

In Proverbs 20:24 Solomon made a pronouncement about *self-reliance:* "Man's goings are of the Lord; how can a man then understand his own way?" Our problem is that we do not have a wide enough perspective. God sees the end from the beginning. He can weigh all the factors and all the forces that come into play when a person makes a decision. As F. W. Boreham once said, "I tremble to think what might have happened to me if one of my ancestors had married the woman he murdered or murdered the woman he married. I might never have got here at all."

Picture a man driving along a narrow country road between rolling hills. He is hedged in on either side. His perspective is very limited. He cannot see around the next corner or over the brow of the next hill. If he has no map and is in unfamiliar territory, he may not have any idea where he is or where he is going. In the dark his understanding will be even more restricted.

Picture another man flying over the same countryside in broad daylight. He can look down and see the motorist. The pilot has a much better idea of his "goings." He can see the road behind and in front of the motorist. The pilot can see every twist and turn of the road and its relationship to other roads. He can see the topography of the entire region and all the terrain through which the road winds. God's perspective is like the pilot's and our perspective is like the motorist's.

Let us consider the leading of the Lord in the choice of a bride for Isaac. Abraham looked at the filthy lifestyle of the wicked Canaanites and decided that he would never find a suitable wife for his son among such rank unbelievers. So he summoned his servant and sent him off to find a wife for Isaac in distant Nahor. Years earlier Abraham's conversion had made an impact and caused a considerable stir there.

The servant had an unenviable task. How would he ever know where to look or how to recognize the right woman when she crossed his path? "How can a man then understand his own way?" he might have asked. He decided that his "goings" would have to be "of the Lord." The servant asked God for guidance:

> O Lord God of my master Abraham, I pray thee, send me good speed this day, and shew kindness unto my master Abraham. Behold, I stand here by the well of water; and the daughters

> of the men of the city come out to draw water: And let it come to pass, that the damsel to whom I shall say, Let down thy pitcher, I pray thee, that I may drink; and she shall say, Drink, and I will give thy camels drink also: let the same be she that thou hast appointed for thy servant Isaac; and thereby shall I know that thou hast shewed kindness unto my master (Genesis 24:12-14).

The servant had not finished speaking when Rebekah arrived at the well and, quite oblivious to the test, met all its conditions. He exclaimed, "I being in the way, the Lord led me" (Genesis 24:27). Several times in the story the same thought is expressed (24:40,48,56).

As we journey through life, how important it is that we come to the One who declares, "I am the way" (John 14:6). Apart from Christ no one can order his way aright.

4. A Man and His Morals (20:25)

"It is a snare to the man who devoureth that which is holy, and after vows to make enquiry." The word translated "devoureth" here can also be rendered "rashly promises." In other words, it is dangerous to consecrate something to the Lord or make a solemn promise to Him and then reconsider or renege.

D. L. Moody used to tell a story about a man to whom he had witnessed. Time and time again the man had put the evangelist off with excuses. Then one day the man became seriously ill and was hospitalized. When Moody went to see him, the man said, "Pray for me, Mr. Moody. Pray that I'll get better. I promise, if I get better, I'll come and get saved."

The man recovered from his illness and the evangelist visited him in his home. Again the man made excuses. "Yes, Mr. Moody," he said, "I certainly intend to get saved. I'll be around to one of your meetings one of these days. Just give me a little more time." No words could persuade him to stop putting off his decision.

Then the man became ill again and once more the diligent soul-winner visited the hospital, but this time Moody's pleadings fell on deaf ears. "It's no use, Mr. Moody," the man said. "My heart is as cold and as hard as that brick wall. I had my chance, and now it's too late."

Moody tried to persuade his friend that it was not too late, that God's mercy was infinite. However, nothing the evangelist said made any difference. He tried to pray, but he felt that his prayers went no higher than the ceiling. "The very heavens seemed as brass," Moody said.

A short while later the man died. "We wrapped him in a Christless shroud, and put him in a Christless coffin," said the evangelist. "We put him in a Christless grave and left him in a Christless eternity." We do not renege on God and get away with it.

There is a line by us unseen
That crosses every path—
The hidden boundary between
God's patience and His wrath.

To pass that limit is to die—
To die as if by stealth;
It does not quench the beaming eye,
Nor pale the glow of health.

The conscience may be still at ease,
The spirits light and gay;
That which is pleasing still may please,
And care be thrust away.

But on that forehead God has set
Indelibly a mark,
(Unseen by man, for man, as yet,
Is blind and in the dark.)

Indeed, the doomed one's path below
May bloom as Eden bloomed;
He did not, does not, will not know,
Or feel, that he is doomed.

He feels, perchance, that all is well,
And every fear is calmed;
He lives, he dies, he wakes in hell—
Not only doomed, but damned.

Oh, where is that mysterious bourn
By which our path is crossed,
Beyond which God Himself hath sworn
That he who goes is lost?

(Alexander)

## D. The King's Policies (20:26-30)

### 1. His Might (20:26-27)

*Displaying practical wisdom,* "a wise king scattereth the wicked, and bringeth the wheel over them" (Proverbs 20:26). (Here "the wheel" refers to a threshing instrument.) In other words, a wise king does not allow the proponents and practitioners of wickedness to congregate, organize, and use the power of their united numbers to threaten the moral foundations and stability of society. He keeps all the strings of power in his own hands.

A wise ruler in our day would smash the power of the Mafia, the drug cartels, the humanist societies, the secret societies, and the political subversives. He would never allow such organized pressure groups to exist and become a threat to the nation.

Today we see moral cowardice and a lack of practical wisdom in the way national leaders deal with sodomy and the way the medical community deals with AIDS. A generation ago people who contracted a dangerous disease would have been isolated in hospitals. Now as the deadly AIDS virus spreads, we are assured that all is well. Every survey shows that the virus is multiplying all over the world and is actually out of control in some countries. Still officials say we face minimal risk.

Behind the weakness of the leaders is the power of a well-organized special-interest group. There was a time when a person who practiced sexual perversion slunk down back alleys and hid his shame because society would not stand for his filthy lifestyle. Now the powers-that-be have allowed sodomites to organize. Having come "out of the closet," they mobilize and march. They chant vile slogans and flaunt their unnatural behavior. They demand that big cities honor them with "gay pride" observances. They speak of their "rights" and penetrate all strata of society. Some of them are our doctors, dentists, lawyers, judges, and mayors. Some of them write textbooks and teach our children. Some of them sit in the halls of Congress and make our laws. Some of them have infiltrated our churches and expect to be allowed to be our pastors and preach from our pulpits. Sodomites wield power.

Solomon wrote Proverbs 20:26, but he himself failed to scatter the wicked. He allowed pornographic religions to take root in his kingdom and the results of his compromising were disastrous. Nevertheless the advice he gave is sound.

In addition to displaying practical wisdom, the wise king increases his might by *developing pondered wisdom.* Proverbs 20:27 says, "The spirit of man is the candle of the Lord, searching all the inward parts of the belly." The word translated "candle" here can also be rendered "lamp." This verse is one of the most useful definitions of the human spirit in the Bible. The spirit of man is his governing principle.

When God created animals, He gave each kind a governing principle we call "instinct" to control their behavior. An animal does what it does because it is what it is. A bee, for instance, always behaves like a bee. It does what a bee does because it is a bee. It has a built-in code that governs all its functions. It can behave no other way.

Emerging from its incubation cell, a bee is fully equipped to perform its function in the hive. Nobody has to teach a bee how to make a honeycomb with perfectly flat surfaces set in straight rows of elegant hexagons. Nobody has to teach a bee how to sense the earth's magnetic field and how to turn the honeycomb to the proper angle in relationship to that field. Nobody has to teach a bee to make each honeycomb cell a hexagonal prism, the best possible shape to hold a given volume of any particular substance while using as little building material as possible.

No one knows how bees construct six perfect 120-degree angles in each honeycomb cell, but they do. They make three or four at a time, tilting each cell back at a grade of 13 degrees and spreading the wax to a uniform thickness of 0.003 inch. The bees build cells in various sizes, depending on their purpose. There are cells for hatching new workers, cells for storing pollen and honey, cells for rearing drones, and cells for raising new queens.

Starting at the top of the comb, the bees begin in two or three places simultaneously. They work with such accuracy and join the various sections with such precision that it is impossible to tell that they were begun separately. All this and much more is done by instinct.

Instinct governs the behavior of each species—except man. When God created Adam, He gave him a different governing principle. True, He gave Adam a body with senses and a soul with faculties of intellect, emotion, and will—gifts that are shared to a lesser extent by many animals. But God did not lock the human race into a behavioral pattern as He did the animal creation. He could have created us so that we would always do what we were supposed to do, but He did not want merely a superior animal. He did not want puppets; He wanted people. So He gave Adam a spirit.

God's intention was that the human spirit control the faculties of man's soul and the senses and functions of his body. More, the human spirit was to be indwelt by the Holy Spirit. The human spirit was to work cooperatively with the Holy Spirit in governing the whole man. Thus controlled, man would willingly, knowingly, and joyfully do those things that please the Father. Thus Solomon wrote, "The spirit of man is the candle [lamp] of the Lord," the lamp being the human spirit and the light of the lamp being the Holy Spirit. Adam, indwelt by God, was to be a perfect expression of God manifested in flesh. And so he was—until the fall.

When sin came in, the Holy Spirit left the human spirit and the light went out. Sinful man has no divine governing principle. He is in the dark—lost, spiritually dead, in desperate need of regeneration. Sinful man may be controlled by his intellect, emotions, will, conscience, or senses—or by a combination of these factors. His human spirit is restless, unsatisfied, ever looking for peace, a prey to false religion, and estranged from God, for without the Holy Spirit, man is still lost and in the dark.

That is why Jesus said to Nicodemus (a religious and moral Pharisee): "That which is born of the flesh is flesh; and that which is born of the Spirit is spirit. Marvel not that I said unto thee, Ye must be born again" (John 3:6-7). When a person accepts Christ, the blood of Christ cleanses him, the Holy Spirit comes back into his human spirit, and the lamp is relit.

2. His Mercy (20:28)

"Mercy and truth preserve the king: and his throne is upholden by mercy." There is to be a definite, if delicate, balance between justice and mercy.

A judge first has to *define the problem:* he has to discover the truth. Is the prisoner guilty or not guilty? What are the extenuating circumstances? Was the crime premeditated or was it a crime of passion? Next the judge has to *decide on the punishment.* All the defendant can do is throw himself on the mercy of the court.

It is possible for a judge to be *too soft.* That is bad for public morale as well as public morals. All too often, when the courts are lenient, the criminal element in society flourishes. Repeat offenders especially need to feel the full weight of the law. On the other hand, it is possible for a judge to be *too severe.*

England's notorious Judge George Jeffreys (1645-1689) was too severe. Born into the Welsh gentry, he was commissioned to enforce the unpopular religious policies of the Roman Catholic king, James II. In 1678 Titus Oates circulated fabricated stories of a popish plot, and during the panic that followed, Jeffreys served as the prosecutor and judge of suspected Catholic conspirators. He became notorious for savagely bullying and ridiculing the defendants.

In 1685 Jeffreys presided over the "Bloody Assizes" that followed the failure of the duke of Monmouth's rebellion. The judge prosecuted the rebels with ferocity, executing as many as two hundred people and ordering hundreds more to be sold into slavery in the colonies.

James II made Jeffreys lord chancellor, but in 1688 James II was overthrown by William of Orange (later known as King William III). Jeffreys disguised himself as a sailor and tried to flee the country, but he was arrested and thrown into the Tower of London, where he died within four months.

The throne is "upholden by mercy," said Solomon. Although there may be times when the full weight of the law needs to be invoked, justice tempered with mercy is the usually the best policy.

3. His Men (20:29)

There are *those who administer:* "The glory of young men is their strength." And there are *those who advise:* "The beauty of old men is the grey head." A king needs both. He needs the power of young men to enforce his decisions and he needs the prudence of old men to enlighten his deliberations.

After the collapse of the Absalom rebellion, David invited old Barzillai to come along to Jerusalem and take his place at the king's table where so many policies were born and nurtured. Barzillai had proven his loyalty to David—and a sane-headed, warm-hearted, far-sighted, open-handed loyalty it was. Many a man had held back during the Absalom rebellion to see which way the wind was going to blow. But the aged Barzillai had loaded up his wagons, harnessed his mules, and headed straight for Mahanaim to put all that he had at David's feet. So now David extended the hospitality of his own table to Barzillai.

Barzillai, however, began to make excuses. He was old, he said, and wedded to his own way of life. He had no interest in what went on at David's table. Besides, a young man named Chimham was eager to go with the king. Maybe David should take him instead (2 Samuel 19:31-40).

David didn't need to be told how old Barzillai was! The king could see the noble chieftain's gray hairs, but David knew he needed more than bright young executives and brawny athletic warriors. He needed a wise mature man of proven loyalty to be one of his counselors. David had just lost Ahithophel—the cleverest counselor in the kingdom, but a scoundrel and traitor as well—so there was an empty seat at the king's table. David yearned to have Barzillai come and fill the vacancy.

David could have taken both Barzillai and Chimham with him—Barzillai with his gray head and Chimham with his youthful strength. David was king enough to appreciate his need for both. So was Solomon.

4. His Method (20:30)

"The blueness of a wound cleanseth away evil: so do stripes the inward parts of the belly." There are times when the king has to take drastic action.

Some injuries require more than a band-aid. They call for painful remedies. Sometimes surgery is necessary; the knife has to cut deep. In certain cases only amputation will suffice. Similarly, there are times when stern measures are needed to cure a person's spiritual ills or to deal with the moral and social ills of an age.

People have often puzzled over God's mandate to Israel, as they stood poised to conquer the promised land, that they utterly exterminate the Canaanites:

> Thou shalt smite them....thou shalt make no covenant with them, nor shew mercy unto them: Neither shalt thou make marriages with them.... thou shalt consume all the people.... thine eye shall have no pity upon them: neither shalt thou serve their gods; for that will be a snare unto thee (Deuteronomy 7:2-3,16).

This case required surgery.

In order to understand the Lord's marching orders to Joshua, we must comprehend the utter vileness of the Canaanite religion. The worship of Asherah, the chief goddess of Tyre, for instance, was wholly detestable to true worshipers of Jehovah (1 Kings 15:13). In the Old Testament she appears as the consort of Baal. Most Biblical references to the goddess associate an obscene sex object with her. It was set up on the high places along with altars of incense and stone pillars that seem to have represented Baal. Asherah was sometimes depicted as a nude woman astride a lion and called

*Qudshu* (which means "the Holiness"). Males consecrated to the cult of *Qudshu* prostituted themselves to her honor and were styled *qedishim* (which means "sodomites"). (See Deuteronomy 23:17; 1 Kings 14:24; 15:12; 22:46). This goddess and her associates specialized in sex and war, and her temples and shrines were houses of legalized vice.

Ashtoreth (the Astarte of the Greeks), a similar Canaanite goddess, was associated with the planet Venus. She was the same as the Babylonian Ishtar—the goddess of sensual love, maternity, and fertility. Licentious acts were part of her worship, which was deeply entrenched at Sidon. Even Solomon succumbed to his wives and served Ashtoreth (1 Kings 11:5; 2 Kings 23:13).

Baal, a chief god of Canaan, was associated with agriculture. His worship was conducted by priests in temples and on the high places. Chambers were provided so that male prostitutes and sacred harlots could help devotees consummate their adoration of the deity in lascivious acts (1 Kings 14:23-24; 2 Kings 23:7). Near the rock altar associated with Baal worship stood a sacred pillar, a lewd symbol of human fertility.[36]

Knowing the character of their gods, we can well imagine what the morals of the Canaanites were. Also, we can well believe that the whole Canaanite population—joined as they worshiped to the temple harlots and sodomites and male prostitutes—must have been riddled with disease. It was therefore necessary, for sanitary as well as spiritual considerations, that radical surgery be performed on the body politic of Canaan. Kindness and holiness, not cruelty, commanded stern measures.

# CHAPTER 2

## Proverbs 21:1–22:10

IV. The Functions of the Throne (21:1–24:34)
- A. His Majesty's Intentions (21:1–22:10)
  1. Presumption (21:1-4)
     - a. Who Really Controls (21:1-2)
       - (1) How God Pursues His Way (21:1)
       - (2) How God Ponders Our Way (21:2)
     - b. What Really Counts (21:3-4)
       - (1) What Is Acceptable to God (21:3)
       - (2) What is Accursed of God (21:4)
  2. Prosperity (21:5-7)
     - a. Getting Rich Wisely (21:5)
     - b. Getting Rich Wickedly (21:6-7)
       - (1) By Fraud (21:6)
       - (2) By Force (21:7)
  3. Purity (21:8)
  4. Peace (21:9-10)
     - a. The Domestic Nagger (21:9)
     - b. The Destructive Neighbor (21:10)
  5. Punishment (21:11-16)
     - a. Sitting in the Court (21:11-13)
       - (1) Judgment Discerned (21:11-12)
         - (a) The Learning Process (21:11)
         - (b) The Looking Process (21:12)
       - (2) Judgment Denied (21:13)
     - b. Settling Out of Court (21:14)
     - c. Standing for the Court (21:15)
     - d. Straying from the Court (21:16)
  6. Pleasure (21:17-19)
     - a. The Wrong Pursuit (21:17)

- b. The Wrong Price (21:18)
- c. The Wrong Partner (21:19)

7. Prudence (21:20-23)
    - a. In the Matter of One's Money (21:20)
    - b. In the Matter of One's Morals (21:21)
    - c. In the Matter of One's Might (21:22)
    - d. In the Matter of One's Mouth (21:23)
8. Pride (21:24)
9. Procrastination (21:25-26)
    - a. Slothful Dreams (21:25)
    - b. Selfish Desires (21:26)
10. Pretense (21:27)
11. Perjury (21:28-29)
    - a. The Doom of the Unscrupulous Man (21:28)
    - b. The Determination of the Unscrupulous Man (21:29)
12. Power (21:30-31)
    - a. A Country and Its Advisers (21:30)
    - b. A Country and Its Armaments (21:31)
13. Priorities (22:1-2)
    - a. The Long-Range Importance of Integrity (22:1)
    - b. The Long-Range Insignificance of Inequity (22:2)
14. Perception (22:3-5)
    - a. Our Future (22:3)
    - b. Our Fortune (22:4)
    - c. Our Footsteps (22:5)
15. Parenthood (22:6)
16. Potentials (22:7-10)
    - a. Sowing and Reaping (22:7-9)
        - (1) In Money Matters (22:7)
        - (2) In Moral Matters (22:8)
        - (3) In Ministry Matters (22:9)
    - b. Scorning and Reproaching (22:10)

Solomon continued with proverbs fit for a king as he discussed various aspects of life, particularly from the viewpoint of the throne. Having talked about the favor, the fury, and the fear of the throne, he next drew attention to *the functions of the throne* (21:1–24:34). He dealt with the king's *intentions* (21:1–22:10), his *intimates* (22:11-29), and his *interests* (23:1–24:34).

## IV. The Functions of the Throne (21:1–24:34)

### A. His Majesty's Intentions (21:1–22:10)

#### 1. Presumption (21:1-4)

##### a. Who Really Controls (21:1-2)

To help us realize afresh who really holds the reins of power, Solomon pointed us to the throne above all thrones—the throne of the King of all kings. In Proverbs 21:1 he showed us *how God pursues His way:* "The king's heart is in the hand of the Lord, as the rivers of water: he turneth it whithersoever he will."

The picture evoked by this proverb is that of an eastern farmer who directs the water in his irrigation channels simply by moving his foot to dam the flow here or release the flow there. It is that simple to make the water run whithersoever he wishes. It is also that simple for God to overrule in human affairs. He makes the very wrath of man to praise Him (see Psalm 76:10).

Even such a violent and evil tyrant as Henry VIII was a tool in the hands of God. Although he was an avid Roman Catholic, he eventually waged war on the papacy and its sources of wealth and power in England.

Henry was six feet tall and powerfully built—a tireless athlete, huntsman, and dancer. He excelled in book learning but rarely allowed academic discussions and the enjoyment of learned conversation to interfere with his pleasures. Ebullient and willful in character, he was determined to have his own way. He was a dangerous man to displease.

Henry earned the title "Defender of the Faith" from the pope in 1521 by writing a book against Martin Luther. Under the influence of two bigoted papists, Gardiner and Bonner, the king enacted the "Six Articles" (also called the "Bloody Statute") that condemned to death all who opposed the dogma of transubstantiation, auricular confession, vows of chastity, and private masses, and all who supported the marriage of the clergy and the giving of the cup to the laity. He was thus responsible for the martyrdom of many true believers. Henry remained a Romanist at heart to the end of his days, and when he died he bequeathed large sums of money for masses to be said for the repose of his soul.

Yet God had access to Henry VIII's wicked heart and turned it to accomplish His will, even while the lustful and lawless king thought he was accomplishing his own will. Consider, for example, the results of Henry's infatuation with Anne Boleyn.

His older brother Arthur died and shortly after his accession to the throne, Henry married Arthur's widow, Catherine of Aragon, who was the daughter of the Spanish sovereigns Ferdinand and Isabella. For seventeen years no question appears to have been raised regarding the validity of this union, although Henry was disturbed because the marriage had produced no male heir. Of the five children (three sons and two daughters) born to the couple, only Mary survived infancy.

Probably the king would have jogged along hoping for the best, had he not fallen for the charms of Anne Boleyn. But having fallen, Henry decided that his marriage to Catherine was illegal and contrary to divine law. From 1527 onward he pursued the goal of a divorce from Catherine. His quest became known as "the king's great matter." Anne was determined to be more than the king's mistress, and his determination grew in proportion to hers. And Henry needed to legitimize his relationship with Anne in order to solve the succession problem.

It took Henry six years to get his way because Pope Clement VII dug in his heels. If he accommodated Henry, the pope would offend Emperor Charles, who was Catherine's nephew—and Clement was more afraid of Charles than he was of Henry. By the time Henry finished fighting with the pope over his divorce, he had separated the English church from Rome and changed the course of history. A Protestant England became, in time, one of the greatest forces for world evangelism.

As God pursues His way, He is not deceived by any man. Proverbs 21:2 states, "Every way of a man is right in his own eyes: but the Lord pondereth the hearts." Solomon was showing us *how God ponders our way*.

The prophet wrote: "The heart is deceitful above all things, and desperately wicked: who can know it? I the Lord search the heart, I try the reins, even to give every man according to his ways, and according to the fruit of his doings" (Jeremiah 17:9-10). We cannot deceive God, but we can deceive ourselves. It is even possible to persuade ourselves that right is wrong and wrong is right. Nothing is more astonishing than the way a person justifies his own actions.

Consider the case of Simon Magus. G. H. Pember quoted the following enumeration of Simon's wonders from the second of the Clementine *Homilies:*

> And they told me that he makes statues walk about; rolls himself upon fire, and is not burnt; and that sometimes he even flies. And he turns stones into loaves; he becomes a serpent; changes himself into a goat; becomes two-faced; and transforms himself into gold. He opens fastened doors, melts iron, and at banquets produces phantoms of every conceivable shape. And lastly: he causes the vessels in his house to be seen moving about, as if spontaneously, to wait upon him, those who are bearing them not being visible. I wondered to hear them speak thus; but they assured me that they had seen many such things done in their presence.

Pember added a story taken from the *Apostolical Constitutions.* It proves that what is now called "levitation" is not new; the concept has been in men's minds for many centuries. The story is about Simon and is supposed to have been told by the apostle Peter:

> Now when he came to Rome, he greatly harassed the Church by subverting many persons, and winning them over to his own party. And he astonished the Gentiles by a display of magic and the operation of demons, insomuch that once he came forward in the middle of the day and, bidding the people drag me also into their theatre, promised that he would then fly through the air. But, while all the multitude was in a state of suspense at this bold offer, I kept secretly praying. And verily he was raised up by demons, and began to fly aloft into the air, crying out, as he rose higher, that he was returning to the heavens, and would bestow blessings upon them from thence. Then, while the people were glorifying him as a god, I lifted up my hands toward heaven with my heart, and entreated God that, for the sake of Jesus our Lord, He would cast down the injurious deceiver, and cut short the power of the demons, since they had used it to mislead and ruin men; that He would smite Simon to the ground, and yet not kill, but only bruise, him. And so, fixing my eyes upon him, I said in answer to his words: "If I be a man of God, a true Apostle of Jesus Christ, a teacher of piety, and no deceiver such as thou art, Simon, I command the wicked powers of the apostate

> from piety, by whom Simon the magician is now being supported and borne along, to let go their hold, that he may be thrown down from on high, and be exposed to the ridicule of those whom he has beguiled." As soon as I had thus spoken, Simon was deprived of his powers, and cast down with a great noise. And, being dashed violently upon the ground, he had his hip and the flats of his feet broken. Then the multitude cried out, saying, "There is one God Whom Peter justly declares to be in very truth the only One." And many of Simon's disciples left him: but some, who were deserving of perdition with him, continued in his evil doctrine. And in this manner the most atheistical sect of the Simonites was first introduced at Rome, and the Devil went on working by means of the rest of the false apostles.[1]

In Scripture we meet this evil, deceitful, and self-deluded man—whose ways were right in his own eyes—in the account of the gospel's first penetration of Samaria. Simon deceived the evangelist Philip, who baptized him as a genuine convert, but he did not deceive the apostle Peter, who saw through him at once (Acts 8:9-24).

b. What Really Counts (21:3-4)

Proverbs 21:3 tells us *what is acceptable to God:* "To do justice and judgment is more acceptable to the Lord than sacrifice." This statement reminds me of King Saul and the Amalekites, descendants of Esau who were confirmed enemies of Israel.

Soon after the Israelites left Egypt, the Amalekites attacked them at Rephidim; the Hebrews under Joshua engaged them in battle and defeated them (Exodus 17:8-16; Deuteronomy 25:17-19). In time the Israelites arrived at Kadesh-barnea, one of the Amalekites' strongholds. There the Hebrews at first refused to go into Canaan. When they changed their minds and in rebellious self-will attempted the invasion, the Amalekites opposed and repulsed them (Deuteronomy 9:23; Numbers 14:43-45). God called for the extermination of the Amalekites as the due reward for their malice and treachery.

After Israel settled in the promised land, the Amalekites continued their unrelenting hostility toward the Hebrew people. They helped Eglon, king of Moab, seize Jericho away from Israel (Judges 3:12-13). Then they allied themselves to the Midianites and oppressed northern Israel (6:3,33).

During the reign of King Saul the nomadic Amalekite tribes roamed a five-hundred-mile stretch of desert extending from Egypt to northern and central Arabia. The prophet Samuel told Saul to make an end of this pernicious and persistent foe (1 Samuel 15:1-3). The instructions were clear. He was to "smite Amalek, and utterly destroy all that they [had]." He was to "slay both man and woman, infant and suckling, ox and sheep, camel and ass." God's patience with the Amalekites was exhausted. (The command is even more understandable when we remember that Amalek in the Old Testament is a type of the flesh.)

Israel's army was victorious, "but Saul and the people spared Agag and the best of the sheep, and of the oxen, and of the fatlings, and the lambs." Although they rigorously destroyed "every thing that was vile," their disobedience in sparing "all that was good" was to cost Saul his throne (15:9-11).

The next morning Samuel arrived in the camp and Saul hastened to make his report. "Blessed be thou of the Lord," he said. "I have performed the commandment of the Lord" (15:13).

Samuel brushed this comment aside. "What meaneth then this bleating of the sheep?" he demanded (15:14).

Saul blamed the people. Then he had a bright idea: "The people spared the best of the sheep and of the oxen, to sacrifice unto the Lord" (15:15).

Samuel was not impressed. He gave the king a lecture:

> Hath the Lord as great delight in burnt offerings and sacrifices, as in obeying the voice of the Lord? Behold, to obey is better than sacrifice, and to hearken than the fat of rams. For rebellion is as the sin of witchcraft, and stubbornness is as iniquity and idolatry. Because thou hast rejected the word of the Lord, he hath also rejected thee from being king (15:22-23).

How well Samuel read Saul's heart! How true was his assessment of the significance of Saul's disobedience! We read of the personal consequences in the story of Saul's involvement with witchcraft (1 Samuel 28:6-19). As for the Amalekites, they were soon back at their mischief-making. Only this time they had David to deal with (1 Samuel 30:1-20).

There is no substitute for obedience. As Solomon said, "To do justice and judgment is more acceptable to the Lord than sacrifice." And as the old hymn says:

> We never can prove the delights of His love
> Until all on the altar we lay;
> For the favor He shows and the joy He bestows
> Are for them who will trust and obey.[2]

Having told us what is acceptable to God, Solomon told us *what is accursed of God:* "An high look, and a proud heart, and the plowing of the wicked, is sin" (Proverbs 21:4).

The "high look" is the sin of looking down on certain people as though they were not worthy of notice. The "proud heart" is the sin of vain conceit, the idea that somehow we are better than other people. People who are born into aristocratic families and are blessed with wealth, good looks, and brains are often wrapped in an armor of self-righteous pride. But even people of humble circumstances and modest gifts can put on airs. In either case there is a gross over-evaluation of their own worth.

"The plowing of the wicked, is sin," Solomon added. A wicked person has no thought for God. He plows and plants as if he himself can make the rain fall, cause the sun to shine, and produce the miracle of germination and growth. That is the height of presumption, the ultimate abuse of God's mercy. God causes the sun to shine on the good and bad alike, but He writes the word *sin* over the lifestyle of a person who lives as though He does not exist. Such a person is ignorant of the fact that God looks upon all that he does—even his ordinary routines and mundane activities, such as plowing his field—as sin. His pride may not take the same form as that of the scornful aristocrat, but it is just as offensive to God.

The classic Biblical example of a proud heart is the prodigal's elder brother. What a stuck-up, self-righteous hypocrite he was! True, he was up with the rooster and off to the barn. He milked his quota of cows before breakfast and prepared the milk for the maids. He said a long grace over the table. He toiled and sweat in the heat of the day. One day he plowed; the next day he cultivated and weeded endless rows of crops; another day he repaired a fence or mended a gate. But all the time black rage welled up in his heart against that scapegrace younger brother of his. The prodigal was the subject of shameful, scandalous stories at the market and in the inn; indeed he had become the song of the drunkard. The family name was now tainted because of him.

At the end of the day the elder brother would come home hot, tired, and angry. Before supper he would have to milk the cows, clean the barn, and fork fresh straw and provender into the manger. He would sit down to eat, but the meal was spoiled by the sight of his father's grief-stricken face and the sound of his brother's name being spoken between sobs during family prayers. Exasperated and bitter, he may even have demanded, "Why don't you just get the family Bible and strike out his name?"

In the sight of God the very plowing of the elder brother was sin. He stayed home, but he carried the far country in his heart, along with pride, envy, malice, and resentment.[3]

There is only one cure for such a case of sinful pride. In *Alice's Adventures in Wonderland* Lewis Carroll gives us a clue as to the remedy.

Alice was lying on the grass one day when a white rabbit went by. He pulled a watch from his vest pocket and said, "Oh dear! I shall be too late." Alice saw him hurrying off and naturally she followed him to see where he went. When he went down a hole, so did Alice.

Once down that hole, she found herself in a large room full of locked doors; there seemed to be no exit. Finally she discovered a fifteen-inch door in a corner of the room. She opened it with a small key she found and peeped through. On the other side was a beautiful garden. She longed to get into it, but she was too big and the door was too small.

Fortunately the author had anticipated her need. On a table in the room was a little bottle. On the bottle was a label. On the label were just two words: "DRINK ME."

Alice picked up the bottle and drank its contents, and as soon as she did, she began to get smaller and smaller until she was only ten inches high. Before long she was able to enter the tiny door and continue the delightful nonsensical adventures that form the basis of the story.

Drawing a parallel, we could say that God has locked the entire human race in a large room labeled "Unbelief." Paul said that God has shut up all men together in unbelief "that he might have mercy upon all" (Romans 11:32). Does Scripture say "that he might condemn all"? Ten thousand times no! It says "that he might have mercy upon all."

God has provided a door out of that room, a door that leads to a full, free, and eternal salvation. Beyond that door lies the garden of God and over that door is written the words, "Except ye be converted, and become as little children, ye shall not enter into the kingdom of heaven" (Matthew 18:3).

But like Alice, and like the elder brother who had a high look and proud heart, we are far too big in our own estimation to get through the door. The door is so low, so strait and narrow, so very small.

But then one day we discover a Book. On the cover are the words *Holy Bible* and inside are some simple instructions: "READ ME." So we who are so self-righteous and have such big ideas of our own importance begin to drink in God's thoughts. And what happens? We get smaller and smaller until we take our stand with the wretched publican and cry, "God be merciful to me a sinner" (Luke 18:13).

Now that God has cut us down to size, we can read what is written on the door: Jesus said, "I am the door: by me if any man enter in, he shall be saved" (John 10:9). With the simplicity of a little child we can believe that Jesus died in our stead. We can receive Him as our personal Savior. We can cross the threshold of that door and enter into all the delights and wonders that await us.

### 2. Prosperity (21:5-7)

#### a. Getting Rich Wisely (21:5)

"The thoughts of the diligent tend only to plenteousness; but of every one that is hasty only to want." The word translated "thoughts" here means "reckonings or calculations." Solomon was saying that the diligent man thinks things through. He makes plans and carries them out in an orderly fashion. He is dedicated to his business, and prosperity usually follows. The hasty man acts on impulse, often irrationally, and then wonders why his efforts never seems to amount to anything.

The incompetent employee or manager accepts problems at face value and makes decisions without weighing all the conditions or objectives involved. He often refuses to seek expert advice in specialized areas. The incompetent person tends to be unrealistically optimistic or pessimistic and is likely to be a worrier, obsessed with details. He also acts too much on sentiment and emotion and does not look to the future. The incompetent man is a doer rather than a thinker and takes pride in that fact. In other words, he is "hasty." The competent man takes time to think.

While Proverbs 21:5 indicates that one's success depends on the proper management of time, Solomon was more concerned here with time's eternal dimension than its temporal dimension. He was reminding us that we have only so much time on this earth and what we do with that time has eternal consequences.

An industrialist used to ask, "What would you do if you had a bank that would credit $86,400 to your account each morning if you agreed to the following stipulations: no balance will be carried over from one day to the next; at the end of the day any leftover cash will be removed from the account; the amount not used will be listed on an accumulating statement of liabilities?"

We have such a bank. We call the currency of that bank "time." Every morning the time bank credits us with 86,400 seconds, and every night it writes off as a liability whatever time we have failed to invest wisely. If we fail to use a day's deposit, the loss is ours. We will be held accountable for the time we waste.

I have in my files a cartoon that depicts an old-fashioned hourglass with time running through it instead of sand. The time in the top glass is labeled "Now." That is the time still available to us. The time in the bottom glass is labeled "Then." The bottom of the hourglass is rapidly filling up and the top is quickly diminishing as "Now" relentlessly turns into "Then." The caption on the cartoon reads, "Time never waits."

Years ago George Hardy, a Vancouver businessman, wrote a little booklet entitled *Countdown.*[4] He began:

> With every living soul, there comes built in a little time fuse. We all have one. Some fuses burn slowly, but then some burn more quickly. Every birth signals the beginning of a countdown which without variation zeroes on an exit. Yet daily we shrug our indifference. Each night we yawn in God's face, roll over, and go to sleep, while our fuse burns ever down.

One of the greatest obstacles to success in life is the mismanagement of time. Too often we devote our time to nonessentials. Many of us would do well to consider the lesson learned by Charles Schwab, a former president of Bethlehem Steel. Schwab asked Ivy Lee, a management consultant, to help him accomplish more each day and promised to pay him for a successful formula.

Lee handed the business tycoon a piece of paper and said, "Write down the things you have to do tomorrow." Schwab made a list.

"Now number these items in the order of their importance." Schwab did as he was told.

"The first thing tomorrow," said Lee, "start working on number one and don't leave it until it is completed. Then take number two and stick with it until it is finished. And so on. Test the idea. If you like it, send me a check for what you think it's worth." A few weeks later Schwab sent Lee a check for $25,000.

b. Getting Rich Wickedly (21:6-7)

Solomon emphasized the wickedness of getting rich *by fraud:* "The getting of treasures by a lying tongue is a vanity tossed to and fro of them that seek death" (Proverbs 21:6).

*The Amateur Gentleman* by Jeffery Farnol provides an illustration of this proverb. The book introduces us to the moneylender Jasper Gaunt, his lesser partner Mr. Quigly, and Farnol's hero Barnabas. Barnabas, who found it necessary to visit the office of these loan sharks, described Jasper Gaunt:

> A tall, slender man he was, with a face that might have been any age,—a mask-like face, smooth and long, and devoid of hair as it was of wrinkles; an arresting face, with its curving nostrils, thin-lipped, close-shut mouth, high, prominent brow, and small, piercingly-bright eyes; quick eyes, that glinted between their red-rimmed, hairless lids, old in their experience of men and the ways of men.

Barnabas, an immensely wealthy young man, was not there to borrow money. He hoped to be able to buy the indebtedness of a friend of his, Ronald Barrymaine, and set him free from the clutches of the moneylender. While waiting for Jasper Gaunt, Barnabas stumbled across another tragedy, a case being managed by the equally rapacious Mr. Quigly. Farnol wrote:

> Now as he sat there waiting, he gradually became aware of a sound that stole upon the quiet, a soft, low sound, exactly what he could not define, nevertheless it greatly perturbed him. Therefore he rose, and approaching that part of the room whence it proceeded, he saw another door. And then, all at once, as he stood before this door, he knew what the sound was, and why it had so distressed him; and, even as the knowledge came, he opened the door and stepped into the room beyond.
>
> And this is what he saw:
>
> A bare little room, or office; the pale, smiling gentleman, who lounged in a cushioned chair, a comb in one hand, and in the other a small pocket mirror, by the aid of which he was attending to a diminutive tuft of flaxen whisker; and a woman, in threadbare garments, who crouched upon a bench beside the opposite wall, her face bowed upon her hands, her whole

> frame shaken by great, heart-broken, gasping sobs,—a sound full of misery, and of desolation unutterable.
>
> At the opening of the door, the pale gentleman started and turned, and the woman looked up with eyes swollen and inflamed by weeping.
>
> "Sir," said the pale gentleman, speaking softly, yet in the tone of one used to command, "may I ask what this intrusion means?" Now as he looked into the speaker's pallid eyes, Barnabas saw that he was much older than he had thought. He had laid aside the comb and mirror, and now rose in a leisurely manner, and his smile was more unpleasant than ever as he faced Barnabas.

Barnabas was not to be bullied. He turned to the woman and, after subduing her fears of her tormentor, extracted her story. She explained:

> Oh, sir,—it's my husband! He's been in [debtors'] prison a whole year, and now—now he's dying—they've killed him. It was fifty pounds a year ago. I saved, and scraped, and worked day and night, and a month ago—I brought the fifty pounds. But then—Oh, my God!—then they told me I must find twenty more—interest, they called it. Twenty pounds! why, it would take me months and months to earn so much.

The woman told how she had been forced to resort to shameful ways to earn the money and then added:

> To-day I brought the twenty pounds, and now—dear God! now they say it must be twenty-three. Three pounds more, and I have no more—and I can't—Oh, I—can't go back to it again—the shame and horror—I—can't, sir!

Farnol continued:

> So she covered her face again, and shook with the bitter passion of her woe.
>
> And, after a while, Barnabas found voice, though his voice was very hoarse and uneven:
>
> "I think," he said slowly, "yes, I think my cane could not have a worthier end than splintering on your villain's back, Mr. Quigly."

In the end Barnabas freed the woman from her debt and faced the even more formidable Jasper Gaunt, whose debtors owed him tens of thousands. And although Barnabas offered to double—even triple—the sum owed by Barrymaine, it was all in vain. The moneylender would not release his victim.

Later in the story the evil man was murdered at his desk. Farnol described what Barnabas saw in the moneylender's den:

> A candle flared and guttered upon the mantel, and by this flickering light he saw an overturned chair, and, beyond that, a litter of scattered papers and documents and, beyond that again, Jasper Gaunt seated at his desk in the corner. He was lolling back in his chair like one asleep, and yet—was this sleep?
>
> Something in his attitude, something in the appalling stillness of that lolling figure, something in the utter quiet of the whole place, filled Barnabas with a nameless, growing horror. He took a step nearer, another, and another—then stopped and, uttering a choking gasp, fell back to the wall and leaned there suddenly faint and sick. For, indeed, this was more than sleep. Jasper Gaunt lolled there, a horrid, bedabbled thing, with his head at a hideous angle and the dagger, which had been wont to glitter so evilly from the wall, smitten sideways through his throat.[5]

Farnol's tale is only a story after all, but it is one that has been enacted often enough in real life. The one who extorts treasure by evil means invites a swift and violent death.

Solomon also emphasized the wickedness of getting rich *by force:* "The robbery of the wicked shall destroy them; because they refuse to do judgment" (Proverbs 21:7). The word rendered "robbery" here can be translated "rapacity." Evil people are undone by their own tyranny. They do not deal justly; instead they use their place of power to oppress. So God, who overrules in the affairs of men and ultimately controls all of life's circumstances, engineers the downfall of the wicked. Their treatment of others finally recoils upon their own heads.

"Thy princes are rebellious [unruly], and companions of thieves," cried Isaiah in his opening blast against Israel and Judah (Isaiah 1:23). In the original Hebrew there is a play on words and the employment of a figure of speech (*paronomasia,* "rhyming words") for solemn emphasis. Isaiah was saying in effect, "Your rulers are unruly!" That was the indictment. The princes were robber barons. "Every one loveth gifts, and followeth after rewards: they judge not the fatherless, neither doth the cause of the widow come unto them," continued the indignant prophet.

Isaiah, a prince among the prophets, was raised in Jerusalem. He was called to his ministry in the year that the leper-king, Uzziah, died. Isaiah preached through the reigns of four Judean kings and committed his oracles to a band of disciples (Isaiah 8:16). No prophet ever had a greater scope of vision. His primary ministry was to Judah and Jerusalem, but he took in Samaria, Israel, and some surrounding nations. Isaiah was as much a statesman as a seer.

To the north, the kingdom of Israel under Jeroboam II was a flickering candle whose flame would soon go out forever. Israel was filled with injustice and even Judah had not escaped the taint. Under King Uzziah, Judah had once again become a powerful military state. It had attained a degree of prosperity not known since the days of David and Solomon. But power, wealth, and luxury had brought with them corruption in the courts, empty form in religion, and the sins of avarice and oppression.

Warnings poured like molten lava from Isaiah's lips. The prophetic names he gave his two sons were intended to reinforce his message that wealth accrued by wickedness brings judgment in its train. The names implied that the Assyrian monarchs, who were already preparing to come and thrash and fleece the Hebrew rulers, would be even more rapacious than the unjust nobles of Israel and Judah.

Isaiah named his first son *Shear-jashub,* which means "a remnant shall return," and his second son *Maher-shalal-hashbaz,* which means "hasten to the spoil, hurry to the prey." The names were symbolic of Assyria's lust for conquest. Both Israel and Judah would feel the weight of the Assyrian arm. Both would be despoiled by this cruel and greedy foe, and Israel would know the added horror of utter ruin and deportation.

As Solomon said, "The robbery of the wicked shall destroy them." In the end there is always someone stronger and more ruthless who is only too eager to get rich by using superior force. Behind all these reverses are the throne and just balances of God, the moral Ruler of the earth.

3. Purity (21:8)

"The way of man is froward and strange: but as for the pure, his work is right." Rotherham's rendering reads, "Crooked is the way of a guilty man." Other translations more or less agree. The evil man's way is not open, straightforward, and simple; it is crooked, stealthy, and underhanded. The path of the pure in heart is direct, straight, and aboveboard.

Unfortunately the "con man" can make his proposition sound very convincing. Agatha Christie introduces us to such a man in her book *Death on the Nile.* The story is about the wealthy heiress Linnet Ridgeway, who has just married Simon Doyle. The couple are in Egypt on a honeymoon cruise up the Nile to Luxor. By crafty design the con man, Andrew Pennington, has also signed up for the cruise. He is the American trustee of a considerable portion of Linnet's fortune. Linnet's English lawyers get wind of the situation. Since they do not trust Pennington and think he plans to get the heiress to sign away her rights to her American property by approaching her at an unguarded moment during her honeymoon, the lawyers arrange for their own agent to join the cruise and keep his eyes open.

When the steamer arrives at Ez-Subûa, the passengers inspect an avenue of sphinxes and a temple, then return to the boat. Back in the ship's observation saloon, Pennington approaches Linnet. He apologizes for having to talk business on her honeymoon, but suggests that because her marriage has changed her status, it might be a good idea to sign the necessary legal papers. Linnet agrees that now would be as good a time as any to attend to the business, so Pennington hurries off to get the papers.

He comes back with a sheaf of documents and spreads them out for her signature. "There's the lease of the Fifth Avenue property...then there are the Western Lands Concessions," he says. He rattles on, rustling papers and setting the stage for the fraud.

At this moment Fanthorp, the English lawyer, comes in. He glances casually at the American and the heiress he is on board to protect and drifts over to a vantage point where he can see and hear what is happening.

"You sign just there," Pennington says and Linnet dutifully signs her name. Fanthorp, still seeming intent on something outside the window, moves closer. "That's just the transfer," Pennington says as he puts down another document. "You needn't read it." The heiress hesitates. "They're all quite straightforward," murmurs the American con man. "Nothing of interest. Only legal phraseology."

"I always read everything through," Linnet replies. "Father taught me to do that. He said there might be some clerical error."

The heiress glances at her playboy husband, who says, "I've never read a legal document in my life. I sign where they tell me to sign on the dotted line—and that's that." His wife comments that such an approach is slipshod. "I've no business head," Simon replies. "I'm a trusting kind of fellow—and it pays, you know." The con man could not have found a better ally.

At that moment the silent Mr. Fanthorp speaks up. "Never to sign a document before you read it through," he says, "is admirable—altogether admirable." Then he apologizes and turns away.

The ploy has failed. "I think perhaps some other time would be better," says Pennington, realizing he has lost this throw of the dice.[6]

That fictional scene has been enacted in essence countless times in real life—often with tragic results. All too often the crooked man succeeds in his crookedness, or so it seems, for all accounts are not always settled in this life. But we can be sure that the evil man will be adequately recompensed at the judgment bar of God. There too the pure person's ways will be weighed, rewarded, and shown to be right.

4. Peace (21:9-10)

Peace can be disturbed by *the domestic nagger:* "It is better to dwell in a corner of the housetop, than with a brawling woman in a wide house" (Proverbs 21:9).

Charles Dickens gave us an illustration of the domestic nagger in *Oliver Twist.* In the novel Mr. Bumble attempted to assert his lordship over his new wife, the former widow Corney. He tried to cow her with that formidable eye of his, an eye that had been known to make many a pauper orphan tremble. Mrs. Bumble, however, was made of sterner stuff than paupers. She refused to be cowed and in fact took the offensive:

> "Are you going to sit snoring there, all day?" inquired Mrs. Bumble.
>
> "I am going to sit here, as long as I think proper, ma'am," rejoined Mr. Bumble; "and although I was *not* snoring, I shall snore, gape, sneeze, laugh, or cry, as the humour strikes me; such being my prerogative."
>
> "*Your* prerogative!" sneered Mrs. Bumble, with ineffable contempt.
>
> "I said the word, ma'am," said Mr. Bumble. "The prerogative of a man is to command."
>
> "And what's the prerogative of a woman, in the name of Goodness?" cried the relict of Mr. Corney deceased.

> "To obey, ma'am," thundered Mr. Bumble. "Your late unfortunate husband should have taught it you; and then, perhaps, he might have been alive now. I wish he was, poor man!"
>
> Mrs. Bumble, seeing at a glance that the decisive moment had now arrived, and that a blow struck for the mastership on one side or other, must necessarily be final and conclusive, no sooner heard this allusion to the dead and gone, than she dropped into a chair, and with a loud scream that Mr. Bumble was a hard-hearted brute, fell into a paroxysm of tears.

The shoe was now on the other foot. Dickens continued:

> But, tears were not the things to find their way to Mr. Bumble's soul; his heart was waterproof. Like washable beaver hats that improve with rain, his nerves were rendered stouter and more vigorous, by showers of tears, which, being tokens of weakness, and so far tacit admissions of his own power, pleased and exalted him. He eyed his good lady with looks of great satisfaction, and begged, in an encouraging manner, that she should cry her hardest: the exercise being looked upon, by the faculty, as strongly conducive to health.
>
> "It opens the lungs, washes the countenance, exercises the eyes, and softens down the temper," said Mr. Bumble. "So cry away."
>
> As he discharged himself of this pleasantry, Mr. Bumble took his hat from a peg, and putting it on, rather rakishly, on one side, as a man might, who felt he had asserted his superiority in a becoming manner, thrust his hands into his pockets, and sauntered towards the door, with much ease and waggishness depicted in his whole appearance.

He was not to get very far. The redoubtable Mrs. Bumble resorted to assault and battery. First Mr. Bumble's hat flew off his head before a hurled missile. Then Mrs. Bumble seized her husband by the throat, beat him, scratched his face, and tore his hair, after which she pushed him over a chair. Mr. Bumble hurried off to the workhouse, thoroughly beaten, to take out his rage on the paupers. He was in the process of abusing and bullying them when his wife showed up. Dickens described the ensuing confrontation:

> "My dear," said Mr. Bumble, "I didn't know you were here."
>
> "Didn't know I was here!" repeated Mrs. Bumble. "What do *you* do here?"

> "I thought they were talking rather too much to be doing their work properly, my dear," replied Mr. Bumble: glancing distractedly at a couple of old women at the wash-tub, who were comparing notes of admiration at the workhouse-master's humility.
>
> "*You* thought they were talking too much?" said Mrs. Bumble. "What business is it of yours?"
>
> "Why, my dear—" urged Mr. Bumble submissively.
>
> "What business is it of yours?" demanded Mrs. Bumble again.
>
> "It's very true, you're matron here, my dear," submitted Mr. Bumble; "but I thought you mightn't be in the way just then."
>
> "I'll tell you what, Mr. Bumble," returned his lady. "We don't want any of your interference. You're a great deal too fond of poking your nose into things that don't concern you, making everybody in the house laugh, the moment your back is turned, and making yourself look like a fool every hour in the day. Be off; come!"
>
> Mr. Bumble, seeing with excruciating feelings, the delight of the two old paupers, who were tittering together most rapturously, hesitated for an instant. Mrs. Bumble, whose patience brooked no delay, caught up a bowl of soap-suds, and motioning him towards the door, ordered him instantly to depart, on pain of receiving the contents upon his portly person.

Mr. Bumble's humiliation was complete. Even the paupers now laughed at him. His surrender, however, was by no means complete. But as Dickens' story continued, Mr. Bumble fell under the sway of his formidable wife and became party to nefarious activities connected with poor Oliver Twist.

In the end Mr. Bumble was brought to account by Mr. Brownlow and Mr. Grimwig, two men who had befriended Oliver. After Mr. Bumble and his wife were exposed, Mr. Brownlow declared his intention of seeing to it that neither of them would ever be employed in a position of trust again. Dickens recounted Mr. Bumble's reaction:

> "I hope," said Mr. Bumble, looking about him with great ruefulness, as Mr. Grimwig disappeared…"I hope that this unfortunate little circumstance will not deprive me of my porochial office?"

> "Indeed it will," replied Mr. Brownlow. "You may make up your mind to that, and think yourself well off besides."
>
> "It was all Mrs. Bumble. She *would* do it," urged Mr. Bumble; first looking round to ascertain that his partner had left the room.
>
> "That is no excuse," replied Mr. Brownlow. "You...indeed are the more guilty of the two, in the eye of the law; for the law supposes that your wife acts under your direction."
>
> "If the law supposes that," said Mr. Bumble, squeezing his hat emphatically in both hands, "the law is...a idiot. If that's the eye of the law, the law's a bachelor; and the worst I wish the law is, that his eye may be opened by experience—by experience."
>
> Laying great stress on the repetition of these two words, Mr. Bumble fixed his hat on very tight, and putting his hands in his pockets, followed his helpmate down stairs.[7]

Deprived of their positions, the Bumbles became paupers themselves and ended up in the same workhouse where they had once lorded it over others. Since the sexes were segregated, Mr. Bumble thereafter lived separate from his shrewish wife. We can at least hope that he found some comfort in that. Mr. Bumble would have agreed with Solomon when he said, "It is better to dwell in a corner of the housetop, than with a brawling woman in a wide house."

Peace can also be disturbed by *the destructive neighbor:* "The soul of the wicked desireth evil: his neighbour findeth no favour in his eyes" (Proverbs 21:10). Bad men are bent on doing harm. It is a terrible thing to have one of them as a neighbor.

The classic Biblical example of the destructive neighbor is King Ahab (1 Kings 21). Pity poor Naboth, Ahab's neighbor who happened to own a vineyard that the king coveted. Naboth rightly refused to sell, but he signed his death warrant when he told Ahab he intended to keep the property in the family where it belonged. Ahab himself earned the death penalty when he went along with Jezebel's murderous plan to acquire the property for him at all costs.

A similar story was developed by Samuel Shellabarger in his book *Captain from Castile.* In Shellabarger's tale the property of Don Francisco de Vargas adjoined that of Diego de Silva. On de Vargas's property was a vineyard that de Silva wanted to buy. De Vargas considered selling the vineyard to obtain the money he needed to enroll his son Pedro as an officer in the army. An old soldier himself, de Vargas wanted Pedro to be trained in the ranks of the famous Señor de Bayard, a French chevalier whose pennon had been displayed on every famous battlefield in Europe. Around his crest blazed the glory of the departing age of chivalry. But it would cost a small fortune for Pedro to become one of de Bayard's lancers, so de Silva's offer was attractive to de Vargas. However, a display of bad manners by de Silva led de Vargas to decide to finance his son's apprenticeship in arms by some other means.

Shellabarger described one scene where the two neighbors were talking in de Vargas's pavilion. De Silva asked de Vargas if he had considered his offer, and then offered even more money. "I do not wish to sell for the present, sir," said de Vargas. Visibly annoyed and inclined to be rude, de Silva carried an air of menace about him. Before long it became evident where his insolence and assurance came from. He told de Vargas that he was an associate member of the dreaded Spanish Inquisition, which exerted absolute power and terrorized the whole country.

The Inquisition was "a kingdom within the kingdom, a power greater than the King's." Until modern times no more dreadful form of terror had been invented. Its dark shadow rested on every home. Its method was "secret denunciation—friend against friend, child against parent, enemy against enemy." Once a person vanished into the dungeons of the Inquisition, all hope was lost. Property was confiscated. Prospects of torture—the whip, the thumbscrew, the boot, the rack, the iron maiden, or the stake—haunted those upon whom the Inquisition cast a speculative eye. No name, however high, was a safeguard.

De Silva proceeded to describe in detail some of the torturing he had observed. Angry, de Vargas cautioned his unwelcome visitor, but de Silva only sneered. He continued his terrible accounts of what it was like to be interrogated by agents of the Inquisition.

Finally de Vargas straightened himself up. The light of battle gleamed in his eyes. In sentences pointed, short, and sharp, he dressed de Silva down. The destructive neighbor rose and took his leave, but his parting words hovered in the air. He promised that they had not heard the last of him.

Soon de Vargas and his family were prisoners of the Inquisition. Their indictment claimed that a great-grandmother of de Vargas had Moorish blood; that he had threatened a member of the Inquisition; and that his son was guilty of other crimes. When asked if he confessed, de Vargas stepped forward and said:

> I confess one crime not mentioned in the bill. Why it was not included, I do not know—perhaps because it has the

distinction of being true and would therefore ill agree with the others. I confess to the black sin of refusing to sell my property outside the walls to Diego de Silva.[8]

How the author extricated his heroes from the clutches of the Inquisition is another story!

5. Punishment (21:11-16)

a. Sitting in the Court (21:11-13)

(1) Judgment Discerned (21:11-12)

Judgment aids *the learning process:* "When the scorner is punished, the simple is made wise: and when the wise is instructed, he receiveth knowledge" (Proverbs 21:11). Solomon acted on this principle in the government of his kingdom.

Early in his reign Solomon had no trouble with the tribes of Israel, although the rift between North and South—between Ephraim and Judah—was always latent. The tribe of Ephraim, descended from Joseph, was envious of the dominant tribe that was descended from Judah, but this rivalry was kept in check by Solomon's firm grasp of the scepter. Following the sage advice of his father David, Solomon sent a warning message to all his people as soon as he ascended the throne: he would not tolerate insurrection. The message came across loud and clear through the executions of Shimei and Joab.

Shimei was a scorner; Joab was a schemer. Both were formidable foes. Shimei was formidable because he was popular with the tribe of Benjamin, and the restless Benjamites were almost as envious of David's dynasty as the Ephraimites were. Saul, Israel's first king, had been a Benjamite, and the Benjamites were resentful over the loss of the throne to Judah.

Joab was formidable because he was a brilliant unscrupulous general. He was also a would-be king-maker, having backed the cause of Adonijah, one of Solomon's brothers. There was always a danger in olden times, as in some countries today, that an ably led military might pull off a palace coup.

In dealing with Shimei, Solomon acted at once. He put Shimei under house arrest and warned him that he would be executed if he ever set foot outside Jerusalem. Shimei lay low for three years, then chased after a couple of runaway servants. He was apprehended, brought before Solomon, and put to death (1 Kings 2:36-46).

Joab walked softly. Then Adonijah made a false move. He persuaded Bath-sheba, the queen mother, to appeal to Solomon to let him marry Abishag the Shunamite, a beautiful widow of David. Although the sacred historian did not give all the details, it seems that Solomon suspected a palace plot; he linked Abiathar (the deposed high priest) and Joab (the deposed military commander-in-chief) with Adonijah's request. "Ask for him the kingdom also," Solomon exclaimed (1 Kings 2:22). Immediately the king issued orders for Adonijah's execution. Joab, realizing that Solomon had implicated him in a plot, fled for the horns of the altar. Little good that did. The murderous old man was dragged away to be executed.

Thus Solomon stamped out the last lingering embers of possible revolution. The people got the message. The king digested the principle behind his firm action and later distilled it into a proverb.

While judgment aids the learning process, *the looking process* aids judgment: "The righteous man wisely considereth the house of the wicked: but God overthroweth the wicked for their wickedness" (Proverbs 21:12). The book of Genesis provides us with an illustration of this proverb.

Two great holocausts were recorded in the book of Genesis. The first was the overthrow of society (which was organized on Cain's principles) by flood. The second was the overthrow of Sodom (which was organized on Canaan's principles) by fire.

When Lot "pitched his tent toward Sodom" (Genesis 13:12), he demonstrated how different he was from Abraham, who "removed his tent" and dwelt in Hebron (13:18). Righteous Abraham wisely considered "the house of the wicked." Lot did not.

All of Canaan was polluted. It was inhabited by the descendants of Canaan, who was the son of Ham and the grandson of Noah. It was colonized and controlled by a foul race of people. Their religion was foul and their rule was foul. But the foulest of the foul lived in Sodom and its sister cities in the Jordan valley. The reputation of these cities was as vile in their day as the reputation of San Francisco is today. What was an occasional reprehensible aberration elsewhere had become a lifestyle in Sodom, the vice capital of the postdiluvian world. When the debauched citizens of Canaan, satiated with ordinary sins, developed an appetite for extraordinary sins, they knew where to go.

Sodom catered to such people. It had gay bars and bathhouses, high-priced establishments and cheap brothels. A person could not walk a city block without being propositioned by a man dressed like a woman or by a woman aping a man. Everyone knew what was for sale. The house of the average wicked citizen of Sodom was worse than a house of ill-repute elsewhere in Canaan. Even in the houses of everyday folk, all kinds of abominations were the norm.

No man—not even a pilgrim and a stranger, as Abraham was content to be—could follow the fertile crescent into Canaan without hearing about Sodom, Gomorrah, and the other three cities of the plain. Abraham and Lot both knew about Sodom and they both knew about Noah, the ark, and the flood. They had their Bible, such as it was—it consisted of only a dozen chapters of Genesis and it was not yet written down, so they carried those chapters in their heads. From the story of the flood, they knew that although God in His grace is marvelously patient, there is a date on His calendar beyond which He will not wait. Beyond that date mercy is replaced by wrath.

As Abraham considered "the house of the wicked," he sensed in his soul that Sodom was no place for a child of God. Yet the first mention in the Bible of a house as a literal place to live is in connection with Sodom and, sad to say, it is Lot's house—the one house where some knowledge of God still lingered, albeit feebly (Genesis 19:2). Abraham considered the facts that Ham's reputation was none too savory, Canaan's was worse, and Sodom's stank to high heaven. So Abraham removed his tent.

Lot, however, decided he could ignore Sodom's pornography and perversions in order to take advantage of the pastures of the plain. It was a fatal choice. Abraham knew that "God overthroweth the wicked for their wickedness," but Lot chose to rationalize that truth. Lot might well have said that since God had taken a long time to visit His wrath on Cain's civilization, He would probably take a long time to visit His wrath on Canaan's.

In any case Lot no doubt planned to stay away from the houses of the wicked. He was interested in their farms, not their fellowship. So he pitched his tent toward Sodom, then moved into Sodom, and then became a senator in Sodom. When God's deadline arrived much sooner than Lot had expected and God overthrew the wicked, Lot barely escaped with his life. The house of the wicked is no place for a saint of God—unless of course he goes there under the call and commission of the Spirit of God and, using the Word of God, proclaims the salvation and certain wrath of God. But that was not why Lot went to Sodom.

### (2) Judgment Denied (21:13)

"Whoso stoppeth his ears at the cry of the poor, he also shall cry himself, but shall not be heard."

The Lord Jesus painted this poor man's portrait in Matthew 18:23-35. Not only was he poor; worse yet, he was in debt. Maybe his son was ill and the doctor's bills had piled up. Maybe he had been obliged to repair his house, or perhaps the landlord had raised the rent. Maybe because of a recent addition to his family, the budget was strained to the breaking point. In any case he had begged one of his affluent fellow servants to lend him a hundred pence. Since in Bible times a man would work all day to earn a penny, the poor man had borrowed a considerable sum. Perhaps he promised to repay his debt at the rate of a penny a week.

Well, the poor man defaulted on a payment. In any era there is hardly a more unhappy person in this world than the poor fellow who owes money he cannot pay, and in Bible times there were no bankruptcy laws—just the debtor's prison.

When the poor man missed a payment, the creditor—evidently a highly-placed and influential manager or overseer—became angry. He went out and "found" the debtor, Jesus said (Matthew 18:28). The word translated "found" means "sought and found." The affluent servant was determined to get his pound of flesh at all costs. He took the debtor by the throat and, throttling him, shouted, "Pay me that thou owest"!

Terrified by his creditor's violence and vindictiveness, the poor man begged for a little more time. Jesus said he "*besought* him, saying, Have patience with me, and I will pay thee all" (18:29, italics added). Since the verb translated "besought" is in the imperfect tense, we understand that the debtor kept on beseeching him.

But by now the creditor's blood was up. He refused to listen to reason or exercise restraint. He called the police, hailed the man before the magistrate, prepared a deposition against him, proved his case, and demanded the full penalty of the law. The unfortunate man was thrown into prison, and his family was left to starve.

This savage, merciless behavior struck a sour note with the rest of the servants. The whole terrible incident became the topic of conversation on the job and the talk of the workers' families at suppertime. Probably the overseer had never been popular. Perhaps he was known for his violent temper and venomous tongue. But this latest display of vindictive malice was too much. As a group the servants approached the king, told him the story, and begged for his help. "You just leave this to me," we can almost hear him saying.

There was a history behind this situation. Prior to this incident, when the overseer was the subject of an audit, his accounts were found to be out of line. We are not told if the man had been stealing money or if he had simply made some bad investments. The fact of the matter was that the auditors discovered a discrepancy in his accounts. Of the funds his lord had entrusted to his care, a total of ten thousand talents was missing. A talent was the heaviest weight in the system of weights and measures used at that time, and ten thousand was the highest number. So ten thousand talents speaks of an enormous debt.

The lord summoned the overseer and asked him to explain the missing money. There was no explanation, so the whole amount was charged to the defaulter. With little hope of ever collecting the debt, the lord determined to salvage what he could. "Well," he said in effect, "I can see nothing else to do but to seize your property and sell it. I will sell you too, for whatever you're worth. I will also sell your wife and children."

Stark ruin stared the overseer in the face. He fell on his face before the king and begged, "Have patience with me, and I will pay thee all" (18:26). Moved by compassion, the lord did much more than that. He canceled the debt in its entirety and sent the overseer home a free man.

It was this same overseer who now so brutally assaulted the poor fellow who owed him a paltry hundred pence. When the group of servants told the story to the king, his anger rose. The next thing the overseer knew, he was back in the lord's presence, his pardon was revoked, his entire indebtedness was revived, and his sentence was pronounced: "O thou wicked servant, I forgave thee all that debt, because thou desiredst me: Shouldest not thou also have had compassion on thy fellowservant, even as I had pity on thee?" (18:32-33) The lord summoned the officers of the law, pressed charges, and demanded the full penalty of the law. Jesus said, "His lord was wroth, and delivered him to the tormentors [jailers], till he should pay all that was due unto him" (18:34). Solomon said, "Whoso stoppeth his ears at the cry of the poor, he also shall cry himself, but shall not be heard."

b. Settling Out of Court (21:14)

"A gift in secret pacifieth anger: and a reward in the bosom strong wrath." Disarming justice by offering a bribe here and a present there was a common practice when this proverb was written. Solomon did not approve of the custom, but he was quick to acknowledge the efficacy of a bribe. In his day, as all too often in ours, palms had to be greased. Even a king's anger could be appeased if the price was right.

The desire for a bribe from Paul damned the soul of Felix, the Roman procurator of Judea. Felix began life as a slave and ended his life as a virtual king, but according to the historian Tacitus, beneath the regal robes there never ceased to beat a slave's heart.

During his governorship in Judea, Felix reveled in every kind of cruelty and lust. He seemed to think that his power and influence at court gave him license to commit any crime. For example, when the high priest Jonathan remonstrated with him for living such a wicked life, Felix conspired with Doras to have Jonathan killed. This assassination encouraged the Sicarii, a league of assassins whose excesses later contributed to the fall of Jerusalem.

Felix became enamored of Drusilla, a daughter of Herod Agrippa I and the wife of Azizus, king of Emesa. Simon the sorcerer persuaded her to live with Felix. When she appeared briefly in the sacred narrative (Acts 24:24), she was still young, but she had already come through enough wickedness to stamp her as one of the worst women of a licentious age. Felix was seated with this adulteress when the apostle Paul was summoned before him to answer charges the Jews had trumped up against him.

Luke gave us an account of the dramatic confrontation. He did not tell us how the interview opened, but he gave us the impression that Paul forgot all about his own chains as he looked at the moral and spiritual chains that bound his wretched judge. Paul "reasoned of righteousness, temperance, and judgment to come" with such effect that "Felix trembled" (24:25). The word translated "trembled" here is *emphobos,* which also means "terrified." The Holy Spirit used that word to indicate that Felix was terrified. Alexander Whyte wrote about his moment of fear:

> If Felix had but sat still a little longer, Paul was just going on to tell him how to get ease to the hell that was beginning to burn in his bosom. But I suspect Drusilla at that moment. I cannot get over my suspicion that it was Drusilla who so suddenly cut short Paul's discourse, and sent him back to his prison. I do not read that Drusilla trembled. My belief about that royal pair is, that had Drusilla not sat beside Felix that day, Felix would have been baptized, and Paul would have been set free, before the sun had gone down. But Drusilla and her sisters have cast into their graves many wounded. Many strong men have been slain to death by them. Their house is the way to hell, and their steps go down to the chambers of death.[9]

"Go thy way for this time," said Felix to Paul. "When I have a convenient season, I will call for thee" (24:25). And so he did—many times. But never again, as far as we know, did Felix tremble. We are left in no doubt as to his motive for his frequent audiences with Paul: "He hoped also that money should have been given him of Paul, that he might loose him: wherefore he sent for him the oftener, and communed with him" (24:26).

In the Roman empire there were stern edicts prohibiting bribery. Nevertheless the wheels of Roman justice ran more smoothly and rapidly if they were properly lubricated. Provincial governors were notoriously venal.

Felix certainly seems to have had the impression that Paul could afford to pay a handsome bribe for his release. No less a scholar than William Ramsay argued that the expenses of Paul's long incarceration and trial during his two years in Caesarea and his two years in Rome were paid from an inheritance that may have come to him during this time. Or perhaps Felix thought that some of Paul's wealthy friends would come through with the cash.

Felix grossly misunderstood the nature of the man whom he was judging. Paul would not make Felix tremble one day by preaching righteousness and judgment, and add to the procurator's damnation the next day by paying him a bribe and confirming him in his sins. Paul, who would rather have died than have Felix's soul on his conscience, had no intention of settling out of court. Felix waited in vain for "a gift in secret."

c. Standing for the Court (21:15)

"It is joy to the just to do judgment: but destruction shall be to the workers of iniquity." Solomon knew there is a great deal of satisfaction to be derived from seeing justice done and from seeing the forces of wickedness put under restraint. *Joy* is not too strong a word, especially when the case is a particularly flagrant one and justice has been defied too long.

Some years ago I visited Madam Tussaud's Royal London Wax Museum. There one gets a glimpse of other worlds. Lifelike portrayals of kings and queens and internationally famous people from various walks of life are displayed in magnificent scenes.

While I was in the museum I followed the crowd into the Chamber of Horrors. As I was walking around making the acquaintance of dozens of gruesome killers, I almost bumped into Charles Manson—hippie, Satanist, car thief, cult leader, and sex maniac. I was thankful it was a wax Manson!

In his book *The Family* journalist Ed Sanders reported on his investigations into the weird world of Charles Manson and his "family," a few young men and about twenty young women who were willing to do anything, any time, anywhere for him. While looking for material for his book, Sanders learned about various occult societies in Los Angeles and the cults of cruelty freaks and those who engage in pain magic. He encountered people who drink dogs' blood, hang rotting goats' heads in their kitchens, and rent corpses to adorn their parties. He came across groups who commit human sacrifice. He found gurus such as Manson who so successfully trap their victims that they actually become tied by invisible bonds to the master, as if they were connected to the same body and will.

Although Manson possessed a measure of good looks and a considerable amount of charisma, his world was dark. He was heavily into drugs and received a considerable amount of his "education" in prison. Manson was guru-oriented and his friends were violent cultists addicted to the worst forms of Satanism, sadism, and sex. Early in his career he was attracted to the Beatles.

Manson snared unsuspecting adherents into the belief that Jesus and His followers were very much like him and his girls, who came from a variety of backgrounds. Believing that women had no souls, Manson used them and abused them. According to him, their duty was to serve men. If the girls really loved him, he told them, they would go out and bring him back others who were prettier and younger. So complying with his wishes, girls came and went. "If you fit in you can stay," he would tell the new recruits. To raise money for "the family" he sent the girls out to sell themselves on the streets. He also loaned them to motorcycle gangs and to men whose money he coveted.

Manson taught his girls to worship him. He created what he called the Final Church and told his followers that he was both Christ and Satan. While she was in prison for murder, Susan Atkins (one of his dupes) told a cellmate how Manson would put himself on a cross and pretend that he was being crucified while girls knelt at the foot of the cross and sacrificed animals and committed abominations before him.

Then he taught them to murder people for him. The most famous murder they committed was that of Sharon Tate, a movie actress who was married to Roman Polanski, a movie producer. Polanski produced films calculated to chill the blood, including *Repulsion,* which was reputed to be one of the most horrifying movies ever made, and *Rosemary's Baby,* which has been called "the greatest advertisement for Satanism ever concocted."

The gruesome details of the Sharon Tate incident have been recounted many times. The bodies of the victims were horribly mutilated. On the way back to report to Manson, the murderers laughed, babbled, and compared notes. They even imitated the moans of their victims. Manson later polled the butchers to see if any of them felt remorse. One by one the girls said no. These murders were followed by others.[10]

Charles Manson made it all the way to prison—and to the Chamber of Horrors. But he escaped the death penalty. His sentence brought *no joy* to many right-minded people. Life imprisonment hardly seems an adequate societal response to Manson's infamous career. For all we know, he might even be paroled. If Solomon were alive today, he would not agree with Manson's sentence or the system that sentenced him (and others of his kind) to so light a punishment.

d. Straying from the Court (21:16)

"The man that wandereth out of the way of understanding shall remain in the congregation of the dead." Here a spiritual history is implied.

We see reflected in the mirror of this proverb a person who at one time had *a chance* to follow the way of understanding. At one time he knew the truth. At one time God spoke to his heart. Perhaps he was raised in a godly home, taken to Sunday school, instructed in the Scriptures, urged to memorize its great passages, and taught God's way of salvation. Such opportunities are not given to everyone, so perhaps God spoke to him through the voice of nature, in a night vision, or by someone's godly life. Perhaps God spoke to him as He spoke to Job, Melchizedek, Balaam, or Abraham.

But then the man in the proverb had to make *a choice.* God never speaks to us so that we can simply say, "How interesting." God demands a response. Nobody can get away with merely giving intellectual assent to revealed truth. The revelation of God always brings a person to a crossroads. The straight and narrow way beckons, and so does the broad highway. The man who "wandereth out of the way" failed to take God's call seriously; he paid lip service to the truth while cultivating the pleasures and promises of the world. The psalmist said that such a person walks in the counsel of the ungodly, stands in the way of sinners, and ends up sitting in the seat of the scornful (Psalm 1:1).

So he ends up with *a chain.* He will "remain in the congregation of the dead." He doesn't realize that the successful businessman he envies, the clever politician he admires, the witty comedian he thinks is so funny, the alluring woman he desires, the brilliant philosopher he reads, and the religious apostate he applauds are "dead," and their meeting place is "the congregation of the dead." To him they seem good companions. He has long since "outgrown" the company of the little flock who gather for Bible study, testimony, and prayer. The "workers of iniquity" have become his people. He laughs at their dirty jokes, supports their vile lifestyles, votes for their godless programs, reads their sin-sodden books, watches their disgusting movies, attends their worldly functions, and in the end shares their lost eternity.

Consider the case of Arius. In his early years he was a pupil of Lucian of Antioch, a celebrated theologian who founded a school dedicated to the literal exegesis of the Scriptures. Lucian made a bold and impressive confession of his faith before the judge and died while being tortured in prison in Nicomedia (A.D. 312). Eusebius of Nicomedia, also one of Lucian's pupils, praised him for the sanctity and purity of his life, for his knowledge of the Scriptures, and for his noble martyrdom. Arius, then, was taught the truth—but he turned his back on it.

Arius has been described as tall, graceful, calm, pale, subdued, popular, and well-mannered. He was known for his acute reasoning and blameless life. But under a humble and mortified exterior he concealed great vanity and ambition.

When Alexander the bishop of Alexandria (312-328) was expounding his strong and orthodox views on the trinity to his presbyters, Arius rose up in the meeting and challenged him. Arius declared that although Jesus was the Son of God, He was not coeternal with the Father. Jesus must be regarded as external to the divine essence. He was only the finest and noblest of those beings whom God the Father had created out of nothing.

Alexander accused Arius of blasphemy. Arius was judged by two councils assembled at Alexandria and cast out of the church. Unabashed and unsubdued, Arius retired to Palestine, where he recruited converts to his cause. He was partially supported by Eusebius the historian of Caesarea (263-339) and strongly supported by Eusebius the bishop of Nicomedia (died about 342), who was a man of vast influence.

Arius, it turned out, had chosen his friends well. Soon Emperor Constantine was drawn into the conflict. He wrote a letter to Alexander and Arius reproving them jointly for contending over "idle issues"! But the controversy continued to rage, so Constantine summoned bishops and clergy from all parts of the empire to meet at Nicaea in Bithynia (A.D. 325) to resolve the dispute. The emperor acted as moderator and the council decided against Arius. Out of this council came the famous Nicene creed, which was signed by the vast majority of the delegates.

Arius was banished to Illyria, but in time he was allowed to return and the controversy continued to rage. A woman sympathizer came to his rescue: Constantia, a sister of Constantine. She persuaded the emperor to invite Arius to court and the crafty Arius presented Constantine with a confession of faith that lulled him into believing that Arius was orthodox enough to be reinstated in the church. The Arians now had the weight of the throne behind them.

Athanasius, who had distinguished himself at the council of Nicaea, defied the emperor's edict that the church receive Arius back into its fellowship. As a result, Athanasius was banished. The aged Bishop Alexander of Constantinople was ordered to admit Arius to holy communion. Alexander said, "Arius has well sworn, if his words have no double meaning: otherwise God will avenge."

For seven days previous to the day appointed for the readmission of Arius, the church of Constantinople—bishop and people alike—fasted and prayed. After a vain endeavor to change the emperor's mind, Alexander resorted to the most solemn form of anathema allowed in the church. With tears he besought the Lord to remove either him or the man who was behind the extended and increasing spiritual evils of the period.

The evening before the day of his anticipated triumph, Arius and his party passed through the streets of the city in an ostentatious manner. Then suddenly he had a stroke and died where he fell. Athanasius reported:

> While the Church was rejoicing at the deliverance, Alexander administered the Communion, praying with all the brethren, and glorifying God greatly; not as if rejoicing over his death, (God forbid!), but because in this event there was displayed more than a human judgment. For the Lord Himself had passed sentence.[11]

Thus Arius wandered out of the way of understanding and remained in the congregation of the dead!

6. Pleasure (21:17-19)

Proverbs 21:17 warns against *the wrong pursuit:* "He that loveth pleasure shall be a poor man: he that loveth wine and oil shall not be rich." Solomon was talking about two lusts: a lust for laughter and a lust for luxury.

Lord Peter Wimsey's improvident nephew (another character in Dorothy Sayers' *Gaudy Night*) loved pleasure, wine, and oil. Young Lord Saint-George, as he was called, was attending Oxford University and living far beyond his means when he was involved in an automobile accident. In one scene we see him as an accident victim recovering from his injuries—sitting up in bed and gazing dismally at piles of bills strewn all around him. His uncle's friend Harriet Vane tried to bring order out of the chaos, since the wealthy Lord Peter had agreed to bail his nephew out of the financial mess.

With bills from exclusive restaurants, notices of fees due for clubs and a polo fraternity, bills accumulated while running around with a fast-living and extravagant crowd, and bills for repairing his wrecked sports car on which he had neglected to pay the insurance, Saint-George certainly was in debt!

Adding to the confusion were gambling debts, doctors' bills, payments due on loans, bills for cigarettes and wine. There were debts incurred for gold-digging girlfriends (he suggested lumping some of these obligations under "sundries" in the hope that his uncle would interpret them to be bills for postage stamps and telephone calls). The young spendthrift could not even recall what he had purchased from some merchants. "Look at this!" he said. "Sixty-nine, fifteen—account rendered; I wonder what it was all about."[12]

Solomon was right. Neither laughter nor luxury comes cheap. Solomon himself loved wine, women, and song, and his extravagant lifestyle was the gossip of the world in his day. But he could afford it. Or could he? His subjects complained that they were taxed oppressively to pay for his opulence. When the account was finally rendered by the exasperated northern tribes, it was Rehoboam who was left to pay the piper. Unfortunately he had already caught the fever for high living and was too blind to see that an empty treasury could not always be filled at other people's expense.

Another warning is found in Proverbs 21:18: "The wicked shall be a ransom for the righteous, and the transgressor for the upright." In the end the wicked will be made to pay. So often the opposite seems true. The wicked steal and defraud. They rob the righteous and revel in their ill-gotten gains. The wicked hold the righteous for ransom and sometimes get the price demanded. But it is *the wrong price,* for it is "the wages of sin" and "the wages of sin is death" (Romans 6:23). Sooner or later, God turns the tables on the wicked. In due time the righteous come into their own.

As we consider Proverbs 21:18, our thoughts go back to the days of Abraham. Ominous news came to the Jordan valley, where the vile cities of Sodom and Gomorrah plied their trade, indulged in bestial vices, and flaunted their filthy lifestyle. Sitting astride the great caravan routes of their day, these cities had grown rich and powerful, but now news came that the kings of the East were on the march.

Soon there was feverish activity in the valley as the five sister cities formed a military alliance to resist the expected invasion. The generals pored over their maps and stationed their troops. The plan was to lure the invaders into the slime pits in the nearby vale of Siddim so that their infantry and cavalry might bog down and be destroyed.

On a distant hill Abraham sat in the doorway of his tent. He too was rich. Moreover his riches were liquid assets, prime booty for an invading army that was eager to grab quick and easy spoils. He was in a dangerous position, but as yet had received no word from God to move. So, righteous man that he was, he was prepared to "stand still, and see the salvation of the Lord" (Exodus 14:13).

The news became progressively worse; the victorious horde was sweeping all resistance aside. Following a well-used trade route running from Damascus to Sodom, the invaders appeared at the headwaters of the Jordan and poured down the eastern side of the river. They concentrated on the lands of Transjordan, and the Rephaims, the Zuzims, the Emims, and even the Horites in their rocky fortress at Petra, fell before them (Genesis 14:5-6). The wealth of centuries was seized.

The cities of the plain must have breathed a sigh of relief when the kings of the East directed their armies to El-paran at the northernmost tip of the gulf of Aqabah. From there they continued in a wide encircling swing to Kadesh-barnea. After thrashing and plundering the Amalekites, the invaders went on to Tamar to despoil the Amorites (14:6-7).

But if Sodom, Gomorrah, and the other three sister cities thought they were spared, they were much mistaken. The victorious armies wheeled around and advanced swiftly to attack the chief prize: Sodom and its confederates. It was time to use the slime-pit tactic, but it didn't work, for the time had come for God to turn the tables on the wicked. Instead of the invaders becoming snared in the slime pits, the panic-stricken people of Sodom and Gomorrah were trapped there. They were rounded up and marched off into captivity, fittingly bespattered and smeared with slime.

The plunder of the invading armies was now so great that the victorious troops did not even bother with Abraham. Thus the wicked were made "a ransom for the righteous, and the transgressor for the upright."

Proverbs 21:19 warns against *the wrong partner:* "It is better to dwell in the wilderness, than with a contentious and an angry woman." Solomon was returning to the theme mentioned in verse 9. We can be sure that one or two of his many wives fit this description. Of course the kind of situation that prompted the proverb does not occur only in a harem or only in a particular age or nation.

Contentious women were even found in Philippi, where the church was about as perfect as a local church could be. Paul's letter to the Philippians was not like some of his other Epistles in which he had to emphasize his authority and apostleship or adopt a tone that warned of censure to come. In his opening remarks to the Philippians he could speak of giving thanks to God upon every remembrance of them. He remembered beloved Lydia, the dear jailer and his family, and so many others. The whole Epistle to the Philippians rang with joy.

The Son of Man had died and risen again only about thirty years before Paul wrote this Epistle, so the Spirit of the Lord Jesus, still so very real, pervaded the church. But there was one blot on the page. Two Christian women, Euodias and Syntyche, were contentious and angry. Their wretched disagreement and quarreling disturbed the entire church in Philippi. One contentious and angry woman is enough to disrupt a house; two are enough to play havoc with the whole house of God.

Notice the repetition of "the Lord" in Philippians 4:1-2. Paul sandwiched the names of the two women between the double reference to the Lord. "The Lord" was the remedy Paul offered to the church.

In a sermon on Philippians 4:1-2, Sam Cathey—a preacher friend of mine—imagined himself arriving in Heaven. Mingling with the throngs on the great golden highways of glory, he met a woman and introduced himself. "I'm Sam Cathey. I used to be a Southern Baptist preacher." He then asked his new acquaintance who she was.

She replied, "I came from Philippi."

"Philippi!" cried Sam. "The Roman colony nine miles from the Aegean sea, on the fertile plain, not far from the gold mines, on the main road to Rome?"

"The very same."

"Well, you must have known Paul."

"Of course I knew Paul. Everyone in Philippi knew Paul. I was a charter member of the church at Philippi."

"Were you indeed? What a joy it is to meet you here in Heaven! Tell me, my sister, what is your name?"

After a momentary pause, she said, "Well, as a matter of fact, my name is Euodias. We made up, you know, Syntyche and I. We became the best of friends. Come along, I'll take you to her place on Joy Plaza near Hallelujah Hill."

My friend imagined that happy ending, but all we really know about Euodias and Syntyche is that they must have glared at each other across the communion table and that they must not have spoken to each other—or they spoke to each other too much, too loudly, and too angrily. If they behaved like that in the house of God, how must they have behaved at home? We can believe that the husband of Euodias grew sick and tired of hearing her berate Syntyche at mealtimes, and the husband of Syntyche heartily wished himself in the wilderness every time his wife got her tongue wrapped around the name Euodias. There could have been little pleasure in the homes of Euodias and Syntyche.

7. Prudence (21:20-23)

Solomon advised prudence first *in the matter of one's money:* "There is treasure to be desired and oil in the dwelling of the wise; but a foolish man spendeth it up" (Proverbs 21:20). It does not take long for a fool to spend a fortune someone else painstakingly accumulated and lived on comfortably, even lavishly, all his days. This proverb reinforces one of Solomon's oft-repeated themes: a fool and his money are soon parted, as we would say today.

Proverbs 21:20 is illustrated in Jeffery Farnol's rollicking story *The Broad Highway.* In the book Farnol's hero, Peter Vibart, tells us of his sundry interesting adventures on the highway along which he meanders in search of his fortune. One day on the road Vibart was hot, dusty, and thirsty. Noticing a wayside tavern, he debated with himself about whether he could afford to stop and buy some refreshments. He decided he could and hurried toward the tavern. In Vibart's words, this is what happened next:

> As I approached I heard loud voices, raised as though in altercation, and a hat came hurtling through the open doorway and, bounding into the road, rolled over and over to my very feet. And, looking down at it, I saw that it was a very ill-used hat, frayed and worn, dented of crown and broken of brim, yet

> beneath its sordid shabbiness there lurked the dim semblance of what it had once been, for, in the scratched and tarnished buckle, in the jaunty curl of the brim, it still preserved a certain pitiful air of rakishness; wherefore, I stooped, and, picking it up, began to brush the dust from it as well as I might.
>
> I was thus engaged when there arose a sudden bull-like roar and, glancing up, I beheld a man who reeled backwards out of the inn and who, after staggering a yard or so, thudded down into the road and so lay, staring vacantly up at the sky. Before I could reach him, however, he got upon his legs and, crossing unsteadily to the tree I have mentioned, leaned there, and I saw there was much blood upon his face which he essayed to wipe away with the cuff of his coat. Now, upon his whole person, from the crown of his unkempt head down to his broken, dusty boots, there yet clung that air of jaunty, devil-may-care rakishness which I had seen, and pitied in his hat.

The man (Peregrine Beverley) picked himself up, thanked Vibart for returning his hat, assumed a happy-go-lucky attitude, and went off down the road. Vibart went into the tavern and ordered something to drink. The landlord demanded payment in advance, explaining angrily that his previous customer, who had been so forcefully expelled, had drained his glass then offered his hat in payment. "An'...wot d'ye think o' that now?" the landlord demanded. Vibart recounted the rest of the conversation:

> "Why, I think you were perhaps a trifle hasty," said I.
>
> "Oh, ye do, do ye?"
>
> "Yes," I nodded.
>
> "An' for why?"
>
> "Well, you will probably remember that the hat had a band round it—"
>
> "Ay, all wore away it were too—"
>
> "And that in the band was a buckle—"
>
> "Ay, all scratched an' rusty it were—well?"
>
> "Well, that tarnished buckle was of silver—"
>
> "Silver!" gasped the man, his jaw falling.
>
> "And easily worth five shillings, perhaps more, so that I think you were, upon the whole, rather hasty." Saying which, I finished my ale and, taking up my staff, stepped out into the sunshine.

Shortly afterward, Vibart met young Beverley, who was sitting in a ditch by the roadside hedge. Vibart offered to share his humble supper of bread and cheese with the vagrant and thereby learned his story. We hear of their discussion from Vibart:

> And after a while, when there nothing remained of loaf or cheese save a few scattered crumbs, my companion leaned back, and gave another sigh.
>
> "Sir," said he, with an airy wave of the hand, "in me you behold a highly promising young gentleman ruined by a most implacable enemy—himself, sir. In the first place you must know my name is Beverley…very much at your service—late of Beverley Place, Surrey, now of Nowhere-in-Particular."
>
> "Beverley," said I…, "I have heard that name before."
>
> "It is highly probable, Mr. Vibart; a fool of that name—fortunate or unfortunate as you choose to classify him—lost houses, land, and money in a single night's play. I am that fool, sir, though you have doubtless heard particulars ere now?"
>
> "Not a word!" said I. Mr. Beverley glanced at me with a faint mingling of pity and surprise. "My life," I explained, "has been altogether a studious one…."
>
> "For my own achievements, hitherto," I continued, "I have…translated the works of Quintilian, with the Satyricon of Petronius Arbiter, and the Life, Lives, and Memoirs of the Seigneur de Brantome…."
>
> "Ha!" exclaimed Mr. Beverley, sitting up suddenly, with his ill-used hat very much over one eye, "there we have it! Who ever heard of Old Quin—What's-his-name, or cared, except, perhaps, a few bald-headed bookworms and withered littérateurs? While you were dreaming of life, and reading the lives of other fellows, I was living it. In my career, episodically brief though it was, I have met and talked with all the wits, and celebrated men, have drunk good wine, and worshipped beautiful women, Mr. Vibart."
>
> "And what has it all taught you?" said I.
>
> "That there are an infernal number of rogues and rascals in the world, for one thing—and that is worth knowing."
>
> "Yes," said I.
>
> "That, though money can buy anything, from the love of a woman to the death of an enemy, it can only be spent once—and that is worth knowing also."
>
> "Yes," said I.
>
> "And that I am a most preposterous fool!—and that last, look you, is more valuable than all the others."[13]

Up to this point Beverley's life illustrates Proverbs 21:20. As Farnol's story goes on, Beverley and Vibart become firm friends.

Next Solomon advised prudence *in the matter of one's morals:* "He that followeth after righteousness and mercy findeth life, righteousness, and honour" (Proverbs 21:21).

Such a man finds much more than he bargains for. He invests in *law.* He seeks righteousness and in turn finds righteousness, honor, and life. It is no wonder that the pursuit of righteousness yields such great rewards. To seek for righteousness means to seek for that which is right in the sight of God, not just in the sight of men. The man who seeks mercy invests in *love,* for that is the root idea behind the word translated "mercy" here. He invests in grace and lovingkindness. In short, the man who invests in law and love—who follows after those things that are dear to the heart of God—finds *life.*

Many noble examples of the man "that followeth after righteousness and mercy" are recorded in history. Not the least of these is the reformer Philipp Melanchthon. Born in Germany in 1497, he enrolled in the University of Heidelberg before he was thirteen. He excelled in Greek and in 1518 became the professor of Greek at Wittenberg.

Melanchthon threw himself behind Luther and the Protestant Reformation. Luther knew that this man was worth pure gold. It was Melanchthon who showed him that the word which had always been translated "penance" really meant "repentance." When Luther died it was Melanchthon who pronounced the historic obituary over his tomb. A few years later Melanchthon was buried in the same grave. They sleep side by side in the old castle church at Wittenberg—the same church where Luther nailed his famous theses to the door.

Melanchthon, Luther's right-hand man, was the real genius behind the Reformation. Luther brought the Reformation to the laity; Melanchthon brought it to the learned. He followed after righteousness and mercy, and placed a more moderate hand on the helm than Luther. Melanchthon was "characterized by moderation, conscientiousness, caution and love of peace."

Visitors to his old house in Wittenberg tell of the inscription high up on the front: "Here lived, taught and died Philipp Melanchthon." He lived for forty years in that house and gathered students around him in his garden each summer. He studied and wrote his books in the upstairs front room. There visitors see another inscription: "Stop, traveller! Against this wall stood the couch on which the venerable Philipp Melanchthon piously and peacefully died, April 19, 1560, at a quarter-past seven o'clock." Outside that study is a message inscribed over the door: *"Si Deus pro nobic, quis contra nos?"*—that is, "If God be for us, who can be against us?" Melanchthon had his pastor read these words to him as he prepared to die, and in dying find eternal life. As Solomon said, "He that followeth after righteousness and mercy findeth life."

Solomon also advised prudence in *the matter of one's might:* "A wise man scaleth the city of the mighty, and casteth down the strength of the confidence thereof" (Proverbs 21:22).

In his early days Joab was a wise man—wise in the ways of war, that is. Never was he more wise than when he took Jerusalem from the Jebusites (2 Samuel 5:8; 1 Chronicles 11:6). He captured the city not so much by brute force as by wisdom. Joab's ambition, which was already in the saddle when he figured how to take that impregnable fortress, was held in check then by his admiration for David.

The classic story about the taking of a city centers around the legendary conflict between the early Greeks and the people of Troy in western Anatolia (Asia Minor) sometime in the twelfth or thirteenth century B.C. No other event so stirred the imagination of the Greeks. The story found its way into Homer's *Iliad* and *Odyssey* and also into Roman literature by way of Virgil's *Aeneid.*

The story tells how Paris, the son of the Trojan king, absconded with Helen, the beautiful wife of Menelaus of Sparta. Agamemnon, brother of Menelaus, raised an army and marched off to seize and sack the city of Troy. That task proved difficult. Indeed Troy held out for ten years.

Since the city could not be taken by conventional tactics of war, a wise Greek soldier suggested an unconventional strategy: make a great wooden horse and conceal a raiding party inside; then withdraw the Greek forces and wait for the Trojans to sally forth, seize the horse, and take it into Troy as their spoil!

The suggested plan was put into action immediately. The Greeks retired from the battle and the Trojans dragged the wooden horse into the city. As soon as the coast was clear, the hidden Greeks descended from the horse's hollow belly and opened the gates of Troy to their comrades, who had returned to the walls. Subsequently the Greeks sacked the city, massacred its men, and carried off its women.

The expression *Trojan horse* has become a byword for any device that can infiltrate the defenses of an enemy or a competitor. One wise man in the Greek army was worth more than the army itself.

In the Middle Ages it was always difficult to capture a city with mighty walls and towers, iron gates, a drawbridge, and a moat. To scale a city with a protected water supply, a loyal population, and enough provisions to withstand a siege was a tough proposition for any invading army—a proposition calling for a wise man like the one in Proverbs 21:22.

Solomon furthermore advised prudence *in the matter of one's mouth:* "Whoso keepeth his mouth and his tongue keepeth his soul from troubles" (Proverbs 21:23). James gave us the best discussion of the evils of the tongue. He called it "a fire" and "a world of iniquity."

By means of a bit in a horse's mouth, a man can control a beast that is bigger and stronger than he is. With a small helm he can steer a ship, even in a stormy sea. But who can control his tongue? Men can tame birds and beasts—even serpents, porpoises, and killer whales—but no one can fully tame his own tongue. At one moment it blesses God, but the next moment it curses God.

Nature obeys the rules of its Creator: fig trees do not bear olives; vines do not yield figs; fountains do not pour out both sweet and bitter water. But the tongue obeys no rules. (See James 3:2-12.)

The author of the Epistle of James was the Lord's half brother. It seems that when he wrote, "If any man offend not in word, the same is a perfect man, and able also to bridle the whole body," he was paying his own personal tribute to the Lord Jesus. James had grown up in the same home as Jesus, but had never heard Him speak a cross word, tell a lie, or answer back. James had never known Him to laugh at anything crude or cruel or say anything that was not pure, kind, just, and good. James had never heard Him raise His voice in anger or say anything that required an apology. Jesus's words had always been full of wisdom, motivated by the highest form of love, and saturated with kindness.

Thinking back over the thirty years or so he had known Jesus, James at last realized just what kind of person Jesus was: the best friend he had ever had; the kindest and noblest big brother he could have had; and the most honest, hard-working, conscientious, cheerful, and generous business partner in the world. As James thought of Jesus in the home, on the highway, in the synagogue, in the school, in the workshop, and around the village, he realized that He epitomized perfection. Solomon never knew Jesus, but he would have most heartily agreed with James.

8. Pride (21:24)

"Proud and haughty scorner is his name, who dealeth in proud wrath." Solomon had the insolent scoffer in mind. The words translated "proud wrath" are sometimes rendered "superfluity of pride."

Among the examples of the type of person described in this proverb are the rationalists who fill scholastic chairs in liberal seminaries and pulpits in liberal churches. They are dedicated to destroying the faith of those who are entrusted to their care. "Proud and haughty scorner" is their name. They reveal their contempt for the Word of God when they set themselves up as its critics. "Higher critics" they call themselves. Their attacks on revealed truth proceed from pride of intellect, and their conclusions about God's inspired and inerrant Word proceed from skepticism, infidelity, and "an evil heart of unbelief" (Hebrews 3:12).

We find a graphic picture of such people in 2 Kings 4:38-41. There we read that the prophet Elisha decided to have a feast day for the sons of the prophets at Gilgal in spite of the fact that a famine raged throughout the land. "Set on the great pot, and seethe pottage," he commanded. So far, so good. But notice what happened next: "One went out into the field to gather herbs, and found a wild vine, and gathered thereof wild gourds his lap full, and came and shred them into the pot of pottage: for they knew them not." As soon as the young men began to eat, they knew something was wrong. "They cried out, and said, O thou man of God, there is death in the pot."

The man who put the wild gourds into the pot was either a great fool or a great criminal. There is something ominous about that faceless individual. Some people today might wish to call him a moderate, but it is hard to see that there is anything moderate about poison. Everything about the man is illustrative of the liberal. The Holy Spirit uses this individual to show us the liberal at work.

Note that this man went into "the field" to find food for the people of God. In one of His parables Jesus shed light on "the field." He said, "The field is the world" (Matthew 13:38). Surely we know what to expect from the man who goes to the world to find his theology. He will glean from Wellhausen, Darwin, Marx, and the like. We need to beware of anything such a man puts into the pot!

Note too that the man in 2 Kings 4:39 gathered fruit from a *wild* vine. Jesus said, "I am the *true* vine" (John 15:1, italics added). Surely then the wild vine represents the lies of the antichrist.

The man who gathered the wild gourds was not moderate in his actions, for he put a whole "lap full" of poison into the pot. This was no small error; this was wholesale apostasy. There was enough poison in the gourds to affect the entire school of prophets.

Note also that the man did not put the poison into the pot in one big clump. If he had, it would have been easy enough to remove the poison as soon as it was detected. But he was more crafty than that—he shredded the poisonous gourds into the pot a little at a time. Consequently the other people "knew them not," said the Holy Spirit. Evidently the man who put "death in the pot" was someone they trusted.

We can see the liberal's poison at work in all the mainline denominations. Eager, unsuspecting young men are sent off to seminaries to be trained for the ministry and there they get their first taste of poisoned pottage. They are immediately introduced to the so-called higher critics, who first try to undermine Moses and the first three chapters of Genesis. If they can persuade the students to rid themselves of belief in God as the Creator and to doubt the true nature of sin, the liberals know they have gone a long way toward getting the poison into the seminarians' souls. Then the rest of the Bible is torn into shreds. Daniel must go, as must Isaiah and Jonah, along with the supernatural Christ of the Gospels and the apostle Paul and his Epistles.

The liberals' attack on the Pentateuch is devilish and determined. According to them, Moses did not write the first five books of the Bible. These books, they say, are a literary mural—a patchwork quilt of ideas woven together over the course of many centuries by unknown authors using various sources.

In explaining the origin of the Pentateuch, the poisoners begin by speaking of a "J" document in which the name *Jehovah* was prominent. The "J" document, so they say, was written centuries after the events it described. Then they refer to an "E" document in which the name *Elohim* was prominent. "E" roughly paralleled "J." These two documents, the liberals assure the astonished young men who are eating from their poisoned pot, happily jogged side by side for a long time. Then somebody combined them by inserting various parts of the newer "E" document into the older "J" document. Later on somebody else wrote what these soul-assassins call the "D" document (which supposedly contained the farewell speeches of Moses) and tacked it onto the end of the imaginary "JE" documents.

Even this patchwork quilt, however, does not satisfy the destructive critics. They hypothesize that a group of priests, about the time of the exile, composed still another document—the "P" document, which supposedly ran parallel with the "JE" documents. Finally, the liberals say, a bright Hebrew innovator cut the "P" document into large and small pieces, spread them out, and inserted appropriate sections into the other documents wherever he saw a similarity. The

Pentateuch is thus robbed by the higher critics of inerrancy, divine revelation, and divine inspiration.

And what do the liberals do with Moses? He remains a problem for them. At one time they brazenly taught that according to the assured results of higher criticism, Moses could not have written the Pentateuch because writing had not been invented in his day! They have had to back off from that position, but they still have many more wild gourds with which to poison pastors and people alike.

The liberals ignore the fact that Jesus, the incarnate Son of the living God, believed in Moses and believed that he could write. Jesus said to His enemies, "Had ye believed Moses, ye would have believed me: for he wrote of me. But if ye believe not his writings, how shall ye believe my words?" (John 5:46-47) That is the bottom line. Who is right—the liberal professors or Christ? Christ is, of course! It is not possible to believe in the incarnation and also believe in liberal theology. It is not Christ the liberals preach, but the antichrist.

Archaeology and other Biblical sciences have long since proved the higher critics wrong. Yet they continue to spew their "high-sounding nonsense,"[14] putting the same wild-vine poison into the seminary and pulpit pot. A "superfluity of pride" is the cause of their attacks on the Word of God.

The Septuagint rendering of Proverbs 21:24 implies that the proud and haughty scorner is a pest, and so he is—to say the least.

9. Procrastination (21:25-26)

Proverbs 21:25 speaks of *slothful dreams:* "The desire of the slothful killeth him; for his hands refuse to labour." The slothful man wants all kinds of things—but he will not work for them. As time goes on he needs all kinds of things—but he will not work for them. He would rather beg, borrow, steal, or starve than work.

The welfare state tends to encourage slothfulness by taking money out of the pockets of the industrious and successful and putting it into the pockets of the indigent and slothful. God does not do that.

Scripture attaches no stigma to being poor, but attaches every stigma to being lazy. I am not talking about the person who cannot work because of illness or disability. First Timothy 5:16 says we are to help those who are "widows indeed." The Bible also commends the orphan and the unfortunate to our care. But if a person will not work, the Bible says he is to be left to lie on the bed he has made.

If we start handing money to a lazy man, he will never learn to be industrious. Even in the garden of Eden, unfallen man was expected to work.

The lazy man's lifestyle leads to death. His mind stagnates. His body—often chronically undernourished and inadequately clothed and housed—becomes susceptible to countless ills. He cannot ward off sickness, the ravages of inclement weather, or the effects of malnutrition. The desire of the slothful is to do nothing, and in the end that desire kills him.

There is an illustration of Proverbs 21:25 in the writings of Dan Crawford who, following in the steps of David Livingstone, penetrated the heart of Africa. In his farewell words to Henry Stanley, Livingstone had said: "On crossing the Lualaba, I shall go direct S.W. to the copper mines of Katanga. Eight days south of Katanga the natives declare the fountains [of the Nile] to be." Livingstone never took that journey, but Crawford did. He told us about it in *Thinking Black*, a fascinating book in which he sought to enter into the African mind.[15]

After a thirty-two-month trek from the coast, he at last passed "through the Western door of Mushidi's empire at the Lualaba." There Crawford was "doomed to drink dirty water for many a day, the potion so putrid that it [was] impossible to drink any that [had] lain overnight."

Mushidi was a tyrant chief. Having studied the horrors of Mushidi's kraal, Crawford defined a tyrant as "a man who finds his happiness in the unhappiness of others." Mushidi refrained, however, from the ultimate horror of savagery in darkest Africa. He assured the missionary that he had not allowed living sacrifices in his capital, whereas in surrounding empires no petty chieftain could be buried without a "red sunset." In other words, the death of a chieftain was generally accompanied by the wholesale slaughter of his womenfolk and often his whole court or even his whole town.

Mushidi, however, had his own brand of terror: "More executions," wrote the missionary, "which means more putrefying skulls and clouds of blue-bottle flies. Skulls heaped on long rustic tables, skulls hanging up on trees like hat-pegs, skulls with yawning mouths that would not shut even in death." Crawford added:

> This Bluebeard business, remember, means hard detective work, and the Emperor spends sleepless nights raiding his own harems. Five hundred (and a fraction) wives and not a padlock in the land. It is on this sorry score blood runs in torrents, for the paramours are legion, and often the true,

> because prior, husbands of the stolen women. Mushidi knows all this and more, knows he must keep running to the red, reckless expedient of killing even on suspicion.

The natives, who disliked the missionary's watch, called it *nsaa* ("sun"). "In this clockless life," wrote Crawford, "you find the real root of his [the native's] happy-go-lucky existence....Time is passing, quickly passing; 'but,' objects the negro, 'why nag out the truth so brutally, why this relentless repetition?'" The Africans hated "the pretensions, too, of this preposterous thing called 'a sun,' still at it after sundown, still bustling on through the night with a tick like a fever pulse."

The lack of a clock was only equaled, the missionary said, by the lack of a calendar. He wrote: "Quite an aged man will tell you blandly that he is ten years of age. Is this calculation correct after all? Does he mean that, sleeping away three-quarters of his life as he does, it is fair only to count the meagre margin that remains of non-slept time?"

Such a lackadaisical existence reminds us of the proverb about the slothful. And Solomon's acute observation applies particularly to the lifestyle of Mushidi, for Arab slave traders had built him what the missionary called "his Castle of Indolence...a cold, cheerless, mud barn, really, the grass roof forbidding a chimney." Crawford continued:

> In the days when I was the only white skin at Bunkeya, I got to size up Mushidi quite closely. Here the five hundred wives stream in on him with well-cooked dainties, for do they not all vie with each other to capture the Chief's citadel, his stomach?...Thus it cometh to pass that, pampered with negro luxury and softened by sloth, strength is forsaking Mushidi's limbs as common sense his skull, and the old tale is once again true that luxury is the conqueror of conquerors.

An epigraph at the opening of chapter XII of Crawford's book certainly applies to the world of Mushidi:

> On that pagan world disgust
> And secret loathing fell;
> Deep weariness and sated lust
> Made human life a hell.

Truly, "the desire of the slothful killeth him."

The next proverb speaks about *selfish desires:* "He coveteth greedily all the day long: but the righteous giveth and spareth not" Proverbs 21:26 is really an extension of 21:25, for the indolent man is full of unsatisfied cravings. He always has his hand out. His eternal desire is to *get.* The industrious man, too, always has his hand out, but his great desire is to *give.* With "bread enough and to spare" (Luke 15:17), he is generous and charitable, full of compassion and eager to help the unfortunate.

This contrast reminds me of the difference between workers and drones in a beehive. They are actually sisters and brothers, hatched from eggs laid by the same queen. But the queen lays both fertilized and unfertilized eggs. Both types hatch, but whereas the fertilized eggs produce females containing genes from both parents, the unfertilized eggs produce males—drones that inherit their genes from the queen alone.

The world inside a beehive is run entirely by females. It is a world for workaholics—a ruthless place of order, efficiency, and drive. The activity inside a hive is ceaseless, but full of purpose.

There are two kinds of worker bees: house bees and field bees. House bees keep the hive clean. If an object is too large to move (for instance, a mouse that has been stung to death for invading the hive), house bees simply mummify it with propolis, a resin gathered from trees. Some house bees serve as undertakers, removing dead bees from the hive. Others serve as air-conditioners, beating their wings near the entrance to keep a cool draft blowing through the hive. There are house bees who build combs to store honey, house bees who repair old combs, house bees who spread wax on newly-finished comb layers, and house bees who construct road systems throughout the hive.

Field bees scout and forage outside the hive. Orienting themselves by means of the sun, they provide precise information to coworkers as to a source of food and its relative quality. They hurry back and forth, gathering pollen in tiny baskets on the outer surfaces of their hind legs and putting nectar into a special honey stomach about the size of a pinhead. Field bees make more than sixty trips and visit more than a thousand flowers just to collect a thimbleful of nectar, yet the foragers in a single hive collect as much as fifteen pounds a day.

At the door of the hive stand the guards who screen every insect entering or leaving the hive. They are ready to kill intruders or fly to the aid of a worker who sounds an alarm.

A special corps of workers constantly groom and protect the queen. She lays the eggs—as many as a million from one impregnation.

The drones, the males who comprise about 5 percent of the hive population, are so lazy that they have to be fed by nurse bees. The one function of the drones is to mate with the queen during her nuptial flight. Pampered, petted, and preserved, they live off the industry of others. But a day of reckoning comes. At the season's end, the surviving drones are dragged from the hive, dumped outside, and left to starve or die of exposure.

Solomon's slothful man is a drone. Solomon's righteous man is a worker. Drones in our society are not simply dumped and left to starve. There is always some hope for them. Human society, after all, is not based on the beehive, but God does expect each person to be industrious and contribute to the well-being of all mankind. That is our common duty.

10. Pretense (21:27)

"The sacrifice of the wicked," wrote Solomon, "is abomination: how much more, when he bringeth it with a wicked mind?" We only have to read the Lord's denunciation of the Pharisees (Matthew 23) to realize how sinful hypocrisy is. And there is no worse hypocrisy than to go through the motions of religion with the deliberate purpose of pretending to be righteous while living unrighteously.

I met some hypocrites during the nearly two years I was stationed in a small military camp on the Haifa docks at the foot of mount Carmel. In those days Palestine was still a mandated territory of the British empire. There were about two dozen of us in that camp and we were a decent group of soldiers until someone had the idea of starting a canteen. After the evening meal the small dining room was converted into a bar and the drinking members of that small community gave themselves over to ribald song, vile behavior, and continual drunkenness. They were joined, as often as not, by sailors from British ships in port.

The man behind all the drinking was an Irishman we called Paddy. Paddy was a Roman Catholic but he never darkened the door of a church except at Christmas. When he was sober he was a friendly fellow. In fact he and I had many discussions about religion. However, he lived for the moment when the canteen would open. He bought the booze, sold the drinks, handled the money, and steered the drunks out of the door in the early hours of the morning. He led the vile songs that made the night hideous and laughed at the men who couldn't hold their liquor and whose resulting vileness disgusted the few who detested the whole canteen scene.

Paddy had two Roman Catholic buddies on the small base, each as hard a drinker as he. The three of them would argue about religion, but they were all first-class hypocrites and habitual drunkards. One December 24th Paddy and his two buddies drank all day long. By eleven o'clock at night they were in a festive mood and quite drunk. Then one of them dredged up from the depths of his drink-drenched memory the fact that the next day was Christmas. "We must go to midnight mass, boys," he said. The last I saw of them, they were off toward the dockyard gates—holding each other up, staggering as they walked, singing crude songs at the top of their lungs as they went to "worship" God. Their sacrifice was an abomination.

Even more abominable in the sight of our holy God, must be the sacrifice of those who practice sodomy. Not long ago the General Assembly of the Presbyterian Church (U.S.A.) presented a report that took three years to prepare. It advocated acceptance of sex outside of marriage for homosexuals, teenagers, and single adults who live together. We can be thankful that the rank and file of the denomination revolted against the leadership and defeated the proposal by a resounding 534 to 31 vote. However, denomination after denomination has faced similar issues—issues that we would have thought were settled once and for all in the Bible.

One church leader has declared, "The apostle Paul would have been more understanding if he knew as much about sexual variance as moderns do." Nonsense! God the Holy Spirit knows all about sexual variance and He bluntly calls it sin. Paul did not originate his teachings against deviant sex. The Holy Spirit did. The fact that such issues even come up for debate shows how deeply apostasy has eaten into the heart of the modern church. God poured fire and brimstone on Sodom and Gomorrah for the practices the Presbyterian report approved. If such behavior in the world called down His wrath, how will God respond when such sexual perversion is condoned by the church? To profess to worship and serve God while practicing sodomy is truly an abomination.

11. Perjury (21:28-29)

Proverbs 21:28 speaks of *the doom of the unscrupulous man:* "A false witness shall perish: but the man that heareth speaketh constantly [that is, always speaks the truth]."

The Bible character Hananiah of Gibeon is an example of the false witness in the proverb. A villain who opposed the prophet Jeremiah, Hananiah uttered false prophecies in the fourth year of Zedekiah's reign. Zedekiah, the last Old Testament king of the Jews, continued to sit on the throne in Jerusalem solely because Nebuchadnezzar, to whom he had sworn allegiance, trusted him to keep his word.

Zedekiah had only been on the throne a brief time when the whole region of Syria began to seethe with plots to throw off the Babylonian yoke. Jerusalem seems to have taken the lead in the planning. In the fourth year of Zedekiah's reign ambassadors from the neighboring kingdoms of Tyre, Sidon, Edom, and Moab visited Jerusalem in order to consult with Zedekiah about the measures they should take (Jeremiah 27:3). That same year Zedekiah went off to Babylon, presumably to throw dust in Nebuchadnezzar's eyes and to assure him of his loyalty (51:59).

Meanwhile the false prophet Hananiah publicly declared in the temple that within two years Jeconiah and his fellow captives, together with the vessels of the Lord's house, would all be brought back from Babylon to Jerusalem. To give his false prophecy more weight, Hananiah took the wooden yoke off Jeremiah's neck (Jeremiah 28:10). Jeremiah had worn this yoke by divine command to signify the certain doom of Judah and Jerusalem (27:2).

Jeremiah at once denounced this false prophecy. He said that the wooden yoke Hananiah had broken would be replaced by yokes of iron and that the whole nation would most certainly serve Nebuchadnezzar. Jeremiah added this:

> Hear now, Hananiah; The Lord hath not sent thee; but thou makest this people to trust in a lie. Therefore thus saith the Lord; Behold, I will cast thee from off the face of the earth: this year thou shalt die, because thou hast taught rebellion against the Lord. So Hananiah the prophet died the same year in the seventh month (Jeremiah 28:15-17).

The plotters, however, ignored Jeremiah—doubtless because they preferred to believe Hananiah's optimistic predictions rather than Jeremiah's prophecies of doom and gloom. So the rebels carried on with their folly.

In the eighth year of Zedekiah, the Babylonians came back to deal with the revolt and Zedekiah's treachery. They speedily subdued all Judah except Jerusalem, Lachish, and Azekah (Jeremiah 34:7). Those inside Jerusalem who favored rebellion were greatly encouraged when the arrival of the supportive Egyptian army caused the Babylonians to lift the siege temporarily. But the next year the Babylonians returned. This time they made a complete end of the Judean monarchy, destroyed both Jerusalem and the temple, and brutally punished the false and foolish Zedekiah.

Meanwhile the man who truly heard from God and always spoke the truth, even when imprisoned, had been thrown into a pit and threatened with a traitor's death. The false witness had been revered, but woe came to those who had listened to him.

Proverbs 21:29 goes on to speak of *the determination of the unscrupulous man:* "A wicked man hardeneth his face: but as for the upright, he directeth his way."

A man's face reveals a great deal about him, as Abraham Lincoln knew. When asked to appoint a certain man to his cabinet, Lincoln replied, "I don't like his face."

The astonished petitioner said, "But the man is not responsible for his face."

"Every man over forty is responsible for his face," the perceptive president replied.

I heard an amusing story about a father who brought his boss home for supper. The boss, a wealthy business tycoon, was very large, very aggressive, very red-faced, and perpetually overbearing. He liked to boast about his achievements and tell about people whom he had outwitted. He was proud of his lack of formal education and his ability to surpass college-trained professionals. Being his usual objectionable self at mealtime, he fixed a belligerent eye on the young son of his employee. "Do you know, son," he boasted, "that I am a self-made man?" The youngster looked the visitor over critically and said, "What did you make yourself like that for?"

A person's face tells us about his character and life story. The general cartography of a face helps tell the tale—the frown lines in the forehead, the humorous crow's-feet at the corners of the eyes, the lines around the mouth, and the set of the chin are all indelible marks. In addition there are indicators of current thought: the eyes, mouth, and brows often betray states of mind ranging from good humor to inquiry to displeasure.

Solomon mentioned the hardening of the face: the obstinate setting of the jaw, the sullen look in the eyes, the scowl darkening the forehead, the set of the mouth in a grim or savage line. These facial expressions, especially once they become habitual, reveal resolution in wickedness, displeasure, and ill will.

Some older editions of John Bunyan's *Pilgrim's Progress* contain remarkable line drawings of various people in the story. The artist was a master at capturing character in his sketches. He recognized the principle that character, sooner or later, is indelibly stamped on the countenance.

Christian, for example, is depicted as being down-at-heel and dressed in rags before finding his way to Calvary. He is carrying his book and his burden, his face is anxious and drawn, and there is a look of mingled hope and fear in his eyes.

Envy appears reasonably well dressed, but there is an air of dissatisfaction captured in the droop of his left arm. His right hand is clutched across his breast, his head is turned slightly, and he is glowering at something he sees. A heavy frown disfigures his brow, his mouth is hard and turned down, and his eyes are fixed on what he sees.

Ignorance has a round, beardless face with big features. His mouth is poised to speak and his eyes, big with curiosity, blandly look out at someone to whom he is evidently talking. The set of his countenance is that of a man who is eager to have his turn to say something even though he has nothing to say. He has the face of an old-fashioned country bumpkin.

As the wicked man hardens his face, God turns *His* face away from him to look at the upright man. "As for the upright," Solomon said, "he [that is, the Lord] directeth his way." The proverb gives us a picture of a humble believer turning an eager, inquiring face toward the Lord. This man is rewarded by the discovery that the Lord's face is turned toward him to point out the good and right way through life.

Such a man was George Muller of Bristol. In my library I have a picture of him in the middle years of life. His face appears resolute and his eyes seem to be accustomed to looking far away across Jordan. Although the line of his lips is firm, at the corners of his mouth one can discern a readiness to smile. It is a good face—a face touched by nobility, the face of a member of the aristocracy of Heaven.

The Lord certainly directed the way of George Muller. One author wrote:

> The volumes of "The Lord's Dealings with George Muller," now compiled into one volume, and the reports issued annually, are a continuous record of answers to prayer in circumstances of varied trial....One incident, coming under

> the writer's notice, may serve as a sample. He had been spending the night at Mr. Muller's house, and at the simple breakfast there was no appearance of lack. On parting he handed Mr. M. a small sum, having no idea how matters might stand with him. When after two years a report was issued, he found at that date an entry to the effect that "a brother had been staying the night with them, and they had enough to put on the table for breakfast not only for themselves but for their guest, but there was nothing left to purchase the next meal. The brother, on leaving, put——— into his hand, and so their wants were supplied for the time."...
>
> Facts like these, of constant occurrence, spreading over so large a space of time, and the deliverances invariably wrought, are such as to silence all the cavils of unbelief.[16]

George Muller's purpose was to prove to a skeptical age that God exists "and that he is a rewarder of them that diligently seek him" (Hebrews 11:6). With the responsibility of providing for a staff of helpers plus 2050 orphans at a time, Muller lived for years literally on a hand-to-mouth basis, often never knowing (humanly speaking) where the next meal was coming from. Yet he always knew that God would supply.

Muller's face, ever turned toward God, must have glowed. His biographer, Arthur T. Pierson, described him like this:

> As we cast this last backward glance at this man of God, seven conspicuous qualities stand out in him, the combination of which made him what he was: Stainless uprightness, child-like simplicity, business-like precision, tenacity of purpose, boldness of faith, habitual prayer, and cheerful self-surrender. His *holy living* was a necessary condition of his *abundant serving,* as seems so beautifully hinted in the seventeenth verse of the ninetieth Psalm: "Let the *beauty of the Lord our God be upon us,* And *establish Thou the work of our hands upon us.*"
>
> How can the work of our hands be truly established by the blessing of our Lord, unless His beauty also is upon us—the beauty of His holiness transforming our lives and witnessing to His work in us?[17]

Solomon observed the *hard* face of the sinner. George Muller had the *holy* face of a saint.

## 12. Power (21:30-31)

Briefly addressing himself to the nation, Solomon spoke of *a country and its advisers:* "There is no wisdom nor understanding nor counsel against the Lord" (Proverbs 21:30). Nobody—be it a man or a nation—who sets out to defy the Lord can ever win. History is strewn with the corpses of men and the wreckage of nations that flaunted their puny might in the face of the almighty God.

Consider the case of Tyre, the ancient Phoenician city on the coast of Canaan. Tyre grew in importance until it ruled the sea as powerfully as Babylon ruled the land. The great commercial center of the ancient world, Tyre was beautiful, rich, and learned. Carthage, Rome's rival, was a mere colony of Tyre. Ships from around the world dropped anchor in Tyre's harbor. Merchants from east and west met to do business in its streets.

When Tyre was at the height of its glory and power, the rising sun would shine on the city until its streets seemed to gleam with gold. But that sun also shone on graven images, altars, and temples dedicated to Baal, Ashtoreth, and Moloch. These gods insulted the Majesty of Heaven.

Moloch, for instance, was a huge, hideous brass idol. His hands, discolored by fire, held a curved tray, one edge of which rested on an opening in his belly. Inside the idol was a cavity where wood and fuel for a fire were placed.

From time to time Tyre staged sacrifices to propitiate this demon god. Thousands of people would throng the courtyard of Moloch, and priests would ignite the fuel inside him. Soon the image would be wreathed in smoke and its brazen belly would glow with fierce heat. White-robed priests would offer prayers, go through rituals, bow before the red-hot image, gash themselves with knives, then catch their blood and cast it into the fire. Wild-eyed seers would utter prophecies and bands of nearly naked women would dance with sensual abandon.

Then silence would fall. A mother would lead a three- or four-year-old child dressed in white and garlanded with flowers toward the grotesque image. The child, suddenly frightened, would cling to his mother's robes, but a priest would snatch him away and drag the struggling youngster to the foot of a little iron ladder, the top of which rested against the outstretched hands of the image. The priest (shielded by protective armor) would hold the terrified child aloft, climb the ladder, and with a yell of triumph throw the screaming child onto Moloch's glowing tray. From there the tortured child would slowly roll down into the red abyss as instruments played, priests sang, and the savage multitude shrieked with delight.

Such was Moloch. Such was Tyre. All its wealth and wisdom were "against the Lord." No wonder Ezekiel proclaimed Tyre's doom (Ezekiel 26).

In time Nebuchadnezzar's armies appeared and after thirteen years of effort took the city and destroyed it. They wreaked vengeance on buildings and people alike, but many of Tyre's citizens escaped to a small island a mile and a half off the coast. There they built a new city, one that soon rivaled the old one. Determined not to be caught again, the people of the new Tyre developed a powerful fleet of warships to patrol their territorial waters. They had a large commercial fleet as well, so they were able to continue to live in luxury, "against the Lord."

When Alexander the Great came to power, Tyre defied him as it had defied all other conquerors. The efficient Tyrian navy and a clever system of underwater obstacles prevented a successful Greek attack by sea. But God had not forgotten His prophecy, and the time had come to fulfill His Word. Tyre's date with doom had arrived. Alexander took what remained of the ruined walls, towers, timbers, and houses of ancient Tyre and used this salvaged material to build a solid causeway to the island city. By the time the causeway was completed, he had actually scraped up the dust from the ruins and thrown it into the sea—just as Ezekiel had prophesied. Then the all-conquering Alexander captured the new city and killed or enslaved its people.

No matter how astute the advisers of a nation's rulers are, if they set themselves against God and insult Him by their lifestyle, in time God will avenge Himself upon that nation and its people.

Continuing the same line of reasoning, Solomon spoke of *a country and its armaments:* "The horse is prepared against the day of battle: but safety is of the Lord" (Proverbs 21:31). A nation's best line of defense is an active trust in God. History abounds with illustrations of this truth.

Consider, for instance, the evacuation of the British army from Dunkirk. Everyone agrees it was a miracle. The bulk of the expeditionary force, which the government feared would be lost, was saved by an armada of tiny vessels that plied the English channel constantly against enormous odds and with remarkably few casualties. The evacuation was possible only because of the weather—and God alone controls the weather.

Lord Gort, who was in command of the British army at Dunkirk, was given permission to capitulate if he thought it best to do so.

Within forty-eight hours after he received this authority from the British war office, however, light began to pierce the dark clouds. When the dikes were opened to flood the low ground to delay the German advance, the wind blew in *from the sea*, greatly aiding this strategy. And during five out of the seven days and nights of the evacuation, the wind blew *from the land*. Without these offshore winds, embarkation in small boats from that dangerous coast would have been impossible.

On June 4, 1940, the British prime minister told the House of Commons: "A fog did its helpful work in screening from the innumerable German aircraft the motley mass of vessels sent to rescue the men; and the swift current of the English Channel gave way to calm waters—a happening almost without precedent at this time of year."

General Sir Beauvoir De Lisle declared at the central hall of Westminster on November 2, 1943, "I believe this war was won on May 26, 1940, the Sunday the King appointed as a Day for National Prayer."

Weather also prevented a German invasion of Britain. The Germans intended to invade England during the weekend of September 16, 1940, because that was the week of the full moon and the harvest moon, when the waters of the English channel are generally smoothest. In fact September 16-20 is the period chosen for the yearly attempts to swim the straits of Dover because the harvest moon prolongs light to a late hour and the weather is usually calm. Having full knowledge of the facts, Churchill told Parliament and the nation that the next ten days would be the most critical in the country's history.

The Germans, who had collected boats at various points on the French coast, waited for the critical time. The weather remained calm right up until September 16 and it seemed that the Germans would have their way. Then on September 17 a gale blew up the channel and the sea became rough. The bad weather lasted until September 29! The Germans could not use their invasion boats and these were soon systematically destroyed by the British air force. Once again, the previous Sunday had been kept as a Day of National Prayer.

The Germans, persistent as ever, set two new target dates. They planned to try again in November or December, when fog usually blanketed the channel. However for the first time in living memory there was no fog that winter in the straits.

Then the Germans set February 15, 1941, as another invasion date. On February 14, however, a submarine earthquake and a hurricane occurred in the Atlantic. The effects of the resulting tidal system around the British Isles were both immediate and prolonged. Ships were driven as far as eighty miles off course. The Germans gave up.[18] Truly, "safety is of the Lord."

13. Priorities (22:1-2)

Proverbs 22:1 speaks of *the long-range importance of integrity:* "A good name is rather to be chosen than great riches, and loving favour rather than silver and gold."

This verse reminds me of the old French count who, because of the spendthrift ways of his ancestors, was reduced to living in a common lodging house in the Paris slums. When his neighbors invited him to join in their lawless expeditions, he pulled himself up to his full height and said, "Thank you, but no! You see, I am a French count, *Noblesse Oblige.* Privilege has its responsibilities. If I were to do as you suggest I should bring dishonor upon the noble name I bear. I pray you, have me excused."

Then there is the story of the little southern boy who, when asked his name, replied, "Ah is George Washington."

The man who had asked his name said: "My! That is a great name. You will have to be careful that you *live* like George Washington."

The little fellow responded: "Of course Ah'll behave like George Washington. Ah *is* George Washington!"

A soldier in the army of Alexander the Great was a habitual offender and a malingerer. When he was brought before the general for punishment, the commander-in-chief looked at the soldier and asked his name. "Alexander," the man replied.

"Look here, soldier," said the conqueror, "you either change your behavior or you change your name."

Booker T. Washington, a former slave, carved his own way to statesmanship. He used to describe his experiences along the way. "Slaves have no names," he would say, "no authentic genealogy, no family history and no ancestral traditions. Therefore they have nothing to live up to." So he invented his own name. He explained:

> I tried to picture myself in the position of a boy or a man with an honored and distinguished ancestry. As it is I have no idea who my grandmother was. The very fact that the white boy is conscious that, if he fails, he will disgrace the whole family is of tremendous value in helping him to resist temptations. And the fact that the individual has behind him a proud family

history serves as a stimulus to help him overcome obstacles when striving for success.

Writers of fiction know the value of names. Think of Bunyan's characters: Mr. Worldly Wiseman and Madam Bubble, for example. Then there was Mr. Brisk, who made an attempt to court Mercy, but Bunyan had his number—Mr. Brisk was "a man of some breeding, and that pretended to religion, but a man that stuck very close to the world."[19] Mercy soon sent him about his business. And what a collection of wretches comprised the jury in the town of Vanity Fair when Faithful was put on trial for his life: Mr. Highmind, Mr. Enmity, Mr. Liar, Mr. Cruelty, Mr. Hate-light, Mr. Implacable, Mr. Blind-man, Mr. No-good, Mr. Malice, Mr. Lovelust, Mr. Live-loose, and Mr. Heady.

Dickens was just as good as Bunyan at naming characters. Who can forget his artful Dodger, or Mr. Fang the magistrate, or Mr. Bumble, or Mr. Grimwig, who offered to eat his head if Oliver did not abscond with the money? And who can forget the terrible Mr. Murdstone, the bane of David Copperfield's early life? Or the execrable Uriah Heep? Or Mr. Stryver, the pushy up-and-coming lawyer? Or Magwitch the convict? How appropriate for a discontented young man to be Pip, and a mean old miser to be Scrooge! Then there was Pecksniff, the arch-hypocrite; Mrs. Gamp, the disreputable old nurse with an indispensable large umbrella; Quilp, "an uglier dwarf than could be found anywhere for a penny"; and Gradgrind, the ruthless utilitarian. The names alert us to what we can expect from the characters.

Solomon, a keener observer than either Dickens or Bunyan, said, "A good name is rather to be chosen than great riches." And have not we who love the Lord been given a good name? There is a whole bevy of good names by which we are known in the New Testament: believers, brethren, saints, disciples. We should be proud of all these names and strive to live up to them. But there is a touch of special genius in the perceptiveness of the pagan people of Antioch who coined the name *Christians.* They chose it for the disciples in the first century and it has stayed with us from that day to this.

In the annals of the Melanesian Mission is the story of a young boy whom Bishop John Selwyn tried to train on Norfolk island. The boy had been raised among one of the most savage cannibal tribes in the South Sea. One day the bishop rebuked the boy for misbehavior and the boy responded by punching him in the face. The bishop quietly turned and walked away. Eventually the boy, who was considered to be beyond hope, was sent back to his own island where he soon returned to the barbarous ways of his people. Years later a missionary on that island visited a seriously ill man, the same person who years before had assaulted his would-be benefactor. The sick man was dying and he asked to be baptized.

When preparing to comply with the request, the missionary asked, "By what name would you like to be known as a Christian?"

"Call me John Selwyn," replied the native. "That is the man who, when I struck him, taught me what Christ was like." The dying man chose a good name.

No Christian group has a greater honor roll than The Salvation Army. Catherine Booth, who helped her husband found the organization, told of a man who breathed and shed abroad the very spirit of the Lord Jesus. He talked of Jesus, and Jesus only, to everyone he met, and his face glowed with the beauty of the Savior. When he was about to die, someone suddenly remembered that there was a paper that needed his signature. Although very weak, he grasped the pen and his hand was guided to the place where he should sign his name. Feebly he wrote, then fell into a coma and died. When his friends looked at his signature, they discovered that he had written *Jesus* where he should have put his name. *Jesus!* What a name! *Christians* (Acts 11:26)! What a name! What a *good* name! Truly a good name is to be desired more than gold.

Proverbs 22:2 speaks of *the long-range insignificance of inequity:* "The rich and poor meet together: the Lord is the maker of them all." As Peter once said, "God is no respecter of persons" (Acts 10:34).

We all are born the same way. We all have the same basic needs. We all will die. We all need the Savior, and we all find salvation on common ground. As we say, "Jack is as good as his master." Nowhere is this truth better displayed than when the rich and the poor meet together.

When the rich and the poor meet together, there is a revelation of character—the rich man's character and the poor man's character. Nathan's parable of the rich man and the poor man revealed injustice (2 Samuel 12:1-9). The Lord's parable of the rich man and the poor man revealed indifference (Luke 16:19-31). The rich man's indifference, which was perpetuated in his brothers' attitude toward social inequity, haunted him in a lost eternity. James saw social inequity and wrote of it twice: in James 2:1-9 he wrote about the rich and the poor in the church in the first century; and in 5:1-8 he wrote about the rich and the poor in the world toward the end of the age.

So the rich and the poor are brought together in Scripture. Their meeting, which is no accident, is occasioned by a sovereign God to give both of them an opportunity to develop character. The rich man is given a chance to develop compassion and the poor man is given a chance to develop contentment. Judas is given a pointed warning when Jesus says, "The poor always ye have with you" (John 12:1-8).

Among the many illustrations of the coming together, for better or for worse, of the rich and the poor is the Old Testament example of Laban and Jacob. Laban was what Charles Dickens would have called "a tight-fisted hand at the grindstone"—Dickens used these words to describe the covetous old miser Ebenezer Scrooge. The first time we meet Laban, he is rubbing his hands with appreciation over the rich gifts Abraham's servant has just bestowed on his sister Rebekah (Genesis 24:29-31).

Laban was a man of means with grown sons to his name and marriageable daughters. A powerful local chieftain, he owned flocks and herds and commanded retainers and servants. He had clout with the authorities and was able to bring pressure to bear on his foes.

Doubtless he was not without foes. When Jacob asked the men at the well, "Know ye Laban?" they said, "We know him" (Genesis 29:5). That simple reply spoke volumes. We can almost catch the cynical inflection in their voices. Anyone who had done business with Laban would not be likely to forget him in a hurry. The men at the well probably eyed Jacob as Laban's next victim. "We know him," they said. Soon enough Jacob would know him too. He would discover what a bargain with Laban was like—full of fine print, hidden clauses, and legal loopholes.

If Laban was the rich man, Jacob was the poor man. True, he had a rich father, but Jacob was also a fugitive from home and evidently very much in need of a job. How many times Rebekah must have wept and prayed for her wayward boy as she remembered what her brother Laban was like! There could have been little doubt in her mind that her dear son was going to be fleeced one way or another. And he was.

First there was the matter of Jacob's wives (Genesis 29:16-30). As soon as Laban discovered which way the wind was blowing between Jacob and his younger daughter Rachel, a gleam came into his eye. He agreed to give Rachel to Jacob in exchange for seven years hard labor, but used a legal loophole as an excuse to give him her older sister instead. So Jacob was beguiled into working an additional seven years for the wife he wanted. The rich and the poor met together and the Lord was the Maker of them both—a fact Jacob remembered (Genesis 31:5) and Laban forgot.

Then there was the matter of Jacob's wages. Laban changed Jacob's wages ten times (Genesis 31:7). We can be quite sure that each time uncle Laban brought nephew Jacob a new contract, it did not provide for a raise in pay. And what could Jacob do but sign? All the power seemed to be on his uncle's side. Laban would not have hesitated to rob Jacob of wealth and wives, fortune and family, and send him home bereaved and bankrupt, as Jacob knew only too well (31:31).

But God was the Maker of them both. He was in sovereign control of the rich man and the poor man, and designed their meeting to teach them both valuable truths. Laban learned about God from Jacob. "I have learned by experience," he confessed in one of his more open moments, "that the Lord [Jehovah] hath blessed me for thy sake" (Genesis 30:27). And Jacob learned about man from Laban: Jacob learned not to put his trust in man. "Your father hath deceived me," he said to his wives (31:7).

The rich man remained largely unchanged by his twenty-year meeting with the poor man. When Laban saw Jacob growing rich too and his power over Jacob diminishing, he planned vengeance. And Laban would have done his nephew harm, had God not prevented him from doing so (Genesis 31:23-29). And what did the poor man learn? He learned many important lessons about the providence, presence, protection, and purposes of God.

We may not be able to read what is being written in the records of eternity as we consider on the purely human level the countless unhappy meetings between the rich and the poor in this sin-cursed world. We will understand better by and by when the books are opened. Then we will praise God for His wisdom, power, and love that we can often barely see from our perspective on earth.

14. Perception (22:3-5)

Solomon would have us be perceptive about *our future:* "A prudent man forseeth the evil, and hideth himself: but the simple pass on and are punished" (Proverbs 22:3).

In Luke's account of the Lord's teaching on the endtimes there is a brief parenthesis (21:20-24) in which the Lord warned the Jews of the coming Roman invasion (A.D. 70). He said:

> When ye shall see Jerusalem compassed with armies, then know that the desolation thereof is nigh. Then let them which

> are in Judaea flee to the mountains; and let them which are in the midst of it [that is, in Jerusalem] depart out; and let not them that are in the countries [that is, fields] enter thereinto. For these be the days of vengeance....Jerusalem shall be trodden down of the Gentiles, until the times of the Gentiles be fulfilled.

The siege of Jerusalem was one of the most terrible events in history. The Roman army took up its position in the Valley of Thorns and built a vast, awesome camp. Then in all their pomp, pride, and power, they moved toward the doomed city and established a second encampment near mount Scopus. One legion marched off to take up a position at the foot of the mount of Olives, and others leveled the entire space between mount Scopus and the city wall. Next the army positioned itself along the northern and western walls; the infantry was in front, the cavalry was in the rear, and the archers were in the middle. Once this impenetrable line was drawn, the Romans moved up their heavy equipment. Titus stationed himself about a quarter-mile from the outer wall near the tower of Psephina and a detachment was posted near the tower of Hippicus, some distance from the army headquarters.

Josephus, now a Roman collaborator, approached Jerusalem and made an impassioned speech to his countrymen. He described the power, bravery, and determination of the Romans and promised clemency from Titus to those who surrendered.

Meanwhile within the city a number of rival factions maneuvered their troops. Simon, the son of Gioras, commanded ten thousand Jewish adherents along with five thousand Idumeans. John of Gischala had six thousand men, and Eleazar held the allegiance of another twenty-four hundred. For the moment these factions were united as they faced the awesome power of the common foe.

Soon the Romans put their catapults and battering rams in place and began assaulting three different parts of the city walls at the same time. From this time on, the aggressors made it a practice to crucify escaping Jews and Jews they caught making sorties. Before long the hills around Jerusalem were black with crosses as Jews were made to suffer the terrible torments their fathers had inflicted on Jesus.

Five days after the Romans took the first wall, they took the second wall, only to lose it again during a fanatical Jewish counterattack. In time the Romans retook the second wall and by then other forces were at work in the city. Famine stalked the streets and the rival factions defending the city fought savagely among themselves.

Titus called a temporary halt to the assault in order to review his troops within sight of the city. The entire Roman army, displaying its best equipment, filed past the wall. It was a brilliant and awe-inspiring spectacle, designed to strike terror into the defenders. The review lasted four days. Then the Romans began to raise up lofty mounds against the towering fortress of Antonia. Titus, however, paused once more, sending Josephus back to urge the city to surrender. Many of the people were moved by the eloquence of the famous historian, but the Zealots were enraged when they discovered that numbers of the miserable populace were deserting to the enemy. John and Simon ruthlessly slaughtered everyone they suspected of harboring thoughts of escape.

The war went on and the Romans continued their crucifixions of those who tried to escape—as many as five hundred were crucified at a time. The terrible sight only strengthened the hand the Zealots held over their wretched countrymen inside the city. The places chosen for the executions were so crowded with crosses, and supplies of wood were so depleted, that the Romans eventually had to desist.

Next Titus decided to encircle the city and starve the garrison into surrender. In three days the Romans completed a five-mile-long trench and embankment. The words of the Lord Jesus—he had said that the enemies of Jerusalem would cast a trench about her and keep her in on every side (Luke 19:43)—were now fulfilled.

And so horror succeeded horror until finally the Romans stormed the doomed city. On August 10, the anniversary of the day the Babylonians destroyed the temple of Solomon, the temple of Herod went up in flames. The Roman army encamped in the sacred precincts, planted their eagles among the smoking ruins, and sacrificed to their false gods. By September 7 the war was over. The victors, thirsting for revenge, rushed through the streets of Jerusalem—slaying, plundering, and ravishing. A vast number of Jews were put to death immediately and thousands more were put in chains so that they could be held for slaughter later in the arenas of the Roman world. The captives numbered ninety-seven thousand and the slain more than one million.

Most of the Christians who had lived in Jerusalem escaped. Believing Jesus' prophetic words, they had seen evil coming and had migrated elsewhere. They were "prudent." "The simple" remained and were punished. Yet the world thinks that those who believe in the Lord Jesus are the simple ones!

Solomon would also have us be perceptive about *our fortune:* "By humility and the fear of the Lord are riches, and honour, and life"

(Proverbs 22:4). Riches, honor, and life are God's gifts. The great counterfeiter—the devil—offers money, fame, and success. They are poor substitutes and all of them can be gained dishonorably. True riches, true honor, and true life are not found on a battlefield, in the political arena, in the halls of commerce, or in the cloisters of a college. They are found at Calvary.

The classic example of Proverbs 22:4 is the apostle Paul. He began life as Saul of Tarsus. Although he was a Jew, he was born to Roman citizenship and raised in a Greek environment. A cosmopolitan, he enjoyed the best of all three worlds.

Saul had the *status of Rome.* We can be reasonably sure that his family moved among the best of society. Doors would be opened to them simply because they were Roman citizens.

Saul had the *scholarship of Greece.* We know that he spoke and wrote flawless Greek and he could quote the Greek poets. Doubtless his far-ranging mind eagerly explored the learning of the Greeks. He easily assimilated what was good and admirable and rejected what was false and superstitious.

Saul had the *Scriptures of Israel.* As a child he had been taught about Moses and the prophets. He knew the Hebrew hymns and poetry by heart. All the great truths of the Bible were at his fingertips. He had been to Jerusalem. He had sat at the feet of Gamaliel, the greatest living rabbi. He had mastered the budding Talmud. Among his peers, he was the young man most likely to succeed. He had money, fame, and success. Committing himself to stamping out the infant church, he made himself available to the Sanhedrin. Doubtless he hoped to become the high priest of Israel some day and he was out to win his spurs.

Then he was converted! He drew up a new balance sheet. All the things he once counted as his greatest assets became his greatest liabilities. He lost his fortune, was cut off from his family, and felt like a sheep prepared for the slaughter. He was hounded and hated by Jews all across the Roman empire. He was chased out of city after city. Even the Christian Jews disliked him. He spent years in prison. Yet he held up his chains and exulted in them as the bonds of Jesus Christ. He rejoiced that he had become a partaker in His sufferings. In spite of persecution he planted churches everywhere he went and wrote much of the New Testament.

But the day came when he could no longer plant churches. Nero was on the rampage and Paul was sentenced to death. He was being held in the terrible Mamertine prison. Its upper cell was gloomy enough, but at least there was light there. Notable prisoners were lowered by rope into a black pit and left to languish there with no candle, no means of telling time, and no glimmer of sunlight. This cell, the dreaded Tullianum, was damp, chilly, and filthy. A bed of straw was one concession to human need, and from time to time guards lowered food through a trap door. But it is said that some wretched prisoners in that dismal hole were eaten alive by rats.

At this point if we had asked Paul, "What have you received in exchange for the wealth, fame, and success that once crowned your brow?" he would have said, "I have exchanged those things for riches, honor, and life. All the riches of Christ are mine! My name is honored by the church of the living God. I have life abundant and eternal." Here are his actual words:

> I am now ready to be offered, and the time of my departure is at hand. I have fought a good fight, I have finished my course, I have kept the faith: Henceforth there is laid up for me a crown of righteousness, which the Lord, the righteous judge, shall give me at that day (2 Timothy 4:6-8).

A short time after writing these words, Paul was executed. Tour guides still point out the execution site to visitors in Rome. The spot is called "the place of the three fountains," for legend has it that Paul's severed head bounced three times before coming to rest and that at each landing a fountain sprang up. We can be sure that whatever happened to his head, his heart was right and he was granted a triumphant entry into Heaven.

True riches! True honor! Eternal life! Not even Nero could rob Paul of these. And he had tribute of gold, silver, and precious stones to lay at Jesus' feet (1 Corinthians 3:12).

Solomon would have us be perceptive, moreover, about *our footsteps:* "Thorns and snares are in the way of the froward [perverse]: he that doth keep his soul shall be far from them" (Proverbs 22:5). "Thorns" are sent by God. They are part of the punishment He has ordained as a result of the fall. "Snares" are devised by men and Satan.

If ever a man's life was characterized by thorns and snares, it was the life of Israel's first king, Saul. He was man's choice for the throne. The children of Israel chose him because he towered head and shoulders above everyone else. Little good his height did him in the valley of Elah when he was face to face with a man who was even taller (1 Samuel 17)!

Thorns and snares were everywhere Saul went and he was always blundering into one or the other. After he was crowned, he made a good enough start because in those early days he was unsure of himself, humble, and teachable. But power corrupts and before long Saul was drinking deeply of that heady wine.

Before long he was *disqualified* for kingship because he intruded himself into the priest's office. A prophet could perform the duties of a priest at times, but a king never. This intrusion was the first of ten downward steps in the life of King Saul.

What were the circumstances surrounding Saul's disqualification? A war with the Philistines was imminent and Saul was afraid to go into battle without some religious exercise. He had been told to wait for Samuel—and Samuel saw to it that Saul did wait, for he was putting him to the test. But when Saul saw that his army was melting away as fear of the Philistines grew in the hearts of his inactive soldiers, he took matters into his own hands. Convinced that Samuel was not coming and persuaded that if he did not act soon he would have no army left, Saul offered a sacrifice himself. He had hardly finished when Samuel appeared. The prophet told Saul that his behavior proved that he was not a fit king for Israel. Indeed God already had another man in mind (1 Samuel 13:5-15).

In Saul's second downward step he was *disinherited.* The prophet told him, "Go and utterly destroy the sinners the Amalekites" (1 Samuel 15:18). God gave Saul a resounding victory over these hereditary foes, but instead of obeying God he spared King Agag and the best of the spoil. Again Samuel denounced Saul, told him that his rebellion was "as the sin of witchcraft," and declared that God had categorically rejected him from being king (15:23).

In the third downward step, not long after the second, Saul was *demented.* "The Spirit of the Lord departed from Saul, and an evil spirit from the Lord troubled him" (1 Samuel 16:14). Only soothing music could give him any relief from this tormenting demon. At this time David was introduced into the court as the king's private musician, and under the influence of David's playing the evil spirit would depart from Saul. Doubtless David sang some of the sacred songs he had composed himself—the same songs we sing when we sing his Psalms.

In the fourth step Saul was *disgraced.* The Philistines and the Israelites were arrayed for battle on the two sides of the valley of Elah. Goliath, the giant of Gath, blasphemed the living God, defied His armies, and dared the Hebrews to find a champion who would fight him in the valley. We can well believe that every eye in the Hebrew army turned to Saul, but all he could do was retire to his tent and wring his hands. He was terrified of Goliath. David, a teenage shepherd boy, did what Saul was afraid to do.

In Saul's fifth downward step he was *defied.* Envy gnawed at the king; bitterly and insanely jealous of David, Saul threw a javelin at the boy while he was attending to his court duties. Saul made up his mind that he was going to kill David, and he set traps for him. To the king's chagrin, however, his own children—Jonathan and Michal—defied him and openly professed their love for David (1 Samuel 18:3,20).

When Saul discovered that he could not kill David, he took the sixth downward step: the king was increasingly *dismayed.* David always escaped—not just because he was too clever to be caught or because he gathered around himself a band of intrepid outlaws, but because he was supernaturally protected. The angel of the Lord encamped "round about" him (Psalm 34:7). All of Saul's plots failed. Even when he called out the whole army to hunt David, Saul was outwitted again and again. It became increasingly obvious to Saul that David was the Lord's anointed.

In the seventh step Saul was *doomed.* When David fled to the Philistines for political asylum, he stopped on the way at the tabernacle at Nob and persuaded the high priest to give him the shewbread from the golden table and Goliath's sword. Saul interpreted the cooperation of the priest as an act of treachery and commanded that the entire priestly community at Nob be massacred. This dreadful order was carried out by Doeg the Edomite (1 Samuel 21–22). From that day on, Saul's conscience must have tormented him by day, and his nights must have been haunted by scenes of the slaughter.

In the eighth downward step Saul was *distraught.* Samuel died (1 Samuel 25:1) and Saul's last link with the God of Israel was severed. Although Saul had long since alienated the prophet, he still looked to him as a symbol of better times in days gone by. Now Samuel was no longer there; all that was left was a grave at Ramah. Soon after Samuel died, Saul resumed his persecution of David. Possibly Saul reasoned that David had lost a friend and protector too. Ironically, the only man left in the kingdom who could have, and would have, helped Saul was David, but he removed himself from Saul's vicinity by returning to the Philistine city of Gath.

Saul was *desperate* when he took the ninth step. Israel was again threatened by war with the Philistines, and Saul knew that he was no match for them. He tried prayer, but the heavens were as brass. His pleas for a vision or dream to guide him in his extremity were met with silence. Grasping at the last straw, he finally went down to Endor and consulted a witch. To the witch's evident fear and astonishment, the ghost of Samuel actually materialized at the seance and read the terrified king's death sentence (1 Samuel 28:6-25).

Taking his tenth downward step, Saul was *damned.* The Israelites lost their battle with the Philistines. The victors hotly pursued Saul, but he committed suicide to avoid being captured alive and then subjected to Samson's fate (1 Samuel 31:1-6). Saul, who was guilty of monstrous crimes, surely passed into a lost eternity.

"Thorns and snares" were ever in the way of this persistently perverse man. David kept his soul and God kept him far from his inveterate enemy. Even when only a hillock or two separated David's and Saul's soldiers, God saw to it that David was as safe as if the waters of the seven seas flowed between them. Maybe Solomon had this history in mind when he wrote Proverbs 22:5.

15. Parenthood (22:6)

"Train up a child in the way he should go: and when he is old, he will not depart from it." A similar Danish proverb reads, "What youth learns, age does not forget." An English proverb says, "As the twig is bent, so grows the tree."

It is important, in considering the great implications of Proverbs 22:6, to remember that there is all the difference in the world between *telling* a child and *training* a child. The Hebrew word translated "train" means "to hedge in." The word suggests a picture of cattle being guided into a pen. Their path is fenced so that there is only one way they can go.

It is no coincidence that "the way" was the usual New Testament word for Christianity. Those who followed Christ were known as "people of the way." We are responsible as parents to guide our children into this way.

The work of training children must begin when they are young. An old saint who had a delightful and remarkably close family of grown children used to say, "If you don't break their will when they first begin to manifest their rebellious sin nature, they will grow up to break your heart."

The Jesuits used to say that if they could have the commanding influence in the life of a child until that child was seven years old, the child was theirs. By then the child's character was formed, his convictions were embedded, and his course was set. No amount of contrary teaching would greatly alter the basic bent of that child.

Years ago a woman needing advice wrote to Jack Mabley, a

columnist for the *Chicago Daily News*. She said she had a seventeen-year-old son who was breaking her heart. He refused to listen to a thing she said. He was rude and defiant. He was abusive and used bad language around the house. He was running around with a bad crowd and sometimes came home drunk. She suspected he was using drugs and he had already been in trouble with the law. What should she do?

Mabley's advice was curt but sadly true. He wrote, "Shrink him down to seventeen months and start all over again." In other words, it was too late to hope to command respect and enforce discipline when her son was in his teens. Training has to begin before a child is out of his crib.

Child training has to be comprehensive and consistent. There are four areas to be reached and ruled. The first area is *the mind*. The entire educational system of our secular society is geared to focus the mind's attention on this world's priorities, philosophies, pleasures, prosperity, programs, principles, and praise. The goal of secular education is to prepare children to succeed in this world, so the system sets this world's art, science, religion, heroes, and idols before the child. The goal of Christian parents must be different. They must teach their children to fix their attention on the world to come.

In Genesis 4 we read a list of Cain's descendants and catch a glimpse of people who lived solely for this world. In Genesis 5 we read a list of Seth's descendants and catch a glimpse of people who lived solely for the world to come. The parting of the ways comes early in the Bible and must also come early in life. The Christian parent must lay a firm foundation with the Bible during the first seven years and then build on that foundation during the next ten years. Since the entire secular-humanist educational system scoffs at the Bible, the Christian parent must make sure that the Word of God is so firmly implanted in the child's mind that no amount of secular influence will challenge the Bible's authority.

In child training the second area to be reached and ruled is *the heart*. The citadel of the emotions has to be stormed and taken for Christ, for self is firmly enthroned from the very beginning. Every child also comes equipped with the capacity to love, hate, laugh, cry, desire, fear, and hope. He is a bundle of emotional contradictions, thanks to the fall. Parents must instill in their children a fear and horror of sin, seek to engage their affections to Christ, and meet their emotional needs. Jesus is the friend of little children and in our efforts to reach their hearts, we have a willing and wondrous ally in the Holy Spirit.

The third area to be reached and ruled is *the will.* Above all, parents must school the will of their children in obedience. Genesis 18:17-19 shows the importance God places on this area of child training: "The Lord said, Shall I hide from Abraham that thing which I do…? For I know him, that he will command his children and his household after him."

The marked decline in parental authority in Abraham's line deserves careful study. Abraham's family was marked by discipline, Isaac's by discord, and Jacob's by depravity.

Parents must command respect, fear, and obedience early, for parents stand in the place of God in the lives of their young children. That stubborn, childish will must learn to obey without argument or the display of temper. Children who do not learn to respect parental authority will learn to defy or challenge all authority.

The fourth area to be reached and ruled is *the conscience.* Conscience—the innate knowledge of right and wrong, the viceregent of God in the human soul—is the only positive legacy we have from the fall. But conscience by itself is a goad rather than a guide, for it can be conditioned—it can be sensitized or seared. That is why it is vital that conscience be bonded to the Word of God. Parents must lay a good moral foundation early in a child's life by instilling the precepts of the Mosaic law. These principles condition the conscience, which the Holy Spirit eventually uses as the instrument for bringing about conviction of sin, and conviction of sin is the great prerequisite to genuine conversion.

"Train up a child in the way he should go." If we neglect this first part of the verse, how can we claim the second part: "When he is old, he will not depart from it"?

It should be added that this verse is *not a promise.* The proverb enshrines a principle, but it is not a blanket guarantee that every child raised in a Christian home will eventually be saved. The book of Proverbs sets before us guidelines and general rules rather than unconditional promises. Those who take Proverbs 22:6 to be an unqualified promise may well be disappointed.

### 16. Potentials (22:7-10)

#### a. Sowing and Reaping (22:7-9)

Solomon gave three applications of the law of sowing and reaping. First he showed that the law applies *in money matters:* "The rich ruleth over the poor, and the borrower is servant to the lender"

(Proverbs 22:7). This principle holds true in all capitalistic systems. Solomon was not commenting on whether the principle is right or wrong; he was only making an observation on the results of borrowing and lending. Communism—as applied wholesale in socialist countries—simply enslaves the worker to the state and ends up bankrupting everybody.

For centuries the Jews were the world's leading capitalists. The love of money entered into the Jewish soul during the days of the Babylonian captivity and the Jews became moneylenders to kings and nobles as well as to ordinary men.

Although the Jews were dispersed throughout three continents and in as many civilizations, they were one people held together by their language, religion, and Talmudic law. The Talmud contained a section dealing with commerce, contracts, oaths, trade, and damages. Chapter upon chapter discussing ethical and legal questions judged moneyhandling in light of Mosaic and rabbinical commands. Jews were as familiar with this section as they were with the rest of the Talmud. The Talmud teaches basic financial common sense and business ethics. However, anyone who believes it to be a master key to modern financial success, big-time banking, or international money-changing has assuredly never read a page of the Talmud. It is simply a primer on business wisdom and, as such, is much like the book of Proverbs.

In medieval times if people or governments needed money, they went to the Jews, who were ready to oblige—for a price. The borrowers became servants to the lenders. By the tenth century the Jews had established widespread commercial enterprises in Europe, North Africa, and the Middle East and opened branches in India and China. The rising middle class in Europe finally broke the Jewish monopoly, but that did not deter the Jews, who continued to increase their hold over international commerce and banking.

In England a Jew named Aaron of Lincoln (1125–1186) amassed a fortune of such magnitude that it was second only to that of the king. Aaron built a network of financial agents across the country and before long Henry II and many of his nobles and high churchmen (including the archbishop of Canterbury) were in Aaron's debt. When Aaron died the king took over all his assets. The total amount involved was so great that a special branch of the royal exchequer had to be set up (it was called the Exchequer of Aaron) to collect all the money owed to Aaron, which of course then fell into the coffers of the crown.

The wealth of the Jews led to the proclamation in 1194 of the

Ordinance of Jewry. This decree required that archives be set up so that the king could be fully informed of the wealth of his Jewish subjects—so that he could confiscate it at leisure. The barons owed the Jews such enormous sums in interest alone that in the tenth clause of the Magna Carta they restricted kings thereafter to collecting only the principal of expropriated Jewish wealth.

In the seventeenth and eighteenth centuries Jewish financial genius was so fully recognized by European monarchs that they realized they could not get along without Jewish counselors at court. Thus "court Jews" were entrusted with the business of kingdoms. They were authorized to borrow money, suggest taxes, control currency, and keep countries solvent. The court Jews made it possible for kings to become independent of their barons and helped bring Europe into the modern age. The emergence of court Jew heralded the approach of capitalism as a means of creating wealth and of carrying on the business of the world.[20]

The villain in Shakespeare's *Merchant of Venice* is a Jew—the medieval Jew was hated because of the firm hold he had over the ruling elite and the common people. But the clutches of the Jew were mild and benevolent compared with the iron grip of the crime syndicate or the loan shark of our day. The loan shark's security is tight, his interest rates are enormous, his deadlines are inflexible, his stranglehold is complete, and his enforcers are ruthless and cruel. To fall into their hands is to find out in a terribly hard way the truth of Proverbs 22:7.

Next Solomon showed that the law of sowing and reaping applies *in moral matters:* "He that soweth iniquity shall reap vanity: and the rod of his anger shall fail" (Proverbs 22:8). The word translated "iniquity" here is *aval,* which means "trickery." "Vanity" means "emptiness."

The classic Biblical example of this proverb is the story of Rebekah. Her marriage was planned in Heaven (Genesis 24) and surely nobody else's marriage got off to a better start—unless it was Eve's. Yet somewhere along the way the marriage went sour. Probably Isaac was much to blame.

The first mention of love in the Bible is significant: "Take now thy son, thine only son Isaac, whom thou *lovest*" (Genesis 22:2, italics added). Here the love of the Father for the Son is prefigured. The second mention of love is equally significant: "Isaac brought her into his mother Sarah's tent, and took Rebekah, and she became his wife; and he *loved* her" (Genesis 24:67, italics added). Here the love of the Son for His bride is mirrored in type. So far, so good. This marriage did what every marriage is supposed to do—it portrayed the relationship of Christ to His church (Ephesians 5:25-28).

However, the love in Isaac's family quickly degenerated. We read that "Isaac loved Esau, because he did eat of his venison: but Rebekah loved Jacob" (Genesis 25:28). The couple played favorites.

The years went by until Isaac, thinking he was going to die, decided to pass on the patriarchal blessing. This blessing included the right to be a progenitor of the Christ. Isaac's carnal mind had no question about who would be the recipient of his blessing—Esau, his favorite of course. So Isaac said to Esau: "Make me savoury meat, such as I love, and bring it to me, that I may eat; that my soul may bless thee before I die" (Genesis 27:4). Rebekah overheard the conversation.

What Isaac was about to do was wrong. Rebekah should have confronted him. Instead she decided to outwit him and she sowed iniquity. She summoned Jacob (to whom the blessing really belonged) and told him to pretend he was Esau. Then she dressed Jacob up to play the part, prepared a spicy dish, and sent him in to deceive his father.

Rebekah helped Jacob secure the blessing by guile and she reaped emptiness. The rod of God's anger fell on both her and Jacob. God does not bless trickery. Jacob's behavior so infuriated his brother that Esau threatened to murder him. Alarmed, Rebekah talked Isaac into sending Jacob off to search for a wife in Padanaram, where her brother Laban lived. She confidently expected the separation from her dear Jacob would not last long, but she never saw her favorite son again. As for Jacob, it took him twenty years of emptiness to learn that God does not condemn sin in the sinner and then condone it in the saint. Jacob reaped what he sowed.[21]

Finally Solomon showed that the law of sowing and reaping applies *in ministry matters:* "He that hath a bountiful eye shall be blessed; for he giveth of his bread to the poor" (Proverbs 22:9). The man who looks out for ways to minister of his substance to the poor will certainly reap God's blessing.

Consider the case of Wenceslas, the patron saint of Bohemia, Czechoslovakia. The son of Duke Wratislaw, Wenceslas was raised by his Christian grandmother Ludmila, who was regent when he acceded to the throne. However, his ambitious and thoroughly pagan mother Dragomir was determined to impose her will on the nation. She murdered Ludmila and installed herself as regent. Eventually her court intrigues and the deep longing of the people for an end to religious strife convinced Wenceslas to take over the reins of government. Devoted to the spread of Christianity, he encouraged the work of German missionary priests throughout Bohemia and was zealous in the practical application of his faith. He is said to have taken a vow of virginity.

In the year 929 Wenceslas was murdered in front of the church door by Dragomir and his younger brother Boleslav. But that was by no means the end of Wenceslas, for there were frequent reports of miracles occurring at the site of his tomb. Boleslav evidently believed the rumors, for he had his brother's remains moved to the Church of St. Vitus in Prague.

Wenceslas must have exhibited extraordinary goodness. His virtues are sung in the well-known Christmas carol that extols the good king's compassion for the poor. He had what Solomon called "a bountiful eye" and his memory has certainly been blessed. I wonder what he would have thought if he had known that a thousand years after his death his generosity would be proclaimed annually around the world? The words of the carol were written by John M. Neale more than a century ago:

Good King Wenceslas look'd out
On the feast of Stephen
When the snow lay round about,
Deep and crisp and even.
Brightly shone the moon that night,
Though the frost was cruel,
When a poor man came in sight,
Gath'ring winter fuel.

"Hither, page, and stand by me,
If thou know'st, telling,
Yonder peasant, who is he?
Where and what his dwelling?"
"Sire, he lives a good league hence,
Underneath the mountain;
Right against the forest fence,
By Saint Agnes' fountain."

"Bring me flesh and bring me wine,
Bring me pine logs hither;
Thou and I will see him dine,
When we bear them thither."
Page and monarch forth they went,

Forth they went together;
Through the rude wind's wild lament,
And the bitter weather.

"Sire, the night is darker now,
And the wind blows stronger;
Fails my heart, I know not how,
I can go no longer."
"Mark my footsteps, my good page,
Tread thou in them boldly:
Thou shalt find the winter's rage
Freeze thy blood less coldly."

In his master's steps he trod,
Where the snows lay dinted;
Heat was in the very sod
Which the saint had printed.
Therefore, Christian men, be sure,
Wealth or rank possessing,
Ye who now will bless the poor,
Shall yourselves find blessing.

b. Scorning and Reproaching (22:10)

Solomon sagely said: "Cast out the scorner, and contention shall go out; yea, strife and reproach shall cease." Solomon certainly was an astute statesman and a profound observer of life.

Some people are born troublemakers. They are scornful of all that is good, right, and desirable. They scoff at holy things and try to subvert constituted authority. They promote wickedness, usually with an eye to their own advancement. One sure way to ensure law and order in a country and to guarantee a measure of peace and quiet is to cast such people out of society by putting them under lock and key. Nowadays, however, we give various rights and liberties to scornful and contentious people. Instead of putting them in prison, we put them on a platform.

"Cast out the scorner," Solomon said, and one day Jesus did just that. The incident occurred in Capernaum on the western shore of the sea of Galilee. The Lord had made Capernaum His headquarters (Matthew 4:13) and Capernaum is called "his own city" (Matthew 9:1). At least three of the Lord's disciples came from here (Peter, Andrew, and Matthew—Mark 1:21,29; Matthew 9:1,9). The paralytic carried to Jesus by his friends had been healed in Capernaum (Mark 2:1-12) and so had Peter's mother-in-law (Mark 1:21,30-31).

Jairus, a ruler of the Capernaum synagogue, had a beloved daughter who had passed childhood and reached the birthday when Jewish law declared a woman to be of age. She was twelve and she was desperately ill.

Not until that hour of supreme need did this father turn to Jesus. We can be sure he knew Jesus, since He frequently visited the synagogue. Jairus probably knew about the healing of the centurion's servant (Matthew 8:5-13), but Jairus's faith did not measure up to that of the Roman. The centurion had said: "I am not worthy that thou shouldest enter under my roof...but say in a word, and my servant shall be healed" (Luke 7:6-7). Jairus, on the other hand, "fell down at Jesus' feet, and besought him that he would come into his house" (Luke 8:41). But Jesus did not demand a certain kind of faith as long as faith was there.

Jesus started out at once, "but as he went the people thronged him" (Luke 8:42). The word translated "thronged" here is a strong word that means "to strangle." Luke wanted us to appreciate how dense and eager the crowds were that day. The multitudes so pressed in upon Jesus that it was very difficult for Him to make any progress. Then the woman with the issue of blood interrupted Him. Poor Jairus! We can imagine he was on tenterhooks and struggling with impatience. After all, when he left home his precious child was *in extremis*—"at the last breath."

Then the blow fell. A messenger came to say it was too late. The child had died. Jesus heard the comment and turned quickly to the stricken man. "Fear not," He said, "believe only, and she shall be made *whole*" (Luke 8:50, italics added). What sparked new hope in the breast of Jairus was that a moment before, Jesus had said to the woman with an issue of blood, "Thy faith hath made thee *whole*" (8:48, italics added).

At last they arrived at Jairus's house. Way down the street they had heard the sounds of mourning: weeping and wailing and doleful flute music. Real mourners and mourners hired for the occasion were already proclaiming the girl's death. The sad preparation for the pageantry of an Eastern funeral was already well underway.

Jesus walked calmly and resolutely into the house. Then He spoke. "Weep not," He said. "She is not dead, but sleepeth" (Luke 8:52). For a moment the mourners looked at Him in astonishment.

Then they "laughed him to scorn, knowing that she was dead" (8:53). After all, they were professionals. No one could fool them!

How was Jairus faring in the meantime? Edersheim wrote:

> The impression which the narrative leaves on the mind is, that all this while the father of the maiden was stupefied, passive, rather than active in the matter. The great fear, which had come upon him when the messengers apprised him of his only child's death, seemed still to numb his faith. He followed Christ without taking any part in what happened; he witnessed the pageantry of the approaching obsequies in his house without interfering; he heard the scorn which Christ's majestic declaration of the victory over death provoked, without checking it. The fire of his faith was that of "dimly burning flax" (Isa. 42:3). But "He will not quench" it.[22]

Once He had put the scorners outside (Mark 5:40), Jesus went to work and "joy unspeakable and full of glory" filled that home (1 Peter 1:8). Those who remained inside watched in amazement, oblivious to the scornful laughter and clamor of growing indignation of those who had been expelled. Jesus took the young girl's hand and spoke. At the sound of His voice the girl blushed back to life and rose from the dead. A few minutes later she was eating a meal!

Scorners understand only one thing: authority that shuts them up and shuts them out. Once they have been silenced, something worthwhile can be done. Solomon understood this fact and One "greater than Solomon" understood it too (Luke 11:31).

# CHAPTER 3

Proverbs 22:11-29

B. His Majesty's Intimates (22:11-29)
   1. His Chosen Friends (22:11-16)
      a. The Person the King Loves (22:11)
      b. The People the King Loathes (22:12-16)
         (1) The Transgressor (22:12)
         (2) The Desecrator (22:13-15)
            (a) The Man Who Diminishes the Stability of the Home (22:13)
            (b) The Woman Who Destroys the Sanctity of the Home (22:14)
            (c) The Child Who Defies the Standards of the Home (22:15)
         (3) The Oppressor (22:16)
   2. His Chief Friends (22:17-23)
      a. The King's Counselor (22:17-21)
         (1) The King Must Court Truth (22:17-18)
            (a) The Request (22:17)
            (b) The Reason (22:18)
         (2) The King Must Cultivate Truth (22:19-21)
            (a) Individual Trust in the Lord (22:19-20)
            (b) Informed Trust in the Lord (22:21)
      b. The King's Conscience (22:22-23)
         (1) Remember! Don't Despoil the Poor (22:22)
         (2) Remember! Don't Displease Their Protector (22:23)
   3. His Chance Friends (22:24-29)
      a. Those He Should Reject (22:24-28)
         (1) The Furious Man (22:24-25)
            (a) A Bad Temper Is Contemptible (22:24)

(b) A Bad Temper Is Contagious (22:25)
(2) The Foolish Man (22:26-27)
(a) His Desire for Bargains (22:26)
(b) His Drift toward Bankruptcy (22:27)
(3) The Fraudulent Man (22:28)
b. Those He Should Receive (22:29)

In writing about his majesty's intentions (21:1–22:10) Solomon reviewed a wide range of subjects about which a king must make up his mind and signify his royal purpose. Narrowing the focus, he began to write about those he allowed to be close to himself (22:11-29). The kind of company a king keeps is of vital importance, not only to himself but also to the people over whom he reigns. For better or for worse, a person—whether a peasant in his cottage or a prince in his court—becomes like the company he keeps.

## B. His Majesty's Intimates (22:11-29)

### 1. His Chosen Friends (22:11-16)

#### a. The Person the King Loves (22:11)

"He that loveth pureness of heart, for the grace of his lips the king shall be his friend."

Second Samuel 15:37 states that Hushai was "David's friend." Likewise the New Testament identifies those who were numbered among the friends of the Lord Jesus: great David's greater Son said, "Ye are my friends, if ye do whatsoever I command you" (John 15:14). Hushai's conduct and conversation qualified him to be David's friend.

Hushai entered the story of David at the time of the Absalom rebellion when the Lord's anointed was being rejected of men. David's fair-weather friends—the opportunists and self-seekers—had left him and thrown in their lot with Absalom. David soon found out who his real friends were. His mighty men stood by him. Ittai the Gittite brought his noble six hundred to David. Zadok and Abiathar the priests, along with a company of Levites, proclaimed their loyalty. Grim Joab remained true. Old Barzillai made his contribution. Poor Mephibosheth would have come to David's aid if he had been able to walk.

The king's small force was engaged in a strategic withdrawal from Jerusalem, and David needed time to gather his forces, choose his spot, plan the battle, and regain the initiative. Then along came Hushai. He must have been somewhat eccentric, for he came to meet David "with his coat rent, and earth upon his head" (2 Samuel 15:32). Such a demonstration was not going to win any battles, but David knew his man.

The cleverest man in the kingdom was Ahithophel, but he turned out to be David's Judas. The second cleverest man in the kingdom was Hushai, David's friend. David knew his friend's worth. Hushai was not the kind of man David would put in the front line, but he was the kind of man David could send down to Jerusalem to defeat the counsel of Ahithophel.

Hushai's coming was an answer to prayer. David had just cleared the top of the mount of Olives when he received word that Ahithophel had openly joined the conspiracy. Then and there David had paused to pray: "O Lord, I pray thee, turn the counsel of Ahithophel into foolishness" (2 Samuel 15:31). God answered David's prayer instantly. Even as he was praying, Hushai showed up.

"Look here, Hushai," David said in effect. "I have just the job for you. Go to Jerusalem, pose as an Absalom sympathizer, insinuate yourself into Absalom's court, and defeat the counsel of Ahithophel." And that is just what Hushai did. He talked so cleverly that he put the fear of David into Absalom. Indeed Hushai talked that vain and foolish young man into following a policy that gave David the time he needed. Hushai's counsel also guaranteed David his choice of battlegrounds and tactics. The words of David's friend brought about the suicide of Ahithophel and lured Absalom to the place of maximum danger where finally he lost his life. Perhaps Solomon had one eye on Hushai when he wrote, "For the grace of his lips the king shall be his friend."

We are living in the days of the King's rejection. The great rebellion of the age is sweeping many into open opposition to the Lord's true Anointed. The Lord Jesus is looking for friends in this world. He is looking for those who are pure of heart, whose lips speak with grace, and who are willing to trust and obey.

### b. The People the King Loathes (22:12-16)

#### (1) The Transgressor (22:12)

Solomon was speaking more and more as a king. Doubtless he had the future king, young Rehoboam, in mind. Solomon warned that a king must beware of the transgressor, the desecrator, and the oppressor.

The first warning is about the transgressor: "The eyes of the Lord preserve knowledge, and he overthroweth the words of the transgressor" (Proverbs 22:12). The word translated "transgressor" means "traitor." We have just seen how David went about overthrowing the words of the traitor Ahithophel. "The eyes of the Lord" is a poetic reference to God's omniscience. He sees all, knows all, and remembers all. Nothing escapes His notice and He knows how to overthrow the treacheries of the perfidious person.

What chance did Judas really have of getting away with his treachery? The eyes of the Lord Jesus read his most secret thought and his most greedy desire. Jesus knew to the penny the total amount that Judas had stolen from the bag. He knew what Judas had done with every last mite. He knew when the first thought of cashing in on his intimate knowledge of Jesus' movements crossed the traitor's mind. Jesus knew when the thought became a decision and when the decision was translated into action. The eyes of the Lord saw Judas when he first knocked at the door of Caiaphas. Jesus saw the money change hands. He saw the image and superscription on each coin. He saw where Judas hid the money. Jesus heard everything the transgressor said.

Jesus told Judas repeatedly that He knew (Matthew 26:23-25; Mark 14:20; John 6:70; 13:26-27). He knew not only from the Scriptures (see Psalm 41:9), which He had memorized and which He believed to the very last jot and tittle. He knew because He was incarnate Omniscience. His heart went out to Judas and to Annas, Caiaphas, and the whole wretched crowd of conniving men who were plotting to betray Him. Their plan was to hand their mighty Maker and long-promised Messiah over to the Romans so He could be crucified. He wanted to save these transgressors. He died that they might live. He shed His blood for them, but for Judas, at least, it was all to no avail.

It is the business of those who rule to identify traitors, but since spies might themselves be traitors, rulers need a higher wisdom than their own. Therefore it behooves kings and all who are in authority to walk close to God, who alone can read men's hearts and know their most secret thoughts.

Solomon knew of an example of a traitor in his father's life: When David received news that the Philistines had attacked the city of Keilah in the lowlands of Judah, he asked the Lord if he should go help the beleaguered city. He received assurance from God that the Philistines would be defeated if he so acted. David went and the citizens of Keilah welcomed him and his men into the city and rejoiced in his spectacular victory.

However, upon hearing that David was in Keilah, Saul gloated because he thought that there he could easily bottle David up and capture him. The citizens of Keilah, it seems, were more afraid of Saul's vengeance than they were grateful for David's deliverance. Indeed they were quite prepared to hand David over to his enemy.

David may have suspected their treachery, but he certainly did not know about it until he asked the Lord, "Will the men of Keilah deliver me up into [Saul's] hand? will Saul come down, as thy servant hath heard? O Lord God of Israel, I beseech thee, tell thy servant." The Lord's answer was brief. "He will come down," He said. "They will deliver thee up" (1 Samuel 23:11-12). This knowledge enabled David to escape. As Solomon said, "The eyes of the Lord preserve knowledge, and he overthroweth the words of the transgressor."

(2) The Desecrator (22:13-15)

The king must also beware of the desecrator who attacks the home. Proverbs 22:13 speaks of *the man who diminishes the stability of the home:* "The slothful man saith, There is a lion without, I shall be slain in the streets." This man is too lazy even to support his family. What an absurd excuse he gives! Sometimes any excuse will do, as long as it gets a person out of going to work. How God must hate our excuses for shirking our responsibility to get busy in His harvestfield.

The sinner makes excuses to God for not responding to the gospel. The Lord Jesus told a story about such excuses (Luke 14:16-24). "A certain man," Jesus said, "made a great supper, and bade many...and they all with one consent began to make excuse." And what silly and insulting excuses they were!

There was the businessman's excuse. He had bought some land, sight unseen, and had to go to see it—the very day of the dinner of course. There was the workingman's excuse. He had bought ten oxen, sight unseen, and had to go to try them out—the very day of the dinner of course. There was the family man's excuse. He had a new bride and had to stay home and play dominoes with her, or go shopping, or prune her roses—the very day of the dinner of course.

Well, God is not mocked and neither was the host in the parable. As the pitiful excuses arrived, the host's wrath grew. "Cancel their invitations," he said in effect. "We'll find people who will come and come gladly."

Some years ago we had neighbors with two little girls the same ages as our own. We persuaded the wife to let her girls come with ours to Sunday school. The neighbor girls liked it and came every Sunday. As the Christmas season drew near and a special program was being planned for the Sunday school children and their parents, our little friends were getting excited. A week before the program we asked them if they thought their daddy could come the next Sunday. Evidently their parents had discussed the possibility already, for the older child didn't hesitate a moment. She announced, as sober as a judge, "Oh, no. My daddy is going to be sick next Sunday." Excuses!

Christians too make silly excuses for not going to church and for not doing church work. I have often wondered what excuse Thomas had for being absent from the meeting in the upper room on resurrection evening. What a day it had been—for everybody except Thomas. And now the time had come for the believers to gather in the place of meeting, and Thomas stayed home. "There is a lion without, I shall be slain in the streets," Thomas might have said. Well of course there was a lion without. There was a whole jungle of lions: Annas, Caiaphas, Herod, Pilate, the caesar, the temple police, and the Roman troops. But God had closed their mouths and bound their claws, just as He had done to the lions in Darius's cage.

Thomas might have had fifty more excuses for not going to the meeting and not getting on with the gospel—excuses very familiar to us and nauseatingly familiar to God. Thomas might have said, "I'm tired." Or "I'm too busy." Or "It's too dangerous." Or "I don't feel too well." Or "I need to stay home with my wife." Or "I'm too discouraged." Or "I think it's going to rain." Or "I don't get anything out of those meetings. I can get more out of staying home and reading my Bible." Or "If Peter's going to be there, I'm not going. After what he did! He'll do all the talking and I sure don't need to hear anything he will say." Excuses!

Proverbs 22:14 goes on to speak of *the woman who destroys the sanctity of the home:* "The mouth of strange women is a deep pit: he that is abhorred of the Lord shall fall therein." The woman in view here was a harlot or an adulteress. Labeled "strange," she was likely a Canaanite who served as a temple prostitute. The Hebrews had been told to exterminate women like her (Numbers 31:14-18), but they had failed to do so. Out of this woman's mouth came seducing words. Some people believe that her seductions were as much theological as they were immoral. Foreigners—often sacred harlots of foreign shrines—were nearly always responsible for the seduction of Israel into the worship of the false, foul, and fierce gods of Canaan.

Unfortunately Solomon didn't take his own advice. He was too broad-minded, too liberal. He was always ready to see the other fellow's point of view. Before long he was defending the other fellow's right to hold that view, even if that view espoused religious error of the most radical kind or immorality of the vilest sort and was flatly condemned by the Word of God. Then in the interest of tolerance and fairness he would concede the other fellow's right to his own lifestyle—that is, his right to practice abominations, as long as he didn't harm anyone else and as long as his partners were consenting adults.

Moral and religious lines became so blurred in Solomon's mind that he forgot that God Himself had spoken to the issues being debated. Even when he remembered, he watered down the absolutes. "Well," we can almost hear Solomon say, "Moses was a radical. He was a fanatic about these things. Mind you, much that Moses wrote was good, but it was for a different age. Times have changed. We must be tolerant. That was a barbarous age. The death penalty for adultery? Even David didn't enforce that, you know. Take the case of Amnon...." By the time Solomon was finished rationalizing, compromising, and tolerating, he had turned Jerusalem into Babylon.

Solomon began falling into the "deep pit" when he married the pharaoh's daughter. Out of a sense of fair play perhaps he allowed her to worship Isis, Osiris, or any of the other Egyptian gods she loved in a private chapel in the palace. *Of course this small concession is only for her and her Egyptian servants,* we can imagine him thinking. *No Hebrew must participate. There must be no proselytizing. But I cannot afford to offend the majesty of the pharaoh by denying his daughter the right to her own religion. Why, the pharaoh might send an army....*

Solomon would have been better off if he had convinced her to worship Jehovah. He would have been even better off if he had never married her in the first place. And it would have been better for him and for Israel if he had never married any of the other "strange" women in his harem. Indeed, since he grew up to marry them, it might have been better if he had never been born, for Solomon's wives finally seduced him. He compromised and compromised until he ended up building public shrines for all their vile gods and even setting an example for Israel by worshiping them himself. He did more to corrupt the nation than any other king who sat on the throne of David.

The man who in his younger days had been great David's greater son and who had built the temple for Jehovah in Jerusalem could be seen prostrating himself before a host of pagan gods. And his idolatries paved the way for the division of the kingdom and its ultimate downfall. Yes, it was a pity that Solomon failed to preach to himself what he so cleverly preached to others.

Following warnings about a man and a woman who attack the home, Proverbs 22:15 speaks of *the child who defies the standards of the home:* "Foolishness is bound in the heart of a child; but the rod of correction shall drive it far from him." Solomon's cure for misbehavior is out of favor with modern psychologists, sociologists, and humanists, but it is strongly recommended by the Holy Spirit. Solomon advocated the use of the "rod of correction"—that is, corporal punishment accompanied by proper instruction.

Nobody in his right mind advocates cruelty to children. Nobody condones bullying and brutality, but old-fashioned spanking has its place. It communicates swiftly and settles a problem in a hurry. The rod of correction must be wielded temperately and by a loving hand, but the rod must be wielded. In today's promiscuous society we are harvesting the fruits of liberal philosophy; we have sown the wind of permissiveness and are now reaping the whirlwind of lawlessness and licentiousness.

No better instruction in parental discipline can be found than that in Jack London's story *White Fang*. White Fang was a wolf cub, born in a cave in the White North. Wrote London:

> Always, in the beginning, before his conscious life dawned, he had crawled toward the mouth of the cave. And in this his brothers and sisters were one with him. Never, in that period, did any of them crawl toward the dark corners of the back-wall. The light drew them as if they were plants; the chemistry of the life that composed them demanded the light as a necessity of being; and their little puppet-bodies crawled blindly and chemically, like the tendrils of a vine. Later on, when each developed individuality and became personally conscious of impulsions and desires, the attraction of the light increased. They were always crawling and sprawling toward it, and being driven back from it by their mother.
>
> It was in this way that the grey cub learned other attributes of his mother than the soft, soothing, tongue. In his insistent crawling toward the light, he discovered in her a nose that with a sharp nudge administered rebuke, and later, a paw, that crushed him down or rolled him over and over with swift, calculating stroke. Thus he learned hurt; and on top of it he

> learned to avoid hurt, first, by not incurring the risk of it; and second, when he had incurred the risk, by dodging and by retreating. These were conscious actions, and were the results of his first generalizations upon the world. Before that he had recoiled automatically from hurt, as he had crawled automatically toward the light. After that he recoiled from hurt because he *knew* that it was hurt.

Later on, London added:

> The cub entertained a great respect for his mother. She could get meat, and she never failed to bring him his share. Further, she was unafraid of things. It did not occur to him that this fearlessness was founded upon experience and knowledge. Its effect on him was that of an impression of power. His mother represented power; and as he grew older he felt this power in the sharper admonition of her paw; while the reproving nudge of her nose gave place to the slash of her fangs. For this, likewise, he respected his mother. She compelled obedience from him, and the older he grew the shorter grew her temper.[1]

That is nature's way. It is God's way too.

### (3) The Oppressor (22:16)

Finally the king must beware of the oppressor: "He that oppresseth the poor to increase his riches, and he that giveth to the rich, shall surely come to want." This proverb underlines the wrongful acquisition and the wrongful outlay of money.

God condemns the practice of getting money by bullying the poor or by bribing the rich. Solomon warned us that God will deal with those who use such methods. Paul said, "The love of money is the root of all evil" (1 Timothy 6:10) and he called money "filthy lucre" (3:8). Some people think that no crime is too great if it will add to their store of riches. The Bible constantly warns of money's corrupting power.

Such corruption is seen in the case of Baron Danglars in Alexandre Dumas's famous story *The Count of Monte Cristo.* Danglars was one of the men who conspired against Edmond Dantès and connived during his unjust trial and incarceration in the dreaded Château d'If. Years later Dantès came back as the fabulous count of Monte Cristo. Rich, powerful, mysterious, and unrecognized, Dantès was dedicated to getting his revenge. By this time Danglars had acquired a vast fortune, so Dantès set about to engineer his ruin.

The count began by dazzling Danglars—now a great Parisian banker and adviser of kings—by a display of wealth beyond anything the baron had imagined. The count talked to Danglars about high finance, impressed him with his knowledge and nerve, and hinted at investments that would be bound to increase the baron's fortune. These investments, of course, would in fact hasten his ruin. Danglars began to lose large sums of money and in the end he absconded with some five million francs from the funds of a Parisian hospital. He had enough money to live in the lap of luxury for the rest of his life, but the implacable count was still on his trail.

Dantès could not forget that Danglars had ruined his life. Because of the baron and his partners, Dantès had spent years in prison. During his incarceration, his father had died of starvation, and his fiancée, thinking him dead, had married his rival. No, the score was not settled yet. Determined that Danglars himself should come to want, the count arranged with a group of bandits to seize the baron and fleece him of what money he had left.

This classic story illustrates Solomon's point: The wrongful acquisition and use of money brings an avenger on its trail.

### 2. His Chief Friends (22:17-23)

#### a. The King's Counselor (22:17-21)

##### (1) The King Must Court Truth (22:17-18)

Solomon made a request and then gave the reason for his request. We note first *the request:* "Bow down thine ear, and hear the words of the wise, and apply thine heart unto my knowledge" (Proverbs 22:17). There is all the difference in the world between hearing the words of a wise man and paying strict attention to what he has to say. And there is all the difference in the world between listening carefully to the counsel of a well-informed man and applying that advice.

When twenty-year-old Ahaz ascended the throne of Judah, he had many strikes against him. Although his father Jotham (the son of the great Uzziah) was a godly king, he did not put a stop to the corrupt practices of the people (2 Chronicles 27:2). So Ahaz received confused signals from Jotham, but he received clear signals from the prophet Isaiah. Isaiah gave Ahaz some very sound advice and his willingness to apply that advice was soon put to the test.

When a combined Syro-Ephraimitic army invaded Judah and besieged Jerusalem, the prophet assured the young king that all he had to do was call on the living God. Isaiah pleaded with this boy in king's clothing not to appeal for foreign aid and offered to show him a sign, any sign, to confirm the words of assurance. Ahaz loftily dismissed the idea of a sign—but he was given one anyway. Isaiah gave him the celebrated prediction of the virgin birth of Christ, a two-edged prophecy that would have a partial and nonmiraculous fulfillment in the near future and another fulfillment in the distant future. To refer to more than one event was a common feature of Old Testament prophecy.

The near fulfillment of Isaiah's prophecy centered on a well-known young woman whose identity, then unmistakable, remains unknown to us. Isaiah foretold that before her baby was old enough to know the difference between right and wrong, the kings of the combined enemy forces would both be dead (Isaiah 7:16).

The prophet coveted the trust of Ahaz, for just over the horizon loomed the awesome, restless power of Assyria (7:17). But talking to the young king was like talking to a brick wall. He had no intention of bowing down his ear to hear the wise words of God's prophet or applying the prophet's knowledge to his heart. Isaiah was an astute counselor, a gifted statesman, and an inspired prophet who had the gift of knowledge, but Ahaz was not impressed. He had already made up his mind.

Ahaz had a taste for idolatry. He was fascinated by the gods of the Canaanites—Baal, Ashtoreth, and Moloch—so he ignored the great man of God who prowled his court. The Bible says of Ahaz that "he walked in the way of the kings of Israel, yea, and made his son to pass through the fire, according to the abominations of the heathen, whom the Lord cast out from before the children of Israel" (2 Kings 16:3).

Ahaz was a born fool. As we would say, "You can take a horse to the river, but you can't make it drink." Likewise you can talk to a fool, but you can't make him listen or do what you say.

Proverbs 22:18 gives *the reason* for Solomon's request that we respond properly to the words of the wise: "It is a pleasant thing if thou keep them within thee; they shall withal be fitted in thy lips."

The Holy Spirit gathered up the words of the wise and placed the collection in the book we call the Bible. The Lord Jesus was incarnate wisdom, the Word made flesh. He exemplified the principle in Proverbs 22:17-18 and even His enemies confessed,

"Never man spake like this man" (John 7:46). They asked, "Whence hath this man this wisdom...?" (Matthew 13:54) Jesus spoke "as one that had authority, and not as the scribes" (Mark 1:22). People recognized that He had a wisdom that was not of this world and they wondered about its source.

The Lord Jesus was truly God in every sense of the word. As God He was omniscient and all-wise, yet as man He had to go through all the stages of growing up. As a boy He had to go to school and learn the alphabet. He who was Alpha and Omega had to learn to read and write. He who was the Word made flesh had to sit at the feet of the rabbis to acquire a knowledge of the Bible.

There is no way we can separate Christ's deity from His humanity. There can be no doubt that He read, studied, memorized, and quoted the Bible. Much of His teaching was firmly based on the Old Testament and His life was governed absolutely by the Word of God.

During His temptation, for instance, Jesus picked up the weapon that Eve so foolishly threw away: the Word of God. When tempted to command stones to become bread, He quoted from His Bible: "Man shall not live by bread alone" (Matthew 4:4; Deuteronomy 8:3). When the devil misquoted the Bible and dared Him to throw Himself down from a pinnacle of the temple, Jesus accurately quoted from His Bible: "Thou shalt not tempt the Lord thy God" (Matthew 4:7; Deuteronomy 6:16). When the devil offered Him the kingdoms of the world if He would worship him, Jesus quoted from His Bible: "Thou shalt worship the Lord thy God" (Matthew 4:10; Deuteronomy 6:13).

When Jesus referred to John the Baptist and Elijah (Matthew 17:10-13), He based what He said on Malachi 4:5-6. When He spoke to the question of divorce (Matthew 19:4-6,8), He referred His critics to Genesis 2:24 and Deuteronomy 24:1. When He accused the leaders of Israel of turning the temple into a den of thieves (Matthew 21:13), He quoted from Isaiah 56:7 and Jeremiah 7:11. When He silenced His critics at the time of His triumphant entry into Jerusalem (Matthew 21:16), He quoted from Psalm 8:2. When He explained why He spoke in parables (Matthew 13:14-15), He quoted from Isaiah 6:9-10. When He called His enemies hypocrites (Matthew 15:7-9), He referred them to Isaiah 29:13. When they accused His disciples of breaking the sabbath and offending their traditions (Matthew 12:1-4), He referred them to 1 Samuel 21:1-6.

The list could go on and on. Jesus, the perfect One, not only bowed down His ear to the wise and applied His heart unto knowledge, but also found it a pleasant thing to keep God's words within Him so that they could always be fitted to His lips. As the sacred ark of the covenant enshrined an unbroken copy of the Mosaic law, so Jesus—God's true ark—enthroned God's Word in His heart. And what was in His heart came out of His mouth.

(2) The King Must Cultivate Truth (22:19-21)

In order to cultivate truth one must have an *individual trust in the Lord:* "That thy trust may be in the Lord, I have made known [God's words] to thee this day, even to thee" (Proverbs 22:19). The bottom line is always trust.

Everything hinges on whom we believe and what we believe. The outcome of the first temptation depended on whom and what Eve believed. God said, "Thou shalt surely die," whereas Satan said, "Ye shall not surely die" (Genesis 2:17; 3:4). Eve chose to believe Satan. In salvation God brings us back to the point of departure, and again everything depends on whom we believe and what we believe.

Salvation is a matter of trust. Basing His plan of salvation on faith, God hinged everything on a factor that is really the common denominator of human activity. Not a day goes by, not a moment passes, in which we do not exercise faith in the everyday transactions of life. A customer who deposits money in a bank exercises faith in the integrity of the institution. A person who boards a bus exercises faith in the competence of the driver. A patient who swallows medicine trusts the judgment of the doctor and the competence of the druggist. A person who enters a building trusts the skill of the architect and the builder. Every time we cite a fact of history we reveal our trust in historians. Most of the things we "know," we have accepted by faith.

Even as I work on this manuscript I am sitting in a plane flying over Oklahoma; I am looking down on a bank of clouds with no concern about the mechanical soundness of the aircraft or the competence of the pilot. I am simply exercising faith. God demands that we exercise the same kind of faith in Him.

We exercise faith in a hundred ways every day. The fact of faith is always there, but the value of it depends on the integrity, dependability, and strength of whom or what we are trusting. Ordinary everyday faith becomes saving faith when it is placed in the Lord Jesus Christ. The difference is not in the *operation* of our faith, but in the *object* of our faith. "That thy trust may be in the Lord," says the Holy Spirit. And the better we know Him, the greater our trust will be.

Someone once said to D. L. Moody, "I can't believe."

The great soul-winner retorted, "*Whom* can't you believe?"

God expects, and has every right to expect, that we will take Him at His word because He is utterly dependable. No greater insult can be offered to God than to say to Him who is the soul of all honor, "I can't trust You." The ultimate folly of the liberal theologian is to say to God, "I can't believe a word You have written." In the end God will say to that man, "I can't hear a word you say."

Trust, of course, involves more than mental assent to a body of beliefs. Trust involves commitment. In each instance of ordinary faith mentioned above, commitment is involved. When we drop a letter into a mailbox, the moment we let the letter go we have made a commitment based on belief. Saving faith also involves commitment.

The difference between intellectual assent and real trust was illustrated years ago at Niagara Falls. The tightrope walker Blondin stretched a cable across the falls and walked on that tightrope over the thundering water many times. He also pushed a wheelbarrow across and performed other daring acts. Then he approached a spectator and asked, "Do you believe I can carry you over that tightrope?"

"I sure do," replied the man.

"Then climb on my back and I'll carry you across," said Blondin.

"Not on your life!" responded the man.

The spectator was probably wise not to place real trust in Blondin, but we can feel safe when we place real trust in the Bible.

Proverbs 22:20 states, "Have not I written to thee excellent things in counsels and knowledge…?" God has written down all kinds of great and marvelous things about Himself in the Bible—excellent things! The Word of God was given by the Holy Spirit: "The prophecy came not in old time by the will of man: but holy men of God spake as they were moved by the Holy Ghost" (2 Peter 1:21). In this verse Peter was telling us that those who wrote the Bible conveyed truth far beyond their own ability to comprehend. Indeed in 1 Peter 1:11 he spoke of them "searching what, or what manner of time the Spirit of Christ which was in them did signify, when it testified beforehand the sufferings of Christ, and the glory that should follow."

In 2 Timothy 3:16 (almost the very last thing Paul wrote) the apostle indicated, "All scripture is given by inspiration of God." The expression "given by inspiration of God" is a translation of one Greek word meaning "God-breathed." The Bible is, as man is, the direct creation of God (Genesis 2:7). Many parts of the Bible make explicit claims to being inspired by God. For example, expressions such as "and God spake" and "thus saith the Lord" occur frequently.

Because of the fact that in the process of breathing out the Scriptures, the Holy Spirit employed men, we can trace differences in style and composition from book to book. But throughout the Bible, God spoke *ex cathedra*—sovereignly, infallibly, inerrantly—preserving what was written from human error. Thus the words, and even the letters that comprise the words, are of God. Each jot and each tittle in the original document were kept free from error. Every part of the Bible perfectly conveys the thoughts and intents of the mind of God in the very words He chose to use.

Under the guidance of the Holy Spirit, the books of the Bible were collected gradually and with great care. The process whereby a book was accepted as canonical was painfully slow. Some books were evaluated for a long time before being admitted to the divine library. Others, such as the Apocryphal books, were never admitted at all because they contained errors, mere legends, or suspicious details. These writings did not ring true. They did not speak with authority.

The Jews divided their Scriptures into three parts: the Law, canonized about 444 B.C.; the Prophets, canonized about 200 B.C.; and the Writings, canonized by 100 B.C. Meticulous in their efforts to preserve the sacred writings from copyist errors, the Jews counted and recounted every word on a page and every letter of every word on every page. So great was their reverence for the Word of God that when a copy of it became too old and frail to be used any longer, they actually interred it and gave it an honorable funeral.

The Lord Jesus, whose knowledge was infinite, put His stamp of approval on the Old Testament Scriptures, quoted them freely as the Word of God, and never once accused the Jews of tampering with them. To Him they were fully authoritative and beyond question. He constantly appealed to them, especially to such books as Genesis, Isaiah, Jonah, and Daniel—books that destructive critics have especially sought to discredit.

The New Testament canon was compiled in a similar way, with the Holy Spirit guiding and overruling each step of the process (2 Timothy 3:16; 2 Peter 1:19-21). The apostles claimed divine authority for their teaching (1 Corinthians 2:7-13; 14:37; 1 Thessalonians 2:13; Revelation 1:1-3) and were entitled to do so because the Lord had guaranteed that the Holy Spirit would lead them into all truth (John 14:26; 15:26-27; 16:12-13a; 16:13b-15). These last four references cover in sequence the Gospels, the book of Acts, the

Epistles, and the book of Revelation. Moreover the apostles called for the public reading of their Epistles (1 Thessalonians 5:27; Colossians 4:16).

The writings of Clement of Rome, Ignatius, and Polycarp show that by the end of the first century and the beginning of the second century several books were in circulation and accepted as authoritative. The idea of a New Testament canon is shown to be generally accepted by the year 200 in the writings of Irenaeus in Asia Minor and Gaul, in the writings of Tertullian in North Africa, and in the writings of Clement of Alexandria in Egypt. By the time of Origen and Eusebius doubtful books were sifted out. By 367 Athanasius could refer to a list of twenty-seven books corresponding to our New Testament.

The Holy Spirit guided the whole process. Moreover He guarded the Word of God. He protected the sacred books from the ravages of wicked men such as Emperor Diocletian, who tried to burn the books, and heretics like Marcion, who tried to distort the books.

"Have not I written to thee excellent things...?" asked Solomon. The things he wrote were far more excellent than he knew, for he was writing a book of the Bible. Solomon's excellent proverbs have given practical help to millions of people for thousands of years.

Confidence in the Bible and individual trust in the Lord are essential in the cultivation of truth. An *informed trust in the Lord* is also essential. Solomon wrote, "Have not I written...that I might make thee know the certainty of the words of truth; that thou mightest answer the words of truth to them that send unto thee?" (Proverbs 22:20-21)

We are not simply to accept the truth of the Word of God; we are to be absolutely certain that the Bible is the Word of God. We are not merely to know with certainty that the Bible is the Word of God; we are to be known for having that conviction. Not only are we to be known as people who have absolute confidence in the inspiration, infallibility, and inerrancy of the Word of God; we must also be able to expound the truth of God's Word to those who come to us for guidance because they know that we are people of the Book.

To whom could King Josiah turn for guidance? He had been shaken to the depths of his soul by the discovery of a copy of the Mosaic Law among the rubble and ruins of the temple. Hilkiah the high priest, Josiah's adviser, could not answer the king's questions. So who could expound the Word of God to him?

Before we answer that question, let's take a good look at Josiah. His grandfather Manasseh had been a royal scoundrel and a disgrace to the human race. Josiah's father Amon had been no better. But in spite of such uncommendable parentage, Josiah opened his heart to God early in his life. "Josiah was eight years old when he began to reign" in Judah (2 Kings 22:1) and when he was still a teenager, he launched a campaign to clean up the moral and religious life of his people.

Josiah's national reformation was greater than that of Luther, Calvin, or Knox. Those iron men had the Bible to spur them on, but Josiah had no Bible. All he had was the voice of a young prophet named Jeremiah, whom almost everyone despised and ridiculed. The young king began by suppressing idolatry and other unlawful forms of worship and in his eighteenth year he took steps to cleanse and repair the neglected temple.

It was while Josiah's workmen were repairing the gaping holes in the temple that Hilkiah discovered the scroll and gave it to Shaphan the scribe to read. He read it privately and then to the king.

So terrible had been the reigns of Amon and Manasseh that the Torah had not only become a forgotten book; it had also been virtually destroyed. Josiah had never heard of it. It is hard for us to believe that the spiritual life of Judah could have fallen so low. The fact remains however that the scroll found by Hilkiah was in all likelihood the last copy of the Mosaic Law left on earth. Had it not been for Josiah, the temple would have been left to rot on its foundation and the buried books of Moses would have crumbled into dust. Truly the watching Spirit of God guarded that last remaining copy until a godly young man sat on the throne of David.

When Josiah heard the commandments and the terrible curses of the Law, he was appalled. He sent his counselors to "enquire of the Lord" (2 Kings 22:13) to see if there was any hope for the nation in view of its horrendous apostasies and sins. We wonder why the king's counselors did not go to Jeremiah, for he had been prophesying for some time prior to the discovery of the scroll (Jeremiah 2–6). Instead they went to a prophetess named Huldah, the wife of Shallum who was the keeper of the wardrobe.

We know nothing about Huldah or why Josiah's counselors consulted her. Perhaps they felt that a second opinion or witness was required in order to establish every word. Josiah would have found words to that effect in the sacred scroll itself (Deuteronomy 19:15). In any case, Huldah soon made known the certainty of God's words of truth. She was quick to answer the questions of the king. The curses recorded in Deuteronomy 28–30 would most certainly fall on the nation, but because of Josiah's personal piety

God would not vent His wrath during his lifetime. Jeremiah wasted no time in confirming the prophecy that judgment would fall (Jeremiah 7–9). Now Josiah had an informed trust in the Lord.

b. The King's Conscience (22:22-23)

Those who wield authority and exercise power—who are in a position either to help or harm others—would do well to mark and memorize Proverbs 22:22: "Rob not the poor, because he is poor: neither oppress the afflicted in the gate." *Remember! Don't despoil the poor.*

People who are at the mercy of those who are more powerful or more clever than they are often feel they have no recourse. Not so! "For the Lord will plead their cause, and spoil the soul of those that spoiled them" (Proverbs 22:23). *Remember! Don't displease their Protector.* The cases of such victims are always referred to the supreme court of the universe. God sends His angels to minister to the afflicted (Genesis 28:10-17; Matthew 18:10; Hebrews 1:13-14).

Solomon's warning can be understood at its lowest level of meaning—as a warning against robbing the poor and helpless simply because they have no apparent means of striking back. While the robbery might be and often is of a material nature, the repayment may be of a spiritual nature. Those who debase their positions of influence and power often pay for their crimes in the coin of a higher realm—the Lord will "spoil the soul." The damage done to the souls of those who abuse others is incalculable.

Solomon's warning, however, must not be restricted to the plane of the material. Proverbs 22:22-23 can also be understood to apply to those who inflict moral harm. Such injury is more severe than material loss, and the retribution is more terrible.

Let's consider the case of Oscar Wilde, the Irish poet, wit, and dramatist. (His real name was Fingal O'Flahertie Wills. His assumed name was probably intended to be symbolic.) Wilde used his position of influence to rob the rags and tatters of morality that clothed the nakedness of humanity's impoverished soul. His whole goal in life (and in this he was by no means alone) was to ridicule morality and the convictions of decent religious people. Today his successors write "comedies" for television and filth for Hollywood and the pornographic press.

Wilde set out to shock the moral conscience of late-nineteenth-century Victorian England. He did not hold people for ransom at the barrel of a gun; his weapon was a venomous pen. In his plays he always sought to bring together an intolerant young idealist and a person who had committed a social sin. The society in which the two met was typically one in which appearances were everything. Wilde's aim was to expose the weakness of the idealist and to preach tolerance and forgiveness. He especially liked to ridicule what he considered to be the hypocrisy of society and the Puritan ethic.

Wilde wrote only one novel, *The Picture of Dorian Gray.* In this melodrama he combined the supernatural elements of a Gothic novel with the vile sins common in decadent French fiction. The novel, which was intended to be an enlarged fable, describes a man whose portrait ages and grows ugly as a reflection of his moral corruption, although his actual appearance always remains the same. Critics saw through the book in a moment and denounced it as essentially immoral in spite of the self-destruction of its central character. Wilde defended himself: "There is no such thing as a moral or immoral book," he said. "Books are well written or badly written. That is all." Today's publishers of pornographic literature would gladly subscribe to that notion. Actually the book was self-revealing, showing the destructive side of devotion to a life of pleasure and exposing the deterioration of the author's soul.

But God is not mocked. Even as Wilde tried to rob society of whatever morals it had left, the rot was going ever deeper into his own soul. For a while he was able to steal from those less witty and clever than himself, but his day of reckoning was coming. Solomon warned that "the Lord will plead their cause," and even while Wilde was delighting in exposing secret sin and indiscretion and maximizing the resulting disgrace, his own soul was being despoiled. He carried with him a personal time bomb of scandal that would soon explode.

The scandal involved his close friendship with Lord Alfred Douglas, the son of the marquis of Queensbury. The marquis was disturbed by the friendship and at last accused Wilde of being a sodomite. Urged on by Douglas, Wilde sued for criminal libel, but his case collapsed in the face of the evidence. He was arrested, ordered to stand trial, found guilty, and sentenced to two years of hard labor. While in prison Wilde wrote a long letter to Douglas that was filled with bitterness against the younger man, whom he accused of encouraging him in his dissipation. After his release from prison Wilde—ruined in health, finances, and creative skill—fled to France where he died of brain inflammation. While only semiconscious he sought solace for his soul by becoming a Roman Catholic. Truly the Lord will "spoil the soul of those that spoiled."

### 3. His Chance Friends (22:24-29)

#### a. Those He Should Reject (22:24-28)

##### (1) The Furious Man (22:24-25)

For the good of their own souls and for the good of society, there are some friendships that those in authority should shun. For example they should avoid friendship with a bad-tempered person. Solomon gave two reasons. First, *a bad temper is contemptible:* "Make no friendship with an angry man; and with a furious man thou shalt not go" (Proverbs 22:24). Second, *a bad temper is contagious:* "Lest thou learn his ways, and get a snare to thy soul" (22:25). Our English proverb says, "You become like the company you keep." We also speak of two people being tarred with the same brush. These proverbs are especially applicable to people of weak character.

In Solomon's words we can almost detect an echo of a quarrel in the palace. Rehoboam may have asked permission to go somewhere with one of his undesirable friends. Solomon, knowing that the friend was a mean-spirited and angry young man, would have put his foot down and replied, "No, I don't approve of your friendship with this man, and that's that."

We can hear Rehoboam whine, "Why can't I go with him? He's my friend. I like him. You don't like any of my friends. Besides, he never loses his temper with me."

And we can see Solomon looking at his son as he said, "Make no friendship with an angry man; and with a furious man thou shalt not go; Lest thou learn his ways, and get a snare to thy soul."

That sound advice did not do Rehoboam any good in the end. As soon as he was free of his father's control, Rehoboam surrounded himself with friends he should have shunned. His failure to follow his father's advice cost him nearly all his kingdom.

When Jeroboam's delegation offered the allegiance of the ten tribes in return for an immediate alleviation of taxation, Rehoboam asked for three days to think about the offer. He conferred with the old men and they advised him to give in and win the hearts of the men of Israel. Then Rehoboam called in his young drinking buddies. Surely his angry friend was among them and his fierce voice raised in strident tones could be heard above the others. We can picture his face red with rage as he shook his fist and said, "You show them, Rehoboam. Show them who gives the orders. Show them who's boss." Forgetting his father's warning, Rehoboam liked what he heard.

The conference reconvened and the wise old men were dismayed to see a thundercloud on Rehoboam's brow. They saw the grim set of his mouth and the raging look in his eyes. "And the king answered the people roughly," the Holy Spirit says (1 Kings 12:13).

We can hear the voice of the angry friend speaking through Rehoboam: "Taxation! You don't know what taxation is. From now on, all taxes are raised. *Raised,* do you hear? And don't you dare complain. You don't know what punishment is. Whips? You'll pray for the whips before I'm finished with you. I'll flay you with scorpions."

Rehoboam enjoyed his triumph just long enough for Jeroboam to catch his breath, but the next moment Rehoboam discovered that his anger had cost him the greater part of his kingdom.

### (2) The Foolish Man (22:26-27)

Those in authority should also avoid friendships with foolish men. Solomon, with one particular foolish person in mind, pointed out *his desire for bargains* and *his drift toward bankruptcy:* "Be not thou one of them that strike hands, or of them that are sureties for debts. If thou hast nothing to pay, why should he take away thy bed from under thee?" (Proverbs 22:26-27). The wise king was repeating his warning concerning the folly of securing another person's loan, especially when one is not in a financial position to do so. "You'll pay for it if you do," Solomon was saying. Our English proverb says, "Better safe than sorry." In effect Solomon's sound business advice was "Don't sign until you are sure."

Years ago I knew a man of great personal integrity who worked for a Christian organization. He was an able preacher and a good administrator, but he knew little or nothing about high finance. An earnest Christian, he was a transparently honest individual. Guileless himself, he was quite sure that others were as honest as he was. It would never have occurred to him that a fellow believer would, or even could, be guilty of any kind of shady deal.

I spent many happy hours in this man's home. He seemed to enjoy talking over the Scriptures and sharing similar tastes in books. But beneath his smiling exterior he carried a terrible burden. One day he revealed to me that he was afraid he might be sent to prison for fraud.

This is his story. When he first accepted a position in the organization, his title was business manager and he simply handled the day-to-day business of the organization. Most of the major financial transactions, including sales of real estate, were handled by his boss. The organization owned some prime property and from time to time the boss would sell a parcel or two of land to individuals who wanted building sites for retirement homes. My friend believed his superior was a good Christian and trusted him completely.

Soon this boss promoted my friend to the position of secretary, increased his salary, and made him a signing officer with full legal powers and responsibilities. Thus my friend took a step up the ladder—or so he thought. In actual fact, he had fallen into a trap.

From time to time the boss put deeds and other documents on my friend's desk. "This is for that property down by the lake, Bill," he would say. "We're selling a piece of it. As secretary you will need to sign where I have marked the papers. I'll take care of all the transfers, titles, and legal details." My unsuspicious friend signed as requested, not for one moment suspecting that anything might be wrong. The bylaws of the organization provided for the sale of property and because he was unskilled in real estate matters, he simply trusted his boss.

After a few years the boss left the organization and moved across the country. At his suggestion the board promoted my friend to the position of general manager. He received an appropriate increase in salary and assumed full responsibility for the organization.

Before long my friend woke up to a terrible reality. He had been systematically deceived into participating in many fraudulent real estate transactions. Property had been sold, all right, but often the same parcel of land had been "sold" to two or three different people. Bogus documents had been issued and my friend, in complete ignorance of what was really going on, had signed them.

"Sign here," he had been told, or "Sign there." Thinking he was doing what he was supposed to do as secretary of the organization, he had signed. Now he was saddled with scores of fraudulent documents for which he was legally responsible. The former boss had absconded with hundreds of thousands of dollars and the victims took legal action against my friend. His name, reputation, and whole life were at stake.

Everyone who knew my friend well, knew that he was as much a victim as the people who had been defrauded, but his innocence did not prevent the lawsuits from being filed. As he faced ruin, my friend said: "The Lord knows. It's in His hands now. I was a fool, but I was an honest fool."

I am glad to say that this story has a happy ending. Another Christian friend of mine took an interest in the case. He was able to persuade a wealthy Christian businessman to put up the money to pay back in full those who had been defrauded. As for the actual thief, his case has been referred to that higher court where all such wrongs will one day be redressed.

(3) The Fraudulent Man (22:28)

Solomon was warning those in authority to shun friendships with fraudulent men when he wrote Proverbs 2:28: "Remove not the ancient landmark, which thy fathers have set."

Nowadays property boundaries, officially surveyed by professionals, are recorded in local courthouses, as are titles, mortgages, and land plots. Surveyors' stakes can be removed, but property boundaries remain unchanged. In ancient times, however, landmarks were of vital importance.

In Israel, to remove an ancient landmark was a serious crime. The whole land had been divided by divine lot among the tribes and families of the nation. Moreover all such property was entailed and could not be permanently sold. The longest lease ran for fifty years, from jubilee to jubilee.

The history of the American West provides us with many illustrations of how important it is for a person to secure a landmark or some other form of official title to the land he owns. James Michener graphically pointed out the importance in his book *Centennial.* Somewhere around the year 1859, according to Michener, Hans Brumbaugh, a settler in Colorado, became disillusioned with prospecting for gold and decided to turn to potato farming instead. Needing land, he asked his friend Levi Zendt how one went about securing a piece of property, for Zendt and his Scottish partner McKeag had staked out a claim many years earlier.

One of their problems in staking a claim was that Colorado was then only a fledgling state and not even an official territory of the United States. Legally the land still belonged to the Indians. Settlers, whatever status they may have imagined was theirs, technically were only squatters on Indian land. The Zendts' stake in the land was more secure, Levi explained, because his wife's mother had been a full-blooded Arapaho Indian. He had bought the land from her and she had given him a paper that said so. Levi had filed that paper in the land office in St. Louis, but even so, there was no guarantee that the claim would be honored when Colorado finally became a state.

Brumbaugh bought some acreage from Zendt and then thought of a plan for enlarging his farm. He dug an irrigation channel from the Platte river through the center of some adjoining arid land. This effort tripled the size of Brumbaugh's arable land. Ownership of water rights was even more touchy than land ownership and it was not until a century later that the Supreme Court of the United States legally recognized the principle that the person who first claimed and used a water source had rights to that water—rights that took precedence over all later claims.

Throughout the rough, turbulent history of the wild West, many bitter fights erupted over the use and ownership of land and water. The rancher with his vast herds of cattle wanted the prairie kept open. The farmer and settler wanted to fence it in. The cowboys referred to the vast plains as "our land," even though they may have actually owned less than .5 percent of it. The railroads, pushing westward, challenged unsubstantiated claims. Settlements grew into towns, which then extended their borders and defied the ranchers.

Most of the wars and feuds during pioneer days revolved around the right to own and fence in land, and many exciting westerns and thrilling movies (*Shane,* for instance) have been written about this theme. Popular authors like Zane Gray and Louis L'Amour have enthralled millions with stories of the old West.

In the promised land battles over property were settled once and for all by use of landmarks, although feuds could still break out with pagan peoples over water rights (Genesis 26:12-33). It was a serious crime to tamper with a landmark and Solomon strictly advised against it. Doubtless as king he had been called on to settle many disputes over landmarks. Those cases must have taxed even his wisdom.

b. Those He Should Receive (22:29)

"Seest thou a man diligent in his business? he shall stand before kings; he shall not stand before mean men."

Abraham Lincoln stood before kings and we can never learn enough about him. He was born in 1809 in a backwoods cabin. The food young Abe ate was coarse and his clothes were made by his mother from the skins of animals that his father shot. The boy rarely went to school because his father, a poor farmer, kept him too busy doing chores.

When Abe was seven, the Lincolns moved to Indiana, where his father built a "half-faced camp"—a log shelter enclosed on three sides. The other side was protected by a fire that kept the animals out and the heat in. Abe's mother died soon after the move to Indiana.

Longing to learn, Abe read everything that came his way. He

practiced arithmetic on a wooden shovel, shaving off the figures to make way for new ones. His father hired him out for six dollars a month. And for a while he split rails to earn cloth for a pair of trousers—four hundred rails for every yard of coarse cloth. He worked hard and was diligent in business.

Yet Abe did not seem to get very far. Everything always seemed to go wrong. He failed in business when he was twenty-two years old. He ran for the Illinois state legislature at age twenty-three and was defeated. He failed in business again at the age of twenty-five. His sweetheart died when he was twenty-six. At twenty-seven he had a nervous breakdown. He was elected to the Illinois state legislature in 1834, but he was defeated for speaker of the house when he was twenty-nine. He was defeated for elector when he was thirty-one and defeated for Congress when he was thirty-four. At thirty-seven he was finally elected to Congress, only to be defeated again when he was thirty-nine. He was defeated for the Senate at forty-six and defeated for vice president at forty-seven. He was again defeated for the Senate at forty-nine. It was not until he was fifty-one that he was elected president of the United States, and early in his second term he was murdered. He was fifty-six years old.

It was after Lincoln was elected president that the crisis over slavery erupted. Refusing to accept his election, the southern confederacy seceded from the Union and prepared for war. After initial hesitation Lincoln rose to the occasion and took charge of the North. His Emancipation Proclamation declared that after January 1, 1863, all slaves would be free. The thirteenth amendment, which abolished slavery forever, followed and the Civil War ended with the surrender of Robert E. Lee on April 9, 1865. Five days later Lincoln was assassinated. A sense of stunned loss swept over the country. The whole nation—North and South—mourned his death.

Abraham Lincoln was heralded as an orator and a statesman, as a man of industry and integrity, as a man of courage and compassion, as a man gifted with humor, and as a man who was able to see the other person's viewpoint. He may not have been very successful in business, but he was determined, diligent, and resourceful, and he stood before kings. Ambassadors and great men of all nations waited upon him when he was president of the United States and since his death millions of people, great and small, have paid him tribute by visiting his impressive memorial in Washington, D.C.

With the great issue of slavery hanging over the United States during his presidency, Abraham Lincoln was as much God's man for the hour as Churchill was in Britain during World War II.

# CHAPTER 4

## Proverbs 23:1–24:34

C. His Majesty's Interests (23:1–24:34)
   1. Words to His Subjects (23:1-14)
      a. A King's Table (23:1-8)
         (1) Beware of Motives (23:1-3)
            (a) Cultivate Alertness (23:1)
            (b) Curb Appetite (23:2-3)
               We should give the king no opportunity to:
               i. Dislike Us (23:2)
               ii. Deceive Us (23:3)
         (2) Beware of Materialism (23:4-5)
            (a) The Desire for Riches (23:4)
            (b) The Deceitfulness of Riches (23:5)
         (3) Beware of Meanness (23:6-8)
            (a) The Invitation (23:6)
            (b) The Insincerity (23:7-8)
               i. The Table Is Spread (23:7)
               ii. The Trap Is Sprung (23:8)
      b. A King's Talk (23:9-14)
         (1) About the Fool (23:9)
         (2) About the Fatherless (23:10-11)
            (a) Their Rights (23:10)
            (b) Their Redeemer (23:11)
         (3) About the Family (23:12-14)
            (a) A Note about Contemplation (23:12)
            (b) A Note about Correction (23:13-14)
               i. A Stringent Command (23:13)
               ii. A Serious Consideration (23:14)
   2. Words to His Son (23:15–24:34)
      a. About Life (23:15-35)

- (1) Comments about Wisdom (23:15-25)
  - (a) A Father's Call (23:15-18)
    - i. A Wise Son Rejoices His Father (23:15-16)
    - ii. A Wise Son Redeems His Future (23:17-18)
  - (b) A Father's Caution (23:19-21)
    - i. Be Guided by Your Father (23:19)
    - ii. Be Guarded in Your Friendships (23:20-21)
      - *a.* Beware of Wild Parties (23:20)
      - *b.* Beware of Waiting Poverty (23:21)
  - (c) A Father's Counsel (23:22-23)
    He gave his son a word about:
    - i. His Mother (23:22)
    - ii. His Mind (23:23)
  - (d) A Father's Comfort (23:24-25)
    - i. In a Righteous Son (23:24)
    - ii. In a Responsible Son (23:25)
- (2) Comments about Women (23:26-28)
  - (a) The Appeal to the Heart (23:26)
  - (b) The Appeal of the Harlot (23:27-28)
    - i. How Dangerous She Is (23:27)
    - ii. How Destructive She Is (23:28)
- (3) Comments about Wine (23:29-35)
  - (a) Look at the Drunkard (23:29-32)
    - i. Strong Drink Stupefies (23:29-30)
    - ii. Strong Drink Stings (23:31-32)
  - (b) Learn from the Drunkard (23:33-34)
    - i. What the Drunkard Desires (23:33a)
    - ii. What the Drunkard Declares (23:33b)
    - iii. What the Drunkard Does (23:34)
  - (c) Listen to the Drunkard (23:35)
    - i. What He Discovers (23:35a)
    - ii. What He Decides (23:35b)

b. About Leadership (24:1-25)
- (1) How to Create Wealth (24:1-4)
  - (a) Be Wary (24:1-2)
    - i. Of Evil Men's Company (24:1)
    - ii. Of Evil Men's Comments (24:2)

(b) Be Wise (24:3-4)
  i. How to Found a Great House (24:3)
  ii. How to Fill a Great House (24:4)
(2) How to Contemplate War (24:5-12)
  (a) Some Substantial Instances (24:5-9)
    i. The Importance of Wise Counselors (24:5-6)
      *a.* For a Nation's Strength (24:5)
      *b.* For a Nation's Safety (24:6)
    ii. The Impotence of Wicked Counselors (24:7-9)
      *a.* The Silent Fool (24:7)
      *b.* The Sinful Fool (24:8)
      *c.* The Scornful Fool (24:9)
  (b) Some Suppositional Inferences (24:10-12)
    i. The Man with No Moral Courage (24:10)
    ii. The Man with No Moral Character (24:11-12)
      *a.* What Such a Man Sees (24:11)
      *b.* What Such a Man Says (24:12)
(3) How to Cultivate Wisdom (24:13-14)
  (a) An Illustration: A Honeycomb Full of Sweetness (24:13)
  (b) An Application: A Heart Full of Satisfaction (24:14)
(4) How to Curb Wickedness (24:15-25)
  (a) Concerning Felony (24:15-18)
    i. The Plot Overheard by God (24:15)
    ii. The Plot Overruled by God (24:16-18)
      *a.* The Fall of the Good Man (24:16)
        *1.* Contemplated (24:16a)
        *2.* Contrasted (24:16b)
      *b.* The Fall of the Godless Man (24:17-18)
        *1.* Rejoicing Is Forbidden (24:17)
        *2.* Rejoicing Is Foolish (24:18)
  (b) Concerning Fretting (24:19-20)

i. Don't Fret (24:19)
ii. Don't Forget (24:20)
(c) Concerning Fickleness (24:21-22)
i. Note the Vacillating Person's Instability (24:21)
ii. Note the Vacillating Person's Insecurity (24:22)
(d) Concerning Favoritism (24:23)
(e) Concerning Fairness (24:24-25)
i. Justifying the Wicked (24:24)
ii. Judging the Wicked (24:25)
c. About Law (24:26-29)
(1) Popularity (24:26)
(2) Priorities (24:27)
(3) Perjury (24:28)
(4) Pardon (24:29)
d. About Laziness (24:30-34)
(1) A Vineyard Seen (24:30-31)
(a) The Character of the Person Involved (24:30)
(b) The Condition of the Property Involved (24:31)
(2) A Vineyard Studied (24:32-34)
(a) The Case Is Reviewed (24:32)
(b) The Conclusions Are Reached (24:33-34)
i. Persistent Indolence (24:33)
ii. Predictable Insolvency (24:34)

As he wrote about topics of particular interest and relevance to those who wield authority, Solomon addressed some wise words to his subjects and some wise words to his son. Because life is complex and full of contradictions and contingencies, the scope of Solomon's observations is wide-ranging. It is not surprising that, as usual, Solomon's thoughts roamed first here, then there. Yet as the outline demonstrates, there is order in the book of Proverbs even where there seems to be disorder, and connection, cohesion, and continuity throughout.

## C. His Majesty's Interests (23:1–24:34)

### 1. Words to His Subjects (23:1-14)

#### a. A King's Table (23:1-8)

#### (1) Beware of Motives (23:1-3)

Solomon offered two pieces of advice for those who receive unexpected or long-sought-for invitations to the king's table. First, he said we should *cultivate alertness* on such occasions: "When thou sittest to eat with a ruler, consider diligently what is before thee" (Proverbs 23:1). Second, he said we should *curb appetite* (23:2-3). If we don't, the king may *dislike us:* "Put a knife to thy throat, if thou be a man given to appetite" (23:2). Or the king may *deceive us:* "Be not desirous of his dainties: for they are deceitful meat" (23:3).

Often a person in a position of authority has ulterior motives when he extends an invitation to lunch or to a banquet. He sometimes uses the occasion to gain information, form an opinion, or make a decision. It is said that when the automobile magnate Henry Ford was considering someone for a promotion, he would invite the prospect to lunch. Ford would watch him when the meal was served. If he put salt on his food before tasting it, Ford would not promote him. If the man would season his dinner before tasting it, Ford reasoned, maybe he would make decisions on the job before ascertaining the facts.

Those in high places often use a banquet or similar occasion to see if a man can curb his appetite, control his use of liquor, handle himself well in society, converse intelligently, and hold his tongue when necessary.

The director of a foreign missionary society used to insist on having a personal interview with each new candidate before the board finally endorsed the applicant. Having spent many years on the field, the director knew of the frustrations, embarrassments, disappointments, and annoyances that awaited any new missionary. The director knew of the stresses and strains to which mission stations are sometimes subjected and he knew of the discourtesy, insolence, and inconsiderate behavior missionaries sometimes have to face. He wanted to determine whether the candidate would be able to cope with such trials.

So the director would send the candidate a letter inviting him to come for an interview and a meal at an unusually early time of day. When the candidate arrived at the specified time, he would find the door locked. There would be no sign of life and no answer to his knock. After waiting outside in the cold for an hour, the candidate would finally get a response to his repeated knocks on the door. He would be invited in by a secretary and asked to wait in an unheated room with spartan furnishings.

An hour would go by, two hours, then three hours. Puzzled, the candidate would look up and down the hallway, but no one would be in sight. A sign reading Private would bar any thought of venturing up the stairs to see what was at the top. Listening at the bottom of the stairs, the candidate would occasionally catch the sound of a distant voice, or laughter, or a telephone, or a radio, but no one would come near the waiting room. Not until mid-afternoon would the secretary reappear, offer a brief apology, and conduct the candidate into the presence of the director.

The whole day was a test. The director would secretly monitor the candidate's arrival and his activities while he waited. The director wanted to evaluate the punctuality and the patience of the candidate because once on the mission field, the new missionary would have to face far worse rudeness and unexplained delays. He would have to put up with more than a cold uncomfortable room and the inconvenience of missing a meal. The director also wanted to know what the candidate would do with time suddenly put at his disposal. Would he spend the time reading and praying? Would he get angry and leave?

In like manner, in olden times an invitation to a royal banquet was not always what it appeared to be on the surface. Solomon himself had sized up many men at his table.

### (2) Beware of Materialism (23:4-5)

Solomon warned against *the desire for riches:* "Labour not to be rich: cease from thine own wisdom" (Proverbs 23:4). We are not to be guided by human wisdom, which places priority on being successful in this world, making a lot of money, and earning a measure of independence.

Solomon also warned against *the deceitfulness of riches:* "Wilt thou set thine eyes upon that which is not? for riches certainly make themselves wings; they fly away as an eagle toward heaven" (Proverbs 23:5). Riches are as illusionary as the fabled pot of gold at the end of the rainbow. A story is told about a company executive who finally made it to the top of the corporate ladder and was earning really big money. He confessed, "I spent all of my life climbing to the top of the ladder, only to discover that it was against the wrong wall." Solomon was saying much the same thing.

Pursuing wealth is like chasing the wind. A man can never get enough of it and it is hard to keep. Wealth is hard to acquire and a man must leave it all behind when he dies. A preacher friend of mine used to say, "If you want treasure in heaven, you'd better give some money to someone who's going there." We can't take it with us, but we can send it on ahead.

Getting rich seems to be the goal of many people. However, this goal is false because it focuses attention on the wrong world. That is one reason God so often allows those who have riches to lose them. When his riches are gone, a man may begin to think about Heaven. His riches kept his thoughts focused on earth. "It is easier," Jesus said, "for a camel to go through the eye of a needle, than for a rich man to enter into the kingdom of God" (Mark 10:25).

The long roll call of Britain's illustrious sons—men who made history and added vast kingdoms to Britain's far-flung domains—includes names such as Wolfe in Canada, Clive in India, Captain Cook in the South Seas, Gordon in the Sudan, Livingstone in Africa, Disraeli in Westminster, and Rhodes in Africa.

Young Cecil Rhodes went out to Africa with one goal in mind: to get rich quick. He was very good at making money. When he was twenty-seven years old, he founded the prestigious De Beers mining company, and by the time he was thirty-five he controlled all of South Africa's diamond mining industry. At thirty-six he became prime minister of Cape Colony. By the time he was forty-one he controlled the gold mining industry of South Africa. When he died, he was probably one of the richest men in the world. His legacy to the British empire was the vast territory of North and South Rhodesia.

It was probably no accident that Rhodes was the personal friend of General Booth, the founder of The Salvation Army and probably one of the poorest men in the world. One day the two men were traveling across England together by train. Booth leaned over and asked the famous statesman and industrialist a question. "Tell me, Rhodes," he said, "are you a happy man?"

Rhodes looked back at the general. "Me?" he said. "Happy? Good heavens, no!"

There are two things money cannot buy, as many people have learned. Money cannot buy happiness, and it cannot buy holiness. So it is often a good thing when riches take wings and fly away.

(3) Beware of Meanness (23:6-8)

Solomon warned us to beware of *the invitation* of the mean person: "Eat thou not the bread of him that hath an evil eye, neither desire thou his dainty meats" (Proverbs 23:6). Solomon also drew attention to *the insincerity* behind the invitation (23:7-8). True, *the table is spread*—"Eat and drink, saith he to thee" (23:7). But before we have time to take the edge off our appetite, *the trap is sprung:* "The morsel which thou hast eaten shalt thou vomit up, and lose thy sweet words" (23:8).

Solomon knew of David's experience with Saul's insincerity. When David was a young shepherd boy, he was chosen by God to be Israel's next king. Soon afterward he became a national hero by killing Goliath of Gath. Thus David's name made the headlines. He was cheered from one end of the country to the other, and black malice and envy seized the soul of King Saul. He "eyed David from that day and forward," wrote the historian (1 Samuel 18:9).

First Saul tried to murder David with a javelin. He missed twice—no wonder he didn't want to fight Goliath! Then, hoping to trap David in an incautious word, Saul proposed to David that he marry into the royal family. Adding a rider to the engagement contract, Saul stipulated that David must provide incontrovertible proof that he had killed a hundred Philistines. Then Saul again tried to murder David with a javelin. Not long afterward David learned of yet another plot to murder him in his bed, and he fled.

It was no fun being a fugitive. We can well believe that David missed many meals. For a while he stayed with his old friend Samuel, the prophet. But before long Saul sent agents to arrest David and finally headed for Samuel's place himself. David fled once more.

Then came the time of the monthly new moon banquet. David, being the king's son-in-law, was expected to attend. The king's table was laid and David's name card was put at his appointed place. But could David trust a king who had already proved that he had an "evil eye"? With this question on his mind, David met clandestinely in the wilds with Jonathan, Saul's son.

David was a healthy young man and no doubt thoughts of the table loaded with the king's dainties danced tantalizingly in his mind. Just thinking about the banquet made his mouth water. So he proposed a test. He would not come to the table and Jonathan would communicate his father's reaction. If Saul took David's absence philosophically and accepted David's excuse, David could safely come and enjoy the king's hospitality for the remainder of the feast. Jonathan agreed and "David hid himself in the field" (1 Samuel 20:24).

On the day of the first banquet Saul sat down at the head table and Jonathan took his place. The guests poured in and Saul eyed them all. At last his evil eye settled on David's empty seat. Saul said nothing the first day, but when David's seat was still empty on the second day, he turned to Jonathan and demanded an explanation. When Jonathan gave the excuse he and David had agreed on, Saul's mask came off. He cursed Jonathan, produced the javelin intended for David's heart, and flung it at his own son (1 Samuel 20:25-34).

David may have desired the king's dainties, but he was too aware of Saul's evil eye to let hunger overrule common sense. We would do well to take Solomon's advice and try to read the secret hearts of those who profess friendship and offer hospitality, especially when we have reason to believe they eye us with ill will.

### b. A King's Talk (23:9-14)

#### (1) About the Fool (23:9)

"Speak not in the ears of a fool: for he will despise the wisdom of thy words." Trying to talk sense into a fool is like talking to a brick wall.

Some time ago I was scheduled to speak in the Sunday evening service at a church in a southern city. It was Sunday afternoon and I was having trouble finding the church. I had exited the interstate and followed the route on the map that the pastor had given me, but it was no use. There was a missing link in the directions. After driving up and down various cross streets, I gave up.

I pulled over to a telephone booth, armed myself with a handful of small change, looked up the pastor's number in my notebook, and dialed the number. A woman answered. I asked for the pastor, and she said, "You've got the wrong number."

There was a tattered telephone book tethered to the booth and I finally found the pastor's listing. The number given was the same as the number in my notebook. I tried again in case I had dialed the number incorrectly the first time. The same woman answered. "May I please speak to Pastor Ken Mitchell?" I asked.

"I told you before, Mister," she said, and her voice had a sharper edge this time. "You've got the wrong number." Evidently his number had been changed.

I decided to call the church. Perhaps someone would be there even if it was Sunday afternoon. I consulted my notebook again and dialed the church's number. A pleasant voice answered: "This is Shirley Waycross of North Shore Baptist Church. The church offices are closed on Sunday. Thank you for calling us.

"If you want information about the time and nature of the various services held at North Shore Baptist Church, at the sound of the tone please dial 102.

"If you want a staff member, at the sound of the tone please dial 103.

"If you want the pastor, dial 104.

"If you want the pastor's assistant, dial 105.

"If you want the minister of music, dial 106.

"If you want the youth pastor, dial 107.

"If you want information about the nursery, dial 108.

"If you want information about our doctrinal statement, dial 109.

"If you want to contact one of our deacons, dial 110.

"If you would like to leave a message, at the sound of the tone press the star button and dial 100.

"Thank you for calling North Shore Baptist Church, your friendly community church. At North Shore you are sure of a warm welcome and the personal touch. This is Shirley."

I groaned. I was in touch with a mindless computer named Shirley!

Well, I wanted the pastor, so at the sound of the tone I dialed 104. Another pleasant voice answered: "This is Betty Bliss, the pastor's secretary. The pastor is not in his office right now. If you would like to leave a message, at the sound of the tone press the star button and dial 100." The recording continued: "The pastor will call you when he gets in, so please give us your name and telephone number. If you would like to be transferred back to the church telephone directory, at the sound of the tone press the star button and dial 101. Thank you for calling North Shore Baptist Church, where you are always sure of a warm welcome and the personal touch. This is Betty."

I groaned again. I desperately needed to talk to someone. I had forgotten all the choices so I pressed the star button and dialed 101. Now I was talking—or listening—to Shirley again:

"This is Shirley Waycross of North Shore Baptist Church. The church offices are closed on Sunday. Thank you for calling us.

"If you want information about the time and nature of the various services held at North Shore Baptist Church, at the sound of the tone please dial 102....

"If you want the pastor's assistant, dial 105."

I dialed 105. A delightful southern drawl announced: "This is Matilda Nightingale, the assistant pastor's secretary. The assistant pastor is not in his office right now. If you would like to leave a message, at the sound of the tone press the star button and dial 111. The pastor's assistant will call you when he gets in, so please give us your name and telephone number." I knew what was coming next: "If you would like to be transferred back to the church telephone directory, at the sound of the tone press the star button and dial 101. Thank you for calling North Shore Baptist Church, where you are always sure of a warm welcome and the personal touch. This is Matilda."

The phone booth was hot. The outside temperature was about 98 degrees and the humidity was about 95 percent. However, I had to reach somebody. After all, the church service was due to start in a couple of hours and I had no idea how to get there. I tried again. I pressed the star button and dialed 101. It was Shirley again: "If you want.... If you want.... If you want...."

I decided to try a deacon and dialed 110. It was Shirley again: "This is Shirley Waycross of North Shore Baptist Church. North Shore Baptist Church is served by a board of twenty-five deacons. Our deacons each serve for a three-year term. At the end of three years each deacon rotates off the board for at least a year, after which he can become eligible for renomination. Our deacons are men who meet the Biblical standards for deacons. They are men who are chosen because they have a heart for lost people and for the flock of God. We will be happy to send you a complete listing of our deacon board along with telephone numbers where they can be reached. Please leave your name and address by pressing the star button and dialing 112. If you would like to be transferred back to the church telephone directory, at the sound of the tone press the star button and dial 101. Thank you for calling North Shore Baptist Church, where you are always sure of a warm welcome and the personal touch. This is Shirley."

I had this frustrating experience about the time I was trying to think of an illustration for Proverbs 23:9! Talking to a fool is like talking to a brick wall or (to bring the analogy up to date) like talking to a computerized answering service. The computer is programmed to parrot set phrases. The voices are sweet and melodious and the information imparted is precise and accurate, but there is no way to get past its complete and impenetrable mindlessness. That is exactly what talking to a fool is like. Solomon had a son who was a fool, and the wise father was frustrated with trying to reason with him.

(2) About the Fatherless (23:10-11)

Speaking of *their rights* in verse 10 and *their Redeemer* in verse 11, Solomon warned: "Remove not the old landmark; and enter not into the fields of the fatherless: For their redeemer is mighty; he shall plead their cause with thee."

Solomon, as we have seen, had issued a similar warning in Proverbs 22:28, but here in 23:10-11 he added the fact that the sin in question is a sin against God. The landmarks in Israel were recorded in the supreme courthouse in Heaven. Those who violated the sanctity of an ancient landmark were inviting divine retribution. The crime is aggravated when the property of orphans is involved. They may look like easy prey, but "their redeemer is mighty."

"Their redeemer is mighty"—the basic principle expressed by these words underlies the book of Ruth. The book of Exodus also deals primarily with redemption, but while Exodus illustrates redemption by power, Ruth illustrates redemption by purchase. We whose Redeemer is mighty have been rescued both ways.

We note ten features of the brief, interesting, and important book of Ruth. First we observe *disorder*. The story took place "in the days when the judges ruled" (Ruth 1:1). The last five chapters of the book of Judges emphasize the religious and moral disarray of Israel during those days.

Then we see *disaster*, for "there was a famine in the land" (Ruth 1:1). Famine was one of the curses pronounced by Moses (see Deuteronomy 28:23-24). He had threatened the nation that if they committed apostasy, the Lord would send such a judgment.

Next we note *dispersal*, for Elimelech took his family into exile in Moab. He hoped to escape the hardships that had come upon *Bethlehem-judah*, "the house of bread and of praise." Elimelech's move was retrogressive and he soon paid a high price for his decision. In the Old Testament God's blessings were centered in a place, the promised land. Even when temporarily suspended while God chastened His children, those blessings were nonetheless sure—but only in that place.

We also observe *disregard*, as Elimelech and his family continued to live in Moab, away from the place where God had put His name and met with His people. For about ten years, while his boys were becoming men, he lived out of fellowship with God's people. Elimelech's testimony for God in Moab must have been negative at best.

Then we see *distress* as death followed death. Elimelech died and his two sons, who had married pagan Moabite women, also died. The high price of backsliding and rebellion was paid under the chastening hand of God.

Next we observe *discovery* when Naomi received word that God had "visited his people" (Ruth 1:6). There was revival back home. Blessing had broken out among God's people. There was "bread enough and to spare" in the place where God had promised to pour out His blessings (see Luke 15:17).

We also note *decision* in the book of Ruth. Naomi made up her mind to go back home. This Old Testament prodigal announced to Ruth and Orpah her determination to be restored to the fellowship of God's people. Two other decisions followed: Ruth decided that she would seek a place among God's people. Orpah decided to go back to the land of the lost, back to Moab, back to her old way of life, back to the demon gods of her people, and back into spiritual darkness.

We see *dispossession* when Naomi found that she had been reduced, by reason of her long backsliding in Moab, to abject indigence. Upon her return home she found poverty in the midst of plenty! The old landmarks had been removed. Her inheritance was in the hands of others. She had the title, but others tilled her land, lived in her house, and claimed what was hers. No one cared about widows (or orphans), especially when caring meant giving up property. Other people had possession of Naomi's land and in those lawless days "when the judges ruled," possession was nine-tenths of the law. So pitiable was Naomi's condition that people hardly recognized her. "Is this Naomi?" they asked. "Call me Mara," she replied. "I went out full, and the Lord hath brought me home again empty" (Ruth 1:19-21).

Then we observe *discernment.* Ruth went out to glean and found the kinsman-redeemer. This poor Gentile woman—a member of a hostile race, a native of a country under a curse, a foreigner raised in pagan darkness, a stranger to the covenants of Israel, an alien with no claim on the promises of God, and an outlaw according to the statute book of Israel—met Boaz! More important, she found grace in the eyes of that great prince of the house of Judah. Her heart was stirred even though she knew nothing about the law of the kinsman-redeemer. All she knew was that this man was mighty—"a mighty man of wealth," as the Bible says (Ruth 2:1).

Finally we note *deliverance.* Boaz did for Ruth what she could not do for herself. He met all the demands of the law, paid the price of her redemption, married her, and brought her into the royal family of Heaven.

Behind this wonderful book with its gospel overtones is the fact that a mighty kinsman-redeemer purchased two things. He purchased both Ruth and her property, and thus the text moves to yet another point of focus. The narrative illustrates not only the story of Christ and His church but also the story of Jehovah and Israel. Like Elimelech, the Israelites left the promised land and found graves in Gentile countries while their own country lay desolate under the judgment of God. Like Naomi, the Israelites have come back in these last days. Though impoverished, Israel is aware that God has again visited His people. Many of the old landmarks have been removed by the Muslims, the Turks, the British, the Palestinians, and the United Nations. The British promised to restore the landmarks, but created the state of Jordan. In trying to force Israel to surrender the West Bank and Jerusalem, even the United States has shown a desire to remove the landmarks. But "their redeemer is mighty."

Israel has not yet met its kinsman-redeemer. It has not yet discovered the grace of our Lord Jesus Christ. But the ancient landmarks are recorded in Heaven and in the Bible. They run all the way from the Nile to the Euphrates (Genesis 15:18-21). Let the Gentile nations take note. Woe betide anyone who removes those landmarks. The mighty Redeemer, who came once to redeem the people of Israel, is coming back to retake their property, which He has likewise bought and paid for (Matthew 13:44). No country on earth, however great and mighty, can afford to enter into a controversy with God over ancient landmarks.

(3) About the Family (23:12-14)

(a) A Note about Contemplation (23:12)

"Apply thine heart unto instruction," Solomon urged, "and thine ears to the words of knowledge." Notice that he said "heart," not "mind." Filling one's mind with facts and figures, truths and maxims, theories and principles, ideas and technicalities, rules and regulations, and concepts is different from allowing them to penetrate one's heart where they become motivating, driving forces of life.

Solomon also referred to "ears." They are the gateway to the mind, which is the vestibule of the heart. Satan always goes after the mind. God goes after the heart.

Ever since the fall when our first parents ate the fruit of the tree of knowledge, our minds have been particularly vulnerable to Satan's suggestions. Paul wrote, "The god of this world hath blinded the minds of them which believe not" (2 Corinthians 4:4). We send our children off to school and right from the start Satan begins to undermine the Word of God through the teaching of Darwinism. We send them off to high school and they are taught humanism. We send them off to college and they are taught relativism or Marxism. From the cradle to the grave, millions of people are blinded by the religious lies of Hinduism, Buddhism, Shintoism, Confucianism, Islam, or some form of cultism. Satan goes after the mind. People will believe arrant nonsense, but refuse even to read the Word of God.

It does little good to argue with people whose minds have been blinded. As our English proverb says, "A man convinced against his will is of the same opinion still."

God never argues. He has no need to, for He goes after the heart. We find that truth in the same passage of Scripture that tells us that Satan goes after the mind. Second Corinthians 4:6 says: "God, who commanded the light to shine out of darkness, hath shined in our hearts, to give the light of the knowledge of the glory of God in the face of Jesus Christ." In that one magnificent statement, Paul referred to the great quests of the Hebrews, Greeks, and Romans of his day.

The passion of the Hebrews was a desire for light. As they followed their quest, they received more and more light. Book after book was added to the Word of God until at last "the Word was made flesh" (John 1:14) and the light of Christ blazed forth upon the world (John 8:12).

The passion of the Greeks was a desire for knowledge. As they pursued their goal, they gave the world a host of philosophers whose writings are still studied today.

The passion of the Romans was a desire for glory. In their attempt to satisfy their thirst for glory, the Romans conquered the world, flung great arterial highways across it, imposed their will on it, and ruled it with a rod of iron.

Paul pointed all three peoples—Romans, Greeks, and Hebrews alike—to Christ. They would find what they were looking for in His face!

Once a person receives the Lord Jesus into his heart, Satan can never get Him out again, although he tries. Such attempts are behind brainwashing techniques, such as those the communists have perfected. But Satan's brainwashing doesn't work on a well-taught Christian who has memorized the Word of God and enthroned it in his heart. The Holy Spirit will minister it to him in time of need.

After sweeping to power in China and Tibet, the communists launched a massive brainwashing campaign to terrorize the people and transform them into Marxists. Geoffrey Bull, a British missionary, was among the numerous foreigners who were incarcerated, accused of spying, and subjected to the most intensive program of political persuasion ever devised by fallen man. He wrote about this experience in his book *When Iron Gates Yield.*

As a means of defense against the constant interrogation, intimidation, and indoctrination, Bull spent his mornings reading his Bible and memorizing Scripture. He spent his afternoons pacing his cell for exercise; sometimes he allowed his mind to roam far and wide and sometimes he used it to compose poems. Thus he, not the communists, took charge of his thoughts. Even so, he found the constant bullying and groundless accusations wearying. Added to his loneliness was the specter of possible torture and execution. Satan tried to bring him into bondage to fear, but the missionary counteracted those attempts by simply resting in the good and acceptable and perfect will of God.

Then the communists took Bull's Bible away and increased the level of pressure. Morning, noon, and night he was provoked and baited. His integrity and self-respect were constantly barraged. His thoughts were constantly probed—day after day, month after month, year after year. He had no privacy; hostile guards spied on him and watched his every move. Officials, wardens, and other prisoners—all of whom feared for their own future—dared not relent. The atmosphere was one of conflict, distrust, and a total lack of love. The purpose of his tormentors was to bring his mind "into absolute submission to the will and indoctrination of the Marxist way of life."[1]

Mental fatigue took over and Bull felt unable to meditate on the Scriptures or pray. It was then that the communists began an all-out attack on his faith. He was brought to the verge of collapse and wished for death. But when his mind was at the end of its tether, a divine voice rang out in his soul: "Thus far and no further."[2] God would not suffer him to be tempted above that which he was able to bear (1 Corinthians 10:13). The pressure suddenly ceased. The peace of God flooded his heart and soul.

The communists then tried a new tactic, putting the missionary under a regimen of total silence and lack of movement. For three years the waves and billows had gone over him. Now in the quietness that the communists hoped would break him, Bull's faith surged back like a flood tide.

The Holy Spirit tells us to apply our *hearts* to instruction, for knowledge of the truth must sink down much deeper than the mind if we are to withstand life's greatest tests.

### (b) A Note about Correction (23:13-14)

Proverbs 23:13 confronts us with *a stringent command:* "Withhold not correction from the child: for if thou beatest him with the rod, he shall not die." Proverbs 23:14 adds *a serious consideration:* "Thou shalt beat him with the rod, and shalt deliver his soul from hell." These two verses make a strong statement. If we believe in the plenary, verbal inspiration of the Scriptures, we need to take the statement seriously, even though modern psychologists, secular humanists, and liberal socialists react to it like a bull responds to a red rag. Corporal punishment may be abused at times in practice, but the principle itself remains true.

First Solomon stated *the rule:* "Withhold not correction from the child." If we love a child, we will not fail to impose discipline on him. Early in life a child has to learn that his will is not the only will in the world. He must learn that he cannot always have everything he wants and always get his own way. He must learn that temper tantrums will be swiftly, surely, and sometimes painfully dealt with. The sooner a child runs into firm, fair, and consistent discipline, the better off that child will be. A person who has not learned to take no for an answer cannot get through life successfully.

After stating the rule, the wise king recommended *the rod:* "If thou beatest him with the rod, he shall not die." In the early years of life nothing communicates as well as physical punishment. Solomon did not have in mind brutal beatings inflicted by an enraged adult. That kind of abuse does occur, but Solomon was not talking about such criminal bullying. When he said, "He shall not die," Solomon was indicating that physical punishment has to be administered rationally and with restraint.

Finally Solomon stated *the reason* for his recommendation: "Thou...shalt deliver his soul from hell." Compared to a child who is neglected or abused, a child who is brought under the firm authority of his parents will be much more easily brought under divine authority. He has a much better start in life and a much better chance for a good ending.

The liberal theologian scoffs at the idea of Hell. The Bible never does. The underlying principle of this proverb is simple and solemn: eternity looms ahead. Every parent should keep that principle in mind as he deals with his child. Every child inherits a fallen nature that manifests itself before the child can even walk or talk. A parent must set limits, form habits, instill truths, implant fear, curb rebellion, command obedience, extend love, and provide direction. A child must be properly rooted and grounded before he is set in a pattern of self-will. The importance of early training is expressed in an old poem:

I took a piece of plastic clay
And gently fashioned it one day,
And as my fingers pressed it still
It moved and yielded to my will.

I came again when days were passed,
That piece of clay was hard at last;
The form I gave it, still it bore
But I could change that form no more.

I took a piece of living clay
And gently formed it day by day,
And molded with my powers and art
A young child's soft and yielding heart.

I came again when days were gone,
It was a man I looked upon.
He still that early impress wore
But I could change him nevermore.

2. Words to His Son (23:15–24:34)

a. About Life (23:15-35)

(1) Comments about Wisdom (23:15-25)

(a) A Father's Call (23:15-18)

In Proverbs 23:15-16 Solomon again reminded his son of a basic parent-child relationship: *a wise son rejoices his father*. He wrote: "My son, if thine heart be wise, my heart shall rejoice, even mine. Yea, my reins shall rejoice, when thy lips speak right things." Sad to say, like many parents, Solomon never did have cause to rejoice in the wise heart of his son. Other parents, however, have experienced the truth of this proverb and have known the joy of seeing their children make right decisions.

Solomon stood midway between two poles: his father's tears and his own fears. He had heard about his father's experiences and knew all about *his father's tears.* David, famous for his wisdom, made one mistake that almost ruined his life. In his early days when he was a man after God's own heart (1 Samuel 13:14), it was written of him again and again that he "behaved himself wisely" (18:5). He was so wise that his archenemy, King Saul, was terrified of him—although David would never have hurt so much as a hair on King Saul's head. Then when David was older, successful, and well established, his heart ceased for one moment to be wise and he tampered with another man's wife. The devil had David entangled.

The Romans used to delight in putting a fully armored and armed gladiator in the arena with a man who was all but naked and armed only with a net and a trident. That man, it seems, would have had no chance when pitted against the seasoned gladiator. But the betting was usually against the gladiator. The man with the net had one goal: to entangle the gladiator in the net and pin him to the ground with the three-pronged spear.

That is how the devil finally entangled David. He caught him with Bath-sheba and pinned him to the ground with the triple spear of adultery, hypocrisy, and murder. Before long David wept in repentance and wrote those tear-drenched Psalms that have meant so much to God's people ever since. David's son knew about those tears.

Solomon, seeing what was happening to his own son, also knew about *his own fears.* Although he too was famous for his wisdom, he also made one mistake. In his early days Solomon, as well as David, was a man after God's own heart. God's name for Solomon was *Jedidiah,* which means "beloved of the Lord." His wisdom was so remarkable that "all the earth sought to Solomon, to hear his wisdom, which God had put in his heart" (1 Kings 10:24). Then in one area of life his heart ceased to be wise. He became involved with a multitude of foreign women.

And now Solomon had fears: fears for the kingdom, soon to be rent asunder; and fears for his son Rehoboam, who had no sense. We can almost hear the king's despair in his last-ditch appeal: "My son, if thine heart be wise, my heart shall rejoice, even mine."

How different was Jacob's experience with Joseph, the son of his love! From the beginning Joseph was wise of heart and eager to know about God. He had early been given "the heavenly vision."

We cannot imagine the despair that flooded Jacob's soul when he heard that Joseph was dead and when he saw the blood-stained coat-of-many-colors. Later, forgetful of Joseph's dreams, Jacob concluded that Joseph had indeed died, but not as the prey of a wild beast; he was convinced that Joseph had been murdered by his brothers (Genesis 42:36). Imagine then the delight that flooded Jacob's heart when he learned that Joseph was alive and God had fulfilled the boy's dreams. Jacob's beloved son was now lord of all the land of Egypt!

"My son...my reins shall rejoice, when thy lips speak right things"—how Jacob must have drunk in the reports of the "right things" Joseph told the pharaoh! "My heart shall rejoice"—how Jacob's old heart must have rejoiced! His delight in Joseph was evident when Jacob was dying and his sons gathered around him. He had many good words for Judah and encouraging words for nearly all of his sons, but when he spoke to Joseph, blessing after blessing poured from the patriarch's lips (Genesis 49:22-26).

His own heavenly vision over, Jacob closed his eyes in death. He crossed over that other Jordan and went to seek his dear Rachel, Joseph's mother, in that "city which hath foundations" (Hebrews 11:10). We can picture them meeting somewhere on the glory side of the river. Jacob has thrown away his staff—he limps no more. He is a pilgrim no longer. He is home with Abraham, Isaac, and Rachel. And what a story he has to tell her about Joseph, whose wise heart made his own heart rejoice!

A wise son not only rejoices his father; *a wise son redeems his future.* Wrote Solomon: "Let not thine heart envy sinners: but be thou in the fear of the Lord all the day long. For surely there is an end; and thine expectation shall not be cut off" (Proverbs 23:17-18).

Because Paul lived in the fear of the Lord, Nero could not intimidate him. What a scene it must have been when Nero (the archetype of the antichrist) eyed Paul (the archetype of an apostle of the Lamb). Paul's notebook provides a sketchy reference to the confrontation:

> Alexander the coppersmith did me much evil.... At my first answer no man stood with me, but all men forsook me: I pray God that it may not be laid to their charge. Notwithstanding the Lord stood with me, and strengthened me...and I was delivered out of the mouth of the lion (2 Timothy 4:14-17).

When Paul first appealed to Rome, Nero was already the caesar. Because Festus was unjust and self-seeking, Paul said, *"Ad Caesarem provoco"* (Acts 25:11). With these words Paul gave Festus a very big headache. How was Festus ever going to explain why this Roman citizen felt it necessary to refer his cause to the emperor?

At the time of Paul's appeal Nero was not the monster he later became. Indeed the first five years of his reign (A.D. 54-59) were promising. His administration was influenced by the Stoic philosopher Seneca, who was Nero's tutor, and by Afranius Burrus, the honest prefect of the praetorian guard. Even in A.D. 59 there was little to herald the coming holocaust of A.D. 64.

Nero was only seventeen when he became emperor. The dark streak in his personality began to show itself very cautiously at first. Coming under the influence of Salvius Otho, Tigellinus, and Pretonius Arbiter, Nero began to plunge into the sinful pleasures offered by the pagan world. In fact he and these close friends would disguise themselves, roam the streets at night, and molest women who took their fancy.

Nero committed his first major crime when he murdered his mother, Agrippina, in A.D. 59. Agrippina had smoothed his way to the throne by killing off his rivals, but she made one big mistake: she tried to control him after he ascended the throne. Then Nero murdered his wife Octavia so that he could steal and marry the Jewess Poppaea Sabina, who was the wife of his friend Otho.

Nero fancied himself to be a great actor, singer, painter, and charioteer. Of course he always won the prize in any competition he entered. The judges had more respect for their necks than to risk offending him. Soon he began to imagine he was God.

In A.D. 64 in the poorer section of Rome a fire broke out and burned fiercely for a week. Many suspected that Nero started the fire to make room for the redevelopment of the city. He wanted to rebuild it in the Greek style and construct a prodigious palace to house his deity. Whether or not he actually started the fire, he is said to have picked up his harp and sung while the city burned. He blamed the Christians for the fire and launched a terrible persecution of them.

When this depraved Roman emperor and the great apostle to the Gentiles finally stood face to face, madness shone out of Nero's eyes, while goodness and holiness shone out of Paul's. The apostle saw nothing to envy in this lost sinner, in spite of his robes and power. Nor did Paul fear him, for the apostle was "in the fear of the Lord all the day long."

We cannot help wondering what Heaven's royal ambassador said to this disgusting young man who so thoroughly disgraced the throne of the world. Did Paul preach to Nero as he had preached to Felix until that Roman trembled? We can be sure the apostle did not waste this golden opportunity to preach Christ.

Paul was condemned to death and when he was duly beheaded in Rome, he went to be with Christ in a far better world. Nero, on the other hand, continued in his wickedness. He kicked his second wife to death and inaugurated a reign of terror. Finally the legions in Gaul, Spain, and Africa revolted against him. Then the praetorian guard sided with the rebels. Thirty-one-year-old Nero was sentenced to death by flogging. When the doomed man was pursued, he took refuge in the dingy basement of a slave's house and cut his own throat.

Would it be better to be a man like Nero or a man like Paul? Surely we would rather be like the man whose heart held no envy for sinners, the man who lived in the fear of the Lord.

Paul had great expectations and he has entered into them now (2 Timothy 4:6-8), "for surely there is an end," wrote Solomon, "and thine expectation shall not be cut off."

The best illustration of a man with great expectations is Abraham. He was a poor lost pagan in Ur when God found him and revealed Himself to him. God said:

> Get thee out of thy country, and from thy kindred, and from thy father's house, unto a land that I will shew thee: And I will make of thee a great nation, and I will bless thee, and make thy name great; and thou shalt be a blessing: And I will bless them that bless thee, and curse him that curseth thee: and in thee shall all families of the earth be blessed (Genesis 12:1-3).

Great expectations indeed!

In due time Abraham arrived in Canaan and once again "the Lord appeared unto Abram, and said, Unto thy seed will I give this land" (Genesis 12:7). Abraham thought that surely now his expectations would be fulfilled. But no! He discovered the unexpected: "There was a famine in the land" (12:10); and "The Canaanite and the Perizzite dwelled then in the land" (13:7). His shock was so great that he moved out of the will of God and detoured into Egypt. The results were disastrous.

When he returned to the promised land, more trouble soon erupted—this time with Lot. Abraham decided to partition the land to put an end to further strife, but he must have wondered how this would affect the fulfillment of his great expectations. In order to strengthen Abraham's faith, God reiterated His promise: "The Lord said unto Abram...Lift up now thine eyes, and look from the place where thou art northward, and southward, and eastward, and westward: For all the land which thou seest, to thee will I give it, and to thy seed for ever" (Genesis 13:14-15).

Not long afterward a coalition of eastern kings invaded the country and Abraham learned how vulnerable, humanly speaking, his tenure was. Still he came through that ordeal and God came to renew the covenant once more.

However, Abraham was depressed because he had no son to be his heir. God reassured him on that point and defined the promised land as stretching from the Nile to the Euphrates, but informed him of another delay in its acquisition: "Know of a surety that thy seed shall be a stranger in a land that is not theirs, and shall serve them; and they shall afflict them four hundred years.... And thou shalt go to thy fathers in peace; and thou shalt be buried in a good old age" (Genesis 15:13-15).

What could Abraham expect? A sentence of death for himself and centuries of suffering for his descendants! How could he cope with this seemingly endless delay? Well, he understood from the start that his real inheritance was not down here. The temporal promises would eventually be fulfilled, but his real inheritance was over there. As we read in Hebrews 11:8-10,

> By faith Abraham, when he was called to go out into a place which he should after receive for an inheritance, obeyed; and he went out, not knowing whither he went. By faith he sojourned in the land of promise, as in a strange country, dwelling in tabernacles with Isaac and Jacob, the heirs with him of the same promise: For he looked for a city which hath foundations, whose builder and maker is God.

Finally Abraham bought the first and only piece of property he ever owned in Canaan: a burying place (Genesis 23). "Surely there is an end," wrote Solomon, "and thine expectation shall not be cut off."

As the children of God, we too have great expectations. There may seem to be no end to the delays and disappointments that come our way; becoming a Christian does not exempt us from disease, disaster, and death. But God promises that "thine expectation shall not be cut off."

### (b) A Father's Caution (23:19-21)

#### i. Be Guided by Your Father (23:19)

"Hear thou, my son, and be wise, and guide thine heart in the way." We cannot help noticing the phrase "my son." Solomon repeated the words again and again (Proverbs 23:15,19,26). His sad lament over Rehoboam echoed David's desolate cry over Absalom.

When David heard the news of the death of his beloved Absalom, a great wail of anguish burst from his broken heart: "O my son Absalom, my son, my son Absalom! would God I had died for thee, O Absalom, my son, my son!" (2 Samuel 18:33) Viewing the torn body of his handsome son and attending the funeral must have been difficult indeed, but worst of all, David was haunted by the knowledge that he was reaping what he had sown. He had sown adultery and murder and now he was reaping the consequences.

Likewise Solomon knew that he too was reaping what he had sown, for Rehoboam's mother was a pagan. Solomon should not have been surprised at his son's penchant for folly since his own behavior was scandalous. From childhood the watchful eyes and open ears of Rehoboam had been exposed to his father's example. Rehoboam had heard Solomon say one thing and had seen him practice something else. Solomon could say, "Hear thou, my son," ten thousand times, but Rehoboam could reply, "I hear you, my father, but what I hear is canceled out by what I see."

Such excuse-making, however, would be discounted in Heaven, for Solomon's bad example did not negate Rehoboam's personal responsibility. Truth is still truth, no matter how inconsistent the messenger may be. God often has to use imperfect instruments to convey divine truth—but there is nothing inconsistent about the truth itself.

"The way" was still the way even though Solomon wandered off it at times. The way was clearly marked in the writings of Moses, Joshua, Samuel, and David. Rehoboam had been instructed in the way, but nobody could choose it for him. When the time of personal accountability and responsibility came, Rehoboam had to decide for himself whether to walk in the way. Solomon, in spite of his faults, gave his son the facts of the faith. It was up to Rehoboam to place faith in the facts and establish a personal relationship with the living God.

I was raised in a Christian home where both parents were earnest believers. In fact, my father was a gifted preacher. From the time I was a babe in arms I was taken to church and I grew up under the teaching of godly men. I was saved when I was ten, baptized when I was twelve, and became a backslider when I was thirteen. My teenage years were a spiritual blank. Then the Lord brought Stephen Olford to my hometown; an anointed servant of the Lord, he impacted my life for the long term. But I still compromised and procrastinated.

Then one day I received a letter. It appeared to be from the king because there was no postage on the envelope and across the top were the words "On His Majesty's Service." I tore the letter open—and found I was mistaken. It was a form letter that said, "Join the army—or else!" I joined. His majesty's government provided me with a train ticket from my home in South Wales to Bradford in the north of England and gave me a date to report for induction into the military.

I can still remember sitting in a corner of the coach on a cold winter's night in February as the train sped on its way. The Lord spoke to me that night. He said, "If your brand of Christianity is not exchanged for My brand of Christianity, you're not going to make it when you get in that barracks with all those godless men." Then and there I made the life-commitment for which the Lord had been waiting so long. That was the night when the Lord said to me, "Hear thou, my son, and be wise, and guide thine heart in the way." Over the years there have been many a stumble and many a fall, but ever since that night I have sought—sometimes with joy, sometimes with tears—to walk in the way.

### ii. Be Guarded in Your Friendships (23:20-21)

Solomon warned his son to *beware of wild parties,* for they have no place in the life of one who must rule over others: "Be not among winebibbers; among riotous eaters of flesh" (Proverbs 23:20). Solomon also warned his son to *beware of waiting poverty:* "The drunkard and the glutton shall come to poverty: and drowsiness shall clothe a man with rags" (23:21).

Drunkenness, gluttony, and laziness are a sure recipe for ruin. They often form a terrible trio, joining forces to bring down even the best, strongest, and cleverest of men. A walk through the slums of any city will attest to the truth of this proverb.

Harold Begbie, who investigated some of the miracles of regeneration wrought in the London slums in the early days of The Salvation Army, recorded the story of Old Born Drunk. In the book *Twice-born Men* Begbie described what happened when another of the Army's converts, a man simply known as the Puncher in deference to his power in the ring, told the local Salvation Army adjutant about Old Born Drunk:

> One day she [the adjutant] was talking to the Puncher in the carriage factory, when he said to her: "I wish you'd have a talk with the man who comes round here with the papers; he's proper low; they call him Old Born Drunk; and he looks it. But I was almost like that myself, not so very long ago. No one can be hopeless, after me. I wish you'd speak to him." Thus early in his conversion did the Puncher...manifest what one calls his "passion for souls."
>
> The little adjutant waited one day to see this man who had the newspaper round, and who visited the carriage factory to serve the workmen with betting news.
>
> She had seen many of the lowest and most depraved people in London, but until she saw Old Born Drunk never had she realized the hideousness and repulsive abomination to which vice can degrade the human body.
>
> This man, the child of frightfully drunken parents, had been born in drink, and was almost certainly, as his name declared, actually born drunk. He had been taught to drink and had acquired an insatiable appetite for drink in earliest childhood. He was now, at the age of five- or six-and-forty, habitually drunk—sodden.
>
> The vileness of his clothing and the unhealthy appearance of his flesh did not strike the adjutant till afterwards. Her whole attention was held in a kind of horror by the aspect of the man's eyes. They were terrible with soullessness. She racks her brain in vain to find words to describe them. She returns again and again to the word *stupefied.* That is the word that least fails to misrepresent what no language can describe. Stupefied! Not weakness, not feebleness; not cunning, not depravity; but stupor. They were the eyes of a man neither living nor dead; they were the eyes of nothing that had ever lived or could ever die—the eyes of eternal stillborn stupor....
>
> For the rest he was a true Miserable, lower than anything to be found among barbarous nations, debased almost out of humanity. He was short, thick-set, misshapen, vile; clothed in rags which suffocated those who blundered near to him—a creature whom ragged children mocked with scorn as he passed down the street.
>
> Civilization had produced this man. He had his place in

London; repulsive as one may find it to contemplate him, he was one of our contemporaries; to the Salvationist he represented a soul.

She said to him, "You don't look very happy. Are you?" He looked, in his dazed fashion, into her clear eyes and kept silence, as though he had lost both the power of speech and the ability to understand it. She said, "Perhaps I could be of some service to you; will you let me try? Will you let me come and see you in your home?"

Old Born Drunk could not speak. She approached quite close to him, bent her kind eyes towards those terrible eyes of stupor, and said, "I want to help you. I know something about your life. They call you Old Born Drunk. Well, Old Born Drunk, let me come and pay you a visit, and make friends with you. There may be many little ways in which I can help you. Let me try."

She made him at last understand. He told her where he lived. Soon afterwards she called upon him.

He occupied a single room, for which he paid seven shillings a week, in a street more notorious for abject destitution than for crime and degradation. She was not in the least afraid of visiting this place, but when she opened the door of the room—good and angelic as she is—the little adjutant almost turned and ran away. Such a smell issued from the den as stifled the lungs and made the spirit heave and shudder with disgust....

In the den of Old Born Drunk there [was] the smell of animals, for the place was like a menagerie.

A dog lifted itself up on the vile coverlet of an unmade bed, and growled at the intruder. A litter of guinea-pigs scuttered across the bare and filthy boards of the floor, disappearing under the bed. Rabbit-hutches, with the dusky shapes of their inmates dimly seen behind wire netting, emitted a thick and stifling smell. There were cats on a sack by the hearth. Hanging from the ceiling in front of the closed window was a cage of doves.

This London interior was dark as well as stifling. A fog seemed to pervade it from dirty wall to dirty wall, from dark ceiling to reeking floor. A figure moved out of this fog, while the dog growled on the unmade bed; it became gradually something that suggested a woman—a creature thin, emaciated, woebegone, clothed almost entirely in sacking. She stood before the Salvationist, in all her wretchedness and

> squalor; a thing really lower than the animals among whom she spent her life; a woman—the woman who loved Old Born Drunk....
>
> ...The adjutant's kindness and humanity did so far appeal to these two Londoners as to induce them to attend some of the services at the local hall. They left their menagerie, and in their poor vile rags came to the evening meetings, and sat with the Miserables at the back of the hall, listening to the band, listening to the hymns, listening to the praying and preaching, feeling the warmth, brightness, and cleanness of the atmosphere—thinking something in their minds of which we have no knowledge.
>
> Both of them appeared stupefied on these occasions. Apparently the service had no meaning for them. In just such a similar manner two owls in a belfry might listen to church music. They came, they sat, they disappeared.
>
> The adjutant began to feel that they had fallen below the depths to which human sympathy can reach. Her officers used to say, in despair, "They don't seem to understand a word that is said to them."

But one day at the end of a service something happened. Begbie continued:

> Several people rose from their seats...and advanced to the penitent form....Some of them said, "God be merciful to me a sinner!" others bowed and were silent; many of the women were crying.
>
> At the back of these penitents came Old Born Drunk and his wife.
>
> The adjutant and her officers were more astonished than all the rest of the people in the meeting. They knew, what the others did not realize, the impenetrable stupefaction of the man's mind, his total obfuscation of soul. For the others, he was only a particularly dirty, particularly vile, particularly drunken one-of-themselves.
>
> The adjutant approached the poor old man as he reached the bench. The small dulled eyes were wet with tears. She put a hand on his arm, and he said to her, in a crying tone, "Oh, I want to be like Joe!"—one of the men who had testified [a man known as the Criminal].
>
> Afterwards he said to her, "While I was listening to Joe, thinking of what he's been, and seeing what he's become, all

> of a sudden it took me that I'd find God and get Him to make me like Joe. It took me like that. I just felt, all of a sudden, *determined* to find God. *Determined!*" he repeated, with energy astonishing in this broken and hopeless creature of alcoholism. "And," he went on, "while I was kneeling, while I was praying, I felt the Spirit of God come upon me. I said, 'Oh, God, make me like Joe!' and while I prayed, I felt the Spirit come upon me. I *knew* I could become like Joe. I know I'm saved."[3]

And so he was. The rest of his story gives evidence of a miracle of grace. But not all such stories have happy endings. Hence the Holy Spirit warns, "The drunkard...shall come to poverty."

(c) A Father's Counsel (23:22-23)

In Proverbs 23:22 Solomon spoke to his son about *his mother:* "Hearken unto thy father that begat thee, and despise not thy mother when she is old."

Solomon lived in a different day and age. His generation was slower-paced, more pastoral, more family-oriented, and kinder than ours. It was a generation that had not been subverted by Darwin, Huxley, Freud, Dewey, Marx, Lenin, the Beatles, the hippies, the yuppies, and television. It was a generation that thought in terms of family relationships and family responsibilities. Children grew up in a world where dad and mom were backed and supported by a whole clan of grandparents, uncles, aunts, cousins, nephews, nieces, brothers, sisters, and other relatives once or twice removed. It was the age of the family. An achievement by one member brought credit to the whole family. A disgraceful act committed by one member brought shame on the whole family. Family members looked out for each other. There was no social welfare. Nursing homes were unknown.

Even a generation ago family responsibilities were taken more seriously. When my wife Jean was a little girl, her mother contracted tuberculosis—a diagnosis that was a long, lingering death sentence. Since her disease was communicable, she was isolated and Jean and her sister were sent to live with an aunt in Vancouver. That aunt had a large family of her own, but she made room for two more. Later Jean went to live with another aunt, a poor widow who lived down the street. Then the depression came and many people found themselves out of work. The one person in Jean's extended family who had a steady job was the aunt with whom she lived. It wasn't much of a job—it involved hard, depressing toil—but at least it was a job. When she was paid her small wage each Friday, she set aside what was needed for rent and life's barest necessities, and with the rest she bought groceries for relatives who had no income at all.

Now we tell our dependents to go on welfare, but Solomon said, "Hearken unto thy father that begat thee, and despise not thy mother when she is old." That is God's idea. When parents grow old, families should pool their resources and take care of their mothers and fathers.

Jesus grew up in a human home where he learned obedience and experienced the joys and sorrows of family life. His family included His mother; Mary's husband Joseph, who stood in the stead of a human father; Jesus' brothers James, Joses, Simon, and Judas (Matthew 13:55); Jesus' sisters (13:56); uncles; aunts; and cousins. Jesus became attached to these people with familial ties, although all such ties were severed by His resurrection, in the interests of a larger family (Matthew 12:46-50).

It is generally thought that Joseph died when Jesus was still young and that the Lord took over the carpenter's shop and shouldered responsibility for the family. His sense of family remained strong even in the hour of death. Seeing His mother and her sister at the cross, the Lord Jesus made one last provision for His family. He gave His mother into the keeping of John, who from that moment took Mary to his own home and treated her as his own mother (John 19:25-27). Thus Jesus set before us the supreme example of family love and care for an aging mother.

In Proverbs 23:23 Solomon spoke to his son about *his mind:* "Buy the truth, and sell it not; also wisdom, and instruction, and understanding."

In the case of Rehoboam we see an illustration of the law of the third generation. David represents the first generation, Solomon the second generation, and Rehoboam the third generation. The third generation always stands in peril. It always needs a Holy Ghost revival.

In the first generation, the truth is discovered. People are willing to die as martyrs for that truth. In its defense, no price is too high to pay. People are willing to fight fiercely for newly discovered truth and they hold onto it tenaciously.

In the second generation, passion for the truth moderates. What was a conviction in the first generation becomes a belief in the second generation. The cutting edge is blunted. People know some of the pioneers who fought for the truth, but are not as fanatical as their forebears. People will profess belief in principles they have inherited and will defend them in debate, but in the second generation there is more tolerance of other views.

In the third generation there is more deterioration. What was a conviction in the first generation, then a belief in the second generation, becomes an opinion in the third generation. Some truth is held casually, but much is up for sale and can be comfortably bartered away.

Think of the great amount of truth David discovered. In his fugitive years, for example, he learned the truth of *sovereignty:* he was the Lord's anointed, God's chosen king, the one from whom the true Sovereign would descend. That truth almost cost him his life; King Saul tried to murder him on two dozen occasions because of it.

David learned the truth about *sin.* As a result of his dark dealings with Bath-sheba and Uriah, he learned what a foul, fearful monster it is. He paid a high price for that lesson!

David learned the truth about *sorrow.* Indeed his tears drench many a page of Holy Writ.

He learned the truth about *salvation.* Not even Paul in his Epistles surpassed David in his Psalms in communicating salvation truth.

David learned the truth about *sanctification.* He prayed that God would not remove His Holy Spirit from him. David, who had seen Saul after the Holy Spirit left him, did not want to be tormented the way Saul was.

David learned the truth about *security* when he went alone to meet Goliath in Elah's vale, and in many flights and forced marches thereafter. Early in life David included the phrase "for thou art with me" in his magnificent twenty-third Psalm.

He learned the truth about *service* as a shepherd in the country and as chief musician in the court. As an outlaw in the cave he was God's servant and learned submission to God. No wonder he became a great king. He learned how to submit to authority. A man who has not learned how to submit to authority is not fit to exercise authority.

While David was a *buyer* in truth's market, Solomon was a *broker.* He knew, for instance, what the Bible said about multiplying wives, and indeed he had a copy of the law in his own handwriting, but he compromised (Deuteronomy 17:14-20). As for Rehoboam, he was a *beggar.* What cared he for truth? He would sell his own soul. When the pharaoh invaded his kingdom, despoiled the temple, and took away the gold shields Solomon had made, what did Rehoboam do?

He replaced them with shields of brass (2 Chronicles 12:1-12). Since brass and gold look much alike, he reasoned, what difference did it make? "Buy the truth, and sell it not," wrote Solomon. Rehoboam did not apply that proverb to his life, nor perhaps do many of us.

(d) A Father's Comfort (23:24-25)

A father finds comfort *in a righteous son:* "The father of the righteous shall greatly rejoice: and he that begetteth a wise child shall have joy of him" (Proverbs 23:24). Parents also find comfort *in a responsible son:* "Thy father and thy mother shall be glad, and she that bare thee shall rejoice" (23:25). Some think that these two verses contain one of the many wise sayings of David that Solomon copied into his notebook and from thence, in due course, into his collection of proverbs. Thus the saying became part of the Bible. It seems that David was speaking first of all *about* Solomon, the much loved son of Bath-sheba, and then *to* Solomon. David saw in Solomon all the qualities he never saw in Amnon, Absalom, and Adonijah.

We can well believe that David grieved over Absalom's folly before he grieved over Absalom's fall. Looking at his tall, dark, and handsome son, David wished with all his heart that he could quicken in Absalom some spark of interest in spiritual things. We can be sure David wanted to make Absalom his heir, but this son was too vain and vengeful. He was too quick to take the law into his own hands, too blind to mitigating circumstances, too easily influenced by the wrong kinds of people, and too hypocritical. These weaknesses became obvious toward the end of Absalom's life, but David was too wise not to detect the hairline cracks in Absalom's character much earlier. David noticed too that although Absalom occasionally paid lip service to religious duties, he was not above using religious forms to further his selfish ends.

When David looked at Amnon, he realized that this son's lusts would surely get him into trouble. And when David looked at Adonijah, he recognized a scheming nonentity. But in Solomon, David saw all the promise of a young man "after God's own heart." As Alexander Whyte so ably put it, "If ever it was said over any child's birth, Where sin abounded, grace did much more abound, it was surely over the birth…of Solomon.[4]

From the day that God named him "Beloved," Solomon felt the pull and tug of Heaven. We can imagine that the composer himself taught young Solomon the words and music of David's Psalms and explained when, where, and why each song was written. As soon as Solomon learned to read and write legibly, his Bible teacher—Nathan the prophet—would have assigned him the task of making his own copy of the Mosaic Law as commanded in Deuteronomy 17:18-19. We can imagine that Solomon went beyond the minimum requirement and also copied Joshua, Judges, Ruth, and Samuel as well as Nathan's notes and commentaries.

Doubtless Solomon was eager to have his father's insights on the sacrifices and offerings. And the young prince would have asked the high priest about the mysteries of the feasts and fasts and his annual visit to the holy of holies. Perhaps Solomon even dreamed of knowing God. "Solomon loved the Lord" and after David's death he had his dream of dreams (1 Kings 3:3,5).

Solomon would have spent long hours with David as they pored over plans for the temple. Probably the youth asked such intelligent questions and was so careful to write down the answers that David's eyes would brim with tears and he would say, "The father of the righteous shall greatly rejoice: and he that begetteth a wise child shall have joy of him."

Solomon's mother also gave him guidance. In spite of her fall, Bath-sheba was a thoroughly humbled and repentant woman, wife, and mother. We can imagine that she had long talks with Solomon about what had happened—from her point of view. No doubt she told him how a sword had pierced her soul and how Solomon's birth was such a token of God's goodness and grace. Pointing out the good and the right way, she would say, "Thy father and thy mother shall be glad, and she that bare thee shall rejoice."

### (2) Comments about Women (23:26-28)

#### (a) The Appeal to the Heart (23:26)

"My son, give me thine heart, and let thine eyes observe my ways" (Proverbs 23:26). We can hear David and Bath-sheba speaking to Solomon in 23:25, but in 23:26 we hear God speaking to him.

God knew what Solomon did not know. God knew his heart. Solomon knew his own mind, but he did not know the weak spot in his heart. So God warned Solomon against having a disloyal heart. These warnings were given in dreams.

Solomon had his first dream right after his marriage to the daughter of the pharaoh (1 Kings 3:1-5). Solomon had his second dream after he had spent seven years building the house of God and thirteen years building his own house and harem (1 Kings 7:1-2; 9:1-10). So Solomon was well-warned, but his eyes affected his heart. Eventually the glorious statement of 1 Kings 3:3, "Solomon loved the Lord," was canceled by the incriminating statement of 1 Kings 11:1, "Solomon loved many strange women."

God demands, "Give me thine heart." God made a number of demands on Abraham, the first and last demands being the most interesting. First God told Abraham to give up his father: "Get thee out of thy country, and from thy kindred, and from thy father's house, unto a land that I will shew thee" (Genesis 12:1). God was saying, "Give me thine heart. I want you to love me more than you love your father."

Abraham's father Terah was a direct descendant of Noah's son Shem, to whom was entrusted the torch of testimony and the progenitorship of the awaited Son of God. Terah however was totally ignorant of God and brought up Abraham to be a pagan. We can think of a thousand ways that Terah could have hindered Abraham from taking his first great step of faith and obedience. But instead of reacting negatively and rebuking Abraham, Terah said in effect, "Let us set out at once."

In Abraham's case a consenting father was more of a problem than a contradicting father. The name *Terah* means "delay" and delay there was. With Terah as a dead weight, Abraham only traveled as far as Haran, where he evidently stayed for a considerable time. Indeed he made no further progress toward Canaan until Terah died. (See Genesis 11:31-32; 12:5.) Even then Abraham did not obey God completely, for he took Lot and Lot's family with him. We know what a constant heartache and hindrance Lot was to Abraham.

God's last demand was that Abraham give up his son: "Take now thy son, thine only son Isaac, whom thou lovest, and get thee into the land of Moriah; and offer him there for a burnt offering upon one of the mountains which I will tell thee of" (Genesis 22:2). This time Abraham was ready. His faith had grown. He fully believed that if he carried out the terrible demand and plunged the knife into Isaac's heart, God would raise Isaac from the dead (Hebrews 11:17-19). Of course God had no intention of allowing Isaac to be harmed. His demand was only a test. As Abraham lifted up the knife, God intervened saying: "Lay not thine hand upon the lad, neither do thou anything unto him: for now I know that thou fearest God, seeing thou hast not withheld thy son, thine only son from me" (Genesis 22:12).

"Let thine eyes observe my ways" is God's postscript to Solomon's proverb. When Abraham "lifted up his eyes, and looked," he saw that God had provided a ram for the burnt offering (Genesis 22:8,13). Abraham also realized that God would provide a Lamb: "In the mount of the Lord it shall be seen," he said (22:14). Abraham's surrendered heart affected his seeing eye. By faith the patriarch saw Golgotha. "Abraham rejoiced to see my day," Jesus said (John 8:56). As Abraham, a human father, had taken his only begotten son to mount Moriah, so the Heavenly Father would take His only begotten Son to mount Calvary.

(b) The Appeal of the Harlot (23:27-28)

Solomon warned *how dangerous she is:* "A whore is a deep ditch; and a strange woman is a narrow pit" (Proverbs 23:27). He also warned *how destructive she is:* "She also lieth in wait as for a prey, and increaseth the transgressors among men" (23:28).

In addition to all the other perils they have always put in the path of their patrons, harlots now offer AIDS. For centuries they have passed along syphilis, gonorrhea, and herpes to their customers, who in turn have passed their infections on to their sweethearts, wives, and paramours. These foul diseases have wiped out whole nations.

The effect of venereal disease is illustrated in *Mutiny on the Bounty*. Authors Nordhoff and Hall tell how Roger Byam revisited the former paradise of Tahiti. As a midshipman he had known it as a lush and friendly island. Then he had been wrongfully arrested, accused of mutiny, and dragged away from his idyllic isle to face a military court. Byam had left behind him a beautiful native wife, but for twenty long years there had been no way to return. Now, twenty years later, as commander of a smart frigate, he was under orders to visit New South Wales, Valparaiso, and Tahiti.

Once during those twenty years he had talked to missionaries who had spent twelve years on Tahiti without making a single convert. They had told him a dismal tale of war and disease plaguing the island and decimating the population.

As the frigate approached Tahiti, Byam could see that the island still "wore the green and smiling aspect" he had cherished in his memory for so many years. He guided the ship through the narrow passage into the bay and dropped anchor, but no canoes put forth to greet the crew. In the old days they would have been besieged by natives swarming aboard. All Byam could see was a few apathetic people on the beach who stared listlessly at the frigate. Finally a small dilapidated canoe embarked, but it was manned by a couple of natives who were little more than beggars with nothing to barter.

Byam had his crew land him ashore alone at sunset. He turned his steps toward the interior. Gone were the merry throngs he had known. Gone was the house of his closest native friend. The gardens were filled with weeds and the path to the temple was overgrown. An old woman told him, "Once Tahiti was a land of men; now only shadows fill the land."

Tahiti was indeed a land of ghosts. Those whom war had spared, pestilence had ravished. Sailors from European ships had brought terrible venereal diseases ashore. These diseases had wrought havoc on the natives, and four-fifths of the Tahitians had been destroyed.

Byam returned to his ship with a broken heart. Everyone he had known was dead. "Suddenly," he said, "the place was full of ghosts,—shadows of men alive and dead,—my own among them."[5]

Pestilence is one of God's many weapons (Deuteronomy 28:35; Ezekiel 14:21; Matthew 24:7). With the AIDS scourge, the latest shell from His arsenal, God has fired a warning shot across the bows of our godless society. Perhaps modern science will find a cure for AIDS, but God has plenty more weapons in reserve. If we do not put the ship of state on a more sensible course, we can expect new judgments from God. To avoid shipwreck we need to make and enforce laws against sodomy, pornography, and prostitution—laws that stipulate severe and mandatory penalties for violations. Some states do have such laws on the books, but where is the determination to implement them? It seems that many of our present politicians do not have enough courage and conviction to pass and/or enforce the laws we need. Political expediency often rules our legislators and other government officials.

(3) Comments about Wine (23:29-35)

(a) Look at the Drunkard (23:29-32)

These verses present an unlovely picture—a full-length portrait of the drunkard. The peril of a nation is great when drunkards are at its helm. Ignoring God's Word, our politicians siphon off a considerable amount of taxpayer money to buy alcoholic beverages to liven their parties and state occasions.

By portraying the drunkard, Solomon was reminding us that *strong drink stupefies*. Half a dozen questions make us think and help us see the drunkard for who he is: "Who hath woe? who hath sorrow? who hath contentions? who hath babbling? who hath wounds without cause? who hath redness of eyes?" (Proverbs 23:29) The answer follows swiftly: "They that tarry long at the wine; they that go to seek mixed wine" (23:30).

A drunkard will sell his baby's shoes and steal from his little girl's piggy bank to obtain drink. "The Plumber" was such a man. His biographical sketch appears in Harold Begbie's *Twice Born Men.* Begbie gives us a picture of the Plumber before his conversion:

> Money easily earned, he quotes with emphatic conviction, is money easily spent, which means beer. He earned pounds every week, and sometimes on Saturday afternoon he was pawning his tools for the evening's finish-up.
>
> "Ah," he says, "to give you an idea of the jolly friends a man gets in that way; not once, but many times, my pals have said to me, 'Put your tools up the spout, old boy, we'll see you through, we'll get 'em out for you,' and after having drunk the money away, when I came to ask them for help, 'Get 'em out yourself,' they'd answer; 'you put 'em up, you get 'em down.' Later on, when I was starving—yes, starving!—those men wouldn't give me a crust, not one of them."
>
> He got married before he was twenty, and he vowed soon afterwards that if his baby was a boy he'd get really drunk to celebrate the event. But he was impatient, and couldn't wait. He began three months before the child was born, and for seven years after he was always profoundly drunk. He lost job after job. In two houses they found him flat on his back in the cellar with the taps of the wine-casks spurting over his face. Ferocity began to manifest itself in his temper. He was strong, and handy with his fists. He fought many a fight with the naked fists. He picked up a foreman who corrected him one day, and threw him through a glass window. He was always in trouble. His private business vanished altogether. He had to go about looking for work.
>
> Then this man, bred from infancy to drink and to steal, uninstructed in the first letters of morality, educated only in sharpness, cunning, and clever dishonesty, but who had preserved all through this base and scurvy career the natural good-humour and cheerfulness of his temperament, became one of those wretches who play the tyrant in the house that they have ruined. The Plumber took to flogging his starved children—one of them, a little girl, said to him in my presence, looking up into his face with a cunning smile, "We've often felt

the buckle-end of your belt, haven't we, daddy?"—took to flogging, kicking, and striking these poor starved children, so that at the first sound of his footsteps on the stair they would run for cover under the bedstead. His wife withstood him. He fought her. He proved himself her master. He went out from the room where she lay, beaten and half stunned, a proud man. But his wife was not cowed. She nagged him. He never came home but she reproached him for his brutality, his drunkenness, his abhorrent cruelty. One day in a fit of ungovernable rage, he seized her, flung her down the flight of stairs, raced down after her, and aimed a blow at her head, which split the top of the banister and scarred his wrist for life. He all but murdered her.

And for drink, everything he could lay his hands on was sold. The furniture went from his home, his tools, the clothes of the children—everything.

He got to the lowest depth but one to which drink can bring a man. He reached that horrible stage where his wife stands with her children at the door of the public-house waiting for the husband to come out. He spent money on beer while the children of his body starved and shivered and cried at the door. He never experienced one pang of remorse. Never once did his conscience upbraid him. He got beer by hook or by "crook"; there for him the universe ended.

One day the news reached him that his oldest mate, the closest companion of all his early depravity, had joined the local corps of the Salvation Army. It made no difference to the Plumber. Drunk at his work, he went straight to the public-house, delivered there on occasion, for the diversion of the company, mock sermons or sang comic songs, and only went out at closing-time, followed home through the rain and the darkness and the cold by his wife with a baby at her breast.

He was in one of his favourite public-houses when his wife opened the door one day, entered, and said to him, "Come out, or give me money for the children's food."

He took no notice. She waited, looking at him—watched by the publican and the potman—and then retired to the door. The Plumber's mates began to say, "I wouldn't have the old woman follow *me* about." He lifted his face from his beer, turned his head, and shouted to the woman at the door to get out, like a dog.

She said that she should wait there till he left.

"Will you?" he cried, with an oath, laying down his pot. And

> in a clumsy stride or two he had delivered a running kick with his hobnail boot at the mother of his children. She moved away, and escaped a fatal injury.
>
> He followed her to the door. "God!" he cried, "if you don't leave me alone, I'll———" He had exhausted blasphemy and menace. He paused for a moment, and concluded, "I'll sign the pledge."
>
> "Oh, you've often done that," she retorted, "and wetted it every time!"

"Now what actual spring worked in his mind at these words it is difficult to say," wrote Begbie. The biographer continued:

> One can find nothing in the man's past to suggest a thesis. But the words of his wife produced an extraordinary effect in his mind. He did not return to the public-house; he did not go home with her; he walked away like a man in a dream. He only knows that he was impelled to walk away. As he passed the big hall occupied by the Salvation Army, he says he suddenly felt himself grow stiff through all his joints, his feet appeared to strike root into the ground, he was unable to move. There he stood, this drunk man—dazed, bewildered, quiet—like a sleepwalker.
>
> While he stood there the thought occurred to him of his old mate who had joined the Salvation Army. Whence came this idea, he does not know; but it came. A desire to see this man made itself felt in the Plumber's heart, and with the desire the tension of his limbs relaxed. He walked forward and made his way up the stairs to the hall door.[6]

Within hours the man was soundly saved and soon his whole life radiated a new life in Christ.

In *Pitcairn's Island*, a sequel to *Mutiny on the Bounty*, Nordhoff and Hall told how strong drink played havoc among the mutineers and Polynesians who had found refuge on the island. Liquor turned the Pacific paradise into a living hell. Terrible were the scenes of drunkenness and debauchery Nordhoff and Hall described. They wrote of fights, of a massacre, and of the flight of women and children to a remote part of the island where they built a fort to protect themselves from drunken husbands and fathers.

Matt Quintal was the worst of the drunkards. Drink turned him into so fierce and savage a madman that he had to be hunted down and killed. William McCoy was responsible for most of the trouble.

He had rigged up a still and had found a way to obtain alcohol from a root plant that grew on the island.

In our society the drunkard is the product of the brewery and the wine shop. From his terrible falls and senseless fights, he brings wounds upon himself, but they are nothing compared to the misery he inflicts on his family. Shame, poverty, terrorism, and savage beatings are part of the misery experienced by the drunkard's wife and children.

The drunkard is a menace not only to his family, but also to the general public, especially on the highways. Some years ago State Farm Mutual Automobile Insurance Company published in an advertisement the actual driving record of a so-called problem drinker. In October he was arrested for speeding. The following August he was arrested for reckless driving. The next July he was arrested for driving while his license was suspended. Two months later he was arrested for driving while intoxicated. Two months after that he was again arrested for driving while his license was suspended. Three years later he was arrested for drunken driving. Four months later his license was again suspended. Six months later he was arrested for reckless driving. The next year he was arrested for driving while intoxicated. Two months later he was again arrested for the same offense, and again had his license suspended. Nine months later he was arrested for reckless driving. Two months later he was arrested for speeding. Four months later he was again arrested for reckless driving. The advertisement labeled this problem drinker "an anti-social drinker." It should have labeled him a criminal.

Think of the toll the drunk driver takes on our highways. Each year in the United States alone, drunk drivers kill thousands of people, injure hundreds of thousands more, and cost society billions of dollars. Nearly half of the Americans aged sixteen to twenty-one who are killed in traffic accidents are legally intoxicated.

Here are some more statistics: 20 percent of freezing deaths in the country are due to alcohol; 25 percent of choking deaths are related to alcohol; 50 percent of deaths from falls are due to alcohol; 52 percent of fire deaths are due to alcohol; 60 percent of suicides are related to alcohol; 64 percent of murders are related to alcohol; 69 percent of drownings are connected with alcohol; 76 percent of aircraft deaths can be traced to alcohol; 72 percent of robberies and assaults are connected with alcohol; 60 percent of rapes are related to alcohol; and 80 percent of criminal court cases involve the use of alcohol.

A victim of a drunkard ought to be able to sue not only the drunkard but also the tavern or liquor store that sold him the alcoholic beverage; the brewery, distillery, or winery that made the beverage; and the media and advertising agencies that promoted its consumption. Yet our society, which insists on calling drunkenness a disease, often absolves breweries, distilleries, and taverns of all responsibility and allows them to spend billions of dollars to promote their deadly wares and to enhance their public image.

Recently I ate in a restaurant where the paper place mats were designed to sell wine. I kept mine as a matter of interest. The bold red-and-white headline—"Who's Afraid to Order Wine?"—was followed by columns of advice. One caption read, "Wine Exists for Food," and the copy stated, "It is not necessary to be concerned about selecting or matching a *particular* wine to a *certain* dish. The enjoyment and fun of having wine with a meal is like adding music." The next caption read, "How Wine Is Served," and the copy went on to demystify wine glasses and carafes. Another caption read, "The Tasting," and the copy told the timid what to do next:

> When the wine is served, the following are the key tests you make before you approve the wine. *Appearance*—Hold the glass of wine by the stem up to the light. Wine should always be "bright," not cloudy or murky. *Smell*—Swirl the wine a bit to give it some air (enable it to breathe), then smell it. It is correct to put your nose in several brief times so that the senses don't become over-exposed. Bouquet is the aroma that is emitted from the wine. *Taste*—After you have really enjoyed the smell, take a good mouthful. Swish it around the mouth. Notice how it tastes as it rolls over the tongue, passing some of your keenest taste buds. A wine should never be sour or bitter.

Following the advice were a listing, description, and pronunciation guide to the red and white wines offered by the restaurant. The whole idea of the place mats, of course, was to lure people into drinking. This is just another example of how people help spread the "disease" of alcoholism.

The brewers and distillers are even more subtle. They pose as champions of the cause of keeping drunks off the road while they spend billions of dollars to persuade drunk drivers to buy their products. *Time* magazine once carried a four-page, full-color advertisement entitled "Who's Responsible for Drunk Driving?" On the first page was a picture of ten cartoon-type people, including a babe in arms. The adults were pointing the finger at someone else while maintaining poker expressions on their faces, and the baby was crying. The copy on the second page introduced a council that claimed to be concerned enough about the problem to contribute millions of dollars to a fund to stop alcohol abuse. The heading on the third page was "Okay, Who Wants to Stop It?" and under the heading the cartoon-type people were again set before the readers. This time the adults were all grinning and raising their hands, and the baby was smiling. The fourth page listed all the brewers, distillers, and grog-shop merchants who were either subscribers to or associate members of the council.[7]

Another advertisement in *Time* showed the deterioration of a person's handwriting as his alcohol consumption increased at a party. When the party began—so the advertisement revealed—the drinker wrote, "I can drink when I drive," in plain, legible handwriting. He wrote the same statement two drinks later, four drinks later, and five drinks later; his handwriting became progressively more difficult to read. After a total of seven drinks he scrawled illegibly. The conclusion was obvious: "When you drink too much, you can't handle a car. You can't even handle a pen." The advertisement was signed "The House of Seagram."

Such clever promotional gimmicks designed by the companies who produce, promote, and sell alcoholic beverages strike me as the epitome of hypocrisy. Alcohol is a deceiver and a destroyer. Yet these companies wring their hands over it on one page and advertise it on the next. One reason the hypocrisy is allowed to continue, of course, is that often people in the legislative, executive, and judiciary branches of government are heavy drinkers. Strong drink stupefies them.

Solomon also reminded us that *strong drink stings:* "Look not thou upon the wine when it is red, when it giveth his colour in the cup, when it moveth itself aright. At the last it biteth like a serpent, and stingeth like an adder" (Proverbs 23:31-32).

Long before he recognized the errors of Rome, Father Chiniquy—the French Canadian Roman Catholic priest—recognized the perils of alcohol. His eyes were opened to the truth of Solomon's proverb by Dr. Douglas, one of the ablest surgeons in Quebec and a founder and governor of the Quebec Marine Hospital. The doctor and the priest became firm friends while Chiniquy was serving as the chaplain of the hospital. Surprised that Chiniquy drank alcoholic beverages, the doctor invited him to attend the autopsy of a sailor who had died suddenly. Chiniquy wrote about what happened:

The next morning I was, at the appointed hour, by the corpse of the dead man, when Dr. Douglas kindly gave me a very powerful microscope that I might more thoroughly follow the ravages of alcohol in every part of the human body.

"I have not the least doubt," said he, "that this man has been killed by a glass of rum, which he drank one hour before he fell dead. That rum has caused the rupture of the aorta."

While talking thus, the knife was doing its work so quickly that the horrible spectacle of the broken artery was before our eyes, almost as the last word fell from his lips.

"Look here," said the doctor, "all along the artery, and you will see thousands, perhaps millions, of reddish spots, which are as many holes perforated through it by alcohol. Just as the muskrats of the Mississippi River, almost every spring, dig little holes through the dams which keep that powerful river within its natural limits, and cause the waters to break through the little holes, and thus carry desolation and death along its shores, so alcohol every day causes the sudden death of thousands of victims by perforating the veins and opening small issues through which the blood rushes out of its natural limits.

"It is not only this big vein which alcohol perforates; it does the same deadly work in the veins and lungs and the whole body. Look at the lungs with attention, and count, if you can, the thousands and thousands of reddish, dark, and yellow spots, and little ulcers with which they are covered. Every one of them is the work of alcohol, which has torn and cut the veins and caused the blood to go out of its canals, to carry corruption and death all over these marvelous organs.

"Alcohol," the doctor continued, "is one of the most dangerous poisons—I daresay it is the most dangerous. It has killed more men than all the other poisons together. Alcohol cannot be changed nor assimilated to any part or tissue of our body, it cannot go to any part of the human frame without bringing disorder and death to it. For it cannot in any possible way unite with any part of our body. The water we drink, the wholesome food and bread we eat, by the laws and will of God are transformed into the different parts of the body, to which they are sent through the millions of small canals which take them from the stomach to every part of our frame. When the water has been drunk, or the bread we have eaten is, for instance, sent to the lungs, to the brain, the nerves, the muscles, the bones—wherever it goes it receives, if I can so speak, letters of citizenship; it is allowed to remain there in peace and work for the public good.

"But it is not so with alcohol. The very moment it enters the stomach it more or less brings disorder, ruin and death, according to the quantity taken. The stomach refuses to take it, and makes a supreme effort to violently throw it out, either through the mouth, or by indignantly pushing it to the brain or into the numberless tubes by which it discharges its contents to the surface through all the tissues. But will alcohol be welcome in any of these tubes and marvelous canals, or in any part or tissue of the body it will visit on its passage to the surface? No! Look here with your microscope, and you will see with your own eyes that everywhere alcohol has gone in the body there has been a hand-to-hand struggle and a bloody battle fought to get rid of it. Yes! Every place where King Alcohol has put his foot has been turned into a battlefield spread, with ruin and death, in order to ignominiously turn it out.

"By a most extraordinary working of nature—or rather by the order of God—every vein and artery through which alcohol has to pass suddenly contracts, as if to prevent its passage or choke it as a deadly foe. Every vein and artery has evidently heard the voice of God: 'Wine is a mocker; it bites like a serpent and stings as an adder!' Every nerve and muscle which alcohol touched trembled and shook as if in the presence of an implacable and unconquerable enemy. Yes, at the presence of alcohol every nerve and muscle loses its strength, just as the bravest man in the presence of a horrible monster or demon suddenly loses his natural strength, and shakes from head to foot."

Father Chiniquy continued:

I cannot repeat all I heard that day from the lips of Dr. Douglas and what I saw with my own eyes of the horrible workings of alcohol through every part of that body. It would be too long. Suffice to say that I was struck with horror at my own folly, and at the folly of so many people who make use of intoxicating drinks.

What I learned that day was like the opening of a mysterious door, which allowed me to see the untold marvels of a new and most magnificent world. But though I was terror-stricken with

> the ravages of strong drink in that dead man, I was not yet convinced of the necessity of being a total abstainer from wine and beer, and a little brandy now and then, as a social habit. I did not like to expose myself to ridicule by the sacrifice of habits which seemed then, more than now, to be among the sweetest and most common links of society. But I determined to lose no opportunity of continuing the study of the working of alcohol in the human body. At the same time I resolved to avail myself of every opportunity of making a complete study of anatomy under Dr. Douglas.

Even more dramatic was the terrible incident that caused Father Chiniquy to give up drink altogether, take the pledge, and preach the cause of temperance far and wide—in spite of fierce opposition from his bishop and fellow priests. He wrote:

> Among my penitents there was a young lady belonging to one of the most respectable families of Quebec. She had a child, a girl, almost a year old, who was a real beauty. Nothing this side of heaven could surpass the charms of that earthly angel. Of course her young mother idolized her; she could hardly consent to be without her sweet angel, even to go to church. She carried her everywhere, to kiss her at every moment and press her to her heart.
>
> Unfortunately that lady, as it was then and is still now too often the case, even among the most refined, had learned in her father's house, and by the example of her own mother, to drink wine at table, and when receiving the visits of her friends or when visiting them herself. Little by little she began to drink, when alone, a few drops of wine; at first by the advice of her physician, but soon only to satisfy the craving appetite, which grew stronger day by day.
>
> I was the only one, excepting her husband, who knew this fact. He was my intimate friend, and several times with tears trickling down his cheeks, he had requested me in the name of God, to persuade her to abstain from drinking. That young man was so happy with his accomplished wife and his beautiful child! He was rich, had a high position in the world, numberless friends, and a palace for his home! Every time I had spoken to that young lady, either when alone or in the presence of her husband, she had shed tears of regret; she had promised to reform, and take only the few glasses prescribed by her doctor. But, alas! that fatal prescription of the doctor was like oil

poured on burning coals; it was kindling a fire which nothing could quench.

One day, which I will never forget, a messenger came in haste and said: "Mr. A. wants you to come to his home immediately. A terrible misfortune has just happened—his beautiful child has just been killed. His wife is half crazy; he fears lest she will kill herself."

I leaped into the elegant carriage drawn by two fine horses, and in a few minutes I was in the presence of the most distressing spectacle I ever saw. The young lady, tearing her robes into fragments, tearing her hair with her hands, and cutting her face with the nails of her fingers, was crying, "Oh! for God's sake give me a knife that I may cut my throat! I have killed my child! My darling is dead! I am the murderess of my own dear Lucy! My hands are reddened with her blood. Oh! may I die with her!"

I was thunderstruck, and at first remained mute and motionless. The young husband, with two other gentlemen, Dr. Blanchet and Coroner Panet, were trying to hold the hands of the unfortunate wife. He did not dare to speak. At last the young wife, casting her eyes on me, said, "Oh, dear Father Chiniquy, for God's sake give me a knife that I may cut my throat! When drunk, I took my precious darling in my arms to kiss her; but I fell—her head struck the sharp corner of the stove. Her brain and blood are there spread on the floor! My child! My own child is dead! I have killed her! Cursed liquor! Cursed wine! My child is dead! I am damned! Cursed drink!"...

After an hour passed in indescribable agony of mind and heart, I attempted to leave and go back to the parsonage. But my unfortunate young friend requested me, in the name of God, to spend the night with him. "You are the only one," he said, "who can help us this awful night...."

I remained, but tried in vain to calm the unfortunate mother. She was constantly breaking our hearts with her lamentations—her compulsive efforts to take her own life....

In vain I tried to speak to her of the mercy of God towards sinners; she would not listen to anything I could say; she was absolutely deaf to my voice. At about ten o'clock she had a most terrible fit of anguish and terror....At about eleven o'clock, when on her knees, clasping her child to her bosom, she lifted her eyes towards me, and said:

"Dear Father Chiniquy, why is it that I have not followed your charitable advice when, still more with your tears than with words, you tried so often to persuade me to give up the use of those cursed intoxicating wines? How many times you have given me the very words which come from heaven: 'Wine is a mocker; it bites as a serpent, and stings as an adder'! How many times, in the name of my dear child, in the name of my dear husband, in the name of God, you have asked me to give up the use of those cursed drinks! But listen now to my prayer....

"Take the blood of my child, and go, redden with it the top of the doors of every house in Canada, and say to all those who dwell in those homes that that blood was shed by the hand of a murderess mother when drunk. With that blood write on the walls of every house in Canada that 'wine is a mocker.' I have cursed that wine which has made me so wretchedly miserable and guilty."

She then stopped, as if to breathe a little for a few minutes. She added: "In the name of God, tell me, can my child forgive me her death? Can she ask God to look upon me with mercy? Can she cause the blessed Virgin Mary to pray for me and obtain my pardon?"

But before I could answer, she horrified us by the cries, "I am lost! When drunk I killed my child! Cursed wine!"

And she fell a corpse on the floor. Torrents of blood were flowing from her mouth on her dead child, which she was pressing to her bosom even after her death!

That terrible drama was never revealed to the people of Quebec. The coroner's verdict was that the child's death was accidental and that the distressed mother died from a broken heart six hours after.

Two days later the unfortunate mother was buried with the body of her child clasped in her arms. Many tears were shed on that tomb, and this dear little child's guardian angel must have written with its blood on that tomb: "Wine is a mocker; look not at it. It biteth like a serpent, and stings like an adder." However, what I had just seen and heard could not be buried and forgotten in the grave. After such a terrible storm I was in need of solitude and rest, but above everything I was in need of praying.

In the middle of that memorable night, when the darkness was most profound, and the stillness fearful, was I awake, was I sleeping? I do not know. But I saw the calm, beautiful, and cherished form of my dear mother standing by me, holding by the hand the late murderess, still covered with the blood of

> her child...and [my mother] said, with power and authority which engraved every one of her words on my soul, as if written with letters of tears, blood and fire: "Go all over Canada; tell every father of a family never to put any intoxicating drink before his children. Tell all the mothers never to take a drop of those cursed wines and drinks. Tell the whole people of Canada never to touch or look at the poisoned cup, filled with those cursed intoxicating drinks."
>
> When the sound of that voice, so sweet and powerful, was hushed, and my soul had ceased seeing that strange vision of the night, I remained some time exceedingly agitated and troubled....
>
> Raising again my mind to God, I said: "O my God, let me know Thy holy will, and grant me the grace to do it. Do the voices I have just heard come from Thee? Hast Thou really sent one of the angels of Thy mercy, under the form of my beloved mother? or is all this nothing but the vain dreams of my distressed mind?"
>
> As quick as lightning the answer was suggested to me: "What I have taught thee in secret, go and tell it on the housetops!" Overwhelmed with an unspeakable emotion, and my heart filled with a power which was not mine, I raised my hands towards heaven and said to my God: "For my dear Saviour's sake, and for the good of my country, O my God, I promise that I will never make use of intoxicating drinks; I will, moreover, do all in my power to persuade the other priests and the people to make the same sacrifice!"
>
> Fifty years have passed since I took that pledge and, thanks be to God, I have kept it.
>
> For the next two years I was the only priest in Canada who abstained from the use of wine and other intoxicating drinks; and God only knows what I had to suffer all that time—what sneers, and rebukes and insults of every kind I had silently to bear! How many times the epithets of fanatic, hypocrite, reformer, half-heretic, have been whispered into my ear, not only by the priests, but also by the bishops.[8]

Even more graphic is the description of the death of an alcoholic, the mutineer William McCoy, on Pitcairn island. In 1808 Alexander Smith, the sole survivor of the seamen who had landed on Pitcairn in 1790, told McCoy's tragic story to Mr. Webber, mate of the *Topaz,* an American sealing vessel that had come to the island in search of fresh water. As he told the whole sad history of the colony, Smith related how one day "he found McCoy huddled down in a corner with the table upset and pulled up close, to hide behind....He had the horrors coming on."[9] McCoy, who was in mortal terror, imagined that one of the natives, Minarii, had come for him. Minarii had been dead and buried for a long time, but McCoy fought and screamed like a madman all night. At the first light of dawn he ran out of the house as though all the devils in Hell were on his track. Straight for the bluffs above the sea he ran. Over he went, and down, down, onto the jagged rocks below.

(b) Learn from the Drunkard (23:33-34)

Proverbs 23:33a states *what the drunkard desires:* "Thine eyes shall behold strange women." There is a well-established link between drunkenness and immorality. A drunken man is often easy prey for the harlot because his senses are muddled and his powers of resistance are eroded. Similarly a drunken woman is easy prey for the lustful man. Many a drunkard has been hastened to an early grave by promiscuous liaisons.

Consider the case of Mary Kelly, who was murdered on Tuesday, November 8, 1888, in a cheap lodging house on Dorset Street in a squalid section of London. She was the fifth and final victim of the notorious Jack the Ripper.

Mary was an attractive, educated, popular, witty, optimistic, and warmhearted woman. She was born, it seems, in Ireland and was married early to a Welsh ironworker who was killed two years later in an explosion. As a destitute widow, Mary was driven to the streets, where she acquired a taste for gin. The rest of her short life she was frequently drunk.

Mary moved to London, where she seems to have taken up with one man after another. Each liaison was terminated because of drink. Her last partner, a young man named Joseph Barnett, worked as a porter in the Spitalfields market. When Barnett was not around, Mary seems to have plied her shameful trade to obtain money for drink. Eventually Barnett moved out too.

Mary found it impossible to pay her rent, but she managed to find money for drink. One authority says that at the time of the Ripper murders a woman of the streets would sell her body for two pence (the price of a wretched bed in a dosshouse was four pence).

Desperate for money on the night of her death, Mary wandered about the streets, haunted the taverns, and accosted a number of men. By midnight she was completely intoxicated. In her drunken state she was picked up by a well-dressed man of medium height—an eyewitness told the police and the press that the man was carrying a small narrow parcel about eight inches long. Mary died of knife wounds about three o'clock in the morning. So terrible were the injuries she suffered—the murderer must have been a madman—that it took a team of six doctors more than six hours to complete the examination of her remains and to account for every organ and piece of hewn flesh.

In London's famous Chamber of Horrors in Madame Tussaud's Exhibition there is no wax model of Jack the Ripper because nobody knows who he was. However, there is a reproduction of a drab, dingy Victorian street in London's East End at the time of the Ripper murders; and on this street is a model of a young woman (perhaps Mary Kelly). One of Jack's potential victims, she waits—standing outside a *tavern,* of course. What an accounting the beer barons and gin giants will have to give at the great white throne when, no longer able to hide behind slick advertising, they are held responsible at last for the misery they have launched upon the world.

Proverbs 23:33b states *what the drunkard declares:* "Thine heart shall utter perverse things." The drunkard blurts out vileness and treachery, words he would never dream of saying when he is sober. Out of the depths of his degenerate heart he dredges up foul oaths, vile stories, and all kinds of blasphemy. He makes promises he cannot keep and utters threats he cannot take back. He may turn sentimental and weep over the death of his goldfish or burst out in a rage, cursing God and defaming the king. Strong drink sweeps away the guard he normally keeps on his tongue, and his mouth becomes an open sepulcher (Psalm 5:9), spewing forth all the rottenness of his heart. His most secret thoughts, feelings, hopes, and ambitions are revealed.

By loosening his tongue, strong drink has handed many a man over to his foes. In the novel *The Holy Flower* Sir Henry Rider Haggard gave us an illustration of a man whose tongue was loosened by alcohol.

In Haggard's story Allan Quatermain and his companions—Stephen Somers, a British horticulturist, and Hans, a native servant of Allan's—were on the first leg of an adventure-packed journey into the interior of Africa. Having been put ashore from the disreputable boat *Maria,* they found themselves in a nest of slave traders, headed by an elderly half-breed who called himself the Beyd Hassan-ben-Mohammed. It did not take Allan and Stephen long to discover that they were in imminent peril of being murdered, but Allan's hints that an English gunboat was in the area saved them.

The travelers were to spend the night in an abandoned mission station that had been taken over by Hassan and his band of cutthroats. When Allan and his companions arrived at the station, they explored the grounds and found an old weed-infested graveyard. Allan suspected that it contained the murdered bodies of the former missionaries. He suspected too that the unsavory Hassan wanted to get rid of his unwelcome guests. The explorers went back to the mission house and Allan related what happened next. He was eager to loosen Hassan's tongue so that he would betray his plans for them, if not his connection with the mission graveyard:

> We returned to the house to find that our meal was ready. Hassan had asked us to dine with him, but for obvious reasons I preferred that Sammy [their cowardly but excellent cook] should cook our food and that he, Hassan, should dine with us. He appeared full of compliments, though I could see hate and suspicion in his eye, and we fell to on the kid that we had bought from him, for I did not wish to accept any gifts from this fellow. Our drink was square-face gin, mixed with water that I sent Hans to fetch with his own hands from the stream that ran by the house, lest otherwise it should be drugged.
>
> At first Hassan, like a good Mohammedan, refused to touch any spirits, but as the meal went on he politely relented upon this point, and I poured him out a liberal tot. The appetite comes in eating, as the Frenchman said, and the same thing applies to drinking. So at least it was in Hassan's case, who probably thought that the quantity swallowed made no difference to his sin. After the third dose of square-face he grew quite amiable and talkative. Thinking the opportunity a good one, I sent for Sammy, and through him told our host that we were anxious to hire twenty porters to carry our packages. He declared that there was not such a thing as a porter within a hundred miles, whereon I gave him some more gin. The end of it was that we struck a bargain, I forget for how much, he promising to find us twenty good men who were to stay with us for as long as we wanted them.
>
> Then I asked him about the destruction of the mission station, but although he was half-drunk, on this point he remained very close. All he would say was that he had heard that twenty years ago the people called the Mazitu, who were

> very fierce, had raided right down to the coast and killed those who dwelt there, except a white man and his wife who had fled inland and never been seen again.
>
> "How many of them were buried in that mound by the church?" I asked quickly.
>
> "Who told you they were buried there?" he replied, with a start, but seeing his mistake, went on, "I do not know what you mean. I never heard of anyone being buried. Sleep well, honoured lords, I must go and see to the loading of my goods upon the *Maria.*" Then rising, he salaamed and walked, or rather rolled, away.[10]

In this case, strong drink loosened the tongue of the villain. It is often the other way around. Strong drink can even stimulate the tongue to speak against a friend.

Proverbs 23:34 states *what the drunkard does:* "Thou shalt be as he that lieth down in the midst of the sea, or as he that lieth upon the top of a mast." The drunkard, in other words, does the most foolish and fatal things imaginable. The reference to a man lying down in the middle of the sea shows the fearful danger to which the drunkard exposes himself. The word "mast" refers to what sailors call the crow's nest, where the lookout is stationed to watch for enemy vessels, treacherous shoals, and distant landfalls. A crow's nest is a foolish place to sleep since a fall from such a height means certain death. And by going to sleep when he should be keeping a watchful eye on the horizon, the drunkard imperils the safety of the whole ship.

Examples of what the drunkard does are found in the life of Tiberius, the caesar who disgraced the throne of Rome at the time Jesus died on a cross on that skull-shaped hill near Jerusalem.

Tiberius became caesar in his fifty-fifth year. Raised beneath the royal standards as the stepson of Augustus, Tiberius had distinguished himself in various wars and was known as an orator and a capable administrator. He seemed to many to be a worthy successor to Augustus.

The historian Suetonius thought otherwise. He wrote, "Even as a young officer he was such a hard drinker that his name, Tiberius Claudius Nero, was displaced by the nickname 'Biberius Caldius Mero'—meaning: 'Drinker of hot wine with no water added.'"[11] His appointment of Pomponius Flaccus to be governor of Syria followed a two-day, one-night drunken orgy.

After becoming caesar, Tiberius swiftly degenerated into a besotted, lecherous, drunken, vengeful, bloodthirsty old man who terrorized friend and foe alike. His lust to see people suffer provoked satires such as the following:

> He is not thirsty for neat wine,
> As he was thirsty then,
> But warms him to a tastier cup—
> The blood of murdered men.[12]

Tiberius was a dreadful monster of a man, yet in Scripture we see wretched Pilate choosing his friendship instead of seeing that justice was done to Christ.

Rome paid for having a man on the throne who, as Solomon put it, "lieth down in the midst of the sea" and "lieth upon the top of a mast." Tiberius retired to the island of Capri to wallow in his disgusting lusts and escape official routines. Suetonius wrote:

> On his return to Capri he let all affairs of state slide: neither filling vacancies that occurred in the Equestrial Order, nor making new appointments to senior military commands in any province. Spain and Syria were left without governors of consular rank for several years. He allowed the Parthians to overrun Armenia; the Dacians and Sarmatians to ravage Moesia; and the Germans to invade Gaul—a negligence as dangerous to the Empire as it was dishonourable.[13]

Many other examples of what the drunkard does could be cited. In May 1988, for instance, a drunkard driving a pickup truck headed down the wrong side of a highway. The truck crashed head-on into a church bus and exploded. Twenty-seven people on board the bus were killed. The truck driver survived and was charged with murder. It wasn't long, however, before some people were excusing his behavior on the grounds that he was drunk—as if drunkenness were a legitimate excuse rather than an added indictment!

(c) Listen to the Drunkard (23:35)

The drunkard has a hangover and is talking to himself. He says, "They have stricken me...and I was not sick; they have beaten me, and I felt it not." Proverbs 23:35a reveals *what he discovers* "the morning after the night before." The drunkard is not sick, but he has a splitting headache. He is black and blue all over, but he cannot remember how he got the bruises. Was he in a fight? Did he fall downstairs? Was he hit by a vehicle? Even when he is sober, his mind is so muddled that he cannot recall how he received his injuries.

Surely, we think, now that the drunkard has discovered the effects of strong drink, he will decide to seek help, get a grip on himself, and break the habit. Surely he will find his way to Calvary and seek the Savior, who can make people whole, break enslaving addictions, impart new life, and fill them with His Spirit (Ephesians 5:18). But listen to *what he decides.* The drunkard says, "When shall I awake? I will seek it yet again" (Proverbs 23:35b). Back to the bottle he goes! "Give me another drink, somebody," he says.

We meet a drunkard, the fierce old sea captain Billy Bones, in Robert Louis Stevenson's *Treasure Island.* Jim Hawkins tells us about this disreputable buccaneer who is hiding at the Admiral Benbow Inn from his former seafaring mates:

> All the time he lived with us the captain made no change whatever in his dress but to buy some stockings from a hawker. One of the cocks of his hat having fallen down, he let it hang from that day forth, though it was a great annoyance when it blew. I remember the appearance of his coat, which he patched himself up-stairs in his room, and which, before the end, was nothing but patches. He never wrote or received a letter, and he never spoke with any but the neighbours, and with these, for the most part, only when drunk on rum. The great sea chest none of us had ever seen open.
>
> He was only once crossed, and that was towards the end, when my poor father was far gone in a decline that took him off. Dr. Livesey came late one afternoon to see the patient, took a bit of dinner from my mother, and went into the parlour to smoke a pipe until his horse should come down from the hamlet, for we had no stabling at the old "Benbow." I followed him in, and I remember observing the contrast the neat, bright doctor, with his powder as white as snow, and his bright black eyes and pleasant manners, made with the coltish country folk, and above all, with that filthy, heavy, bleared scarecrow of a pirate of ours, sitting far gone in rum, with his arms on the table. Suddenly he—the captain, that is—began to pipe up his eternal song:
>
> Fifteen men on the dead man's chest—
> Yo-ho-ho, and a bottle of rum!
> Drink and the devil had done for the rest—
> Yo-ho-ho, and a bottle of rum!
>
> At first I had supposed "the dead man's chest" to be that

identical big box of his up-stairs in the front room, and the thought had been mingled in my nightmares with that of the one-legged seafaring man. But by this time we had all long ceased to pay any particular notice to the song; it was new, that night, to nobody but Dr. Livesey, and on him I observed it did not produce an agreeable effect, for he looked up for a moment quite angrily before he went on with his talk to old Taylor, the gardener, on a new cure for the rheumatics. In the meantime, the captain gradually brightened up at his own music, and at last flapped his hand upon the table before him in a way we all knew to mean—silence. The voices stopped at once, all but Dr. Livesey's; he went on as before, speaking clear and kind, and drawing briskly at his pipe between every word or two. The captain glared at him for a while, flapped his hand again, glared still harder, and at last broke out with a villainous, low oath: "Silence, there, between decks!"

"Were you addressing me, sir?" says the doctor; and when the ruffian had told him, with another oath, that this was so, "I have only one thing to say to you, sir," replies the doctor, "that if you keep on drinking rum, the world will soon be quit of a very dirty scoundrel!"

The old fellow's fury was awful. He sprang to his feet, drew and opened a sailor's clasp-knife, and, balancing it open on the palm of his hand, threatened to pin the doctor to the wall.

The doctor never so much as moved. He spoke to him, as before, over his shoulder, and in the same tone of voice; rather high, so that all in the room might hear, but perfectly calm and steady:—

"If you do not put that knife this instant in your pocket, I promise, upon my honour, you shall hang at next assizes."

Then followed a battle of looks between them; but the captain soon knuckled under, put up his weapon, and resumed his seat, grumbling like a beaten dog.

Sometime later, after receiving a shock, the captain suffered a stroke. It so happened that Dr. Livesey was present at the time. He and Jim Hawkins helped the old villain to his bed. The doctor practiced some rough minor surgery on Billy Bones and left him with a parting shot: "Now, mind you, I clear my conscience—the name of rum for you is death." Jim continued:

And with that [Dr. Livesey] went off to see my father, taking me with him by the arm.

"This is nothing," he said, as soon as he had closed the door. "I have drawn blood enough to keep him quiet a while; he should lie for a week where he is—that is the best thing for him and you; but another stroke would settle him."

About noon I stopped at the captain's door with some cooling drinks and medicines. He was lying very much as we had left him, only a little higher, and he seemed both weak and excited.

"Jim," he said, "you're the only one here that's worth anything; and you know I've been always good to you. Never a month but I've given you a silver fourpenny for yourself. And now you see, mate, I'm pretty low, and deserted by all; and Jim, you'll bring me one noggin of rum, now, won't you, matey?"

"The doctor—," I began.

But he broke in cursing the doctor, in a feeble voice, but heartily. "Doctors is all swabs," he said; "and that doctor there, why, what do he know about seafaring men? I been in places hot as pitch, and mates dropping round with Yellow Jack, and the blessed land a-heaving like the sea with earthquakes—what do the doctor know of lands like that?—and I lived on rum, I tell you. It's been meat and drink, and man and wife, to me; and if I'm not to have my rum now I'm a poor old hulk on a lee shore, my blood'll be on you, Jim, and that Doctor swab"; and he ran on again for a while with curses. "Look, Jim, how my fingers fidges," he continued, in the pleading tone. "I can't keep 'em still, not I. I haven't had a drop this blessed day. The doctor's a fool, I tell you. If I don't have a drain o' rum, Jim, I'll have the horrors; I seen some on 'em already. I seen old Flint in the corner there, behind you; as plain as print, I seen him; and if I get the horrors, I'm a man that has lived rough, and I'll raise Cain. Your doctor hisself said one glass wouldn't hurt me. I'll give you a golden guinea for a noggin, Jim."[14]

Well, the captain got his grog—and in a day or so he was dead. It was back to the bottle for him, just as Solomon said.

b. About Leadership (24:1-25)

(1) How to Create Wealth (24:1-4)

(a) Be Wary (24:1-2)

As he talked about leadership, Solomon offered sound advice for those aspiring to positions of authority and power. They should, he said, be wary *of evil men's company:* "Be not thou envious against evil men, neither desire to be with them" (Proverbs 24:1). Those aspiring to leadership positions should also be wary *of evil men's comments:* "For their heart studieth destruction, and their lips talk of mischief" (24:2).

The Hebrew word translated "evil" in 24:1 means "wicked or injurious" and refers to the breaking up of all that is good and desirable. The equivalent Greek words, *poneros* and *kakos,* underline the moral depravity, corruption, and lewdness of evil people. Their influence is wholly destructive. They have no moral standards. They want the laws against immoral behavior to be lenient and permissive. Today the phrase "evil men" refers to the kind of people who want abortion on demand, oppose stiff laws against drunk driving, demand so-called gay rights, favor the legalization of prostitution and drugs, champion the rights of pornographers to publish and peddle their filth, and hate the evangelical and fundamentalist arm of the church.

By sheer weight of numbers such people may, especially in a democratic society, be able to win a great deal of freedom under the law; but they are pitiable slaves to their lusts. We are not to envy their imagined freedom, said Solomon, and we should avoid their company. After all, we become like the company we keep.

Absalom is an example of an evil man. David was very fond of his handsome, charming, and persuasive son. So were the people. However, Absalom was like King Saul: he had the outward appearance of a born leader, but his character was flawed. Whatever his father might have privately wished, Absalom was not the right man to sit on David's throne. Absalom's heart was host to pride, ambition, lust, rage, resentment, and revenge. The rank and file could not see the hairline crack in Absalom's soul, but God saw it clearly. David saw it too, but he chose to turn a blind eye to it until it was too late. By the time David faced the truth about his son, Absalom had already stolen "the hearts of the men of Israel."

We do not know for sure why David lost his grip on the kingdom after the Bath-sheba affair. No doubt that scandal cost him much of his popularity, and men like Shimei and Ahithophel were quick to use the scandal to their own advantage. A clue to the reason for David's uncharacteristic neglect of his governmental duties can be found in some of his penitential Psalms. They indicate that after his great sin, David became deathly sick. He did not say what the illness was, but we can infer from some of his remarks that he may have been smitten with leprosy.

Whatever the reasons for David's weakness were, Absalom wasted no time in cashing in on it. Believing he had a legitimate grievance against his father, and urged on by that prize scoundrel Ahithophel, Absalom made plans to seize the throne for himself. Truly he was a man whose heart studied destruction and whose lips talked mischief. First he capitalized on his good looks, charm, and princely status. Then he posed as a friend and protector of the people and their civil rights. The sacred historian wrote:

> And it came to pass after this, that Absalom prepared him chariots and horses, and fifty men to run before him. And Absalom rose up early, and stood beside the way of the gate: and it was so, that when any man that had a controversy came to the king for judgment, then Absalom called unto him, and said, Of what city art thou? And he said, Thy servant is of one of the tribes of Israel. And Absalom said unto him, See, thy matters are good and right; but there is no man deputed of the king to hear thee. Absalom said moreover, Oh that I were made judge in the land, that every man which hath any suit or cause might come to me, and I would do him justice! And it was so, that when any man came nigh to him to do him obeisance, he put forth his hand, and took him, and kissed him. And on this manner did Absalom to all Israel that came to the king for judgment: so Absalom stole the hearts of the men of Israel (2 Samuel 15:1-6).

Absalom was very successful for a while. Many people flocked to his standard when he raised the banner of rebellion. "The conspiracy was strong," the Holy Spirit said (2 Samuel 15:12).

What kind of man was this rebel Absalom? He was a man filled with self-importance (2 Samuel 17:11-14). He was shameless and lewd enough to rape ten of his father's wives and to do it publicly and openly where everyone could see him (16:21-22). He was dastardly enough to plot his father's murder (17:1-4).

Should we be envious of a man like Absalom, a man born with a silver spoon in his mouth? He possessed rank and riches, good looks and charm, popularity and personality—and a heart full of violence and vice. Should we envy Absalom who, having been caught by his hair in the branches of an oak tree, swung helplessly and painfully to and fro until Joab came with his darts? (2 Samuel 18:9-15) Never!

Absalom was twenty-four years old at the time of the rebellion. David was fifty-six and Solomon was six. Solomon was old enough to remember the panic, the flight from Jerusalem, David's horror at the news that Ahithophel had sided with the conspirators, the desperate hours when everything hung in the balance, and Absalom's funeral. Remembering it all, Solomon was wise enough to be wary of other evil men.

(b) Be wise (24:3-4)

A leader must be wary and wise to create wealth. Solomon showed the aspiring leader *how to found a great house:* "Through wisdom is an house builded; and by understanding it is established" (Proverbs 24:3). Solomon also showed *how to fill a great house:* "By knowledge shall the chambers be filled with all precious and pleasant riches" (24:4).

Perhaps the Lord Jesus had Proverbs 24:3-4 in mind when He stressed the importance of building one's life on His words (see the parable of the wise and foolish builders in Matthew 7:24-29). He told the parable after giving the Hebrew people the laws of the kingdom of Heaven in the sermon on the mount (Matthew 5–7). What magnificent laws they are! What a foundation to build on!

In the sermon on the mount Jesus took the Mosaic law—that pure, white light from Heaven—and passed it through the prism of His brilliant intellect and burning heart, breaking the light up into its pristine colors. Again and again He said, "Ye have heard that it hath been said...but I say unto you." Moses dealt with adultery; Jesus dealt with lust. Moses dealt with murder; Jesus dealt with anger. Moses dealt with the fruit; Jesus dealt with the root. Jesus took the law of Moses, which dealt with the outward aspects of human behavior, and lifted it to the heights of Heaven. The beatitudes alone leave us breathless (Matthew 5:1-12), but they were just the beginning of the sermon.

Jesus went on to examine the law, extol the law, then exalt the law. He put it on a plane beyond the reach of even the most zealous Jew. The righteousness of the scribes and Pharisees, according to Jesus, did not measure up (and in fact was a hindrance to entering the kingdom of Heaven). The law of Moses had been beyond the capacity of fallen man to keep, and only the Holy Spirit could enable one to keep the laws of the kingdom.

Christ taught on the mount that almsgiving, praying, and fasting are all well and good—if done in absolute secrecy. Food, clothes, and shelter, He said, were necessary, but not nearly as important as the kingdom of God and His righteousness.

Jesus' fine sayings are not pious platitudes and expressions of wishful idealism. On the contrary, they are the down-to-earth, solid-granite, bedrock, foundational precepts of the coming kingdom of Christ. By these laws Christ, at His second coming, will rule His global empire. He is coming to found a house. That house will be built on knowledge, understanding, and wisdom. That house will be filled with precious and pleasant riches. Imagine a world ruled by such a King and such a house!

Think of Jesus' knowledge. He knows all the laws that are known to science and all the laws not yet known to science. He knows them not because He has investigated them, but because He invented them. The discoveries and wonders of the present century will be totally eclipsed when Jesus places the key to all science in the hands of His servants and when science becomes what it was always intended to be: the handmaid of His glory.

Think of Jesus' understanding! He knows and understands the heart, mind, will, holiness, love, omniscience, omnipotence, and omnipresence of God—because He is God. God the Son is coequal, coeternal, and coexistent with God the Father and God the Holy Spirit. Jesus is God, blessed forevermore, in every sense of the word.

At the same time Jesus is truly man. He was born into this world. He grew up, went to school, made friends, worked, traveled, and taught. Although He was sinless, He was tempted, tested, and tried. He grew tired, became hungry and thirsty, wore clothes, lived in a house, and rode a donkey. He loved, laughed, wept, and prayed. He was praised and persecuted, loved and loathed, blessed and betrayed. And then He died—and such a cruel death it was. Jesus fully understands man because He is a man Himself. Someday a King who understands man will have control of the affairs of men!

Think of Jesus' wisdom. He never made a mistake, never had to apologize, never acted or reacted inappropriately. He is wiser far than Solomon. His words are an inexhaustible fountain of wisdom. His contemporaries said, "Never man spake like this man" (John 7:46). They asked, "Whence hath this man this wisdom?" (Matthew 13:54) They marveled, "How knoweth this man letters, having never learned?" (John 7:15) Jesus' wisdom was evident when His enemies tried to trap Him; when Herod, Caiaphas, Annas, and Pilate tried to bully Him; and when the soldiers mocked and murdered Him. As He was dying He said, "Father, forgive them; for they know not what they do" (Luke 23:34).

Jesus' wisdom, His parables, His teaching, and His prophecies are recorded in the Gospels. For two thousand years the world's cleverest and wisest men have studied, loved, and revered His flawless words. What a world it will be when such a King and such a house rule over all! God speed the day.

(2) How to Contemplate War (24:5-12)

(a) Some Substantial Instances (24:5-9)

i. The Importance of Wise Counselors (24:5-6)

As Solomon continued to talk about leadership, he stressed the vital importance of wise counselors *for a nation's strength:* "A wise man is strong; yea, a man of knowledge increaseth strength" (Proverbs 24:5). He also stressed the importance of wise counselors *for a nation's safety:* "For by wise counsel thou shalt make thy war: and in multitude of counsellors there is safety" (24:6). A sensible ruler surrounds himself with wise counselors. With their help he can study the facts and count the cost before he declares war. The decision is difficult because victory does not always go to the big battalions.

Alexander's armies, for example, were far smaller than Persia's armies, but Alexander was a military genius and Darius was not. Indeed Alexander soon had the Persian emperor on the run. "The great king," as Darius was called, tried to make a stand at Gaugamela. He had 34,000 front-line cavalry, compared to Alexander's 7,250.[15] Still the Persian king feared because he had been beaten so often. Darius tried to subvert Alexander's men by offering fabulous rewards to anyone who would kill or betray Persia's foe. When that failed, Darius made his third and final attempt to negotiate a settlement. He offered Alexander all the territories west of the Euphrates, thirty thousand talents as ransom for his mother and daughter, the hand of one daughter in marriage, and the retention of his son Ochus as a permanent hostage. "If I were Alexander," Parmenio, Alexander's general, declared, "I should accept." "So should I," retorted Alexander, "if I were Parmenio."

Alexander was a personally gifted general. He knew when to take advice and when to reject it. Solomon's son Rehoboam, however, needed all the wise counsel he could get—not that he would admit it. His failure to listen to good advice cost him the ten northern tribes.

We can imagine Rehoboam's thoughts when Jeroboam flung the gauntlet in his face and marched off with the bulk of the kingdom: *I'll show that rebellious upstart! Jeroboam may have made off with most of the tribes, but I still have the loyalty of Judah and Benjamin, the toughest of the tribes. Besides, Jeroboam is no king. He's a good talker, perhaps, and a clever organizer, but what does he know about waging war?*

Jeroboam probably knew more than Rehoboam, for Jeroboam had spent time in Egypt at the court of the warrior pharaoh

Shishak. Rehoboam had spent his life in the court of Solomon, a man of peace who never once put an army on a battlefield.

Confident that he could quickly crush the rebellion before Jeroboam could muster his men, Rehoboam raised an army of 180,000 men—"which were warriors," the Holy Spirit added (2 Chronicles 11:1). But the war was never fought. The prophet Shemaiah, called "the man of God" in Scripture, intervened and this time wisdom saved Rehoboam from making an even bigger fool of himself.

Shemaiah was one of a noble company of only seven people in the Old Testament who were named and given the title "man of God": Moses (Deuteronomy 33:1); Samuel (1 Samuel 9:6); David (Nehemiah 12:24); Elijah (1 Kings 17:18); Elisha (2 Kings 4:7); Shemaiah (2 Chronicles 11:2); Igdaliah (Jeremiah 35:4). The names of four others who were called "man of God" are known only to God (see 1 Samuel 2:27; 1 Kings 13:1; 20:28; 2 Chronicles 25:7).

Shemaiah stepped forward and gave Rehoboam a bold, brief, and blunt message: "Thus saith the Lord, Ye shall not go up, nor fight against your brethren: return every man to his house: for this thing is done of me" (2 Chronicles 11:4). Rehoboam complied with this uncompromising divine mandate. Probably he had no other option. His army simply melted away. "They obeyed the words of the Lord," the Holy Spirit said, "and returned from going against Jeroboam." If Rehoboam commanded the demobilization of his army, we are not told so. If he did, he was behaving uncharacteristically, for it seems he was rarely willing to take advice.

Alarmed by the speed with which Jeroboam consolidated his power and fearful of an attack by the rival kingdom, Rehoboam wasted no time in fortifying Jerusalem and fifteen other cities. It seems that these cities were built up to create a line of defense against Egypt because of Jeroboam's influence with the pharaoh, but these fortifications did Rehoboam little good when Shishak invaded Judah.

Foolish Rehoboam had already destroyed his first line of defense—trust in God and obedience to His Word—and when Egypt took the offensive, Shemaiah once again appeared at court with a divine message. "Thus saith the Lord," he said, "Ye have forsaken me, and therefore have I also left you in the hand of Shishak" (2 Chronicles 12:5). Rehoboam should have listened to his father's advice and surrounded himself with the right kind of counselors.

All too often a dictator surrounds himself with sycophants and toadies who are ever willing to tell him what he wants to hear. Without realistic counsel, he unwisely involves his people in wars.

Antiochus the Great, the famous Syrian king, must have received unwise counsel or rejected all counsel when he decided to tangle with the rising Roman empire.

Having successfully concluded the second Punic war, the Romans had just negotiated a treaty with Egypt, a country Antiochus wanted to control. He deliberately provoked the Romans by outfitting a fleet of three hundred vessels and attacking the coastline and islands of Asia Minor. When the Romans protested, Antiochus contemptuously told them that they had no interest in Asia, that he was not their vassal, and that he had every right to recover lands that had once belonged to Lysimachus, one of Alexander the Great's successors. Antiochus may as well have waved a red rag at a bull. Defeated at the battle of Magnesia, Antiochus barely escaped with his life and the Romans imposed a heavy tribute on him.

The Syrians however still imagined that they could play games with Rome. When Antiochus Epiphanes ascended the throne, he continued his father's suicidal policies. Again unwise counselors, or the lack of counselors, proved fatal.

In the spring of 168 B.C. Antiochus Epiphanes marched against Egypt, but when he was four miles from Alexandria he received a sudden check: a Roman fleet was anchored in the bay. He did not have to wait long to learn what that fleet portended. Caius Popilius Laenas presented him with an ultimatum from the Roman senate. Antiochus was commanded to stop molesting the friends of the Roman people, to return to his own realm, and to stay there. He replied that he would consult with his advisers and come to a decision. Laenas, well aware of the worthlessness of his enemy's advisers, drew a circle in the sand around Antiochus. "Before you step out of that circle," the Roman said, "you will give me an answer that I can report to the senate." Thus the empire that Alexander had established was forced to bow to the new masters of the world. Mastery, it seems, was a matter of counselors.

The outcome of the Absalom rebellion was also a matter of counselors. If Absalom had had any common sense, he would have listened to Ahithophel, wily old fox that he was, rather than Hushai, who was known as David's friend (see 2 Samuel 17).

### ii. The Impotence of Wicked Counselors (24:7-9)

Solomon warned against listening to the advice of three kinds of fools: the silent fool, the sinful fool, and the scornful fool.

Proverbs 24:7 introduces us to *the silent fool:* "Wisdom is too high for a fool: he openeth not his mouth in the gate." In accordance with the Peter Principle, this man has been promoted beyond the level of his competence. He has a position among the mighty, but he is completely out of his depth. He dares not open his mouth "in the gate" because the discussion is over his head. He does not have the faintest idea what the wrangling is all about. As a counselor this kind of fool is useless.

This proverb applies to all walks of life—in the field of pathology, for instance. My brother, who is an expert on diseases of the human liver, wrote a book entitled *The Liver: An Atlas and Text of Ultrastructural Pathology*. I opened the book at random and read:

> In the liver biopsy of a 21-day-old patient with Jeune syndrome (Asphyxiating Thoracic Dystrophe) who had marked hyperbilirubinemia, intense bile ductular proliferation associated with poital febrosis, inflammation and edema was found. The hepatic ultrastructure revealed lysosomal retention of bile pigment.... Other changes included proliferation of the membranes of the smooth endoplasmic reticulum with glycogen body formation, mildly dilated rough endoplasmic reticulum.[16]

I felt like I was reading a foreign language! If I were asked to review that book for a medical journal, I would be wise to decline. The height of wisdom would be to keep my mouth shut and ply my pen in a field where I have some measure of competence. The medical wisdom displayed in my brother's book is too high for me. It would be folly for me to open my mouth "in the gate" where diseases of the liver are discussed. It would be equally foolish for my brother to keep his mouth shut if in such a discussion someone began advancing incompetent ideas on a liver disease.

More foolish than the man who keeps his mouth shut is the man who blurts out nonsense and displays his ignorance. Years ago when I was conducting services on a Caribbean island, I learned about a man who liked to add new words to his vocabulary even when he did not know their meanings. If he liked the sound of a word, he would use it. During one meeting in his church a prayer request was made for a brother who was going into the hospital for an operation. The man who liked new words jumped to his feet to lead the congregation in prayer. "O Lord," he prayed, "You have heard the request for our dear brother who is facing a critical operation in the hospital tomorrow morning. O Lord, we pray that You will give our brother a successful *post mortem!*"

Solomon was more concerned about the man who took his place

at the king's council table, but had nothing to say. The problem was that he was occupying a seat in which a competent counselor might have sat.

Proverbs 24:8 introduces us to *the sinful fool:* "He that deviseth to do evil shall be called a mischievous person." The word translated "mischievous" here means "a genius at plots."

I was writing my commentary on this verse while I was in Orlando, Florida, where I was visiting the church of a pastor who is an American Indian. As I rode with the pastor in his car, I read the verse to him and asked, "How would you illustrate this proverb, Robert?" He replied:

> As a lad I grew up in Chicago and ran with a street gang. In the gang there were a few types known as "gators" (a contraction of the word "instigators"). These were the gang leaders. They were the ones who had the ideas. The idea may have been to trash someone's car or to murder someone. The "gators" came up with the idea, made the plans, spelled out the details, told the various gang members their specific duties, and instigated the action. We all looked up to them. They were the heroes.

Whether or not there were street gangs in Solomon's day, the population doubtless included criminal types, including organized bands of robbers. Crime is nothing new. Certain criminal types are born leaders. Lesser criminal types have always looked up to them and followed their lead. Solomon realized the folly of allowing such leaders to get anywhere near the reins of government.

Nazi Germany illustrates what happens when people from the gutter become the leaders of the government. The Nazi leaders were a gang of thieves and mass murderers. They lied, cheated, and bullied their way to power. They launched the nation on a course of crime and conflict. Their crimes against humanity almost defy description.

Summing up the findings of the Nuremberg trials, Sir Hartley Shawcross of the British delegation described the atrocities committed in the concentration camps. People were worked, beaten, and starved to death—if they were not murdered on arrival. Human hair was baled for commercial purposes and used for stuffing mattresses. Tattooed human skin was made into lampshades. Human fat was used to make soap. Gold teeth were extracted from corpses, melted into ingots, and shipped to the Reichsbank. Said Sir Hartley, "Mass murder had become a state industry, with by-products."[17]

In the Nazi regime those in authority devised to do evil. And they gave their countrymen and the world fair warning of what they intended to do. Hitler even spelled it out in *Mein Kampf.*

Proverbs 24:9 introduces us to *the scornful fool:* "The thought of foolishness is sin: and the scorner is an abomination to men." What a definition of sin! God declares the very thought of foolishness to be sin in His sight—and He reads the secret, unspoken thoughts of our hearts (Matthew 9:3-4; 12:24-25; Luke 9:46-47).

The word rendered "foolishness" in Proverbs 24:9 actually indicates a lax or careless habit of mind. Solomon could not imagine either a person with a slack mind or a person with a scornful mind being allowed to hold a leadership position in his administration. Thus he probably would not have been impressed with the democratic principle of one man, one vote. As soon as the masses realize their power, they use their numbers to deliver the governmental process into their own hands or the hands of those who will pass the kind of laws they want.

On Pitcairn island power fell by popular vote into the hands of those who had slack or scornful minds. When some surviving mutineers and some Polynesians landed on this lonely island to start a new life, these colonists had to make some major decisions. First they had to decide what to do with the *Bounty.* According to Nordhoff and Hall, most of the mutineers wanted her to be burned and scuttled so no damning evidence could be found if a king's ship should penetrate those remote seas. Two of the mutineers objected, but in the end the majority ruled. Fletcher Christian, who had led the mutiny, then made the fateful announcement: "In matters of importance that concern us as a community, every man, from this day on, shall have his vote. All questions shall be decided by the will of the majority."[18]

The trouble began when McCoy discovered he could distill alcohol from ti roots. McCoy obtained his ti from a glade, the only place on the island where it grew plentifully. One day he found a fellow mutineer clearing the ti patch in order to plant yams. Wanting to make sure that no one else trespassed on his precious patch of ti roots, McCoy broached the idea to Quintal, another mutineer, that the land should be divided up among the men. Quintal was for dividing the land, but only among the seamen. He did not want to give any land to the Polynesians. "Give 'em land," he said, "and they'll not work for us."[19] Quintal's idea was to enslave the natives.

Matters came to a head when McCoy saw Minarii, one of the Polynesians, clearing the ti patch. McCoy rounded up his cronies and made sure he had enough for a majority vote. Then the mutineers congregated at Christian's house. Christian heartily agreed to a fair division of the island, but he was astounded when McCoy demanded that the island be divided among the white men only. There was a heated debate, but the McCoy faction had enough votes to overrule the others. Christian, however, declared the matter to be so serious and so fraught with fatal consequences that the final vote should be postponed. It was unthinkable to him that the whites should expect the Polynesians, two of whom had been chiefs and landowners on their native islands, to submit tamely to serfdom. Christian hoped that some of McCoy's supporters would come to their senses.

As it turned out, the Polynesians heard about the proposal, took matters into their own hands, and attempted a wholesale massacre of the white men. Attempting to seize power by sheer weight of numbers, McCoy and his cronies led the idyllic Pitcairn community into a terrible orgy of hatred and bloodshed. Their thought of foolishness was sin indeed.

(b) Some Suppositional Inferences (24:10-12)

Solomon, still writing about the kinds of people who should not be allowed to get their hands on the machinery of government, paused here to make some suppositional inferences. "If...If...If...," he wrote.

i. The Man with No Moral Courage (24:10)

"If thou faint in the day of adversity, thy strength is small." The last kind of person who ought to be in a position of power is the man who caves in before opposition. In this world, opposition is the name of the game. No matter what the project or the proposal is, there are always those who raise objections—or even veto an idea if they can. When we are involved in a project, we must make sure that we have God's mind on the matter, be sure that we are in God's will, and then go forward in spite of opposition.

We admire the spirit of Lord Nelson, Britain's great naval hero who sailed into battle against a numerically superior force. When one of his officers observed more enemy ships approaching from another direction, he became alarmed and pointed Nelson to that part of the horizon. Nelson simply put his telescope to his blind eye and calmly replied, "Ships? I see no ships!"

Nelson knew how to deal with that kind of opposition. He knew that the French fleet, for the most part bottled up in harbor because of the British blockade, was no match for the British fleet. The French captains were demoralized by years of constant defeat at sea; the British captains were veterans of many victories. The French sailors, who had been scraped together from here and there to form crews, were poorly trained; the British sailors had been well-drilled at sea. The French were brave enough, but the British were more skilled and handier at the hundreds of tasks required to maneuver sailing ships and take advantage of the wind. The British sailors, who could service their guns twice as fast as the French, could fire two shots to every one of the French. The British sailors' accuracy was as superior as their speed. Napoleon might rule Europe, but his authority stopped at the water's edge. Britain ruled the seas.

So Nelson refused to be deterred by more opposition. The greater the odds, he reasoned, the greater the victory. He told the captains who served under his flag: "Gentlemen, in the heat of battle, it may well be that you will not be able to discern signals from the flagship. But no captain can go wrong if he puts his ship alongside that of the enemy."[20]

It is the duty of those who are entrusted with power to make sure that their policies are right and then pursue them in spite of the opposition of foes, interest groups, and vacillating friends. The time of adversity is no time to faint.

ii. The Man with No Moral Character (24:11-12)

Solomon didn't want the man without moral character anywhere near the seat of power. He drew attention first to *what such a man sees:* "If thou forbear to deliver them that are drawn unto death, and those that are ready to be slain" (Proverbs 24:11). Then Solomon drew attention to *what such a man says:* "If thou sayest, Behold, we knew it not; doth not he that pondereth the heart consider it? and he that keepeth thy soul, doth not he know it? and shall not he render to every man according to his works?" (24:12)

Solomon was uncompromisingly condemning the doctrine of *laissez faire* that is so common in this world's diplomacy. All too often politicians lack the moral character to take the necessary steps to do what is right. Because it is so much easier to do what is expedient, they ignore terrible wrongs that need righting—or simply apply bandaids. Consider the following illustrations of the consequences of a *laissez-faire* attitude.

When Hitler sent his troops to occupy the Ruhr, the overwhelming French and British power could have stopped him in his tracks and toppled his evil regime. Instead the Allies turned a blind eye on the situation and in their spinelessness hoped for the best. They refused to take action again and again until it was almost too late and they paid a terrible toll for their *laissez-faire* policy.

When the Soviet Union refused to liberate Eastern Europe and put up the iron curtain right after World War II, the West should have given the Kremlin an ultimatum. The United States, which had the necessary military might, could have saved millions of people from the nightmare of communism. But the United States took the easy way out—and paid for the decision.

The classic Biblical illustration is the outcome of Pilate's confrontation with Christ. Pilate knew, we are told, "that for envy they had delivered him" (Matthew 27:18). Moreover Pilate knew that the Lord Jesus was completely innocent of all the charges brought against Him. "I find in him no fault at all," he told the Jews (John 18:38; also see John 19:4,6 and Luke 23:4,14). And Pilate was warned by his wife to beware of what he did with Jesus. (His wife, Claudia Procula, was the daughter of the third wife of the reigning emperor Tiberius and the granddaughter of the illustrious Augustus.)

So Pilate faced a simple choice. Would he do what was right, or would he do what was expedient? He tried to dodge the decision by sending Jesus to Herod. Herod mocked Christ and sent Him back. Pilate tried to reason with the Jews, but the Sanhedrin was obdurate. They wanted Jesus crucified, and quickly. Then Pilate tried offering them the choice of Jesus or Barabbas. He hoped they would choose a good man rather than a bad man, but they chose Barabbas and whipped the mob into a fury. Next Pilate tried offering to scourge Jesus and let Him go. He hoped that the terrible torture of a Roman scourging would satisfy their hate, but the Jews only howled louder for Christ's death. In one more attempt to satisfy them, he showed them Christ—crowned with thorns, bruised, and bleeding. All this time Pilate should simply have let Jesus go.

The final choice could not be put off any longer. By this time the Sanhedrin had the measure of their man. "If thou let this man go," they said, "thou art not Caesar's friend" (John 19:12). So that was it: whose friendship would Pilate choose? He could befriend the meek and lowly, friendless and forsaken, but evidently innocent man who stood so silently before him—and Pilate had superstitious doubts about whether He was merely a man. Or he could befriend that suspicious, abominably wicked tyrant in Rome.

There was another factor in the equation. Pilate was aware of the power and widespread influence of the Jews. He knew that if he let Jesus go, the Jews in Rome would whisper to the emperor that his Judean procurator had freed a man whom the Sanhedrin had formally charged with claiming to be a king. With that realization, Pilate caved in. It was easier to do what was expedient than to do what was right.

We cannot help wondering...How did Pilate receive the report of the centurion in charge of the crucifixion? Did the centurion speak of his own personal conviction that the man they had murdered was the Son of God? What did the procurator think when he heard that Jesus had died of His own volition and that His death was attended by astonishing miracles? What did Pilate say to his wife, and what did she say to him? What did he think when three days later the guards reported that the tomb was empty and that Jesus was risen from the dead? What happened to this man with a *laissez faire* attitude? Did he indeed reap any benefits from what he sowed?

History tells us how Pilate's administration came to a sudden end in A.D.36. When he received word that a horde of Samaritans were assembling on mount Gerizim, Pilate thought it expedient to make a display of Roman power, so he ordered out the troops. Had he stopped to investigate, he would have discovered that these people were merely the dupes of a Samaritan impostor who had told them he could show them where Moses had hidden the golden vessels of the tabernacle. These people were harmless treasure hunters, not traitors planning insurrection.

In the interest of expediency, however, Pilate seized all the access routes to Gerizim and sent in the infantry and the cavalry. There was a general massacre and those who were not killed were rounded up and sent to the executioner. The Samaritans appealed to Vitellius, the Roman legate of Syria. He deposed Pilate and sent him to Rome to explain himself to the caesar. By the time Pilate arrived, Tiberius—the man he had chosen for his friend—was dead. According to tradition, Pilate was banished to Vienne on the Rhone in southern France and may have committed suicide.

Some people have no business being anywhere near the corridors of power.

(3) How to Cultivate Wisdom (24:13-14)

Those who would rule over their fellow men must cultivate wisdom. Solomon wanted to tell his son how to develop this essential quality. First the king gave *an illustration: a honeycomb full of sweetness.* "My son," he wrote, "eat thou honey, because it is good; and the honeycomb, which is sweet to thy taste" (Proverbs 24:13). Solomon followed up the illustration with *an application: a heart full of satisfaction.* He wrote, "So shall the knowledge of wisdom be unto thy soul: when thou hast found it, then there shall be a reward, and thy expectation shall not be cut off" (24:14).

Honey is sweet to the taste and good for food. God described the promised land as "a land flowing with milk and honey" (Exodus 3:8). Evidently Solomon's son Rehoboam was fond of honey. It is doubtful that he ever kept a beehive or even thought about the process of beekeeping. He just liked the taste of honey. Probably Solomon had often seen him dipping into the honey pot.

Since honey represents natural sweetness, God forbade the Jews to add it to their animal sacrifices (Leviticus 2:11). Salt could be added, but not honey or leaven. Leaven could be added to the loaves of Pentecost, but honey was forbidden. God wants no mere natural sentiment to be offered to Him as part of worship. He wants supernatural sweetness: the fruit of the Spirit.

Solomon likened wisdom to honey. Like honey, wisdom is gathered slowly, carefully, knowingly, arduously, and sometimes painfully. But since honey represents natural sweetness, the wisdom that is compared to honey is natural wisdom. We must carefully distinguish between natural wisdom that can be acquired and spiritual wisdom that is divinely bestowed.

Spiritual wisdom is a gift from God. James wrote, "If any of you lack wisdom, let him ask of God, that giveth to all men liberally, and upbraideth not; and it shall be given him" (James 1:5). When Solomon was given this wisdom, it manifested itself instantly and awed his people (1 Kings 3).

In time Solomon added a great deal of natural wisdom to his store of spiritual wisdom. He became a shrewd observer of human psychology and natural history. He became skilled in statecraft and took a keen interest in architecture, horticulture, and international trade. Solomon even took an interest in comparative religion. But sweet and satisfying as natural wisdom may be, it—like honey—is swift to ferment.

James contrasted the two kinds of wisdom. Of natural wisdom he said, "This wisdom descendeth not from above, but is earthly, sensual, devilish" (James 3:15). Of spiritual wisdom he said, "The wisdom that is from above is first pure, then peaceable, gentle, and easy to be intreated, full of mercy and good fruits, without partiality, and without hypocrisy" (3:17). As Solomon grew older, he displayed a great deal of earthly, sensual, and devilish wisdom in his private life and public worship (1 Kings 11:1-9).

Those who would rule need all the knowledge they can acquire. They also need the wisdom of God. Abraham Lincoln is said to have stated that often during the great crises of his presidency he turned to God because there was nowhere else to go. The wisdom needed by those who rule can be found in the Word of God, where God speaks to all our needs. Happy is the nation whose leaders know, read, and believe the Word of God.

### (4) How to Curb Wickedness (24:15-25)

#### (a) Concerning Felony (24:15-18)

##### i. The Plot Overheard by God (24:15)

"Lay not wait, O wicked man, against the dwelling of the righteous; spoil not his resting place." In this verse a wicked man who is plotting a felony is overheard by God, who warns him not to proceed with his plans.

God knows how to protect His people. Dr. John G. Paton, a missionary to the cannibals in the New Hebrides, experienced His protection in a confrontation he had with the savages in a certain village on the island of Tanna. Three witch doctors, he recounted, "declared they did not believe in Jehovah, nor did they need His help, for they had the power to kill my life by Nahak (*i.e.,* sorcery or witchcraft), if only they could get possession of any piece of the fruit or food that I had eaten." Accepting their challenge, Paton took a bite from each of three pieces of fruit and gave the rest to the three medicine men.

As the ritual of Nahak began, the other natives fled in terror, but Paton watched. Slowly burning the fruit and waving it in the air and around their heads, the sorcerers chanted their incantations with the expectation that the missionary would be destroyed. When the spell didn't work, the witch doctors decided they would call for the help of all the other "Sacred Men" on the island and threatened that together they would kill the white man with their black arts before the next sabbath. In his autobiography Paton wrote, "Sabbath dawned upon me peacefully, and I went to that village in more than my usual health and strength." The three medicine men acknowledged defeat. "On being questioned, why they had failed," Paton wrote, they replied "that my God being the stronger had protected me from their Gods."[21]

Paton's story contrasts *the resilience* of the good man with *the ruin* of the evil man. God protects His people more often than we will ever know until we get to Heaven. The cunning of the wicked man is no match, in the end, for the character of the good man. When it seems as if the evil man is triumphing, we need to remember that we have not heard the end of the story—as the book of Job illustrates so well.

ii. The Plot Overruled by God (24:16-18)

*a.* The Fall of the Good Man (24:16)

In Proverbs 24:16a the fall of the good man is *contemplated:* "A just man falleth seven times, and riseth up again"—notice his resilience. In 24:16b his fall is *contrasted:* "But the wicked shall fall into mischief." The word translated "mischief" can also be rendered "calamity."

The classic example of Proverbs 24:15-16 is the story of David and King Saul. King Saul was the man who lay in wait "against the dwelling of the righteous." After Saul threw a javelin at David and missed, David escaped and made his way home. First Samuel 19:11-15 tells us what happened next:

> Saul also sent messengers unto David's house, to watch him, and to slay him in the morning: and Michal David's wife told him, saying, If thou save not thy life to night, to morrow thou shalt be slain. So Michal let David down through a window: and he went, and fled, and escaped. And Michal took an image, and laid it in the bed, and put a pillow of goat's hair for his bolster, and covered it with a cloth. And when Saul sent messengers to take David, she said, He is sick. And Saul sent the messengers again to see David, saying, Bring him up to me in the bed, that I may slay him.

David, on the other hand, was the just man who fell seven times, only to rise up again. In spite of all his faults and failings, David loved the Lord. Let's enumerate his seven falls.

First, he lied to Ahimelech and conned the priest into helping him. For this fall the unfortunate priest paid with his life (1 Samuel 21:1-10; 22:9-19).

Second, when David fled to Gath, he was afraid of being exposed as the one who had killed Goliath, so he shamed himself and dishonored the Lord by pretending to be mad (1 Samuel 21:11-15).

Third, enraged by Nabal's insults, David mobilized his men and marched toward Nabal's house with the intent to kill him. And David would have killed Nabal if Abigail had not intervened (1 Samuel 25:10-35).

Fourth, David temporarily lost faith (1 Samuel 27). Convinced that Saul's campaign of persecution would one day be successful, David went back to Gath to seek political asylum with the enemy. There he systematically lied and deceived the Philistine king.

Fifth, David lolled at home when he should have been in battle, cast lustful eyes on Bath-sheba, and seduced her (2 Samuel 11:1-4).

Sixth, when he discovered that Bath-sheba was pregnant, David tried to shift the apparent paternity of the child to her husband. When that failed, David had Uriah murdered and married his widow (2 Samuel 11:5-27).

Seventh, David insisted in a moment of pride on numbering the Hebrew people in a way contrary to the Mosaic law and in spite of Joab's protests (2 Samuel 24).

Each time David fell, he recovered himself. He was often bruised by falling, but his tender conscience and willingness to confess and ask for God's forgiveness led to restoration. Deep down in his heart David was "a just man," a genuine believer who was justified before God (Romans 4:5-8).

*b.* The Fall of the Godless Man (24:17-18)

The godless man is bound to fall in the end. King Saul carried on in his lawless way, again and again trying to murder David, but Saul died a wretched suicide, guilty of resorting to witchcraft and defeated in battle.

Should we rejoice over the fall of such a man? No, *rejoicing is forbidden:* "Rejoice not when thine enemy falleth, and let not thine heart be glad when he stumbleth" (Proverbs 24:17). Not only is rejoicing expressly forbidden by a God whose heart weeps over the fallen. *Rejoicing is foolish* too: "Lest the Lord see it, and it displease him, and he turn away his wrath from him [to thee]" (24:18).

A young Amalekite tried to cash in on Saul's suicide. He plundered the corpse and, bringing Saul's crown and bracelet to David, claimed that he had killed Saul. David's reaction was not what the man expected. David burst into tears for his fallen enemy. The Amalekite must have been astonished. He probably thought that

David would rejoice in the death of the man who had so often tried to murder him. We get the distinct impression from Scripture, however, that David never did dislike Saul. David had wanted to be Saul's friend and serve him as a loyal subject and soldier.

David mourned, wept, and fasted for the remainder of the day. Then with the swiftness of lightning the wrath of God was transferred from Saul to the Amalekite as David turned on him. Like a thunderbolt, the judgment fell. "How wast thou not afraid to stretch forth thine hand to destroy the Lord's anointed?" David demanded (2 Samuel 1:14). Then he called for an executioner to put the Amalekite to death.

The execution was followed by one of the most remarkable eulogies on record (2 Samuel 1:17-27). David burst into a poetic chant of praise for Saul and Jonathan, a hymn that came from the depths of his heart. He called Saul "the beauty of Israel." He cried, "Saul and Jonathan were lovely and pleasant in their lives, and in their death they were not divided: they were swifter than eagles, they were stronger than lions." Weeping over the death of his good friend Jonathan, David declared, "Thy love to me was wonderful." David's lament was not mere hyperbole. "Out of the abundance of the heart the mouth speaketh," Jesus said (Matthew 12:34). Again David has provided us with the best Old Testament example of a man who lived out what is essentially a New Testament truth.

How different from David were the Edomites! Having descended from Jacob's twin brother Esau, the Edomites were kin to the children of Israel, but they were not on good terms. Their enmity could be traced to Jacob's determined, unscrupulous, and successful campaign to secure the birthright and the blessing from Esau. Under normal circumstances these would have been given to the elder son, Esau, who was born minutes before Jacob. The blessing that Esau lost and Isaac bestowed on Jacob was comprehensive:

> God give thee of the dew of heaven, and the fatness of the earth, and plenty of corn and wine: Let people serve thee, and nations bow down to thee: be lord over thy brethren, and let thy mother's sons bow down to thee: cursed be every one that curseth thee, and blessed be he that blesseth thee (Genesis 27:28-29).

Prosperity, power, pre-eminence, and protection were all bestowed on Jacob. Esau had to take what was left. The desert was to be his portion. The sword would be his trust. Esau was to serve Jacob, although Isaac did prophesy that in time Esau would break Jacob's yoke from off his neck (27:40). Esau went out from his father's presence vowing vengeance.

Several of Israel's and Judah's kings fought against Edom, and David thrashed the Edomites thoroughly. They revolted in the days of Joram, but were again brought into subjection by Amaziah, who treated them with barbarous cruelty. In the reign of Ahaz they retaliated against Judah and when Nebuchadnezzar destroyed Jerusalem, the Edomites cheered him on. "Rase it, rase it, even to the foundation thereof," they cried (Psalm 137:7). Moreover they captured fleeing Jews and handed them over to the Babylonians. The Edomites were roundly rebuked by the prophet Obadiah, who joined other prophets in foretelling Edom's doom. Thus the Lord saw the Edomites' delight in the downfall of their enemy and transferred His wrath to them.

### (b) Concerning Fretting (24:19-20)

Solomon offered a double-barreled piece of advice: *don't fret* and *don't forget.* Proverbs 24:19 tells us not to fret: "Fret not thyself because of evil men, neither be thou envious at the wicked." The next verse tells us what not to forget: "There shall be no reward to the evil man; the candle of the wicked shall be put out" (24:20).

It is likely that when Solomon distilled this advice into a maxim, he had in mind his father's Psalm 37 and Asaph's Psalm 73. These two Psalms and Solomon's proverb urge us to take the long view of things. The prosperity of a wicked man is short-lived, even if it lasts his whole lifetime. There will be a day of reckoning on the other side of the grave.

Consider the case of Iosif Vissarionovich Dzhugashvili. He adopted the pseudonym *Stalin* ("man of steel") after becoming a Bolshevik leader in 1913. Stalin was probably the greatest mass murderer in history. Historians say it is unfair to compare him with Genghis Khan, Tamerlane, or Ivan the Terrible because Stalin was far worse than any of them. He exterminated more people than any other tyrant in history. He was responsible for wars, famines, purges, mass deportations, and campaigns of terror.[22]

Neither a Slav nor a Russian, Stalin was a Georgian. He was Asiatic, anti-Western, and antisemitic to the core. His mother, a Georgian peasant, wanted him to become a priest in the Russian Orthodox Church. His father was a drunken cobbler who beat his son. Filled with a burning contempt for all authority, Stalin was expelled from seminary in 1899.

Before Lenin died in 1924, he planned to get rid of Stalin and appoint Trotsky as his successor. Trotsky, who later said that Stalin poisoned the ailing Lenin, was himself murdered in 1940 in Mexico City by a Stalinist agent.

An estimated 10 million people perished during Stalin's drive to collectivize the farms of Russia. Another 25 million were deported to industrial areas and forced to work in factories. In the Ukraine more than 10 million peasants disappeared. Another 4.8 million died of starvation. The secret police shot and hanged whole villages. In Byelorussia (Belorussia) more than 1.5 million people lost their lives. In Soviet Central Asia an estimated 1.5 million people were exterminated. Mass repressions in Caucasus, Azerbaijan, and Armenia led to the exile or murder of hundreds of thousands of people.

In December 1934 a new law in Stalin's Soviet Union legalized the arrest and execution of anyone. All the secret police needed to enforce the law was a simple allegation that a person was an "enemy of the people." In addition to issuing daily death lists, the secret police would arbitrarily order local detachments across the Soviet Union to execute a thousand, two thousand, or ten thousand people in their cities at once. There were party purges and "show trials" in Moscow. The entire leadership of the Red Army was shot. An estimated thirty thousand Soviet military officers were brought home and executed in 1937 alone.

After World War II, Stalin launched the cold war and spread new waves of terror throughout the captive nations of eastern Europe. More than a million Lithuanians, Latvians, and Volga Germans were deported to Siberia. Khrushchev later admitted that whole nations in northern Caucasus were deported or shot. The only reason the Ukrainians did not suffer the same fate, Khrushchev said, was that there were too many of them. More than three million Jews vanished from Russia, the Baltic states, and Soviet-occupied Poland during and immediately following the war. More than a million Poles disappeared.

Roy Medvedev, in his book *Let History Judge,* wrote that Stalin and his secret police chief would spend hours poring over the lists of people to be approved for execution. There were hundreds of names, and the two men would go over each name on the list with relish. Stalin, Medvedev said, was fond of lavishing kindness on personal friends he had slated for execution or torture. Members of the tyrant's own inner circle were always at risk. For instance Stalin ordered the arrest and torture of the wife of Mikhail Kalinin while her husband continued in his post as president.[23]

Toward the end of his life Stalin became increasingly afraid of a plot against him. He planned to get rid of all his most faithful henchmen: Molotov, Voroshilov, Khrushchev, Beria, and others. New purges were heralded by the infamous "doctor's plot." On January 13, 1953, the Communist press announced that a sinister plot had been discovered among the Kremlin doctors. Nine had been arrested, of whom six were Jews. The Kremlin doctors were said to have conspired under the direction of a Jewish-American-British intelligence group against the Soviet political and military high command. Stalin appointed Semyon Ignatiev as the new commissar of state security and told him to beat confessions out of the alleged plotters. Then Stalin decided to get rid of the older members of the politburo and to trump up charges against all remaining Jews in the Soviet Union.

If ever there was an evil man, it was Stalin, and his "candle" was put out. Some think he was murdered by his comrades. His daughter Svetlana said that at the end her father refused to have any doctors near him and that he "died horribly and with difficulty, slowly suffocating to death." One thing is certain: Lavrenty Beria, the head of the KGB and Stalin's old accomplice, immediately dismissed all of Stalin's personal attendants. Some were shot, some were exiled, and some committed suicide. Beria himself was executed in 1953. Now in a lost eternity Stalin reaps the due reward of his deeds.

### (c) Concerning Fickleness (24:21-22)

Here Solomon pointed us to the vacillating person—the weathercock, the fair-weather friend, the man who trims his sails to the prevailing political or religious wind. Having no permanent loyalty, he is only concerned about his selfish interests and personal safety. We are to *note the vacillating person's instability:* "My son, fear thou the Lord and the king: and meddle not with them that are given to change" (Proverbs 24:21). We are also to *note the vacillating person's insecurity:* "For their calamity shall rise suddenly; and who knoweth the ruin of them both?" (24:22).

Solomon warned his son not to trust a man who has turned traitor once. He might betray his king again. Of course anyone—commoner or king—can be a human weather vane, and the consequences of fickleness can come swiftly to either one. Solomon traced unstable behavior to a failure to keep God in the picture. The fear of the Lord cancels out the fear of man, a major cause of vacillation.

Solomon's proverb concerning fickleness reminds me of the satirical poem about the turncoat vicar of Bray:

In good King Charles's golden days,
When loyalty no harm meant,
A zealous high-churchman was I,
And so I got preferment.
To teach my flock I never missed:
Kings were by God appointed,
And lost are those that dare resist
Or touch the Lord's anointed.
*And this is law that I'll maintain*
*Until my dying day, sir,*
*That whatsoever king shall reign,*
*Still I'll be the Vicar of Bray, sir.*

When royal James possessed the crown,
And popery grew in fashion,
The penal laws I hooted down,
And read the Declaration;
The Church of Rome I found would fit
Full well my constitution;
And I had been a Jesuit
But for the Revolution.
*And this is law, etc.*

When William was our king declared,
To ease the nation's grievance,
With this new wind about I steered,
And swore to him allegiance;
Old principles I did revoke,
Set conscience at a distance;
Passive obedience was a joke,
A jest was non-resistance.
*And this is law, etc.*

When royal Anne became our queen,
The Church of England's glory,
Another face of things was seen,
And I became a Tory;
Occasional conformists base,
I blamed their moderation,
And thought the Church in danger was,

By such prevarication.
*And this is law, etc.*

When George in pudding-time came o'er,
And moderate men looked big, sir,
My principles I changed once more,
And so became a Whig, sir;
And thus preferment I procured
From our new Faith's defender,
And almost every day abjured
The Pope and the Pretender.
*And this is law, etc.*

The illustrious house of Hanover,
And Protestant succession,
To these I do allegiance swear—
While they can keep possession;
For in my faith and loyalty
I nevermore will falter,
And George my lawful king shall be—
Until the times do alter.
*And this is law that I'll maintain*
*Until my dying day, sir,*
*That whatsoever king shall reign,*
*Still I'll be the Vicar of Bray, sir.*
(author unknown)

(d) Concerning Favoritism (24:23)

"These things also belong to the wise. It is not good to have respect of persons in judgment." Those in power should take Solomon's warning against favoritism seriously.

The impartiality of a judge will be tested when he presides over a case involving one party who is rich, powerful, and influential and another party who is poor, unprotected, and friendless. Because impartiality is essential in court, we depict justice as a *blindfolded* woman holding a sword in one hand and a pair of scales in the other.

We all have bias toward our friends, the members of our caste or club, and those who share our creed. An illustration of natural bias can be seen in the game of lawn bowling. The green, made of well-manicured grass, is about 120 feet square and is surrounded by a shallow ditch and a small embankment. The green is divided into lanes, each 20 feet wide. At the far end of each lane is a small, white, earthenware ball about 2-1/2 inches in diameter. The bowling balls are wooden, measure 5 inches in diameter, and weigh up to 3-1/2 pounds. Each player has two or four bowling balls. His objective is to place his bowling balls as close to the white ball as possible. He can use his balls to knock an opponent's ball away from the target ball or to guard a teammate's ball. What makes the game difficult is that each wooden ball has a bias caused by the fact that one side of the ball is larger than the other. A ball will curve unless it is sent down the green at great speed. A slow-rolling ball will curve as much as 6 feet from a straight line. Great skill and much practice are required to overcome the natural bias of each bowling ball. No less skill and no less patience are required to overcome our natural bias when we face a situation or judge a case.

Justice is often subverted by bias, as in the case of poor James of the Glen, whose story appears in Walter Scott's fine tale *Catriona.* James was falsely accused of murdering Colin Roy Campbell of Glenure, commonly called the Red Fox. David Balfour witnessed the murder and was able to testify that James of the Glen was innocent. Balfour's testimony, however, was not wanted. In fact he was abducted so that he could not appear in court.

When Balfour first told his side of the story to Prestongrange, the Lord Advocate, he was bluntly told his testimony was irrelevant. A Campbell had been murdered in the glen and the head of the College of Justice was the duke of Argyle, a Campbell. "This is a political case," Prestongrange said quite frankly. "Ah, yes, Mr. Balfour! Whether we like it or not, the case is political." Later on Balfour learned the bitter truth: a Campbell had died, a Campbell judge was determined to avenge the death, and poor James of the Glen was the scapegoat. Balfour was told, "This is not a case, ye see. This is a conspiracy."

Walter Scott summed up the results of the bias: "In course of time, on November 8th, and in the midst of a prodigious storm of wind and rain, poor James of the Glen was duly hanged a Lettermore by Ballachulish." Balfour reflected on the politics involved:

> So there was the final upshot of my politics! Innocent men have perished before James, and are like to keep on perishing (in spite of all our wisdom) till the end of time. And till the end of time young folk (who are not yet used with the duplicity of life and men) will struggle as I did, and make heroical resolves, and take long risks; and the course of events will push them upon the one side and go on like a marching army. James was hanged; and here was I dwelling

> in the house of Prestongrange, and grateful to him for his fatherly attention. He was hanged; and behold! when I met Mr. Simon in the causeway, I was fain to pull off my beaver to him like a good little boy before his dominie. He had been hanged by fraud and violence, and the world wagged along, and there was not a pennyweight of difference; and the villains of that horrid plot were decent, kind, respectable fathers of families, who went to kirk and took the sacrament!
>
> But I had had my view of that detestable business they call politics—I had seen it from behind, when it is all bones and blackness; and I was cured for life of any temptations to take part in it again.

Yes, favoritism is dangerous, but Solomon's warning has all too often fallen on deaf ears.

(e) Concerning Fairness (24:24-25)

Solomon also warned against *justifying the wicked:* "He that saith unto the wicked, Thou art righteous; him shall the people curse, nations shall abhor him" (Proverbs 24:24).

History is full of illustrations of this proverb. We find examples everywhere because of the sad condition of the world in which we live. Think of the gang of thugs Hitler brought to power in Germany. Think of how he stacked the courts, the legislature, and his administration with men who justified the wicked. Think of the decent men he corrupted. Think of the men who passed the Nuremberg laws that launched the horrors of full-blown Nazi antisemitism.

Hitler gave the world ample warning of what was to come. On September 15, 1935, the Nuremberg laws were passed by the Reichstag, which had become a rubber stamp for Hitler's decrees. From that time on, the Jews were systematically deprived of German citizenship and forbidden to marry or employ Aryans. The Nuremberg laws were soon supplemented by some thirteen decrees that completely restricted the Jews. By the summer of 1936 when Germany hosted the Olympic games and charmed visitors from the West, the Jews had already been practically eliminated from most activities. They were excluded from public office, the civil service, the media, the theater, and the stock exchange. Eventually they were eliminated from the legal and medical professions and prevented from engaging in business. In many towns stores carried signs forbidding Jews to enter. Many communities displayed signs reading, "Jews Strictly Forbidden in This Town."

Hitler viewed himself as the great lawgiver. He laid down the law arbitrarily and absolutely. He was a master liar, an art he cultivated to perfection. Insensitive to the torments and tortures he caused, he liked to be regarded as absolutely pitiless. He said to Herman Rauschning, "They regard me as an uneducated barbarian. Yes, we are barbarians. It is an honorable title."

Hitler began his career of mass murder by killing Germans. The old, the sick, and the insane were systematically eliminated to free up hospital beds. Then came the gas chambers and the furnaces. It was not enough for Hitler that Jews should die by the millions—he wanted them to die in agony. Himmler evolved the idea of shipping Jews to the concentration camps in boxcars in which the floors were coated with quicklime that produced terrible burns.

Germany justified these wicked men. Hitler, Himmler, and their cohorts were cheered on their way by a deluded nation.

Outside their own country the Nazis waged war with reckless disregard for international law and human life. Towns like Coventry in England were bombed flat. London was set ablaze from end to end. Nation after nation was overrun or sucked into the vortex. Eventually Hitler was hated and vilified around the world. "Nations shall abhor him," said Solomon, and how right he was.

When at last the Allies began to give Berlin, Stuttgart, Hamburg, and other German cities a taste of saturation bombing, the German people began to have second thoughts about the monster they had once cheered.

After warning against justifying the wicked, Solomon wrote about *judging the wicked:* "To them that rebuke him shall be delight, and a good blessing shall come upon them" (Proverbs 24:25).

Consider the illustration in Scripture of the prophet Jeremiah and wicked Zedekiah, the last king of the Jews. Zedekiah had a court official named Pashur, the son of Malchiah. Presumably it was into this Malchiah's dungeon that Jeremiah was eventually lowered when the king decided to punish him for his unpopular prophecies. In that dread hole he was to sink into the mire. Indeed he would have perished had it not been for the kindness of an Ethiopian (Jeremiah 38:1-13).

But we must go back to the time when the Babylonian army was on the march and Zedekiah sent Pashur to consult with the prophet of God. Perhaps, he thought, Jeremiah would now change his tune. Little did the king know the prophet if he thought that was a possibility, for Jeremiah was the kind of person who did not hesitate to rebuke the wicked—even if he was a king.

Having heard from God, Jeremiah was ready when the king's godless representative appeared. The prophet delivered his message to Pashur, who was to relay it to Zedekiah. No more uncompromising and unwelcome prophecy has ever scalded the ears of a wicked king.

Jeremiah indicated that the military preparations of Zedekiah were worse than useless because God had already determined to defeat them and indeed had allied Himself with the enemy. In addition God would unleash His own weapons: pestilence and famine, for instance. Those who escaped these inflictions would fall by the sword. The Babylonians would have no pity and would show no mercy. The sensible thing to do would be to flee Jerusalem before the invading armies arrived and to seek asylum with the king of Babylon. Jerusalem was doomed. Wicked King Zedekiah would reap the due reward of his deeds (Jeremiah 21).

Jeremiah, needless to say, was branded a traitor and treated accordingly by the Jews. But he was, as we can well imagine, a delight to Nebuchadnezzar. The Babylonian king "gave charge concerning Jeremiah to Nebuzar-adan the captain of the guard, saying, Take him, and look well to him, and do him no harm, but do unto him even as he shall say unto thee" (Jeremiah 39:11-12). Accordingly the Babylonians rescued Jeremiah from the prison where Zedekiah had kept him incarcerated. He was invited to come to Babylon as an honored guest. If he preferred, he could settle anywhere he liked in his native land. Certainly he would not be deported to Babylon against his will, as were most of the Jews (39:13-14; 40:1-4).

Concerning those who would speak out against injustice, Solomon wrote, "A good blessing shall come upon them." So now Jeremiah is blessed beyond his wildest earthly dreams. He is seated with the aristocracy of Heaven. But his earthly lot was one of weeping and woe. Centuries later Jesus would say: "Blessed are ye, when men shall revile you, and persecute you, and shall say all manner of evil against you falsely, for my sake. Rejoice, and be exceeding glad: for great is your reward in heaven" (Matthew 5:11-12).

c. About Law (24:26-29)

Proverbs 24:26 speaks about *popularity:* "Every man shall kiss his lips that giveth a right answer." Solomon of course was writing in an oriental setting. Today we would say that everyone wants to shake the hand of—or give a round of applause or a standing ovation to—

the man who gives a right answer. (Speaking in colloquial English, we might say that popularity comes to the man who knows how to hit the nail on the head.) Most of us appreciate a word fitly spoken.

Robert Clive knew how to give a right answer. In the heyday of British empire-building, no name ranked higher than his. Clive's involvement with colonialism started early. When he was seventeen years old, his family shipped him off to India with the British East India Company. Either he would make his fortune in India or die there of fever. He hated India and twice pointed a pistol at his head. Both times the pistol misfired, so he decided there must be some purpose for his life after all. At the time Britain and France were fighting for control of the Indian subcontinent, and Clive joined the army.

As the struggle for India proceeded, an Indian nabob shut up 146 British captives in a prison chamber only twenty feet square. This cell became infamous as the Black Hole of Calcutta. After a night of stifling tropical heat only 23 people were still alive. Clive marched to avenge this outrage. He had only 600 British soldiers and 800 native sepoys, but he won a resounding victory against overwhelming odds. Later he fought the battle of Plassey, which gave India to Britain for the next two centuries. When the spoils of the battle were divided, Clive took £160,000. He was hailed as a hero at home, was made an Irish peer, took the title of Baron Clive of Plassey, and secured a seat in the House of Commons.

Such successes do not come without cost however and along the way Clive made some enemies, one of whom tried to have him impeached. Accused of taking bribes from the rajahs, Clive indignantly defended himself. He told a spellbound audience how after the battle of Plassey he fell heir to a treasure in gold, silver, and jewels piled as high as the ceiling, and he was invited to help himself. "I am accused," he said, "of taking a paltry one hundred and sixty thousand pounds! I could have taken millions! I stand astonished at my own moderation!" It was a word fitly spoken.

Solomon said, "Every man shall kiss his lips that giveth a right answer," and the House of Lords evidently agreed with Solomon, for it found that "Robert, Lord Clive, did render great and meritorious service to his country."

Proverbs 24:27 speaks about *priorities:* "Prepare thy work without, and make it fit for thyself in the field; and afterwards build thine own house." In giving this sound advice Solomon was simply telling us to work for what we want and to save so that we can afford to buy it.

Credit is the lifeblood of modern business. Most of us have grown up in an environment where almost everyone has a few credit cards.

Borrowing money in order to buy a house, a car, furniture, or even an overseas vacation is common practice. As long as the loans are sensible, properly secured, and within one's means to repay, borrowing money is probably legitimate enough. Even so, I can remember a world where the word *credit* was unknown.

After high school I went to work for a large British bank that loaned money to business customers, but the cautious bankers made sure that the debt was well secured and that the prospects were good for its repayment. An ordinary private citizen was required to fill out an application form and supply two reliable character references just to open a checking or savings account. Overdrafts were nipped in the bud and credit cards unheard of.

In those days people worked hard, saved their money, and paid cash for at least all of the ordinary purchases. The world was simpler then. Students of economics learned only a few basic principles, such as the law of supply and demand.

Today we have easy credit and people are in a mood to spend rather than to save. At the same time high-powered advertising—often subliminal—is pitched to the emotions rather than the head. We also have an astronomical national debt, endless budget deficits, adverse international balances of payment, and the constant threat of runaway inflation—not to mention crowded bankruptcy courts made popular by advantageous bankruptcy laws. This is the environment in which I met a man I'll call Harry Baldwin, although that is not his real name. He was a professing Christian with a charming manner, a college degree, and a land development business.

Baldwin would drive around town and country looking for undeveloped land. What he wanted to buy was property that offered good prospects for future development. If he spotted a tract of land near a small city, he would consider all the possibilities. Maybe a super highway that was on the drawing boards would come close to that property and make it desirable for small businesses, gas stations, motels, stores, shopping centers, or housing projects. Maybe a new factory or giant business enterprise was being considered for the area and property values were likely to soar. Maybe the local city council was planning to enlarge its borders and annex all the property in the area. Maybe there were plans to rezone the area to attract new businesses.

Land with potential for development was the kind of property Baldwin wanted. He also wanted to buy houses that had been repossessed by banks or dilapidated houses that could be renovated and resold at much higher prices. The problem was that although he had a good eye for such property, he had no money. But he didn't need money as long as he could talk people into investing in his projects. What Baldwin offered the unwary was a limited partnership.

For instance he might find a farm that could be bought for half a million dollars. Located close to a booming town, the farm could be developed into a housing complex—a bedroom community worth many millions. The land would have to be purchased, zoning agreements would have to be secured, the property would have to be subdivided into home sites, and water lines, roads, curbs, and fire hydrants would have to be provided. It would all take money—money Baldwin did not have. He might rent the farm with an option to buy. Or he might scrape up a down payment. More likely he would con other people into investing by way of a limited partnership.

Harry put very little of his own money into such projects and he often had a dozen or more of them going at one time. Gullible people would put up money and in return for their investments receive legal-looking forms stating the terms of the limited partnership. The agreement was that a property would be bought, developed, and sold in Baldwin's name. If the property sold for a profit, the partners would receive their shares. They would also receive interest on their investments. Baldwin took money from anyone. I knew of one instance when he took the meager life savings of a preacher's widow and paid her quarterly interest with bad checks.

For a while money rolled in. Times were good. The economy was growing rapidly. Everyone was happy. Baldwin sold more and more partnerships, bought more and more property (with mortgages)—and went deeper and deeper into debt. He once boasted to me that he owed over a million dollars. He also juggled funds. If an investor to whom he owed money complained too loudly, he would take new money invested by a new partner for a new project and use it to buy off the crisis in the ongoing project. He was trying to keep more and more financial balls in the air at the same time.

Then the Middle East oil crisis caused runaway inflation. Interest rates went through the roof. Contractors and land speculators went bankrupt. Banks seized housing subdivisions, shopping centers, and real estate holdings and sold them for a song. Baldwin cynically salted away cash in financial shelters where the courts could not touch it and filed for bankruptcy. The limited partnerships became practically worthless. Baldwin's business, built on borrowed money, collapsed and some of his partners lost almost all the money they had invested. Baldwin told a friend of mine that he had "a good bankruptcy." How good that bankruptcy will seem at the judgment seat of Christ is another matter. Perhaps Solomon's advice to pay as we go is better than we think.

Proverbs 24:28 speaks about *perjury:* "Be not a witness against thy neighbour without cause; and deceive not with thy lips." Solomon was advising us not to volunteer to be a witness against a neighbor. In other words, he was counseling us to mind our own business.

The word translated "deceive" here is *pathah,* which can also be rendered "delude." In the book of Proverbs *pathah* is one of eight different words used to convey the concept of deception. The thought conveyed in Proverbs 24:28 seems to be that even when a witness tells the truth, he can create a wrong impression that can lead to a wrong verdict. So his desire to be officious and important can have grave consequences for his neighbor. The consequences could eventually come home to roost with the informer too. Solomon was advising us not to be busybodies and not to put ourselves up by putting someone else down.

An author is particularly vulnerable to the officious person who takes the form of a biased book reviewer. Some reviewers like to pontificate. They will tear a book and an author to shreds simply because of personal dislike or doctrinal bias. They can be highhanded and dictatorial. They can be patronizing when they approve and punishing when they don't. Over the years I have fared fairly well at the hands of book reviewers, but on occasion a book of mine has been reviewed by the kind of person Solomon had in mind in Proverbs 24:28.

When my book *Exploring Genesis* was first published, a Christian magazine printed a thoroughly biased review. The reviewer did not like my alliterated outline, a hallmark of my books. He ridiculed the outline by the way he wrote his review: for about a quarter of a column he began each word with the same letter.

When I write a Bible commentary, I start by doing a structural analysis of the text and then I create an alliterated outline. The process is slow and painstaking. It took the best part of a year to create the outline of *Exploring Genesis.* There was nothing haphazard, strained, or artificial about that outline. To the best of my knowledge it was comprehensive, grammatically correct, and accurately correlated to the text. Over the years thousands of preachers have found my outlines to be helpful and they have told me so.

The reviewer did something else that was worse than belittling my outline. He said, "Phillips evidently has no trouble believing in Noah's ark." Well, I don't. Jesus, the incarnate Son of the living

God, had no trouble believing in Noah's ark, so why should I? In His Olivet discourse the Lord Jesus referred to the flood, Noah, and the ark in a way that showed that He believed the Genesis record to be historical and accurate (Matthew 24:37-39).

The reviewer went on and on in a caustic tone. As I read his remarks I could only conclude that he was not interested in being a fair witness; he was more concerned with putting himself up by putting me down. I chose not to retaliate, and time has vindicated me. *Exploring Genesis* has been reprinted numerous times and I have received countless testimonies from those who have been helped and blessed by the book. I am thankful that the Holy Spirit has chosen to overrule the witness of that reviewer.

Proverbs 24:29 speaks about *pardon:* "Say not, I will do so to him as he hath done to me: I will render to the man according to his work."

"Eye for eye, tooth for tooth" was the principle of the law (Exodus 21:23-25). This principle was embodied in the imprecatory Psalms (Psalm 109:1-20, for example). So we are astonished to find the contrary principle enshrined in Proverbs 24:29. There Solomon was urging his readers not to invoke the law when wronged.

Solomon told us what not to do. The New Testament ethic, of course, goes further. He who described Himself as a "greater than Solomon" told us what to do instead of invoking the law (Matthew 12:42; 5:38-48). Jesus translated the proverb from the negative into the positive. Solomon said, "Don't!" Jesus said, "Do!" Solomon was saying, "Don't do to others what they have done to you." Jesus was saying, "Do to others what you would like them to do to you." Abraham Lincoln said, "If I make a friend out of my enemy, have I not destroyed my enemy?"

The New Testament ethic is a high standard. It calls us to react to mistreatment the way Paul and Silas did. At Philippi they were mobbed, rushed before the magistrates, condemned without a hearing, and sentenced to a beating (Acts 16:22).

"Beat them with rods," the magistrates said in effect. The English expression "to be beaten with rods" is a rendering of the original word *rhabdizo,* which occurs in Scripture only in Acts 16:22 and in Paul's testimony in 2 Corinthians 11:25 (note that "with rods" is omitted from the King James version of Acts 16:22, but is included in some other translations). The lictors, who attended the magistrates in Roman courts and carried rods for the express purpose of executing such a sentence, stripped Paul and Silas and beat them forcefully. Luke said that they "laid many stripes upon them" (Acts 16:23).

Then, as if that thorough thrashing were not enough, the missionaries were thrust "into the inner prison" and their feet were made "fast in the stocks" (Acts 16:24). There they were left in agony—their backs bruised and bleeding and their legs knotting up with cramps.

Paul and Silas might have wept and moaned. They might have cursed and threatened because, after all, they were Romans. Instead "at midnight Paul and Silas prayed, and sang praises unto God: and the prisoners heard them" (Acts 16:25). What a testimony!

The expression "sang praises" is particularly interesting. It is a translation of the word *humneō*, which can be literally rendered "were hymning." Paul and Silas were singing hymns. *Humneō* only occurs elsewhere in Scripture in Matthew 26:30, Mark 14:26, and Hebrews 2:12. The verses in Matthew and Mark refer to the Lord singing the Great Hallal in the upper room just before going to Gethsemane and Calvary—He probably sang the second set of hallelujah Psalms (Psalms 115-118). Thus it is likely that Paul and Silas sang the same hymns that Jesus sang on His way to the scourging and the cross. If so, here are some of the words the astounded prisoners heard echoing within those dank and dreary prison walls in Philippi:

> Ye that fear the Lord, trust in the Lord: he is their help and their shield (Psalm 115:11). What shall I render unto the Lord for all his benefits toward me? I will take the cup of salvation, and call upon the name of the Lord (116:12-13). The Lord is on my side; I will not fear: what can man do unto me? The Lord is my strength and song, and is become my salvation. This is the day which the Lord hath made; we will rejoice and be glad in it. O give thanks unto the Lord; for he is good: for his mercy endureth for ever (118:6,14,24,29).

Surely such a song had never been sung in such a place at such a time by such a couple to such an audience!

Then came the earthquake! The foundations of the prison shook. All the doors burst open and the chains that bound the prisoners fell to the floor. There should have been a stampede to escape, but the other prisoners were riveted to their bunks by the awesome power of the Holy Spirit. Shaken awake, the jailer saw that the prison doors were open and presumed that the prisoners were all gone. Thinking his life was forfeited, he prepared to commit suicide.

The jailer had been none too gentle with Paul and Silas the night before, but their attitude toward him was in keeping with the Lord's teaching and Solomon's proverb. *We will not do so to him as he hath done to us,* they thought. *He has an immortal soul to save.* Paul saw the flash of the sword and called out to save the jailer from suicide. A few minutes later the apostle led the astounded man to Christ!

Solomon never met Paul, but he did have the example of David to ponder. Time and time again David spared the life of his enemy King Saul and later showed the kindness of God to a surviving member of King Saul's family (1 Samuel 24; 26; 2 Samuel 9).

### d. About Laziness (24:30-34)

#### (1) A Vineyard Seen (24:30-31)

Remembering some neglected property he had seen, Solomon thought about *the character of the person involved:* "I went by the field of the slothful, and by the vineyard of the man void of understanding" (Proverbs 24:30). Solomon drew our attention to *the condition of the property involved:* "It was all grown over with thorns, and nettles had covered the face thereof, and the stone wall thereof was broken down" (24:31).

The condition of the property tells us much about the character of its owner. It had once been cared for; for instance someone had built a wall around it. Properly cultivated, that property could have brought a fortune to its owner, for it consisted of a field and a vineyard. Solomon did not have to meet the current owner of the property to know that he was lazy and stupid.

The condition of this slothful man's field and vineyard teaches a lesson to the evolutionist. The theory of evolution says that nature is gradually moving upward, that the survival of the fittest and the processes of natural selection guarantee the march of life from protoplasm to paradise. The lazy man's garden exposes the lie in that theory. Left to themselves, the forces of nature do not build up; they tear down. The vineyard degenerates into a jungle. The wall, succumbing to wind and weather, crumbles and falls. What prevails in the wild is not the law of regeneration but the law of degeneration.

It is not some hypothetical evolutionary law that rules in the wild, but the second law of thermodynamics. This law states that although the total amount of energy in the cosmos remains constant, the amount of energy available to do useful work is always getting smaller. Suppose for instance there is a stream of water coming from the top of a mountain. That water possesses kinetic energy that can be put to use as it flows down the mountain. For example it can be channeled through turbines to generate electricity. Once that water reaches sea level, however, it has no more kinetic energy available to develop electrical current. The mass of water remains the same, but its kinetic energy changes and decreases as the water loses altitude.

The same is true of all the energy in the cosmos. The total energy remains the same, but the available energy is constantly diminishing. We can convert matter into energy, as in the case of a nuclear reactor or an atomic bomb, but the total quantity of matter plus energy remains unchanged.

The energy available for work is relentlessly decreasing while the amount of unavailable energy (entropy) is steadily increasing. In nature, in other words, everything is constantly moving toward greater probability. (It is improbable that water will stay on top of a mountain. It is always likely to move to an area of greater probability nearer sea level.) Everything in the physical universe tends to move toward the area of highest entropy or greatest probability.

Translating this principle into everyday language, we could say that everything tends to move in the direction of the least orderliness, the greatest chaos, or the maximum "spentness." Order is not only improbable; it tends to disintegrate into disorder. Solomon astutely observed this principle at work in his slothful neighbor's garden.

We would see this principle at work if we put a brand-new luxury car under a tree in a forest and left the vehicle there unattended for twenty or thirty years; at the end of that period the car would be useless.

Or let's suppose that we are flying over a city in a plane. We have on board fifty thousand white index cards neatly stacked in orderly piles, with a thousand cards in each pile. As we fly over the city square, we open a door and dump all fifty thousand cards out of the plane. As they slowly begin to fall toward the city, the wind blows them this way and that. Would we expect those cards to fall in neat piles in the city square and arrange themselves in such a way that the stacks spelled out the name of the city? Impossible! The falling cards would be spread out at random over a vast area. They would lose all semblance of their original order and become ever more random in their distribution as time goes by. As the second law of thermodynamics declares, order degenerates into chaos.

According to the wholly untenable theory of evolution, the exact opposite occurs: non-living atoms of carbon, hydrogen, nitrogen, and so on have slowly arranged and organized themselves into complex, energy-rich, orderly forms. The theory is incredible and contrary to fact. The chance that protein molecules—complex enough to function as enzymes and bear life—could arrange themselves thus by accident is astronomically remote.

Nobody can explain how life, by chance, arose from non-living matter. Yet evolutionists blandly assume that, given long enough periods of time, anything can happen. It is as if they are saying that, given enough time, the fifty thousand index cards, blown far and wide through city and countryside, could organize themselves into something meaningful and productive. The contrary of course is the truth.

(2) A Vineyard Studied (24:32-34)

We note that *the case is reviewed:* "I saw, and considered it well: I looked upon it, and received instruction" (Proverbs 24:32). We note also in 24:33-34 that *the conclusions are reached.* Solomon, having observed life and the forces of nature, concluded that *persistent indolence* (24:33) produces *predictable insolvency* (24:34). He wrote, "Yet a little sleep, a little slumber, a little folding of the hands to sleep: So shall thy poverty come as one that travelleth; and thy want as an armed man." Solomon was repeating what he had already written in a previous proverb (6:10-11).

The law of entropy, as we have seen, states that everything begins to run down, rust, and decay. Engineers throw a bridge across a river and at once it begins to rust; nature is tearing it down. Man builds a skyscraper and nature sends wind, rain, and frost to open cracks, exploit weak spots, and pull the building down. Man builds a superhighway and the sun melts the tar and buckles the surface, water gets in the cracks and freezes, and the ice produces potholes. Constant maintenance is needed. There is no time for laziness.

An unused limb atrophies. "Use it or lose it" is the unwritten law. The law of laziness applies as much in the spiritual realm as it does in the physical realm. I could see that law at work in a church that had stagnated. When I was speaking there, the leaders asked me to share some observations about growing churches in the United States. I recounted some ordinary dynamics of growth and described how some other churches had put them into practice. When I mentioned that a church near Atlanta had successfully used buses to reach its wider neighborhood, one man said, "Oh, we had a bus and tried that once, but it didn't work."

"Well," I said, "the church I know in Atlanta has twenty buses. They have a bus captain and twenty drivers. Nobody gets to be a bus driver in that church who is not prepared to make a solemn commitment to be faithful to that ministry and to work at it. Once a driver has made a commitment, he is given training and then assigned a route. Every Saturday morning he meets with the bus captain for prayer, sharing ideas and experiences, and fellowship. Sometime during that morning he must also drive along his assigned route and call on all his regular passengers, follow up leads for new prospects, and make friendly contacts with the people he is hoping to serve.

"On Sunday morning," I continued, "rain or shine, he drives his route. He picks up children and adults, speaks to each person by name, and shows friendship and interest. After the morning services he delivers all his charges back to their homes. He is always alert for an opportunity to share a personal word about Christ. The driver may not get home for his lunch until midafternoon.

"Tell me," I added, "is that how you ran your bus program?"

"No," the man answered. "Our driver just drove the bus on Sundays to pick up the handful of regulars we had scraped together."

"Well," I said, "it wasn't the bus that didn't work, was it? It was you!" No wonder their bus ministry didn't work.

I occasionally visit a particular church that is remarkable for its dynamic leadership and phenomenal growth. This church has two pastors. One is a born organizer; the other is a gifted expositor. One of these godly men summed up the secret of their church's growth: "Our people love the Lord, they love each other, and they love lost people."

Their church has a large body of spiritually minded deacons as well as a large, consecrated staff. No man qualifies to be a deacon there unless he is a soul-winner. The young people are motivated and taught to be soul-winners. A spirit of caring, enthusiasm, and expectancy breathes through the Sunday school (from the earliest grades up), the choir, the various ministry outreaches, the senior citizens, and the pastors. The church is a worshiping church, a witnessing church, and a working church. People get involved. They make commitments. They pull their weight. God blesses and the church continues to grow.

A local church, like a garden, must be tended, or it will soon decline in size and spirituality. In a growing church attention is paid to the *wall*, to keep things out that don't belong there; and attention is paid to the *weeds*, to make sure no unsound doctrine or unspiritual attitude can take root.

When I was a boy I attended a church that had one of the largest Sunday schools in the British Isles. It was blessed with a number of gifted men who could make the Bible live and with soul-winners who had a vision for making a dynamic impact on the community with city-wide gospel crusades. That was more than forty years ago. When I went back as a guest speaker, the congregation was only a handful of people. Gone was the big Sunday school. Gone were the great Bible teachers. Gone were the programs to reach the lost. The leading elder, who was showing his years, shook his head sadly. "After I'm gone," he said, "I don't know who'll carry on." Like Solomon, "I saw, and considered it well: I looked upon it, and received instruction."

# CHAPTER 5

Proverbs 25:1–26:28

Section 2: Proverbs of Solomon—Edited by Hezekiah (25:1–29:27)

- I. The King and His Subjects (25:1–27:27)
  - A. Those of Whom to Beware (25:1–26:28)
    - 1. Beware of Sovereigns (25:1-7)
      - a. Some Are Wise (25:1-2)
        - (1) A Royal Example (25:1)
        - (2) A Royal Exercise (25:2)
      - b. Some Are Wily (25:3)
      - c. Some Are Wicked (25:4-5)
        - (1) How God Searches Motives (25:4)
        - (2) How God Stabilizes Monarchs (25:5)
      - d. Some Are Wary (25:6-7)
        - (1) So Beware of Self-Assertion (25:6)
        - (2) So Beware of False Assumption (25:7)
    - 2. Beware of Sinners (25:8–26:12)
      - a. Look Well to Your Fellows (25:8-20)
        - (1) Those Who Cause Trouble (25:8-10)
          - (a) Being Unable to Control Their Tempers (25:8)
          - (b) Being Unable to Control Their Tongues (25:9-10)
            - i. We Should Resist Temptation If We Can (25:9)
            - ii. We Will Reap Trouble If We Can't (25:10)
        - (2) Those with Convincing Talk (25:11-15)
          - (a) Fit Words (25:11-12)
            - i. The Picture (25:11-12a)
            - ii. The Point (25:12b)

(b) Faithful Words (25:13)
(c) Forceful Words (25:14-15)
i. The Person Whose Profession Is Empty (25:14)
ii. The Person Whose Persuasion Is Effective (25:15)
(3) Those We Cannot Trust (25:16-20)
(a) People Who Cannot Draw the Line (25:16-17)
i. In the Matter of Food, They Become Nauseated (25:16)
ii. In the Matter of Friendships, They Become Nuisances (25:17)
(b) People Who Cannot Desist from Lies (25:18-19)
i. Those Who Make False Pronouncements (25:18)
ii. Those Who Make False Promises (25:19)
(c) People Who Cannot Depart from Levity (25:20)
b. Look Well to Your Foes (25:21-22)
(1) How to Treat Them (25:21)
(2) How to Trust Them (25:22)
c. Look Well to Your Friends (25:23-24)
(1) The Blowing Wind (25:23)
(2) The Brawling Woman (25:24)
d. Look Well to Your Feelings (25:25-28)
(1) The King's Position (25:25-26)
(a) When Good News Comes (25:25)
(b) When Grim News Comes (25:26)
(2) The King's Pride (25:27)
(3) The King's Passions (25:28)
e. Look Well to Your Follies (26:1-12)
(1) How to Assess a Fool (26:1-2)
(a) By the Calamity He Brings (26:1)
(b) By the Curse He Brings (26:2)
(2) How to Admonish a Fool (26:3)

(3) How to Answer a Fool (26:4-5)
(a) The Need to Be Careful (26:4)
(b) The Need to Be Comprehending (26:5)
(4) How to Appear a Fool (26:6-9)
(a) By Expressing Confidence in One (26:6)
(b) By Exercising Credence in One (26:7)
(c) By Expecting Competence from One (26:8)
(d) By Explaining Concepts to One (26:9)
(5) How to Appraise a Fool (26:10-12)
(a) By His Condemnation (26:10)
(b) By His Character (26:11)
(c) By His Conceit (26:12)
3. Beware of Sluggards (26:13-16)
a. What the Sluggard Says (26:13)
b. Where the Sluggard Stays (26:14)
c. Why the Sluggard Starves (26:15)
d. Whom the Sluggard Scorns (26:16)
4. Beware of Self-Importance (26:17-28)
a. The Man Who Tries to Stop Something (26:17)
b. The Man Who Tries to Stir Something (26:18-23)
(1) The Man Full of Guile (26:18-19)
(a) His Portrait (26:18)
(b) His Pretense (26:19)
(2) The Man Full of Gossip (26:20-22)
(a) The Strife He Causes (26:20-21)
(b) The Sorrow He Causes (26:22)
(3) The Man Full of Gall (26:23)
c. The Man Who Tries to Start Something (26:24-28)
(1) Rage (26:24-26)
(a) Hatred Dissembled (26:24)
(b) Hatred Diagnosed (26:25)

(c) Hatred Discovered (26:26)
(2) Retribution (26:27)
(3) Review (26:28)

The best way to learn a skill is to watch an expert at work. If I wanted to learn how to make pottery, I would find a potter, visit his shop, ask him questions, watch him prepare and shape the clay, and find out how to fire, color, and glaze the finished vessel. Having discovered all the tricks of the trade, I would observe how the potter displays and sells his wares.

Solomon learned the skill of governing by watching his father. There was much to learn, for statecraft is both a political science and a fine art involving all ranks and conditions of men and all areas of human learning and activity. Solomon learned much from David, but Rehoboam refused to learn anything from Solomon.

Generations later, when Hezekiah came to the throne, he had to unlearn most of what his ungodly father had taught him. We can imagine that in order to discover how to rule aright, Hezekiah spent many long hours poring over the writings of Moses, the story of David, and the proverbs of Solomon. In these writings Hezekiah could see the masters at work. We can also imagine his delight when he discovered another collection of Solomon's sage sayings that were not as yet incorporated into Scripture. No doubt Hezekiah sat up all night reading and rereading them and spent days arranging and rearranging them. Then he had the sayings copied and, under the guidance of the Holy Spirit, he put them into the book of Proverbs.

We can divide the proverbs of Solomon that were edited by Hezekiah into three major categories: *the king and his subjects* (Proverbs 25:1–27:27); *the king and his sins* (Proverbs 28:1–29:14); and *the king and his sons* (Proverbs 29:15-27).

## I. THE KING AND HIS SUBJECTS (25:1–27:27)

### A. Those of Whom to Beware (25:1–26:28)

#### 1. Beware of Sovereigns (25:1-7)

#### a. Some Are Wise (25:1-2)

This section begins with *a royal example:* "These are also proverbs of Solomon, which the men of Hezekiah king of Judah copied out"

(Proverbs 25:1). No greater king than Hezekiah ever occupied the throne of David. Hezekiah's father Ahaz was a weak ruler and his son Manasseh was an almost unbelievably wicked monarch, but Hezekiah was a wise leader. There were other good kings, but Hezekiah stands majestically, like a massive snow-clad peak, towering above them all.

The great prophet Isaiah was Hezekiah's friend, counselor, guide, and (some think) father-in-law. A tremendous religious revival took place during Hezekiah's reign and, under his guidance, temple worship was restored and a great Passover was kept. Hezekiah outlawed the idolatries of former kings and stood firm when the northern kingdom of Israel fell in ruins before the Assyrians and its people were marched away into captivity. The Assyrian tide of conquest inundated much of Judah and lapped up to the walls of Jerusalem, but Hezekiah saw God work a mighty miracle of deliverance (2 Kings 19).

Hezekiah's noblest work, however, was in connection with the holy Scriptures. He not only edited some of Solomon's previously unpublished proverbs and added them to the sacred text; he also added a number of Psalms—for instance the fifteen "songs of degrees" (Psalms 120-134). The number fifteen corresponds with the number of years that were added to Hezekiah's life. He seems to have written ten of the fifteen himself. The number ten corresponds with the number of degrees that the shadow of the sun went backward on the sundial of Ahaz (2 Kings 20:1-11). Among the other five Psalms were one by Solomon (127, in the very center of the fifteen) and four by David (122, 124, 131, 133).[1] Hezekiah's additions to the Bible were made under the direction of the Holy Spirit.

The phrase "the men of Hezekiah" (Proverbs 25:1) seems to refer to a special guild of scribes employed by the king to edit, copy, and arrange various Old Testament books. Many human hands were at work in the gradual compilation of the sacred text, but one divine hand was in control. Here a book was written; there a Psalm was composed. Here a piece of divine history was recorded; there a burst of prophecy was inspired. Here a new piece of legislation was mandated; there a new letter was written or a collection of wise sayings was added. Thus the Word of God expanded. And all the while the hand of God was controlling the human hands that penned the words. As a result the original, finished, autographed documents were perfect and complete, inerrant and inspired, right down to every jot and tittle—just as Jesus said (Matthew 5:18). The Bible grew under the hand of the same God who makes all living things grow.

The people who wrote the Bible came from various walks of life. They were separated from one another by hundreds of miles and hundreds of years. All kinds of literary styles and historical, cultural, and geographical backgrounds are reflected in the pages of Scripture. Yet the Bible is not a miscellaneous assortment of occidental and oriental beliefs; it is an organic whole. Any single part of the Bible can only be properly explained in reference to the Bible as a whole—just as the role of any single part of the human body can only be properly explained in reference to the body as a whole.

The process by which each part of the Bible came to be included in the whole was not haphazard, but long, slow, and painstaking. The Holy Spirit superintended the compilation as directly and as actively as He inspired the writing of each part. By the time of Christ the various books that make up our Old Testament had already been gathered into a single collection. The Lord Jesus, who was God manifested in the flesh, stamped the finished product with His unique imprimatur. He referred to the Law, the Prophets, and the Writings as divinely authoritative and canonical.

As custodians of the Old Testament, the Jews were meticulous. Indeed they were virtually superstitious in their veneration of the sacred text. The Masoretes for instance invented a system to safeguard against scribal errors: they counted the number of times each letter of the alphabet occurred in each book of the Old Testament; they figured out the middle letter of the Torah and the middle letter of the entire Hebrew Bible; they used memory devices that stimulated quick recall of Biblical facts. When a copy of the Scriptures was too old and worn for further use, the Masoretes retired it and stored it in a special room attached to the synagogue. The storage room was called a *genizah,* which literally means "a hiding place." Eventually the old copy was given an honorable burial.

Moving on to Proverbs 25:2, we read of *a royal exercise:* "It is the glory of God to conceal a thing: but the honour of kings is to search out a matter." A wise king encourages learning, backs exploration, helps finance research, and supports scientific discovery.

We live in a complex universe. The more we know, the less we know. The field of medicine provides an example. A doctor who was an expert on diabetes said to a group of medical men he was addressing at a convention some years ago, that in spite of all the research he and others had done, they really knew little about the disease. He confessed to his colleagues, "Every time I get the answer to one question I have about this disease, it only raises another hundred questions to which I do not have the answer." When he sat down, the chairman thanked his learned colleague for "casting so much darkness on the subject." God conceals; man seeks out the answers.

God conceals the secrets of the atom, and man seeks them out. We know that the center of the atom is made up of positively charged protons. But according to Coulomb's law, simply stated, like charges repel. This law can be easily demonstrated by trying to bring together the positive poles of two magnets. Since they always push apart, it seems that the center of the atom should disintegrate—but it doesn't. For many years scientists referred to the force that holds the center of the atom together as unknown and mysterious. Physicists are on the track of that force now, but it took a great deal of research just to discover some clues.

The greatest of all the mysteries that God has concealed is the mystery of life itself. In seeking out the answers, man has discovered that each human body contains more than a million million (1,000,000,000,000) cells; that each living cell contains as many as two hundred trillion tiny groups of atoms called molecules; that the nucleus of each cell is less than four-thousandths of an inch in diameter; and that each cell's components are enclosed in a membrane only one-half of a millionth of an inch thick. Man has explored the master plan—that is, the code of life or blueprint carried by DNA. He has probed deeper and discovered chromosomes and genes. He has learned that genes contain instructions for making the particular kinds of protein that are the building blocks of life. He has even learned how to make artificial protein, manage genetic engineering, clone, and mutate life. Man has discovered much, but thousands of questions remain unanswered.

God conceals; man seeks out the answers. This premise is as true for us as it was for Solomon's contemporaries, although we now have access to information that would have made their minds whirl.

### b. Some Are Wily (25:3)

"The heaven for height, and the earth for depth, and the heart of kings is unsearchable." Just as man cannot ascend to the highest height of the heavens nor descend to the deepest depth in the core of the earth, he cannot figure out the heart of a king.

The heart of anyone is unfathomable. Of all the complexities in the universe, nothing is more complex than a human being's mind or motives. Just when we think we have someone figured out, he does something quite out of character; unexpectedly revealing another side of his complex personality, he completely destroys the neat little model we have built.

The heart is complex—and it is also deceitful. Jeremiah 17:9-10 says, "The heart is deceitful above all things, and desperately wicked: who can know it? I the Lord search the heart, I try the reins [thoughts and affections], even to give every man according to his ways, and according to the fruit of his doings." In other words, only God can read the heart and understand its ways.

Who would have thought that Noah would get drunk? Who would have thought that Abraham, having lied about his wife and disgraced himself in Egypt, would turn around and do the same thing all over again in Gerar? Who would have thought that Moses, the man of God who led Israel out of Egypt, would be locked out of Canaan for losing his temper and saying foolish things? Who would have thought that Aaron, chosen by God to be Israel's first high priest, would make the golden calf? Who would have thought that Miriam, the sweet singer of Israel and Moses' dear sister, would have such a sour and acid tongue that God would decide to turn her into a leper for seven days?

If the heart of an ordinary person is unsearchable, how unfathomable must be the heart of a king whose wealth and power tend to make him completely unpredictable! A king can change in a moment from smiles to scowls. His petted and pampered favorite of today may be the prisoner under sentence of death tomorrow.

Who would have thought that King David—famous for his spirituality, tender conscience, justice, and sense of fair play—would seduce another man's wife, murder her husband, and play the hypocrite before his people?

Who would have thought that King Solomon—who received wisdom as a gift from God and was renowned for that wisdom around the world—would be so foolish as to make an Egyptian woman his queen? Who would have thought that he would marry a legion of pagan women, tolerate their idolatries, and grovel at the feet of their graven images? Who would have thought that Solomon would imagine that he could prevent God's judgment from falling by murdering Jeroboam (1 Kings 11:40)?

"The heart of kings is unsearchable" indeed. We find another illustration of this proverb in the story of the Zulu emperor Chaka in Sir Henry Rider Haggard's *Nada the Lily.* Chaka had the military genius of Napoleon and the blood lust of Nero. Like Nero, Chaka murdered his mother. Often he killed just for the enjoyment of seeing people die. Like a monstrous black widow spider, he had no mercy. No one was safe. Chaka killed every child born to him to make sure that he would not raise a possible rival for the throne. His brothers lived in mortal fear.

Haggard began *Nada the Lily* with some words of explanation:

> The writer of this romance has been encouraged to his task by a purpose somewhat beyond that of setting out a wild tale of savage life. When he was yet a lad,—now some seventeen years ago,—fortune took him to South Africa. There he was thrown in with men who, for thirty or forty years, had been intimately acquainted with the Zulu people, with their history, their heroes, and their customs. From these he heard many tales and traditions, some of which, perhaps, are rarely told nowadays, and in time to come may cease to be told altogether. Then the Zulus were still a nation; now that nation has been destroyed, and the chief aim of its white rulers is to root out the warlike spirit for which it was remarkable, and to replace it by a spirit of peaceful progress. The Zulu military organisation, perhaps the most wonderful that the world has seen, is already a thing of the past; it perished at Ulundi. It was Chaka who invented that organisation, building it up from the smallest beginnings. When he appeared at the commencement of this century, it was as the ruler of a single small tribe; when he fell, in the year 1828, beneath the assegais of his brothers, Umhlangana and Dingaan, and of his servant, Mopo or Umbopo, as he is called also, all south-eastern Africa was at his feet, and in his march to power he had slaughtered more than a million human beings.

Haggard told the story of Chaka through the lips of Mopo, one of the king's chief counselors. Mopo tells us that after Chaka murdered his mother, he became ever more wicked and cruel. And Mopo gives us this illustration:

> Eight-and-twenty days went by, my father, and on the nine-and-twentieth it befell that Chaka, having dreamed a dream in his troubled sleep, summoned before him certain women of the kraal, to the number of a hundred or more. Some of these were his women, whom he named his "sisters," and some were maidens not yet given in marriage; but all were young and fair. Now what this dream of Chaka's may have been I do not know, or have forgotten, for in those days he dreamed many dreams, and all his dreams led to one end, the death of men. He sat in front of his hut scowling, and I was with him. To the left of him were gathered the girls and women, and their knees were weak with fear. One by one they were led before him, and stood

> before him with bowed heads. Then he would bid them be of good cheer, and speak softly to them, and in the end would ask them this question, "Hast thou, my sister, a cat in thy hut?"
>
> Now, some would say that they had a cat, and some would say that they had none, and some would stand still and make no answer, being dumb with fear. But, whatever they said, the end was the same, for the king would sigh gently and say: "Fare thee well, my sister; it is unfortunate for thee that there is a cat in thy hut," or "that there is no cat in thy hut," or "that thou canst not tell me whether there be a cat in thy hut or no."
>
> Then the woman would be taken by the slayers, dragged without the kraal, and their end was swift. So it went on for the most part of that day, till sixty-and-two women and girls had been slaughtered. But at last a maiden was brought before the king, and to this one her snake had given a ready wit; for when Chaka asked her whether or no there was a cat in her hut, she answered, saying that she did not know, "but that there was a half a cat upon her," and she pointed to a cat's-skin which was bound about her loins.
>
> Then the king laughed, and clapped his hands, saying that at length his dream was answered; and he killed no more that day.

Then Mopo tells the story that illustrates the unpredictability of a king's heart:

> When we had sat a little while in the kraal, certain men came in bearing cranes' feathers, which the king had sent them to gather a month's journey from the kraal Duguza, and they were admitted before the king. These men had been away long upon their errand, and Chaka was angry with them. Now the leader of the men was an old captain of Chaka's, who had fought under him in many battles, but whose service was done, because his right hand had been shorn away by the blow of an axe. He was a great man and very brave.
>
> Chaka asked the man why he had been so long in finding the feathers, and he answered that the birds had flown from that part of the country whither he was sent, and he must wait there till they returned, that he might snare them.
>
> "Thou shouldst have followed the cranes, yes, if they flew through the sunset, thou disobedient dog!" said the king. "Let him be taken away, and all those who were with him."
>
> Now some of the men prayed a little for mercy, but the

captain did but salute the king, calling him "Father," and craving a boon before he died.

"What wouldst thou?" asked Chaka.

"My father," said the man, "I would ask thee two things. I have fought many times at thy side in battle while we both were young; nor did I ever turn my back upon the foe. The blow that shore the hand from off this arm was aimed at thy head, O King; I stayed it with my naked arm. It is nothing; at thy will I live, and at thy will I die. Who am I that I should question the word of the king? Yet I would ask this, that thou wilt withdraw the kaross from about thee, O King, that for the last time my eyes may feast themselves upon the body of him whom, above all men, I love."

"Thou art long-winded," said the king, "what more?"

"This, my father, that I may bid farewell to my son; he is a little child, so high, O King," and he held his hand above his knee.

"Thy first boon is granted," said the king, slipping the kaross from his shoulders and showing the great breast beneath. "For the second it shall be granted also, for I will not willingly divide the father and the son. Bring the boy here; thou shalt bid him farewell, then thou shalt slay him with thine own hand ere thou thyself art slain; it will be good sport to see."

Now the man turned grey beneath the blackness of his skin, and trembled a little as he murmured, "The king's will is the will of his servant; let the child be brought."

But I looked at Chaka and saw that the tears were running down his face, and that he only spoke thus to try the captain who loved him to the last.

"Let the man go," said the king, "him and those with him."

So they went glad at heart and praising the king.

I have told you this, my father, though it has not to do with my story, because then, and only then, did I ever see Chaka show mercy to one whom he had doomed to die.[2]

### c. Some Are Wicked (25:4-5)

Since power corrupts, it is important for a king to guard well the approaches to his throne and to his thoughts. Proverbs 25:4 tells *how God searches motives:* "Take away the dross from the silver, and there shall come forth a vessel for the finer." And 25:5 tells *how God stabilizes monarchs:* "Take away the wicked from before the king, and his throne shall be established in righteousness."

The impurities found in silver ore have to be removed before it yields the bright shining metal that can be used to make vessels fit for the table of a king. The ore has to be heated in a crucible and transformed into a molten state so that the dross can rise to the surface and be skimmed off. The process is repeated again and again. It is slow, but it is sure.

Likewise a king must bring to bear all the white-hot heat of the throne to force the lawless elements in society to rise to the surface so that they can be removed from the place where they harm and degrade society. It should be noted here that the word translated "the wicked" in Proverbs 25:5 can also be rendered "the lawless one."

A great wave of lawlessness swept over the western world in the 1960s. It was orchestrated by the political left and international forces that were dedicated to the downfall of the free world in the interests of Soviet communism. Soviets provided financial aid and every encouragement. The movement was oriented toward the drug culture and inspired by a new music form that was dedicated to ridiculing and removing the establishment and everything that was moral, decent, normal, and Christian. Lyrics that were drilled into the minds and hearts of the youth, scoffed at patriotism and authority and glorified rebellion, Satan, drugs, and sexual immorality.

Once launched upon the world, this wave of lawlessness gathered force. The movement claimed to be antiwar and pro-civil rights. It organized large-scale marches and demonstrations. Its devotees burned the American flag and fought the police. Its apostles were the hippies who sported unkempt beards and long uncombed hair and reveled in being dirty, wearing disgusting clothes, and expressing themselves in obscenities.

Countless thousands of youths translated ordinary teenage rebellion into antiestablishment lawlessness. Many left good homes and flocked to faraway cities where they lived in dirty communes, smoked pot, and graduated to hard drugs. These young people lived in open immorality, promoted decadent sex proclivities, organized rock concerts, and held massive drug-fests. They defied the authorities, gathered to protest whatever they disliked, embraced oriental cultic religions, cheered communism, and hated their native land.

In America (and elsewhere) a stunned establishment failed to act promptly and decisively. As a result, the forces of decency, law and order, morality, and Christianity met opposition at every turn. The lawless ones captured the goodwill of a left-leaning media, and liberal sentiments prevailed in the universities, courts, and

Congress. There was neither the conviction nor the courage to do anything to stem the ever-rising tide of lawlessness in society.

The dross was not removed from the silver. The wicked were not dealt with by Congress and the courts. As a result, disrespect for law and order steadily grew and public morals steadily declined. Patriotism, strong convictions about old-fashioned virtues, the Judeo-Christian ethic, and the very foundations of Western civilization were all eroded.

Having sown the wind, our culture is now reaping the whirlwind. We have abortion on demand. We have marching sodomites demanding and getting more and more concessions from society. We have pornography channeled into millions of homes via cable television. We have epidemic divorce, a breakdown in morality, a weakened educational system, gang warfare in our big cities, upsurges in crime, and a horrendous drug problem. We have legislators who are unabashed by charges of sodomy, drunkenness, bribery, and corruption. We have government officials who are guilty of scandals in their private lives. At one time such scandals would have guaranteed censure, disgrace, and dismissal from office; now the guilty officials often simply run for re-election when their terms expire and get voted back into office.

Nothing short of a genuine, nationwide, life-transforming, society-cleansing, God-enthroning, Christ-exalting, Holy Ghost revival can now stem the tide. That is the only kind of fire that can "take away the wicked from before the king." Whether or not such a revival will take place remains to be seen. It is more likely that instead of *revival,* we will experience *rapture.* The church will be gone and *ruin* will engulf the globe. Then "the lawless one" will bring the rising storm of lawlessness to its consummation.

d. Some Are Wary (25:6-7)

Since members of a royal family are trained to keep distance between themselves and commoners, Solomon gave a word of advice to those whose social climbing brings them within notice of the throne: "Put not forth thyself in the presence of the king, and stand not in the place of great men" (Proverbs 25:6). In other words, the king's favor cannot be taken for granted, *so beware of self-assertion.* Solomon added, "Better it is that it be said unto thee, Come up hither; than that thou shouldest be put lower in the presence of the prince whom thine eyes have seen" (25:7). In other words, the king's favor cannot be taken for granted, *so beware of false assumption.*

The gap between the throne and the throng is illustrated in

Jeffery Farnol's novel *The Amateur Gentleman.* Farnol's hero is Barnabas Barty, the son of an innkeeper. The story is set in England in the days when the British aristocracy was the richest, most powerful, and most exclusive club in the world. Blood, birth, and breeding were all that mattered. Those not born into the nobility stood no chance of acceptance. Thus Barnabas stood little chance of being admitted into that closed society even though he was the sudden heir of fabulous wealth. His father, John Barty, the unbeaten heavyweight boxing champion of England, tried to persuade his son not even to try to associate with the aristocrats.

But Barnabas was undaunted. He adopted his mother's name of Beverley, which he considered to be more euphonious than Barty, and sallied forth on his adventures. Barnabas was young, rich, and personable and he made friends with some of the younger sprigs of the nobility. Concealing his humble origins, he won their acceptance.

Barnabas became more well-known when he bought and tamed a savage horse that had just thrown a member of the nobility. Later he won a critical and highly publicized steeplechase and a banquet attended by royalty was held in his honor. The blue blood of England gathered to toast its new idol. When Barnabas arrived, he was given the seat of honor. Farnol described the scene:

> Never had White's, that historic club, gathered beneath its roof a more distinguished company; dukes, royal and otherwise, elbow each other on the stairs; earls and marquises sit cheek by jowl; viscounts and baronets exchange snuff-boxes in corners, but one and all take due and reverent heed of the flattened revers and the innovation of the riband.
>
> Yes, White's is full to overflowing for, to-night, half the Fashionable World is here, that is to say, the masculine half; beaux and wits; bucks and Corinthians; dandies and macaronis; all are here and, each and every, with the fixed and unshakable purpose of eating and drinking to the glory and honor of Barnabas Beverley, Esquire....
>
> Forthwith the banquet begins and the air hums with talk and laughter punctuated by the popping of corks; waiters hurry to and fro, dishes come and dishes vanish, and ever the laughter grows, and the buzz of talk swells louder.

Barnabas was toasted and loudly lauded in speech after speech until at last he rose to reply. Farnol continued:

> And as Barnabas stands there, an elegant figure, tall and

> graceful, all eyes may behold again the excellent fit of that wonderful coat, its dashing cut and flattened revers, while all ears await his words. But, or ever he can speak, upon this silence is heard the tread of heavy feet beyond the door and Barnabas glances there...but the feet have stopped and...he begins:
>
> "My Lords and gentlemen! So much am I conscious of the profound honor you do me, that I find it difficult to express my ——"
>
> But here again a disturbance is heard at the door—a shuffle of feet and the mutter of voices, and he pauses...whereat his auditors cry angrily for "silence!" which being duly accorded, he begins again:
>
> "Indeed, gentlemen, I fear no words of mine, however eloquent, can sufficiently express to you all my ——"
>
> "Oh, Barnabas," cries a deep voice; "yes, it *is* Barnabas!" Even as the words are uttered, the group of protesting waiters in the doorway are swept aside by a mighty arm, and a figure strides into the banqueting-room, a handsome figure, despite its country habiliments, a commanding figure by reason of its stature and great spread of shoulder, and John Barty stands there, blinking in the light of the many candles.

The innkeeper-prizefighter father of Barnabas had arrived at the banquet, having been sent there by an enemy of Barnabas for the purpose of exposing Barnabas as an impostor. Most of the noble guests at the banquet thought the interruption was a joke. Some thought the commoner was trying to gate-crash the banquet. Several lords of the sporting type were for pitching the intruder down the stairs. Others wanted to take him on with bare fists. In the meantime John Barty stood there bewildered. Then as the Marquis stepped forward to challenge the intruder, Barnabas regained his manhood. Farnol continued his description of the debacle:

> But as he [the Marquis] advanced, Barnabas lifted his head and staying him with a gesture, turned and beheld his father standing alone, the centre of an angry circle. And John Barty's eyes were wide and troubled, and his usually ruddy cheek showed pale, though with something more than fear as, glancing slowly round the ring of threatening figures that hemmed him in, he beheld the white, stricken face of his son. And, seeing it, John Barty groaned, and so took a step towards the door; but no man moved to give him way.
>
> "A—a mistake, gentlemen," he muttered, "I—I'll go!" Then,

> even as the stammering words were uttered, Barnabas strode forward into the circle and, slipping a hand within his father's nerveless arm, looked round upon the company, pale of cheek, but with head carried high.
>
> "My Lords!" said he, "gentlemen! I have the honor—to introduce to you—John Barty, sometime known as 'Glorious John'—ex-champion of England and—landlord of the 'Coursing Hound' inn—my father!"
>
> A moment of silence! A stillness so profound that it seemed no man drew breath; a long, long moment wherein Barnabas felt himself a target for all eyes—eyes wherein he thought to see amazement that changed into dismay which, in turn, gave place to an ever-growing scorn of him. Therefore he turned his back upon them all and, coming to the great window, stood there staring blindly into the dark street.
>
> "Oh, Barnabas!" he heard his father saying, though as from a long way off, "Barnabas, lad, I—I—Oh, Barnabas—they're going! They're leaving you, and—it's all my fault, lad! Oh, Barnabas,—what have I done! It's my fault, lad—all my fault. But I heard you was sick, Barnabas, and like to die—ill, and calling for me,—for your father, Barnabas. And now—Oh, my lad! my lad!—what have I done?"
>
> "Never blame yourself, father, it—wasn't your fault," said Barnabas with twitching lips, for from the great room behind him came the clatter of chairs, the tread of feet, with voices and stifled laughter that grew fainter and fainter, yet left a sting behind.[3]

Only two of the noble company remained behind, both of them close personal friends of Barnabas. As for the rest, they believed that they had taught the commoner his place. How Barnabas won his way back, on different terms, is the rest of the story.

The gap between the throne and the throng can rarely be bridged from below, although occasionally it has been bridged from above. In Luke 14:1-11 Christ applied Proverbs 25:6-7 to the Pharisees and advised them to "sit down in the lowest room" at a wedding so that the host could say, "Friend, go up higher."

In Christ the greatest gulf of all has been spanned—the gulf between the highest pinnacle of Heaven and the guilty sinner in his squalor, the gulf between the holiness of God and the vileness of the lost. The Lord Jesus says to the lost, "Come up higher!" That invitation is surely the greatest ever to fall on the ears of a fallen sinner of Adam's ruined race.

### 2. Beware of Sinners (25:8–26:12)

#### a. Look Well to Your Fellows (25:8-20)

##### (1) Those Who Cause Trouble (25:8-10)

###### (a) Being Unable to Control Their Tempers (25:8)

"Go not forth hastily to strive, lest thou know not what to do in the end thereof, when thy neighbour hath put thee to shame." Solomon was saying that we should beware of picking quarrels lest we pick one too many.

This principle is illustrated again and again in that popular genre of fiction known as the western. Few westerns have enjoyed greater popularity than *Shane* by Jack Schaefer. The background of the story is the long-running feud between the cattlemen (who wanted the range left open so their cattle could roam) and the settlers (who wanted to fence the land in for their farms).

The setting was Wyoming. The year was 1889. Fighting to survive, the farmers were already locked in a life-and-death struggle against the cattle kings. News came to a peaceful valley, which had become home to a dozen farms, that Luke Fletcher was back and that he wanted to get rid of the farms. He would buy them for what he considered a fair price—or else. So the farmers had a meeting. A few of them wanted to sell out. The tougher farmers, led by Joe Starrett, refused to be bullied.

Soon mysterious fires broke out. Barns went up in smoke; flames destroyed farmhouses. Then the shooting started. Worse, the Fletcher gang hired a sharpshooting braggart, Stark Wilson, to pick quarrels with the farmers, one by one, as they rode into town for supplies. Like the man Solomon had in mind, Wilson would pick a fight with anyone. He was a confident killer, able to shoot equally well with either hand. The quarrels always ended the same way: the gun-toting tough fought a duel with the farmer and killed him. Fear gripped the settlers. They were terrorized by that swaggering, cold-eyed, broad-shouldered stranger with two big businesslike .45s in his low-slung holsters.

Into the valley and into the quarreling rode Shane. He drew rein at Starrett's homestead and asked for water. Shane stayed for supper and agreed to stay longer and do some chores. He was dusty and trail-worn, just a drifter it seemed, but he was a quiet, reserved kind of man who exuded a sense of power. Shane made the settlers' problem his own when Fletcher and his hired gunman rode over to the Starrett homestead and gave the farmer an ultimatum: accept his final cash offer by the next day or face his hired gunman the next time he rode into town.

The showdown came in the town saloon that night. It was not Starrett who had come to deal with Fletcher and his hired gun. It was Shane. The men in the saloon froze as Shane entered.

"Where's Fletcher?" Shane demanded. His eyes took in every face, every detail, every corner where a Fletcher hand might be lurking with a gun. "Where's Fletcher?" he demanded again.

"Where's Starrett?" The answer to Shane's question came in the form of a question. The speaker, Stark Wilson, exuded pride and arrogance. He was sure of himself. He felt in charge. *This farmhand is an easy mark,* he thought. But Wilson had finally met his match. Shane goaded him and suddenly shots rang out. Wilson's right arm hung useless and he reached for his other gun with his left hand. Shane's next bullet took him in the chest and the duel ended. It was the end of the Fletcher gang and the end of the menace. Shane rode away into the night, leaving only a wondering memory behind.[4]

Schaefer's story is a rattling good yarn and it makes Solomon's point: the quarrelsome man meets his match in the end.

(b) Being Unable to Control Their Tongues (25:9-10)

Since trouble is caused when people are unable to control their tongues, Solomon offered us some sound advice. He said that *we should resist temptation if we can:* "Debate thy cause with thy neighbour himself; and discover not a secret to another" (Proverbs 25:9).

A man was urged by his friends to share some spicy piece of gossip. He said to them, "Can you keep a secret?" They assured him they could. "So can I," he said, and refused to say any more. We smile at his wise words.

Solomon's advice was that when we have a disagreement with a neighbor, we should go to him, sit down with him, and try to resolve the problem with him. Involving a third party only enlarges the problem and may cause the disagreement to degenerate into a feud.

Joseph followed this principle in his dealings with his brothers when they came to Egypt—even though their dealings with him had been scurrilous. Their problem was jealousy. Joseph was the firstborn of Rachel and therefore the firstborn of Jacob's heart.

When Joseph was a teenager he wore a young chieftain's coat, a clear advertisement of Jacob's intention to set him over his brothers. Joseph told his brothers his dreams, which advertised God's intention to set him even higher. The brothers resented Joseph's morals and his pure life. They resented his courage, integrity, and honesty. They could not speak peaceably to him, but we can imagine that they often spoke about him to each other, feeding the deep resentment they harbored.

The jealousy and resentment all spilled out at Dothan. When his brothers saw Joseph coming toward them, they decided to get rid of him once and for all. Their plan was to kill him, but they settled for selling him into slavery.

Years passed and God kept His word. Joseph became the grand vizier of Egypt, second in power only to the pharaoh. Then the famine came—and the family came. Joseph recognized his brothers at once, but they did not recognize him because he looked so much like the other great lords of Egypt. After he engineered circumstances so that at last he had his brothers in his power, he realized the time had come to reveal himself. Would the guilty brothers now face the retribution they deserved for all the wrongs they had committed against Joseph, or would they experience godlike forgiveness?

What did Joseph do? Did he summon the palace guards? Did he call for the jailer? Did he denounce these men before the pharaoh? No! As far as Joseph was concerned, the terrible secrets would remain family secrets. "Cause every man to go out from me," he said. The Holy Spirit added: "And there stood no man with him, while Joseph made himself known unto his brethren" (Genesis 45:1).

"I am Joseph," he said. They were stunned into silence. "I am Joseph," he said again, "your brother, whom ye sold into Egypt." As he explained further he added, "Ye sold...God did send." They remained silent and he talked to them quietly, graciously, and reassuringly. He embraced his younger brother Benjamin then each of the others. "After that," we read, "his brethren talked with him." (See Genesis 45:3-15.)

Thus Joseph won his brothers over. Had he acted otherwise, the results would have been far different. There is no knowing what an angry, resentful, and vengeful Joseph might have done. There is no knowing what ten desperate, frightened men might have done. The whole Bible story might have ended then and there. Instead Joseph brought his cause to his brothers and discovered not his secret to another.

We may be sorely tempted to cause trouble with our tongues. But Solomon advised us that we should resist temptation if we can, for *we will reap trouble if we can't:* "Lest he that heareth it put thee to shame, and thine infamy turn not away" (Proverbs 25:10). The word translated "shame" here can carry the meaning of disgrace, so

Solomon was saying that if we enlarge a quarrel and involve other people, we might come out looking worse than our neighbor. We may lose a great deal of credit with others if we do not control our tongues. A stigma that can never be erased might be attached to our names.

My dad used to tell a story about a man he knew who ruined his reputation by quarreling in public with another believer at the Lord's table. In that church the Lord's supper was celebrated weekly and brothers in Christ were free to take part by leading in prayer, suggesting an appropriate hymn, or ministering from the Scriptures. My father's friend had been a missionary in a difficult country and he had the reputation of being a godly man. He could give extraordinary accounts of specific and miraculous answers to prayer. He was a published author and translator, a popular preacher, and a keen-minded apologist. But he held an odd view on the rapture of the church and it was that view which brought him into disagreement with his brethren. For the most part, however, he held this view in check and his brethren were willing to tolerate this one aberration for the sake of his other good teaching.

As the man grew older he became increasingly obsessed with his deviant view and it became increasingly prominent in his preaching. Invitations to preach dwindled, but he still had one platform he could not be denied: the Lord's table in his own home church. Another brother in his church, however, greatly objected to the man's views and when the man injected these views into comments during the Lord's supper, the other brother would contradict him. The elders tried to talk to the former missionary privately, but he was too clever for them. He had juggled his favorite texts so often that he could outwit them in debate. So the elders tried to talk to the other brother. He insisted that the former missionary was out of order—he was in error and was abusing his right to speak at the Lord's table by introducing his erroneous views there. The wrangling continued and in the end the elders silenced both men; they were forbidden to participate audibly at the Lord's table. Thus a man who had once been an honored servant of the Lord was disgraced because he did not know how and when to hold his tongue.

(2) Those with Convincing Talk (25:11-15)

(a) Fit Words (25:11-12)

After writing about how the tongue can be used to cause trouble, Solomon wrote about how the tongue can be used to speak fitting words. First he drew *the picture:* "A word fitly spoken is like apples of gold in pictures of silver. As an earring of gold, and an ornament of fine gold" (Proverbs 24:11-12a). Then he made *the point:* "So is a wise reprover upon an obedient ear" (25:12b).

An amusing story is told about a budding artist who aspired to be a great and famous painter. Unfortunately his talent did not rise to greatness. He produced a succession of poor paintings on indifferent themes. Critics sneered at his work, his pictures remained unsold, and he lived in poverty.

Out of compassion a wealthy friend bought one of his paintings, poor as it was, and tried to overcome its limitations by having it framed in an expensive, ornate, gold-inlaid, hand-wrought frame. He hung the picture in one of the lesser-used rooms of his mansion. Shortly afterward a thief broke into the mansion, but the burglar alarm went off before he could steal very much.

The rich man told his painter friend what happened. "Do you remember that picture I bought from you a few weeks ago? That was the only thing the thief was able to lay his hands on before the alarm sounded."

"Is that so?" said the delighted artist, thinking that the publicity would be good for his reputation.

"Yes!" said his friend, "but he tore it out of the frame."

"My fortune's made!" exclaimed the painter, thinking of the impact this sensational piece of news would have in artistic circles. *Well,* he thought, *the reviewers never appreciated me. Now maybe they will.* Rosy dreams filled his vision. He could see the headlines: UNKNOWN ARTIST'S PICTURE STOLEN FROM RICH MAN'S HOME. EXPENSIVE FRAME DISCARDED BY DISCERNING THIEF.

A moment later the painter's bubble was burst. His rich friend continued, "Yes, he tore the picture out of the frame, threw it into a corner of the room, and made off with the frame!" The frame was not appropriate for the picture.

"Apples of gold in pictures of silver," rhapsodized Solomon, who in spite of his faults certainly had an eye for beauty. He probably was referring, judging from the context, not to a framed picture, but to expensive jewelry—sculptured golden fruit on silver trays. Pointing to the rarity of the golden apples and the appropriateness of their setting, Solomon intended to point to the rarity of a fitting word being spoken at an appropriate time.

Most people can appreciate an appropriate verbal response to a situation, whether the words convey an insult or a compliment. George Bernard Shaw, the English playwright, entertained a spiteful dislike for Winston Churchill. On one occasion Shaw offered the great prime minister a gratuitous insult. He sent Churchill two tickets to the opening night of one of his plays. The tickets were accompanied by a note that read, "Come and bring a friend—if you have one." Churchill acknowledged the tickets and the note with these words: "Thank you for the tickets to the opening night's performance of your new play. I shall come the second night—if there is one."

Many appropriate responses have been given on the spur of the moment. Surely the greatest example is the one recorded in Matthew 22:15-22. The Herodians, joining forces with the Pharisees, set a trap for Jesus. They "took counsel how they might entangle him in his talk," wrote Matthew. First they offered a word or two of flattery and then they sprung their trap. "Tell us," they said, "Is it lawful to give tribute unto Caesar, or not?" (It was a trick question—like "Have you stopped beating your wife yet?") If Jesus said yes, He would be in trouble with the Sanhedrin; if He said no, He would be in trouble with the caesar.

His answer has gone down in history as a classic. Probably nobody appreciated it more than Matthew, a former tax collector for the hated Roman government and a despised publican. "Show me the tribute money," Jesus said. When they brought Him a penny, He asked, "Whose is this image and superscription?"

Jesus' opponents answered, "Caesar's."

Then the Lord said, "Render therefore unto Caesar the things which are Caesar's; and unto God the things that are God's." Christ's words were "fitly spoken" indeed!

Matthew added, "When they had heard these words, they marvelled, and left him, and went their way".

To make the picture perfect, the words of the "wise reprover" must fall upon "an obedient [attentive] ear." The "obedient ear" receives the words fitly spoken and wears them as an ornament of value and beauty, to be prized and exhibited.

When Paul reproved Peter, Peter had an attentive ear. It would be hard to find two men who were more opposite. Peter was a fisherman; Paul was a polished scholar. Peter was a Galilean and as such was despised by the sophisticated Jerusalem Jews; Paul, a Roman citizen and a well-educated, cosmopolitan, Hellenist Jew from a well-to-do family, was equally at home in the synagogue or the senate. Peter was impulsive; Paul was impressive. Peter had known Christ according to the flesh (indeed it is likely that Peter's Capernaum home had been Christ's home for months on end); Paul had only known Jesus as the Lord from Heaven. Peter was intimidated by James; James felt threatened by Paul. Peter was the apostle to the narrow, exclusive Jewish world centered in Jerusalem; Paul was the apostle to the Gentiles, a missionary to the regions beyond. Peter was often inhibited by the Judaism in which he had been raised; Paul had jettisoned Judaism in Arabia, soon after he was saved.

The confrontation between the two came when Peter visited the dynamic, fully integrated church at Antioch, where Paul and Barnabas had ministered mightily among both Jews and Gentiles. Peter had a grand time. He was lionized, being invited here, there, and everywhere. He accepted requests to speak at this service and to come to that home. Then some of James' crowd arrived in town. Cowed by these visitors from Jerusalem, Peter refused to accept any more invitations from the Gentiles or to mingle with them. The James faction even intimidated Barnabas.

When Paul learned what had happened, he exploded! He challenged Peter in front of the Gentile believers who had been offended by his "dissimulation" (Galatians 2:13; the Greek word translated "dissimulation" is *hupokrisis,* which means "hypocrisy"). "I withstood him to the face," Paul later recounted. "I said unto Peter before them all, If thou, being a Jew, livest after the manner of Gentiles, and not as do the Jews, why compellest thou the Gentiles to live as do the Jews?" (2:11,14).

Paul was a "wise reprover" and Peter had an "obedient ear." Later Peter wrote warmly of Paul as one who confirmed his own teaching: "Even as our beloved brother Paul also according to the wisdom given unto him hath written unto you; As also in all his epistles, speaking in them of these things; in which are some things hard to be understood" (2 Peter 3:15-16). Solomon would have approved of them both.

(b) Faithful Words (25:13)

"As the cold of snow in the time of harvest," wrote Solomon, "so is a faithful messenger to them that send him: for he refresheth the soul of his masters."

A man in the Roman empire, if he was wealthy enough, would often refresh the guests at his table with drinks iced by snow that was brought at enormous cost and great speed from distant snow-clad peaks. Perhaps Solomon did the same, for the snowy summit of mount Hermon was not that inaccessible. But such a refreshment must have been as rare as it would have been relished. In his proverb Solomon was likening a faithful messenger to ice-cold drinks brought to perspiring laborers in a harvest field!

To be a messenger charged with delivering a highly unpopular message to a powerful, despotic king could be a dangerous business, as the unfortunate Adoram discovered. When the ten northern tribes rallied to the banner of Jeroboam and rebelled against Rehoboam over the tax issue, Rehoboam tried to assert his authority. He sent Adoram, the detested chief of the Internal Revenue Service, to enforce Rehoboam's right to levy taxes on Jeroboam's supporters. First Kings 12:18 records the fate of the messenger: "King Rehoboam sent Adoram, who was over the tribute; and all Israel stoned him with stones, that he died." Rehoboam, afraid that he would be next, fled to the relative security of stone-walled Jerusalem.

God's prophets were rare, faithful messengers like the one praised in Solomon's proverb. Many faced extreme danger. Most were unpopular with those to whom they were sent. All discharged their commissions well. Some paid the high price of martyrdom.

Moses is one example. Armed with might and miracle, he stood before the haughty pharaoh of Egypt and demanded in the name of the Lord, "Let my people go!" Pharaoh sneered, "Who is the Lord?...I know not the Lord, neither will I let Israel go" (Exodus 5:1-2). In spite of this negative response, Moses remained adamant and determined.

Samuel is another example. He faithfully confronted the weak and disobedient Saul with this message: "Because thou hast rejected the word of the Lord, he hath also rejected thee from being king....The Lord hath rent the kingdom of Israel from thee this day, and hath given it to a neighbour of thine, that is better than thou" (1 Samuel 15:23,28).

After recovering from a bad start, the prophet Jonah stalked through the streets of sin-stained, bloodthirsty Nineveh and proclaimed this uncompromising message: "Yet forty days, and Nineveh shall be overthrown" (Jonah 3:4). If we had accosted Jonah on his way to Nineveh and asked whether he was afraid to preach in Nineveh, he would have told us that he had already been in enough trouble for *not* preaching in Nineveh!

Faithful Elijah, braving hundreds of false prophets who had been imported by Jezebel into Israel, challenged them to a showdown on mount Carmel. "The God that answereth by fire," he thundered, "let him be God." Then as the false prophets lashed themselves into a religious frenzy, cut themselves with knives and lances, danced around their altar, and cried aloud to Baal, Elijah mocked them. "Cry aloud," he jibed, "for he is a god; either he is talking, or he is pursuing, or he is in a journey, or peradventure he sleepeth, and must be awaked" (1 Kings 18:24, 27).

Jeremiah, the hated and persecuted Old Testament "man of sorrows," dared to confront evil King Jeconiah. The prophet contemptuously and significantly cut the king down to size by calling him "Coniah." Jeremiah then delivered the Lord's message: "Write ye this man childless, a man that shall not prosper in his days: for no man of his seed shall prosper, sitting upon the throne of David, and ruling any more in Judah" (Jeremiah 22:30).

Daniel was a faithful messenger in the banquet hall of the despicable and dissolute Belshazzar. Walking in, Daniel saw the evidence of the royal drunkard's contempt for the living God of Israel: the golden vessels stolen from the temple on mount Moriah had been desecrated and were strewn about. Daniel also saw disheveled guests and writing on the wall. Then he heard the king's offer: "Read that writing, Mr. Prophet, if you can," he said in effect, "and I'll make you third ruler in the kingdom." The fearless old prophet answered swiftly: "Keep your gifts, oh king," he said in effect. "There is no kingdom to rule." Then Daniel preached a sermon that must have made the king squirm and finally read the writing on the wall and interpreted the message to be one of doom. (See Daniel 5.)

Another of God's prophets was John the Baptist. He told the religious leaders of his day that they were a "generation of vipers" (Matthew 3:7) and dared to tell Herod that his liaison with Herodias was an affront to the laws of God (Matthew 14:1-12).

We think of all these examples of prophets who were faithful messengers. But above all we think of Jesus who poured out denunciation after denunciation into the ears of the scribes and Pharisees. Their resentment and rage defies description. By delivering His message He was signing His own death warrant (see Matthew 23).

(c) Forceful Words (25:14-15)

In Proverbs 25:14 Solomon turned his attention to *the person whose profession is empty:* "Whoso boasteth himself of a false gift is like clouds and wind without rain." The word translated "false" here means "pretended." The kind of person Solomon had in mind pretends to be someone he isn't, or claims to have skills, abilities, and insights he doesn't have, or makes promises he cannot keep. Such a man may bluff his way for a while, but in the end he will be exposed as a fraud. The apostates who will fill the pulpits and seminary classrooms in the last days fit into this category (Jude 4,14-15).

Zedekiah, the son of Chenaanah, is an example of a person who "boasteth himself of a false gift." A false prophet, Zedekiah was much favored by wicked King Ahab and came into prominence at the end of Ahab's reign. While Ahab reigned in Israel, Jehoshaphat reigned in Judah. Jehoshaphat, who seems to have had a fatal fascination with the evil King Ahab and the even more evil Queen Jezebel, took a trip to Samaria and made a fatal *military* alliance with Ahab. Jehoshaphat had already made a fatal *matrimonial* alliance with Israel's wicked royal family and later he made a fatal *maritime* alliance with them (2 Chronicles 18:1; 20:35-37).

The city of Ramoth-gilead (a Levitical city of refuge in the territory of Gad and once the home of the judge Jephthah) had fallen into the hands of Syria, so Ahab proposed to Jehoshaphat that Israel and Judah mount a joint expedition to recapture the city. King Jehoshaphat agreed readily, but was cautious enough to propose that they first ask the Lord for guidance. Ahab, on the other hand, proposed that they consult the four hundred false prophets he kept about him.

Knowing full well which side of their bread was buttered, the false prophets were unanimous in their advice: "Go up; for the Lord shall deliver it into the hand of the king," they said. Ahab was satisfied, but not Jehoshaphat. He asked, "Is there not here a prophet of the Lord besides, that we might enquire of him?" Ahab reluctantly acknowledged there was such a prophet: Micaiah the son of Imlah. Candidly enough Ahab added, "But I hate him; for he doth not prophesy good concerning me, but evil." (See 1 Kings 22:6-8.)

Ahab summoned Micaiah while the false prophets were still chanting their favorable auguries. Among them was Zedekiah, who made horns of iron and dramatically pushed with them as if he were a bull. "Thus saith the Lord," he said, "With these shalt thou push the Syrians, until thou have consumed them" (1 Kings 22:11).

Ahab's messenger turned to Micaiah and demanded in effect, "What do you say? And for once why don't you be agreeable and try to be positive?" If all Ahab wanted was a rubber-stamp endorsement of the false prophets' predictions, Micaiah was willing to oblige. "Go, and prosper: for the Lord shall deliver [Ramoth-gilead] into the hand of the king" he said (22:15). However, something about the look on his face or in the tone of his voice made it obvious, even to Ahab, that Micaiah was being sarcastic.

Then he burst out with the truth: "I saw all Israel scattered upon the hills, as sheep that have not a shepherd." With those words Micaiah pronounced the sentence of death on Ahab if he proceeded with his plans. Ahab pouted and said to Jehoshaphat, "Did I not tell thee that he would prophesy no good concerning me, but evil?" (22:17-18) Courageous Micaiah continued his prophecy:

> Hear thou therefore the word of the Lord: I saw the Lord sitting on his throne, and all the host of heaven standing by him on his right hand and on his left. And the Lord said, Who shall persuade Ahab, that he may go up and fall at Ramoth-gilead? And one said on this manner, and another said on that manner. And there came forth a spirit, and stood before the Lord, and said, I will persuade him. And the Lord said unto him, Wherewith? And he said, I will go forth, and I will be a lying spirit in the mouth of all his prophets. And he said, Thou shalt persuade him, and prevail also: go forth, and do so (22:19-22).

Then Micaiah made the pointed application, one that cost him dearly a few minutes later. He said, "Now therefore, behold, the Lord hath put a lying spirit in the mouth of all these thy prophets, and the Lord hath spoken evil concerning thee" (22:23).

This was more than that empty windbag Zedekiah could stand. He smote God's true prophet on the cheek and said, "Which way went the Spirit of the Lord from me to speak unto thee?" (22:24) Zedekiah put on a great show complete with iron horns and proud words, but he was like "clouds and wind without rain."

Micaiah looked Zedekiah in the eye and answered, "Behold, thou shalt see in that day, when thou shalt go into an inner chamber to hide thyself" (22:25).

Ahab did not know it, but his last day had come. He chose to believe his lying prophets, who were led by Zedekiah. Ahab summoned the guard and ordered: "Take Micaiah, and carry him back unto Amon the governor of the city, and to Joash the king's son; And say, Thus saith the king, Put this fellow in the prison, and feed him with bread of affliction and with water of affliction, until I come in peace" (22:26-27). If Ahab thought he had silenced the prophet of God, he was much mistaken. The indomitable Micaiah had one last parting shot: "If thou return at all in peace, the Lord hath not spoken by me" (22:28). Raising his voice so that everyone in the place—King Jehoshaphat, the four hundred false prophets, Zedekiah, the guard, the courtiers, the attendants—could hear, he called out, "Hearken, O people, every one of you." Within twenty-four hours everyone knew who was the true prophet and who was a mere windbag, an empty cloud without substance.

Providing a contrast to the person whose profession is empty, Solomon set before us *the person whose persuasion is effective:* "By long forbearing is a prince persuaded, and a soft tongue breaketh the bone" (Proverbs 25:15). This proverb means that no one will by being bossy persuade a king to act. Patience and self-control are needed, no matter how great the provocation.

An old fable describes what happened when the sun, the wind, and the frost got into an argument about which of them was the strongest. The frost said, "I can break the mountains and pulverize the most massive rocks. All men are afraid of me."

The wind said, "I am the master of the storm. I can flatten forests. I can pick up the waves of the sea and hurl them with hurricane force against the land. I can create tornadoes and plow paths through mighty cities."

The sun, insisting that he was the strongest, proposed a test. "Look at that man over there," he said. "Let's see which of us can get the coat off his back."

The frost tried. It dug its damp icy fingers into the fabric of the coat until every fiber was stiff and uncomfortable. The coat was nothing but a frozen lump of ice. The man shivered and although the coat was no longer warm, he pulled it closer to his body, hoping to thaw the garment out so he could gain some comfort from it.

Next the wind tried. It howled and blustered and tore at the coat. When that didn't work, the wind put its fingers under the hem of the garment and tried to force it over the man's head. Then the wind tried to rip the buttons off and cut the coat into shreds, but all was in vain.

Then the sun's turn came. It simply smiled down on the man with all its strength. Within two minutes he was perspiring and in another two seconds he had taken off his coat!

A smile accomplishes more than a scowl. A soft tongue is more persuasive than threats and angry words. It is foolish to argue with a judge and even more foolish to display anger in front of him. Calmness, reasonableness, and patience have more power to achieve results.

Elijah needed to learn a lesson about power. He was a prophet of fire and force, but after his magnificent victory on mount Carmel he sank into a deep depression. Queen Jezebel was thirsting for his blood and had put a price on his head, so he fled south about two hundred miles. At last he found himself beneath the shadow of

Horeb, the mount of God, and spent the night there in a cave. Then the Lord challenged his being there when he was needed in the north where Ahab and Jezebel were corrupting the people of God. Elijah complained that he was the only prophet of God left, that his zeal for God seemed to have done little good, and that Jezebel was now calling for his death.

God then proceeded to teach Elijah a lesson about power. He told Elijah to leave the cave and stand on the mountain. First Kings 19:11-12 tells us what happened next:

> And, behold, the Lord passed by, and a great and strong wind rent the mountains, and brake in pieces the rocks before the Lord; but the Lord was not in the wind: and after the wind an earthquake; but the Lord was not in the earthquake: And after the earthquake a fire; but the Lord was not in the fire: and after the fire a still small voice.

The Hebrew expression translated "a still small voice" in the King James version can also be translated "a sound of stillness." The phrase used in the Septuagint can be rendered "a gentle breeze." In other words, the greatest force in the world is the gentle breeze of the Word of God. Thus the miracle-working prophets (Elijah and Elisha) were replaced by the writing prophets. The prophets who made the greatest impact on Israel and the world were not those who could call down fire from heaven and surround themselves with spiritual chariots of fire, but those who wrote the great prophetic books of the Old Testament.

Likewise when God sent His Son into the world, He did not come blazing with brightness and armed with fire, famine, plague, and pestilence. He did not ride on the wings of the storm, hurl thunderbolts across the world, and demand instant surrender to His might and majesty. He came with the still small voice of a baby and announced Himself to be the Word of God made flesh.

"Long forbearing" is the Lord's way. Gentle persuasion is His style. His soft tongue "breaketh the bone"; it can overcome the most stubborn will. In this age of grace, God's method is persuasion. "Behold, I stand at the door, and knock," Jesus says. "If any man hear my voice, and open the door, I will come in to him, and will sup with him, and he with me" (Revelation 3:20).

But one of these days He will knock and call no longer. Then He *will* be in the wind, the earthquake, and the fire that shook, shocked, and seared the mountain where Elijah stood.

(3) Those We Cannot Trust (25:16-20)

(a) People Who Cannot Draw the Line (25:16-17)

People who cannot draw the line tend to tire of life. For instance *in the matter of food, they become nauseated.* Proverbs 25:16 says, "Hast thou found honey? eat so much as is sufficient for thee, lest thou be filled therewith, and vomit it." In other words, it is possible to have too much of a good thing.

I once toured a chocolate factory in Pennsylvania. All about me were fancy candies that, when packaged and sold, would bring high prices. My mouth watered, but none of the employees in the factory seemed to be the least bit tempted. The tour guide explained:

> When a new employee joins the staff, he is invited—even encouraged—to eat all the chocolates he wants. He is not allowed to take any out of the factory, but there are no limits placed on how many he may eat while he is at work. Usually a new employee will indulge his love for chocolates to the full—for the first few days. After a while, however, he becomes sick of the very sight of them. Indeed in a few weeks' time he rarely so much as tastes one. He is satiated.

Likewise a little honey is good, but too much makes a person sick. Honey is used in Solomon's proverb as an illustration of the "law of satiation." The hymn writer acknowledged the operation of this law in the spiritual realm when he wrote these words:

> I tried the broken cisterns, Lord,
> But ah! the waters failed!
> E'en as I stooped to drink, they'd fled,
> And mocked me as I wailed.
>
> Now none but Christ can satisfy,
> None other name for me;
> There's love, and life, and lasting joy,
> Lord Jesus, found in Thee.[5]

In the Bible honey represents *natural* sweetness. We soon tire of the sweets this world offers because they all cloy in the end. This fact is the theme of the book of Ecclesiastes, in which Solomon lamented that there is nothing new under the sun. He had tried all that the world has to offer; he had tried it over and over again until he was sick of it all. He wrote:

> The sun also ariseth, and the sun goeth down, and hasteth to his place where he arose. The wind goeth toward the south, and turneth about unto the north; it whirleth about continually, and the wind returneth again according to his circuits. All the rivers run into the sea; yet the sea is not full (Ecclesiastes 1:5-7).

Wit and wisdom, wine and wealth, works and women—Solomon had tried them all. He had thrown moderation to the winds. When he found honey, he "made a pig of himself," as some would say. He had to have more and more until his whole soul revolted, and yet he went back for more...until he became sick of life itself. Finally Solomon's appetite for the sweets of this world was satiated. He plunged into depression and caught himself on the brink of insanity. He even contemplated suicide and confessed that he was weary of life.

When Solomon wrote Proverbs 25:17, he was still thinking about people who cannot draw the line. His thought was that *in the matter of friendships, they become nuisances.* He learned a lesson from observing them and passed it on to us: "Withdraw thy foot from thy neighbour's house; lest he be weary of thee, and so hate thee."

We all have met people who overstay their welcome. I remember meeting just such a person in a church not far from my home. I had been preaching and at the close of the service a woman came forward and introduced herself as a friend of a colleague of mine who was a well-known preacher and radio personality. The mention of his name gave her a measure of instant acceptance and credibility. This woman and I talked for a while and she expressed an eager desire to know more about the Bible. She claimed to be an ex-Catholic nun. When most of the people had left the church, I gave her my telephone number and suggested she call my wife.

Not long afterward we received not a phone call, but a visit. The ex-nun, dressed in dowdy clothes, drove up in a small car. Of course we invited her in, little realizing she had come to stay for as long as she could. The visit lasted about a week.

The woman had a fascinating story to tell of contacts within the higher echelons of the Roman church. She said she had been a traveling emissary of the church, had held the rank of Mother Superior, and had had considerable authority over many convents. The details of her conversion, however, were somewhat sketchy and vague.

Day followed day and she showed no signs of leaving. We began to be suspicious, so I called my preacher friend. Yes, he knew who she was. No, he had no factual knowledge about the woman. She had showed up at his office one day and asked for spiritual counsel. He did not know if there was any truth to her claims.

The woman continued to tell us stories about her former role as Mother Superior. She evidenced some desire to know more about the Bible, so I gave her an annotated study Bible. She asked questions and listened politely to the answers. She also talked about men she had met and often her conversation was quite entertaining. Her stories were disjointed, but the general impression was that she had been everywhere and met everyone. We wondered how long she intended to stay, what her real motives were, and how much of her story was true.

Then one day the woman was transformed. Her dowdy clothes were gone. She appeared in a stylish, expensive suit, her hair was swept up in the latest fashion, and her makeup was impeccable. She looked every inch the part of a successful woman of the world. Her new look gave some credibility to her stories of past rank, responsibility, and privilege in the Roman church. At the same time her worldly-wise air awakened more suspicions in my wife's mind. Who was this woman? Why was she here? What did she really want?

Our visitor still showed no signs of leaving, although we wished she would. Finally we devised a strategy: I stayed away from the house as much as possible; when I was home I shut myself up in my study and avoided all conversation with her; when I had to be present for a meal, my conversation was polite, but cool and distant; all the "entertaining" was done by my wife, who also adopted a busy schedule and a distant manner.

Before long our uninvited guest became restless. In the end she requested permission to use the phone, made a few calls, and announced that she had to be on her way. At last she withdrew her foot from our house. Her departure was only just in time, for we were almost out of patience.

Solomon was quite right. A person can overstay his welcome.

### (b) People Who Cannot Desist from Lies (25:18-19)

Those who cannot desist from lies are to be avoided even more than those who cannot draw the line. Some dishonest people make false pronouncements and others make false promises. Proverbs 25:18 refers to *those who make false pronouncements:* "A man that beareth false witness against his neighbour is a maul, and a sword, and a sharp arrow." A maul, which is a large wooden hammer or club, bruises; a sword cuts and wounds; an arrow pierces to the heart. False witnesses inflict terrible wounds on their victims. They can cause a person to lose his reputation, possessions, or life.

To tell lies under oath is perjury, which is rightfully treated as a crime. We can be sure that many people had perjured themselves in Solomon's court. His first case—the case that established his reputation for wisdom and made him famous—involved a false witness (1 Kings 3:16-28).

The classic Biblical example of one who made false pronouncements is Ziba, a scoundrel if there ever was one. Perhaps Solomon had him in mind when he wrote Proverbs 25:18. Ziba had been a servant of King Saul, but in David's regime he had twenty servants of his own and a large family of fifteen sons (2 Samuel 9:10). David appointed him and his household to be the servants of Mephibosheth and ordered Ziba to till the land David had bestowed on the lame son of Jonathan. David showed Mephibosheth "the kindness of God" (9:3) and, treating him as one of the king's own sons, gave him a seat at the royal table.

Then came the Absalom rebellion and David's forced flight from Jerusalem. Mephibosheth, lame in both feet, ordered Ziba to saddle an ass for him so that he could accompany David into exile. But Ziba betrayed Mephibosheth (2 Samuel 19:25-27). He saddled a couple of asses all right, but instead of lifting the poor lame man onto one of them, he loaded them up with supplies and hurried off to David to see if he could ingratiate himself with the king at Mephibosheth's expense. When Ziba caught up with David, he threw so much mud on Mephibosheth's reputation that he deceived the very elect.

Second Samuel 16:3 records Ziba's false pronouncement: "The king said, And where is thy master's son? And Ziba said unto the king, Behold, he abideth at Jerusalem: for he said, To day shall the house of Israel restore me the kingdom of my father." Ziba's calumnious story was so convincing that David, acting uncharacteristically, hastily transferred the title of Mephibosheth's property to Ziba. Unctuously Ziba responded, "I humbly beseech thee that I may find grace in thy sight, my lord, O king" (16:4).

Ziba deceived even so astute a judge of character as Alexander Whyte. First this gifted expositor agreed that there is a problem: "Was Mephibosheth," he asked, "a heartless, selfish, contemptible time-server, while Ziba, his servant, was a prince beside him? Or, was Ziba a lying scoundrel, and Mephibosheth a poor, innocent, ill-used, lameter saint?"[6] But then, having succinctly stated the question, this usually penetrating commentator came down hard on Mephibosheth and helped Ziba rob him of his reputation.

However, it is Ziba who looks like the scoundrel when we weigh carefully—far more carefully than David did—Ziba's story that Mephibosheth had opted to stay in Jerusalem in anticipation of being unanimously hailed as the rightful king of Israel. Could Mephibosheth have believed that Absalom arranged his deep plots, suborned Ahithophel, subverted the rank and file of the nation, and mobilized his men for war against David just to install Mephibosheth as king? Never! Ziba glibly circulated the lie he had forged in order to ruin Mephibosheth and advance the fortunes of his own house!

When David returned to Jerusalem after the collapse of the Absalom rebellion, Mephibosheth found a more faithful attendant to help him get to the king. The lame man bore in his deliberately neglected appearance the evidence of his personal grief over David's sorrows. He told David that Ziba had deceived him and the king went halfway toward making amends. Mephibosheth understood David's predicament—Ziba was a powerful man allied to the Benjamite faction—and disclaimed all interest in the property. Mephibosheth acted royally, hailing the return of David as his all-sufficient joy.

But Ziba's deceptions had done their deadly, poisonous work only too well. Mephibosheth was still the loser in terms of material things.

Proverbs 25:19 refers to another kind of dishonest people, *those who make false promises:* "Confidence in an unfaithful man in time of trouble is like a broken tooth, and a foot out of joint." To suffer one of these afflictions is bad enough, but to suffer both at the same time is intolerable. Each brings gnawing, nagging, crippling pain. A person cannot bite with a broken tooth and he cannot walk with a broken foot. Both let their victim down painfully at a point of need. So does an unfaithful man. His friends think they can trust his promises and then they discover his broken promises.

Sometimes people who make false promises are sincere, but they promise more than they can perform. Sometimes right from the start they have no intention of fulfilling their promises.

Zedekiah, the last king of the Jews, made the fatal mistake of trusting the promises of one who was unable to deliver what he had promised. The Babylonians at that time were the new world superpower, moving in to fill the geopolitical vacuum left by the collapse of Assyria. Nebuchadnezzar, the Babylonian king, had subdued Judah and installed Zedekiah as his puppet regent. The fiercely independent Jews and Zedekiah were anxious to regain their independence. So what if he had sworn fealty to the Babylonian king? When hope of independence loomed on the horizon, Zedekiah seized it.

Egypt had been watching the westward wash of the Babylonian tide with increasing apprehension. So the pharaoh mobilized and sent ambassadors to Jerusalem with the message that if Zedekiah rebelled, he could rely on Egyptian support. Egypt would put on the battlefield an army that was able to defeat the Babylonians if the pharaoh could be assured of Judah's cooperation. He could not afford to fight the Babylonians if Judah remained loyal to Nebuchadnezzar. The pharaoh could not allow a hostile Judah to sit astride his supply lines.

The pharaoh reasoned along these lines: Why should Egypt waste its strength subduing Judah as a preliminary step to fighting Babylon? Why not conserve Egypt's strength for the real foe? Better still, why not add Judah's strength to Egypt's strength? Egypt alone could fight Babylon, but if Egypt were allied to Judah, the odds for a successful outcome would be greatly increased. Egypt wants to remain free. Judah wants to be free. Why shouldn't Judah trust the mighty Egyptian arm?

The Jews were always too quick to overestimate Egypt's strength. Egypt was all glitter and glamour, all outward show. Years before, at the time of the Assyrian invasion, Rabshakeh had described Egypt as "a broken reed." "Lo," he had said, "thou trustest in the staff of this broken reed, on Egypt; whereon if a man lean, it will go into his hand, and pierce it: so is Pharaoh king of Egypt to all that trust in him" (Isaiah 36:6). The great days of the Egyptian empire-building pharaohs were gone. All that remained was bluff, bluster, and a third-rate army that was no match for a real superpower.

Zedekiah, however, put his trust in the pharaoh. Then he sent a messenger to the prophet Jeremiah to ask him to pray for this dubious, dishonorable enterprise. The prophet, who had more sense than his king, warned Zedekiah that the Egyptian army would be of no use to him: "Behold, Pharaoh's army, which is come forth to help you, shall return to Egypt into their own land. And the Chaldeans shall come again, and fight against this city, and take it, and burn it with fire. Thus saith the Lord; Deceive not yourselves" (Jeremiah 37:7-9).

Zedekiah learned the hard way not to trust a man who cannot make good on his promises in a time of crisis. Having confidence in Egypt was like having a broken tooth and a broken foot. Later Zedekiah had plenty of time to reflect on his folly, for his eyes were put out and he was bound in fetters, carried off to Babylon, and put in prison, where he stayed for the rest of his life.

(c) People Who Cannot Depart from Levity (25:20)

Solomon warned us to beware of people whose behavior is inappropriate. He wrote, "As he that taketh away a garment in cold weather, and as vinegar upon nitre, so is he that singeth songs to an heavy heart."

"He that taketh away a garment in cold weather" could refer to the heartless creditor. Some commentators rephrase the first part of the proverb to read "he that decketh himself out in winter." According to their interpretation, the person Solomon had in mind was more concerned about his appearance than he was about his comfort and health. Such a person is typical of many in a fashion-conscious society. Some women would rather suffer agony in high heels than wear shoes with flat heels. A friend of mine refuses to wear a topcoat, even on a bitter winter's day, because he thinks he appears more macho without one. Some people would rather bumble around half blind than wear glasses. Whichever interpretation we accept, the action is condemned.

The second part of the proverb is "vinegar upon nitre." In Solomon's day nitre (natron), a natural alkali that contains carbonate of soda, was used in cooking and washing. Natron effervesces when combined with acid—vinegar for instance. To pour natron into vinegar would be foolish, spoiling the usefulness of both substances. Natron was only useful in its alkaline state. And of what use is effervescence to vinegar?

In the third part of the proverb, "so is he that singeth songs to an heavy heart," Solomon made his point. Grief, he was saying, has its place. Grief is appropriate in the dark winter of the soul. Frivolity is inappropriate. Only a fool sings songs to a broken heart. Such behavior is as foolish as pouring natron into vinegar; the result is froth and fizz. To rob a person of his grief when he has been bereaved is like robbing him of his coat in winter.

Joab robbed David of his grief when his heart broke over the death of Absalom (2 Samuel 18:33; 19:1-7). Joab was too pragmatic. What he said to David may have been true, but Joab was brusque and rude. It is doubtful that David ever forgave him. Indeed, not long afterward, David made an unsuccessful attempt to have Amasa replace Joab as head of the army (20:1-23).

One of the most poignant instances of misplaced frivolity is found in James Hilton's great story *Good-bye Mr. Chips.* Mr. Chips was the Latin master at Brookfield, a private school for boys. His first ordeal was supervising the homework session of a bunch of rowdy boys in Big Hall. Discipline had never been one of his strong points, so he almost ruined his career at the outset by being overly severe. He liked the boys, but had difficulty with them.

In the spring of 1896 when he was forty-eight, while doing some mountain-climbing in the English lake district, Mr. Chips met the outgoing, adventuresome, young, and beautiful Katherine Bridges. She swept him off his feet, married him, revolutionized his life, filled it with joy and wonder, transformed his relationship with the boys, and made him a general favorite with students and masters alike.

Then on April 1, 1898, his wife and newborn child died. "Half struggling to escape into an outside world where the sun still shone," he made his way in a daze to his classroom, assigned some Latin grammar, and sat down at his desk in a trance. One of the boys spoke to him. "Please, sir," he said, "there are a lot of letters for you."[7] Mr. Chips hadn't noticed the letters; he hadn't noticed anything. His wife was dead; his child was dead; he wished he were dead. Numbly he opened one of the letters. Inside the envelope was a blank sheet of paper. The next one was the same; they were all the same. It did not dawn on him until afterward that the letters were an April Fools' joke. All he knew was that it was April 1 and his wife and child had died that morning. Nobody else knew yet. The boys did not know. His life was a blank.

The joke had gone wrong. The levity was like singing songs to a heavy heart.

### b. Look Well to Your Foes (25:21-22)

Solomon wrote, "If thine enemy be hungry, give him bread to eat; and if he be thirsty, give him water to drink: For thou shalt heap coals of fire upon his head, and the Lord shall reward thee." This statement, written by a man who was not without enemies, anticipated Christ's sermon on the mount (Matthew 5:44; also see Romans 12:20). The precept in Proverbs is similar to the precept in Matthew. The difference is that Jesus (who described Himself in Matthew 12:42 as "a greater than Solomon") practiced what He preached. Solomon didn't (1 Kings 11:26-40).

The best Old Testament illustration of the application of Solomon's noble and magnificent proverb is found in the story of Elisha. In many ways Elisha stands in contrast to Elijah. Elijah, the great prophet of the law, habitually called down fire on his foes (1 Kings 18:24; 2 Kings 1:1-15). Elisha, on the other hand, was the prophet of grace. In 2 Kings 6:1-23 we see that Elisha handled threats to his life in an altogether different way.

We read there that again and again the king of Israel had been able to avoid ambushes set for him by the king of Syria. The enraged Syrian king demanded that someone tell him who was spying for Israel. He was astonished when he was told that God's prophet Elisha could report to the king of Israel everything the king of Syria said—even what he whispered in the privacy of his bedroom. Reacting immediately, the king of Syria sent contingents of his army to seize Elisha. The prophet was fully aware of the Syrian king's intentions, but Elisha was undisturbed. He simply remained where he was.

When the Syrian army arrived, Elisha prayed that God would smite his enemies with blindness. The prophet then led them into downtown Samaria. When Elisha asked God to open their eyes, they saw that they were in the heart of the enemy's capital—and at the mercy of the king of Israel. The king of Israel rubbed his hands. Now one command could wipe out the entire enemy contingent. Turning to Elisha, the king said, "My father, shall I smite them? shall I smite them?"

The angry prophet replied: "Thou shalt not smite them: wouldest thou smite those whom thou hast taken captive with thy sword and with thy bow? set bread and water before them, that they may eat and drink, and go to their master." So the king of Israel prepared a banquet, treated his enemies as honored guests, then sent them home. As a result the hostilities ended and the historian wrote, "So the [marauding] bands of Syria came no more into the land of Israel."

The lofty concepts incorporated in Solomon's proverb—and later in the sermon on the mount—are not just idealistic dreams. When put into practice, they work!

c. Look Well to Your Friends (25:23-24)

Next we can learn a lesson from *the blowing wind:* "The north wind," Solomon wrote, "driveth away rain: so doth an angry countenance a backbiting tongue" (Proverbs 25:23). Job made a similar observation: "Fair weather cometh out of the north" (Job 37:22). The ancients called the north wind "the heavenly one" because it brightened up the sky. The lesson in the proverb is that an angry look can still a gossiping or backbiting tongue. The person with a hot temper and threatening scowl can often impose his will on others.

The redoubtable Widow Trapes was like the north wind. We meet her in Jeffery Farnol's book *The Definite Object.* Mrs. Trapes was honest, eagle-eyed, and a good friend. She was fearless and to be feared for her quick temper, sharp tongue, and acidulous countenance.

Mrs. Trapes was poor and lived on the top floor of a malodorous high-rise tenement. Across the hall from her lived the lovely young Hermione Chesterton and her brother Arthur (or Spike, as he preferred to be called). Into the widow's home came Geoffrey Ravenslee, a millionaire posing as a poor man looking for work. Ravenslee was determined to help Spike get out of the clutches of Bud M'Ginnis.

Spike admired M'Ginnis, a flashy gangster who controlled a gang of thieves and thugs. M'Ginnis was handsome, tough, and a mean fighter. He recognized no law and had the police in his pocket. M'Ginnis wanted to marry Hermione and used Spike's weaknesses as a powerful lever to bully and threaten her.

Ravenslee also wanted to marry Hermione. Among his other accomplishments, he was a trained boxer, able to hold his own against the best fighters. Most people were afraid of M'Ginnis, but Ravenslee was not one of them. Neither was Mrs. Trapes.

The author described how Spike first introduced Ravenslee to the formidable Mrs. Trapes:

> "Say, Geoff," said he, "I've seen Mrs. Trapes, an' she wants you to go over so she can pipe you off. 'N' say, you're sure up against a catty proposition in her; if you don't hit it off on the spot as soon as she gets her lamps onto you, it'll be nix for you, Geoff, an' nothin' doin'!"
>
> "Lucid!" said Ravenslee, yawning, "and sounds promising!"
>
> "Why, y' see, Geoff, she's got a grouch on because I was out last night, so, if she gives you the gimlet eye at first, just josh her along a bit. Now slick yourself up an' come on." Obediently Mr. Ravenslee arose and having tightened his neckerchief and smoothed his curly hair, crossed the landing and followed Spike into the opposite flat, a place of startling cleanliness as to floors and walls, and everything therein; uncomfortably trim of aspect and direfully ornate as to rugs and carpet and sofa cushions.
>
> Mrs. Trapes herself was elderly; she was also a woman of points, being bony and sharp featured, particularly as to elbows, which were generally bare. Indeed, they might be said to be her most salient and obtrusive features; but her shrewd,

sharp eyes held an elusive kindliness at times, and when she smiled, which was very rarely, her elbows and her general sharpness were quite forgotten.

She was awaiting them in her parlour, enthroned in her best easy chair, a chair of green velvet, where purple flowers bloomed riotously, her feet firm-planted upon a hearthrug cunningly enwrought with salmon-pink sunflowers. Bolt upright and stiff of back she sat, making the very utmost of her elbows, for her sleeves being rolled high (as was their wont) and her arms being folded within her apron, they projected themselves to left and right in highly threatening fashion. Sphinx-like she sat, very silent and very still, while her sharp eyes roved over Mr. Ravenslee's person from the toes of his boots to the dark hair that curled short and crisp above his brow. Thus she looked him up and she looked him down, viewing each garment in turn; lastly, she lifted her gaze to his face and stared at him—eye to eye.

And eye to eye Mr. Ravenslee, serene and calm as ever, met her look, while Spike, observing her granite-like expression and the fierce jut of her elbows, shuffled, and glanced toward the door. But still Mrs. Trapes glared up at Mr. Ravenslee, and still Mr. Ravenslee glanced down at Mrs. Trapes wholly unabashed.

After the interview Spike exclaimed, "She sure gave you the frosty-face, Geoff, but it didn't seem to joggle you any!"

Ravenslee admitted he wasn't "joggled." He said, "I like her."

"Like Mrs. Trapes?" Spike responded. "You an' Hermy are about the only ones then; most every one in Mulligan's hates her an' gets scared stiff when she cuts loose!"

Later on in the story Ravenslee took Spike to the theater one evening. The next day Mrs. Trapes talked with Ravenslee about Spike:

Mrs. Trapes sniffed. "Anyway, it's a good thing you had him safe out o' the way, as it happens."

"Why?"

"Because that loafer M'Ginnis was hanging around for him all the evenin'. Even had the dratted imperence to come in here an' ask me where he was."

"And what did you tell him?"

"Tell him?" she repeated. "What did I not tell him!" Her voice was gentle, but what words could convey all the quivering

> ferocity of her elbows! "Mr. Geoffrey, I told Bud M'Ginnis just exactly what kind o' a beast Bud M'Ginnis is. I told Bud M'Ginnis where Bud M'Ginnis come from an' where Bud M'Ginnis would go to. I told Bud M'Ginnis the character of his mother an' father, very plain an' p'inted."
>
> "And what did he say?"
>
> "He say! Mr. Geoffrey, I didn't give him a chance to utter a single word, of course. An' when I'd said all there was to say, I picked up my heaviest flatiron, as happened to be handy, an' ordered him out; and Mr. Geoffrey, Bud M'Ginnis—went!"
>
> "Under the circumstances," said Ravenslee, "I'm not surprised that he did."[8]

Solomon was quite right. An angry countenance can be a useful weapon at times.

His next proverb refers to *the brawling woman:* "It is better to dwell in the corner of the housetop, than with a brawling woman and in a wide house" (Proverbs 25:24).

I met a brawling woman years ago when I was speaking at a couples' retreat. I was billeted in an old home that had been converted into a guesthouse. Some of the larger rooms had been divided into two smaller bedrooms and the partitioning walls were very thin. I was assigned to just such a room.

I was alone and had just settled down at a desk to do some writing when a couple moved into the room next-door. There was the usual bang and clatter as suitcases were opened and clothes were stowed away in the closet. There were also occasional acrimonious remarks. I realized that I was going to have a grandstand seat to quite a "conversation." It was more like a monologue. The woman began to harp on some grievance in a bitter, rasping voice that carried through the partitioning wall loud and clear:

> I don't know what's the matter with you, William, and that's the truth. You drag me all the way downtown. We go into that hardware store and there's that iron I have been wanting for years and you say we don't need it. It's too expensive. It's not a General Electric. You're just too cheap to part with the money. That's what's the matter with you. Well, I've had it with that old iron. I'm just going to send your shirts to the laundry, that's all, or you can iron them yourself.
>
> I've never known anyone so tight with money as you. You begrudge me every nickel. Let me tell you, I work just as hard as you do. And another thing: why did we have to have this

> cheap room? It only costs a few dollars more to stay in one of the cottages down by the lake. But, oh no! You want to save a few miserable nickels. When was the last time I bought a new dress? And look at your shoes. I'm ashamed to be seen out with you. Here we were in the shoe shop the other day and you couldn't make up your mind. Couldn't find a pair to fit or the right color. I know what it was. You couldn't bear the thought of parting with the money. But you're just like your mother. A regular old miser she was. I'll never forget the time we visited her in Chicago and she gave us canned pork and beans to eat.
>
> Look how I had to nag you just to come up here this weekend. You'd think, considering the way I slave for you, you could take me somewhere once in a while without making so much fuss over it. You always say you are retired and we have to cut back. What about all that severance pay you got when you left General Electric? It's as much my money as yours. And anyway, you never took me anywhere before you retired unless I nagged you into it. Well, I've made up my mind. Right after lunch you're going to take me back downtown and I'm going to get that iron. If you think I'm going to be satisfied with another cheap one you're mistaken. The last cheap one didn't last three months before the steamer stopped working.

And so the monologue continued. I was reminded of the man who was asked if he had ever considered divorce as a solution to frequent family squabbles. "No," he said, "but I've often considered murder!"

As it turned out, I knew the couple in the room next-door. They had always struck me as an agreeable couple, but after that memorable weekend, I thought the man deserved a medal for heroism! He was married to a brawling woman and no house in the world would have been wide enough for him to escape her nagging tongue.

d. Look Well to Your Feelings (25:25-28)

(1) The King's Position (25:25-26)

Solomon described what it is like *when good news comes:* "As cold waters to a thirsty soul, so is good news from a far country" (Proverbs 25:25).

This proverb reminds me of Jacob when he received news from Egypt. We can picture him sitting in his home in Canaan. All his boys have gone away. His beloved Joseph is dead. Simeon is in a prison somewhere in Egypt. Now even dear Benjamin is gone.

The ominous vizier of Egypt suspected Jacob's sons of being spies, claimed they had lied, and demanded that Benjamin—the brother they had inadvertently mentioned—be brought to Egypt as proof that they were telling the truth. We can hear Jacob's sorrowful cry when the brothers first returned from Egypt with the news about Simeon and Benjamin: "Me have ye bereaved of my children: Joseph is not, and Simeon is not, and ye will take Benjamin away: all these things are against me" (Genesis 42:36). And as the brothers loaded up their mules and headed toward Egypt with Benjamin, we can hear Jacob's fatalistic wail: "If I be bereaved of my children, I am bereaved" (43:14).

So we see him brooding over his misfortunes. He mopes about, nursing his memories and grievances, lifting his hands to Heaven in desperate prayer, pleading for God to intervene. The patriarch thinks of his many mistakes. He stayed too long in Padan-aram. He was too eager to make money and too crafty in his dealings with Laban. He was too slack in controlling his boys and now they are all gone. His beloved Rachel is dead and her maid Bilhah has been disgraced. Egypt seems so far away and utterly alien and pagan. Jacob is lonely and afraid.

No doubt he is wondering, *What is going to happen to my boys? Who is that mysterious and mighty minister of state? Why did he have to ask for Benjamin? Why, oh why, did they have to tell him about Benjamin in the first place? Suppose those prodigal sons of mine land in more trouble, and in Egypt of all places. Abraham warned me about Egypt.*

After many sleepless nights and fear-haunted days, Jacob went as usual to his lookout on top of the nearby hill. Straining his old eyes toward the south, he saw a caravan approaching. Surely, like the father of the prodigal of Luke 15, Jacob saw his sons while they were yet a great way off and ran and fell on their necks and kissed them. They blurted out the news: "Joseph is yet alive, and he is governor over all the land of Egypt" (Genesis 45:26). The old man fainted. When he revived he saw the wagons and the ten asses "laden with the good things of Egypt," which his great grand-vizier son in Egypt had sent him.

Good news turned Jacob into a new man. "As cold waters to a thirsty soul, so is good news from a far country."

It is much different *when grim news comes:* "A righteous man falling down before the wicked is as a troubled fountain, and a corrupt spring" (Proverbs 25:26). The word translated "troubled" here can be rendered "trampled" or "fouled." In eastern lands where water is scarce and a fountain is a treasure, only an evil man will trample and foul a spring. Everyone suffers when that happens. Likewise it is bad news for everyone when an evil man triumphs over a righteous man. It is a setback for society.

The same is true when a fool triumphs over a wise man. Consider the case of Galileo. When he was a seventeen-year-old medical student at Pisa, he noticed that the chandelier hanging over the altar in the cathedral was swinging. He observed something never before noticed: although the length of the swing was slowly decreasing, each swing took the same amount of time. Each swing was shorter and slower. The decrease in speed was compensated by the decrease in distance. Galileo had discovered the law of the isochronism of the pendulum.

Galileo switched his field of study from medicine to mathematics. He was tutored in the subject for only a short time, but his keen mind went on to master Euclid and all the mathematics known in his day. In fact Galileo became a lecturer in mathematics at the University of Pisa.

From the famous leaning tower of Pisa, Galileo demonstrated another principle of physics. He dropped two weights simultaneously. One weighed one pound; the other weighed ten. Both weights hit the ground at the same time, disproving Aristotle's theory that a heavy body falls faster than a light one. Galileo figured out that an object, regardless of its weight, falls sixteen feet the first second and thirty-two additional feet in each succeeding second. He went on to discover the basic laws of motion and to invent the thermometer.

Then Galileo heard that a Dutch lens maker, Jan Lippershey, had invented a telescope. Galileo worked out the optical theory and made a true telescope by mounting lenses in a tube. He went on to build a telescope that had a magnification of thirty diameters. Then he turned it toward the moon and saw its mountains and valleys.

Galileo began to study the sun and the stars. He challenged the old Ptolemaic system, which postulated that the earth was the center of the universe and the sun moved around the earth. But the pope forbade him to teach any such heresy. The Roman pontiff sat on his throne in St. Peter's and pronounced *ex cathedra* that the sun went around the earth. This infallible decree was signed by Cardinals Felia, Guido, Desiderio, Antonio, Bellingero, and Fabriccio. It read:

> In the name and by the authority of Jesus Christ, the plenitude of which resides in his Vicar, the Pope, that the proposition that the earth is not the centre of the world [universe] and that it moves with a diurnal motion, is absurd, philosophically false, and erroneous in faith.

In 1632 Galileo published his most famous work, *Dialogue Concerning the Two Chief World Systems,* and brought down the wrath of Pope Urban VIII. So Galileo was summoned to Rome and tried by the Inquisition. On June 22, 1633, in order to escape a cruel death, Galileo was obliged to fall on his knees and sign a retraction: "I abjure, curse and detest the error and heresy of the motion of the earth." But the pope did not have the last word. As Galileo rose from his knees, he muttered under his breath, *"E pur si muove"* (This will not prevent the earth from moving).[9]

(2) The King's Pride (25:27)

"It is not good to eat much honey: so for men to search their own glory is not glory." Solomon may have been thinking of the glory of kings, but his proverb is also good advice for anyone else who likes to "blow his own trumpet." Just as people can become sick of honey, they can become sick of a man who continually draws attention to himself and imagines himself to be much more magnificent than he really is.

Diotrephes is the classic New Testament example of a man who worked for his own glory. He and Gaius were prominent in a church somewhere in the Roman province of Asia. Gaius was a faithful, loving brother whose children walked with God; he was an elder and he was given to hospitality. The apostle John wrote his third Epistle to Gaius.

John had written another letter to Gaius's church, but Diotrephes, who had set himself up as some sort of pope, intercepted the letter and refused to allow it to be read (3 John 9). Diotrephes disliked John because John was a threat to him. Having been one of the twelve, John exercised the power and authority of an apostle. John had known Jesus from boyhood and had been like a son to the Lord's mother. Everyone loved John because he reminded them of Jesus. John was a sweet, saintly man, given to apocalyptic vision. In short, John was everything that Diotrephes wasn't.

So Diotrephes, who imagined himself to be some great one, spoke against John maliciously. Diotrephes refused to receive people into the fellowship of the church unless they bowed to his authority. He excommunicated those who opposed him and those who entertained members of his opposition (3 John 10).

But John "had his number," as we would say. The apostle wrote to Gaius and said in effect: "One of these days I'm likely to show up. If and when I do, I will remember Diotrephes' words and deeds." Even such a loving and tender apostle as John would only need to show up to prick this man's balloon.

(3) The King's Passions (25:28)

"He that hath no rule over his own spirit is like a city that is broken down, and without walls." In other words, such a person is highly vulnerable. A man who gets drunk, loses his temper on the slightest provocation, or cannot control his lusts is like a city with broken walls. His enemies soon get to know his weak spot and exploit it.

In modern times Austria was handed over to Hitler partly because Dr. Kurt von Schuschnigg, the Austrian chancellor, was addicted to tobacco! Throughout 1937, after the Nazis had already won far-reaching concessions from the Austrian government, the Austrian Nazis, financed and inspired by Berlin, kept up a campaign of terror. They had plans to assassinate Schuschnigg and create a climate for armed German intervention in Austria. Mussolini and Hitler had forged the Rome-Berlin axis. Britain and France were seeking appeasement. Then Hitler summoned Schuschnigg to a meeting in the palace at Berchtesgaden on February 12, 1938.

The wily Franz von Papen, Hitler's special ambassador to Vienna, met Schuschnigg and his party at the frontier and dropped a hint. He told him on the way to the conference that the führer had three generals with him: Keitel, the chief of the German army; Reichenau, who commanded German forces on the Austrian frontier; and Sperrle, who commanded the German air force in the area. Schuschnigg, a Jesuit-trained intellectual, became alarmed when he heard that Hitler had his military advisers with him, for Austria was in no condition to argue with generals, but Von Papen assured the Austrian that Hitler was in a good mood.

Wearing the uniform of a storm trooper, Hitler greeted the polite Austrian chancellor, who soon found himself alone with the dictator in the second-floor study, which commanded a breathtaking view of the snow-clad Alps and Austria. When Schuschnigg made a general remark about the view and the weather, Hitler rudely cut him short and broke into a tirade that continued for two hours.

Schuschnigg never had a chance. The pedantic Austrian reminded Hitler of the school professors he had detested in his boyhood and he took delight in hectoring, threatening, bullying, and shouting at him. The führer kept using the chancellor's personal name instead of his title and watched for the first sign of weakness, the first hint of fear. Full of rage and venom, Hitler reminded his nervous visitor of Austria's isolation and helplessness, called for General Keitel, and issued his ultimatum.

The führer allowed the Austrian no time to compose his thoughts and during the crucial morning session he refused the wretched man permission to smoke. Schuschnigg was a chain smoker, so he was not only assailed psychologically; he was also tortured by a desperate craving for tobacco. Thus tortured, before the day was done he was willing to sign anything. In the end Schuschnigg signed a new agreement with Hitler and, along with it, the death warrant of Austria. Truly, "he that hath no rule over his own spirit is like a city that is broken down, and without walls."

e. Look Well to Your Follies (26:1-12)

(1) How to Assess a Fool (26:1-2)

Solomon returned to one of his most urgent topics: watch out for the fool. One way to assess a fool, Solomon taught, is *by the calamity he brings:* "As snow in summer, and as rain in harvest, so honour is not seemly for a fool" (Proverbs 26:1). The snow, rain, and honor in this proverb are all rare, exceptional, and out of place. They are the result of freak conditions. Honor for instance is inappropriate for a fool; he deserves dishonor.

Honor was given to a fool in the case of King Uzziah, for he allowed his early successes to go to his head. When Uzziah (Azariah) was sixteen years old, he was made king instead of his father, who had suffered a humiliating defeat at the hands of the king of Israel (2 Kings 14:8-14;19-21). The shame of the defeat must have burned into the boy's soul, for he steered his course toward greatness and honor. At some point Uzziah must have thrown off the intolerable yoke of Israel's King Jeroboam II, who had captured and dismantled the defenses of Jerusalem, maintained it as a vassal state, and held hostages to make sure Judah complied with the terms of surrender. Uzziah put an end to that unbearable state of affairs.

Once Judah was free of that galling and shameful bondage to Israel, Uzziah must have said to himself, "Never again!" He set about reorganizing and rebuilding his army and strengthening fortifications throughout Judah. There was nothing wrong with Uzziah's wits when it came to war. He gave his troops new weapons and military machines and warred successfully against the Philistines, the Arabs, and the Ammonites. Having enough wisdom to give a boost to agriculture, build towers, dig wells, and uphold the ancestral faith, Uzziah recovered much of Judah's lost strength.

But in spite of all his might, he was a fool and the honor he received was "as snow in summer, and as rain in harvest." After achieving success, Uzziah did the most incredibly foolish thing a man could do. He decided that the time had come to end the long-standing, God-ordained separation of "church" and "state." Among God's chosen people the priesthood was reserved exclusively for the tribe of Levi and the family of Aaron. Only the priests had the prerogative to perform the rites and rituals of the Hebrew faith. The Judean kings descended from the tribe of Judah and the family of David and were therefore barred from the priesthood. A man could be a king and a prophet, or a priest and a prophet, but he could never be a priest and a king. That prohibition became increasingly intolerable to Uzziah. Why should he have to share power with the priests? He decided to put an end to this vexing division of power.

So one sorry day Uzziah, filled with a sense of his own importance, armed himself with censer and incense and intruded into the temple. He was determined to burn incense on the golden altar in the holy place in front of the temple veil. The high priest Azariah could hardly believe his eyes. Even the most degenerate Judean king had never attempted to burn the incense. Azariah summoned his colleagues and, backed by eighty valiant men, stood in the king's way and said: "It appertaineth not unto thee, Uzziah, to burn incense unto the Lord, but to the priests the sons of Aaron, that are consecrated to burn incense: go out of the sanctuary; for thou hast trespassed; neither shall it be for thine honour from the Lord God" (2 Chronicles 26:18).

Uzziah, now in the grip of his folly, lost his temper. "And while he was wroth with the priests, the leprosy even rose up in his forehead" (26:19). The horrified priests pushed the king toward the door and as soon as Uzziah realized what had happened to him, he fled. He spent the rest of his life in an isolated house where he had plenty of time to think about honor and folly.

Another way to assess a fool is *by the curse he brings:* "As the bird by wandering, as the swallow by flying," Solomon wrote, "so the curse causeless shall not come" (Proverbs 26:2). Nothing happens in a vacuum. There is a law of cause and effect.

This proverb is illustrated in the story of the menace of Goliath. War was in the air. The powerful Philistine army had invaded Israel and drawn up their forces on the hill overlooking the valley of Elah, about fifteen miles southwest of Bethlehem. King Saul's army was encamped on the other side of the valley.

Meanwhile David was minding sheep at the family farm. Three of his older brothers—Eliab, Abinadab, and Shammah—were conscripts in Israel's army and naturally their father Jesse was concerned. With stories of the Philistine giant circulating throughout the country, there was anxiety everywhere. Old Jesse called David in from the field, gave him some supplies for his brothers and their captain, and sent him off to the front.

David arrived just as the two armies were forming in battle array. He found his brothers and was talking to them when the Philistine giant appeared. Goliath, who was nearly twelve feet tall, was fully clad in heavy armor that gleamed in the sun and he carried a spear like a weaver's beam. When his voice sounded across the valley, David stared and pricked up his ears. Goliath shouted in effect:

> Hear ye! Hear ye! I have an offer, a fair offer it seems to me. Why should so many good men die? Am not I a Philistine? Are you not servants of Saul? Choose one man and let him come down to me. If he fights with me and kills me, then the Philistines will be your servants. If I prevail against him and kill him, then you will be our servants, and serve us (see 1 Samuel 17:8-9).

Goliath paused, then added an insult. He cursed Israel's God and roared, "I defy the armies of Israel this day; give me a man that we may fight together" (17:10). David looked around and saw fear on every soldier's face.

King Saul was the proper man to fight Goliath. He was a giant of a man himself (1 Samuel 9:2). He had been anointed king, but had been chosen by the people in self-will (1 Samuel 8:4-9; 10:17-24). Worse still, he was a failure. Two years into his reign he had proved himself unfit to rule when he had his first confrontation with the Philistines, for it was Jonathan, not Saul, who saved Israel and defeated the Philistines. Saul's behavior had been despicable. The curse had not causeless come.

Now the Philistines were back and they had a giant on their side. They were thirsting for revenge, for the total humiliation and demoralization of the Hebrews. Saul was deathly afraid of that giant and so were Prince Jonathan, General Abner, and David's brothers.

First Samuel 17:11 tells us, "When Saul and all Israel heard those words of the Philistine, they were dismayed, and greatly afraid."

Israel had demanded a king, and God had given them a king. They wanted Saul because he was big, and God had given them Saul because they wanted him. Now they discovered that he was not nearly big enough. They had trusted in bigness, and all the enemy had to do was produce someone bigger. Saul was only big on the outside. David was little on the outside, but bigger than a giant on the inside.

David, who was astonished by Goliath's defiance, listened to what the soldiers were saying:

> And the men of Israel said, Have ye seen this man that is come up? surely to defy Israel is he come up: and it shall be, that the man who killeth him, the king will enrich him with great riches, and will give him his daughter, and make his father's house free in Israel (1 Samuel 17:25).

Eager to get the facts straight, David went from one man to another. "Who is this uncircumcised Philistine," he demanded, "that he should defy the armies of the living God?" (17:26)

Presently Eliab, David's oldest brother, butted in. He had had enough of David and his questions. "Why camest thou down hither? and with whom hast thou left those few sheep in the wilderness?" Eliab angrily asked. "I know thy pride, and the naughtiness of thine heart; for thou art come down that thou mightest see the battle" (17:28). Eliab's words revealed that he didn't know David at all. All he saw was his baby brother. True, Samuel the prophet had recently visited the farm and secretly anointed David to be Israel's next king. But remembering the prophet's visit only increased the brother's anger, because Samuel had looked Eliab over and dismissed him.

By now David was used to his older brothers and their pride. He had a short answer for Eliab: "What have I now done?" David said. "Is there not a cause?" (17:29) Then he turned his back on Eliab and continued to question and challenge the people.

"Is there not a cause?" Of course there was a cause. There always is, and God intends for us to link the curse with the cause. There was for example a cause for Job's sufferings, although he could not identify it for a considerable length of time; the cause was much deeper and far more complex than he or his friends had imagined. Likewise Eliab never imagined that when Goliath defied Saul's army, Israel was reaping what it had sown.

Another cause that Eliab never thought of was God's intention to introduce His newly anointed king to Israel. Before long Goliath was dead and soon his slayer's name became a household word in Israel.

(2) How to Admonish a Fool (26:3)

In Proverbs 26:3 Solomon taught us the only way to get any sense into the head of a fool: "A whip for the horse, a bridle for the ass, and a rod for the fool's back." The "rod" (which does not always have to be a piece of wood) is the only way to get a fool to do what he is supposed to do. Wiser, more tractable people do not need forceful curbs and incentives.

A whip makes the horse go, or go faster. A bridle reins the ass in and slows him down. Some people need both whip and bridle. Peter is one example. He was always running ahead or lagging behind.

On one notable occasion Peter and the other disciples were with the Lord at Caesarea Philippi, a city at the foot of towering, snow-clad mount Hermon. Nestled within an angle of the Jordan's lush valley, the city was noted for its adoration of the Roman god Pan. Herod Philip had beautified the town and named it Caesarea in honor of the Roman emperor Tiberius Caesar.

In this vicinity the Lord asked His disciples to tell Him what people thought about Him. Then He challenged them to state what they thought. Simon Bar-jona spoke up: "Thou art the Christ, the Son of the living God" (Matthew 16:16). The Lord acknowledged the correctness of this statement, changed Simon's name to Peter, told him God Himself had revealed the truth to his heart, and promised him a leading role in the church.

Then Jesus began to reveal to the disciples that, far from heading toward a coronation, He was heading toward a crucifixion. This information was too much for Peter. At once he showed how far he lagged behind the Lord in his grasp of God's purposes and plans. "Then Peter took him," we read, "and began to rebuke him, saying, Be it far from thee, Lord: this shall not be unto thee" (Matthew 16:22). In turn, he received a stunning rebuke from the Lord.

A week later on the mount of transfiguration Peter again blurted out his carnal thoughts and interrupted the conversation that the glorified Lord Jesus was having with Moses and Elijah, who had come back from the glory land. While Peter was talking, the shekinah cloud overshadowed them and a voice said, "This is my beloved Son, in whom I am well pleased; hear ye him" (Matthew 17:5). The extraordinary meeting was over. Peter's carnality had spoiled it. On this occasion he had rushed ahead of the Lord. Peter's reference to "three tabernacles" suggests that Peter had in mind the feast of tabernacles, the annual Jewish feast that anticipates the millennial reign of Christ. That's how far Peter was ahead of the Lord.

We see him rushing ahead again after the disciples left the upper room. Jesus said, "All ye shall be offended because of me this night: for it is written, I will smite the shepherd, and the sheep of the flock shall be scattered" (Matthew 26:31). Peter hurriedly protested, "Though all men shall be offended because of thee, yet will I never be offended" (26:33). When the Lord told Peter that he would actually deny Him three times before daybreak, he at once said, "Though I should die with thee, yet will I not deny thee" (26:35).

Then in Gethsemane the Lord asked Peter, James, and John to "watch and pray" (26:41), and Peter—like the others—fell asleep. When the mob came Peter was brave enough, but he rushed ahead again by using his sword.

As the mob led the Lord to the house of Caiaphas, "Peter followed him afar off" (26:58). When John secured a place for him in the courtyard, Peter warmed his hands at the world's fire and ended up cursing, swearing, and denying the Lord.

After the resurrection when the disciples had gone back home to Galilee and Peter had announced that he was going back to fishing, the Lord revealed Himself on the shore and reined Peter in. The Lord also told Peter how he would die and Peter at once wanted to know His plans for John. Peter had to be told to mind his own business. (See John 21.)

In those days Peter was always in need of spur or rein. He was just like so many of us who need the whip and the bridle. We all show our folly at times and often reveal our need to be corrected.

### (3) How to Answer a Fool (26:4-5)

Solomon alerted us to *the need to be careful:* "Answer not a fool according to his folly, lest thou also be like unto him" (Proverbs 26:4). Solomon also alerted us to *the need to be comprehending:* "Answer a fool according to his folly, lest he be wise in his own conceit" (26:5).

You cannot reason with a fool. No matter what you say, you only confirm him in his folly. If you don't answer him, he will think he is more clever than you are. If you do answer him in the same vein, you will only inflate his good opinion of himself because he will think that you are a fool for saying foolish things. Even if you are only being sarcastic, he will take what you say literally. Doubtless Solomon had tried both methods on his son—ignoring him and ridiculing him—only to discover that Rehoboam was complacently confirmed in his own conceit.

The consequences can be serious when a man is "wise in his own conceit"—as serious as the tragic sinking of the *Titanic.*

The ship's captain, a seasoned veteran of the White Star fleet and a patriarch of the seas, was due to retire once the *Titanic's* maiden voyage was over. He was polished, urbane, and very much in command—a born leader of men. He was adored by passengers and crew alike and had a considerable following among the rich and famous, who made it a point to be booked on ships he was sailing.

But surely only a man who was "wise in his own conceit" would have recklessly driven that floating hotel across ice-littered seas at full-steam-ahead. No doubt he had his reason. The *Titanic* outclassed everything else afloat. She displaced 66,000 tons, was 883 feet long, could carry 3,000 passengers, and could make 24-25 knots. With such a ship, the captain must have wanted to establish a new record for crossing the Atlantic. Why else would he have ignored all the warnings he received that fateful April day?

The ship's log told its own tale:

| | |
|---|---|
| 9:00 a.m. | The *Caronia* reported ice—Latitude 42° North, Longitude 49° to 51° West. |
| 1:42 p.m. | The *Baltic* reported ice—Latitude 41° 51' North, Longitude 49° 52' West. |
| 1:45 p.m. | The *Amerika* reported ice—Latitude 41° 27' North, Longitude 50° 8' West. |
| 7:00 p.m. | Temperature given as 43°. |
| 7:30 p.m. | Temperature given as 39°. |
| 7:30 p.m. | The *Californian* reported ice—Latitude 42° 3' North, Longitude 49° 9' West. |
| 9:00 p.m. | Temperature given as 33°. |
| 9:30 p.m. | Lookouts warned to keep a sharp watch for ice. |
| 9:40 p.m. | The *Mesaba* reported ice—Latitude 42° North to 41° 25' North, Longitude 49° to 50° 30' West. |
| 10:00 p.m. | Temperature given as 32°. |
| 10:30 p.m. | Temperature of the sea given as 31°. |
| 11:00 p.m. | The *Californian* warned of ice, but her message was cut off before she could give the location. |
| 11:40 p.m. | The *Titanic* struck by an iceberg—Latitude 41° 46' North, Longitude 50° 14' West. |
| 12:15 a.m. | First radio call for help. |

Surely only a man "wise in his own conceit" could have been so disdainful of the warnings. The captain was sure that nothing could harm the *Titanic.* In case of trouble all he had to do was press a button and all the ship's compartments would be closed, making the *Titanic* virtually unsinkable. But it turned out that it was not unsinkable after all. With a three-hundred-foot gash in her side and the first five compartments already full of water, the great ship was doomed.

What was Captain Smith thinking as he issued orders to abandon ship? He must have been haunted by his folly. He had been warned repeatedly. The evidence was in the log. He had ignored the messages warning of icebergs and he had ignored the dropping of the thermometer.

The wireless operator, J. G. Phillips, must have been equally "wise in his own conceit." All day Sunday he had been receiving messages of ice in the water and relaying those messages to the bridge. But he was tired and when the *Californian* sent her last warning at 11:00 p.m., he was exasperated. He cut her off with a curt reply: "Shut up, shut up! I am busy." He did not even wait to hear the location of the icebergs or bother to relay the warning to the bridge. As a result of this folly, the radio operator on the *Californian* tuned the *Titanic* out and consequently did not even hear the first call for help.

Smith, Phillips, and the rest of the crew placed their faith in the superior construction of the *Titanic.* They thought that modern shipbuilding techniques had produced a vessel immune to disaster. Before the *Titanic* left Southampton, Mrs. Albert Caldwell asked one of the deck hands if the ship was really unsinkable. "God Himself could not sink this ship," he told her.

So, wise in their own conceit, the officials of the White Star Line, Captain Smith, and his crew loaded 2,207 people on board that ship, which was about to sail to its doom, and provided lifeboat space for only 1,178 people. There were no boat drills and the passengers were given no boat assignments. The crew were assigned duties in case of disaster, but they failed, for the most part, to find out what those duties were.[10]

(4) How to Appear a Fool (26:6-9)

A person can appear to be a fool *by expressing confidence in one:* "He that sendeth a message by the hand of a fool cutteth off the feet, and drinketh damage" (Proverbs 26:6). A man who cuts off his own feet renders himself helpless.

It is the height of folly to entrust important business matters to a person who is wholly incompetent to handle them. David once made this mistake by expressing confidence in Amasa.

In the wake of the Absalom rebellion, David, although restored to the throne, was still vulnerable. The speed with which Absalom had been able to subvert the kingdom must have shocked the king. David, who had once reigned supremely and securely in the affections of his people, had completely underestimated the damage he had done to his fund of national goodwill by seducing Bath-sheba and murdering Uriah. In particular David had miscalculated the malice of Ahithophel, the grandfather of Bath-sheba.

So after a nasty civil war in which twenty thousand Israelites lost their lives, David had been escorted back to his throne by all the men of Judah, but only half the men of Israel (see 2 Samuel 19:40). Indeed a squabble broke out almost immediately between the men of Judah and the men of Israel over the question of loyalty to David, and another civil war resulted. The Benjamites, still nursing resentment over the fact that King Saul's dynasty (he was a Benjamite) had been replaced by a Judean dynasty, followed the call of Sheba, who blew a trumpet to herald a new rebellion. Again the response was overwhelming. All the tribes except Judah went over to the side of Sheba.

Once he was back in Jerusalem, David had to turn his attention to putting down this new rebellion. Still smarting over Joab's rough words to him at the time of his bereavement, David made an almost fatal mistake. He deposed Joab and made Amasa commander-in-chief with responsibility for conducting the new civil war. (According to 1 Chronicles 2:17 Amasa was the son of David's half-sister Abigail and the Ishmaelite Jether, and according to 2 Samuel 17:25 Amasa was also Joab's cousin.) Amasa had been the captain of Absalom's army, but David forgave Amasa and even though he had just proved his military incompetence, put him in Joab's place. It was an incredibly foolish decision and we can only conclude that appointing Amasa was David's way of getting back at Joab. By commissioning Amasa to deal with Sheba, David was, so to speak, sending a message by the hand of a fool. He nearly cut off his own feet in the process.

David's instructions were clear. Amasa had three days to assemble an all-Judean army and report back to the throne. When the deadline came and went and Amasa failed to show up, David became alarmed. He realized too late how serious his mistake was. He turned to one of his mighty men, Joab's brother Abishai, and burst out, "Now shall Sheba the son of Bichri do us more harm than did Absalom: take thou thy lord's servants, and pursue after him, lest he get him fenced cities, and escape us" (2 Samuel 20:6). Fortunately for David, Joab took the initiative and made short work of both Amasa and Sheba. Had it not been for Joab, David would have made a fool of himself by expressing confidence in one.

A person can also appear to be a fool *by exercising credence in one:* "The legs of the lame are not equal: so is a parable in the mouth of fools" (Proverbs 26:7). The expression translated "are not equal" can also be rendered "are lifted up." Solomon's idea was that just as clothes are lifted up to reveal lame legs, a fool exposes his folly by attempting to expound a parable.

Parables, by their very nature, are the most difficult Scripture passages to exegete. Some of the Lord's parables, such as the parable of the vineyard in Matthew 21:33-45, are intended to *reveal* truth. But others, such as the mystery parables of Matthew 13, are intended to *conceal* truth (see 13:10-17).

An axiom of hermeneutics says, "You cannot make a parable run on all fours." In other words, when you are interpreting a parable, you need to identify the main truth that the story is intended to teach. Not all the details of a parable have symbolic significance. Some details are just window dressing, setting the stage or providing background scenery. Trying to explain every single detail is foolish and leads to ridiculous conclusions.

Even some renowned church fathers have been guilty of wild exegesis. An illustration of the foolish handling of a parable is Augustine's interpretation of the parable of the good Samaritan. He said the "certain man" who "went down from Jerusalem to Jericho" represents Adam. Jerusalem stands for the heavenly city of peace. It was from the blessedness of peace that Adam fell. Jericho is the moon, which symbolizes our mortality because it waxes, wanes, and dies. The thieves are the devil and his angels, who stripped the sojourner of his immortality. They beat him—that is, they persuaded him to sin—and left him half dead. He is half dead because in the measure man can know and understand God, he is alive, and in the measure he is spoiled and oppressed by sin, he is dead. The priest and the Levite who "passed by on the other side" represent the priesthood and service of the Old Testament, which had no salvation to offer. The Samaritan is Christ, the guardian. By binding the man's wounds, the Lord restrains sin. The oil is the comfort and hope that Christ brings. The wine is the fervent work of the Holy Spirit. The beast upon which the good Samaritan placed the wounded wayfarer is the flesh, or the humanity of Christ! The placing of the man on the beast symbolizes belief in the incarnation of Christ. The inn is the church, where travelers are refreshed during their return from their pilgrimage to their heavenly home. The "morrow" is the time after the resurrection of Christ. The two pence are the two commandments of love: to love God supremely and to love one's neighbor as oneself. Or perhaps the two pence represent the promises for this life and the life to come. The innkeeper is the apostle Paul!

When a person tries to make a parable run on all fours, his interpretation is lopsided indeed.

A person can appear to be a fool *by expecting competence from one:* "As he that bindeth a stone in a sling, so is he that giveth honour to a fool" (Proverbs 26:8). To bind a stone in a sling defeats the purpose of a sling. A stone should be placed so that it can easily be released at the right moment and sent swiftly along its ordained trajectory. Binding a stone in a sling is foolish and entrusting a fool with a position of honor and responsibility is just as foolish.

British history provides a classic example of the truth of this proverb. In 1854 Great Britain declared war on Russia to prevent further Russian expansion and interference in the affairs of Turkey. One of the engagements in this Crimean war was the battle of Balaklava. The British and their allies easily captured this seaport on the Black Sea and established a base there. The Russians, in turn, sent a large naval force from Sevastopol, about eight miles to the northwest, but failed to recapture Balaklava. Both sides suffered heavy losses. During the battle the Russians occupied strategic heights overlooking a valley near Balaklava. Lord Raglan and his staff, who were based on the heights above Sevastopol, observed the Russians removing guns from the captured artillery posts and sent orders to the Light Brigade to disrupt them. The orders received by Lord Cardigan, who headed the brigade, were garbled and he led his small brigade of British cavalry in a charge upon the strong Russian position. The charge was not only useless; it was suicidal. Less than a third of approximately six hundred cavalrymen survived this charge into "the jaws of Death,"[11] the blazing maws of the Russian cannons.

The incident caught the imagination of British poet Alfred Lord Tennyson. In his day the officer corps was made up of titled sprigs of the British nobility. These men of wealth and privilege were frequently quite unqualified to lead troops into battle. Lord Raglan was one of these inexperienced and incompetent commanders. He was blamed for the campaign's lack of progress, for the terrible suffering of his troops who lacked adequate supplies and shelter during the winter, and for the stupid order that sent the Light

Brigade to its death. Tennyson underlined Raglan's blunder in the famous poem, "The Charge of the Light Brigade." One stanza reads:

> "Forward, the Light Brigade!"
> Was there a man dismay'd?
> Not tho' the soldier knew
> Someone had blundered:
> Theirs not to make reply,
> Theirs not to reason why,
> Theirs but to do and die:
> Into the valley of Death
> Rode the six hundred.

Someone had promoted Lord Raglan to a level beyond his competence. Someone had put power into the hands of a bungler. Someone had given honor to a fool. Someone had bound a stone in a sling. At the critical moment others had to pay for the man's foolish order.

Finally a person can appear to be a fool *by explaining concepts to one:* "As a thorn goeth up into the hand of a drunkard, so is a parable in the mouth of fools" (Proverbs 26:9). A drunkard, of course, can become so bereft of his senses that he does not even know that he has a thorn in his hand. Although the palm of the hand is very tender, the drunkard can be oblivious to the sharp point of the thorn that has pierced it. Likewise a fool fails to grasp the point of even the plainest teaching. He will twist the truth and think that he is very clever.

In *Nada the Lily* Sir Henry Rider Haggard wrote about a missionary who lived near Umgugundhlovu, the seat of the Zulu chief Dingaan, who was the brother and successor of the terrible Chaka. Dingaan had all of his brother's vices, but none of Chaka's greatness. Mopo told the tale:

> Now the mind of Dingaan was heavy, and he sought something to lighten it. Presently he bethought him of the white praying man, who had come to the kraal seeking to teach us people of the Zulu to worship other gods than the assegai and the king. Now this was a good man, but no luck went with his teaching, which was hard to understand; and, moreover, the indunas did not like it, because it seemed to set a master over the master, and a king over the king, and to preach of peace to those whose trade was war. Still, Dingaan

sent for the white man that he might dispute with him, for Dingaan thought that he himself was the cleverest of all men.

Now the white man came, but his face was pale, because of that which he had seen befall the Boers, for he was gentle and hated such sights. The king bade him be seated and spoke to him saying:—

"The other day, O White Man, thou toldest me of a place of fire whither those go after death who have done wickedly in life. Tell me now of thy wisdom, do my fathers lie in that place?"

"How can I know, King," answered the prayer-doctor, "who may not judge of the deeds of men? This I say only: that those who murder and rob and oppress the innocent and bear false witness shall lie in that place of fire."

"It seems that my fathers have done all these things, and if they are in this place I would go there also, for I am minded to be with my fathers at the last. Yet I think that I should find a way to escape if ever I came there."

"How, King?"

Now Dingaan had set this trap for the prayer-doctor. In the centre of that open space where he had caused the Boers to be fallen upon he had built up a great pyre of wood—brushwood beneath, and on the top of the brushwood logs, and even whole trees. Perhaps, my father, there were sixty full wagon-loads of dry wood piled together there in the centre of the place.

"Thou shalt see with thine eyes, White Man," he answered, and bidding attendants set fire to the pile all round, he summoned that regiment of young men which was left in the kraal. Maybe there were a thousand and half a thousand of them—not more—the same that had slain the Boers.

Now the fire began to burn fiercely, and the regiment filed in and took its place in ranks. By the time that all had come, the pyre was everywhere a sheet of raging flame, and, though we sat a hundred paces from it, its heat was great when the wind turned our way.

"Now, Doctor of Prayers, is thy hot place hotter than yonder fire?" said the king.

He answered that he did not know, but the fire was certainly hot.

"Then I will show thee how I will come out of it if ever I go to lie in such a fire—ay, though it be ten times as big and fierce. Ho! my children!" he cried to the solders, and, springing up,

"You see yonder fire. Run swiftly and stamp it flat with your feet. Where there was fire let there be blackness and ashes."

Now the White Man lifted his hands and prayed Dingaan not to do this thing that should be the death of many, but the king bade him be silent. Then he turned his eyes upward and prayed to his gods. For a moment also the soldiers looked on each other in doubt, for the fire raged furiously, and spikes of flame shot high toward the heaven, and above it and about it the hot air danced. But their captain called to them loudly: "Great is the king! Hear the words of the king, who honours you! Yesterday we ate up the Amaboona—it was nothing, they were unarmed. There is a foe more worthy of our valour. Come, my children, let us wash us in the fire—we who are fiercer than the fire! Great is the king who honours us!"

Thus he spoke and ran forward, and, with a roar, after him sprang the soldiers, rank by rank. They were brave men indeed; moreover, they knew that if death lay before them death also awaited him who lagged behind, and it is far better to die with honour than ashamed. On they went, as to the joy of battle, their captain leading them, and as they went they sang the Ingomo, the war-chant of the Zulu. Now the captain neared the raging fire; we saw him lift his shield to keep off its heat. Then he was gone—he had sprung into the heart of the furnace, and but little of him was ever found again. After him went the first company. In they went, beating at the flames with their ox-hide shields, stamping them out with their naked feet, tearing down the burning logs and casting them aside. Not one man of that company lived, my father; they fell down like moths which flutter through a candle, and where they fell they perished. But after them came other companies, and it was well for those in this fight who were last to grapple with the foe. Now a great smoke was mixed with the flame, now the flame grew less and less, and the smoke more and more; and now blackened men, hairless, naked, and blistered, white with the scorching of the fire, staggered out on the farther side of the flames, falling to earth here and there. After them came others; now there was no flame, only a great smoke in which men moved dimly; and presently, my father, it was done: they had conquered the fire, and that with but very little hurt to the last seven companies, though every man had trodden it. How many perished?—nay, I know not, they were never counted; but what between the dead and the injured that regiment was at half strength till the king drafted more men into it.

> "See, Doctor of Prayers," said Dingaan, with a laugh, "thus shall I escape the fires of that land of which thou tellest, if such there be indeed; I will bid my impis stamp them out."
>
> Then the praying man went from the kraal saying that he would teach no more among the Zulus, and afterwards he left the land.[12]

Trying to teach that Zulu savage the truth of God was useless. All the missionary received for his pains was a thorn in his hand.

(5) How to Appraise a Fool (26:10-12)

Solomon gave three ways to sum up a fool: *by his condemnation, by his character,* and *by his conceit.*

Proverbs 26:10 draws attention to a fool's condemnation: "The great God that formed all things both rewardeth the fool, and rewardeth transgressors." The word translated "fool" here is *kesil,* which means "dense" or "stupid" and refers especially to that form of stupidity which expresses itself in impiety. The impious fool is as bad as the transgressor and God's judgment awaits both. This kind of fool says that there is no God or lives as though there is no God.

Psalm 14, which paints a portrait of this kind of fool, indicates that his disregard of God is linked not so much to his mind as to his morals. The problem is not that a person *cannot* believe in God, but that he *will not* believe in God. And his disbelief can be traced to his love of sin.

Such foolishness is evident in a man like T. H. Huxley, who popularized Darwin's theory of evolution because he saw it as a working hypothesis for atheism. The theory gave him, or so he imagined, a way of explaining the universe without God. The fact that the theory of evolution is as full of holes as a sieve made no difference to this confirmed atheist.

Consider also the case of Wilder Smith and "the pink professor." The professor, who was a Marxist and a convinced atheist, overheard Wilder Smith say to another student that he saw no reason not to believe in God just because man's scientific instruments had not detected him. The professor exploded. He launched into a tirade, a typical "intellectual" attack on God. He described a cat playing with a mouse—clawing it and letting it get away, only to pounce on it again and again until the mouse finally died. The professor ridiculed the kind of God who made the mouse so helpless and the cat so fiendish. He pointed to situations such as a young mother dying of cancer, the lifetime of suffering to which the starving millions in India are born, and the torture resulting from the transmission of the malarial parasite. "Your God is my Devil," he sneered. "If he is almighty, then he is not good; if he is good, then he is not almighty. Either way, no intelligent man has any use for him. Don't tell me," he continued, "that you attribute war, disease, oppressions and all the world's woes to the devil. If your God is not almighty with regard to the devil, then he is no God at all."

The professor thought of himself as very modern and clever because he had paraded these enigmas that are as old as sin itself. The denseness of his mind, however, was in itself proof of the power of sin and Satan. The fact that the professor had a brain at all was proof that an omniscient and omnipotent God exists.

The human brain contains some thirty billion nerve cells, or neurons, each one connected with the others as many as sixty thousand times. Neurons are complicated structures. Their dendrites pick up signals from adjacent neurons, pass them to the body of the cell, which in turn passes the signals along a filament at speeds up to 225 miles per hour. After each signal passes, the filament takes 1/2000th of a second to recharge itself chemically. The brain has five to ten times as many glial cells as it does neurons.

No computer exists that can duplicate all the myriad functions of a brain. Yet "the pink professor" imagined that his brain just happened by chance. Solomon described the professor's denseness exactly. He had the kind of denseness that expresses itself in impiety.

The true explanation for the existence of evil in the world is found in the Bible and nowhere else. The existence of Satan, the fall of man, and the reign of self-will and sin in the universe, all figure in the explanation and all were scoffed at by that professor.[13]

Proverbs 26:11 turns our attention to a fool's character: "As a dog returneth to his vomit, so a fool returneth to his folly." Such a man was the pharaoh who was king of Egypt at the time of the Hebrew exodus. He seemed incapable of staying away from his suicidal policy.

God gave the pharaoh an ultimatum and God's ambassador presented his credentials. Moses directed Aaron to cast his rod to the ground and the rod became a serpent. When the magicians of Egypt duplicated the miracle, Aaron's serpent swallowed up theirs (Exodus 7:9-13). The significance would not have been lost on a man who wore a symbolic serpent on his brow, but the pharaoh simply hardened his heart.

Moses then turned the waters of the Nile to blood—and the

waters of the tributaries, canals, ponds, and reservoirs as well. But the magicians were able to duplicate this miracle also, and the pharaoh hardened his heart again (7:14-25). Next came the plague of frogs. Once again the magicians were able to duplicate the miracle and once again the pharaoh hardened his heart (8:1-15).

Then suddenly, without warning, the plague of lice came. This time the magicians confessed themselves beaten and told the pharaoh, "This is the finger of God." But the pharaoh, like a dog returning to its vomit and a fool to his folly, once more hardened his heart (8:16-19).

Next came the plague of flies. The pharaoh discussed terms with Moses and promised to let God's people go, but as soon as the flies were gone the pharaoh went back to his old ways and hardened his heart (8:20-32).

Another plague killed all the cattle of the Egyptians. When the pharaoh heard that none of the cattle of the Hebrews had died, he hardened his heart again (9:1-7).

Then Moses took ashes from the furnace and threw them toward heaven. Perhaps the ashes were the residue of human sacrifices offered by the Egyptians to propitiate the god Typhon and thus avert the plagues. But the sacrifices were to no avail, for Moses used the ashes to produce another unannounced plague: the terrible plague of boils (9:8-12). This time the magicians could not even stand before the pharaoh because they themselves were covered with boils. And this time, as a warning, *God* hardened the pharaoh's heart. God confirmed him in his folly.

Next the plague of hail smote "all that was in the field" throughout Egypt (9:13-35). Every herb was smitten and every tree was broken, except in Goshen. And as soon as the plague was removed, the pharaoh returned to his folly—for the last time by his own volition. At this point he crossed an unseen line and became the captive of his own habitual stubbornness. Now it was inevitable that he would automatically harden his heart. Three more plagues followed—the locusts (10:1-20), the terrifying darkness (10:21-29), and the deaths of all the firstborn (11:1–14:8)—and again and again the pharaoh returned like a dog to his vomit and hardened his heart. His foolishness had become culpable folly.

Proverbs 26:12 turns our attention to a fool's conceit: "Seest thou a man wise in his own conceit? There is more hope of a fool than of him." This proverb is well illustrated in Samuel Shellabarger's book *Prince of Foxes*. The story revolves around the determination of a peasant, who had assumed the name of Andrea Orsini, to make his way in the world and become a prince of Italy.

At one stage in his career, while serving as an agent of the crafty and determined Cesare Borgia, Andrea found himself in the service of the duke of Ferrara. Andrea's task was to persuade the duke, who hated and feared Borgia, that it would be in the duke's best interest to come to terms with the ominous Borgian conqueror. Replying to Andrea's overtures with counterproposals, the duke agreed to listen to Andrea's proposals if Andrea would go to the city of Viterbo and persuade the city's living patron saint, Suora Lucia Brocadelli da Narni, to move to Ferrara.

Lucia was renowned because she bore in her hands, it was said, the stigmata of Christ. She also received visions and could perform miracles. She was a prodigy of holiness, as holiness was understood in medieval Europe. The duke wanted Lucia to come to Ferrara because he thought her presence would add a dimension of holiness to his city, and he assured Andrea that Lucia wanted to come. The problem was that the people of Viterbo refused to let her go.

Andrea and his accomplice, the sinister Mario Belli, went to Viterbo, secured an audience with the saintly Lucia, arranged to smuggle her out of the city, and prepared for action. At the critical moment, however, Andrea was arrested and taken to the city magistrate, His Excellence Julio Vettori. Andrea was accused of acting in the interest of Ferrara to remove Sister Lucia from Viterbo, and he knew he would have to talk his way out of this predicament. Andrea also knew that he would have to buy time so that while he was holding the attention of Vettori, Belli could abduct Lucia.

Andrea found himself talking to "a man wise in his own conceit." Andrea had been warned that Vettori was incorruptible, but Andrea was not convinced. He began telling Vettori what a pleasure it was to meet so great a magistrate.

"I am not susceptible to flattery, Messer Andrea," the magistrate replied.

"How often have I heard that said of you, my lord!" Andrea offered, "and no later than last week by the illustrious Duke Cesare himself."

Vettori took the bait and Andrea played on his own relationship to Borgia. Andrea claimed to be one of Borgia's most trusted emissaries and behind the claim was a threat: Vettori was not dealing with a spy from Ferrara, but with an agent of Borgia, whose father was the pope and whose long arm reached across half of Italy. Andrea touched a chord of alarm in Vettori's breast, for the Borgias were more to be feared than the duke of Ferrara, and Cesare Borgia's accredited special envoy had been arrested in his town.

Andrea reassured Vettori, but he had the measure of the man now: he was poor, disappointed, proud of his honesty, proud of his striking profile, and acting a role.

Andrea then appealed to Vettori's vanity. Noting the magistrate's remarkable features, Andrea ventured, "May I ask whether you have ever had a medal struck to commemorate your term of office?…No? It's a pity, sir, a great pity."

Next Andrea talked the politics of statecraft. It was heady wine for the magistrate of a small, unimportant town to be given a glimpse of what went on behind the scenes of the stage where important diplomatic decisions were made. Andrea drew back the curtain veiling high intrigue and talked of his mission to Ferrara, the desired alliance between the house of Borgia and the duke of Ferrara, the desire of the pope to humor the illustrious duke of Ferrara in this matter of the venerable Lucia, and how it would bode ill for Viterbo to stand in the way of such formidable actors. Borgian displeasure could mean poverty, disgrace, or worse.

When Andrea got around to answering the charge of conniving in the transfer of the saint to Ferrara, he asked Vettori if he knew that the general of the Dominicans had ordered Lucia Brocadelli to go to Ferrara and that her reverence desired to obey. Would Vettori support the people of Viterbo in their lawless determination to keep her a prisoner?

As a final sop to the Vettori's vanity, Andrea hinted at the gratitude of the duke of Ferrara and Borgia and dangled before Vettori the prospect of becoming magistrate of the far more important city of Ferrara.[14]

Vettori, wise in his own conceit, fell for Andrea's flattery. There was more hope for a fool than for Vettori.

### 3. Beware of Sluggards (26:13-16)

Solomon returned to a theme he discussed frequently—the sluggard—and told us what the sluggard says, where he stays, why he starves, and whom he scorns.

We note first *what the sluggard says:* "The slothful man saith, There is a lion in the way; a lion is in the streets" (Proverbs 26:13). Any kind of excuse will do. If a lazy man doesn't want to go to work, he phones in sick. Or he says, "I can't get my car started." Or "It's been snowing and my driveway is covered." People will make up extraordinary excuses for neglecting their duty. They will say most anything to get out of doing what they don't want to do.

Excuses for not getting a job done did not fool Abraham Lincoln.

He was an astute president and many stories are told about his penetrating wit. Once he was asked how many men the Confederate army had in the field. Lincoln replied, "According to the best authority, they have twelve hundred thousand."

His questioner was astounded. "More than a million men?" he exclaimed.

"Yes, sir," repeated Lincoln, "twelve hundred thousand, no doubt about it." He paused and then added, "You see, all of our generals, when they lose a battle, say that the enemy outnumbers them from three or five to one. We have four hundred thousand men in the field, and three times that makes twelve hundred thousand men."

Another story reveals Lincoln's sense of honor and love for hard work. A prospective client called at his law office with a case involving a claim worth six hundred dollars, a princely sum in those days. Lincoln was sure he could win the case, but winning it would ruin a widow and bring extreme hardship to her children, so he refused to take the case. "I am quite sure I can win the case for you," he said to the client, "but there are some things which, though they may be legally right, are not morally right. Now, if you like, I will give you some advice for which I will charge you nothing. I strongly advise an able-bodied, intelligent, healthy man like you to try your hand at making six hundred dollars in some other way."

Inaction irked Lincoln. At one time during the American Civil War, General George B. McClellan, then in command of the Union forces, was conducting a waiting campaign. Indeed he was being so careful to avoid making mistakes and was making so little progress that Lincoln wrote him a letter: "My dear McClellan," he wrote, "if you don't want to use the Army, I should like to borrow it for a while. Yours respectfully, A. Lincoln."

After the battle of Antietam, when McClellan's army lay idle for no accountable reason, Lincoln was equally sarcastic. He and his friend O. M. Hatch of Illinois went to the front to see the situation for themselves. They stood on a hill from which they could see the vast army camp. "Hatch," demanded Lincoln, "what's that over there?"

"Why," exclaimed Hatch, "that's the army of the Potomac!"

Replied Lincoln, "You're wrong, Hatch. That is General McClellan's bodyguard!"

We note also *where the sluggard stays:* "As the door turneth upon his hinges, so doth the slothful upon his bed" (Proverbs 26:14). A door swings this way and that way, but it does not go anywhere. Likewise the activity of the slothful man, even when he can manage to drag himself out of bed, is aimless and does not get him anywhere. He just stands idle, like a door on its hinges, moving only when someone gives him a push this way or that. More energetic people pass him by on their way in and out as they get on with the business of life.

For years the Ripley "Believe It or Not" cartoon was a favorite in America's newspapers. Ripley museums still dot the country. The last time I was in the one in Gatlinburg, Tennessee, I noticed an exhibit of old tombstones with odd or humorous inscriptions. One inscription (found on a tombstone in a cemetery in Ruidoso, New Mexico) read, "Here lies Tom Yeast. Pardon me for not rising!" Solomon would have liked to place that tombstone on the bed of the sluggard who was too lazy to get up and go to work.

Few prescriptions have been more commonly given than "bed rest," but doctors have re-examined this old cure-all. They have found that too much bed rest can be harmful. In one experiment, healthy young volunteers were immobilized for weeks in plaster casts. When these volunteers were released, they swayed on their feet, their bones were depleted of calcium, and their muscles were flabby and useless.

World War II brought about a radical change in attitudes toward bed rest. Spurred by the urgent need for hospital beds for war casualties, doctors began to try early ambulation of women after childbirth and of patients after surgery. The results were dramatic. For example postoperative complications such as blood clots decreased. Nowadays even patients who undergo open-heart surgery are often up and walking in a matter of days. We can conclude that the sluggard, who is addicted to massive, voluntary doses of bed rest, not only misses out on life, but also courts death.

We note moreover *why the sluggard starves:* "The slothful hideth his hand in his bosom; it grieveth him to bring it again to his mouth" (Proverbs 26:15). Using a sarcastic hyperbole, Solomon pictured the slothful man as being too lazy to feed himself. The sluggard wants to be supported by someone else and to be indulged in every way.

At the zoo we have all seen lazy polar bears, sitting up on their haunches, waiting for people to throw them tidbits. Too indolent to move, they just wave their gaping maws to and fro, hoping for a morsel to fall right in. In our national parks, rangers warn visitors against feeding the animals. They explain that deer can become so used to handouts that they actually lose their ability to fend for themselves. Bears, the rangers say, can come to believe that handouts are their due and will become quarrelsome—even violent—if they do not get what they want. Smaller animals such as chipmunks and squirrels gravitate to places where people feed them, thus upsetting the proper balance of nature.

So nature teaches us that giving too many handouts is not a good idea. A right-minded society does not make it easy for people to live on the dole. A healthy and compassionate society makes work available and refuses to support all but the sick, the incapacitated, and the hopelessly handicapped.

Finally we note *whom the sluggard scorns:* "The sluggard is wiser in his own conceit than seven men that can render a reason" (Proverbs 26:16). In other words, the sluggard is the original know-it-all. He is far too lazy to study, but he thinks he knows more than those who do. Other men spend their lifetimes studying, painstakingly forming opinions and coming to conclusions on a subject. Right or wrong, they can at least back up their opinions by appealing to the sources they have studied and to the work they have done in the field. But the sluggard considers his own half-baked ideas to be just as good or even better than theirs.

In the realm of religious belief, everyone considers himself to be an expert. When a preacher who has been in the ministry for forty years and is widely respected by his peers makes a statement regarding the sovereignty of God, eternal security, the second coming of Christ, the cessation of certain gifts of the Spirit, or the creation narrative of Genesis, he can almost count on what will happen afterward. Someone with not half his years, not a tithe of his experience, and none of his expertise in the subject, will challenge him. Often the challenger will be someone who has an ax to grind, or someone who has had some dubious experience, or someone who has uncritically accepted a contradictory statement, or someone who has strung together a few texts taken out of context. I have met them all!

Even if seven men can give a reason for their opinion, the sluggard believes his shallow opinion is better than theirs. The wise man of old must have met many slothful men. He did not tell us what to do about them; he just told us to look out for them.

## 4. Beware of Self-Importance (26:17-28)

### a. The Man Who Tries to Stop Something (26:17)

"He that passeth by, and meddleth with strife belonging not to him, is like one that taketh a dog by the ears." In other words, the meddler is asking for trouble. Often the people fighting each other will join forces against an intruder.

Solomon raised two related issues in this proverb: When does strife become a situation to meddle with? When does it become a matter of honor and personal integrity to interfere deliberately?

Years ago one of the bravest men I have ever known in the ministry told me of an incident in which interference was necessary. My friend was an itinerant missionary in the backwoods of northern Canada. He was well able to take care of himself if he faced physical violence, but first and foremost he was a man of God.

One day he walked into a cafe in a rough frontier town and sat down at a table. A group of men, tough logging types, were sitting nearby. Their conversation was punctuated with oaths and obscenities, but my friend was used to that. Presently, however, his ears heard words that made his hackles rise. One of the men was teaching a teenager in the group to blaspheme the Holy Ghost. My friend pushed back his chair and deliberately walked over to their table. "Excuse me," he said to the men. Then he turned to the lad. "Son," he said, "don't do that. Blasphemy against the Holy Ghost is a damnable offense in the sight of God. I would advise..."

The man who had been blaspheming suddenly pushed his chair back. "See here, mister," he said, "you mind your own business or I'll smash your face in."

My friend said, "This *is* my business. I am a minister of the gospel. This is very much my business."

The logger glared at the minister, but noted his impressive physique and quailed before the look in his eye.

"Son," my friend added as he turned toward the boy, "God's Word says that all manner of sin can be forgiven, but blasphemy against the Holy Ghost cannot be forgiven, either in this life or the next. You just remember that." He eyed the now-silent men at the table, and returned to his seat.

There is a time when interference is right. Most often, however, it is best to leave matters alone. If you must interfere, remember that there are better ways to take hold of a dog than by the ears! If it is necessary to intervene in someone else's affairs, know what you are doing and do not act out of a sense of self-importance.

### b. The Man Who Tries to Stir Something (26:18-23)

#### (1) The Man Full of Guile (26:18-19)

Turning his thoughts to the man who is full of guile, Solomon first showed us *his portrait:* "As a mad man who casteth firebrands, arrows, and death" (Proverbs 26:18). Then Solomon showed us *his pretense:* "So is the man that deceiveth his neighbour, and saith, Am not I in sport?" (26:19) All too often the guileful man is responsible for the ruin of other people. But when caught and confronted, he says, "It was just a joke. I was only kidding." The victims do not think his joke was funny.

Charles Dickens' character, "the old Jew" Fagin, was a man full of guile. When little Oliver Twist was first introduced to Fagin's boys, he did not know that they were a gang and he was in a den of thieves. He was just grateful to be off the streets and he hoped that Fagin would be his benefactor and help him make his way in the world. Fagin however had other plans. Oliver's fresh, young, innocent face would be invaluable to him in some of his nefarious schemes. So he gave Oliver some supper and bundled him off to bed. Dickens described what happened next:

> It was late next morning when Oliver awoke, from a sound, long sleep. There was no other person in the room but the old Jew, who was boiling some coffee in a saucepan for breakfast, and whistling softly to himself as he stirred it round and round, with an iron spoon. He would stop every now and then to listen when there was the least noise below: and when he had satisfied himself, he would go on, whistling and stirring again, as before....
>
> When the coffee was done, the Jew drew the saucepan to the hob. Standing, then, in an irresolute attitude for a few minutes, as if he did not well know how to employ himself, he turned round and looked at Oliver, and called him by his name. He did not answer, and was to all appearance asleep.
>
> After satisfying himself upon this head, the Jew stepped gently to the door: which he fastened. He then drew forth: as it seemed to Oliver, from some trap in the floor: a small box, which he placed carefully on the table. His eyes glistened as he raised the lid, and looked in. Dragging an old chair to the table, he sat down; and took from it a magnificent gold watch, sparkling with jewels.
>
> "Aha!" said the Jew, shrugging up his shoulders, and distorting every feature with a hideous grin. "Clever dogs! Clever dogs! Staunch to the last! Never told the old parson where they were. Never peached upon old Fagin! And why should they? It wouldn't have loosened the knot, or kept the drop up, a minute longer. No, no, no! Fine fellows! Fine fellows!"
>
> With these, and other muttered reflections of the like

nature, the Jew once more deposited the watch in its place of safety. At least half a dozen more were severally drawn forth from the same box, and surveyed with equal pleasure; besides rings, brooches, bracelets, and other articles of jewellery, of such magnificent materials, and costly workmanship, that Oliver had no idea, even of their names.

Having replaced these trinkets, the Jew took out another: so small that it lay in the palm of his hand. There seemed to be some very minute inscription on it; for the Jew laid it flat upon the table, and, shading it with his hand, pored over it, long and earnestly. At length he put it down, as if despairing of success; and, leaning back in his chair, muttered:

"What a fine thing capital punishment is! Dead men never repent; dead men never bring awkward stories to light. Ah, it's a fine thing for the trade! Five of 'em strung up in a row, and none left to play booty, or turn white-livered!"

As the Jew uttered these words, his bright dark eyes, which had been staring vacantly before him, fell on Oliver's face; the boy's eyes were fixed on his in mute curiosity; and although the recognition was only for an instant—for the briefest space of time that can possibly be conceived—it was enough to show the old man that he had been observed. He closed the lid of the box with a loud crash; and, laying his hand on a bread knife which was on the table, started furiously up. He trembled very much though; for, even in his terror Oliver could see that the knife quivered in the air.

"What's that?" said the Jew. "What do you watch me for? Why are you awake? What have you seen? Speak out, boy! Quick—quick! for your life!"

"I wasn't able to sleep any longer, sir," replied Oliver, meekly. "I am very sorry if I have disturbed you, sir."

"You were not awake an hour ago?" said the Jew, scowling fiercely on the boy.

"No! No, indeed!" replied Oliver.

"Are you sure?" cried the Jew: with a still fiercer look than before: and a threatening attitude.

"Upon my word I was not, sir," replied Oliver, earnestly. "I was not, indeed, sir."

"Tush, tush, my dear!" said the Jew, abruptly resuming his old manner, and playing with the knife a little, before he laid it down; as if to induce the belief that he had caught it up, in mere sport. "Of course I know that, my dear. *I only tried to frighten you* [italics added]. You're a brave boy. Ha! ha! you're

> a brave boy, Oliver!" The Jew rubbed his hands with a chuckle, but glanced uneasily at the box, notwithstanding.
>
> "Did you see any of these pretty things, my dear?" said the Jew, laying his hand upon it after a short pause.
>
> "Yes, sir," replied Oliver.
>
> "Ah!" said the Jew, turning rather pale. "They—they're mine, Oliver; my little property. All I have to live upon, in my old age. The folks call me a miser, my dear. Only a miser; that's all."
>
> Oliver thought the old gentleman must be a decided miser to live in such a dirty place, with so many watches; but, thinking that perhaps his fondness for the Dodger and the other boys, cost him a good deal of money, he only cast a deferential look at the Jew, and asked if he might get up.
>
> "Certainly, my dear, certainly," replied the old gentleman. "Stay. There's a pitcher of water in the corner by the door. Bring it here; and I'll give you a basin to wash in, my dear."
>
> Oliver got up; walked across the room; and stooped for an instant to raise the pitcher. When he turned his head, the box was gone.[15]

"Am not I in sport?" says the man full of guile. "I only tried to frighten you," said Fagin, whose heart was full of guile and wickedness.

(2) The Man Full of Gossip (26:20-22)

Solomon wrote next about the gossip and drew our attention to *the strife he causes:* "Where no wood is, there the fire goeth out: so where there is no talebearer, the strife ceaseth. As coals are to burning coals, and wood to fire, so is a contentious man to kindle strife" (Proverbs 26:20-21).

The gossip, who likes to stir up trouble, is a moral arsonist. He is only too willing to provide fuel to feed the fire of strife. We meet a classic example of a talebearer in *Tom Sawyer.* One hot summer afternoon Tom's Aunt Polly suspected that Tom had played hooky from school and had gone for a dip in the swimming hole. Mark Twain told us what happened:

> Tom did play hooky, and he had a very good time. He got back home barely in season to help Jim, the small colored boy, saw next-day's wood and split the kindling before supper—at least he was there in time to tell his adventures to Jim while Jim

did three-fourths of the work. Tom's younger brother (or rather, half-brother) Sid, was already through with his part of the work (picking up chips) for he was a quiet boy, and had no adventurous, troublesome ways.

While Tom was eating his supper, and stealing sugar as opportunity offered, Aunt Polly asked him questions that were full of guile, and very deep—for she wanted to trap him into damaging revealments. Like many other simple-hearted souls, it was her pet vanity to believe she was endowed with a talent for dark and mysterious diplomacy, and she loved to contemplate her most transparent devices as marvels of low cunning. Said she:

"Tom, it was middling warm in school, warn't it?"

"Yes'm."

"Powerful warm, warn't it?"

"Yes'm."

"Didn't you want to go in a swimming, Tom?"

A bit of a scare shot through Tom—a touch of uncomfortable suspicion. He searched Aunt Polly's face, but it told him nothing. So he said:

"No'm—well, not very much."

The old lady reached out her hand and felt Tom's shirt, and said:

"But you ain't too warm now, though." And it flattered her to reflect that she had discovered that the shirt was dry without anybody knowing that that was what she had in her mind. But in spite of her, Tom knew where the wind lay, now. So he forestalled what might be the next move:

"Some of us pumped on our heads—mine's damp yet. See?"

Aunt Polly was vexed to think she had overlooked that bit of circumstantial evidence, and missed a trick. Then she had a new inspiration:

"Tom, you didn't have to undo your shirt collar where I sewed it, to pump on your head, did you? Unbutton your jacket!"

The trouble vanished out of Tom's face. He opened his jacket. His shirt collar was securely sewed.

"Bother! Well, go 'long with you. I'd made sure you'd played hooky and been a swimming. But I forgive ye, Tom. I reckon you're a kind of a singed cat, as the saying is—better'n you look. *This* time."

She was half sorry her sagacity had miscarried, and half glad that Tom had stumbled into obedient conduct for once.

But Sidney said:

"Well, now, if I didn't think you sewed his collar with white thread, but it's black."

"Why, I did sew it with white! Tom!"

But Tom did not wait for the rest. As he went out at the door he said:

"Siddy, I'll lick you for that."

Saturday came and Tom was sentenced to whitewash thirty yards of board fence, nine feet high. How he conned his school friends into giving him special treasures in exchange for being allowed to do his chore, comprises one of the great passages of literature. Three coats of whitewash were put on the fence while Tom lolled in glorious idleness, receiving the toll and tribute of the junior section of the village. Tom then summoned his aunt to inspect the finished job and release him from his punishment. Mark Twain wrote:

> Then he skipped out and saw Sid just starting up the outside stairway that led to the back rooms on the second floor. Clods were handy and the air was full of them in a twinkling. They raged around Sid like a hail-storm; and before Aunt Polly could collect her surprised faculties and sally to the rescue, six or seven clods had taken personal effect, and Tom was over the fence and gone. There was a gate, but as a general thing he was too crowded for time to make use of it. His soul was at peace, now that he had settled with Sid for calling attention to his black thread and getting him into trouble.[16]

Sid was the kind of talebearer Solomon had in mind. Even though what Sid said was true, his words stirred up trouble and caused strife.

Next Solomon, writing more about the gossip, drew our attention to *the sorrow he causes:* "The words of a talebearer are as wounds, and they go down into the innermost parts of the belly" (Proverbs 26:22). Such words hurt; they do damage deep within a person and can cause untold harm.

This proverb is illustrated by an incident in Jeffery Farnol's book *The Broad Highway.* The hero of the story, Peter Vibart, was living in the woods in a disused cottage that had the reputation of being haunted. He befriended the lovely Charmian Brown and shared with her his poverty, along with a high sense of integrity and impeccable good manners. Not knowing she was a fabulously wealthy heiress, Peter became increasingly fond of his mysterious guest while she, in turn, became increasingly curious about him.

Charmian was curious about the fact that he said his name was Smith, the fact that he read Virgil in Latin, and the fact that the name on the flyleaf of the book was Peter Vibart. She knew Peter Vibart's cousin, Maurice Vibart, in high society—to which she belonged and to which she suspected "Smith" also belonged in spite of his poverty and present employment as a village blacksmith.

An unpleasant peddler, known by the picturesque title of Gabbing Dick, tried to lay claim to the cottage in the woods, but was sent about his business in a hurry by Peter. Later Gabbing Dick spied Charmian questioning a stranger about the Virgil book. (The stranger had worked for Peter as a groom before Peter had been overtaken by poverty.) The malicious peddler saw his chance to cause trouble and get his revenge. He accosted Peter as the blacksmith was making his way back to the cottage at the end of a day's work. Peter retold their conversation. The peddler began by making general disparaging remarks about women, their slyness, and their underhandedness:

> "Oceans of good blood's been spilt all along o' women, from the Eve as tricked old Adam to the Eve as tricks the like o' me, or say—yourself." Here he regarded me with so evil a leer that I turned my back in disgust.
>
> "Don't go, young cove; I ain't done yet, and I got summ'at to tell ye."
>
> "Then tell it!" said I, stopping again, struck by the fellow's manner, "and tell it quickly."
>
> "I'm a-comin' to it as fast as I can, ain't I? Very well then! You're a fine, up-standin' young cove, and may 'ave white 'ands (which I don't see myself, but no matter) and may likewise be chock-full o' taking ways (which, though not noticin', I won't go for to deny)—but a Eve's a Eve, and always will be—you'll mind as I warned you again' 'em last time I see ye?—very well then!"
>
> "Well?" said I impatiently.
>
> "Well," nodded the Pedler, and his eyes twinkled malevolently. "I says it again—I warns you again. You're a nice, civil-spoke young cove, and quiet (though I *don't* like the cock o' your eye), and, mind, I don't bear you no ill-will—

though you did turn me from your door on a cold, dark night—"

"It was neither a cold nor a dark night!" said I.

"Well, it might ha' been, might n't it?—very well then! Still, I don't," said the Pedler, spitting dejectedly into the ditch, "I don't bear you no 'ard feelin's for it, no'ow—me always makin' it a pint to forgive them as woefully oppresses me, likewise them as despitefully uses me—it might ha' been cold, and dark, wi' ice and snow, and I might ha' froze to death—but we won't say no more about it."

"You've said pretty well, I think," said I; "supposing you tell me what you have to tell me—otherwise—good night!"

"Very well then!" said the Pedler, "let's talk o' summ'at else; still livin' in the 'Oller, I suppose?"

"Yes."

"Ah, well! I come through there today," said he, grinning, and again his eyes grew malevolent.

"Indeed?"

"Ah!—indeed! I come though this 'ere very arternoon, and uncommon pretty everythin' was lookin', wi' the grass so green, and the trees so—so—"

"Shady."

"Shady's the word!" nodded the Pedler, glancing up at me through his narrowed eyelids, and chuckling. "A paradise you might call it—ah! a paradise or a—garden of Eden, wi' Eve and the serpent and all!" and he broke out into a cackling laugh. And, in the look and the laugh, indeed about his whole figure, there was something so repellent, so evil, that I was minded to kick and trample him down into the ditch, yet the leering triumph in his eyes held me.

"Yes?" said I.

"Ye see, bein' by, I 'appened to pass the cottage—and very pretty that looked too, and nice and neat inside!"

"Yes?" said I.

"And, bein' so near, I 'appened to glance in at the winder, and there, sure enough, I see—'er—as you might say, Eve in the gardin. And a fine figure of a Eve she be, and 'andsome wi' it—'t ain't often as you see a maid the likes o' 'er, so proud and 'aughty like."

"Well?"

"Well, just as I 'appened to look in at the winder, she 'appened to be standin' wi' an open book in 'er 'and—a old, leather book wi' a broken cover."

> "Yes?" said I.
>
> "And she was a-laughin'—and a pretty, soft, Eve's laugh it were, too."
>
> "Yes?" said I.
>
> "And—*'e* were a-lookin' at the book—over 'er shoulder!" The irons slipped from my grasp, and fell with a harsh clang....
>
> "Ketches ye, does it, my cove?" he repeated; "turn me away from your door on a cold, dark night, would ye (not as I bears you any ill-will for it, bein' of a forgivin' natur')? But I says to you, I says—look out!—a fine 'andsome lass she be, wi' 'er soft eyes and red lips, and long, white arms—the eyes and lips and arms of a Eve; and Eve tricked Adam, didn't she?—and you ain't a better man nor Adam, are ye?—very well then!" saying which, he spat once more into the ditch, and, shouldering his pack, strode away.
>
> And, after some while, I took up my iron bars, and trudged on towards the cottage. As I went, I repeated to myself, over and over again, the word "Liar." Yet my step was very slow and heavy, and my feet dragged in the dust; and, somewhere in my head, a small hammer had begun to beat, soft and slow and regular, but beating, beating upon my brain.

Peter lost all appetite for his supper. "Supper," he said, "was a very ghost of a meal.... The very food grew nauseous and seemed to choke me."[17]

How the incident brought a trail of twists and turns to the story is a tribute to the novelist's art. Dark suspicion took over Peter's mind, soured his soul, and led him into folly. The words of the malicious peddler had done their work. They illustrate Solomon's observation that "the words of a talebearer are as wounds, and they go down into the innermost parts of the belly."

(3) The Man Full of Gall (26:23)

"Burning lips and a wicked heart are like a potsherd covered with silver dross." A silver covering could give a clay pot some value, even though the glitter and shine would probably be temporary since metal and clay do not mix or adhere. But a covering of silver *dross* would give the pot no value. Some people are like clay pots covered with silver dross. They are flashy and at first sight they may appear to be clever or strong or successful—people to be envied. But the impression they make is all empty show.

Cesare Borgia—duke of Valentino and the son of Pope Alexander VI—had a wicked heart overlaid with sham glitter. He held the rank of duke of the Romagna, and as captain general of the armies of the church, he capitalized on his father's papacy to attempt the conquest of central Italy. His duplicity and ruthlessness led Machiavelli to eulogize him as an example of the new "prince." Cesare's mother was the pope's most famous mistress.

Cesare was educated for a career in the church. At the age of seven he was made an apostolic prothonotary and canon of the cathedral of Valencia. He studied law and was named bishop of Pamplona at age sixteen. After his father became the pope, seventeen-year-old Cesare was made archbishop of Valencia. Two years later he became a cardinal.

Cesare had a brilliant mind and enjoyed the reputation of being the handsomest man in Italy, but he was just "a potsherd covered with silver dross." He was more famous for his hunting parties, amorous intrigues, and gorgeous apparel than for any attention he paid to his religious duties. In fact he gave up his cardinalate at age twenty-three to devote himself to the conquest of the cities of the Romagna and the Marches. Ambitious and arrogant, he was determined to establish himself as an Italian prince before his father died and he lost the political and financial support of the papacy. Egotist that he was, he adopted the motto Either Cesare or Nothing.

Cesare's policy was to trick and countertrick, betray and double-deal. These methods were not simply the commonplace tactics of Borgia's political game; they were the very texture of his policy. They were to be expected. If they proved to be successful, they were to be admired.

Cesare had the full backing of his father, who subordinated his position as the vicar of Christ to his position as prince of the church. Pope Alexander VI ruled over provinces and cities, had armies on his payroll, contracted alliances, and ruled as a secular sovereign. Cesare was the pope's military arm to carry out his schemes of conquest. No one knew what went on behind Cesare's mask. He could present a tender, menacing, ardent, or imperious front—as the occasion required.

Cesare's strategy was to put pressure on a man or a city to do the impossible, then take the refusal as a pretext for an all-out attack. For a while everything went his way. In 1501 he joined France in an attack on Naples. In 1502-1503 he conducted his third Romagna campaign using methods typical of his style: a lightning-swift attack on the unsuspecting city of Urbino led to its capitulation without a shot being fired; then Cesare turned on Camerino, which also quickly surrendered. He brought many of the city-states of Italy under his control.

Cesare's growing personal power alarmed his commanders, who conspired against him. The papal purse, however, enabled him to rebuild his army in spite of the defection of former colleagues. At the same time, he conspired against the conspirators. Having weakened their coalition, he proposed a peace conference with them. When they came, he isolated them from their troops and executed them. Once again he had the army behind him and once again his success seemed assured.

But Cesare's success was all gloss and glitter covering an earthenware pot. Within a year his father died, Cesare himself became ill, and the new pope became his determined enemy. Through the years Cesare had made too many enemies. His dukedoms dissolved like sand castles before the rising tide, and the Borgia bully with the burning lips and the wicked heart was revealed as a potsherd covered with silver dross.

c. The Man Who Tries to Start Something (26:24-28)

(1) Rage (26:24-26)

This passage teaches us about the rage of the man who tries to start something. Proverbs 26:24 shows us *hatred dissembled:* "He that hateth dissembleth with his lips, and layeth up deceit within him." In other words, while this man's heart is boiling with rage, he presents a smiling face to the world and even to those he hates the most. Proverbs 26:25 shows us *hatred diagnosed:* "When he speaketh fair, believe him not: for there are seven abominations in his heart." In other words, this man should not be taken at face value. Proverbs 26:26 shows us *hatred discovered:* "Whose hatred is covered by deceit, his wickedness shall be shewed before the whole congregation." In other words, this man's mask will sooner or later be ripped off.

The false prophet of the Apocalypse is such a man. He looks like a lamb (Revelation 13:11), but his appearance is deceptive. He has "two horns like a lamb," but they are deceptive too, for they are mere toys compared to the formidable horns of a full-grown wild ram of the mountains.

When the false prophet finally speaks, however, he gives himself away to the wary, for he speaks like a dragon. In Scripture the dragon is the evil one himself (Revelation 12:3-9). He is plainly identified as "the Devil" (the slanderer) and "Satan" (the adversary). The dragon has an offspring who bears the family likeness and is commonly called the antichrist (Revelation 13:1). To him the devil gives both his power *(dunamis)* and authority *(exousia).* The antichrist shares that power and authority with the false prophet. The purpose of this diabolical trinity—the devil, the antichrist, and the false prophet—is to deceive the whole world (Revelation 13:14). The fact that Satan (in John's vision) has been cast out of the heavenlies and his activities are restricted to the earth, greatly intensifies his efforts to achieve his goal of deception.

The coming age is pre-eminently an age of deception (2 Thessalonians 2:1-12). The purpose of the false prophet is to lull the world into a false sense of security and well-being. He is the close ally and soul-twin of the antichrist, who understands "dark sentences" and causes "craft [deceit] to prosper" (Daniel 8:23-25).

Deep within the hearts of all three—the devil, the antichrist, and the false prophet—is an implacable hatred of mankind. Satan hates the human race with a bitterness and malice that defies description. His desire is to wreak his envy, spite, and loathing on us. That is why he taught our first parents to sin. That is why he summons countless legions of fallen angels and evil spirits to hold this world in thrall. That is why he plagues us with lies, diseases, and disasters, and gloats over the reign of sin and death on this once fair planet.

In the revelation given to John, the false prophet comes with sugar-coated lies. He tells a plague-wracked, war-ravished, famine-stricken, ecologically-ruined planet (Revelation 6) that there is an answer—there is a man who can bring order out of chaos, solve the world's problems, and usher in an age of prosperity and peace. The one the false prophet champions is the antichrist, who indeed seems to be the savior. He is handsome, clever, personable, and full of charisma and charm. He is a born leader. To the Germans, Hitler appeared to be just such a leader; and to the Russians, Lenin appeared to be just such a savior.

The book of Proverbs warns, "When he speaketh fair, believe him not," and in the book of Revelation the false prophet is eloquent. We can imagine that as he speaks before the United Nations, he charms the people of France with his elegant French, the Muslims with his flawless Arabic, the British with his Oxford accent, and the Japanese with his absolute command of their idioms. He carries all his audiences on the soaring wings of his oratory. Sometimes he whips groups of people into mass hysteria and other times he influences people individually. He speaks to a Sudanese peasant in his mother tongue and to a highlander in broad Scots. In a single sentence he solves an investment problem for a business tycoon. He gives a microbiologist an equation that unlocks a riddle in genetics. He gives a word of consolation to an orphaned child. In every situation he speaks deceitfully. Whether he flatters, or threatens, or woos, or warns, his golden tongue always promotes one man—the antichrist.

Solomon wrote about a man with "seven abominations in his heart." The false prophet fits the description, for in his heart are lust and lies, malice and murder, idolatry, hatred, and hell itself. These abominations—skillfully veiled when appropriate, or artfully revealed when suitable—pander to man's lusts and win hearts to the man of sin. Revelation 13:12-14 says that the false prophet

> causeth the earth and them which dwell therein to worship the first beast, whose deadly wound was healed. And he doeth great wonders, so that he maketh fire come down from heaven on the earth in the sight of men, And deceiveth them that dwell on the earth by the means of those miracles which he had power to do in the sight of the beast; saying to them that dwell on the earth, that they should make an image to the beast, which had the wound by a sword, and did live.

As soon as the image is made, the false prophet takes off his mask and speaks like a dragon. Truly his "hatred is covered by deceit." The treaty he persuaded the Jews to sign with the antichrist is torn up. The temple he enabled them to build is seized, probably on the occasion of some great Jewish feast when "the whole congregation" is there. The imperial guard cordons off the area. The image of the antichrist is brought into the outer court of the temple in the sight of the horrified Jews. We can imagine television cameras capturing the drama, as the whole world watches. And suddenly the image comes to life. It walks, goes into the temple, rends the veil, and sits down on what was supposed to be the mercy seat. And Revelation 13:15 tells us that those who refuse to worship the image are killed.

(2) Retribution (26:27)

"Whoso diggeth a pit shall fall therein: and he that rolleth a stone, it will return upon him." This proverb too is illustrated by the false prophet.

At first all goes well for him and his fellow conspirators. The antichrist himself takes over the Jewish temple. Second Thessalonians 2:4 tells us that he "opposeth and exalteth himself above all that is called God, or that is worshipped; so that he as God sitteth in the temple of God, shewing himself that he is God." New edicts are issued from the temple. For example Revelation 13:16-17 tells us that the false prophet "causeth all, both small and great, rich and poor, free and bond, to receive a mark in their right hand, or in their foreheads: And that no man might buy or sell, save he that had the mark, or the name of the beast, or the number of his name." Spiritually enlightened people recognize the ominous portent of the hour and flee to the mountains (Matthew 24:15-22).

God however is still very much in control. He has set a time limit of 1,290 days on the activities of the Satanic trinity (Daniel 7:25; 12:6-12). So the age of terror lasts that long and then retribution comes. Christ returns and seizes the antichrist and the false prophet; He hurls them headlong into the lake of fire (Revelation 19:19-21). Satan is incarcerated in the abyss for a thousand years, and afterward is flung into the lake of fire where he joins his fellow conspirators (Revelation 20:1-10). If there is only one thing we learn from the book of Revelation, it is this: God is still on the throne!

Like the man in Proverbs 26:27, the false prophet digs a pit and falls in it; the antichrist rolls a stone and it hits his own head. As Longfellow phrased the old adage, "The mills of God grind slowly, yet they grind exceeding small."

(3) Review (26:28)

Summing up, Solomon wrote, "A lying tongue hateth those that are afflicted by it; and a flattering mouth worketh ruin." This proverb has proved true in all ages. Victims sometimes find it in their hearts to forgive perpetrators. But perpetrators rarely ask forgiveness. On the contrary, they usually hate their victims.

The classic Biblical example is Amnon, the son of David and Ahinoam, the Jezreelitess. Amnon fell in love with his half sister Tamar, but he could not get close to her even though she was a relative, because in those days the women of the palace were segregated and guarded, usually by eunuchs, and all the ladies' activities were closely chaperoned. Amnon told his friend Jonadab (the son of David's brother Shammah or Shimeah as he is sometimes called) about his predicament. Jonadab understood the problem and suggested that Amnon pretend to be sick, so that when David came to see him, he could ask for Tamar to be his nurse.

Amnon followed through with the plot. Tamar came in response to David's order and started to make some pancakes for the patient.

He eyed her lustfully while she innocently went about her task. Then when the food was ready, Amnon suddenly dismissed all his servants, and as soon as he and Tamar were alone, he seized the young woman and propositioned her. She protested, pointing out the sin and shame of what he suggested. She begged him, perhaps stalling for time, to ask David for her hand in marriage. Tamar pleaded, but Amnon was not to be denied and he raped her.

After he committed the crime, Amnon was consumed by the same kind of revulsion that Solomon described in his proverb. "Then," says the Holy Spirit, "Amnon hated her exceedingly; so that the hatred wherewith he hated her was greater than the love wherewith he had loved her" (2 Samuel 13:15). Exhibiting his hatred in deeds, Amnon callously ignored Tamar's cries and had her thrown out of his house. When David heard of the incident, he hesitated to execute Amnon for his shameful behavior, but Absalom—Tamar's full brother—was not slow to act. He took matters into his own hands and had Amnon murdered.

Often wrongdoing does not produce a guilty conscience, and no forgiveness is sought. Instead the situation turns sour and breeds hatred of the one who has been wronged.

# CHAPTER 6

Proverbs 27:1-27

B. Thoughts on How to Behave (27:1-27)
  1. Regarding Glaring Faults (27:1-4)
    a. Beware of Presumption (27:1)
    b. Beware of Pride (27:2)
    c. Beware of Petulance (27:3)
    d. Beware of Prejudice (27:4)
  2. Regarding Good Friends (27:5-10)
    a. Comparing Friendships (27:5-6)
      (1) The Cautious Friend (27:5)
      (2) The Courageous Friend (27:6)
    b. Cultivating Friendships (27:7-8)
      (1) Prove Your Friendships (27:7)
      (2) Protect Your Friendships (27:8)
    c. Comprehending Friendships (27:9-10)
      (1) Develop the Right Climate (27:9)
      (2) Develop the Right Contacts (27:10)
  3. Regarding Glad Fathers (27:11)
  4. Regarding Great Folly (27:12-16)
    a. The Folly of Having Too Little a Mind (27:12-13)
      (1) Failure to Read Obvious Signs (27:12)
      (2) Failure to Regard Ordinary Sense (27:13)
    b. The Folly of Having Too Large a Mouth (27:14-16)
      (1) Extravagant Compliments (27:14)
      (2) Endless Contentions (27:15-16)
        There is no way to:
        (a) Shut a Nagging Woman Up (27:15)
        (b) Shut a Nagging Woman In (27:16)
  5. Regarding Growing Finances (27:17-27)
    a. The Question of Integrity (27:17-22)

- (1) Diligence Discussed (27:17-18)
  - (a) Mutual Help (27:17)
  - (b) Mutual Harmony (27:18)
- (2) Vigilance Discussed (27:19-21)
  - (a) Look Out for People (27:19)
  - (b) Look Out for Prospects (27:20)
  - (c) Look Out for Praise (27:21)
- (3) Ignorance Discussed (27:22)

b. The Question of Industry (27:23-27)
- (1) When One Gives Up Being Diligent (27:23-24)
  - (a) The Warning Introduced (27:23-24a)
  - (b) The Warning Illustrated (27:24b)
- (2) When One Goes On Being Diligent (27:25-27)
  - (a) Look at the Fields (27:25)
  - (b) Look at the Farm (27:26)
  - (c) Look at the Food (27:27)

In Proverbs 27, which contains proverbs edited by Hezekiah, Solomon continued to pursue a series of thoughts on *the king and his subjects* (25:1–27:27). Having provided a long and varied list of *those of whom to beware* (25:1–26:28), he began to express his *thoughts on how to behave* (27:1-27). Again his mind ranged far and wide, in a manner reminiscent of a hummingbird that darts from one flower to another. The bird hovers for a moment over one bright blossom, barely sips nectar from another, then is attracted to still another fragrant flower. This constant darting here and there makes the book of Proverbs interesting to read—and a challenge to outline!

## B. Thoughts on How to Behave (27:1-27)

### 1. Regarding Glaring Faults (27:1-4)

Solomon's first piece of advice is to *beware of presumption:* "Boast not thyself of to morrow; for thou knowest not what a day may bring forth" (Proverbs 27:1).

This proverb reminds me of an incident that took place in the coal-mining area of south Wales. I was raised in a town on the edge of the district. Each valley had a coal mine and a population of miners who lived in cottages on the terraced hillsides. The colliery dominated the view, the economy, the way of life, and usually the politics of the valley. Another prominent feature of the landscape was the slag heap.

Slag was a waste substance that the miners brought out of the underground galleries along with the coal. The mine owners had no use for the slag and certainly had no intention of diluting their profits by paying the miners to put it back where it came from. Nor would the owners waste good money on shipping the slag away so that it could be used for landfill elsewhere. They simply put the slag on long conveyer belts, moved it from the mine to the mountain, and dumped it. So outside each mining village was an ugly heap of slag. The villagers simply accepted these manmade mountains of ugliness as part of the scenery.

One such village, named Abervan, had its coal mine, its church, its fading memories of the Welsh revival, its narrow streets and crowded cottages, its small shops, its view of sheep dotting the mountains—and its slag heap. The pattern of life had been unchanged for generations. One Monday morning in October 1968 the children of the village climbed out of bed, ate breakfast, put on their coats, and headed off for school as usual. And as usual the miners were already at work. The boys and girls and their teachers arrived at school, went to their classes, and began their daily routine. A steady rain had fallen for days, but no one took notice—in Britain it nearly always rains.

Unknown to anyone in the village, the rain had undermined the slag heap. Suddenly with a roar it gave way, came hurtling down on the village, and buried the schoolhouse. About 116 boys and girls and their teachers were buried alive. A call for help rang out across the nation. Miners descended in droves on that village and dug like frantic fiends to get into that school. They got in, but they were too late.

The villagers went to the local cemetery, dug a trench eighty feet long, and buried all those children and their teachers. Today a visitor to Abervan can walk down the length of that communal grave. The walk is long, sad, and sobering. At regular intervals he will see a slab of stone bearing the name of a boy or girl. Occasionally the visitor will see a stone enshrining the picture of a child, or a stone carrying a message or a line or two of poetry. Proverbs 27:1 might well have been written on every slab.

Solomon's words could also have been applied to Abner (2 Samuel 3:27); to Benhadad (1 Kings 20:1-30); to Ahab (1 Kings 22:19-37); to Haman (Esther 5:12; 7:1-10); to Nebuchadnezzar (Daniel 4:30-33). Solomon's words belong pre-eminently to the rich fool (Luke 12:20) and they need to be applied to us. The strongest man, the most beautiful woman, the liveliest boy or girl, the most bitter atheist, the most devout believer, the wisest man, or the world's silliest scoffer is only a heartbeat away from eternity. "Boast not thyself of to morrow."

My wife and I walked down the length of that Abervan graveyard and read the inscriptions. One stands out in my mind to this day. A brokenhearted mom and dad had written:

> Some day we'll understand it,
> And know the reason why;
> The saddest thing of all is,
> We never said "Good-bye."

Next Solomon warned us to *beware of pride:* "Let another man praise thee, and not thine own mouth; a stranger, and not thine own lips" (Proverbs 27:2).

Every few years we who live in the United States are exposed to the undignified spectacle of congressional and presidential election campaigns. They seem to be conducted for the purpose of determining who can crow about himself the longest and the loudest. Candidates for high office rent billboards and paste up giant pictures of themselves. They buy radio and television time and they buy space in the press in order to publicize how wise, honest, generous, and admirable they are. Even Muhammad Ali, who in the days of his boxing fame boasted, "I am the greatest!" seems reserved compared with these politicians. They organize armies of people to shout their praises. They hand out brochures about themselves. They interrupt our favorite television programs to tell us why they are the greatest. Solomon would have laughed aloud at the whole performance or sadly shaken his head. "Let another man praise thee."

The classic Biblical example of humility is John the Baptist. He was the Lord's first cousin, but he never said so. He was the prophet who broke the silence of four hundred years, but he never mentioned that. He was born and bred to the priesthood, but he never referred to his upbringing. With his gifts, abilities, determination, godliness, and command of the crowd, he could have become the high priest. But he was not interested in position. John could have mounted a milk-white horse, dwelt in a palace, worn scarlet and ermine, and lived like a lord. Instead he wore a hairy shirt, lived in the desert, and ate locusts and honey.

Enormous crowds flocked from all parts of the country to hear him preach in the wilderness and denounce their sins. Even the Sanhedrin sent a delegation. "Who are you?" they demanded in effect. "Are you Elijah? Are you the prophet foretold by Moses? Are you the Messiah?"

"No!" he said. "No! No! No!"

"Then who *are* you?" they insisted.

"I am the voice of one crying in the wilderness," he replied (see John 1:19-23).

John did not praise himself, but Jesus praised John. When the Baptist was in prison (he would soon be executed by Herod to satisfy a woman's spite), Jesus eulogized His forerunner:

> He began to speak unto the people concerning John, What went ye out into the wilderness for to see? A reed shaken with the wind? But what went ye out for to see? A man clothed in soft raiment? Behold, they which are gorgeously apparelled, and live delicately, are in kings' courts. But what went ye out for to see? A prophet? Yea, I say unto you, and much more than a prophet. This is he, of whom it is written, Behold, I send my messenger before thy face, which shall prepare thy way before thee. For I say unto you, Among those that are born of women there is not a greater prophet than John the Baptist (Luke 7:24-28).

No man has ever received greater praise or praise from a greater source.

Another warning from Solomon is to *beware of petulance:* "A stone is heavy, and the sand weighty; but a fool's wrath is heavier than them both" (Proverbs 27:3). Although a stone and sand are hard to move, it is well nigh impossible to move a fool, especially an angry fool.

Nabal was an angry fool. His very name means "fool." His anger added to his folly and exposed him to imminent danger; his drunkenness added to his folly and bade fair to be his doom.

David's men had thrown a blanket of protection over Nabal's flocks and herds—a valuable service in those wild and lawless days. Nabal was rich—he had three thousand sheep and a thousand goats—but David would not allow his men to take tribute from Nabal's flocks. On the other hand, David did not think that Nabal should go scot-free. So David sent a deputation to ask Nabal to contribute something toward the upkeep of David's band.

Nabal foolishly refused to contribute anything in acknowledgment of services rendered and thus keep the goodwill of this powerful group of men who were roaming in the vicinity of his farm and fields. He angrily sneered at David and his deputation and sent the men away filled with his angry words.

David reacted at once. With four hundred men at his back, he marched out of his camp to deal with Nabal once and for all. Doubtless he would have done so, had he not been met by Nabal's wife Abigail. Her voluntary contribution and wise, humble, and reasoned words averted her husband's doom.

When Abigail returned home, she found her husband feasting like a king and as drunk as a lord. She went off to bed, but first thing next morning, as soon as Nabal was sober, she told him what she had done and how close had been his brush with death. Then "his heart died within him, and he became as a stone," the historian wrote (1 Samuel 25:37). Perhaps Solomon was remembering the story of Nabal when he wrote, "A stone is heavy... but a fool's wrath is heavier."

Solomon also warned us to *beware of prejudice:* "Wrath is cruel, and anger is outrageous; but who is able to stand before envy?" (Proverbs 27:4) Once envy takes root, woe betide its victim. Envy knows no logic and no mercy. There is no end to its gall and guile. Wrath and anger can be appeased, but not envy.

Joseph was a victim of envy. The trouble was that Jacob loved Rachel. Rachel was the only wife he had wanted. Leah, Bilhah, and Zilpah had all been more or less forced on him. Jacob wished that all his children could have been Rachel's children. Joseph was Rachel's firstborn, so Joseph was the firstborn of Jacob's heart. So what if Reuben was really his firstborn? So what if Simeon, Levi, and Judah were all born to Leah long before Joseph was born to Rachel? So what if Bilhah and Zilpah bore Dan, Naphtali, Gad, and Asher before Joseph was born? So what if Leah bore Issachar and Zebulun before Joseph was born? Jacob wrote them all off. Joseph was his beloved boy, his pride and joy. The others could take the leftovers of his love. Joseph ruled supreme in Jacob's heart.

The coat of many colors was proof of Jacob's favoritism. The older boys had suspected it, of course, but when young Joseph was arrayed in the robe of a chieftain, Reuben was outraged, Simeon sharpened his cruelty, Levi collected his wits, and Judah counted up what it would cost him if Joseph were given the family fortune.

In short, the sons of Leah, Bilhah, and Zilpah ganged up against Joseph. "When his brethren saw that their father loved him more than all his brethren, they hated him, and could not speak peaceably unto him" (Genesis 37:4). They did their best to make Joseph's life miserable. As long as Rachel was alive, that was all they dared to do. When Joseph told his brothers his dreams, "they hated him yet the more" (37:8). At last the Holy Spirit tells us bluntly, "His brethren envied him" (37:11).

Then circumstances delivered Joseph into his brothers' hands. The ten older boys were in Shechem, and Jacob had good cause to worry about them (34:25-30), so he decided to send Joseph to find out how they were (37:13-14). By the time Joseph arrived at Shechem, the brothers had moved on to Dothan, which was on the high road to Egypt. Genesis 37:18-20 states:

> When they saw him afar off, even before he came near unto them, they conspired against him to slay him. And they said one to another, Behold, this dreamer cometh. Come now therefore, and let us slay him, and cast him into some pit, and we will say, Some evil beast hath devoured him: and we shall see what will become of his dreams.

Reuben made a tentative effort to save Joseph. Reuben either had some qualms of conscience or was terribly afraid of his father's wrath (from 35:22 we know that he had reason to be afraid). But Reuben lost out to Judah, who proposed selling Joseph as a slave to some Ishmaelites who were passing by. So outrageous is envy that the brothers steeled their hearts against Joseph's anguished cries (42:21). Wrath and anger are hot sins, but envy is cold-blooded, calculating, and cruel.

## 2. Regarding Good Friends (27:5-10)

### a. Comparing Friendships (27:5-6)

Proverbs 27:5 presents *the cautious friend:* "Open rebuke is better than secret love." True love is big and strong, fearless and at times formidable, honest and frank when needful, and always kind. Secret love is timid and shy, weak and retiring, and anxious not to offend; it is hardly love at all.

Henry Drummond, in a magnificent sermon that is still read and quoted although it was first given nearly a hundred years ago, said that love is "the greatest thing in the world." After reading 1 Corinthians 13 to the congregation, he commented:

> We have been accustomed to be told that the greatest thing in the religious world is Faith. That great word has been the keynote for centuries of the popular religion; and we have easily learned to look upon it as the greatest thing in the world. Well, we are wrong. If we have been told that, we may miss the mark. I have taken you in the chapter which I have just read, to Christianity at its source; and there we have seen, "The greatest of these is Love." It is not an oversight. Paul was speaking of faith just a moment before. He says, "If I have all Faith, so that I can remove mountains, and have not Love; I am nothing." So far from forgetting he deliberately contrasts them, "Now abideth Faith, Hope, Love," and without a moment's hesitation the decision falls, "The greatest of these is Love."
>
> And it is not prejudice. A man is apt to recommend to others his own strong point.
>
> Love was not Paul's strong point. The observing student can detect a beautiful tenderness growing and ripening all through his character as Paul gets old; but the hand that wrote "The greatest of these is Love," when we meet it first, is stained with blood.
>
> Nor is this letter to the Corinthians peculiar in singling out Love as the *summum bonum.* The masterpieces of Christianity are agreed about it. Peter says, "Above all things have fervent love among yourselves." *Above all things.* And John goes farther, "God is love." And you remember the profound remark which Paul makes elsewhere, "Love is the fulfilling of the law." Did you ever think what he meant by that? In those days men were working their passage to Heaven by keeping the Ten Commandments, and the hundred and ten other commandments which they had manufactured out of them. Christ said, I will show you a more simple way. If you do one thing, you will do these hundred and ten things, without ever thinking about them. If you love, you will unconsciously fulfill the whole law. And you can readily see for yourselves how that must be so. Take any of the commandments. "Thou shalt have no other gods before Me." If a man love God, you will not require to tell him that. Love is the fulfilling of that law. "Take not His name in vain." Would he ever dream of taking His name in vain if he loved Him? "Remember the Sabbath day to keep it holy."

> Would he not be too glad to have one day in seven to dedicate more exclusively to the object of his affection? Love would fulfill all these laws regarding God. And so, if he loved Man you would never think of telling him to honor his father and mother. He could not do anything else. It would be preposterous to tell him not to kill. You could only insult him if you suggested that he should not steal—how could he steal from those he loved? It would be superfluous to beg him not to bear false witness against his neighbor. If he loved him it would be the last thing he would do.
>
> And you would never dream of urging him not to covet what his neighbors had. He would rather they possessed it than himself. In this way "Love is the fulfilling of the law." It is the rule for fulfilling all rules, the new commandment for keeping all the old commandments, Christ's one secret of the Christian life.

Drummond continued by showing how Paul contrasted love with "other things that men in those days thought much of":

> [Paul] contrasts it with eloquence. And what a noble gift it is, the power of playing upon the souls and wills of men, and rousing them to lofty purposes and holy deeds. Paul says, "If I speak with the tongues of men and of angels, and have not love, I am become as sounding brass, or a tinkling cymbal." And we all know why. We have all felt the brazenness of words without emotion, the hollowness, the unaccountable unpersuasiveness, of eloquence behind which lies no Love.
>
> He contrasts it with [prophecy]. He contrasts it with mysteries. He contrasts it with faith. He contrasts it with charity. Why is Love greater than faith? Because the end is greater than the means. And why is it greater than charity? Because the whole is greater than the part. Love is greater than faith, because the end is greater than the means. What is the use of having faith? It is to connect the soul with God. And what is the object of connecting man with God? That he may become like God. But God is Love. Hence Faith, the means, is in order to Love, the end. Love, therefore, obviously is greater than faith. It is greater than charity, again, because the whole is greater than a part. Charity is only a little bit of Love, one of the innumerable avenues of Love, and there may even be, and there is, a great deal of charity without Love. It is a very easy thing to toss a copper to a beggar on the street; it is generally

> an easier thing than not to do it. Yet Love is just as often in the withholding. We purchase relief from the sympathetic feelings roused by the spectacle of misery, at the copper's cost. It is too cheap—too cheap for us, and often too dear for the beggar. If we really loved him we would either do more for him, or less.

Drummond continued, speaking particularly to prospective missionaries in the congregation:

> Then Paul contrasts [love] with sacrifice and martyrdom. And I beg the little band of would-be missionaries...to remember that though you give your bodies to be burned, and have not Love, it profits nothing—nothing! You can take nothing greater to the heathen world than the impress and the reflection of the Love of God upon your own character. That is the universal language. It will take you years to speak in Chinese, or in the dialects of India. From the day you land, that language of Love, understood by all, will be pouring forth its unconscious eloquence. It is the man who is the missionary, it is not his words. His character is his message. In the heart of Africa, among the great Lakes, I have come across black men and women who remember the only white man they ever saw before—David Livingstone; and as you cross his footsteps in that dark continent, men's faces light up as they speak of the kind Doctor who passed there years ago. They could not understand him; but they felt the Love that beat in his heart.... You may take every accomplishment; you may be braced for every sacrifice; but if you give your body to be burned, and have not Love, it will profit you and the cause of Christ *nothing.*

After analyzing the "ingredients" of love, Drummond spoke of "Paul's reason for singling out Love as the supreme possession":

> It is a very remarkable reason. In a single word it is this: *it lasts.* "Love," urges Paul, "never faileth."...He runs over the things that men thought were going to last, and shows that they are all fleeting, temporary, passing away.
>
> "Whether there be prophecies, they shall fail." It was the mother's ambition for her boy in those days that he should become a prophet. For hundreds of years God had never spoken by means of any prophet, and at that time the prophet was greater than the King. Men waited wistfully for another

> messenger to come and hung upon his lips when he appeared as upon the very voice of God. Paul says, "Whether there be prophecies, they shall fail." This book is full of prophecies. One by one they have "failed"; that is, having been fulfilled, their work is finished; they have nothing more to do now in the world except to feed a devout man's faith.
>
> Then Paul talks about tongues. That was another thing that was greatly coveted. "Whether there be tongues, they shall cease." As we all know, many, many centuries have passed since tongues have been known in this world. They have ceased.

Think for a moment with Drummond and Paul about tongues. All languages have a life of their own. New words are constantly coined and added to the language and from time to time words become archaic and drop out of circulation. If the process of renewal stops for any reason, the language dies.

In view of the craving in many quarters for the gift of tongues, let us bring the issue up to date. Speaking in tongues was a temporary phenomenon. It flared up for a generation, then died away. The gift was only intended to be a sign to unbelieving Jews and as soon as it had served its purpose, it was withdrawn. The fall of Jerusalem, the final debacle of the Bar Kokhba rebellion, and the global dispersion of the Jews who then learned to speak the tongues of the Gentile world, made the sign of tongues redundant.

Drummond continued:

> Then Paul goes farther, and with even greater boldness adds, "Whether there be knowledge, it shall vanish away." The wisdom of the ancients, where is it? It is wholly gone. A schoolboy today knows more than Sir Isaac Newton knew. His knowledge has vanished away. You put yesterday's newspaper in the fire. Its knowledge has vanished away. You buy the old editions of the great encyclopaedias for a few pence. Their knowledge has vanished away. Look how the coach has been superseded by the use of steam. Look how electricity has superseded that, and swept a hundred almost new inventions into oblivion.

If Drummond were living today, he would have to add: "Now we have nuclear power and are tapping also the very energy of the sun itself." He continued:

> One of the greatest living authorities, Sir William Thompson, said the other day, "The steam-engine is passing away." "Whether there be knowledge, it shall vanish away." At every workshop you will see, in a back yard, a heap of old iron, a few wheels, a few levers, a few cranks, broken and eaten with rust. Twenty years ago that was the pride of the city. Men flocked in from the country to see the great invention; now it is superseded, its day is done. And all the boasted science and philosophy of this day will soon be old. But yesterday, in the University of Edinburgh, the greatest figure in the faculty was Sir James Simpson, the discoverer of chloroform. The other day his successor and nephew, Professor Simpson, was asked by the librarian of the University to go to the library and pick out the books on his subject that were no longer needed. And his reply to the librarian was this: "Take every textbook that is more than ten years old, and put it down in the cellar." Sir James Simpson was a great authority only a few years ago: men came from all parts of the earth to consult him; and almost the whole teaching of that time is consigned by the science of today to oblivion. And in every branch of science it is the same: "Now we know in part. We see through a glass darkly."
>
> Can you tell me anything that is going to last?...The only immortal things are these: "Now abideth faith, hope, love, but the greatest of these is love."
>
> Some think the time may come when two of these three things will also pass away—faith into sight, hope into fruition. Paul does not say so. We know but little now about the conditions of the life that is to come. But what is certain is that Love must last. God, the Eternal God, is Love. Covet therefore that everlasting gift, that one thing which it is certain is going to stand, that one coinage which will be current in the Universe when all the other coinages of all the nations of the world shall be useless and unhonored.[1]

The kind of love described by Paul and Drummond is quite different from the secret love mentioned in Proverbs 27:5. Nicodemus displayed an almost furtive kind of love. Even when he did speak up for Christ before the Sanhedrin, his voice was thin and his protest was couched in generalities. It took Calvary to transform his love (compare John 7:50-51 and 19:38-42). Peter's love was boastful and blustering as long as he was with his own crowd, but his love faded into sad denials while he was warming his hands at the world's fire. It took Pentecost to change his love.

Secret love, which is partly self-love, can never bring itself to utter an open rebuke to a loved one. Consider the example of Eli's love for his sons. He was Israel's high priest toward the end of the dark days of the judges. We have no idea how he became the high priest, because that position belonged to the Aaronic family of Eleazar, and Eli came from the family of Ithamar, a younger branch of the Aaronic family. Eli functioned as high priest and judge, and he was a thoroughgoing failure in both roles.

He spoke sharply to poor Hannah when he rebuked her for drunkenness. (Actually she was not drunk and when Eli realized his mistake, he tendered her a half apology.) But he found it impossible to deliver an open rebuke to his own sons. His sons made themselves vile and, abusing the priestly office, seized even the Lord's portion of the sacrifices. They also seduced women who came to worship. Yet the strongest words of rebuke that Eli could muster were:

> Why do ye such things? for I hear of your evil dealings by all this people. Nay, my sons; for it is no good report that I hear: ye make the Lord's people to transgress. If one man sin against another, the judge shall judge him: but if a man sin against the Lord, who shall intreat for him? (1 Samuel 2:23-25)

Eli's sons simply ignored his mild rebuke. He should have taken a whip and cleansed the tabernacle of such vile priests, even if they were his sons.

Since Eli's love was a self-indulgent love, he could never bring himself to discipline his sons. Eli's kind of love eventually led to the death of his sons. Eli is the father of all parents who are unable to deliver an open rebuke to their children and back it up with firm punishment.

In contrast to the cautious friend is *the courageous friend:* "Faithful are the wounds of a friend; but the kisses of an enemy are deceitful" (Proverbs 27:6).

Nathan was a courageous, faithful friend to David after David's terrible sin with Bath-sheba. Nathan bearded the lion in his den and boldly informed David of God's active displeasure (2 Samuel 12:1-12).

Ahithophel, on the other hand, was an enemy whose kisses were deceitful. He professed friendship for David even as he put strength and backbone into Absalom's cause (Psalm 41:9; 2 Samuel 15:10-12).

Joab, David's general, was a strange mixture. He was a true friend to David in many ways. His words were rough, but this tough old general had David's best interests in mind when he bluntly advised him to lay aside his extravagant grief over the death of Absalom and pay more attention to his throne, which was still perilously insecure (2 Samuel 19:1-7). Faithful indeed were the wounds of that friend that day, although it seems that David never forgave Joab for them.

In contrast to this example of Joab's faithfulness, Joab's treatment of Abner was treacherous in the extreme. Abner, who had been King Saul's general, had brought eight hundred thousand fighting men and their families over to David's side. And it was Abner who had taken the initiative in ending the civil war between the house of Saul and the house of David. So Abner posed a threat to General Joab. Wasting no time, Joab caught up with Abner at Hebron and "took him aside in the gate to speak with him quietly" (2 Samuel 3:27). The moment Abner was off guard, Joab stabbed him.

Joab's treatment of Amasa was even more callous. After the death of Absalom, David had every intention of deposing Joab. The king reasoned that if Amasa proved himself, he could take Joab's place as general. So Amasa also posed a threat to Joab.

When they were both pursuing the rebel Sheba, Joab caught up with Amasa "at the great stone which is in Gibeon" (2 Samuel 20:8). As Joab approached the stone, his sword fell out of its sheath, possibly by design; he picked it up and still had it in his hand when he came close to Amasa. Scripture tells us what happened next:

> And Joab said to Amasa, Art thou in health, my brother? [Amasa was Joab's cousin.] And Joab took Amasa by the beard with the right hand to kiss him. But Amasa took no heed to the sword that was in Joab's hand: so he smote him therewith in the fifth rib, and shed out his bowels to the ground, and struck him not again; and he died" (20:9-10).

Although we can cite many illustrations of Proverbs 27:6, none can compare with the example of Jesus. Think of the wounds Jesus deliberately gave to the scribes and Pharisees in Jerusalem a few days before His death. Eight times the terrible words "Woe unto you" rang in their ears (Matthew 23). Again and again He cut them to the heart.

The scribes and Pharisees did not want the kingdom of heaven and they did their best to bolt and bar it to everyone else. Woe to them indeed! They victimized poor widows and covered their crimes with long prayers. Woe! They made a mockery of sacred vows. Woe! They were scrupulous in religious externals such as tithing, but neglected the realities of the faith. Woe! They cleaned up on the outside, but were dirty and vile on the inside. Woe! They paid lip service to the murdered prophets of the past, but were as bad as the people who had martyred them. Woe again! The scribes and Pharisees were a generation of vipers on their way to Hell. Utter desolation lay ahead for their beloved Jerusalem. Nobody had ever spoken to them like that before, except John the Baptist.

"Faithful are the wounds of a friend," and what a friend Jesus is! Jesus wounded people because He loved them enough to die for them. He loved them enough not only to wound them but also to be wounded Himself, even unto death (Isaiah 53:5), to provide salvation for them.

As for the kisses of an enemy, who ever planted a more deceitful kiss on a human cheek than Judas? He had sold out to Christ's enemies and guided the mob and the soldiers to the garden. The Bible says, "Now he that betrayed him gave them a sign, saying, Whomsoever I shall kiss, that same is he: hold him fast. And forthwith he came to Jesus, and said, Hail, master; and kissed him" (Matthew 26:48-49). That deceitful kiss has ever after been synonymous with treachery and shame.

b. Cultivating Friendships (27:7-8)

Is it possible to have too many friends? You probably have times when you crave solitude. Enough is enough, even of one's friends. Conversely, if you do not have any friends, you may so crave companionship that you are glad to see almost anyone, even those who are not really friends at all. In that case Solomon's advice is to *prove your friendships:* "The full soul loatheth an honeycomb; but to the hungry soul every bitter thing is sweet" (Proverbs 27:7).

Fagin, understanding the principle behind this proverb, used loneliness in his attempts to make a life of crime palatable to young Oliver Twist. The old schemer was determined to turn Oliver into a thief, but Fagin (whom Dickens referred to as "the Jew") was up against a formidable problem: poor, orphaned, unfortunate Oliver was not only innocent; he was good. Fagin would have to break down the barrier of Oliver's innate integrity and he explained the difficulty of his task to the young villain Monks. Dickens told of their conversation, beginning with Monk's reflections:

> "I tell you again, it was badly planned. Why not have kept him here among the rest, and made a sneaking, snivelling

pickpocket of him at once?"

"Only hear him!" exclaimed the Jew, shrugging his shoulders.

"Why, do you mean to say you couldn't have done it, if you had chosen?" demanded Monks, sternly. "Haven't you done it, with other boys, scores of times? If you had had patience for a twelvemonth, at most, couldn't you have got him convicted, and sent safely out of the kingdom; perhaps for life?"

"Whose turn would that have served, my dear?" inquired the Jew humbly.

"Mine," replied Monks.

"But not mine," said the Jew, submissively. "He might have become of use to me. When there are two parties to a bargain, it is only reasonable that the interests of both should be consulted; is it, my good friend?"

"What then?" demanded Monks.

"I saw it was not easy to train him to the business," replied the Jew; "he was not like other boys in the same circumstances."

"Curse him, no!" muttered the man, "or he would have been a thief, long ago."

"I had no hold upon him to make him worse," pursued the Jew, anxiously watching the countenance of his companion. "His hand was not in. I had nothing to frighten him with; which we always must have in the beginning, or we labour in vain. What could I do? Send him out with the Dodger and Charley? We had enough of that, at first, my dear; I trembled for us all."

Fagin, in his attempts to break Oliver, had first threatened to have the boy falsely accused and hanged, and then had tried starving Oliver of companionship. Dickens wrote:

Little Oliver's blood ran cold, as he listened to the Jew's words, and imperfectly comprehended the dark threats conveyed in them. That it was possible even for justice itself to confound the innocent with the guilty when they were in accidental companionship, he knew already; and that deeply-laid plans for the destruction of inconveniently knowing or over-communicative persons, had been really devised and carried out by the old Jew on more occasions than one, he thought by no means unlikely, when he recollected the general nature of the altercations between that gentleman and Mr. Sikes: which seemed to bear reference to some foregone conspiracy of the kind. As he glanced timidly up, and met the Jew's searching look, he felt that his pale face and trembling limbs were neither unnoticed nor unrelished by that wary old gentleman.

The Jew, smiling hideously, patted Oliver on the head, and said, that if he kept himself quiet, and applied himself to business, he saw they would be very good friends yet. Then, taking his hat, and covering himself with an old patched greatcoat, he went out, and locked the room-door behind him.

And so Oliver remained all that day, and for the greater part of many subsequent days, seeing nobody, between early morning and midnight, and left during the long hours to commune with his own thoughts. Which, never failing to revert to his kind friends, and the opinion they must long ago have formed of him, were sad indeed.

After the lapse of a week or so, the Jew left the room-door unlocked; and he was at liberty to wander about the house.

It was a very dirty place. The rooms up stairs had great high wooden chimney-pieces and large doors, with panelled walls and cornices to the ceilings; which, although they were black with neglect and dust, were ornamented in various ways. From all of these tokens Oliver concluded that a long time ago, before the old Jew was born, it had belonged to better people, and had perhaps been quite gay and handsome: dismal and dreary as it looked now.

Spiders had built their webs in the angles of the walls and ceilings; and sometimes, when Oliver walked softly into a room, the mice would scamper across the floor, and run back terrified to their holes. With these exceptions, there was neither sight nor sound of any living thing; and often, when it grew dark, and he was tired of wandering from room to room, he would crouch in the corner of the passage by the street-door, to be as near living people as he could; and would remain there, listening and counting the hours, until the Jew or the boys returned.

In all the rooms, the mouldering shutters were fast closed: the bars which held them were screwed tight into the wood; the only light which was admitted, stealing its way through round holes at the top: which made the rooms more gloomy, and filled them with strange shadows. There was a back-garret window with rusty bars outside, which had no shutter; and out of this, Oliver often gazed with a melancholy face for hours together; but nothing was to be descried from it but a confused and crowded mass of house-tops, blackened chimneys, and gable-ends.

Then Fagin had some of his young thieves stop in to break Oliver's loneliness and to talk about the benefits and enjoyments of their profession. "To the hungry soul every bitter thing is sweet," wrote Solomon. Poor Oliver was hungry for companionship. Even the company of thieves now seemed to him better than no company at all. Dickens continued:

> "Look here!" said the Dodger, drawing forth a handful of shillings and half-pence. "Here's a jolly life! What's the odds where it comes from? Here, catch hold; there's plenty more where they were took from. You won't, won't you? Oh, you precious flat!"
>
> "It's naughty, ain't it, Oliver?" inquired Charley Bates. "He'll come to be scragged, won't he?"
>
> "I don't know what that means," replied Oliver.
>
> "Something in this way, old feller," said Charley. As he said it, Master Bates caught up an end of his neckerchief; and, holding it erect in the air, dropped his head on his shoulder, and jerked a curious sound through his teeth: thereby indicating, by a lively pantomimic representation, that scragging and hanging were one and the same thing.
>
> "That's what it means," said Charley. "Look how he stares, Jack! I never did see such prime company as that 'ere boy; he'll be the death of me, I know he will." Master Charles Bates, having laughed heartily again, resumed his pipe with tears in his eyes.
>
> "You've been brought up bad," said the Dodger, surveying his boots with much satisfaction when Oliver had polished them. "Fagin will make something of you, though, or you'll be the first he ever had that turned out unprofitable. You'd better begin at once; for you'll come to the trade long before you think of it; and you're only losing time, Oliver."...
>
> From this day, Oliver was seldom left alone; but was placed in almost constant communication with the two boys, who played the old game with the Jew every day: whether for their own improvement or Oliver's, Mr. Fagin best knew. At other times the old man would tell them stories of robberies he had committed in his younger days: mixed up with so much that was droll and curious, that Oliver could not help laughing

heartily, and showing that he was amused in spite of all his better feelings.

In short, the wily old Jew had the boy in his toils. Having prepared his mind, by solitude and gloom, to prefer any society to the companionship of his own sad thoughts in such a dreary place, he was now slowly instilling into his soul the poison which he hoped would blacken it, and change its hue forever.[2]

Solomon's next piece of advice is to *protect your friendships.* In our mobile society it is difficult to heed this advice. We are like the man in Proverbs 27:8: "As a bird that wandereth from her nest, so is a man that wandereth from his place."

Each person has his rightful place in life. He is born into a given family. Most likely he grows up surrounded by relatives and friends. He has associations with a host of familiar people and places: neighbors, church, school, playgrounds, vacation spots, college, business connections.

A person's place in life was even more specifically defined in Solomon's day. Society was agrarian; it was rooted to the land, to the extended family, to Jerusalem, and to the temple. Outside the walls of Solomon's society was a hostile world of warlike neighbors, false religions, and pagan ideas. Solomon tried to breach these walls by marrying foreign women, adapting to pagan ideas (especially the idea that kings had the right to be as polygamous as they pleased), and compromising with heathen religions. Like a bird wandering from its nest, he wandered from his rightful place in life and the results were disastrous to himself and his people.

In our day the ancient landmarks have been removed and people have difficulty recognizing their place. Big business demands a man's soul and in return offers him a promotion, a pension, and many places to which he can—or must—move.

I have personally experienced the effects of moving again and again. When I first came to North America I left my place. I did not really want to leave. Necessity dictated the move. Actually I had already left my place when I entered military service. My three years in the British army began a cycle of loss. I was constantly moved from post to post and constantly forced to make new friends, only to lose them again. Then when at last my tour of duty in the Middle East was over, I could not really return to my place, because while I was away, my parents had sold their home and business and gone to the mission field. I came home to an empty nest.

When I was inducted into the army, I was working for a large

British bank. When I was discharged from the army, the bank told me it was chronically overstaffed; I could come back for a year, but no longer. That was bad news in postwar Britain, for it was almost impossible to find work.

I had lost my home and my place at the bank, and I started wandering. Once I thought I found a place to settle in Britain, but it was only a dream. Time was getting on and something had to be done, so I decided to emigrate. I went to London and sought employment at a large Canadian bank that hired me on the condition that I would go to Canada. So I said my last goodbye and traveled to Montreal. I wandered far away from my nest.

At the Montreal branch cold eyes looked me up and down. Calculating minds evaluated the new recruit and handed down the verdict: "We are sending you to Vancouver." I traveled across the continent and thousands of miles farther from Britain. I was lonely and entered into the misery of the psalmist when he lamented, "I watch, and am as a sparrow alone upon the house top" (Psalm 102:7).

On the north shore of Vancouver I met new business associates, found a church, and lodged with kind Christians who took me in and treated me kindly. Eventually I married and I thought I had found a new place. But not so! The bank, which ruled more than a thousand branches across Canada, moved me again and again. Each move was like wandering from another nest.

The bank's policy was simple: sell us your soul and we'll see that you get on. The bank expected its bright young executives to join service organizations and civic clubs, become active in the community, work long hours, further their education after office hours, and, above all, be prepared to move at a moment's notice.

The bank gave no thought to this young executive's housing problems. *Should we rent or buy?* we wondered. *Should we buy only to sell again a few years later?* The bank simply wanted us to move, and move fast. It gave no thought to my wife and children or to the sense of rootlessness bred by constant moving.

Each move marked one more rung up the corporate ladder, but in the end I decided that the price was too high. I left the bank to build a nest of my own. I can still see the look of incredulity on the face of the branch manager when I put my resignation on his desk. "But what about your pension?" he asked, even though I was forty years away from retirement at the time!

Corporate America also says, "Move, move, move! Up, up, up! Work, work, work! Join, join, join!" As a result our nation has forgotten the past that made it great. Families are scattered far and wide—parents here, children there, grandparents somewhere else, aunts and uncles and cousins rarely seen and scarcely known. Divorce is rampant. Immorality is a way of life. Loyalties are eroded. Deep friendships are virtually impossible to maintain. Abortion is accepted and drugs are prevalent. That is the lifestyle of millions of mainstream Americans. True, some have remained in the eddies and backwaters as they cling to the old values. Most, however, have wandered from their nests. Solomon would have been appalled to see how far we have strayed.

Of course some moves are part of that "good, and acceptable, and perfect, will of God" of which Paul wrote in Romans 12:2. Stagnation is no better than fermentation. Whether a move is in the will of God depends on whether the move is prompted by obedience, as in the case of Abraham, or by disobedience, as in the case of Cain. Abraham moved because he had deliberately assumed a pilgrim character in response to the will of God for his life. He became "a stranger and a sojourner" in this world (Genesis 12:1-4; 23:4). Cain moved because he was under the judgment of God, who sentenced him to be "a fugitive and a vagabond...in the earth" (Genesis 4:12).

c. Comprehending Friendships (27:9-10)

Continuing his discussion of friendship, Solomon advised us to *develop the right climate*—to bring the right atmosphere into our relationships. As Proverbs 27:9 states, "Ointment and perfume rejoice the heart: so doth the sweetness of a man's friend by hearty counsel." "Hearty counsel"—counsel that comes from the heart—has a fragrance all its own. It is genuine and its rarity and worth is recognizable.

The counsel found in the teaching of the Lord Jesus is rich and rare. It carries the sweet perfume of the holy anointing oil that is spoken of in the Old Testament. That oil was to be used only for anointing the tabernacle and its vessels and God's priests, prophets, and kings. It is no accident that Jesus is known as "the Lord's anointed." He fulfilled all the rich typology of the tabernacle and He alone was God's true Prophet, Priest, and King. No wonder His counsel exudes a unique fragrance.

Let's think about that fragrant anointing oil. In Exodus 30:22-33 we read:

> The Lord spake unto Moses, saying, Take thou also unto thee principal spices, of pure myrrh five hundred shekels, and of

> sweet cinnamon half so much, even two hundred and fifty shekels, and of sweet calamus two hundred and fifty shekels, And of cassia five hundred shekels, after the shekel of the sanctuary, and of oil olive an hin: And thou shalt make it an oil of holy ointment, an ointment compound after the art of the apothecary: it shall be an holy anointing oil....Upon man's flesh shall it not be poured, neither shall ye make any other like it, after the composition of it: it is holy, and it shall be holy unto you. Whosoever compoundeth any like it, or whosoever putteth any of it upon a stranger, shall even be cut off from his people.

The uniqueness of the oil speaks of the absolute uniqueness of Christ. The myrrh speaks of Jesus as *the Lamb of God.* The cinnamon and calamus together speak of Jesus as *the Word of God.* The cassia speaks of Jesus as *the holy One of God.* The olive oil speaks of Jesus as *the Christ of God.* The myrrh points to Christ's *passion.* The cinnamon and calamus together point to His *person.* The cassia points to His *perfection.* The olive oil points to His *position.* Whether we think of Jesus as the Lamb of God, the Word of God, the holy One of God, or the Christ of God, the perfume of His anointing—His consecration—pervades our thoughts. Whether we consider His passion, His person, His perfection, or His position, we are aware of an inimitable fragrance. God combined all these aspects of the Lord Jesus into one luxurious, unique, aromatic blend.

The quantities stipulated in the formula for preparing anointing oil are also significant. All the spices were weighed by the measure of the sanctuary. In Israel half a shekel was required from each individual for ransom money, so a full shekel would indicate that a ransom for sin had been more than fully provided. Thus five hundred shekels of myrrh, the spice used for burying, implied that the measure of redemption provided by Christ is so vast and comprehensive that only God Himself can fully appreciate it. The death of Christ was like the free-flowing gum that pours out of a myrrh-producing tree when incisions are made in its trunk. The wounded tree pours perfume over the violence done to it, just as Christ poured the sweet fragrance of His life over the appalling crime of Calvary, which reeked of human and Satanic wickedness. As we stand by the cross and listen to His gracious words, we breathe in the fragrance He poured over the violence done to Him by sinful man.

The sweet cinnamon and the sweet calamus were carefully weighed so that equal amounts—250 shekels of each spice—were used. Taken together, mixed and merged, they made up a whole.

The two spices were so perfectly blended that one could not be separated from the other. Similarly the two natures of Christ were blended into one. The Lord Jesus was both God and man. One nature did not outweigh the other, nor would one suffice without the other. We cannot tell where the humanity of Jesus ends and His deity begins, or where His deity ends and His humanity begins. The human and the divine were perfectly mixed and blended.

The cinnamon came from an evergreen tree—ever fresh, ever luxuriant, ever verdant. Thus this spice reminds us that the life the Lord Jesus laid down on the cross was an eternal life. The cinnamon was taken from the bark of the tree. The bark, which is just the surface of the tree, reminds us that we cannot penetrate beyond the mere surface of understanding when we try to comprehend the deity of Christ.

The fragrance of calamus was obtained by crushing an aromatic cane that grew in the mire. This plant was essentially a reed, a tall grass with a woody stem, so it symbolizes the Lord's humanity, especially His humility. A reed stands in contrast to a great spreading tree (see Daniel 4:19-27).

The cassia tree belongs to the same family as the cinnamon tree, and therefore cassia also points to the essential deity of Christ. Growing in places not suitable for other plants, the cassia was extremely pungent. The five hundred shekels of cassia added a special strength to the blend of ingredients in the holy anointing oil. "All thy garments smell of...cassia," exclaimed the psalmist (Psalm 45:8). Likewise everything about Christ is redolent of His deity and holiness.

In addition to the shekel, the formula for the anointing oil mentions the hin. The word *hin* is of uncertain meaning, but it derives from a word meaning "to be wealthy or full or sufficient." The hin of olive oil points to the Holy Spirit. The olive oil was used to blend the myrrh, the cinnamon, the calamus, and the cassia into an ointment to be used for anointing (the words *ointment* and *anoint* are kin to each other). As Prophet, Priest, and King, the Lord Jesus knew the full and unstinted anointing of the Holy Spirit. The titles *Messiah* and *Christ* actually mean "the anointed."

The Lord Jesus carried the fragrance of the anointing with Him all His life—at all times, in all places, under all circumstances. He shed abroad the perfume of His presence everywhere. He filled every place He visited with the aromatic blend of His divine and human natures. He carried into every relationship the ointment of His blessed being. He brought with Him the climate and atmosphere of Heaven.

In his discussion of friendship, Solomon went on to suggest that we *develop the right contacts:* "Thine own friend, and thy father's friend, forsake not; neither go into thy brother's house in the day of thy calamity: for better is a neighbour that is near than a brother far off" (Proverbs 27:10). Today we would say, "There are no friends like old friends." We should keep old friends, for they are tried and tested. In times of calamity a friend close at hand is better than a brother who lives halfway across the country. We should cultivate friendships with our neighbors, for we never know when we might need them, or they us.

A friend in need is a friend indeed, as the wounded man in Luke 10:30-37 discovered. He was attacked by thieves as he was traveling from Jerusalem to Jericho. Jerusalem, perched on a triad of hills on the crest of the central ridge of Palestine, was some 2,450 feet above sea level and was surrounded on three sides by deep ravines. Jericho, situated west of the Jordan and about five miles north of the Dead Sea, was about seventeen miles from Jerusalem and about 825 feet below sea level.

The man headed steadily downhill. Behind him was "the city of the great King" (Matthew 5:35) and the temple, the religious heart of the nation. Below him was Jericho, the city of the curse (Joshua 6:26). Soon he was overwhelmed by disaster. He "fell among thieves, which stripped him of his raiment, and wounded him, and departed, leaving him half dead" (Luke 10:30).

Now he needed a friend. We can suppose that the man had brothers and friends, but the nearest of these would have been far away—in Jerusalem or Jericho—and he needed a friend close by.

The sun was hot. Already the vultures could be seen hovering in the sky. Faint and in pain, the wounded man was lying in the dust. When he heard footsteps approaching, he opened his eyes. Then he groaned in despair and closed his eyes again, for he saw that the passerby, a priest, was hurrying along on the other side of the road. The priest represents *the rites of religion,* which are of little benefit to a fallen man. The priest was no friend to the man in need.

When the wretched man heard more footsteps, hope reared up in his heart, for he saw that the passerby, a Levite, was crossing over to his side of the road. But hope faded, for the Levite turned away, leaving the wounded man lying in the dust. The Levite represents *the rules of religion,* which are of little benefit to a fallen man. The Levite was an expert in the law, but he was no friend to the man in need.

Despair was again closing in when the sound of a donkey's hoofbeats broke through the wounded man's departing consciousness.

He did not stir, for he had no hope left. When he heard an exclamation, he made a final mental note that this newcomer was a Samaritan. *I can expect no help from him,* the thieves' victim no doubt thought. *Jews have no dealings with Samaritans.* But the Samaritan spoke kindly to him and examined his wounds! He poured in oil to soothe and wine to cleanse. The Samaritan took the fallen man in his arms, put him on the donkey, accompanied him to an inn, paid the cost of his care, and promised to come back again before long. The Samaritan was truly "a neighbour that is near," to use Solomon's words. The psalmist would say he was "a very present help in trouble" (Psalm 46:1).

Jesus is our "neighbour that is near." He does for us poor, fallen, robbed, and ruined members of Adam's race what we cannot do for ourselves. He does for us what the rites and rules of religion cannot do. He comes to where we are, puts His arms around us, pays the price of our care, and promises to come back again. Thank God for such a friend!

### 3. Regarding Glad Fathers (27:11)

"My son, be wise, and make my heart glad, that I may answer him that reproacheth me." This proverb is the plea of a frustrated father. A father who occupies any position at all—whether at work, in the church, or in the community—has a name to uphold. If he is a person of proven character, ability, and integrity, he himself is usually invulnerable to criticism or attack. However, he can become vulnerable to his enemies if his son is foolish or wicked. Even a wise man becomes vulnerable if his son is a fool. Even a good man becomes vulnerable if his son is wicked. Even a successful man becomes vulnerable if his son is incompetent. Even a brave man becomes vulnerable if his son is a coward.

Samuel, the last of the judges and the first of the prophets, was a man of sterling integrity, but he was vulnerable to criticism. When the people of Israel cried out for a king, Samuel felt keenly that their rejection of the theocracy was an attack on himself. He gave them the king they wanted, but he called the tribes together and made a speech:

> Now, behold, the king walketh before you: and I am old and grayheaded; and, behold, my sons are with you: and I have walked before you from my childhood unto this day. Behold, here I am: witness against me before the Lord, and before his anointed: whose ox have I taken? or whose ass have I taken? or

> whom have I defrauded? whom have I oppressed? or of whose hand have I received any bribe to blind mine eyes therewith? and I will restore it to you. And they said, Thou hast not defrauded us, nor oppressed us, neither hast thou taken ought of any man's hand. And he said unto them, The Lord is witness against you, and his anointed is witness this day, that ye have not found ought in my hand. And they answered, He is witness (1 Samuel 12:2-5).

Few men had been as diligent as Samuel. Like John the Baptist, Samuel had been used to break a centuries-long silence; God spoke through him and "all Israel from Dan even to Beer-sheba knew that Samuel was established to be a prophet of the Lord" (1 Samuel 3:20). Samuel had led Israel into battle, giving them a taste of victory over their hereditary foes, the Philistines (7:7-14). He had established a regular circuit, going from Ramah to Beth-el, Gilgal, and Mizpeh, and for years he had emphasized the importance of divine worship (7:15-17). What then made this great man so vulnerable to criticism? His sons! We read:

> And it came to pass, when Samuel was old, that he made his sons judges over Israel. Now the name of his firstborn was Joel; and the name of his second, Abiah: they were judges in Beer-sheba. And his sons walked not in his ways, but turned aside after lucre, and took bribes, and perverted judgment (8:1-3).

Samuel had a stainless character, but his sons did not. Solomon had the same problem. He was world-famous for his wisdom, but Rehoboam was a fool. Many fathers have echoed Solomon's plea: "My son, be wise [good, brave, diligent], and make my heart glad, that I may answer him that reproacheth me."

4. Regarding Great Folly (27:12-16)

a. The Folly of Having Too Little a Mind (27:12-13)

Solomon warned against *failure to read obvious signs:* "A prudent man foreseeth the evil, and hideth himself; but the simple pass on, and are punished" (Proverbs 27:12). The expression translated "and are punished" can also be rendered "and pay the penalty."

The Hebrew people could not foresee evil. The walls of Jerusalem seemed impregnable to the Jews of Jesus' day. Indeed in one incident cited in the Gospels, the disciples proudly pointed out to Jesus the courts, halls, colonnades, towers, and various wings of the temple. These were part of Jerusalem's great fortification system. The Lord was not impressed: "There shall not be left here one stone upon another, that shall not be thrown down," He said (Matthew 24:2).

Pompey had captured Jerusalem in 63 B.C. and had broken down part of the city wall. That should have warned the Jews that trouble was coming. Crassus despoiled the temple nine years later. That should have warned the Jews. The Parthians plundered Jerusalem in 40 B.C. and it was captured again in 37 B.C. by the Idumean King Herod. That should have warned the Jews. But the Jews were impervious to warnings of any kind.

When Herod was firmly seated on the Jewish throne, he repaired the walls of Jerusalem and adorned the city with many great buildings. He also rebuilt the temple on a scale and with a magnificence undreamed of by the Jews. By the time of his death, two walls encircled the city. Then Herod Agrippa began a third wall in A.D. 42, about a decade after the crucifixion. All this activity only confirmed to the Jews, in their folly and pride, that their city was impregnable.

But in A.D. 70 the Roman general Titus captured Jerusalem after a long, stubborn siege. He was much more impressed with the walls than Jesus had been. Titus deliberately broke them all down, except for a part of the west wall and three towers (Hippicus, Phasael, and Mariamme), which he left so that future generations could admire the military genius that had overthrown such mighty fortifications.

In A.D. 33 the Lord Jesus, on His way to the cross, had warned the Jews not to trust those walls:

> When ye shall see Jerusalem compassed with armies, then know that the desolation thereof is nigh. Then let them which are in Judaea flee to the mountains; and let them which are in the midst of it depart out; and let not them that are in the countries [fields] enter thereinto. For these be the days of vengeance, that all things which are written may be fulfilled. But woe unto them that are with child, and to them that give suck, in those days! for there shall be great distress in the land, and wrath upon this people (Luke 21:20-23).

And so there was, just as Jesus had said. The prudent man living in Jerusalem in those days foresaw the evil coming. He heard the blare of the trumpets as they echoed in the hills. He looked out from the city's turrets and saw the standards and eagles of seemingly endless Roman legions drawing ever nearer. He gathered his family and fled—as Noah had fled to the ark and as Lot had fled to the hills. Meanwhile the simple man looked at the massive walls of Jerusalem, listened to the boasts of the zealots, and entered the city, where he paid the penalty for his folly.

The words of Proverbs 27:12 have an evangelistic ring. A day of judgment is coming. The great white throne is ready and the date of that judgment is set. There is however a place of refuge. The road to that place runs by way of Calvary and an empty tomb to the arms of Jesus. As Solomon said, "A prudent man foreseeth the evil, and hideth himself; but the simple pass on, and are punished."

Next Solomon warned against *failure to regard ordinary sense:* "Take his garment that is surety for a stranger, and take a pledge of him for a strange woman" (Proverbs 27:13). The word translated "stranger" here is readily rendered "apostate." The phrase "a strange women" refers to a temple prostitute. The gist then of this proverb is that you shouldn't back an apostate or trust a whoremonger because you'll pay dearly if you do.

In the book of Proverbs Solomon warned repeatedly that it is foolish to provide surety for anyone. And in 27:13 he made it clear that it is the height of folly to provide surety for an apostate. We must not under any conditions back an apostate. A man who has denied the truth is not to be trusted. A man who has lost his reputation with a temple prostitute is not to be trusted either. He is immoral and therefore capable of most anything. Both men stand discredited by their behavior and it is best to leave them to themselves.

This proverb reminds me of Abner and the investment he made in Ish-bosheth. Abner, the son of Ner, was King Saul's general, and Ish-bosheth was one of King Saul's younger sons. Ish-bosheth somehow escaped the slaughter that followed the fateful battle of Gilboa. When the victorious Philistines came to plunder the bodies of the slain, they found Saul and his three other sons, including Jonathan, dead on the battlefield and with spiteful arrogance nailed the royal bodies to a wall in Beth-shan.

We would like to know more about the young prince who escaped, but we have to rely for the most part on what can be gleaned from his names. In the Old Testament names are highly significant, often giving important clues to characters, careers, or conditions associated with individuals.[3]

Originally this son of Saul was called *Esh-baal* (1 Chronicles 8:33; 9:39), which means "the Lord's man." This name suggests that at one time he professed to belong to the Lord. Later his name was changed to *Ish-bosheth,* which means "man of shame." This name of shame, replacing the earlier name of fame, strongly suggests that, Saul-like, he turned his back on the Lord. We do not know how, when, where, or why he turned his back on the Lord, but we know he did. No longer "the Lord's man," Ish-bosheth was a picture of the apostate.

The Bible gives us several examples of name changes. Abram was changed to Abraham; Jacob was changed to Israel; Simon was changed to Peter; Saul was changed to Paul. The change was always significant in terms of the life change that accompanied it. In each of these examples the change was for the better, but in the case of Ish-bosheth the change was for the worse.

Abner evidently had his dealings with Ish-bosheth after the name change (2 Samuel 2:8-10). The new, unlovely name ought to have served as a warning to Abner. But Abner's ambitiousness affected his common sense. Having been King Saul's commander-in-chief, he now aspired to be a king-maker in Israel—the real power behind the throne. So Abner, hoping to make his fortune, decided to provide surety for Ish-bosheth. Abner backed this apostate's questionable claims to the throne and as a result civil war broke out.

For years neither side seemed able to win a decisive victory. But "David waxed stronger and stronger," we read, "and the house of Saul waxed weaker and weaker" (2 Samuel 3:1). Abner realized that Ish-bosheth wasn't winning; he had backed a loser. Second Samuel 3:7-10 tells us what happened next:

> Saul had a concubine, whose name was Rizpah, the daughter of Aiah: and Ish-bosheth said to Abner, Wherefore hast thou gone in unto my father's concubine? Then was Abner very wroth for the words of Ish-bosheth, and said, Am I a dog's head, which against Judah do shew kindness this day unto the house of Saul thy father, to his brethren, and to his friends, and have not delivered thee into the hand of David, that thou chargest me to day with a fault [iniquity] concerning this woman? So do God to Abner, and more also, except, as the Lord hath sworn to David, even so I do to him; To translate the kingdom from the house of Saul, and to set up the throne of David over Israel and over Judah, from Dan even to Beer-sheba.

So Abner cut his losses and left "the man of shame" to himself, but Abner never lived to enjoy his new investment in David. During his days of backing Ish-bosheth, Abner had unfortunately killed Asahel, Joab's brother (2 Samuel 2:18-23). Abner had tried in vain to disentangle himself from the wretched situation. However, he never would have become involved at all if he had not invested in Ish-bosheth. That involvement proved to be costly, for it caused Abner to lose not only his garment (today we would say he lost his shirt) but also his life. Joab murdered Abner to avenge Asahel's death. Truly it does not pay to back an apostate.

b. The Folly of Having Too Large a Mouth (27:14-16)

(1) Extravagant Compliments (27:14)

"He that blesseth his friend with a loud voice, rising early in the morning, it shall be counted a curse to him." In other words, look out for the man who professes friendship too loudly and offers too many compliments. Such ostentation is offensive, shallow, and suspect. The man who takes overblown compliments at face value is foolish.

Years ago it was common for an African chief to keep a retainer whose job it was to sing the chief's praises. In his books on Africa and the Zulus, Sir Henry Rider Haggard gave numerous examples of this practice. In *Allan Quatermain* the hero of the story was the subject of such praise.

The old hunter was about to embark on his last adventure, a journey far into the interior of Africa to search for a rumored and mysterious white race. Needing porters, he had approached some Wakwafi Askari who had just returned from a trek, but they had refused to join him. About that time he came across an old acquaintance: a former Zulu chieftain who was a renowned warrior and a descendant of Chaka, the Zulu Napoleon. Haggard described the meeting of Quatermain and the chieftain. Quatermain is speaking:

> The tall man (who among his own people was commonly known as the "Woodpecker," and also as the "Slaughterer") started, and almost let the long-handled battle-axe he held in his hand fall in his astonishment. Next second he had recognized me, and was saluting me in an outburst of sonorous language which made his companions the Wakwafi stare.
>
> "Koos" (chief), he began, "Koos-y Pagate! Koos-y-umcool!" (Chief from of old—mighty chief). "Koos! Baba!" (father). "Macumazahn, old hunter, slayer of elephants, eater up of

> lions, clever one! watchful one! brave one! quick one! whose shot never misses, who strikes straight home, who grasps a hand and holds it to the death" (i.e., is a true friend). "Koos! Baba! wise is the voice of our people that says, 'Mountain never meets with mountain, but at daybreak or at even man shall meet again with man.' Behold! a messenger came up from Natal. 'Macumazahn is dead!' cried he. 'The land knows Macumazahn no more.' That is years ago. And now, behold, now in this strange place of stinks I find Macumazahn, my friend. There is no room for doubt, the brush of the old jackal has gone a little grey; but is not his eye as keen, and are not his teeth as sharp? Ha! ha! Macumazahn, mindest thou how thou didst plant the ball in the eye of the charging buffalo—mindest thou—"
>
> I had let him run on thus because I saw that his enthusiasm was producing a marked effect upon the minds of the five Wakwafi, who appeared to understand something of his talk; but now I thought it time to put a stop to it, for there is nothing that I hate so much as this Zulu system of extravagant praising—"bongering," as they call it. "Silence!" I said. "Has all thy noisy talk been stopped up since last I saw thee that it breaks out thus, and sweeps us away? What doest thou here with these men—thou whom I left a chief in Zululand?"[4]

The classic Biblical example of extravagant compliments is found in the story of King Hezekiah. A black shadow hung over Judea and Jerusalem because the Assyrian army was on the march. Sargon had captured the city of Samaria in 722 B.C., and the ten tribes had been deported into captivity. By 701 B.C. Sennacherib and the Assyrian army were penetrating deeply into Hezekiah's realm. At this critical time in his nation's history, when a strong hand was needed on the helm, Hezekiah fell deathly ill. Indeed the prophet Isaiah told him to put his house in order because he was going to die. In answer to Hezekiah's prayer, however, the Lord granted the godly king a fifteen-year extension to his life and gave him the remarkable sign of the sundial. (See 2 Kings 20:1-11.)

Shortly after his recovery Hezekiah received at his court ambassadors from Babylon who brought with them "letters and a present"—a form of "bongering" (Isaiah 39:1-8; also see 2 Chronicles 32:31). The Babylonians flattered, congratulated, and praised Hezekiah and made him feel as though he were someone important. The truth was that the Babylonians were as apprehensive of the Assyrian army as everyone else was and they were anxious to find allies. If Judah and Egypt could be persuaded to put up a stiff resistance, that would take the heat off Babylon.

The flattery, which concealed an ulterior motive, went to Hezekiah's head. Little Judah was being invited to join the international heavyweights. And Babylon would be a good ally to have. Carried away by all the attention, Hezekiah decided to show off for these important ambassadors:

> Hezekiah...shewed them all the house of his precious things, the silver, and the gold, and the spices, and the precious ointment, and all the house of his armour, and all that was found in his treasures: there was nothing in his house, nor in all his dominion, that Hezekiah shewed them not (2 Kings 20:13).

He should have recalled one of the proverbs he was preparing to add to the sacred collection: "He that blesseth his friend with a loud voice, rising early in the morning, it shall be counted a curse to him." Babylonian envoys "blessed" Hezekiah with all the polished charm and eloquence of oriental diplomats, and he swallowed the bait. It would have been better for him if they had come to curse him and declare war on him. Then at least he would have been on his guard. As it was, the ambassadors returned to Babylon with a thorough inventory of Jerusalem's treasures. Doubtless this information excited the cupidity of the Babylonian king and an official note was made: When the time comes for Babylon to replace Assyria as the superpower, Jerusalem will be well worth seizing.

Before long Hezekiah had occasion to regret his folly in succumbing to the flattery of his guests, for he had to listen to a blistering attack on his senseless behavior from the lips of his good friend Isaiah, who certainly wasted no time "bongering" the king.

(2) Endless Contentions (27:15-16)

In these verses Solomon pointed out two truths related to the home. First, there is no way to *shut a nagging woman up:* "A continual dropping in a very rainy day and a contentious woman are alike" (Proverbs 27:15). Second, there is no way to *shut a nagging woman in:* "Whosoever hideth her hideth the wind, and the ointment of his right hand, which bewrayeth itself" (27:16). In other words, a man might as well try to restrain the wind as try to restrain this kind of woman. He can no more stop her from advertising herself, her temper, and her loud mouth than he could conceal the fact if he had just dipped his hand in a jar of perfume! Her shrewish voice follows him from room to room. Then off she goes to broadcast her grievances to the neighbors and the whole community.

These truths remind me of Washington Irving's character Rip Van Winkle. Irving drew attention to his hero's wife:

> [Rip Van Winkle] was a descendant of the Van Winkles who figured so gallantly in the chivalrous days of Peter Stuyvesant, and accompanied him to the siege of Fort Christina. He inherited, however, but little of the martial character of his ancestors. I have observed that he was a simple, good-natured man; he was, moreover, a kind neighbor, and an obedient, hen-pecked husband. Indeed, to the latter circumstance might be owing that meekness of spirit which gained him such universal popularity; for those men are most apt to be obsequious and conciliating abroad, who are under the discipline of shrews at home. Their tempers, doubtless, are rendered pliant and malleable in the fiery furnace of domestic tribulation; and a curtain lecture is worth all the sermons in the world for teaching the virtues of patience and long-suffering. A termagant wife may, therefore, in some respects, be considered a tolerable blessing; and if so, Rip Van Winkle was thrice blessed.
>
> Certain it is that he was a great favorite among all the good wives of the village, who, as usual, with the amiable sex, took his part in all family squabbles; and never failed, whenever they talked those matters over in their evening gossipings, to lay all the blame on Dame Van Winkle....
>
> Rip Van Winkle, however, was one of those happy mortals, of foolish, well-oiled dispositions, who take the world easy, eat white bread or brown, whichever can be got with least thought or trouble, and would rather starve on a penny than work for a pound. If left to himself, he would have whistled life away in perfect contentment; but his wife kept continually dinning in his ears about his idleness, his carelessness, and the ruin he was bringing on his family. Morning, noon, and night, her tongue was incessantly going, and everything he said or did was sure to produce a torrent of household eloquence. Rip had but one way of replying to all lectures of the kind, and that, by frequent use, had grown into a habit. He shrugged his shoulders, shook his head, cast up his eyes, but said nothing. This, however, always provoked a fresh volley from his wife; so that he was fain to draw off his forces, and take to the outside

> of the house—the only side which, in truth, belongs to a hen-pecked husband.
>
> Rip's sole domestic adherent was his dog Wolf, who was as much hen-pecked as his master; for Dame Van Winkle regarded them as companions in idleness, and even looked upon Wolf with an evil eye, as the cause of his master's going so often astray. True it is, in all points of spirit befitting an honorable dog, he was as courageous an animal as ever scoured the woods—but what courage can withstand the ever-during and all-besetting terrors of a woman's tongue? The moment Wolf entered the house his crest fell, his tail drooped to the ground, or curled between his legs, he sneaked about with a gallows air, casting many a sidelong glance at Dame Van Winkle, and at the least flourish of a broomstick or ladle, he would fly to the door with yelping precipitation.
>
> Times grew worse and worse with Rip Van Winkle as years of matrimony rolled on; a tart temper never mellows with age, and a sharp tongue is the only edged tool that grows keener with constant use. For a long while he used to console himself, when driven from home, by frequenting a kind of perpetual club of the sages, philosophers, and other idle personages of the village; which held its sessions on a bench before a small inn, designated by a rubicund portrait of His Majesty George the Third....
>
> From even this stronghold the unlucky Rip was at length routed by his termagant wife, who would suddenly break in upon the tranquillity of the assemblage and call the members all to naught; nor was that august personage, Nicholas Vedder himself, sacred from the daring tongue of this terrible virago, who charged him outright with encouraging her husband in habits of idleness.
>
> Poor Rip was at last reduced almost to despair; and his only alternative, to escape from the labor of the farm and clamor of his wife, was to take gun in hand and stroll away into the woods. Here he would sometimes seat himself at the foot of a tree, and share the contents of his wallet with Wolf, with whom he sympathized as a fellow-sufferer in persecution.

After Rip Van Winkle's remarkable twenty-year sleep, he returned to the village and his "heart died away" when he heard of all the changes that had taken place. In the midst of his bewilderment he met his grown-up daughter. Rip made some inquiries and their conversation continued. Irving wrote:

Rip had but one question more to ask; but he put it with a faltering voice:

"Where's your mother?"

"Oh, she too...died but a short time since; she broke a blood-vessel in a fit of passion at a New England peddler."

There was a drop of comfort, at least, in this intelligence.[5]

Although much could be said in favor of Rip Van Winkle's long-suffering wife, the fact remains that her shrewish tongue drove her husband to despair.

5. Regarding Growing Finances (27:17-27)

a. The Question of Integrity (27:17-22)

(1) Diligence Discussed (27:17-18)

The remainder of Proverbs 27 is concerned mostly with matters of money. As Solomon started to write about how to make money grow, he brought up the subject of *mutual help:* "Iron sharpeneth iron; so a man sharpeneth the countenance of his friend" (27:17). Underlying all true prosperity is integrity of character and scrupulous honesty in dealings with other people. Our friends and partners are important. We learn from one another; we take character and color from one another. Our character eventually shows in our faces.

When I joined the staff of the Moody Bible Institute, I saw how well staff members there work together, providing mutual help. I was put in charge of developing the courses offered by the correspondence school—and over the years I wrote most of the testing instruments that transformed their books into courses. I soon discovered that it was not as easy to write a common multiple-choice question as it first appeared.

A multiple-choice question consists of two parts: the *lead statement,* which is followed by at least three (and preferably four or more) *alternative statements,* only one of which correctly completes the lead statement. The person writing the question has to be sure that only one of the alternative choices is correct and complete and that the wrong alternatives are highly plausible. The wrong alternatives must be different from each other, not obviously wrong, not ambiguous, and not incongruous. The writer must not assume that the student knows more than he has been taught.

Well-constructed multiple-choice questions look easy to answer.

But some are highly sophisticated and demand research as well as recall on the part of the student. For example a question may require the student to work out an exercise in which he draws conclusions before he tackles the question; he can answer the question correctly only if he has reached proper conclusions in the exercise. Another multiple-choice question may test the student's ability to recognize principles taught in the text and his ability to recognize those principles when they are put in a different context.

Over the years I became adept at writing multiple-choice and other kinds of objective questions that test a student's comprehension, memory, and proficiency. My skills were honed in a hard process. Every question in every course had to run the gauntlet of two eagle-eyed staff members.

The first reviewer was the director of the correspondence school, a college-trained educator who understood all the techniques of objective testing. He would read each question and challenge it if he thought it was unfair, poorly constructed, or too obvious. I would try to defend what I considered to be good questions—sometimes successfully, sometimes futilely. Truly iron sharpened iron, for he learned some Biblical truths from me, and I learned some educational principles from him.

The second reviewer was the head instructor, whose evaluation was even more thorough than the director's. The head instructor had to keep in mind that once the course was published, weak questions would generate complaints that would land on his desk. Complaints meant work! Letters had to be answered; allowances had to be made; comments had to be written on students' test papers; questions had to be rewritten when the course was reprinted. So the head instructor was fussy. He tried to make sure that all the perceived, possible, or imagined flaws in my questions were eliminated. Sometimes a question became the subject of considerable debate and might even have to be referred to the director for arbitration.

In the review process we all learned something, including mutual respect for each other's special abilities. Iron sharpened iron. Eleven years of this kind of sharpening within an exact discipline developed my other writing skills as well.

After pointing out the value of mutual help, Solomon stressed the importance of *mutual harmony:* "Whoso keepeth the fig tree shall eat the fruit thereof: so he that waiteth on his master shall be honoured" (Proverbs 27:18). In other words, a reward can be expected for diligent and competent service. Just as a man who tends a fig tree can look forward to tasting the sweetness of its fruit, a man who serves his employer well can usually look forward to a sweet reward when the time comes.

Think of the high honor that attaches to the memory of Abraham's "eldest servant" (Genesis 24:2). We can assume that this servant was "Eliezer of Damascus," whom Abraham once proposed to make his heir (15:2-3). However, the Holy Spirit leaves the servant unnamed in Genesis 24, which records the greatest of all the services he ever rendered to his master.

Abraham, who was getting on in years, thought it was time for his grown son Isaac to marry. The question was where he would find a suitable bride for the heir to the promises of God, the one chosen to be a direct progenitor of Christ. It would be unthinkable for Isaac to marry a Canaanite and become entangled in the gross immorality of Canaanite religion. So Abraham decided to send a servant back to Mesopotamia to see if a suitable wife could be found among Abraham's own people. At least his people knew something about the true God. His own testimony had been lively enough to ensure that. So Abraham summoned his chief steward, properly equipped him, gave him the strictest instructions, and sent him back to the Euphrates valley.

When the servant arrived at his destination, he did not have the faintest idea of where to look for the prospective bride, so he prayed. He asked the God of Abraham to guide him and proposed a simple but unusual test (Genesis 24:14). Then he tethered his camels and sat down by a well near the city of Nahor and waited. Immediately Rebekah came out to draw water, fulfilled to the letter the terms of the test (24:18-19), and revealed herself to be a descendant of Terah, Abraham's father. The servant rewarded Rebekah for watering his camels, resumed his seat by the well and waited some more.

Before long Rebekah's brother Laban, greatly impressed by the magnificent gifts that had been given to his sister, came hurrying out to the well and invited Abraham's servant into their home. Once inside, the servant told his story and requested that Rebekah's hand be given to Isaac in marriage. Laban and his father agreed to the proposal and when Rebekah was asked if she would go, she answered simply, "I will go" (Genesis 24:58).

During the long journey to Isaac, we can be sure that the servant told Rebekah much about Abraham and Isaac. Doubtless the servant recounted what had happened at mount Moriah. Likely enough he helped her understand what it meant for Isaac to be heir to the Abrahamic covenant and the promises of God.

Clearly this servant waited on his master well. But since he was not even named, how can we say that he was highly honored? The answer lies in the fact that the whole story has deep significance. Abraham, the father, is a type of God the Father. Isaac, the son, is a type of God the Son. What happened at mount Moriah is a picture of Calvary (Genesis 22). Rebekah is a type of the church, the bride of Christ. And the unnamed servant is a type of the Holy Spirit.[6] What greater honor could he have? Not only is his faithful service written up by the Holy Spirit and incorporated for all eternity in the Word of God; he himself is set before us as one of the greatest Biblical pictures of the Spirit of God at work in the world today.

(2) Vigilance Discussed (27:19-21)

Proverbs 27:19 warns us to *look out for people:* "As in water face answereth to face, so the heart of man to man." In other words, we see ourselves reflected in other people. They reflect our thoughts and feelings, hopes and ambitions, lusts and desires, sins and follies, aspirations and goals. The Scottish bard Robert Burns expressed the idea well in the lines he jotted down after sitting behind a well-dressed woman in church and observing a louse on her bonnet:

> Ha! whare ye gaun, ye crowlan ferlie!
> Your impudence protects you fairly:
> I canna say but ye strunt rarely,
> Owre gawze and lace;
> Tho' faith, I fear ye dine but sparely
> On sic a place.
>
> Ye ugly, creepan, blastet wonner,
> Detestet, shunn'd, by saunt an' sinner,
> How daur ye set your fit upon her,
> Sae fine a Lady!
> Gae somewhere else and seek your dinner,
> On some poor body.
>
> . . . . . . . . . . . . . . . . . . . . . . . .
>
> O wad some Pow'r the giftie gie us
> To see oursels as others see us!
> It wad frae monie a blunder free us
> An' foolish notion:
> What airs in dress an' gait wad lea'e us,
> An' ev'n Devotion![7]

The classic Biblical example of face answering to face and heart answering to heart is seen in the story of Jacob and Laban. Set a thief to catch a thief, we say, and certainly we see God doing just that in this story. Jacob and Laban were two of a kind, cut from the same piece of cloth.

Before the wily uncle and nephew ever met, Jacob had deceived his blind old father Isaac and cheated his twin brother Esau out of birthright and blessing. Not long after the uncle and nephew met, Laban cheated Jacob in the matter of wives and in the matter of wages. Jacob responded by multiplying his own flocks at Laban's expense but within the literal terms of their agreement. When Laban planned to rob Jacob of his family and his flocks, Jacob stole a march on him and escaped. For twenty years God thus held Laban up before Jacob as a mirror and said in effect: "There you are, Jacob. Take a good look at yourself. You and he are a pair well matched."

We should, indeed, look out for people. We are mirror images of each other and it often happens that the sins we are quick to spot and condemn in others are the sins of which we are most guilty ourselves.

Proverbs 27:20 warns us to *look out for prospects:* "Hell and destruction are never full; so the eyes of man are never satisfied." The Hebrew word translated "Hell" here is *Sheol* (the Greek translation is *Hades*), meaning the underworld of the dead. The word translated "destruction" means "the abyss." So the proverb personifies the grave, which is never satisfied, never full. The human eye is also insatiable. Indeed 1 John 2:16 refers to "the lust of the eyes." In this proverb the eyes stand for all the senses and their inability ever to be satisfied.

The lusts of the lost cannot be assuaged either in this life or in the life to come. The Apocalypse makes a terrible pronouncement: "He which is filthy, let him be filthy still" (Revelation 22:11). Death does not curb, cure, or crucify lust any more than it extinguishes life. Lusts indulged on earth are carried into eternity. The rich man awoke in Hell to a craving that was heated beyond all endurance by the tormenting flame (Luke 16:24). Men who develop cravings for drugs, tobacco, drink, women, perverted sex, power, fame, money, and recognition find that these things cannot satisfy in this life and they become dragon lusts in eternity.

Years ago a beloved preacher-friend of mine was traveling on a bus to a distant city. Because he had arrived at the bus station early just to make sure he could get a seat in the no-smoking section, he was dismayed when the woman in the seat in front of him deliberately ignored the no-smoking sign and lit up a cigarette. Like most nonsmokers, he disliked the smell of cigarette smoke and hated what it did to his hair, clothes, and lungs.

The thoughtless woman ignored the black looks she received from other passengers and went on puffing on her cigarette and blowing smoke all over her neighbors. When she came to the end of one cigarette, she promptly lit another from the stub of the previous one. She worked her way through a pack, tossed it into the aisle, and opened another.

One discarded pack landed at my friend's feet. He looked at it with distaste, noting the brand and the advertising slogan printed in bold letters. "Smoke Whiffies," the package proclaimed. "They *Satisfy*." My friend said to me later, "I felt like tapping the woman on the shoulder and saying, 'Lady, tell me—how *many* does it take?'"

The desires of men are never satisfied on earth because God engineered us for eternity. He made us for Himself. Only Christ is big enough to satisfy the longings of our hearts. David, having prayed that God would deliver him from wicked people who live to satisfy their cravings in this life, declared: "As for me, I will behold thy face in righteousness: I shall be satisfied, when I awake, with thy likeness" (Psalm 17:15). At that time the restless eye will have found what it is looking for at last!

Proverbs 27:21 warns us to *look out for praise:* "As the fining pot for silver, and the furnace for gold; so is a man to his praise." Silver and gold are tested by the heat of fire, which brings all the dross to the surface so that it can be removed. The refiner is never satisfied until he can see his own face reflected perfectly in the molten metal in the crucible.

What the fire does to silver and gold, praise does to us. There can be no truer indication of a person's character than how that person responds to praise. Some people do not know how to accept compliments. When they are praised, they begin to depreciate themselves and their accomplishments. Other people bask in praise. They cannot get enough of it and they swell visibly with pride and satisfaction when they do get it. Still others are completely ruined by praise. It goes to their heads and intoxicates them with an exaggerated sense of their own importance. This third type of response is characteristic of dictators.

C. S. Forester described such a dictator in his novel *The Happy Return.*[8] In the book the British admiralty sent naval hero Captain Horatio Hornblower to the lonely waters of the Pacific to contact a Nicaraguan rebel named Don Julian Alvarado. Hornblower was to put his warship *Lydia* at the disposal of this rebel and help him create as much trouble as possible in the Spanish domains of Central America. After seven months at sea, during which Hornblower carefully avoided all contact with the land, he made a perfect landfall, brought his frigate into a bay in the gulf of Fonseca, and mused over his sealed orders.

Because Spain had sided with Napoleon against England, Spanish domains overseas were fair game. So Hornblower was to supply Alvarado with arms and ammunition. He was to do everything in his power to ensure the success of Alvarado's rebellion. He could present the rebel with guns from his own ship and he had fifty thousand guineas in gold, which he could use at his discretion. Hornblower was to go so far as to recognize Alvarado's sovereignty over any land he might conquer, provided Alvarado would sign a treaty with Britain. The captain's orders also mentioned a Spanish ship named the *Natividad.* This two-decked ship of fifty guns was known to be in the area and Hornblower was to "take, burn, sink or destroy" it.

The British naval hero put on his resplendent uniform, appeared on deck, and commanded his lieutenant to "beat to quarters" and "clear for action." It was best to be well prepared. Who could tell when the Spanish ship might show up? As the din of preparing for action rang through the ship, Hornblower's attention was drawn to a small boat that had put off from shore. Alvarado's representative was on the boat and Hornblower received him aboard the *Lydia.*

The man was a somewhat swarthy, ragged individual and when he introduced himself, Hornblower got the first of many shocks that lay ahead. "I am Manuel Hernandez," the representative said, "lieutenant general of el Supremo (the Almighty One)." Hornblower temporized, saying that his orders concerned an individual of quite a different name. Hernandez loftily announced that the lord, el Supremo, had been known as His Excellency Don Julian Maria de Jesus de Alvarado y Montezuma, but now he was el Supremo and it would go ill with anyone who forgot it.

Ashore, the messenger led Hornblower through forest trails to the dictator's home. The route was lined with corpses and anguished men bound to stakes and dying of thirst. Around them hovered a circle of vultures. Hernandez explained that these were "the unenlightened," people who had failed to recognize the deity of el Supremo.

Later on, after he had captured the *Natividad,* Hornblower was obliged to welcome the dictator aboard the *Lydia* so they could plan a joint expedition that was to be mounted against El Salvador. Hornblower put on his ceremonial uniform and prepared to receive the dictator with proper honors. The first person to come aboard was a young man who wore gold earrings, boots of soft brown leather, and patched white trousers. He declared himself to be Vice Admiral Don Cristobal de Crispo. Hornblower received another shock when the young man announced that a twenty-three gun salute was proper for the petty, would-be conqueror. That was more recognition than the king of England was accorded! And so it went on. All Alvarado wanted was praise and more praise until, like some caesar of old, he claimed all the rights and honors of a god.

In the end Spain broke with Napoleon and declared itself to be an ally of England. The last time Hornblower saw the dictator, el Supremo was a prisoner on a Spanish ship. In chains and awaiting execution, he was still suffering from delusions of grandeur and deity.

(3) Ignorance Discussed (27:22)

"Though thou shouldest bray a fool in a mortar among wheat with a pestle, yet will not his foolishness depart from him." The process alluded to here is much more painstaking than ordinary threshing, and the point of the proverb is that no matter what pains you take to correct a fool, your efforts will do no good. An obstinate, self-willed, opinionated, and unprincipled man cannot be corrected. A leopard's spots cannot be changed and a fool will remain a fool, as Solomon well knew from bitter personal experience.

One of the greatest fools mentioned in Scripture is Esau, Jacob's twin brother. Esau was born into a family with every earthly and heavenly advantage. True, God had sovereignly decreed that Jacob would receive the birthright and the blessing, but Esau was still left with enormous advantages over the rest of mankind. His father was Isaac. His grandfather was Abraham. Esau, like his illustrious forebears, could have sought that city "whose builder and maker is God" (Hebrews 11:10).

But Esau lacked imagination. He had no eye for the unseen, the spiritual, and the eternal. He had no interest in those "exceeding great and precious promises" that God had given to Abraham and confirmed to Isaac and his seed (2 Peter 1:4). Esau was a born fool. He is the father of all who are born into the homes of believers, but fail to benefit from their advantage.

Esau quickly developed a love for this world. He became a skilled hunter. He had an eye like a hawk, he could steal through tall grass like a leopard, and his arrow never missed. He was bold, brave, rugged, hairy, and sunburned, but he was a heathen. Alexander Whyte described him as "all body and no soul...a profane person, who failed of the grace of God."[9]

Esau's preoccupation with this world blinded him to the world to come. So he sold his birthright, which was never his to sell, then wept bitter tears when Jacob stole what really was already his: the undiluted blessing of God. The pestle and mortar were busy enough that day. Esau "cried with a great and exceeding bitter cry," the Holy Spirit recorded in Genesis 27:34. But Esau was a fool and soon forgot what he had been taught.

He drifted away from the old homestead to find more congenial friends among the vile Canaanites. In many a home Esau was welcome because of his haunch of venison or long string of fresh-caught fish and because of his hunting yarns and spicy tales. Alexander Whyte wrote:

> Esau, alas! was all the time himself a true Canaanite at heart. Son of Isaac and Rebekah, and grandson of Abraham and Sarah, as he was, Esau had nothing of his forefathers or his foremothers in him, unless it was some of the dregs of their remaining vices.[10]

What a shock and disappointment it must have been to Isaac and Rebekah to learn that Esau was going to marry "Judith the daughter of Beeri the Hittite, and Bashemath the daughter of Elon the Hittite" (Genesis 26:34). Indeed the Bible says that these godless marriages "were a grief of mind unto Isaac and to Rebekah" (26:35). Now this believing couple had two raw pagans in their covenantal camp. Isaac and Rebekah's disapproval put the pestle and mortar to work again, but Esau was too big a fool to profit much from his mistake and its consequences.

One day Esau overheard his mother say to his father: "I am weary of my life because of the daughters of Heth: if Jacob take a wife of the daughters of Heth, such as these which are of the daughters of the land, what good shall my life do me?" (Genesis 27:46). Then Esau saw Jacob leave home to seek a wife among his mother's people in Mesopotamia. Finally it dawned on Esau that his marriages had broken his parents' hearts. So what did he do? He did what a born fool would do. The sacred text tells us:

> When Esau saw that Isaac had blessed Jacob, and sent him away to Padan-aram to take him a wife from thence; and that as he blessed him he gave him a charge, saying, Thou shalt not take a wife of the daughters of Canaan; And that Jacob obeyed his father and his mother, and was gone to Padan-aram; And Esau seeing that the daughters of Canaan pleased not Isaac his father; Then went Esau unto Ishmael, and took unto the wives which he had Mahalath the daughter of Ishmael Abraham's son...to be his wife" (28:6-9).

The thought never occurred to Esau that Ishmael was as pagan as the Canaanites and that a marriage to a daughter of Ishmael would no more please his parents than his marriages to Judith and Bashemath.

After that there was no more pestle and mortar. The fool was left to his folly. But other fools might have thought that Esau was a sensible fellow. After all, he got on well in this world. He settled in mount Seir and became the patriarch of the formidable Edomite race. One of his grandsons, Amalek, founded another nation that was bitterly hostile to Israel. And the Edomite race spawned Herod the Great, the infamous ruler who massacred the babes of Bethlehem in an attempt to murder the infant Christ of God.

### b. The Question of Industry (27:23-27)

#### (1) When One Gives Up Being Diligent (27:23-24)

Writing from the viewpoint of a son of a caring shepherd, Solomon advised, "Be thou diligent to know the state of thy flocks, and look well to thy herds" (Proverbs 27:23). Flocks of sheep demand a great deal of care. They readily stray, easily get lost, have no means of self-defense, and are easy prey for their enemies.

We can learn more about sheep and their care from Walter Godfrey Bowen's book *Why! The Shepherd.*[11] Bowen, a highly successful New Zealand sheep rancher, served as field director for the New Zealand wool board for many years. He was awarded one of Britain's highest decorations for his services to the sheep industry.

Bowen maintained that no other animal is as useful as a sheep. It provides wool, meat, fertilizer, and lanolin. Wool keeps out extremes of heat and cold, absorbs moisture without becoming clammy, breathes and moves with the body on which it is worn, and keeps its shape. The tensile strength of wool is very high and it is more fire-resistant than any other fiber.

However, a sheep needs constant care. It is the only animal that can get lost within sight of its home. Within its own range it has adequate skills, but once it wanders beyond that range, it has no orientation whatsoever. It will walk around in circles, often calling continually to advertise its panic.

A sheep would quickly starve to death or die of thirst were it not for the shepherd. Most animals can smell water on the wind from afar, but a sheep cannot. When it has devoured the grass on its own range, it cannot seek new feeding grounds. It wanders around eating stubble even though abundant pastures may be only a few miles away. Left to itself, a domestic sheep may eat poisonous plants because it cannot tell the difference between good plants and harmful ones.

A sheep cannot keep itself clean either. Its fleece contains grease and attracts dirt, seeds, and vegetation carried by the wind. A sheep is prey to lice, ticks, and similar pests. An infected sheep cannot lie still. It constantly rubs itself against anything it sees and will even try to eat its own wool to obtain relief. A sheep is particularly prone to infectious diseases that are easily spread.

Not strong, swift, or smart, a sheep is the most defenseless of all animals. It panics easily. Although a ram will often try to protect its ewes and lambs, it is no match for a determined predator. Weak-spirited, a sheep is soon demoralized by pain. It will not fight back when attacked, and when it is only slightly wounded, it will lie down and await death. If a sheep with a full fleece rolls over on its back in a hollow, it will not make a determined effort to get back on its feet.

Bowen recounted many other interesting facts about sheep. One statement however stands out above the rest. He said that when you see a diseased, dirty, or endangered sheep, you should not blame the sheep; you should blame the shepherd. You shouldn't say, "Poor sheep." You should say, "Poor shepherd." The condition of the sheep is a reflection on the shepherd.

So the shepherd's son wrote, "Be thou diligent." Then, writing from the viewpoint of a wise king, Solomon added, "For riches are not for ever" (Proverbs 27:24). Even the most prosperous sheep farmer can lose his wealth if his flocks—the foundation of his fortune—are neglected. Thus 27:23-24 is another of Solomon's oft-repeated warnings against laziness and taking wealth for granted.

This warning ends with a rhetorical question: "Doth the crown endure to every generation?" (27:24) Everyone familiar with history knows the answer. Royal dynasties change frequently. The history of the northern kingdom of Israel amply illustrates the need for diligence to avoid a coup d'état.

Indeed the northern kingdom of Israel began with a coup. In spite of Solomon's repeated efforts to teach diligence to his son, Rehoboam never learned his lesson. He had hardly taken office when Jeroboam snatched away ten of the twelve tribes. After that beginning there was one change after another.

Jeroboam's dynasty continued through the reign of his son Nadab, who was killed by Baasha. Baasha reigned for two dozen years. He was succeeded by his son Elah, who lasted only two years, for he was murdered by Zimri in a palace coup. Zimri had no chance of founding a dynasty because he lasted only a week!

Then came the powerful Omri dynasty, of which Ahab was the most notable and notorious king. He was followed on the throne by his son Ahaziah and grandson Jehoram (Joram). That disgraceful dynasty was brought to an end by Jehu.

Jehu was followed on the throne by his son Jehoahaz, grandson Jehoash (Joash), great-grandson Jeroboam II, and great-great-grandson Zachariah. Jehu's dynasty was powerful enough while it lasted, but it too came to an end. Zachariah reigned only a scant six months before being murdered by Shallum.

Dynasty followed dynasty in rapid succession. Shallum lasted a month; he was murdered by Menahem. Menahem reigned for ten years and was followed on the throne by his son Pekahiah. Pekahiah lasted for two years; he was murdered in a palace coup by Pekah. Pekah hung onto the throne for twenty years, but in the end was murdered by Hoshea. Hoshea's inglorious dynasty, along with the northern kingdom itself, was terminated by the Assyrians. The fact that a man sits on a throne is no guarantee that he will remain there.

It is no accident that Solomon links the work of a shepherd with the duties of a king. The will of God for His people was that their king should be their pastor, the shepherd of God's flock. David, the ideal Old Testament king, was taken from the sheepfold to be the shepherd-king of Israel.

(2) When One Goes on Being Diligent (27:25-27)

Coming back to the theme of financial matters, Solomon gave some final advice about how to make money. Pointing to the success of those who persevere, he told us to *look at the fields* of the diligent: "The hay appeareth, and the tender grass sheweth itself, and herbs of the mountains are gathered" (Proverbs 27:25). Next Solomon told us to *look at the farm* of the diligent: "The lambs are for thy clothing, and the goats are the price of the field" (27:26). Then Solomon told us to *look at the food* of the diligent: "And thou shalt have goats' milk enough for thy food, for the food of thy household, and for the maintenance for thy maidens" (27:27). We can learn from what we observe.

Note that in these verses there is no mention of animals being killed for food. In Solomon's day, meat was probably not a prime item in the peasants' diet. Meat was eaten on high days and holy days or to honor a guest.

The picture presented in Proverbs 27:25-27 is one of rural prosperity and peace. There are no internal dangers and no external wars. Such a delightful, ideal condition existed in Israel during the reign of Solomon and was the direct result of having a king on the throne who was, on the whole, a true shepherd of his people; he was diligent in promoting their welfare. This picture of Solomon's reign is intended to be a preview of the millennial reign of Christ.

What a reign that will be! There will be no more war. Swords will be converted into plowshares and tanks into tractors. There will be no more natural disasters, no more droughts, no more deserts. The whole world will become a garden of Eden. New insights into the nature and structure of living things will open up vast new horizons in productivity. Modern experiments in genetic engineering give us a hint of the dramatic changes that will take place when Jesus reigns and all such research is guided by His almighty hand.

# CHAPTER 7

Proverbs 28:1–29:14

II. The King and His Sins (28:1–29:14)
  A. The King and the Law (28:1-14)
    1. The Stability of Government (28:1-2)
      a. A Nation's Defenses (28:1)
      b. A Nation's Dynasties (28:2)
    2. The Statutes of God (28:3-14)
      a. Those Who Forsake Them (28:3-5)
        (1) No Sense of Material Justice (28:3)
        (2) No Sense of Moral Justice (28:4)
        (3) No Sense of Magisterial Justice (28:5)
      b. Those Who Follow Them (28:6-7)
        (1) The Honest Poor (28:6)
        (2) The Happy Parent (28:7)
      c. Those Who Forget Them (28:8-14)
        (1) The Heartless Man (28:8)
        (2) The Heedless Man (28:9)
        (3) The Heinous Man (28:10)
        (4) The Haughty Man (28:11)
        (5) The Harmful Man (28:12)
        (6) The Hypocritical Man (28:13)
        (7) The Hard Man (28:14)
  B. The King and His Life (28:15–29:1)
    1. The Wicked Ruler and His People (28:15)
    2. The Wicked Ruler and His Perceptions (28:16-17)
      a. Avoiding Vain Policies (28:16)
      b. Avoiding Violent Policies (28:17)
    3. The Wicked Ruler and His Perversity (28:18)
    4. The Wicked Ruler and His Priorities (28:19-22)
      a. His Goals (28:19)

b. His Guilt (28:20)
c. His Guile (28:21)
d. His Greed (28:22)
5. The Wicked Ruler and His Problems (28:23-27)
a. His Critics (28:23)
b. His Crimes (28:24)
c. His Conceit (28:25-26)
(1) Where It Will Lead Him (28:25)
(2) Where It Will Land Him (28:26)
d. His Curse (28:27)
6. The Wicked Ruler and His Power (28:28)
7. The Wicked Ruler and His Punishment (29:1)
C. The King and His Land (29:2-14)
1. The Strains of the Throne Assessed (29:2-13)
a. Beware of the Sinful Man (29:2)
b. Beware of the Sensual Man (29:3)
c. Beware of the Seductive Man (29:4-6)
(1) The Man Who Seduces with His Money (29:4)
(2) The Man Who Seduces with His Mouth (29:5)
(3) The Man Who Seduces with His Morals (29:6)
d. Beware of the Selfish Man (29:7)
e. Beware of the Scornful Man (29:8-9)
(1) He Brings Ruin to the State (29:8)
(2) He Bestows Ridicule on the Sage (29:9)
f. Beware of the Spiteful Man (29:10)
g. Beware of the Stupid Man (29:11-13)
(1) He Who Talks Freely (29:11)
(2) He Who Tells Falsehoods (29:12-13)
(a) To the Prince (29:12)
(b) To the Poor (29:13)
2. The Stability of the Throne Assured (29:14)

Kings are often guilty of flagrant sin. They are exposed to special temptations that come to those who wield almost absolute power. David used his position and power to cover up his grievous adultery by murdering Uriah. David also used his position and power to protect Amnon and then Absalom from the due rewards of their sinful deeds. So Solomon, with the example of his father David ever before him, wrote about *the king and the law* (Proverbs 28:1-14), *the king and his life* (28:15–29:1), and *the king and his land* (29:2-14).

## II. The King and His Sins (28:1–29:14)

### A. The King and the Law (28:1-14)

#### 1. The Stability of Government (28:1-2)

The strength of a nation lies in its citizens. Thus when Solomon wrote about *a nation's defenses,* he mentioned two kinds of people: those who are cowardly and those who are courageous. He observed, "The wicked flee when no man pursueth: but the righteous are bold as a lion" (Proverbs 28:1).

If anyone ever fled when no one was pursuing, it was Mephibosheth's nurse. Mephibosheth was the son of Jonathan, who was slain by the Philistines. Jonathan's father died the same day. After Saul died, civil war raged between Abner (Saul's general) and David until Abner defected from Ish-bosheth (Saul's son) to David. Much to David's dismay, Joab (David's general) murdered Abner, and David promptly and publicly disassociated himself from this crime. Then the sons of Rimmon the Beerothite murdered Ish-bosheth in his bed. (They came from a Hivite town possessed by the tribe of Benjamin.) David was innocent of this crime too and wasted no time in executing the two murderers.

When all this happened, Mephibosheth was only five years old. His nurse panicked as soon as she heard that Saul and Jonathan were dead. She seized the young boy and fled, but in her haste she dropped him, leaving him permanently lame. She picked him up and continued her flight to distant Lo-debar in Gilead (2 Samuel 4:4; 9:1-4).

Why did she panic? Did she not know that David was Jonathan's best friend, that Jonathan had made a covenant with David, and that David had for many years resolutely refused to raise a hand against Saul even though Saul persistently tried to murder him? How could she think that David would harm a hair of Mephibosheth's head? Her lack of knowledge about David was culpable and her lack of trust in him was criminal.

Who was this woman? How was she raised? How long had she been Mephibosheth's nurse? Was she a relative of King Saul? We certainly see in her a great deal of Saul's chronic disbelief in David, the Lord's anointed. Would it be going too far to say that she was wicked? Had she grown so attached to Mephibosheth that she wanted to keep the little fellow's affection focused on herself? Was she afraid that he might be taken away from her and raised, as a ward of the king, by tutors and court officials? We can conclude from her flight when no one was pursuing that she had a mistrustful, unbelieving heart as far as David was concerned. Having such an attitude toward David in those days was almost like having an unbelieving attitude toward great David's greater Son today.

We can think of many other Bible characters who, unlike Mephibosheth's nurse, were "bold as a lion." Moses was bold before the pharaoh; David before the lion, the bear, and the giant; Elijah before Ahab; Shadrach, Meshach, and Abed-nego before Nebuchadnezzar; Daniel before Darius; John the Baptist before Herod and Herodias; Peter and John before the Sanhedrin; Stephen before his murderers; and Paul before Nero. Centuries later Luther was bold before the Diet of Worms and John Knox was bold before Mary, Queen of Scots. Such men are a nation's first line of defense—inspiring fellow citizens and upholding the cause of national righteousness, without which no country can long withstand its foes.

Solomon also considered *a nation's dynasties:* "For the transgression of a land many are the princes thereof" (Proverbs 28:2, which is an expansion of 27:24). Constantly recurring coups and civil wars make a nation vulnerable to its foes. The entire history of the northern kingdom of Israel illustrates the truth of these two proverbs.

God, in His providential sovereignty over nations, often uses dynastic change as a punishment. When a nation descends into apostasy and moral decadence, it becomes a prey to pretenders and partisans who keep it in turmoil. Then change comes and a new regime imposes new policies, new taxes, new laws, and new burdens. We who live in a democratic society tend to effect changes, for better or for worse, by means of the ballot rather than the bullet. Even so, we are not exempt from assassinations, terrorists' plots, and revolution.

In Proverbs 28:2 Solomon completed his thought about a nation's dynasties by adding, "But by a man of understanding and knowledge the state thereof shall be prolonged." In other words, stability is ensured in a country when those in power are willing to hear and heed the counsel of wise, experienced statesmen. Joseph was a counselor to the pharaoh; Daniel to Nebuchadnezzar; and Isaiah to Hezekiah.

Once the voices of Elijah and Elisha were stilled, the northern kingdom of Israel never produced such an elder statesman to take their place. The southern kingdom of Judah, on the other hand, was well served by a whole succession of able, godly, brilliant men who backed or confronted the throne as the occasion required. Surely it is no accident that although both kingdoms had the same number of kings, the southern kingdom outlasted the northern kingdom by about 135 years.

Winston Churchill was "a man of understanding and knowledge." At the very moment France was collapsing in ruins before the Nazi onslaught, he hurled defiance at Hitler and rallied the British people to fight to the finish.

On the night of May 13, 1940, Churchill, who had just been made prime minister, spoke to his people. Britain was woefully unprepared for war. Years of pacifism and appeasement had practically beggared the country of any means of self-defense. The miracle of Dunkirk would soon rescue most of the British expeditionary force that was trapped on the continent, but nearly all its arms and equipment would be abandoned. The so-called home guard, made up of old but still able-bodied men, drilled with broom handles because there were no rifles. The gruff, deliberate voice of Churchill, however, put new heart into the nation:

> I have nothing to offer but blood, toil, tears and sweat.... You ask, what is our policy? I will say: It is to wage war, by sea, land and air, with all our might and with all the strength that God can give us; to wage war against a monstrous tyranny, never surpassed in the dark, lamentable catalogue of human crime. That is our policy.

Churchill was born at Blenheim palace, the magnificent home presented to his famous ancestor, the first duke of Marlborough, for his victory at Blenheim in 1704. Young Churchill did not shine as a scholar and barely made it into Sandhurst, the British military academy. After his school years he saw service in India and the Sudan, and took part in Kitchener's famous triumph at Omdurman. Churchill then became a journalist and went to South Africa to cover the Boer War. Later he went into politics, where he honed his wit and oratorical skills. During World War I he served in the admiralty.

Churchill was one of the first to warn the world about Hitler. People called him a scaremonger and he was refused the right to use the radio to tell his story. He deplored Britain's connivance at German rearmament and denounced Mussolini's rape of Ethiopia. Churchill opposed the policies of Neville Chamberlain, who danced back and forth to appease Hitler and finally returned from Munich waving a worthless treaty and proclaiming, "Peace in our time!"

After Dunkirk, when Britain stood braced for invasion, Churchill again rallied the nation:

> We shall not flag or fail. We shall go on to the end.... We shall defend our island, whatever the cost may be, we shall fight on the beaches, we shall fight on the landing grounds, we shall fight in the fields and in the streets, we shall fight in the hills; we shall never surrender.

This "man of understanding and knowledge" was able to prolong the existence of his land.

### 2. The Statutes of God (28:3-14)

#### a. Those Who Forsake Them (28:3-5)

People who violate the laws of God have no sense of material, moral, or magisterial justice. Proverbs 28:3 refers to those who have *no sense of material justice:* "A poor man that oppresseth the poor is like a sweeping rain which leaveth no food."

In this proverb two different words are rendered "poor." The first (in the phrase translated "a poor man that oppresseth") means "needy." The second (in the phrase translated "that oppresseth the poor") means "weak" and can be translated "impoverished" or "reduced." The word translated "man" here means "strong man." A situation in which a needy but strong man oppresses a weaker impoverished man is abhorrent to God. He likens such a man to a sweeping rain that leaves food for no one.

In the world of nature often a dominant male or female achieves its coveted position by its brute strength or its cunning as a fighter. Then it has to fight off all comers to keep its place on top of the heap. The defeated creature takes out its frustrations on weaker members of the community, who in turn pick on even weaker members. At the bottom of the heap is the wretched creature who has no one to pick on. The phenomenon is so evident in the henhouse that we have borrowed the terminology of "the pecking order" and now refer to a man who is bullied by his wife as "henpecked."

Being at the top of the heap, even if it is only a dung heap, all too often brings out the worst in a person. Being *near* the bottom, but not *at* the bottom, also brings out the worst in a person.

Of all the villains invented by Charles Dickens, surely the lowest of the low was not old Fagin, or the despicable Uriah Heep, or the cad Steerforth, or even the terrible dwarf Quilp. The most despicable was Noah Claypole, who worked for Sowerby the undertaker. Noah oppressed and bullied young Oliver Twist when the poor orphan was apprenticed to Sowerby. Wrote Dickens:

> Noah was a charity-boy, but not a workhouse orphan. No chance-child was he, for he could trace his genealogy all the way back to his parents, who lived hard by; his mother being a washerwoman, and his father a drunken soldier, discharged with a wooden leg, and a diurnal pension of twopence-halfpenny and an unstateable fraction. The shop-boys in the neighbourhood had long been in the habit of branding Noah, in the public streets, with the ignominious epithets of "leathers," "charity," and the like; and Noah had borne them without reply. But, now that fortune had cast in his way a nameless orphan, at whom even the meanest could point the finger of scorn, he retorted on him with interest. This affords charming food for contemplation. It shows us what a beautiful thing human nature may be made to be; and how impartially the same amiable qualities are developed in the finest lord and the dirtiest charity-boy....
>
> One day, Oliver and Noah had descended into the kitchen at the usual dinner-hour, to banquet upon a small joint of mutton—a pound and a half of the worst end of the neck—when Charlotte being called out of the way, there ensued a brief interval of time, which Noah Claypole, being hungry and vicious, considered he could not possibly devote to a worthier purpose than aggravating and tantalising young Oliver Twist.
>
> Intent upon this innocent amusement, Noah put his feet on the table-cloth; and pulled Oliver's hair; and twitched his ears; and expressed his opinion that he was a "sneak;" and furthermore announced his intention of coming to see him hanged, whenever that desirable event should take place; and entered upon various other topics of petty annoyance, like a

malicious and ill-conditioned charity-boy as he was. But, none of these taunts producing the desired effect of making Oliver cry, Noah attempted to be more facetious still; and in this attempt, did what many small wits, with far greater reputations than Noah, sometimes do to this day, when they want to be funny. He got rather personal.

"Work'us," said Noah, "how's your mother?"

"She's dead," replied Oliver; "don't you say anything about her to me!"

Oliver's colour rose as he said this; he breathed quickly; and there was a curious working of the mouth and nostrils, which Mr. Claypole thought must be the immediate precursor of a violent fit of crying. Under this impression he returned to the charge.

"What did she die of, Work'us?" said Noah.

"Of a broken heart, some of our old nurses told me," replied Oliver: more as if he were talking to himself, than answering Noah. "I think I know what it must be to die of that!"...

"Yer know, Work'us," continued Noah, emboldened by Oliver's silence, and speaking in a jeering tone of affected pity: of all tones the most annoying: "Yer know, Work'us, it can't be helped now; and of course yer couldn't help it then; and I'm very sorry for it; and I'm sure we all are, and pity yer very much. But yer must know, Work'us, yer mother was a regular right-down bad 'un."

"What did you say?" inquired Oliver, looking up very quickly.

"A regular right-down bad 'un, Work'us," replied Noah, coolly. "And it's a great deal better, Work'us, that she died when she did, or else she'd have been hard labouring in Bridewell, or transported, or hung; which is more likely than either, isn't it?"

Crimson with fury, Oliver started up, overthrew the chair and table; seized Noah by the throat; shook him, in the violence of his rage, till his teeth chattered in his head; and, collecting his whole force into one heavy blow, felled him to the ground.

Later in the story Noah (with Charlotte) arrived in London and put himself under the tutelage of Fagin. It took some time for the Jew and his new recruit to agree on his sphere of operations. Dickens described their negotiations:

"Um!" said Noah. "What's the wages?"

"Live like a gentleman—board and lodging, pipes and spirits free—half of all you earn, and half of all the young woman earns," replied Mr. Fagin.

Whether Noah Claypole, whose rapacity was none of the least comprehensive, would have acceded even to these glowing terms, had he been a perfectly free agent, is very doubtful; but as he recollected that, in the event of his refusal it was in the power of his new acquaintance to give him up to justice immediately (and more unlikely things had come to pass), he gradually relented, and said he thought that would suit him.

"But, yer see," observed Noah, "as she will be able to do a good deal, I should like to take something very light."

"A little fancy work?" suggested Fagin.

"Ah! something of that sort," replied Noah. "What do you think would suit me now? Something not too trying for the strength, and not very dangerous, you know. That's the sort of thing!"

"I heard you talk of something in the spy way upon the others, my dear," said Fagin. "My friend wants somebody who would do that well, very much."

"Why, I did mention that, and I shouldn't mind turning my hand to it sometimes," rejoined Mr. Claypole slowly; "but it wouldn't pay by itself, you know."

"That's true!" observed the Jew, ruminating or pretending to ruminate. "No, it might not."

"What do you think, then?" asked Noah, anxiously regarding him. "Something in the sneaking way, where it was pretty sure work, and not much more risk than being at home."

"What do you think of the old ladies?" asked Fagin. "There's a good deal of money made in snatching their bags and parcels, and running round the corner."

"Don't they holler out a good deal, and scratch sometimes?" asked Noah, shaking his head. "I don't think that would answer my purpose. Ain't there any other line open?"

"Stop!" said Fagin, laying his hand on Noah's knee. "The kinchin lay."

"What's that?" demanded Mr. Claypole.

"The kinchins, my dear," said Fagin, "is the young children that's sent on errands by their mothers, with sixpences and shillings; and the lay is just to take their money away—they've always got it ready in their hands,—then knock 'em into the

> kennel, and walk off very slow, as if there were nothing else the matter but a child fallen down and hurt itself. Ha! ha! ha!"
>
> "Ha! ha!" roared Mr. Claypole, kicking up his legs in an ecstasy. "Lord, that's the very thing!"
>
> "To be sure it is," replied Fagin; "and you can have a few good beats chalked out in Camden Town, and Battle Bridge, and neighbourhoods like that, where they're always going errands; and you can upset as many kinchins as you want, any hour in the day. Ha! ha! ha!"
>
> With this, Fagin poked Mr. Claypole in the side, and they joined in a burst of laughter both long and loud.[1]

Certainly Noah Claypole illustrates Proverbs 28:3. He was a poor man eager to oppress the poor and, consequently, worse than a blighting storm.

Proverbs 28:4 refers to those who have *no sense of moral justice:* "They that forsake the law praise the wicked: but such as keep the law contend with them." This proverb reminds me of Herod Antipas, who murdered John the Baptist and mocked Jesus.

This Herod was educated in Rome with his half brother Philip. Herod became the tetrarch of Galilee and Perea and married a daughter of Aretas, king of the Nabataean Arabs, whose capital was at Petra. On a visit to Rome, Herod fell under the spell of Philip's wife Herodias and urged her to abandon her husband and come with him. She agreed on the condition that Herod divorce his wife and marry her. He followed the law of his lust and forsook the law of God.

Herod's liaison with Herodias involved him in endless complications. His former father-in-law declared war on him. The fearless prophet John the Baptist publicly denounced Herod. Then Herodias and her sensual daughter Salome incited him to murder John.

Herod eyed the remarkable career of Jesus with a mixture of curiosity, fear, and superstition. His guilty conscience caused him to imagine that Jesus was John the Baptist resurrected from the dead. Herod was consumed with a desire to see one of Jesus' miracles, and hoped he would while he was in Jerusalem for the Passover holiday.

Herod must have followed the events of passion week with considerable interest. The Sanhedrin made its move—swiftly, illegally, and under cover of night. Herod soon learned that Jesus had been arrested, that the Sanhedrin had condemned Him to death, and that Pilate was expected to ratify the sentence. Then came some astounding news. The haughty Roman procurator, ever jealous of his own position, power, and prerogatives, did something unexpected and extraordinary: he deferred the case of Jesus of Nazareth to Herod because Jesus was a Galilean. Now Herod thought he would get to see a miracle! But he saw nothing of the kind, for Jesus simply ignored him.

When Jesus faced Pilate and Herod, something else happened. Luke 23:12 tells us that "the same day Pilate and Herod were made friends together: for before they were at enmity between themselves." Two wicked men, both in contempt of God's holy law, shook hands over their mutual rejection of Christ. Of all their acts of infamy, this was the most despicable. As Solomon said, "They that forsake the law praise the wicked."

Solomon's verse continues, "But such as keep the law contend with them" (Proverbs 28:4). John the Baptist is a good illustration of this statement, for he paid with his life for contending with Herod.

Proverbs 28:5 refers to those who have *no sense of magisterial justice:* "Evil men understand not judgment: but they that seek the Lord understand all things." The evil man so rationalizes his wickedness that he actually comes to believe that his evil is good. We see that illustrated in our own society by gay-rights activists and by those who, calling themselves "pro-choice," advocate the wholesale massacre of babies in the womb.

Such distortions of what is right and what is wrong are simply the results of humanism. Humanists deny the existence of God and regard the universe as self-existing. They believe that modern science has fully accounted for the universe. Since there is no God, any supernatural or human standard of values is unacceptable. Human values are to be determined by means of intelligent inquiry and are to be related to human needs.

According to humanistic thought, man is simply a part of nature, the product of mechanistic evolutionary forces. The soul does not exist apart from the body, so death terminates conscious existence. An individual is largely the product of his culture, and his religion—like his civilization—is also the product of gradual development. Humanists have no use for evangelical Christianity or what they call "God-intoxicated believers."

For the humanist, religion has nothing whatsoever to do with belief in the supernatural. There is no room for the artificial distinction between the sacred and the secular. Religion is only acceptable to the extent that it reflects human labor, art, science, philosophy, love, friendship, and recreation; and religious institutions and their activities must be restructured accordingly. Religious emotions should heighten a sense of personal life and spur cooperative efforts to promote social well-being and mental health.

The humanist's goal lies in the realization of his personality and in the development and fulfillment of his life here and now. He believes that a satisfactory life must be established on earth. Man, and man alone, is responsible for the realization of the world for which he longs. Old religious hopes and ideas are dismissed by humanists as so much wishful thinking. They believe it is up to men themselves to foster creativity and achievement. Man has within himself all that he needs to achieve utopia: a global socialistic order that ensures an equitable distribution of materials, goods, and services.

Humanists maintain that there are no absolutes, either good or evil. Man can create his own moral standards as he goes along, changing them whenever necessary. And because humanists do not believe in absolutes, they embrace abortion and wholesale divorce; they advocate sexual diversity and endorse homosexuality and other forms of deviant sex; they are permissive regarding illegal drug use; they support the right of AIDS victims to suppress the truth about their condition. As Solomon said, "Evil men understand not judgment."

We can be sure that although Solomon was liberal in many ways, he would have been shocked by the humanistic values so prevalent in modern society. Humanists do not comprise a majority in our country, but they are organized and vocal and they dominate the courts, the media, the public schools, and the halls of Congress. No wonder we have an epidemic of poor judgment, which results in high rates of alcoholism, crime, and other kinds of immoral behavior.

Evil men have no sense of right and wrong, but "they that seek the Lord understand all things." They understand the origin and destiny of the universe. They understand the fall and the degenerate condition of mankind. They understand the root and remedy of our sinful behavior. They understand who we are, where we came from, why we are where we are, and where we are going. The liberal, humanistic segment of society may laugh Christians out of court, but they will not have the last laugh. God will (Psalm 2:4).

"They that seek the Lord" believe the Bible. Therefore they understand *creation.* The theory of evolution, the pursuit of which has cost so much money and has led into so many blind alleys, has captured the thinking of many people, but it is a myth. The ten edicts of Genesis 1 contain more truth about the origin and nature of the material universe than whole libraries devoted to the false and foolish theory of evolution.

"They that seek the Lord" understand *conduct.* The speculative world of psychology is based, more or less, on humanistic concepts of human personality. Entire schools are devoted to competing theories; the mysteries of human behavior are explained this way by some, that way by others. Yet, for the most part, doctor and patient alike wander in the dark, down blind alleys, for they ignore one basic and comprehensive law of human behavior. The Bible calls it "the law of sin and death" (Romans 8:2).

We do what we do because we are what we are. The Bible says that we are lost sinners; therefore we live sinful lives. We are lost and need to be directed to a Savior, to Christ. A mechanistic psychologist may unearth some underlying stratum of guilt that produces aberrations in behavior, but what can he do about it? The only place where guilt can be removed is Calvary, and that is the last place the Freudian psychologist wants his patient to go.

"They that seek the Lord" understand *conversion:* They understand what Peter bluntly told the leaders of the Sanhedrin about man's need for Christ: "Neither is there salvation in any other: for there is none other name under heaven given among men, whereby we must be saved" (Acts 4:12).

Every child of Adam's ruined race needs to be saved. Aristocratic, religious Nicodemus needed to be saved. The sin-stained woman at the well needed to be saved. Greedy, thieving Zacchaeus needed to be saved. Zealous, ambitious Saul of Tarsus needed to be saved. The tough Philippian jailer needed to be saved. The devout, earnest Caesarean centurion needed to be saved. The dying thief needed to be saved.

The righteous understand the universal need of all people in all places and at all periods of time to be saved. Muslims need to be saved, Buddhists need to be saved, Hindus need to be saved, atheists need to be saved, and Catholics and Protestants need to be saved. Rich and poor, bond and free, good and bad, wise and foolish—all need to be saved.

"They that seek the Lord" also understand *condemnation.* They understand that people don't get away with sin—that God has appointed a day on which He will judge the world. They know that the judgment seat of Christ awaits every blood-bought child of God and that the great white throne awaits the rest of mankind. "They that seek the Lord" have inside information on God's plans and purposes concerning the second coming of Christ and how world affairs point steadily toward a violent and climactic consummation of the age.

b. Those Who Follow Them (28:6-7)

After considering those who forsake God's statutes, Solomon turned his attention to those who follow His statutes. Included among those who follow are *the honest poor.* Solomon wrote, "Better is the poor that walketh in his uprightness, than he that is perverse in his ways, though he be rich" (Proverbs 28:6).

John D. Rockefeller, for instance, lost his health in the process of acquiring a fortune. This founder of the Rockefeller dynasty was a millionaire at the age of thirty-three. At fifty-three he was the world's first billionaire. Making a million dollars a week, he became the richest man in the world. Rockefeller set out to make Standard Oil of Ohio a monopoly that would control all the production, refining, distribution, and marketing of oil in the United States. He ruthlessly forced competitors out of business and his compatriots considered him a criminal. When new antitrust laws were passed, Standard Oil was split up, but the change made little difference to Rockefeller's profits.

This rich man paid for his perverse ways, however. Rockefeller had traded health for wealth. He suffered from alopecia, which caused him to lose all his hair, including eyelashes and eyebrows. He ate only crackers and milk, enjoyed nothing, and at age fifty-three looked like a decrepit old man. He could not sleep and he never went out, but he was a billionaire.

Then Rockefeller discovered the grace of giving. He was like Dickens' Scrooge, who was a new man after the Christmas Eve hauntings. Rockefeller gave and gave. When he discovered that existing charities considered his money to be tainted, he set up the Rockefeller Foundation to handle his charitable donations, the General Education Board to provide scholarships, and the Rockefeller Institute of Medical Research. The more he gave away, the more money flowed into his pockets.

One biographer wrote, "Between his retirement in 1896 and his death in 1937 [Rockefeller] gave away three times as much as he had taken into retirement."[2] He recovered both his health and his character. People no longer called him an octopus and an anaconda. His popularity grew; he was loved and applauded. Sargent, who painted his portrait, called him a saint, a modern Francis of Assisi. The man who looked like death itself at the age of fifty-three lived to be ninety-seven!

Also included among those who follow God's statutes is *the happy parent.* Solomon had both the happy and the unhappy parent in mind when he wrote Proverbs 28:7: "Whoso keepeth the law is a wise son: but he that is a companion of riotous men shameth his father."

"A certain man had two sons," Jesus said, and then He went on to tell His matchless story of the prodigal son and his older brother (Luke 15:11-32). In the Old Testament we can find many parallels. Adam and Eve for example had Cain and Abel. Abraham had Ishmael and Isaac. Isaac had Esau and Jacob. Noah had both his Ham and his Shem.

Moses, one of the few people in the Bible who were given the title "man of God," had two sons. They were born during the years Moses wandered as a shepherd in the desert. The name of the older son was *Gershom,* which means "a stranger here"; the name of the younger son was *Eliezer,* which means "God is my helper." Beyond this we know little about them.

However, we can infer much from a few Biblical notes. We have a note in 1 Chronicles 23:17 that "the sons of Eliezer were, Rehabiah the chief. And Eliezer had none other sons; but the sons of Rehabiah were very many." An only child often grows up to be close to his parents, so we can infer that young Rehabiah delighted in his parents. We can imagine too that he was a favorite of his illustrious grandfather Moses. In the absence of any word to the contrary, it would be fair to assume that Rehabiah, because of the influence of his father and his law-giving grandfather, was a man who kept close to the law. In any case, Rehabiah had "very many" sons, often a sign of divine approbation in Old Testament times (Psalm 127:3-5; 128:3-6). So we picture Moses rejoicing in his younger son and in his grandson.

Quite a different picture emerges when we trace the line of Gershom. In the Bible the flesh often appears to dominate an older son. The principle that "the elder shall serve the younger" is by no means restricted to Esau and Jacob (Genesis 25:19-23). It is an Old Testament characteristic with New Testament implications—for instance the replacement of "the old man" with "the new man" (Colossians 3:9-10).

Something seems to have gone wrong with Gershom. Maybe he was closer to his mother than his father and shared her resentment over the rite of circumcision that was imposed on him when his family headed toward Egypt (Exodus 4:20-26). Perhaps Gershom was always somewhat willful and showed an increasing tendency to pull against the law.

Full-blown rebellion characterized Gershom's son Jonathan. Moses must have looked askance at this grandson. God mercifully called Moses home before Jonathan became a "companion of riotous men" that "shameth his father." If Moses had lived longer, he would have sentenced the young man to death, grandson or not.

We read about Jonathan in Judges, where he takes his place as a leader of apostasy in Israel. The incident recorded in Judges began when Micah, a man from mount Ephraim where Joshua had lived and was buried, stole some money from his mother. Later, when Micah restored the money to his mother, she took part of the silver and had it cast into a graven image, in flagrant violation of the second commandment (Exodus 20:4-6). This action alone called for the death penalty under the Mosaic law.

Not content with his mother's graven image, Micah made a shrine for it, made imitation holy garments, and consecrated one of his sons to be his priest. About that time an unemployed Levite from Bethlehem wandered to mount Ephraim. Micah offered him his keep, along with ten shekels of silver a year, and a suit if he would remain in mount Ephraim and become a priest of the idol. The Levite succumbed to the temptation and sold his soul for a mess of this world's pottage.

Presently five men from the tribe of Dan stumbled across Micah's shrine. Some time later they returned with an armed contingent, stole the graven image, and suborned the Levite to abandon Micah and come with them. "Is it better for thee to be a priest unto the house of one man, or that thou be a priest unto a tribe and a family in Israel?" they demanded. "And the priest's heart was glad," commented the Holy Spirit (Judges 18:19-20).

Thus the tribe of Dan officially introduced idolatry into Israel and the Levite became a "companion of riotous men." And who was this young man? He was Jonathan, the son of Gershom and grandson of Moses. Jonathan brought such shame to his father and grandfather that the Jews did something almost unprecedented in all their history: they tampered with the sacred text. And so we read, "The children of Dan set up the graven image: and Jonathan, the son of Gershom, the son of *Manasseh,* he and his sons were priests to the tribe of Dan until the day of the captivity of the land" (Judges 18:30, italics added). Jonathan was not the grandson of Manasseh; he was the grandson of Moses. *The Companion Bible* offers the following explanation in a marginal note:

> Manasseh. This word is one of the four that has a suspended letter. Here the letter (נ), *nun* (n), is written partly in the line

> and partly above the line, to show that originally it formed no part of the word, but was put in to make it spell "Manasseh" instead of "Moses". Jonathan was the grandson of Moses (his contemporary Phinehas, the grandson of Aaron, being mentioned in 20.28). This was done for two reasons: (1) to spare the honour of Moses' memory and name; (2) to put the sin upon one who committed so gross a sin. The Talmud gives this latter as the reason. Jonathan's name is omitted in 1 Chron. 23.15,16, and 26.24. The Chald. paraphrase says that "Shebuel", there substituted, is meant for Jonathan after his repentance and restoration. Shebuel = "he returned to God".[3]

So Jonathan brought shame to his father. But Solomon doubtless would prefer that we meditate on the happy parent of "a wise son" who "keepeth the law." Doubtless too Solomon wished that he had a wise son.

c. Those Who Forget Them (28:8-14)

Solomon next gave seven illustrations of people who ignore God's Word. First he mentioned *the heartless man:* "He that by usury and unjust gain increaseth his substance, he shall gather it for him that will pity the poor" (Proverbs 28:8).

People still make money by usury. Big credit-card companies, which put credit in the hands of the unwary and careless, first tempt people to buy and then to buy beyond their means so that they will have to pay finance charges. The credit-card companies penalize these consumers with high interest rates that border on usury. Then there are the crime syndicate's loan sharks, who charge skyrocketing interest rates and send bullies armed with knives, bludgeons, and guns to enforce collection. We should feel outraged when we read about this kind of usury.

The Bible says that a person who gets rich by such means may indeed amass a fortune, but in the end that fortune tends to find its way back to the poor. Nowadays the Internal Revenue Service sometimes uncovers "unjust gain" and the taxes and fines imposed by the IRS go into the government's capacious coffers. A good percentage of that tax money is distributed to the poor through government-financed social service programs.

This idea of robbing the robbers in order to give to the poor is the basis of the perennial popularity of the stories of Robin Hood and his merry men who cavorted in Sherwood forest in Lincoln green. It was the practice of these outlaws to waylay the treasure caravans of the rich and powerful of the nation and the church. Robin would seize local barons and bishops who had extorted money from the poor and hold these rich men for ransom; when he had squeezed the money out of them, he would give it back to the poor. If Robin had wanted a text to give some air of respectability to his activities, Proverbs 28:8 would be as good as any.

The distribution of wealth has always brought windfalls to some and downfalls to others. Capitalism has created the new rich and the terribly poor. Feudalism did the same. Communism was supposed to redress the wrongs against the working class. The basic idea sounded sane and compassionate: "To each according to his need, from each according to his ability." In practice, however, communism produced one of the worst tyrannies the world has ever known.

Marxism failed because it was *philosophically* wrong. Its driving force was a vision of man without God. "Religion is the opiate of the people," raved Marx and Lenin. They regarded religion as a capitalistic device for keeping the downtrodden masses content with their lot in life. Consequently the communists said terrible things about God and His Son. Vowing to abolish God from heaven and earth, the communists went about getting rid of religion with a high and heavy hand. For a while they had astounding success, spreading atheism around the world. Atheism however is poor fare for an immortal soul and in the end it did not prevail.

Marxism failed because it was *morally* wrong. The communists' creed was to plunder the rich to please the poor. Although it is no more right to rob a rich man by government decree than to rob him at gunpoint, the communists nationalized everything. Their idea was that the state is supreme and therefore everything belongs to the state. All men, they thought, must be reduced to the same level, and the "undesirable" elements in society must be eliminated.

Stalin imposed communism on his countrymen, regardless of who was hurt. He massacred millions of peasants in his drive to collectivize the farms of the Soviet Union. Entire populations were shot or deported to slave camps. The rich, the religious, the educated, the politically undesirable, the officer corps of the army, those unable or unwilling to work, the diseased, and the addicts were all marked for extermination. If communism is to work, he reasoned, there must be no opposition. There must be an absolute dictatorship of the proletariat. People must do what they are told. There must be five-year plans to improve industrial output. This farm must plant potatoes; that one must cultivate corn. This factory must produce tanks; that one must produce tractors. There must be spies and informers; a ruthless, omnipresent police force; and a vast subversive military.

Under Stalin an elite group of planners decided who would do what and who would go where. So out of his wholly immoral communistic system grew another upper class of party bosses and another lower class of deprived laborers. No wonder the system did not work!

Marxism failed because it was *economically* wrong. The system broke down because nobody is smart enough to make all the detailed decisions involved in making a modern industrial, agricultural, social economy work. Moreover the workers themselves refused to work. Faced with an ever-increasing breakdown of the system and robbed of their savings, they were living in poverty, unable to buy the bare necessities of life and cut off from all hope of luxuries. The workers were outraged that the privileged elite had bread to spare while the proletariat perished with hunger. When the workers did work, they produced shoddy results. Many turned to drink.

At last Gorbachev had to come begging, hat in hand, to the Big Seven—the successful, wealthy western capitalist nations. He asked for an astronomical $250 billion in aid. By then the ruble was worthless as a medium of international exchange. Of 220 consumer items that we take for granted in the West, at that time no less than 200 were difficult or even impossible to get in the Soviet Union. Marxism in the end bankrupted the Soviet Union and created an economic nightmare.

One day, as prophesied in the Bible, God will impose His plan for the economic well-being of mankind. The resources of this planet will be put into the hands of Jesus, who will inaugurate economic and ecological miracles and establish a reign of peace and universal prosperity. Those who rob and oppress the poor will be banished from the world, and the poor will be poor no more.

*The heedless man* too ignores God's Word. Solomon mentioned him in Proverbs 28:9: "He that turneth away his ear from hearing the law, even his prayer shall be abomination."

Prayer is the most mysterious force in the universe. We are familiar with the laws of nature that underlie such phenomena as electricity, light, sound, magnetism, and gravity. Every scientific discipline has a distinctive set of highly complex laws, some of which we understand, some of which we understand partially, and some of which we don't understand at all. Prayer is another law of the universe. We really have no idea how prayer works; we only know that it does. In His administration of the universe, our omniscient, omnipresent, and omnipotent God takes all the laws of nature, science, and prayer into account. He weighs the prayer factor along with all the others.

Some time ago I was the guest speaker at a church in Tennessee. I was housed in a large, comfortable hotel where I was picked up every day before services. On the last day I brought my luggage down to the hotel lobby and went toward the counter to check out.

Normally I carry three pieces of luggage when I travel: a garment bag, a suitcase, and a shoulder bag. In the shoulder bag I keep items that would be difficult or impossible to replace. I never put that bag down, except at my feet. On this particular occasion my shoulder bag contained my preaching notes for fifty conference-style messages; some books that would be difficult, expensive, or impossible to replace; and extensive notes on the book of Proverbs, including fifty manuscript pages I had composed during my stay at the hotel. I parked my luggage in a handy spot about ten feet from the counter and, for some unexplainable reason, left the shoulder bag with the garment bag and suitcase. No one was in the lobby except two employees who were running vacuum cleaners over the carpet.

The process of turning in my key and waiting for a receipt took about three minutes. Then I turned to pick up my bags—and they were gone, including the all-important shoulder bag. I could not believe my eyes. I stood and stared at the empty spot where I had placed my bags.

I looked up and down the lobby. There was no one there except the two women who were still busy vacuuming. I hurried to the door of the hotel. An airport limousine was parked there and the driver was lounging against his vehicle. He had not seen anyone leaving the hotel. No one else was in sight, so I ran out to the parking lot. No one was in sight there either. Stunned, I went back to the lobby and announced my loss to the clerk at the counter. The hotel security guard was summoned, but he seemed to be as perplexed as everyone else and all he could do was give me a claim form.

Some financial remuneration might be forthcoming from the hotel's insurance, but nothing could replace that shoulder bag. I visualized the monumental task of trying to reconstruct the lost material and, naturally, lifted up my heart to the Lord. Just then an associate pastor from the church arrived to take me to the church for the closing message and then to the airport. He saw right away that something was wrong and as soon as I explained what had happened, he said, "Let's pray!" He offered a brief prayer for the return of the bags.

When we opened our eyes we saw a tall, thin man coming toward us. He was carrying my three pieces of luggage. "Have you lost these?" he asked. Offering no explanation and making no comment, he put the bags down and walked away, vanishing as mysteriously as he had appeared. Needless to say, that young pastor and I had a praise meeting then and there!

Who can explain such answers to prayer? Who can explain the equally mysterious occasions when prayer is seemingly unanswered?

We can, however, comprehend certain basic laws that operate in the sphere of prayer. Prayer must be offered in the power of the Holy Spirit and in accordance with the will of God. It must be offered in the name of the Lord Jesus Christ. It must be appropriate—we cannot expect God to give us what we want just to satisfy our lusts.

We know that unconfessed sin hinders prayer, as does a man's inconsiderate treatment of his wife. We learn from Proverbs that the person who ignores God's Word cannot expect God to answer his prayer either; in fact the heedless man actually insults God with his prayer. "His prayer shall be abomination," wrote Solomon. A graphic illustration of this "abomination" is found in the book of Revelation:

The seals have been broken and the world has been reduced to utter chaos by war, famine, pestilence, persecution, and outright panic. The trumpets have sounded and the world has come under the direct control of Satan, the antichrist, and the false prophet. Economic and ecological disasters have reached an unprecedented magnitude and a demon-inspired drug culture has emerged. The unspeakable horrors of the great tribulation have been in full force for about three and a half years.

The time has come for God to close His ears to the heedless man's prayer. God sent His two witnesses, and they were murdered. He sent his 144,000 witnesses, and millions of their converts were massacred. He even sent an angel to give a final gospel call.

Now the seven angels who are commissioned to pour out the bowls of God's wrath have assembled. They emerge from the heavenly temple clothed in pure, white linen and golden girdles. And just before the angels pour out the bowls, something ominous takes place: "The temple [is] filled with smoke from the glory of God, and from his power; and no man [is] able to enter into the temple, till the seven plagues of the seven angels [are] fulfilled" (Revelation 15:8).

Why is no man able to enter? Because wicked men's prayers are an abomination to God. Now that His wrath is brimming over, He deliberately closes the way to enter into His presence. He refuses to hear the prayers of heedless men.

We can well imagine that when these final horrors actually begin to overtake the world, men will cry out to God, but it will be too late. Their prayers will not enter His temple. He will close the door and say in effect, "Praying time is over. Call all you want. I refuse to listen to you anymore. Your prayer is an abomination."

God's Word is also ignored by *the heinous man,* who is mentioned in Proverbs 28:10: "Whoso causeth the righteous to go astray in an evil way, he shall fall himself into his own pit: but the upright shall have good things in possession." This proverb tells us that someone who sets up an essentially righteous person for a fall will not reap any lasting benefit from his lapse. On the contrary, the heinous man will fall into a worse pit and become entangled in his own evil. Moreover the good man who fell will eventually realize his condition, fully recover, and be more wary and watchful thereafter.

Lot and his daughters provide an illustration of this proverb. We know little about the girls, except that they were brought up in Sodom. Two were single and their sisters were married to Sodom's sons. Their mother seems to have grown attached to the vile city. Their father's business interests kept him in Sodom, but he was never happy there and he lamented the filthy lifestyle of its people. Lot was a righteous man. We would hardly gather that from his history, but the Holy Spirit assures us that this was so (2 Peter 2:7-8).

We can imagine that Lot would sometimes speak nostalgically about the time when he, like Abraham, had been a pilgrim and a stranger. Now he was entangled in Sodom. Not even the terrible fright of being taken captive by the invading armies from the East could pry him loose from the accursed city. (If his Uncle Abraham had not acted promptly and fearlessly to save him and his family, they would have been carried away to the slave markets of Mesopotamia.) After Lot was rescued he could have returned to the fellowship of God's people, but he was unable to resist the king of Sodom's offer to give him the keys to the city and a seat in the gate.[4] Lot went back to Sodom and in time even his two unmarried girls became more and more like the people of that polluted place.

Lot and his unmarried daughters escaped the horrifying events of Sodom's last night "by the skin of their teeth." Then these two girls caused him "to go astray." Lot may have been weak, but he was not wicked. There is no evidence that he was a drunkard or an immoral person. He seems to have been a family man and the

Holy Spirit tells us that he was greatly disturbed by "the filthy conversation of the wicked." But his daughters were bereft of all morality. They had thoroughly imbibed Sodom's manner of life. Accordingly on two successive nights they made their father drunk and committed incest with him (Genesis 19:30-38). As a result, each gave birth to a son.

By causing righteous Lot "to go astray," they fell into their own pit, for the son of one daughter was Moab (the father of the Moabites) and the son of the other was Ben-ammi (the father of the Ammonites). The Moabites and the Ammonites became two of the most inveterate and bitter enemies of God's people in Old Testament times.

For about two thousand years, readers of the holy Scriptures were left to think the worst of Lot. But Genesis 19 was not the last word. The last word was 2 Peter 2:7. Peter rescued Lot's name from infamy and, under the inspiration and revelation of the Holy Spirit, restored to Lot the best possession a man could have—the integrity of his name. Truly, "the upright shall have good things in possession."

*The haughty man* too ignores the Word of God: "The rich man is wise in his own conceit; but the poor that hath understanding searcheth him out" (Proverbs 28:11).

We have no trouble picturing the two men in this proverb. The first one is rich, purse-proud, arrogant, full of conceit and self-importance, and cocksure of his opinions. The second one is poor, obliged to grapple daily with the hard facts of life, pragmatic, down-to-earth, and a realist; his common sense is proverbial. The second man has no trouble seeing through the first man's facade, yet the first man looks down his nose at the second man. The second man is a fundamentalist who deals with the great basic issues of life. The first man is a fool. It is astonishing how many rich people think they are far more clever than they really are, especially if they have simply inherited wealth and power, and have not earned it.

C. S. Forester, in his *Captain Horatio Hornblower* series, contrasted a poor man's son (Hornblower) with a rich man's son (Admiral Leighton). It was Hornblower's misfortune to serve under Leighton, who was only a year or so older than the captain.

Hornblower, who was a competent seaman, a veteran of a number of naval battles, a first-class navigator, and a strategic thinker, was worthy of higher rank. Yet he had to take orders from an incompetent who owed his rank to his wealth, social position, and marital alliance with the powerful Wellesley faction in government.

The marquis of Wellesley was the foreign Secretary; Henry Wellesley was the ambassador in Spain; Sir Arthur Wellesley, the duke of Wellington, was commander-in-chief in the Iberian peninsula. Leighton (in the story, at any rate) was married to Lady Barbara, sister to the all-powerful Wellesleys. That was why he was an admiral and Hornblower was only a captain.

Hornblower brought his ship, the *Sutherland,* to his squadron's rendezvous off Palamos point in the Mediterranean sea. There was no sign of the flagship or the admiral. When another ship of the fleet arrived, its captain invited Hornblower, an old friend of his, to come aboard and have supper with him. Captain Bolton had come up through the ranks and had none of the pretensions of the sprigs of the nobility who commanded so many of His Majesty's ships. Indeed Hornblower was startled by his friend's bluntness: "Now," said Bolton, "we must await, in idleness, the arrival of Sir Mucho Pomposo, Rear Admiral of the Red."[5] Much as Hornblower disliked Sir Percy Leighton, he never would have voiced his personal feelings in such terms. Bolton continued, airing his opinion of the new admiral's competence: Noting the wind, Bolton observed that if the admiral had not passed the straits of Gibraltar two days ago, he would not show up for another week. Moreover if he did not leave all navigation to his captain, the flagship would never show up at all!

Hornblower and Bolton tossed a coin to see who would remain on station to await the admiral's arrival and who would reconnoiter the French and Spanish coastline. Hornblower won the toss and departed in search of adventure. He arrived back flushed with a number of victories and full of news and valuable suggestions. In the meantime the admiral had arrived and he impatiently summoned Hornblower aboard the flagship. Leighton brushed aside Hornblower's victories, gave him a warning scowl when he ventured to suggest a possible move to follow up his successes, and then expressed annoyance because Hornblower had not been on station to greet him when he arrived.

Later the admiral almost wrecked the flagship in a storm and had to be towed away from a threatening lee shore by the *Sutherland.* Then the admiral commanded an ill-advised and poorly-planned land action and blamed Hornblower for its inevitable failure. Eventually the admiral was killed in a battle off the French coast, but that did not do Hornblower much good. Thanks to the admiral's incompetence, at the end of Volume II, Hornblower was a prisoner awaiting a certain death sentence from Napoleon.

Forester's tale is only a story, but it well illustrates Solomon's words about the rich man who is "wise in his own conceit" and the poor man who possesses understanding. The despised man often puts the lionized man to shame. It is the theme of many stories and not at all uncommon in real life.

Also among those who forget the statutes of God is *the harmful man*. When the harmful are in power, good people have to hide themselves to escape danger. As Proverbs 28:12 states, "When righteous men do rejoice, there is great glory: but when the wicked rise, a man is hidden." This verse paints a word picture of a festive occasion celebrating the coming to power of a righteous man after a period of misrule.

The proverb is amply illustrated in the histories of King Saul and King David. King Saul was the first man to sit on the throne of Israel, a throne that was about ten times too big for him. King Saul wore royalty about as badly as David wore Saul's massive armor (1 Samuel 17:38-39). We can well imagine that righteous men in Israel rejoiced when David finally came to the throne.

David was in the tenth generation of Judah's successors. There seems to be some significance in the tenth generation, for it crops up often in Scripture. Jesse, David's father, was in the tenth generation of the descendants of Jacob. The line from Adam to Noah spanned ten generations, and so did the lines from Shem to Abraham, Solomon to Uzziah, and Uzziah to Zedekiah.

We know nothing about David's mother and little about his father. The story of David's early years revolves around four centers. We see him first *in the country*. There he grew up as the unspoiled youngest of eight brothers (1 Samuel 16:10-11). He was a shepherd and an exceedingly good one, fearless in the defense of his flock. Out on the lonely hills he would tune his harp and sing hymns he composed himself. Even after the aged Samuel anointed David to be Israel's future king, he was quite content to go back to minding his sheep.

Next we see David *in the camp*. There, in the valley of Elah, in full view of two armies, David won his spurs. His victory over Goliath made him famous overnight. Thus God drew the attention of the Israelites to their future king—and the attention of the Philistines to their future nemesis.

We see David next *in the court*. He had been recommended to King Saul for his skill as a harpist. The hope was that David's music might calm the king's shattered nerves and quiet the evil spirit that possessed him. Instead Saul, who was jealous of David's victory over Goliath and suspicious of David's popularity with the people, began to plot his murder. After several narrow escapes, David was forced to flee.

Thus we see him next *in the cave.* David was a constant fugitive from Saul's malicious, unrelenting, and single-minded persecution. "When the wicked rise, a man is hidden," wrote Solomon, surely remembering the many stories his father had told him about Saul. The cat-and-mouse game went on—now David hid in the cave, now he fled to the Philistines, now he was back in the cave, now he fled to the mountains with Saul's army at his heels. Saul continued his pursuit until he died.

With this ordeal ended, David ascended the throne and he reigned in "great glory." Solomon knew all about the glory, for he was heir to it. By the time Solomon ascended David's throne, no nation in the Middle East dared to raise a finger against Israel. Israel had enjoyed years of prosperity and peace, and the religious life of the nation had been revived. David had amassed vast amounts of money and materials for the building of the temple. The treasury was overflowing, and equity and justice were available to all. Glory was the order of the day as Psalm 45:3 so magnificently declares: "Gird thy sword upon thy thigh, O most mighty, with thy glory and thy majesty." (Some think that Solomon wrote Psalm 45 to celebrate his marriage to the pharaoh's daughter.)

Such glory eluded King Saul, who, forgetting the statutes of God, was a harmful man. The harmful man ignores God's Word, as does *the hypocritical man.* Proverbs 28:13, referring to the hypocrite, warns that "he that covereth his sins shall not prosper: but whoso confesseth and forsaketh them shall have mercy."

People who cover their sins often seem to prosper at first. Such was the case of M. de Villefort in Alexander Dumas's famous story *The Count of Monte-Cristo.* Villefort, a lawyer, had Edmond Dantès sentenced unjustly to life imprisonment. Fully aware of Dantès' innocence, Villefort pressed the case solely to protect himself from certain incriminating information that Dantès possessed.

The lawyer went on from one success to another until he became the royal prosecutor of France. But Villefort had another secret—more personal and even darker than the secret Dantès knew. The lawyer had once had an adulterous affair with a young woman, and a child was born of their union. Trying to avoid scandal and thinking that the baby was stillborn, Villefort buried the infant in the garden outside the house where the amorous intrigues had been clandestinely conducted. However, the secret burial was observed by a spy. Thinking that Villefort had been hiding treasure, the spy dug up the box—and discovered it contained a still-living child. The treasure-hunter adopted the baby, who grew up to be a vicious criminal.

By the time the child reached adulthood, the royal prosecutor had long since suppressed all thoughts of that most sinful episode in his life. He had no idea that the baby he had buried was alive and had become a notorious villain. Villefort had covered his sins, or so he thought.

In the meantime, Dantès escaped from prison and fell heir to a fabulous fortune. In prison his appearance had changed and he had been educated by a fellow inmate who was a priest. So an unrecognizable Dantès burst upon Parisian society as the count of Monte-Cristo. The count thirsted for revenge against the men who had wronged him, but hated the king's prosecutor most of all. Dantès unearthed the secret of Villefort's son, found him in prison, rescued him, groomed him, dressed him, put money at his disposal, and introduced him into society as Andrea Cavalcanti, the wealthy son of an Italian nobleman. Monte-Cristo knew his protégé as Benedetto, an unscrupulous and clever rogue.

The story came to a climax when Cavalcanti committed a brutal murder. All Paris was interested in his trial. As far as the prosecutor Villefort knew, Cavalcanti was simply a criminal to be brought to justice and punished by death. Dumas told the story of the trial as follows:

> "Accused," said the president, "your name and surname?"
>
> Andrea rose.
>
> "Excuse me, M. le Président," he said, in a clear voice, "but I see you are going to adopt a course of questions through which I cannot follow you. I have an idea, which I will explain by-and-by, of making an exception to the usual form of accusation. Allow me, then, if you please, to answer in different order, or I will not do so at all."
>
> The astonished president looked at the jury, who themselves looked upon the procureur du roi. The whole assembly manifested great surprise. But Andrea appeared quite unmoved.
>
> "Your age?" asked the president; "will you answer that question?"
>
> "I will answer that question as well as the rest, M. le Président, but in its turn."
>
> "Your age?" repeated the president.

"I am twenty-one years old; or rather I shall be in a few days, as I was born the night of the 27th of September 1817."

M. de Villefort, who was busy taking down some notes, raised his head at the mention of this date. [It was the date he had buried the child.]

"Where were you born?" continued the president.

"At Auteuil, near Paris."

M. de Villefort a second time raised his head, looked at Benedetto as if he had been gazing at the head of Medusa, and became livid [for Auteuil was the place where Villefort had committed the crime].

As for Benedetto he gracefully wiped his lips with a fine cambric pocket-handkerchief.

"Your profession?"

"First I was a forger," answered Andrea, as calmly as possible; "then I became a thief, and lately have become an assassin."

A murmur, or rather storm, of indignation burst from all parts of the assembly. The judges themselves appeared stupefied, and the jury manifested tokens of disgust for a stoicism so unexpected from a fashionable man.

M. de Villefort pressed his hand upon his brow, which, at first pale, had become red and burning; then he suddenly rose, and looked around as though he had lost his senses—he wanted air.

"Are you looking for anything, M. le Procureur du Roi?" asked Benedetto, with his most pleasing smile.

M. de Villefort answered nothing, but sat, or rather threw himself down again, upon his chair.

"And now, prisoner, will you consent to tell your name?" said the president. "The brutal affectation with which you have enumerated and classified your crimes calls for a severe reprimand on the part of the court, both in the name of morality, and for the respect due to humanity. You appear to consider this a point of honour, and it may be for this reason you have delayed acknowledging your name. You wished it to be preceded by all these titles."

"It is quite wonderful, M. le Président, how entirely you have read my thoughts," said Benedetto, in his softest voice and most polite manner. "This is, indeed, the reason why I begged you to alter the order of the questions."

The public astonishment had reached its height. There was no longer any deceit or bravado in the manner of the accused.

The audience seemed like some thundercloud about to burst over the gloomy scene.

"Well!" said the president, "your name?"

"I cannot tell you my name, since I do not know it; but I know my father's, and will pronounce it."

"Repeat your father's name," said the president.

Not a whisper, not a breath was heard in that vast assembly; every one waited anxiously.

"My father is the procureur du roi," replied Andrea calmly....

"Gentlemen?" said Andrea, commanding silence by his voice and manner; "I owe you the proofs and explanation of what I have said."

"But," said the irritated president, "you called yourself Benedetto, declared yourself an orphan, and claimed Corsica as your country."

"I said anything I pleased, in order that the solemn declaration I have just made should not be withheld, which otherwise would certainly have been the case. I now repeat that I was born at Auteuil on the night of the 27th September 1817, and that I am the son of the procureur du roi, M. de Villefort. Do you wish for any further details? I will give them. I was born in No. 28 Rue de la Fontaine, in a room hung with red damask. My father took me in his arms, telling my mother I was dead, wrapped me in a napkin marked with an H and an N, and carried me into a garden, where he buried me alive."...

"The proofs! the proofs!" said the president, "remember this tissue of horrors must be supported by the clearest proofs."

"The proofs?" said Benedetto, laughing, "Do you want proofs?"

"Yes."

"Well, then, look at M. de Villefort, and then ask me for proofs."

Every one turned towards the procureur du roi, who, unable to bear the universal gaze now riveted on him alone, advanced staggering into the midst of the tribunal, with his hair dishevelled, and his face indented with the mark of his nails. The whole assembly uttered a long murmur of astonishment.

"Father!" said Benedetto, "I am asked for proofs; do you wish me to give them?"

"No, no, it is useless!" stammered M. de Villefort, in a hoarse voice—"no, it is useless!"

> "How useless?" cried the president; "what do you mean?"
> "I mean that I feel it impossible to struggle against this deadly weight which crushes me! Gentlemen, I know I am in the hands of an avenging God! We need no proofs; everything relating to this young man is true."[6]

Truly, "he that covereth his sins shall not prosper," as so many people have discovered, and often too late.

In the Old Testament, God provided an acceptable way for sins to be covered. On the annual day of atonement two goats were presented to the Lord. One goat was slain and its blood was taken into the holy of holies, where it was sprinkled on the mercy seat. Over the head of the other goat all the sins of the people were confessed. It was then taken into the wilderness, symbolically bearing away the people's sins, and left there to perish, out of the sight of everyone except God. The word translated "atonement" in the Old Testament is derived from a word that means "to cover."

Summing up the rites and rituals of Old Testament religion, the Holy Spirit said in Hebrews 10:11, "Every priest standeth daily ministering and offering oftentimes the same sacrifices, which can never take away sins." The entire sacrificial system was one great cover-up. But what a change Calvary wrought! Hebrews 10:12 explains, "But this man, after he had offered one sacrifice for sins for ever, sat down on the right hand of God."

Now God cleanses sin. "If we confess our sins," wrote John (picking up Solomon's words "whoso confesseth and forsaketh them shall have mercy"), "he is faithful and just to forgive us our sins, and to cleanse us from all unrighteousness" (1 John 1:9). If we confess our sins, they are not covered; they are canceled! In the Old Testament God was willing to cover the sins of repentant sinners, but now, because of Calvary, He can blot their sins out forever!

Concluding his illustrations of people who forget the statutes of God, Solomon mentioned *the hard man:* "Happy is the man that feareth alway: but he that hardeneth his heart shall fall into mischief" (Proverbs 28:14).

The classic Biblical example of the hard man is the pharaoh who ruled Egypt at the time of the exodus. The apostle Paul referred to this wicked and stubborn king in the Epistle to the Romans.

Having dealt with the three great issues of sin, salvation, and sanctification, Paul turned his attention to the problem of the Jews' rejection of the gospel.[7] He had been raised as a Jew and was filled with compassion and concern for the Hebrew people. Although God had given them mighty, marvelous promises, they had murdered their Messiah. Worse, instead of repenting, the nation had rejected the Spirit of God as stubbornly as it had rejected the Son of God.

Now where did the Jews fit into the purposes of God? Did their rejection affect God's promises to Abraham and David? Paul wrestled with the problem in Romans 9–11. In chapter 9 he wrote about the sovereignty of God and His past dealings with Israel. In chapter 10 Paul wrote about the salvation of God and His present dealings with Israel. In chapter 11 Paul wrote about the sincerity of God and His promised dealings with Israel.

In Paul's famous discourse on the sovereignty of God in Romans 9:14-24, we cannot miss the repeated references to God's will in such expressions as "I will," "he will," and "his will." Paul observed that God asserts His sovereignty over all human activity, as in the case of the pharaoh. The apostle wrote, "For the Scripture saith unto Pharaoh, Even for this same purpose have I raised thee up, that I might shew my power in thee, and that my name might be declared throughout all the earth. Therefore hath he mercy on whom he will have mercy, and whom he will he hardeneth" (9:17-18).

God's sovereignty, it should be noted, does not preclude man's free will. God created human beings to be volitional and morally accountable, fully responsible for our behavior and answerable to Him. He could have locked us into a behavior pattern from which there was no escape and in which there was no choice—as in the animal creation. But then He would not have created people; He would have created puppets.

The apparent clash between divine sovereignty and free will is resolved in the story of Moses' confrontation with the pharaoh. The Biblical account of the historical incident contains twenty references to the hardening of pharaoh's heart. Ten times the hardening is attributed to pharaoh; ten times it is attributed to God. Three different Hebrew words are translated "harden" and the same three words that are used to describe pharaoh's action in hardening his heart are used to describe God's action in hardening pharaoh's heart. Some of the references to God's action were prophetic. He simply told Moses in advance what to expect: pharaoh would not listen, pharaoh would harden his heart, and God would harden pharaoh's heart.[8]

It was not until after the sixth plague that God actually did harden pharaoh's heart. After the seventh plague God gave pharaoh one more chance to exercise his free will and again he hardened his own heart. From the eighth plague onward pharaoh's heart was hardened by God; he had no more opportunity to repent, for he had crossed an unseen line in his stubborn unbelief. As Solomon said, "He that hardeneth his heart shall fall into mischief." Pharaoh discovered that God is not to be mocked.

Unlike the hard man, "the man that feareth alway" is happy. The first part of Proverbs 28:14 is one of the eight beatitudes found in the book of Proverbs (3:13; 8:32,34; 14:21; 16:20; 20:7; 28:14; 29:18). The unsaved often look upon the Christian life as a list of negatives, a life of denial and unhappiness. Not so! The Christian life is blessed with love, joy, and peace. The man who fears God does not need to fear anybody or anything else. For example Joseph's fear of God led him to reject politely but firmly the amorous advances of Potiphar's wife. He may not have considered the immediate outcome to be very happy, but eventually God vindicated him, set him on high, gave him a wife and children, and restored his lost father and brothers to him. Then his cup was full and running over.

## B. The King and His Life (28:15–29:1)

This series of proverbs concentrates on the wicked ruler. Anyone who studies history will learn that all too often nations have been governed by wicked men.

### 1. The Wicked Ruler and His People (28:15)

The series begins with Proverbs 28:15: "As a roaring lion, and a ranging bear; so is a wicked ruler over the poor people." In other words, poor people are almost defenseless against a wicked ruler.

Philip II of Spain was a wicked ruler. In the mind of this Roman Catholic zealot, the rise of Lutheranism on the European continent called for bitter persecution. After the writings of Luther, Erasmus, Melanchthon, and Zwingli were brought into Spain, the Inquisition prepared an *Index Expurgandorum.* Every book on the list was banned, including the Bible in the common tongue. Philip wanted any lingering remnant of Protestant teaching uprooted from his domain.

When Philip II came to the throne in 1556, he urged the Inquisition on to extreme measures. He took great delight in the public burning of heretics after soldiers of the Inquisition had finished twisting and torturing their bodies. He was eager to attend each auto-da-fé.

Each auto-da-fé began with a procession from the church to the square. The familiars of the holy office and their attendants sallied forth in triumphal array carrying large, white, lighted tapers. In their midst was a bier covered by a black pall. Following them were the heretics, and bringing up the rear were a band and a choir.

Among the heretics, the terrified penitents were closely shaved and arrayed in demeaning garb. Those condemned to die at the stake wore sacks of black canvas adorned with painted flames and fool's caps decorated with coarse pictures of devils in flames. All along the route of the procession these unfortunates were assailed with ceaseless exhortations to repent. They were promised that repentance would be rewarded: they would be strangled at the stake before the flames touched them.

When the procession reached the square, there was a sermon. Then all the people had to swear an oath, pledging support of the Inquisition. Finally the sentences were pronounced. All penalties carried with them civil repercussions. When penance was imposed, it took various forms. One person might be required to fast once a week and recite a specified number of prayers. Another person might be required to appear at church on Sundays with a halter around his neck. Still another might be scourged in the city. Many people were burned alive at the stake, and the blood of their descendants was considered to be tainted.

King Philip watched with relish as nine victims were martyred at an auto-da-fé held on Trinity Sunday at Valladolid on May 21, 1559. He rose from his seat, drew his sword, and brandished it as he swore to uphold and honor the holy office. Not content with being a spectator, Philip visited the various stakes and ordered his bodyguard to help the familiars of the Inquisition pile up wood around the sufferers.

Philip II married Mary I of England and became joint sovereign of England until her death in 1558. He wrote to his ambassador in Rome that "rather than suffer the least damage to religion and the service of God I would lose all my states and an hundred lives, if I had them; for I do not propose nor desire to be the ruler of heretics."

In 1588 Philip launched the Armada against England. The Armada—a vast fleet of 130 galleons with thousands of sailors and infantrymen—was proclaimed to be invincible. Philip's goal was to subjugate England so that he could turn loose the Inquisition on the English people, but by the mercy of God, his army never reached England. The Armada was completely outclassed by the smaller English vessels. What havoc the superb English seamen did not wreak on the cumbersome ships of the Armada, the weather did. Only 76 Spanish ships reached home. The English lost no ships at all and only one hundred men.

What defense do poor, long-suffering people have against roaring lions and ranging bears such as Philip II? In the short run, not much. In the long run, God always sways the balance of justice against tyranny. And sometimes He acts quickly, as in the case of England, which was committed to a righteous cause.

## 2. The Wicked Ruler and His Perceptions (28:16-17)

### a. Avoiding Vain Policies (28:16)

"The prince that wanteth understanding is also a great oppressor: but he that hateth covetousness shall prolong his days." What the oppressor fails to grasp is that his behavior provokes the passions of those he so ruthlessly holds down. He underestimates the depth of hatred nursed against him. In the end the plots he espoused come home to roost.

Nicolae Ceausescu, the former president of Romania, was an oppressor who lacked understanding. In the early 1930s he was a member of the Romanian communist youth movement and he came up through the ranks. Ceausescu was imprisoned in 1936 and again in 1940 for his communist activities. After the communists seized power in 1947, he served as head of the ministry of agriculture and then as deputy minister of the armed forces. In 1965 he assumed leadership of the communist party in Romania and in 1967 became president of his unfortunate country.

Under Ceausescu's regime, Romania became a nightmare state. Hunger was widespread, malnutrition rose dramatically, and beggars multiplied. Official rations were paltry: a pint of cooking oil and one or two pounds of meat per person per month. Even that meager amount was often not available. A typical dinner consisted of boiled cabbage and onions. The allocation of electricity for a one-room apartment was barely sufficient to boil two kettles of water a day. In 1988 factories lengthened the workweek to seven days and imposed pay cuts of up to 30 percent on employees who failed to meet quotas.

Ceausescu launched plans to raze up to eight thousand of his country's thirteen thousand villages and settle the displaced villagers in five hundred concrete-block agro-industrial centers. He saddled Romania with more than ten billion dollars in foreign debt and squandered most of the loans on senseless projects. He demolished much of central Bucharest to erect a new national palace complex and in the process swept away many churches and historic monuments and the homes of more than forty thousand residents. Similar projects tore the centers out of provincial towns. The Romanian people suffered much during the time Ceausescu was president. Not the least of their troubles was the spread of AIDS to thousands of children.

In 1945 Ceausescu established the dreaded Securiate. This omnipresent security apparatus was a kind of praetorian guard for the communist party's central committee and the sinecured members of Ceausescu's family. The Securiate had up to three million informants (one for every eight people). One branch specialized in torturing prisoners.

Then came the coup of December 22, 1989. Ceausescu was arrested and forced to face a military tribunal. It took the dictator's accusers only two hours to find him and his wife, who shared power with him, guilty of genocide with "more than 60,000 victims, and of gross abuse of power." At dusk on Christmas Day the pair were placed against a wall of the Boteni army barracks outside Bucharest and executed without blindfolds. One news report said that no less than three hundred people volunteered to be part of the three-man firing squad. The crimes of "the prince that wanteth understanding" caught up with him.

b. Avoiding Violent Policies (28:17)

"A man that doeth violence to the blood of any person shall flee to the pit; let no man stay him." The thought behind this proverb is that a murderer will be oppressed by the guilt of his crime. Even if society fails to apprehend, try, convict, and execute such a person—even if he literally gets away with murder—he will be his own tormentor. At times he will be unable to stand the haunting of his conscience and may even confess his crime to the authorities.

In *Payment Deferred* by C. S. Forester, William Marble was his own tormentor. Marble, a wretched bank clerk, was chronically in debt. He owed money to the grocer, the butcher, the baker, friends at the office, and everyone who had been foolish enough to loan him a few pounds. Marble's wife could not understand that things bought on credit had to be paid for eventually. His superiors at the bank eyed him with disfavor because he habitually asked for an advance on his pay.

In one of Forester's word-pictures we see Marble as he sat one night in his dismal home; he was hunched over, adding up his debts. A crisis was pending and he feared he would soon lose his job.

Then came the unexpected knock at the door. The visitor turned out to be Marble's rich nephew from Australia. Marble noted his bulging wallet, expensive clothes, and other evidences of wealth. The young man was alone in the world; his parents were dead. Nobody knew he was in town. He had left his luggage in the baggage room at the train station and had not checked into his hotel. He had come straight from the train to the home of the only relative he had in the world.

Mr. Marble packed his wife and children off to bed, brought out the whiskey, and proceeded to make his nephew drunk. At first Marble thought he would ask for a loan, but when the young man shied away from even the most tentative advance along that line, a more sinister idea took shape in the uncle's mind. Before the night was over Marble had poisoned his nephew, appropriated the money in the bulging wallet, and buried the body in the garden.

For a while life looked brighter. Marble paid his creditors and restored his financial equilibrium. Then he invested in the international money market and was able to pull off a suspicious but highly successful deal that made him independently wealthy. He lost his job at the bank, but he was now rich enough to take that setback in stride.

Soon, however, the crime Marble had committed began to haunt him. He took to excessive drinking and became increasingly obsessed by the garden where the corpse lay buried. Marble could not tear himself away from a tiny, seldom-used sitting room that commanded a view of that garden at the back of the house. He felt he had to mount guard over that piece of land with its terrible secret. Marble would sit down to his evening meal and then suddenly push away from the table and hurry into that tiny back room to peer through the window.

Marble was afraid to have anyone in the house. He upset his wife by telling her she could no longer have the washer woman in on Mondays to help with the laundry. He drank more and more and took to reading books on crime. He became suspicious of anyone who came anywhere near the house and then a new fear haunted him: What if a neighbor's dog were to nose around that muddy plot where the body lay concealed? Other questions plagued him. What if he lost his lease and had to move? What if the new tenant were to dig in the barren flower bed?

Marble had done violence to the blood of his nephew and not even the pit was big enough to hide him from his fears. He hated being away from home, even for an hour. Every moment he was away from the house he was haunted by his obsession: What if someone were interfering with his garden? His fits of panic worsened until his wife could no longer endure them. In the end she committed suicide by swallowing some of the same poison that her husband had administered to his nephew. Appropriately Marble was accused of poisoning his wife and hanged. The pit yawned for him at last. Sin carries a high price tag.

3. The Wicked Ruler and His Perversity (28:18)

"Whoso walketh uprightly," Solomon wrote, "shall be saved: but he that is perverse in his ways shall fall at once." The second part of this proverb can also be rendered, "He that is perverse and walketh in double ways shall fall in one of the two." A perverse person is like someone who is trying to sit on two three-legged stools at the same time. He will fall off one or the other.

Judas thought he could have the best of both worlds.[9] His story is scattered here and there, like fragments of a shipwreck, across the pages of the four Gospels and the book of Acts. Judas was an opportunist who coldly calculated that Jesus of Nazareth was going somewhere. Anyone who could turn water into wine, feed thousands with a little lad's lunch, and command the forces of nature was bound to have a future. Judas had rosy visions of Jesus swiftly bringing the tribes of Israel to His feet, of Jesus leading a triumphant Israel against Rome, of Jesus sitting on the throne of the world. Who could stand against a man of such might and miracle? So Judas jumped on the Messianic bandwagon.

It did not take long for Judas to become disillusioned. Jesus seemed to be more interested in healing sick folk and preaching idealism than marshaling an army. He went out of His way, it seemed to Judas, to antagonize the ruling Jewish elite in Jerusalem instead of courting their favor and support. Jesus went about establishing a kingdom and an empire in a strange way.

When the Lord fed the five thousand, the delighted people tried to force His hand and make Him a king. But the Lord's moral power was as great as His miracle power. He simply sent the multitude home. That was the last straw for Judas. He concluded that maybe he had made a mistake in following Jesus.

Still Judas was reluctant to make a complete break. Determined to salvage something from his association with Jesus, he began to help himself to money from the bag and quietly salt away his ill-gotten gains. Then he had his "bright" idea. He *could* have the best of both worlds. He had seen how easily Jesus avoided the mob at Nazareth. He had seen officers sent by the Sanhedrin to arrest Him simply walk away, overwhelmed by His teaching. Judas knew that the Sanhedrin was afraid of Jesus' undeniable supernatural power as well as His popularity with the common people. So Judas, we can infer, decided on a simple but diabolical plan: He would secretly sell Jesus to His enemies. Then when they came to arrest Him, He would no doubt do what He had done before—simply walk away from them. Thus Judas could both pocket his fee and continue to be a disciple. And if the time did come for Jesus to use His powers to advance His fortunes, Judas would still be in a position to cash in on that eventuality too.

At first it seemed that Judas's sordid scheme was going to work. When the mob and the military arrived at Gethsemane, Jesus "went forth, and said unto them, Whom seek ye? They answered him, Jesus of Nazareth. Jesus saith unto them, I am he" (John 18:4-5). The result was spectacular: "As soon then as he had said unto them, I am he, they went backward, and fell to the ground" (18:6). The Lord's enemies had to be taught that they indeed had no power over Him at all.

Then Judas's plans collapsed. When Peter drew a sword and tried to defend the Lord, Jesus simply told him to desist and deliberately healed the man Peter had wounded. And to Judas's astonishment, Jesus allowed Himself to be taken away, to be tried, to be falsely accused, and to be crucified. Judas went out and hanged himself, fulfilling Solomon's saying that "he that is perverse in his ways shall fall at once."

4. The Wicked Ruler and His Priorities (28:19-22)

Proverbs 28:19 speaks to us of the wicked ruler and *his goals:* "He that tilleth his land shall have plenty of bread: but he that followeth after vain persons shall have poverty enough." The prosperity or poverty of a nation depends largely on the character of its citizens and the use the authorities make of its natural and human resources. Solomon wrote in terms of the individual, for a nation is simply a collection of individuals.

The history of Israel in the days of the judges illustrates the principle behind this proverb. As soon as the Hebrews were rescued from one disaster, they set the stage for another. We are repeatedly told that they "did evil in the sight of the Lord." The nature of that evil can easily be discerned: they followed after "vain persons" or "vanities," as Solomon's original word can also be rendered. What those "vanities" were can be gathered from Moses' use of the term in his farewell address to Israel: "They provoked him to jealousy with strange gods....They sacrificed unto devils, not to God; to gods whom they knew not....They have moved me to jealousy with that which is not God; they have provoked me to anger with their vanities" (Deuteronomy 32:16-21). The sin of idolatry, which Moses so roundly condemned, came to full flower and fruit in the days of the judges. And so we read in Judges 6:1-6:

> The Lord delivered them into the hand of Midian seven years. And the hand of Midian prevailed against Israel: and because of the Midianites the children of Israel made them the dens which are in the mountains, and caves, and strong holds. And so it was, when Israël had sown, that the Midianites came up, and the Amalekites, and the children of the east, even they came up against them; And they encamped against them, and destroyed the increase of the earth, till thou come unto Gaza, and left no sustenance for Israel, neither sheep, nor ox, nor ass. For they came up with their cattle and their tents, and they came as grasshoppers for multitude; for both they and their camels were without number: and they entered into the land to destroy it. And Israel was greatly impoverished because of the Midianites.

Because the Israelites had followed vanities, God let them become impoverished. They tilled their fields, but they did not have plenty of bread. The enemy stole all their grain. They had to learn again the folly of trusting in vanities.

Gideon had more sense than the others. He had been able to salvage some wheat from the pillage and was threshing it in the winepress so that the enemy could not see him. The angel of the Lord appeared to him and called him a "mighty man of valour" (Judges 6:12). Gideon, who thought the angel was mocking him, demanded an explanation for the terrible impoverishment of God's people. Actually he needed to look no further than his own back doorstep to find the reason.

His father had in his garden an altar to Baal and an *'ashērah* (translated "grove" in Judges 6:25; it was an offensive sex symbol). That "vanity" was the reason Gideon had to confess, "Behold, my family is poor in Manasseh" (6:15). When they turned from Baal to the Lord, they had "plenty of bread"—like the man in Solomon's proverb who tilled his land. As the historian put it: "Thus was Midian subdued before the children of Israel, so that they lifted up their heads no more. And the country was in quietness forty years in the days of Gideon" (Judges 8:28).

Throughout the book of Judges we see the principles of the Palestinian covenant illustrated. That covenant (Deuteronomy 27–28) promised that obedience to the Mosaic law would bring blessing on the land in the form of peace and plenty (28:1-14). Failure and apostasy would bring cursing—war, famine, pestilence, drought, plague, exile, and gnawing fear (28:15-68). Thus it was in the days of Gideon. Once Gideon brought the nation back to God, all was well. But when even his well-intentioned effort to restore the national religion went awry (Judges 8:24-27), the stage was set for further disaster in the shape of civil war (Judges 9). Israel certainly did follow after a "vain person" when they fell in with the ambitious plans of Gideon's son Abimelech.

The next proverb refers to the wicked ruler and *his guilt:* "A faithful man shall abound with blessings: but he that maketh haste to be rich shall not be innocent" (Proverbs 28:20).

Get-rich-quick schemes frequently involve some kind of criminal activity, some form of gambling, or speculation on the stock market. People who get rich by playing the stock market always do so at someone else's expense. Corporate raiders, who speculate with millions and even billions of dollars, prowl the boardrooms of giant corporations. Looking for those they can devour, these raiders initiate hostile takeovers. Once they acquire a victim company, they strip away its assets. So what if people lose their pensions, their life savings, their investments, and their jobs? So what if the new acquisition goes bankrupt? Bankruptcy can be a useful tool for shedding unwanted creditors and unions. The raiders' idea is not to acquire a desirable company by fair means in order to increase its efficiency and productivity. Their idea is to manipulate the company's assets for the benefit of a handful of conspirators.

In Proverbs 28:20 the expression translated "not be innocent" can also be translated "not go unpunished." All too often man's laws are not adequate; wicked people do go unpunished here on earth. However, we must remember that all accounts will be settled at the judgment bar of God on the shores of a coming eternity. The books will be opened, the truth revealed, and adequate punishment decreed (see Revelation 20:12).

Achan in the Bible made haste to be rich. His story is told in Joshua 7. After the conquering Hebrew people had dealt with their enemies on the east bank of the Jordan, they had crossed the river and come upon Jericho on the west bank. Jericho, one of the cities described by the spies as "great and fenced" and "walled up to heaven," stood 825 feet below the level of the Mediterranean sea and enjoyed a tropical climate. Jericho was a garden city, strong and rich, commanding the valley of the lower Jordan and the passes into the western mountains.

As Joshua's well-disciplined army stood poised to take the city, the great general addressed the troops. He knew that Jericho was doomed to destruction by divine decree. The city was morally foul and God had put a curse upon it. Joshua instructed the people that when Jericho fell, no one was to be spared except Rahab and those who were inside her house. No doubt he pointed to one house on the wall and in the window of that house could be seen a scarlet cord. That cord was the token of Rahab's faith. Joshua added that all the spoils were dedicated to God. Let every man beware of helping himself to any of the wealth.

Jericho fell and the soldiers of Israel went about their grim task of executing God's sentence against this vile city. Only one man disobeyed orders. As he moved among the ruins and rubble of the city, he furtively picked up a luxurious Babylonian garment, a bar of gold, and a bag of silver and hid them in the folds of his capacious robe. He successfully avoided being observed. Heavy-laden, the man returned to his tent, somewhere in the Judean regiment. He swore his family to silence, dug a hole in the ground, buried his loot, and went about his business. He was Joshua's Judas.

The disobedient man's riches did him little good. The defeat at Ai and the revelation from God that someone had broken the commandment concerning the spoils called for an inquiry. Swiftly the accusing finger was pointed at Achan who, once he was found out, confessed.

The Holy Spirit recorded the terrible sequel in Joshua 7:24. Notice the use of the polysyndeton (the repetition of the word "and," which emphasizes each specific item): "And Joshua, and all Israel with him, took Achan the son of Zerah, and the silver, and the garment, and the wedge of gold, and his sons, and his daughters, and his oxen, and his asses, and his sheep, and his tent, and all that he had: and they brought them unto the valley of Achor." There Israel executed the whole family, then burned them, buried them, and raised a warning memorial over them. "He that maketh haste to be rich shall not go unpunished," wrote Solomon.

Unlike Achan, Salmon was a faithful man who abounded with blessings. He too was in the Judean regiment on the day Jericho fell. Salmon was probably one of the two spies Joshua had sent to assess conditions in Jericho—that is, one of the two men who had been saved by Rahab (Joshua 2). They made it their business to rescue Rahab from the ruins of Jericho (6:22-23), and Salmon ended up marrying her.

How could marrying Rahab have been a blessing? She had been a pagan and a harlot, but the *saved* Rahab was a different woman. Marrying Rahab was a blessing indeed, for she became one of the women in the genealogy of Christ (Matthew 1:5) and her faith is praised in Hebrews 11 along with that of the great heroes of the Old Testament.

The next proverb refers to the wicked ruler and *his guile:* "To have respect of persons is not good: for for a piece of bread that man will transgress" (Proverbs 28:21).

When Jeroboam, the first king of the separated northern kingdom of Israel, set up his false religion, God sent an unknown and unnamed prophet to denounce the king and his false altar (1 Kings 13). This young prophet from Judah was under the strictest injunction: He must not eat or drink with anyone. He must go to Beth-el, deliver his message, and leave.

The prophet fulfilled his commission. He cursed the false altar, worked a miracle, and prepared to leave. Jeroboam was shocked, but recovering quickly, he saw at once that he had to save face. He had been publicly rebuked and humiliated. What could he do to salvage something from this whole awkward incident? Invite the prophet to the palace and get him to compromise!

So Jeroboam offered the prophet the hospitality of the palace. The prophet was not supposed to have fellowship with anyone, but a man does not receive an invitation to be a guest at the table of a king very often. Most men, if invited, would "have respect of persons." After all, is not a royal invitation akin to a royal command? But the prophet was unimpressed. He did not see a ruler; he saw a reprobate. He had no respect at all for the king. The invitation was no sooner given than it was refused.

Shortly afterward, temptation came from a different quarter. Not far off, down some back street in Beth-el, lived an old prophet. His sons, who had seen the confrontation, hurried home to tell their father the whole story. The old man decided to find the young prophet and invite him home for supper.

Meanwhile the young prophet had flung himself down under an oak tree. The hours after a great spiritual victory are always fraught with peril. Often after the excitement of action—when the nerves have been keyed up and the adrenalin has been flowing—there is a reaction. Elation is followed by depression. So we should not be surprised that the young prophet was lonely, tired, and hungry. It was getting dark and he could hear a lion roaring on the nearby hills.

Suddenly, we can imagine, he heard the braying of a donkey. He looked up and saw an old man coming his way. When the old man reached the oak tree, he said in effect: "I say, young man, how about some supper? My boys told me all about you. You're absolutely fantastic! You can't come home with me? Nonsense! Of course you can. What you don't know is that I am a prophet like you. I've been in the ministry much longer than you have. You're not the only one God speaks to, you know. He used to speak to me quite often years ago, but I've been retired now these many years. But I felt the moving of the Spirit again—less than an hour ago, right after my boys came home. God told me that you have fully discharged your duty and that your refusal to go with the king was magnificent! Now He has rescinded His orders. You can come home with me and eat and drink in my house. Coming home with me is not the same as going home with the king, for we are brethren, you and I. I didn't even send my boys to give you this message. I came myself."

The young prophet weakened. In the end he had "respect of persons." He foolishly respected the backslidden, reprobate prophet who was so friendly, so chatty, and so persuasive. When the old prophet mentioned home, supper, and an opportunity to share the things of God with his boys, the young prophet gave in. "For a piece of bread" he transgressed, and his disobedience cost him his life (1 Kings 13:24).

The next proverb refers to the wicked ruler and *his greed:* "He that hasteth to be rich hath an evil eye, and considereth not that poverty shall come upon him" (Proverbs 28:22).

Ebenezer Scrooge is a literary example of the greedy man.[10] In *A Christmas Carol* author Charles Dickens told us what "a tight-fisted hand at the grindstone" Scrooge was. Getting rich was all that mattered to him. He did not care whom he had to hurt or what scurrilous tricks he had to play, as long as he became rich in the process.

The haunting of Scrooge by the various ghosts was intended to show the mean old miser how wretchedly poor he had become. He could have lived like a lord, but he lived in a "gloomy suite of rooms" up a long flight of stairs. He had no friends. His partner was dead. He despised his poor but cheerful nephew.

The first of the three Christmas ghosts took the old skinflint back into his past. The ghost showed Scrooge a Christmas party where as a young man he had been given a remarkably good time by old Fezziwig, his employer. Scrooge recalled how generous Fezziwig had been and how much the old man had been loved. The contrast to the scurvy way Scrooge had treated his poor clerk that very afternoon, when Bob Cratchit had asked to have Christmas Day off, was obvious. And Fezziwig's unselfishness was so different from the scurrilous way Scrooge had treated the two businessmen who asked him to contribute to a fund to help the poor!

Then the ghost of the past reminded Scrooge of the young woman he had once courted. She had finally broken off their engagement because he had grown to love money more than he loved her. The spirit took him to see her—happily married and surrounded by loving children and an adoring husband—and Scrooge thought of his own loneliness, utterly bereft of domestic joys.

Next the Ghost of Christmas Present appeared. He left Scrooge appalled, but the miser suffered most at the hands of the ghost of the future, who made him aware of death and its horror. This ghost led Scrooge to the heart of the city where the business associates of someone who had died were talking.

One said, "I thought he'd never die."

Another asked, "What has he done with his money?"

Someone answered, "I haven't heard.... He hasn't left it to *me*." The reply was greeted with cynical mirth.

Someone else asked if anyone was going to the funeral, and a gentleman replied, "I don't mind going if a lunch is provided." Apparently the group decided that the funeral would not be worth attending.

On another street two more businessmen met. One said to the other, "Old Scratch has got his own at last, hey?"

The scene changed and Scrooge saw the corpse, "plundered and bereft, unwatched, unwept, uncared for." Thieves had pawned its clothes for a few meager shillings.

Becoming increasingly aware that the terrible corpse was his own, Scrooge asked the ominous, silent ghost of the future if anyone in all that great city showed some emotion over his death. In response the ghost showed him a family living in poverty. The husband had borrowed money from Scrooge and needed more time to repay the loan. Did the couple feel any emotion when they heard that he was dead? Yes, they were glad!

"Let me see some tenderness connected with a death," said Scrooge, and the ghost took him to Bob Cratchit's house, where the memory of poor little Tiny Tim was kept very much alive. The child had died because his father's stingy employer did not pay him enough to provide the little invalid with proper medical care.[11]

Ebenezer Scrooge had plenty of money, but in every other way he was poorer than the most destitute beggar on the city's streets. "He that hasteth to be rich...poverty shall come upon him."

Solomon would have approved of Dickens' tale—especially the end, when Scrooge learned to be generous.

5. The Wicked Ruler and His Problems (28:23-27)

a. His Critics (28:23)

"He that rebuketh a man afterwards shall find more favour than he that flattereth with the tongue."

We can be quite sure that plenty of people flattered Belshazzar of Babylon. He was the firstborn son and coregent of Nabonidus, the last king of the neo-Babylonian empire. Belshazzar's mother is thought to have been Nebuchadnezzar's daughter and in typical Old Testament fashion he is called the son of Nebuchadnezzar.

Nabonidus, in the third year of his reign, conquered Taima and afterward adorned it and made it his principal residence. He installed Belshazzar in Babylon, the capital of the empire, and left most of the administrative duties to him. Nabonidus had other interests and rarely bothered visiting the capital.

Then war broke out. Cyrus led the Persian army westward, crossed the Tigris, and conquered the fabulously wealthy Croesus, the Lydian king. Then Cyrus defeated the Ionian Greeks and by the end of 545 B.C. he had subdued all of Asia Minor. In 539 he defeated the Babylonians at Opis, took Sippar, and was ready to take the capital. The Babylonians, however, thought that Nebuchadnezzar's walled and mighty capital was impregnable.

We can picture proud Belshazzar driving in his chariot around the massive walls. We can see his flattering courtiers sneering at the Persian army far below. We can follow the king in our imaginations to his great banqueting hall, and we know what happened next. The drunken king, doubtless egged on by his flatterers, decided to glorify the images and gods of Babylon. He toasted them with wine poured into the sacred vessels once dedicated to the temple of the living God in Jerusalem. After all, Jerusalem had been destroyed and mighty Babylon was thriving! Which god was stronger: Jehovah of the Jews or Bel of Babylon?

Then that ghostly hand appeared and wrote mysterious letters on the wall. Belshazzar announced that he would share his realm with anyone who could make sense of that ominous script. When Belshazzar's advisers could not read the writing, he summoned Daniel, and the king himself tried flattery:

> The wise men, the astrologers, have been brought in before me, that they should read this writing, and make known unto

> me the interpretation thereof: but they could not shew the interpretation of the thing: And I have heard of thee, that thou canst make interpretations, and dissolve doubts (Daniel 5:15-16).

Then the king promised a promotion and rewards, but Daniel was not impressed. He told the king to keep his gifts or give them to someone else. Then Daniel gave the king a lecture in which he reminded Belshazzar that it was God who had given the empire to Nebuchadnezzar. God had raised him up to the pinnacle of power, but Nebuchadnezzar had forgotten that fact. When he had boasted in the pride of his heart about the great Babylon he had built, he had been smitten with insanity. Nebuchadnezzar did not regain his sanity until once again "he knew that the most high God ruled in the kingdom of men" (5:21). Daniel continued:

> And thou his son, O Belshazzar, hast not humbled thine heart, though thou knewest all this; But hast lifted up thyself against the Lord of heaven; and they have brought the vessels of his house before thee, and thou, and thy lords, thy wives, and thy concubines, have drunk wine in them; and thou hast praised the gods of silver, and gold, of brass, iron, wood, and stone, which see not, nor hear, nor know: and the God in whose hand thy breath is, and whose are all thy ways, hast thou not glorified" (5:22-23).

Having thus scalded the ears of this wicked king, Daniel read him his doom, as it was written on the wall.

Belshazzar died that night. Darius the Mede "took the kingdom" (5:31), brought Daniel out of retirement, and advanced him to the highest executive post in the realm (6:1-3). And so it was that he that rebuked a man afterward found more favor.

b. His Crimes (28:24)

"Whoso robbeth his father or his mother, and saith, It is no transgression; the same is the companion of a destroyer." Prince Absalom is a case in point. While he did not actually rob his father of cold cash, he robbed him of something infinitely more precious. We read that "he stole the hearts of the men of Israel," subverting their loyalty to David (2 Samuel 15:6). Almost at once Absalom became "the companion of a destroyer" by the name of Ahithophel. Ahithophel had once been David's most astute counselor (16:23).

The advice this wicked man gave Absalom was clever but diabolical (16:21; 17:1-4) and God did not allow it to prosper.[12]

The principle behind Proverbs 28:24 can be seen at work in the lives of ordinary people too. Presumably individuals who rob their parents and then justify themselves imagine that their parents owe them something and that they are only taking that which is rightfully theirs. But Solomon said they are like murderers. Indeed murder sometimes goes hand-in-hand with this kind of robbery. A son (or daughter) can build up so much resentment against his parents that he will murder to get what he wants.

This proverb reminds me of the celebrated case of Lizzie Borden, whose activities were satirized as follows:

> Lizzie Borden took an axe
> And gave her mother forty whacks;
> When she saw what she had done
> She gave her father forty-one.[13]

Of course Lizzie and her sister Emma never did regard Abby Durfee Gray, their father's second wife, as their mother. Andrew Borden met the thirty-eight-year-old spinster at church and married her because he needed someone to care for the household. But the arrangement didn't work. Emma hated her stepmother from the start. Emma viewed Abby as a threat and turned Lizzie against her. As the two girls grew older, remained unmarried, and became increasingly dependent on their father's money, their hatred of the unhappy Abby increased. Yet all four lived under the same roof for thirty years before the explosion came.

Borden was reputed to be the wealthiest man in Fall River, Massachusetts, the largest cotton manufacturing center in America. He was a director of the Globe Yarn Mill Company and other corporations, took over the Union Savings Bank, and bought and sold property—always earning a handsome profit. His prize possession, a new complex on Main Street, covered a city block and bore his name: the A. J. Borden Building. He was never much bothered by scruples, but he was obsessed by thrift. Borden was known around town as a brusque, dour, and miserly man.

Lizzie was Borden's favorite child. He spoiled her, but he was incapable of giving her real affection. He took her on long walks, introduced her to his god—money—and talked to her about business.

As though it were not bad enough for their father to marry again and jeopardize their share of his fortune, Lizzie and Emma learned that he had given a house to Abby's sister. The girls felt betrayed. Moreover they discovered that he was thinking about giving their farm to his wife. (Ever since Lizzie and Emma were little girls, they had gone to the farm for their summer vacations and fished in the stream that ran through it.) And they suspected that their father was contemplating a new will that would cut them out of the bulk of his fortune.

One hot August morning in 1892 Lizzie Borden (so it was claimed) crept upstairs, stole along the thickly carpeted floor to Abby's bedroom, and cut her down with repeated blows of an ax. Later that morning Borden came home. Not feeling well, he stretched out on the couch in the living room. That was the last thing he ever did. Lizzie (so it was said) sneaked up to the couch and battered his face with an ax. The jury found her not guilty, but a cloud of suspicion hung over her and her sister until they died. Most likely, Lizzie and Emma set out to rob their father and stepmother by the most effective means they knew: murder. Greed turned Lizzie (or was it Emma?) into a destroyer.[14]

c. His Conceit (28:25-26)

Proverbs 28:25 says, "He that is of a proud heart stirreth up strife: but he that putteth his trust in the Lord shall be made fat." Solomon's words cause us to think about the evil ruler's conceit and *where it will lead him.* The contrast in the proverb is best illustrated by the contrast between Satan and Christ.

Satan, who once occupied a position near the throne of God, was the highest and most brilliant of all created beings. He was the choirmaster of Heaven and the anointed cherub. Known as Lucifer—the son of the morning—he was full of wisdom, perfect in beauty, and resplendent with precious stones (Ezekiel 28:12-15). Then his heart was lifted up with pride. The words of Isaiah 14:13-14 are addressed to him:

> For thou hast said in thine heart, I will ascend into heaven, I will exalt my throne above the stars of God: I will sit also upon the mount of the congregation, in the sides of the north: I will ascend above the heights of the clouds; I will be like the most High.

Lucifer never attained his goal, for he and his followers were thrown from Heaven (Isaiah 14:12-20; Ezekiel 28:1-19). From that time he has been known as Satan or the devil and he has been stirring up strife. He has not only led a rebellion of angelic beings (no less than a third of them—see Revelation 12:3-4); he has also invaded our world and led the human race in rebellion. Satan is behind all the discord on this planet. He delights in stirring up trouble. He incited Cain to murder Abel and he filled the earth with violence in the days of Noah. Satan has his hand in every domestic, political, religious, regional and global war. In the book of Revelation we see him waging war in Heaven itself, only to be flung from the skies to stir up more strife on earth (Revelation 8:10–9:1).[15]

In a coming day Satan will battle the saints. He will mobilize men by the millions and march them to Megiddo, there to stage the penultimate war of human history. After the millennial reign of Christ, when Satan is released from the abyss, he will incite war again. For that he will be thrown headlong into the lake of fire. Truly, "he that is of a proud heart stirreth up strife."

The contrasting statement—"He that putteth his trust in the Lord shall be made fat"—means that a person who trusts the Lord will prosper. When the Lord Jesus came to earth, he demonstrated this trust. He was the eternal, uncreated, self-existing, creator of the universe, the sustainer of all things, the second person of the godhead, God the Son, God over all, blessed forevermore. Yet He came to be born of the virgin Mary, to live, to die, and to rise again. He demonstrated the kind of life that God had planned for Adam and his race.

God always intended for man to be inhabited by Himself. The human spirit was to be indwelt by the Holy Spirit, who would bring man's intellect, emotions, will, and senses into harmony with Heaven. Man was created to love God, to trust Him, to obey Him, and to enjoy Him forever. But when sin, then death, entered the world, the harmony was ruined.

Jesus came to be man as God intended man to be. Every moment of every day He loved and trusted His Father with all His mind, heart, soul, and strength. Jesus had implicit, unquestioning faith in His Father. Even in Gethsemane, with Golgotha only hours away, He could still say, "Thy will be done."

And Jesus certainly "prospered." He dealt with sin to God's eternal satisfaction. He conquered death and ascended on high. In glory now, He sees the results of the travail of His soul and is satisfied. Every man, woman, boy, and girl who comes to love and trust Him adds to His joy. Paul wrote, "God also hath highly exalted him, and given him a name which is above every name: That at the name of Jesus every knee should bow...And that every tongue should confess that Jesus Christ is Lord" (Philippians 2:9-11).

Now it is our turn to trust in the Lord and prosper. Through the miracle of regeneration, the Holy Spirit indwells us, and the way lies open before us to walk as Jesus walked. As 1 John 4:17 states, "As he is, so are we in this world."

Solomon's next words cause us to think about the evil man's conceit and *where it will land him:* "He that trusteth in his own heart is a fool: but whoso walketh wisely, he shall be delivered" (Proverbs 28:26). The contrast in this proverb is illustrated by the contrasting behavior of Peter and John in Caiaphas's courtyard on the night of Jesus' trial.

Peter often trusted in his own heart. He was too sure of himself. On one occasion he even went so far as to take the Lord Himself to task because He spoke of His upcoming death on the cross. The Lord had to rebuke him sharply.

When the Lord warned all His disciples that they would be offended because of Him—that they would deny Him and forsake Him—Peter was indignant. "Not me, Lord," he said in effect. "Everyone else perhaps, but not me" (see Matthew 26:33). Peter was trusting in his own impulsive, treacherous heart. At one point the Lord had to warn him, "Satan hath desired to have you" (Luke 22:31).

In Gethsemane Peter trusted in his own heart again. Determined to make good on his boast, he drew a sword to defend the Lord against the mob. Jesus had to tell him to put the weapon away.

Shaken but manfully trying to quell his fears, Peter followed Jesus, at a distance, to Caiaphas's house. Still trusting in his own heart, Peter slipped through the garden gate and looked around. He could see the priests bullying Jesus. Suddenly he realized that he could be arrested too if his identity became known. His treacherous heart let him down as his courage evaporated and cold panic seized his soul. Within the hour he denied any knowledge of or connection with Jesus three times. Once he even employed the coarse language his heart had kept in storage since his conversion. Peter would come to agree with Solomon: "He that trusteth in his own heart is a fool."

John ran away from Gethsemane. "All the disciples forsook him, and fled," Matthew recalled (26:56). However, John seems to have recovered his nerve. His love for the Lord drew him, like Peter, to Caiaphas's house, but John conducted himself wisely. He stayed away from the attendants around the fire in the courtyard and he seems to have made himself known at the door as an acquaintance of the high priest (John 18:15). Because John walked wisely, he was delivered. He was not arrested and he did not make a fool of himself as Peter did.

At Calvary John was in the company of that faithful little band of women who loved the Lord so much. John acted so wisely that he was able to perform one of the last and most precious services ever rendered to the Lord during His earthly pilgrimage. It was to John that Jesus turned when He was concerned about providing for His mother. The Lord asked John to be a son to His mother and told His mother to go home with John and regard him as her son.

d. His Curse (28:27)

"He that giveth unto the poor shall not lack: but he that hideth his eyes shall have many a curse." As a boy I saw the first part of this proverb fulfilled almost weekly.

When the World War II broke out in Britain, my father had a small car dealership in south Wales. Car dealerships were practically non-existent during the war years because gasoline was heavily rationed, new cars were channeled almost exclusively to the military, and spare parts were almost impossible to obtain. Yet my father's business survived. He had a few customers, mostly farmers, whose vital war work entitled them to vehicles, spare parts, extra gasoline, and extra supplies.

At that time clothes and food were rationed, travel was restricted, buses ran on a curtailed schedule, and coal was scarce; life was a struggle, but somehow we managed. Our family of seven pooled our food coupons, enabling my mother to buy at least a chicken or a small roast for Sunday dinner.

The church we attended owned a home that was kept for the use of visiting missionaries. One impoverished missionary family occupied that home all through the war years. Hardly a week went by when my parents did not extend the hospitality of our home to that family for Sunday dinner. My mother would prepare potatoes (which were plentiful), greens, bread, and roast chicken stuffed to the bursting point with dressing. My father would carve that chicken with the skill of a surgeon and everyone—seven of us and five of them—had a helping. When every dish had been scraped clean and all that was left of the chicken was bare bones, there would be a dessert of some kind. That miracle went on Sunday after Sunday.

My parents gave to the poor and never lacked. To this day, I don't know how they did it. There always seemed to be enough, even if it was only just barely enough during the war years. The Lord took good note of my parents' hospitality and when they went overseas as missionaries themselves after the war, they never lacked then either.

The Lord knows what it is like to be poor and He takes note of people who look the other way when the needs of the poor are pointed out. There is no blessedness for people who hide their eyes. There is only a curse. The seriousness of that curse is obvious in the Lord's parable of the sheep and the goats (Matthew 25:31-46).

6. The Wicked Ruler and His Power (28:28)

"When the wicked rise," Solomon wrote, "men hide themselves: but when they perish, the righteous increase." The wicked and the righteous have diametrically opposed perspectives on all the great issues of life. Once wicked people seize the reins of government, righteous people are well advised to hide.

When Ahab and Jezebel ruled Israel, a new dimension of apostasy was introduced. Jeroboam, the first king of the northern kingdom, is called "the son of Nebat, who made Israel to sin." But his sin, bad as it was, was nothing compared to Ahab's. Jeroboam made a golden calf and instituted a false worship of the true God. He added a dimension of idolatry to the worship but, ostensibly at least, it was still supposed to be the worship of God. What Jeroboam introduced was heresy. What Ahab introduced was apostasy.

Ahab and Jezebel swept away all pretense of worshiping Jehovah. They inaugurated the outright worship of Ashtoreth, "sacred" prostitution, and a pagan priesthood. The result was utter demoralization of the national character. The true people of God opposed the innovations, but Jezebel—the real power behind the throne—was ruthless and determined. She persecuted God's people and forcibly put down all resistance to the new religion.

Ahab, wicked though he was, had a valued, trusted steward named Obadiah. Obadiah "feared the Lord greatly" (1 Kings 18:3), but he was also deathly afraid of Jezebel, and with good reason, for she "cut off the prophets of the Lord." Nevertheless when the persecution was underway, Obadiah did what he could: he "took an hundred prophets, and hid them by fifty in a cave, and fed them with bread and water" (18:4). This scene has many parallels in history—"When the wicked rise, men hide themselves."

When the great tribulation bursts upon the world, the righteous will know from God's Word that they should take heed of the activities of the Roman dictator and flee to the hills (Matthew 24:15-18).

When wicked men are in power, God has two ways of dealing with the situation. Sometimes He sends *ruin*. He overthrows the wicked with swift and terrible judgment, as He did in the days of Noah and Lot. The wicked perish. Sometimes He sends *revival*, as He did in England about the time of the French revolution.

The French revolution was a time of terror. The nobility of France were rounded up, given drumhead trials, and sent to the guillotine. Woe betide anyone suspected of harboring any resistance to the revolution!

Social conditions in England were little better than those in France. An arrogant aristocracy held on to its wealth, privilege, and power while the common people were poor, downtrodden, and given to every vice. Drunkenness was epidemic. Everyone feared a revolution like the one in France, but instead of revolution, God sent revival. The Wesleys came, the righteous increased, and conditions improved!

### 7. The Wicked Ruler and His Punishment (29:1)

"He, that being often reproved hardeneth his neck, shall suddenly be destroyed, and that without remedy." Nowhere is this proverb better illustrated than in the history of Israel, in which we see a pattern of constant reproof and hardening. Stephen made this history the theme of his defense before the Sanhedrin (see Acts 7).

We can see the pattern even in a brief overview of Hebrew history. The patriarchs rejected Joseph. Then famine came and they were forced to buy bread in Egypt. Joseph recognized them and deliberately dealt with them in ways that would reprove them and quicken their consciences. They had put him in a pit, so he put Simeon in prison. They had sold him for cold cash, so he put money in their sacks until they feared and hated the sight of cash. They had been jealous of him because of his coat of many colors, so at dinner he gave Benjamin more food than he gave to them. At last they confessed their guilt and were forgiven.

Time passed and the Hebrews found themselves in bondage in Egypt. God sent Moses to deliver them, but they resented his connection with the Egyptian court and rejected him. Because of their rejection of Moses, they were obliged to suffer in bondage for another forty years. Then Moses returned, armed with might and miracle. Because the pharaoh did not respond immediately to

Moses' demands, the Hebrews turned on their great kinsman. Eventually they were emancipated, but almost immediately they began to murmur. They complained because they were thirsty. They complained because they were hungry. God sent them manna from heaven and they demanded meat. When Moses turned his back, they made a golden calf. They traveled as far as Kadesh-barnea, but refused to go on to Canaan when they heard about the giants in the land. Then when God told them that they could not enter Canaan, they said that they would. Condemned to wander for forty years in the wilderness, the Hebrews backed a rebellion led by Moses' cousin Korah. The Israelites were often reproved—by plague, by defeat in battle, by earthquake, by fiery serpents. Still they hardened their hearts.

Moses died and Joshua took his place. The Hebrews crossed the Jordan river and captured Jericho. Then Achan stole what belonged to God and the Israelites were reproved at Ai. They conquered Canaan, but they did not exterminate the vile inhabitants of the land. And the Israelites left the coastline in the hands of the Philistines and the Phoenicians. God reproved the Israelites for not conquering the coastline: in time the Philistines conquered the Hebrews and the Phoenicians corrupted them.

During the four hundred years under the judges, the Israelites were repeatedly reproved for their foolish infatuation with the foul, fierce gods of the Canaanites. The Hebrews were sold to Chushan-rishathaim, king of Mesopotamia; smitten by Eglon, the repulsive king of Moab; and sold to Jabin, king of Canaan, who had nine hundred iron chariots. After that, Midian, then the Amorites and the Ammonites oppressed the Israelites. Finally the Philistines rose up to crush them.

When the Israelites rejected the theocracy, God reproved them by giving them what they wanted: a king of their own choosing. Then came David and a new dynasty, and the Israelites rebelled against him. Worse yet, David's son Solomon sank so deeply into sin that upon his death the nation was divided into two kingdoms.

Right from the start the northern kingdom was headed for apostasy. Jeroboam instituted the worship of two golden calves and he was reproved. Ahab instituted the worship of Baal and Ashtoreth and he was reproved. Prophet after prophet reproved the nation of Israel until at last there was no remedy. God sent the Assyrians to uproot the northern tribes and scatter them abroad.

The southern kingdom followed much the same path but, thanks to a sprinkling of godly kings and an occasional revival, at a slower pace. Judah too was often reproved. There were repeated judgments, including invasion. A growing number of prophets raised their voices and plied their pens in vain. Finally God sent the Babylonians to destroy Jerusalem and the oft-defiled temple. The defeated people were deported to Babylon.

In Babylon the Jews fell in love with the world and learned to make money. When a new superpower arose and the Persian emperor magnanimously decreed that the Jewish people could go home and rebuild their temple, the majority elected to stay in Babylon.

Even the repatriated Jews had to be reproved by Ezra, Nehemiah, and the last three Old Testament prophets. In response these Jews hardened their hearts. Instead of walking in the light of the law, they invented what they called the oral law and gave birth to rabbinical Judaism and the beginnings of the Talmud. God simply left them to themselves in a silence that lasted four hundred years. During those years the little land of Judah became an international political football. The Jews were kicked here and there—now by Syria, now by Egypt—until at last they fell into the hands of Antiochus Epiphanes, who was a veritable antichrist. Even so, Hellenism flourished among the Jews. At the same time Pharisaism and Sadduceeism took deep root in the land.

God sent John the Baptist to break the silence and announce the coming of Christ. Jesus came and lived as no man had ever lived, taught as no man had ever taught, and did what no man had ever done. He demonstrated deity in humanity. He reproved the Jews and told them, both prophetically and parabolically, what to expect. His warnings made no difference: they murdered Him and the Jewish nation was cut off without remedy.

Jesus rose from the dead. The Holy Spirit came. The church was born. The voice of the apostles rang clear at home and throughout the diaspora. Yet the Jewish nation rejected the Spirit of God as bitterly as it had rejected the Son of God.

As the proverb says, "He, that being often reproved hardeneth his neck, shall suddenly be destroyed, and that without remedy." There was no way for the Jewish nation to avoid destruction. In A.D. 70 the Romans took Jerusalem and destroyed the temple. In A.D. 135 at the time of the Bar Kokhba rebellion, the Romans banished Jews from Palestine.

For two thousand years the Jews as a nation have persisted in their unbelief, and for two thousand years in land after land they have been persecuted without remedy. Indeed the Jews are a flesh-and-blood commentary on the accuracy and inspiration of the Word of God. When Frederick the Great asked a Christian to defend the truth of the Bible, all the believer had to say was one word: *Israel.*

## C. The King and His Land (29:2-14)

### 1. The Strains of the Throne Assessed (29:2-13)

#### a. Beware of the Sinful Man (29:2)

Now Solomon introduced the first of seven types of people of whom the king should beware. The king should avoid appointing the sinful man to a position of authority. Proverbs 29:2 explains, "When the righteous are in authority, the people rejoice: but when the wicked beareth rule, the people mourn." The word translated "in authority" here means "increase," and the word translated "wicked" means "lawless." A nation suffers when lawless people increase in authority. Indeed a nation is on the road to ruin when people devoid of moral principles rise to high office and wield great influence over governmental decisions.

In a few tumultuous decades a handful of men in the United States Supreme Court gained control of the decision-making process and changed the character and course of the nation. In 1956 the Supreme Court invalidated sedition laws in forty-two states. The next year it ruled that a person could not be prosecuted for advocating the theoretical overthrow of the government by force unless he also advocated action to accomplish the goal. The same year the Court liberalized rules against obscene publications. In 1958 it ruled that the State Department could not withhold passports from suspected communists. In 1961 the Court declared that evidence obtained by illegal search or seizure was inadmissible in state prosecutions, even when the evidence was reliable.

During the two-year period of 1961-1963 the Court ruled against religion in schools and elsewhere. The Court declared that states cannot require public officials to declare their belief in God; ruled that state officials may not compose prayers to be recited in public schools; and mandated that public schools cannot require pupils to repeat the Lord's prayer or read the Bible. On June 25, 1962, the Court voted six-to-one to deny New York school children the right to open the school day with a nonsectarian prayer. To add insult to injury, that same day the Court decided that pornographic literature designed to appeal to homosexuals was not obscene and indecent and could therefore be distributed via United States mail.

In 1965 the Court ruled that members of the communist party

cannot be compelled to register with the Subversive Activities Control Board. In 1967 the Court ruled that electronic eavesdropping is unconstitutional; that a property owner does not have the right to sell his property to whomever he pleases; and that an American cannot be stripped of his citizenship even if he deserts the armed forces in time of war or votes in a foreign election.

These and many other decisions detrimental to the national interest were pushed through the Court by a handful of justices. Deaths and retirements gave President Franklin D. Roosevelt his chance to control the Supreme Court. He appointed four justices: Hugo Black, Felix Frankfurter, Stanley Reed, and William O. Douglas. None of the four had any judicial experience. They joined forces to reverse dozens of previous court decisions. During his first twenty-five years on the bench, Justice Black voted in favor of the communist position 102 times in 102 cases, as did Justice Douglas in 97 of 102 cases. Practically all legal restraints against communism and subversion in the United States were destroyed at a time when communism was a real and present danger to the United States and the world.

Congressional leader Gerald Ford led an unsuccessful effort to have one of the justices impeached. Ford had the backing of 105 bipartisan members of the House. Charges ranged from inciting anarchy to conflict of interest and from dealing with criminals to condoning hard-core pornography.

Solomon said, "When the wicked beareth rule, the people mourn," and we have cause for mourning today. In this country sodomy is condoned as an alternate lifestyle. Women can have abortions on demand. Slaughter on the highways by drunken drivers is treated with astonishing leniency. The criminal's rights are often given more consideration than those of his victim. A guilty man can fight his conviction in court after court and often evade punishment altogether or obtain an early release from prison. Scandals are commonplace. Divorce is epidemic. Organized crime flourishes. Addiction to drugs is increasing. Men of proven decadence are being elected to high offices. The death penalty, a healthy deterrent for crime, is frequently not invoked and rarely implemented. Many of society's ills can be traced to Supreme Court decisions that were made by "the wicked," as Solomon would not hesitate to call them.

### b. Beware of the Sensual Man (29:3)

"Whoso loveth wisdom rejoiceth his father: but he that keepeth company with harlots spendeth his substance."

David's deathbed was greatly eased by the knowledge that his heir, Solomon, was a wise man. David warned the young prince against two culpable and dangerous men—Joab and Shimei—and advised his son to execute the pair of them. Regarding the case of Joab, David said to Solomon, "Do therefore according to thy wisdom" (1 Kings 2:6). Regarding the case of Shimei, David made a similar comment to the prince: "Thou art a wise man" (2:9). Solomon lived up to his reputation for wisdom in both cases. David rejoiced in the knowledge of that wisdom.

How different was the heir of good King Hezekiah! We wonder how long it took Hezekiah to realize that even though Manasseh was born of a miracle, he was a good-for-nothing son. His bent nature must have betrayed itself at a very early age, for when Manasseh came to the throne at the age of twelve, he at once plunged into all kinds of wickedness. He reveled in the sex- and sodomy-saturated Canaanite religions (2 Kings 21:1-9; 2 Chronicles 33:1-9). At the shrines harlots were employed by the hundreds to assist in the consummation of "worship." How far astray Manasseh went can be seen in the scope of Josiah's reforms (2 Kings 23). The cost of Manasseh's behavior was high. He was made to taste of captivity (2 Chronicles 33:10-13) and his kingdom never recovered from his debaucheries. Within a few decades the Babylonians robbed the morally and spiritually bankrupt nation of all it possessed (2 Kings 25:1-21).

The truths expressed in Proverbs 29:3 also apply to ordinary folks. Wang Lung is an example. Pearl Buck told us about him in her novel *The Good Earth.* He was a poor peasant who owned a small piece of land. In a time of great famine he and his family were forced to become refugees in a southern city. During an insurrection in the city his wife took part in the looting of a rich man's house, and Wang returned to his farm with a purse full of gems. Cautiously he began to buy more land. A series of good harvests increased his wealth. Finally he became rich and had servants. Time hung on his hands and he viewed his wife with increasing disfavor. Repeated childbirths and backbreaking labor in the fields beneath the burning sun had left their mark. She looked old and ill.

Then in town Wang discovered the new shop where men drank tea, gambled, and hired women of ill-repute. Such an establishment had always filled him with horror before, but now, driven by his restlessness, he visited the new place. At first he was embarrassed and sat silently in a corner, sipping his tea. Then he began to look furtively at the pictures of women lining the walls of the shop. The madam, a woman called Cuckoo, interpreted the look in his eye and glided up to him. She told him that the pictures were portraits of the women upstairs. If he was willing to pay, he could pick out the one he would like to visit. He chose a woman named Lotus.

Wang became besotted with the woman. More and more of his money poured into the hands of Cuckoo and Lotus. Eventually he purchased Lotus from the tea shop and added a court and rooms to his house for her. She came to him riding in a closed sedan chair of bamboo.

But Wang was not happy. He was angered by the knowing grins of the laborers who carried the sedan chair. He was angry because his uncle's wife, who had arranged the transaction, smirked and told him that Lotus was not nearly as young as she looked. He was disturbed by his wife's scorn and sullen looks.

Wang discovered that he had taken a viper into his bosom, for the harlot he had purchased easily lost her temper and made unremitting demands for this and that. Worst of all, when his old father stumbled across the painted woman, "he cried out in his shrill cracked voice, 'There is a harlot in the house!'...He shouted over and over, 'There is a harlot here!'"[16] And Wang's troubles and expenditures had only just begun.

The whoremonger spends not only his substance, but also his health and his joy. Solomon deliberately contrasted him with the man who "loveth wisdom" and thus "rejoiceth his father."

### c. Beware of the Seductive Man (29:4-6)

A ruler should beware of *the man who seduces with his money*. Solomon believed, as his father David had believed, that a throne should be noted for its inflexible and impartial justice. For a good reason we depict justice as a blindfolded woman with both hands already full (she holds a set of balances in one hand and a sword in the other). Proverbs 29:4 warns, "The king by judgment establisheth the land: but he that receiveth gifts overthroweth it."

The principle underlying this proverb is integrity. Integrity should be the mark of all three branches of government. The legislative branch should be noted for passing wise, fair laws and for setting appropriate, meaningful penalties for lawbreakers. The executive branch should be noted for fair, evenhanded administration. The judiciary branch should be noted for impartiality in making justice available to all.

Integrity should mark the way a nation handles both internal and international matters. A nation should be noted for the way it honors its treaty obligations, practices equity in international trade, and requires integrity of its ambassadors, ministers, agencies, and services. Integrity should characterize all of a government's representatives, from highest-level appointees to the most junior officials.

Solomon, in the early days of his reign, came close to establishing the ideal kingdom. He inherited from his father a stable domain. Internationally there was not a foe in sight. The troubles that had plagued David's reign after the Bath-sheba incident had subsided. The nation was at peace and prosperous. Along with stability, Solomon inherited sagacity. His natural gifts of observation and deduction were greatly augmented by the wisdom that God bestowed on him in response to his prayer.

Within a year of his enthronement, Solomon had dealt with Shimei, Joab, and Abiathar and had executed Adonijah. Solomon had nipped in the bud any possibility of insurrection and everyone had seen the fairness of his dealings with these past and prospective troublemakers. His actions sent a strong message to the tribes that although he was a man of peace rather than a man of war like David, he was not to be trifled with. The new king could and would act decisively. Solomon's handling of the disagreement between the two harlots crowned his reputation for wisdom. By judgment he established the land. Everyone knew that no one could pull the wool over Solomon's eyes.

Then with the vast treasure David had accumulated for the purpose, Solomon built the temple according to divine specifications and dedicated it with great pomp and ceremony. Now the nation had a central place of worship and the entire Levitical code could be upheld. The shekinah glory cloud hovered over the temple to signify to one and all that God was in residence, enthroned among His people. God was in His temple and all was well with the land.

Religion was established as a key ingredient in the nation's health. The entire Mosaic law with its 613 firm but fair edicts became the law of the land. (The king had made a copy for himself with his own hand.) Precepts and punishments alike, all of the commands were upheld. Sacrifices, offerings, feast days, and fast days were observed. Israel enjoyed a situation as ideal as it will ever be until the millennium.

However, the first crack in the picture of perfection soon appeared. Acting as if there were not enough good and beautiful women in Israel, Solomon married a pagan Egyptian. That event was the beginning of the end.

The Mosaic law, anticipating the day when the theocracy would be replaced by a monarchy, codified three things a king must not do:

> He shall not multiply horses to himself, nor cause the people to return to Egypt, to the end that he should multiply horses: forasmuch as the Lord hath said unto you, Ye shall henceforth return no more that way. Neither shall he multiply wives to himself, that his heart turn not away: neither shall he greatly multiply to himself silver and gold (Deuteronomy 17:16-17).

Solomon broke all three injunctions. If he was forbidden to go to Egypt to buy horses, whatever made him think he could go there with God's blessing to look for a queen?

The crack in the picture of perfection widened. Noting the ominous word "but," we read what the Holy Spirit said about the completion of the temple: "In the eleventh year, in the month Bul, which is the eighth month, was the house finished throughout all the parts thereof, and according to all the fashion of it. So he was seven years in building it. *But* Solomon was building his own house thirteen years" (1 Kings 6:38–7:1). In the Bible the number thirteen is associated with apostasy and rebellion.

Money completed Solomon's corruption. Proverbs 29:4 warns, "He that receiveth gifts overthroweth [the land]," and we read in 1 Kings 10:24-25: "All the earth sought to Solomon....And they brought every man his present." First Kings 10:23 tells us that "king Solomon exceeded all the kings of the earth for riches and for wisdom." Soon the wisdom departed and only the money was left. And he spent the money faster than it came in, so he wanted more and more. Toward the end he was not too scrupulous about how he acquired money and, taxing his people unmercifully, he lost the good will of ten of the tribes (1 Kings 12:1-4). Solomon was evidently much better at coining and collecting proverbs than he was at heeding them.

A ruler should beware of the corrupting power of money. He should also beware of *the man who seduces with his mouth:* "A man that flattereth his neighbour spreadeth a net for his feet" (Proverbs 29:5). Saul tried to trick David with flattery.

The trouble began when, under the control of an evil spirit, Saul prophesied (1 Samuel 18:10). (Prophetic utterance is no proof that the Holy Spirit is at work.) David had been hired to minister in music to Saul, especially on such occasions, so David was present at the time. He felt awkward because he knew that Saul hated him. When the prophetic fit was over, Saul sat there eyeing David and playing with a javelin, and then suddenly threw it at him. Saul meant to pin David to the wall, but he missed. In fact he missed twice. Now Saul was afraid of David (18:12), so he dismissed David from his post as court musician and made him an army captain. In his new post David became even more popular and Saul became even more fearful (18:15-16).

Hoping to trick David into falling into a trap by saying an incautious word, Saul tried flattery. "David, you are a valiant man," Saul said in effect. "Now then, if you use your valor for me, I'll let you marry Merab, my elder daughter. How would you like to be a king's son-in-law?" David, who had learned to be cautious, sidestepped the flattery and disclaimed any personal ambition. "Who am I?" he said, "and what is my life, or my father's family in Israel, that I should be son in law to the king?" (18:18) Saul waited to see what David would do and then suddenly gave Merab to someone else, but David held his peace.

Then Saul told David that he still intended to make him his son-in-law and offered him Michal, a younger daughter. Saul summoned his servants. "Flatter David," he said in effect. "Tell him that I love him, that everybody likes him, and that it would be a fine thing for him to be a king's son-in-law. Then come back and tell me what he says." David's response was to depreciate himself.

Flattery had failed, so Saul next tried guile. He set the snare he had been preparing for David. "Tell David," he said in effect to his servants, "that the king realizes he is a poor country lad who cannot come up with a suitable dowry. Tell him that the king will settle for courage instead of cash. Tell him that all he needs to do is bring the king hard evidence that he has killed two hundred Philistines." Saul hoped of course that David would fail in his attempt to win his dowry and that the Philistines would kill David in the process.

David had not fallen for flattery, and he did not fall to the foe. He reached his quota, gave the king his dowry, and married Michal. Saul allowed the marriage to proceed because he hoped to use Michal to snare David. (Saul evidently had some strong hold over Michal.) Perhaps Solomon had this story in mind when he wrote Proverbs 29:5.

A ruler should beware of being corrupted by flattery as well as by money. He should also beware of *the man who seduces with his morals:* "In the transgression of an evil man there is a snare: but the righteous doth sing and rejoice" (Proverbs 29:6). A wicked man's lifestyle can be infectious. Those who spend time with an immoral man risk becoming like him. Those who go along with his transgressions forget that there is always a snare.

The evil man does not tell his imitators of the diseases he has contracted or the guilt that gnaws away in his innermost soul. He does not talk about the torment of addiction. He does not reveal the haunting fear that someone he has wronged will seek revenge. The evil man does not speak of how he cringes at the sight of the police or how he awakens at night, terror-stricken by thoughts of the certain judgment of God. Instead he drinks and carouses, laughs and sneers, mocks and blasphemes, cheats and lies. The evil man seems to be carefree, successful, popular, and clever. But he is caught in a snare. His life is a sham.

Some time ago a leading news magazine printed an interview that one of its reporters had had with Nicholas Caramandi, a member of the underworld. This mobster, known as "The Crow," had been a killer for a Mafia boss. Caramandi told the reporter about the treatment he had enjoyed when he was riding high, wide, and handsome as a hit man. If he sneezed, he was handed a dozen handkerchiefs. If it rained, umbrellas popped open for him everywhere. When Christmas came, gifts were showered on him. If he walked into a restaurant, the best table—occupied or not—was cleared for him. Women threw themselves at him. He had a stake in everything: gambling, loan-sharking, drugs, unions, politics, shakedowns. Work was for suckers!

But Caramandi had lived in fear. Everybody in the underworld feared everybody else, and everybody was deathly afraid of the boss. The boss held grudges. "If you didn't say hello to him 20 years ago, he never forgot," said Caramandi. "When you're around the boss, don't drink. See, when a guy drinks, his feelings come out." The boss would try to get "The Crow" drunk so he would talk.

When he made the mistake of getting arrested, the boss put out a contract on his life. Caramandi had lied, cheated, and killed for the boss and had brought in millions of dollars for the organization, but now the boss wanted him to be killed because he knew too much. Most anyone in that prison could be his executioner.

Caramandi was scared to death, so he called the FBI, asked for protection and a new identity, turned state's evidence, and betrayed the mob. He testified in eleven trials that resulted in fifty-two convictions. The FBI moved him to another city and set him up as an ordinary citizen.

Caramandi still remembers the killing and treachery of his thirty years in the mob. "There's no security," he said. "You're never safe."

He described his new life as "a dog's life." He lives in constant fear and doesn't dare make any friends. His wife has disowned him and nobody likes him. What does he do with his time? He has become a sucker, he says. He works.[17]

Caramandi knows that the proverb is true: "In the transgression of an evil man there is a snare." But Solomon didn't stop there. He added, "The righteous doth sing and rejoice." The world thinks that the believer lives a wretched life—going to church, singing hymns, declining the pleasures of sin, reading the Bible—but the believer knows that his life is full of rejoicing. What a life indeed!

d. Beware of the Selfish Man (29:7)

"The righteous considereth the cause of the poor: but the wicked regardeth not to know it."

Concern for the poor seems to be a somewhat rare trait among kings, even in Bible times. David is one of the outstanding exceptions. His concern doubtless stemmed from his outlaw years when he attracted the poor to himself (1 Samuel 22:2). Perhaps Solomon had David's treatment of Mephibosheth in mind when he wrote Proverbs 29:7.

Mephibosheth's situation was deplorable. He had once been in succession to the throne, but when he was five years old, his dreams of becoming crown prince and then king were dashed by the death of his father and the downfall of Saul's dynasty. When David discovered that this son of Jonathan was still alive, Mephibosheth was a fugitive, dependent on the charity of others. He was living in a bleak town called *Lo-debar,* which means "the place of no pasture," and because he was lame, he had little hope of bettering his lot in life. The Holy Spirit delights to tell us how David sought Mephibosheth and brought him to himself. David gave him back his lost estates and made room for him at his own table (2 Samuel 9).

Various other Biblical illustrations of Proverbs 29:7 come to mind. We think of Paul and how he befriended Onesimus, Philemon's runaway slave. We think of the good Samaritan and we contrast his righteous behavior with the wicked behavior of the priest and the Levite. We think of the story Jesus told about the rich man and Lazarus.

Jesus knew all about being rich. His wealth was greater than any we could ever imagine. In His country the streets are paved with gold, the walls are built of jasper, and the gates are made of pearl. His city is the city that haunted Abraham's dreams, the "city which hath foundations, whose builder and maker is God"

(Hebrews 11:10). The city's twelve foundations are ablaze with precious stones and its main boulevard runs through an arcade formed by the arching branches of the tree of life. The palaces are ivory, the servants are angels, and from the throne of God flows the crystal river of the water of life.

Jesus knew all about being rich and He also knew all about being poor. He was born in a cattle shed. His first bed was made of straw, strewn in a manger from which cows normally fed. He was so poor He sometimes had to borrow what He needed. He borrowed Simon Peter's boat, a little lad's lunch, a penny, a donkey, an upper room, a cross,[18] and a tomb. During His last three years His only earthly possessions were the clothes He wore; He had no home of His own, no means of transportation, no money, and no visible means of support.

He who once gave up being rich so that He could become poor has now given up being poor and has gone back to being rich.

Since Jesus knew all about both wealth and poverty, we can be sure that when He told the story about the rich man and Lazarus, He knew what He was talking about. This story was much more than a parable. It was an account of an incident that actually happened. Jesus did not name the people He mentioned in His parables, but He named two of the people in this story (Lazarus and Abraham). Jesus knew Lazarus and it is likely that He knew the rich man and his five brothers as well. None of them had any use for Lazarus—or Him. The six brothers probably knew Abraham as a historical figure and nothing more. It never occurred to them that Abraham was still very much alive—on the other side of death. After the rich man died he saw Abraham, but he was never able to get anywhere near him. The despised Lazarus, however, was very near Abraham.

Applying Solomon's proverb, we could say that Jesus considered the cause of the poor, but the rich man did not regard it. No doubt the rich man lived in a mansion and owned valuable land. He had servants, butlers, footmen, and gardeners. He had horses, stables, cattle, and barns. He lived like a lord and wore expensive clothes. He sat down at a great oak table laden with good food.

According to Luke 16:19 the rich man "fared sumptuously every day," whereas Lazarus sat at his gate, beggar bowl in hand, and starved. Scavenger dogs, regarded with the utmost abhorrence by every conscientious Jew, were kinder to poor Lazarus than the rich man was. They "came and licked his sores" (16:21). The rich man went to bed at night in an elegant room filled with expensive furniture; his servants turned down the bedspread and turned off the lamp. Lazarus wrapped his threadbare cloak around him and slept on a hard, cold floor.

When with fanfare of trumpets and a retinue of servants the rich man rode away from his mansion, he would see Lazarus at the gate. The rich man would not actually look at him; he would just see him out of the corner of his eye. The rich man could easily have told his servants to chase the unsightly beggar away, but he let him stay. Perhaps occasionally the rich man told his cook to send some kitchen scraps to the gate. Doubtless he imagined he was doing a good work—acquiring merit, laying up treasure in Heaven—and thus he salved his conscience.

For all practical purposes, he really ignored Lazarus. If the rich man had been righteous, he would have walked down his driveway and introduced himself. He would have given the beggar some clean clothes, called a doctor to put salve on his sores, bathed him, given him a spare room in the servants' quarters at least, and found him a job on his estate. The rich man would have shown Lazarus what David showed Mephibosheth: the kindness of God.

But the rich man never considered the cause of the poor. He preferred to know nothing about it. He despised the poor because they were poor. In studiously refusing to consider poor Lazarus, the rich man revealed his attitude toward Jesus, for in those days Jesus was poor. The rich man was essentially wicked, and when he died he went to Hell. Only the righteous go to Heaven.

Solomon did not care for the poor. He was rich, but he taxed the poor—taxed them more and more until in his son's reign they revolted. We rejoice that a greater than Solomon has come. What He said is far more important than Solomon's proverb:

> When the Son of man shall come in his glory, and all the holy angels with him, then shall he sit upon the throne of his glory....And he shall set the sheep on his right hand, but the goats on the left. Then shall the King say unto them on his right hand, Come, ye blessed of my Father, inherit the kingdom prepared for you from the foundation of the world: For I was an hungred, and ye gave me meat...Naked, and ye clothed me: I was sick, and ye visited me.... Then shall the righteous answer him, saying, Lord, when saw we thee an hungred...or thirsty...or sick?...And the King shall answer and say unto them, Verily I say unto you, Inasmuch as ye have done it unto one of the least of these my brethren, ye have done it unto me. Then shall he say also unto them on the left hand, Depart from

me, ye cursed, into everlasting fire, prepared for the devil and his angels: For I was an hungred, and ye gave me no meat: I was thirsty, and ye gave me no drink...naked, and ye clothed me not: sick...and ye visited me not. Then shall they also answer him, saying, Lord, when saw we thee an hungred, or athirst...or naked, or sick...and did not minister unto thee? Then shall he answer them, saying, Verily I say unto you, Inasmuch as ye did it not to one of the least of these, ye did it not to me. And these shall go away into everlasting punishment: but the righteous into life eternal" (Matthew 25:31-46).

e. Beware of the Scornful Man (29:8-9)

A king should beware of the scornful man because he brings ruin to the state and bestows ridicule on the sage. First, *he brings ruin to the state:* "Scornful men bring a city into a snare: but wise men turn away wrath" (Proverbs 29:8).

The Jebusites, secure in their mighty fortress, ridiculed David's handful of men down below. The scoffers said in effect, "We can hold this place with our blind and our lame" (see 2 Samuel 5:6). Not long afterward the stronghold was in David's hands.

Even as scornful Belshazzar was boasting and blaspheming, the military engineers in the Persian army were diverting the flow of the Euphrates, giving them the riverbed as a highway into the city of Babylon. Truly, "scornful men bring a city into a snare."

Just as surely, "wise men turn away wrath." In the case of Abel-Beth-maachah, a fortified town in the tribal territory of Naphtali, a wise woman saved the people from Joab's wrath. This remote town on the northern frontier of Israel became famous because of the following incident.

Right after the Absalom rebellion had been crushed, another insurrection, led by a Benjamite named Sheba, broke out. Seeing an opportunity to capitalize on the wavering loyalty of the ten northern tribes, Sheba blew a trumpet and called on the men of Israel to renounce, once and for all, their allegiance to David. Sheba secured an immediate following. Indeed his rebellion soon became as serious as Absalom's had been.

Before long, however, Joab had the situation well in hand. Sheba and his adherents fled northward. Like a bloodhound on the trail, Joab and his men followed the rebels. Finally the insurrectionists burst into the town of Abel.

Joab was an old hand at taking walled cities and in no time he had Abel surrounded. When its citizens gazed over the walls, they were dismayed by what they saw. Joab's veterans were making warlike preparations with the utmost speed and efficiency. Before long they had cast up a great mound against the wall and battering rams began pounding away.

The siege and sack of a city was no pleasant prospect, but the people of Abel were "between the devil and the deep blue sea." They had Sheba and his men on the inside and Joab and his men on the outside. So a wise woman asked Joab to come near. Hostilities ceased as Joab bravely enough approached the city wall. After the usual preliminary civilities, which enabled the woman to make sure she was dealing with Joab himself, she began to speak.

"You must have heard of our town," she said in effect. "Abel has an old reputation, you know. We have a history of settling matters peacefully and with common sense. Indeed there used to be a saying, 'Ask counsel at Abel.' Why then are you so determined to attack us? Abel is 'a mother in Israel.' Attacking us is like attacking your own mother" (see 2 Samuel 20:18-19).

Joab denied that he had any desire to destroy Abel. He explained that Abel was harboring Sheba, a traitor to King David. Joab said he would make a deal: if Abel would hand the rebel over to Joab, he would withdraw his forces. The woman promised to throw Sheba's head over the wall and Joab reined in his troops to await developments.

"Then," said the Holy Spirit, "the woman went unto all the people in her wisdom" (2 Samuel 20:22). We are not told what she said, but evidently she was persuasive.

"Who is this man Sheba anyway?" she may have argued. "What has he ever done for Israel? Why should so many people suffer just to bolster his ambitions? What chance will anyone have once Joab's forces are within the walls? There will be killing, raping, pillaging, and all the other horrors attendant to a siege. And for what purpose? David may have his faults, but after all he is Israel's rightful king, constitutionally crowned by the tribes. And think of what David has done for the nation! What would this fellow Sheba do for it? He is an upstart and a pretender. Why should anyone die for him? Why should anyone be afraid of him? When he arrived at Abel, he was out of breath from running away! Joab is much more to be feared than Sheba." Perhaps the woman added that if they were afraid to cut off Sheba's head, she would do it herself!

So before long, over the wall came Sheba's head, and Joab blew a trumpet to call off his troops. We could call Sheba's insurrection "the war of the trumpet," for it began with Sheba blowing a trumpet and ended with Joab blowing a trumpet (2 Samuel 20:1,22). The rebellion was over, thanks to a wise woman who turned away wrath instead of bringing her city into a snare.

The scornful man not only brings ruin to the state. *He bestows ridicule on the sage:* "If a wise man contendeth with a foolish man, whether he rage or laugh, there is no rest" (Proverbs 29:9). A wise man attempting to get a point across to a fool may try anger, sarcasm, and mockery, but not even these approaches will have the desired effect. It is easier to storm a strong city than to penetrate the mindset of a fool.

As we have seen in Solomon's other proverbs regarding the fool, here we see again the shadow of Rehoboam. Solomon had evidently tried beating some sense into the young man's head, but that had done no good. He had also tried holding Rehoboam up to ridicule, but that had done no good either.

When I was a boy, the school system tried both methods on the "dunce," as the unfortunate slow learner was called in those days. The schoolmaster freely used a bamboo cane on the "dunce" and just as frequently made the "dunce" stand in the corner with his face to the wall. His punishment was supposed to be an object lesson to the rest of us; we knew what to expect if we gave dumb answers to questions. Such methods may have been salutary for fools who were not paying attention, but probably did not help the truly backward student.

Elijah used both rage and laughter in his attempts to penetrate the defenses of Ahab. When it was evident that Ahab and his wicked wife were determined to impose Baal worship and its accompanying immoralities on Israel, the prophet tried anger. Elijah left his home in Gilead and went to Samaria to confront the king. Wasting no words, the prophet simply made a pronouncement: "As the Lord God of Israel liveth, before whom I stand, there shall not be dew nor rain these years, but according to my word" (1 Kings 17:1). Elijah left just as abruptly as he had come, but the lash of his words rankled in Ahab's soul (18:17).

The prophet vanished across Jordan. Ahab and Jezebel scoured the land for him as the heavens became as brass, as famine tightened its grip on Israel, as men tightened their belts and perished with hunger. Elijah was not to be found, for the wrath of the prophet was swallowed up in the wrath of God.

But Elijah's rage was unavailing. Ahab was a fool and all he did was bitterly blame the man of God for the ever-worsening drought. The drought lasted for three and a half years, and as that Old Testament "great tribulation" followed its fearful course, we can be sure that Ahab and Jezebel told each other what they would do to Elijah once they got their hands on him. In the meantime they vented their rage on lesser prophets when they could find them (1 Kings 18:4).

Then Elijah tried ridicule. He confronted the wicked king again and told him to summon the people and Baal's false prophets to a contest on Carmel. Elijah proposed that the false prophets build an altar and prepare a sacrifice to Baal, and he would build an altar and prepare a sacrifice to the Lord. The God who answered by fire would be proved to be the true and living God. Elijah let the false prophets have prime time—they could have the benefit of the heat of the day. He would call upon Jehovah when the evening shadows lengthened. We read in 1 Kings 18:26-27:

> [The prophets of Baal] took the bullock which was given them, and they dressed it, and called on the name of Baal from morning even until noon, saying, O Baal, hear us. But there was no voice, nor any that answered. And they leaped upon the altar which was made. And it came to pass at noon, that Elijah mocked them, and said, Cry aloud: for he is a god; either he is talking, or he is pursuing, or he is in a journey, or peradventure he sleepeth, and must be awaked.

Elijah's scorn and sarcasm were not lost on the false prophets and they doubled their efforts. His mocking laughter was certainly not lost on Ahab and Jezebel, but Ahab just went on from bad to worse and Jezebel swore that she would take Elijah's life. Trying to get truth into a fool's head is indeed futile. Ahab continued on his foolish way until he met his death and had to answer to God for his crimes.

f. Beware of the Spiteful Man (29:10)

"The bloodthirsty hate the upright: but the just seek his soul."

Classic Biblical examples of kings who fell foul of spiteful people are Saul and Ahab. Saul kept the bloodthirsty Doeg the Edomite on his staff and the result was one of the worst massacres in Bible times (1 Samuel 22). Ahab married the notoriously wicked Jezebel, who spurred him on in the terrible matter of Naboth, an upright man whom Ahab hated (1 Kings 21). Saul and Ahab would have done well to beware of people such as Doeg and Jezebel. How different the histories of their reigns would have been! Saul could have found a good counselor in his son Jonathan, who sought to preserve the "soul" of David (1 Samuel 19:4), and Ahab could have found a just counselor in Obadiah (1 Kings 18:4).

Our attitude toward the upright reveals our own nature. Good people take sides with the upright. As Proverbs 29:10 declares, wicked people dislike the upright intensely. That is why Simon Legree hated his black slave, Uncle Tom. We read about these opposite personalities in Harriet Beecher Stowe's story *Uncle Tom's Cabin.*

It was an unhappy day for Uncle Tom when he fell into the clutches of the cruel Legree. Tom had been used to a kind master, but now he was in the hands of a fiend. Legree stripped Tom of the good clothes he had worn in the slave market and furnished him with rags. Tom managed to keep his cherished Bible, but Legree found Tom's Methodist hymnbook and reacted characteristically:

> "Humph! pious, to be sure. So, what's yer name,—you belong to the church, eh?"
>
> "Yes, Mas'r," said Tom, firmly.
>
> "Well, I'll soon have *that* out of you. I have none o' yer bawling, praying, singing niggers on my place; so remember. Now, mind yourself," he said, with a stamp and a fierce glance of his gray eye, directed at Tom, "*I'm* your church now! You understand,—you've got to be as *I* say."

The slave caravan reached Legree's plantation on the Red river. Stowe described the scene:

> The house had been large and handsome. It was built in a manner common at the South; a wide verandah of two stories running round every part of the house, into which every outer door opened, the lower tier being supported by brick pillars.
>
> But the place looked desolate and uncomfortable; some windows stopped up with boards, some with shattered panes, and shutters hanging by a single hinge,—all telling of coarse neglect and discomfort.
>
> Bits of board, straw, old decayed barrels and boxes, garnished the ground in all directions; and three or four ferocious-looking dogs, roused by the sound of the wagon-wheels, came tearing out, and were with difficulty restrained from laying hold of Tom and his companions, by the effort of the ragged servants who came after them.

> "Ye see what ye'd get!" said Legree, caressing the dogs with grim satisfaction, and turning to Tom and his companions. "Ye see what ye'd get, if ye try to run off. These yer dogs has been raised to track niggers; and they'd jest as soon chaw one on ye up as eat their supper. So, mind yerself!"

The author continued:

> It took but a short time to familiarize Tom with all that was to be hoped or feared in his new way of life. He was an expert and efficient workman in whatever he undertook; and was, both from habit and principle, prompt and faithful. Quiet and peaceable in his disposition, he hoped, by unremitting diligence, to avert from himself at least a portion of the evils of his condition. He saw enough of abuse and misery to make him sick and weary; but he determined to toil on, with religious patience, committing himself to Him that judgeth righteously, not without hope that some way of escape might yet be opened to him.
>
> Legree took silent note of Tom's availability. He rated him as a first-class hand; and yet he felt a secret dislike to him,—the native antipathy of bad to good. He saw, plainly, that when, as was often the case, his violence and brutality fell on the helpless, Tom took notice of it; for, so subtle is the atmosphere of opinion, that it will make itself felt, without words; and the opinion even of a slave may annoy a master. Tom in various ways manifested a tenderness of feeling, a commiseration for his fellow-sufferers, strange and new to them, which was watched with a jealous eye by Legree.

A little later on Legree approached Tom:

> "And now," said Legree, "come here, you Tom. You see, I telled ye I didn't buy ye jest for the common work; I mean to promote ye, and make a driver of ye; and to-night ye may jest as well begin to get yer hand in. Now, ye jest take this yer gal and flog her; ye've seen enough on't to know how."
>
> "I beg Mas'r's pardon," said Tom; "hopes Mas'r won't set me at that. It's what I an't used to,—never did,—and can't do, no way possible."
>
> "Ye'll larn a pretty smart chance of things ye never did know, before I've done with ye!" said Legree, taking up a cowhide,

and striking Tom a heavy blow across the cheek, and following up the infliction by a shower of blows.

Then Legree handed Tom over to two "gigantic Negroes," who thrashed him to within an inch of his life. The next day Legree talked to Tom again:

"Well, my boy," said Legree, with a contemptuous kick, "how do you find yourself? Didn't I tell yer I could larn yer a thing or two? How do yer like it,—eh? How did yer whaling agree with yer, Tom? An't quite so crank as ye was last night. Ye couldn't treat a poor sinner, now, to a bit of a sermon, could ye,—eh?"

Tom answered nothing.

"Get up, you beast!" said Legree, kicking him again.

This was a difficult matter for one so bruised and faint; and, as Tom made efforts to do so, Legree laughed brutally.

"What makes ye so spry, this morning, Tom? Cotched cold, may be, last night."

Tom by this time had gained his feet, and was confronting his master with a steady, unmoved front.

"The devil, you can!" said Legree, looking him over. "I believe you haven't got enough yet. Now, Tom, get right down on yer knees and beg my pardon, for yer shines last night."

Tom did not move.

"Down, you dog!" said Legree, striking him with his riding-whip.

"Mas'r Legree," said Tom, "I can't do it. I did only what I thought was right. I shall do jest so again, if ever the time comes. I never will do a cruel thing, come what may."

"Yes, but ye don't know what may come, Master Tom. Ye think what you've got is something. I tell you 'tan't anything,—nothing 'tall. How would ye like to be tied to a tree, and have a slow fire lit up around ye;—wouldn't that be pleasant,—eh, Tom?"

"Mas'r," said Tom, "I know ye can do dreadful things; but,"—he stretched himself upward and clasped his hands,—"but, after ye've killed the body, there an't no more ye can do. And O, there's all ETERNITY to come, after that!"

ETERNITY,—the word thrilled through the black man's soul with light and power, as he spoke; it thrilled through the sinner's soul, too, like the bite of a scorpion. Legree gnashed on him with his teeth, but rage kept him silent; and

> Tom, like a man disenthralled, spoke, in a clear and cheerful voice.
>
> "Mas'r Legree, as ye bought me, I'll be a true and faithful servant to ye. I'll give ye all the work of my hands, all my time, all my strength; but my soul I won't give up to mortal man. I will hold on to the Lord, and put his commands before all,—die or live; you may be sure on't. Mas'r Legree, I an't a grain afeard to die. I'd as soon die as not. Ye may whip me, starve me, burn me,—it'll only send me sooner where I want to go."

With consummate skill Stowe drew the contrast between Simon Legree and Uncle Tom. She wrote:

> Tom's whole soul overflowed with compassion and sympathy for the poor wretches by whom he was surrounded. To him it seemed as if his life-sorrows were now over, and as if, out of that strange treasury of peace and joy, with which he had been endowed from above, he longed to pour out something for the relief of their woes. It is true, opportunities were scanty; but, on the way to the fields, and back again, and during the hours of labor, chances fell in his way of extending a helping-hand to the weary, the disheartened and discouraged. The poor, worn-down, brutalized creatures, at first, could scarce comprehend this; but, when it was continued week after week, and month after month, it began to awaken long-silent chords in their benumbed hearts. Gradually and imperceptibly the strange, silent, patient man, who was ready to bear every one's burden, and sought help from none,—who stood aside for all, and came last, and took least, yet was foremost to share his little all with any who needed,—the man who, in cold nights, would give up his tattered blanket to add to the comfort of some woman who shivered with sickness, and who filled the baskets of the weaker ones in the field, at the terrible risk of coming short in his own measure,—and who, though pursued with unrelenting cruelty by their common tyrant, never joined in uttering a word of reviling or cursing,—this man, at last, began to have a strange power over them; and, when the more pressing season was past, and they were allowed again their Sundays for their own use, many would gather together to hear from him of Jesus.[19]

Eventually Legree murdered Tom, but the cruel slave owner did not get rid of the kind Christian gentleman, for the author introduced Tom's ghost. Haunted by the ghost and his conscience, Legree drank recklessly and he died of his excesses. Tom's ghost continued to witness to his former master until, at his death, divine amnesty was withdrawn. Legree was a bloodthirsty man who hated the upright, whereas Tom was a just man who sought after the soul of his hateful tormentor.

g. Beware of the Stupid Man (29:11-13)

(1) He Who Talks Freely (29:11)

"A fool uttereth all his mind: but a wise man keepeth it in till afterwards." There are times when it is wise not to tell all we know. Some comments should be made "afterwards"—in a private conversation after a more public debate. Many a person has said too much and lived to regret it. Shimei and Nabal are prime Biblical examples of such a fool.

Our supreme example of a wise man is the Lord Jesus Christ. Although He had complete knowledge of all facts and all truth, He often did not tell all that He knew. He kept some of His knowledge for "afterwards." For instance, even after three and a half years of constant instruction, the Lord's disciples were quite unprepared to receive certain truths. They could not handle truths such as those concerning His impending crucifixion and subsequent resurrection. So how could He possibly tell them about the age-long postponement of kingdom truth and the substitution of church truth during the postponement? He mentioned the church once or twice (Matthew 13:45-46; 16:17-19; 18:15-20; 24:37-41), but the concept was foreign to them. He said: "I have yet many things to say unto you, but ye cannot bear them now. Howbeit when he, the Spirit of truth, is come, he will guide you into all truth" (John 16:12-13).

Some of that truth became plain on the day of Pentecost, but some of it was not made clear until the coming of the apostle Paul. Paul unfolded three great mystery truths that were entrusted to him: the truths concerning Christ's cross (see Romans), Christ's church (see Ephesians) and Christ's coming (see 1 and 2 Thessalonians). To the end of his days Peter never fully grasped some of these truths (2 Peter 3:14-16).

After the transfiguration the Lord said to Peter, James, and John, "Tell the vision to no man, until the Son of man be risen again from the dead" (Matthew 17:9). The Lord had taken these three disciples up the snow-clad slopes of mount Hermon, where He had revealed to them His glory and the coming kingdom age. The Lord had been transfigured, Moses and Elijah had arrived, and the vision had ended (it ended when Peter, overwhelmed and utterly destitute of spiritual comprehension, had broken into the Lord's conversation with His two heavenly visitors). The disciples had been full of eager questions as they had started down from the mount.

It was while they were coming down that the Lord gave them his charge not to reveal the incident until "afterwards." He did not want any more premature attempts to make Him a king by force. He was on His way to a cross, not a crown. After the resurrection Matthew, Mark, Luke, Peter, and John would all mention the transfiguration (Matthew 17:1-13; Mark 9:2-13; Luke 9:28-36; 2 Peter 1:15-19; John 1:14; 1 John 1:1-2).

(2) He Who Tells Falsehoods (29:12-13)

Solomon said to beware of the stupid man who tells falsehoods *to the prince:* "If a ruler hearken to lies, all his servants are wicked" (Proverbs 29:12). History has known many rulers who were not concerned about right and wrong. They surrounded themselves with evil men—flatterers, time-servers—who told them just what they wanted to hear. Ahab had the prophet Zedekiah (1 Kings 22:10-28); King Zedekiah had the prophet Hananiah (Jeremiah 28). How foolish King Ahab and King Zedekiah were!

Do you remember Hans Christian Andersen's fairy tale about the emperor's new clothes? One day some weavers told the emperor and his court that they knew a secret that enabled them to make clothes that were visible only to the wise. The clothes were invisible to stupid people. The emperor was quite taken in and agreed to pay an outrageous fee for a suit of these rare and wonderful garments.

The weavers measured the emperor and they flattered the emperor. They set up their looms in the palace and ran their looms at full speed as they wove the invisible cloth from which the royal robes would be made. The emperor's courtiers came to inspect the looms and assured him that the invisible cloth was all that the weavers declared it to be.

Then the weavers became tailors. They cut that invisible cloth and stitched it with invisible thread. On the day of the fitting the emperor said that the clothes seemed very light. In fact he couldn't feel them at all. "Naturally," the tailors told him, "invisible cloth is practically weightless. All the better for comfort."

A date was set for the emperor to parade himself before his people so that they could admire his marvelous invisible clothes. The tailors went through the process of arraying the emperor. One of them paused to put in an imaginary tuck here. Another halted the robing to let out a seam there. At last the emperor was ready. The sycophants admired and praised and applauded their monarch, and the emperor sallied forth to display his new magnificence. The people cheered themselves hoarse and the emperor swelled with pride. Then the parade turned a corner and an honest little boy looked at the emperor and shrilled out, "But he doesn't have anything on!"

The weavers had made a fool of the emperor—and it served him right. Such is the folly of a prince who surrounds himself with liars. In the end he believes the lies he is told.

The stupid man tells falsehoods not only to the prince. He also lies *to the poor:* "The poor and the deceitful man meet together: the Lord lighteneth both their eyes" (Proverbs 29:13). "The poor" is a needy man who needs help. He is the usurer's prey, his easy victim. "The deceitful man" is crafty. He is an oppressor such as a creditor or usurer. The phrase "the deceitful man" is a translation of a word that occurs in the plural only here in Scripture. The plural was used for emphasis.

The word translated "meet together" means "to meet unexpectedly." We might well ask how, when, and where this unexpected meeting will take place. Surely the oppressor and his victim will meet at the great white throne when the books will be opened and the dead will be judged according to their works. The eyes of both men will be opened then.

In this proverb is comfort for the poor man and a warning for the crafty oppressor. In this world right seems to be forever on the scaffold, and wrong forever on the throne. But this world is not all there is. Any unfinished business will be referred to a higher court on the shores of eternity.

The Hebrew word translated "meet together" in Proverbs 29:13 is first used in Scripture in Genesis 32:17 in reference to Jacob and Esau, who had some unfinished business to take care of.

Jacob had left Padan-aram in a hurry, hotly pursued by the indignant and vengeful Laban. There is no knowing what harm Laban would have done to Jacob, had it not been for direct divine intervention. Jacob certainly seems to have feared the worst. His crafty and callous father-in-law was quite capable of robbing him of flocks and family alike.

However, another matter was causing Jacob even more concern. He had an angry Laban behind him and an angry Esau before him. Twenty years earlier Jacob had robbed his twin brother and as far as Jacob knew, Esau was still threatening to kill him. So once the danger from Laban was averted, Jacob prepared to disarm the hostility of Esau.

"Jacob was greatly afraid," we read in Genesis 32:7. He prayed that the God who had protected him from Laban would protect him from Esau. News that Esau was coming with four hundred men added a fine edge to Jacob's prayer.

He prayed, but he made his own preparations, as we so often do. Jacob set aside "two hundred she goats, and twenty he goats, two hundred ewes, and twenty rams, Thirty milch camels with their colts, forty kine, and ten bulls, twenty she asses, and ten foals"—more than five hundred valuable animals altogether (Genesis 32:14-15). He divided them into three batches and assigned trusted servants to lead each batch. He sent the first batch on its way to Esau. After allowing suitable space between droves, he sent the second batch and then the third. The batches were to be given to Esau as presents from Jacob in his last crafty act.

The oily obsequiousness of Jacob during his encounter with Esau must have been a sight to behold. We can picture Jacob bowing to Esau seven times as he approaches him. It is "thy servant" this and "my lord" that. "The poor and the deceitful man meet together." Only now neither man is poor and Jacob is about through with his deceitfulness.

The Lord did indeed enlighten both brothers. Each said to the other, "I have enough" (Genesis 33:9,11). Jacob and Esau were well matched, even though they were about as opposite as the poor man and the oppressor in Proverbs 29:13. There is all the difference in the world between a man who has gotten on well in the world and a man who has had an encounter with the world to come.

Years earlier Esau and Jacob had quarreled over money, but Esau had long since ceased to fret and fume about that. He had enough wealth. Why would he want Jacob's presents? The animals were a peace offering of course, but Esau did not need them. Suddenly he was "enlightened." It dawned on him that he had succeeded in the world by the force of his own character and competence. He was now a prince of Edom; he had a country of his own and troops to do his will. He had become rich and successful without the aid of either birthright or blessing.

What need did Esau have for such ethereal, spiritual things? In his heart he had always known that the birthright and the blessing were based on religious superstition—pie in the sky by-and-by. So the Lord allowed Esau to see what he wanted to see. When he said, "I have enough," he was saying in effect, "I have made it on my own. I don't need God." No wonder centuries later one of Esau's descendants tried to murder Christ.

Jacob had wanted Esau to accept his gifts because oriental custom dictated that acceptance would be tantamount to signing a peace treaty; Jacob would no longer need to fear Esau. But when Jacob said, "I have enough," he had just seen a vision of angels and wrestled with God (Genesis 32:1-2,24-32). He bore in his body the mark of Jesus Christ. Jacob's feet were now planted on higher ground. He had been enlightened and he offered a word of testimony: "Take, I pray thee, my blessing that is brought to thee; because God hath dealt graciously with me, and because I have enough" (33:11).

Jacob's statement was remarkable indeed. Boldly, Jacob offered *his* blessing, for now he stood where Isaac had once stood. As the direct heir of Abraham, Jacob was the custodian of the blessings of God and the one in whom all families of the earth would be blessed (Genesis 12:1-3; 32:24-29). Jacob could now see the great gulf fixed between him and his successful twin brother. Esau once wept because he had lost the blessing of his father and the blessing of God (27:34), but now he no longer cared. Jacob's heart went out to Esau, and Jacob tried in vain to awaken a sense of spiritual lack in his brother's life.

Esau did not even acknowledge God, but Jacob said he owed everything he had to the Lord. Jacob said in effect, "I have the blessing of God and I am satisfied." He had become a prophet; Esau had become a pagan. Both could say, "I have enough," but Esau's "enough" would end at the tomb. Jacob's would last for all eternity.

2. The Stability of the Throne Assured (29:14)

"The king that faithfully judgeth the poor, his throne shall be established for ever." Evidently God uses the poor as a litmus test. A nation's rulers reveal much about themselves by the way they treat their poor people.

When poor people are mistreated, they may rise up against their oppressors and exact a terrible vengeance. Or a nation that neglects or oppresses its poor may be sold by God into the hands of an invader.

Thus ended the reign of Zedekiah, the last of the Old Testament Judean kings. He was a poor apology for a king, although he had been given a good start in life. His father was Josiah, one of the godly, reforming kings of Judah. Josiah and the prophet Jeremiah had been good friends.

Zedekiah had come to the throne of Judah in a roundabout way. When Josiah was killed at the battle of Megiddo, the Jews put Jehoahaz, a younger son of Josiah, on the throne. Jehoahaz lasted only three months—long enough for his evil tendencies to become evident. The Egyptians deposed him and deported him in chains to Egypt. Pharaoh Necho put Jehoiakim, the oldest son of Josiah, on the throne in place of Jehoahaz.

Jehoiakim was originally called Eliakim, but the pharaoh changed his name. Jehoiakim sat on the throne for eleven years and was quite unlike his godly father. The realm was greatly impoverished by the heavy tribute Jehoiakim had to pay to Egypt. He soon clashed with Jeremiah, whose threatening scroll he treated with contempt. During Jehoiakim's reign the Babylonians first began to hammer at the doors of Jerusalem. Thus the king who began as the vassal of Egypt ended as the vassal of Babylon. Jehoiakim came to an inglorious end and was given "the burial of an ass" (Jeremiah 22:19; 36:30). This figure of speech means that he had no burial at all. His body was simply dumped outside the gate of Jerusalem, a fate worse than death in Jewish eyes.

Jehoiakim was succeeded on the throne by his son Jehoiachin. He lasted only three months and ten days (2 Chronicles 36:9), after which he was deported to Babylon by Nebuchadnezzar. The prophet Jeremiah debased Jehoiachin's name to Coniah, and all Jehoiachin's descendants were barred from the Davidic throne.

Zedekiah succeeded Jehoiachin. One would think that Zedekiah would have learned, from the doom of his predecessors, the abysmal folly of ignoring God. (He was a son of Josiah, the uncle of Jehoiachin, and the brother of Jehoahaz and Jehoiakim.) But neither Zedekiah nor his counselors paid the slightest heed to the Word of God or to the prophet Jeremiah. The country descended into political insanity, religious apostasy, moral depravity, and social injustice. The poor became everyone's lawful prey. Zedekiah did not judge the poor faithfully, but Jeremiah gave him one last chance. We read:

> Thus saith the Lord; Go down to the house of the king of Judah, and speak there this word, And say, Hear the word of

> the Lord, O king of Judah, that sittest upon the throne of David, thou, and thy servants, and thy people that enter in by these gates: Thus saith the Lord; Execute ye judgment and righteousness, and deliver the spoiled [robbed] out of the hand of the oppressor; and do no wrong, do no violence to the stranger, the fatherless, nor the widow, neither shed innocent blood in this place. For if ye do this thing indeed, then shall there enter in by the gates of this house kings sitting upon the throne of David, riding in chariots and on horses, he, and his servants, and his people. But if ye will not hear these words, I swear by myself, saith the Lord, that this house shall become a desolation (Jeremiah 22:1-5).

Jeremiah announced the litmus test, but Zedekiah ignored him. The oppression continued, so God decided that the Babylonians would be better for the poor of Palestine than their own Judean kings.

The most basic duty of a ruler—to protect and help the poor and the weak—is acknowledged when an English sovereign is enthroned. Preceded by the swords of mercy and justice and the great sword of state, he enters Westminster Abbey. The new king wears the robes of a peer of Parliament and—after ceremonies involving the orb and the golden bracelets and spurs—the massive gem-studded crown of St. Edward is placed on his head. Other elaborate and gorgeous rituals follow. Then the archbishop hands the sword of state to the king and says: "With this sword do justice, stop the growth of iniquity, defend widows and orphans, restore the things that are gone to decay, maintain the things that are restored, punish and reform what is amiss, and confirm what is in good order." During the rest of the coronation ceremonies that sword is carried before the king. It is a symbol of a divine principle: "The king that faithfully judgeth the poor, his throne shall be established for ever."

# CHAPTER 8

## Proverbs 29:15-27

III. The King and His Sons (29:15-27)
  A. Wise Words about Discipline (29:15-17)
    1. A Tragedy (29:15)
    2. A Trend (29:16)
    3. A Truth (29:17)
  B. Wise Words about Discernment (29:18)
  C. Wise Words about Duty (29:19)
  D. Wise Words about Diplomacy (29:20)
  E. Wise Words about Devotion (29:21)
  F. Wise Words about Disorder (29:22)
  G. Wise Words about Dishonor (29:23)
  H. Wise Words about Dishonesty (29:24)
  I. Wise Words about Deity (29:25-26)
    1. The Fear of Man (29:25)
    2. The Favor of Monarchs (29:26)
  J. Wise Words about Détente (29:27)

### III. THE KING AND HIS SONS (29:15-27)

### A. Wise Words about Discipline (29:15-17)

In Proverbs 29:15-17 Solomon painted three pictures. First he portrayed *a tragedy:* "The rod and reproof give wisdom: but a child left to himself bringeth his mother to shame" (29:15). What a word of caution for today's parents whose work takes them away from home.

In recent years neglect of children has become a worldwide epidemic. Brazil provides a prime example. Brazilians call their neglected and abandoned little ones *abandonados,* which means "nobody's children." *Time* magazine reported that "in Rio de Janeiro alone, more than 100 children under three years old are abandoned each month."[1] Throughout Brazil three million *abandonados* now scramble to survive. In addition there are twenty million *marginalizados,* youngsters who have only minimal contact with their families. One-half of Brazil's children under age fifteen are growing up unsupervised, uneducated, and unwanted.

One small twelve-year-old was thrown out of the shack where he lived with thirteen brothers and stepbrothers. His father, who could not afford to support him, simply gave him his bus fare and told him to go to the city and support himself. *Time* magazine reported that "millions of peasant families have fled the countryside in search of factory jobs in the cities. For most, the effort has been futile. Lacking skills and education, they have settled for poverty-level employment at best—and in all too many instances, no job at all. By working ten hours a day, six days a week, an ambitious woman might earn about $75 per month, scarcely enough to survive in a wooden and tin-can hovel, let alone support her children."[2] The annual inflation rate in Brazil is about 80 percent.

Brazil's abandoned and neglected children roam the streets in bands and sleep wherever they can. Their mattresses are torn newspapers; their clothes are rags; their occupations are hustling, petty crime, and prostitution.

Police offer "protection" if young thieves will engage in drug traffic. Waifs on the streets have had to pay off the police from their scanty earnings or else be driven away from the better spots. Some of the children are killed by death squads.[3]

Many girls between the ages of ten and seventeen are forced into prostitution. There are reports that boys and girls picked up by the police are forced to commit homosexual acts and in prison they are raped by guards. Some boys are injected with female hormones.

The authorities shrug their shoulders as the situation worsens. The population is growing by more than 2.8 percent a year and a population of two hundred million is anticipated by the year 2000. Then there will be eighty million children under the age of fifteen.

Such problems are not restricted to Brazil. A father in northern Thailand sold his ten-year-old daughter to a Bangkok brothel for $400. The unfortunate girl will earn the madame $40 a night until her freshness fades. In New Delhi children work eleven-hour shifts breaking rocks in a quarry and are paid $.85 a day. In Mexico City children can earn $2.80 a day scavenging in the municipal dumps. A United Nations' World Summit for Children considered the plight of 150 million children under the age of five suffering from malnutrition and 30 million living in the streets.[4]

Even in the affluent United States, 25 percent of children under age six are said to live in poverty.[5] Infant mortality rates are worse than in seventeen other developed countries. Although programs for the elderly are on the rise, and spectacularly so, programs for children are reported to be declining.[6] Child abuse statistics continue to soar. In 1989 alone some 2.4 million cases were reported.[7] A growing number of American children are said to be living in home environments that are "hostile to healthy emotional growth."[8]

Neglect and indifference have terrible consequences. The instability of many families breeds insecurity and a sense of guilt. An increasing number of children have emotional and mental problems. Broken homes and remarriages add to the problems. Psychologists warn that when neglected children grow up, they can be expected to turn in rage on the society that neglected them.[9]

If Solomon were alive today, he would be appalled. He wrote Proverbs 29:15 for a stable society where a strong home life was the norm. What would he have written for a society like today's?

With many mothers entering the work force, increasing numbers of small children are placed in day-care centers or in the hands of private baby sitters. Before long, it is said, nearly 50 percent of children under six will require daytime supervision because there will be no one at home to take care of them. High-quality day-care is often unaffordable. According to a United States Census Bureau report titled "Who's Minding the Kids?" 37 percent of preschool children of working mothers spend their days in someone else's home. Some ten million preschoolers in the United States spend their days with caregivers other than their mothers.

Professional counselors are changing their minds about the desirability of placing small children with baby sitters, even when they provide reasonably good care. It is now thought that many day-care children are victims of anxiety and that they are likely to remain anxious even after their parents take them home. It is estimated that babies who spend more than twenty hours a week with people other than their mothers are likely to develop insecure attachments to their mothers and to become uncooperative and aggressive in the early school years. Solomon was right, of course, on the subject of child rearing.

We are raising an insecure generation of latchkey children and teenagers who come home from school to empty houses and fend for themselves until a parent returns. Too often television is their baby sitter, counselor, entertainer, and guide. Having no supervision and no enforced standards, these young people develop their own patterns of behavior.

We can learn a lesson from Mary, the Lord's mother, who was present at Calvary. She could not stop the crucifixion. She could not stop the suffering and pain or the mob's jeers and sneers. But she was there. Great is the value of a mother's "just being there" when her children are very small and when at all ages they come home from school. Woe to the generation that robs its children of that loving support.

Next Solomon portrayed *a trend:* "When the wicked are multiplied, transgression increaseth: but the righteous shall see their fall" (Proverbs 29:16).

We find an illustration of this proverb in the Lord's Olivet discourse, in which he takes us back to the days of Noah. Seven characteristics of those days come to mind:

They were days of *spiritual decline.* The faith was first delivered to Adam. The martyr Abel shed his blood for it, but Cain distorted it into a false gospel. For generations the faith was upheld by a handful of saints in the line of Seth, but by the days of Noah that godly line was almost extinct.

They were days of *social dilemma.* The days of Noah were marked by a tremendous increase in the world's population and a corresponding increase in crime.

They were days of *shameless depravity.* "God saw that the wickedness of man was great in the earth, and that every imagination of the thoughts of his heart was only evil continually" (Genesis 6:5).

They were days of *scientific development.* The godless line of Cain spurred great advances in science, technology, and engineering.

They were days of *strong delusion.* Jesus significantly says that the people "knew not" (Matthew 24:39).

There was no excuse for their ignorance, however, for those days were marked by *some devotion.* The more degenerate the times are, the more definite the testimony will be. Noah, we are told, was "a preacher of righteousness" (2 Peter 2:5). Moreover the ark itself was a monumental testimony of judgment to come.

Finally the days of Noah were days of *sudden destruction.* As Jesus says, "The flood came, and took them all away" (Matthew 24:39).[10]

It was "when men began to multiply" that the extraordinary wickedness of the antediluvians was seen (Genesis 6:1-5). As Solomon said, "When the wicked are multiplied, transgression increaseth." By sheer weight of numbers the godless descendants of Cain overwhelmed the forces of righteousness. Society became pornographic and the deceptions of the occult world were added to the depravity of the ordinary world. There was nothing left for that society but judgment.

Jesus says, "As the days of Noe [Noah] were, so shall also the coming of the Son of man be" (Matthew 24:37). And today's world is much like Noah's world: we are experiencing a population explosion of unprecedented magnitude and record-setting crime waves!

Pornography and perversion have become the alternate lifestyle for millions of people. Divorce is epidemic, broken homes are commonplace, and casual sexual liaisons are accepted as the norm. Drug use has become a craze, causing wholesale mayhem in our inner cities. Weird religious cults have multiplied and the New Age movement has plunged countless souls into pre-Christian paganism. In many countries terrorists defy the establishment, and the mob is bigger than the government. The voice of the church is barely heard and rarely heeded. The Bible is banished from classrooms. And a burgeoning population is making ever-increasing demands on the world's ever-decreasing natural resources. Truly the trend is for the wicked to multiply and transgressions to increase.

Finally Solomon portrayed *a truth:* "Correct thy son, and he shall give thee rest; yea, he shall give delight unto thy soul" (Proverbs 29:17).

Our children become either a source of constant anxiety or a source of rest and contentment. It depends a lot on how they were raised, but not altogether. When we observe two children from the same home, we may see that one becomes a credit to his parents while the other throws off all restraints. Out of Abraham's home came an Ishmael and an Isaac. Out of Isaac's home came an Esau and a Jacob. Out of Noah's home came a Ham and a Shem. Out of David's home came an Absalom and a Solomon.

The supreme example of the application of the principle underlying Proverbs 29:17 is the way God corrects His children. He is far too wise a Father to let us get away with disobedience. Consider, for instance, the extraordinary incident recorded in Exodus 4:

First God met with Moses at the burning bush when he was shepherding the flock in the desert. There He called him and commissioned him to be the kinsman-redeemer of Israel. After overcoming all of Moses' excuses, He armed him with divine power and warned him about what to expect.

Moses went back to Jethro to resign his position as shepherd and to request his father-in-law's permission to take his family to Egypt. Jethro gave his blessing and Moses—accompanied by his wife

Zipporah and his sons Gershom and Eliezer—set out for Egypt. On the way God met with Moses again and encouraged him. Again He told Moses what to do, what to say, and what to expect. Then we read in Exodus 4:21-26:

> The Lord said unto Moses...thou shalt say unto Pharaoh, Thus saith the Lord, Israel is *my* son, even *my* firstborn: And I say unto thee, Let *my* son go that he may serve me: and if thou refuse to let him go, behold, I will slay *thy* son, even *thy* firstborn. And it came to pass by the way in the inn, that the Lord met him [Moses], and sought to kill him [Eliezer]. Then Zipporah took a sharp stone, and cut off the foreskin of *her* son [Eliezer], and cast it at his [Moses'] feet, and said, Surely a bloody husband art thou to me. So he [God] let him [Eliezer] go: then she said, A bloody husband thou art, because of the circumcision (italics added).

The casual reader will infer from this passage that the Lord sought to kill Moses. That interpretation, however, makes little sense. A more careful reader will conclude that God sought to kill his son—and for a good reason. The pronouns make it clear that the passage concerns God's son, the pharaoh's son, and Moses' son.

To better understand this incident and how it illustrates Solomon's proverb, we need to consider the background of the story. The seal and sign of circumcision, which was the mark of the Abrahamic covenant, was given to the patriarch under the most solemn circumstances and was absolutely binding on all of Abraham's seed who were to be part of that covenant. There were to be no exceptions: "The uncircumcised man child...that soul shall be cut off from his people; he hath broken my covenant" (Genesis 17:14). Abraham's obedience in this matter was prompt and comprehensive.

It seems that the practice of circumcision was unknown to Jethro's people. When Gershom was born, Moses apparently circumcised him as required by the Abrahamic covenant. The result was a family squabble in which Zipporah triumphed. She resolutely refused to let Moses repeat the painful, messy operation on Eliezer when he was born, and Moses gave in. For years he lived in disobedience with his younger son cut off from the covenant. Now Moses was going to Egypt to demand obedience from the pharaoh and to threaten his son; at the same time Moses was being disobedient regarding the circumcision of his own son. How could Moses reasonably demand that the pharaoh obey God when he himself was not being obedient to God?

Moses never forgot the lesson of Exodus 4. God corrected Moses and thereafter was able to delight in him. How great that delight was is seen in the unusual and honorable burial He gave Moses when his work on earth was done. God also showed His delight by reserving a place of honor for him on the mount of transfiguration so that Moses could meet *His* Son.

### B. Wise Words about Discernment (29:18)

"Where there is no vision," Solomon wrote, "the people perish: but he that keepeth the law, happy is he." The missionary vision comes from "the law" (the Bible). When it is obeyed, people find Christ, adjust their lives to the Word of God, and find the secret of a happy life (Psalm 1).

The modern missionary movement was born on May 31, 1792, when William Carey preached his great sermon at Nottingham. His text was Isaiah 54:2-3: "Lengthen thy cords, and strengthen thy stakes; For thou shalt break forth on the right hand and on the left; and thy seed shall inherit the Gentiles, and make the desolate cities to be inhabited." One listener thought the audience would dissolve into tears as Carey charged the church with criminal neglect. However, they did not weep; they simply rose up to leave. "Call them back!" Carey cried. "Call them back!" The result was that a missionary society was formed and Carey became its missionary.

Although Carey was a humble cobbler by profession, he was an extraordinary man. By the time he was in his teens he had learned Latin, Greek, Hebrew, French, and Dutch. He could read his Bible in half a dozen languages. He avidly followed the activities of David Brainerd among the American Indians. Carey devoured the *Voyages* of Captain Cook and kept a homemade leather map of the world on the wall where he worked.

Soon after preaching his revolutionary sermon, "Expect Great Things from God; Attempt Great Things for God," Carey set sail for India. He landed at Calcutta on November 11, 1793, the very day that French revolutionists tore the cross from the Notre Dame cathedral in Paris, smashed it on the pavement, and denied Christianity. After working as the superintendent of an indigo factory in Calcutta for five years, Carey purchased a factory in 1799 and launched his mission. In 1800 he moved to Serampore, located in Danish territory not far from Calcutta, because the East India Company resented his missionary activities.

Carey baptized his first converts in 1800. In 1831 he became professor of oriental languages in the newly founded Fort William College in Calcutta and began to translate the Bible. Under his direction the press at Serampore issued the Bible, or parts of it, in some thirty-six languages, making the Bible accessible to more than three hundred million people.

Tireless, Carey and his colleagues preached; translated; prepared grammars and dictionaries in various languages; opened mission stations in many parts of India, Burma, and the East Indies; and established schools. Carey's influence helped end the horrific practice of burning child widows. As a sideline he greatly advanced horticulture and agriculture in India.

Carey had a single vision, the vision of a world in peril. He could not rest until he had done what he could and until the church was awakened to the plight of lost people. "Where there is no vision, the people perish," said Solomon, who would have appreciated William Carey. Perhaps the two have met in Heaven! We can almost hear Carey saying, "I caught your vision, Solomon."

"I wish I had caught it myself," we can imagine Solomon replying. "You know, friend William, I came pretty close to it once when the queen of Sheba came to see me, but I missed my chance."

The missionary task remains incomplete. Untold millions are still untold. Truly, "where there is no vision, the people perish."

## C. Wise Words about Duty (29:19)

"A servant will not be corrected by words: for though he understand he will not answer." The servant who "will not answer" is surly as well as stubborn.

Mere words are sometimes insufficient to secure a desired response from an intractable employee. Sterner measures may be needed. Such an employee understands what is expected of him but has no interest in doing what he is told. He drags his feet or deliberately botches the job. We can be sure that Solomon, who employed large numbers of men (many of them conscripts) to work on his numerous building projects, had ample opportunity to study such recalcitrant behavior.

We have all been inconvenienced by more sophisticated methods of "foot dragging." The last time I was in London, the Underground employees pulled a wildcat strike, making it virtually impossible to travel within the city. Buses and cabs, already full, rolled past the boarding places. The last time I was in Toronto, the air-traffic controllers pulled a similar stunt, jamming the airport and backing up flights for hours. Once when I was in Windsor, Ontario, truckers with a grievance practically closed the bridge between Windsor and Detroit. The methods are modern, but the mood of the employees is as old as work itself.

The Lord Jesus understood the problems of employer-employee relationships as perfectly as He understood everything else. He showed his understanding in a story He told in response to a somewhat worldly question posed by Peter. The story was recorded only by Matthew; this former tax collector was always interested in the subject of money.

The Lord had just told the rich young man that he had too much money to get into Heaven. His money stood in his way. He needed to get rid of it because it was blinding him to spiritual realities.

The Lord then turned to His disciples and said, "It is easier for a camel to go through the eye of a needle, than for a rich man to enter into the kingdom of God" (Matthew 19:24). This statement was so contrary to the thinking of the day that the disciples were amazed. Peter put two and two together and asked his question: "Behold, we have forsaken all, and followed thee; what shall we have therefore?" (19: 27). The Lord answered Peter's question and then told the following story.

A householder went out at daybreak to hire laborers to work in his vineyard. He and the laborers came to an agreement: so much per hour for so many hours. Knowing who the real Householder is, we can be sure that the terms of the agreement were more than fair; they were generous.

During the day the householder stopped by the employment market time and again—at the third hour, the sixth hour, the ninth hour, and the eleventh hour. Each time he saw unemployed men who were willing to work, and he offered to hire them. They had families to support and jumped at the opportunity to put in some time so they would not return home empty-handed at the end of the day. They demanded no contract; they simply trusted the integrity of the owner of the vineyard. "Whatsoever is right, that shall ye receive," he said (Matthew 20:7). That promise was good enough for them.

At the end of the day the owner settled with his employees. He began with the unfortunate men who had been looking for work all day and had not been hired until the eleventh hour when the day was almost over. To their joy and astonishment he gave them a full day's pay. The householder paid the same amount to the men who had been hired in the third, sixth, and ninth hours. Finally those who had been working since daybreak approached the owner of the vineyard. They fully expected to get a big bonus, but they only received the wage they had agreed upon—no more, and no less. They were furious and complained bitterly.

The householder listened to their grievances. They argued that they had put in a twelve-hour day and should be paid more than those who had worked only half a day or only the last hour of the day. Then the employer reminded the angry employees of their agreement. We can hear him say, "Didn't I pay you the amount we agreed on? Yes? Then take your wages and be satisfied. I have not robbed you. I have given you what I said I would."

But "a servant will not be corrected by words," said Solomon. Turning sullen, the men took their money and, casting malicious looks at the employer they had hailed for his generous terms that morning, went home to their wives. We can imagine that their supper gave them indigestion and their wine turned to vinegar in their stomachs.

Notice that the husbandman did not try to reason with the angry laborers. He knew that it would be futile to offer an explanation to men who "will not be corrected." If they had been willing to trust him instead of demanding a contract at the beginning of the day, he would have dealt with them too on the basis of grace. They served on the basis of law, and law is what they received when their work was done.

Had they been disposed to listen, the householder would have explained his grace to them. "Those other poor fellows," he would have said, "they have families too, you know. Could you support your family on a half or a twelfth of the going wage? You couldn't? Neither can they! As for the money I gave them, did I rob you to pay them? No, I robbed myself. Take your money. I am good and you are evil. Grumble all you want to. I'll be back at the job market tomorrow. You can please yourself. If you want to work for me again, choose your terms—law or grace."

The primary lesson of the story is that we should not drive bargains with the real Householder. Do we serve Him for reward? If so, let us beware.

"What do we get out of it?" Peter demanded in effect.

"Wait and see," Jesus said.

The secondary lesson of the story is that our attitudes are as important as our motives. Both affect the way we serve, whether we work in the sacred realm or the secular realm.

### D. Wise Words about Diplomacy (29:20)

Proverbs 29:20 says, "Seest thou a man that is hasty in his words? there is more hope of a fool than of him."

The classic Biblical example of a man who was "hasty in his words" is Jephthah. Jephthah was born under the cloud illegitimacy. His father Gilead had a number of sons by his wife, but Jephthah was the son of a harlot. His cheeks were often made to burn for what was not his fault. (Perhaps that is why he became such a tough fighter.) When company came, Jephthah was probably sent to the fields to be out of the way. In the end his half brothers threw him out of the family altogether.

Before long Jephthah knew everyone for miles around who was in debt, discontented, or in distress. He welcomed the dropouts of society and turned them into a troop of mighty men. Word soon spread that Jephthah was the leader of a band of outlaws. He was making a name for himself.

Then the Ammonites from the wilderness side of Jordan invaded the land. When they descended on the glades and glens of Gilead, the people reluctantly thought of Jephthah's tough outlaws and appealed to him for aid. By this time the Spirit of God had singled out Jephthah and come upon him and he agreed to fight the Ammonites. As he prepared for the critical battle, he hastily spoke fateful words:

> Jephthah vowed a vow unto the Lord, and said, If thou shalt without fail deliver the children of Ammon into mine hands, Then it shall be, that whatsoever cometh forth of the doors of my house to meet me, when I return in peace from the children of Ammon, shall surely be the Lord's, and I will offer it up for a burnt offering" (Judges 11:30-31).

Of all the hasty words a man could speak, surely Jephthah's were among the most foolish. Before long Jephthah would bitterly regret having made that rash vow. To this day we are not sure how he fulfilled that foolish promise.

Jephthah won a resounding victory over the Ammonites, then returned home. Judges 11:34-35 tell us what happened next:

> Behold, his daughter came out to meet him with timbrels and with dances: and she was his only child; beside her he had neither son nor daughter. And it came to pass, when he saw

her, that he rent his clothes, and said, Alas, my daughter! thou hast brought me very low, and thou art one of them that trouble me: for I have opened my mouth unto the Lord, and I cannot go back.

Jephthah may have been "hasty in his words," but compared with the men of Ephraim, he was as slow as a glacier. Jephthah had appealed to this neighboring tribe to help him fight against the Ammonites, but he had appealed in vain. After the victory was won, however, the Ephraimites accused Jephthah of not asking for their help. They said he had slighted them and hastily vowed to burn up his house.

The Ephraimites had picked on the wrong man. Jephthah wasted no time. He and his men thrashed the Ephraimites and caught those who tried to escape to the other side of the Jordan. The Gileadites seized everyone seeking to cross the river and demanded, "Art thou an Ephraimite?" If he said no, they said to him, "Say now Shibboleth." If he said, "Sibboleth," they knew he was an Ephraimite, for the Ephraimites could not pronounce the word correctly. If the fugitive could not say "Shibboleth," the Gileadites slew him (Judges 12:5-6). Many Ephraimites fell that day because they had spoken hastily to the wrong man.

## E. Wise Words about Devotion (29:21)

"He that delicately bringeth up his servant from a child shall have him become his son at length." We can see the truth of this proverb in the relationship Abraham developed with his servant Eliezer.

Eliezer of Damascus was one of Abraham's 318 "trained servants, born in his own house" (Genesis 14:14). The Hebrew word translated "trained" means "initiated" or "instructed" and probably refers to their being introduced to the worship of the living God. We note that Solomon used the identical Hebrew word in Proverbs 22:6: "Train up a child in the way he should go: and when he is old, he will not depart from it."

The "trained servants" probably were "the souls that they had gotten in Haran" (Genesis 12:5), who joined Abraham in his pilgrimage to the promised land. Later God took Abraham into His confidence because of his diligence in winning his servants to Him. "The Lord said, Shall I hide from Abraham that thing which I do...? For I know him, that he will command his children and his household after him, and they shall keep the way of the Lord, to do justice and judgment" (Genesis 18:17-19).

Eliezer is introduced by name in Genesis 15:2. *Eliezer* means "God is my helper." The title "of Damascus" is not explained. It may simply imply that Eliezer's father or forebears came from Damascus. Maybe there was more than one Eliezer in Abraham's great establishment and the title was used to differentiate this Eliezer from another Eliezer.

At any rate, Eliezer was born in Abraham's household and raised under the eye of the patriarch. Evidently Eliezer distinguished himself in Abraham's service. Abraham was childless so it was natural for him to take a paternal interest in this particular bright boy. As Eliezer's character and capabilities increased, Abraham came to regard him almost as a son. The patriarch thought so highly of Eliezer that at one time he intended to make him his heir.

When the kings of the East captured Lot, Abraham "armed his trained servants...and pursued them" (Genesis 14:14). After the battle was won and Lot was rescued, God once more appeared to Abraham to confirm the covenant. The patriarch responded: "Lord God, what wilt thou give me, seeing I go childless, and the steward of my house is this Eliezer of Damascus?...Behold, to me thou hast given no seed: and lo, one born in my house is mine heir" (Genesis 15:2-3). God ruled out that option, but we can still see the truth of Proverbs 29:21 in the story of Abraham and Eliezer.

## F. Wise Words about Disorder (29:22)

"An angry man stirreth up strife, and a furious man aboundeth in transgression."

Demetrius, the silversmith of Ephesus, was an angry man. Having noted a drop in sales for the silver images of the goddess Diana, he rightly attributed the decrease to the preaching of the gospel. Furious, he called a meeting of his guild, stirred up his colleagues against Paul, and precipitated a riot of ominous proportions. Only the daring and diplomatic intervention of the townclerk prevented serious consequences (Acts 19:24-41).

Simeon and Levi were also angry men. These two sons of Jacob became enraged when they discovered that Shechem, a young Hivite, had violated their sister Dinah. Shechem and his father Hamor entered into negotiations with Jacob to see if the situation could be remedied. Shechem would marry Dinah and no reasonable reparations would be refused.

Then Simeon and Levi took over the negotiations and craftily demanded that Hamor's whole clan be circumcised. As bait, Jacob's sons offered trade and intermarriage. The pagan clan just as craftily agreed, fully expecting to swamp the Hebrews by sheer weight of numbers after the circumcision.

The painful operation was performed. Then Simeon and Levi betrayed their true character. Before the Hivite men were healed, these two sons of Jacob armed themselves and massacred Shechem's village.

Jacob was horrified by the mass murder. He first learned about it when the exultant brothers arrived home. Seeing the women, children, and cattle they had seized as the spoils of war, Jacob cried: "Ye have troubled me to make me to stink among the inhabitants of the land.... And I being few in number, they shall gather themselves together against me, and slay me; and I shall be destroyed, I and my house" (Genesis 34:30). As Solomon said, "An angry man stirreth up strife."

Jacob spoke even more indignantly on his deathbed: "Simeon and Levi are brethren; instruments of cruelty are in their habitations.... Cursed be their anger, for it was fierce; and their wrath, for it was cruel: I will divide them in Jacob, and scatter them in Israel" (Genesis 49:5-7).

Nikita Khrushchev was another angry man. The son of a miner and the grandson of a serf, Khrushchev began working as a pipe fitter at age fifteen. He joined the Red Army in 1919 and served as a political commissar. In the early 1930s he consolidated his hold on the Moscow cadres of the communist party. He zealously supported Stalin and participated in the dictator's purges of the party's leadership. Somehow Khrushchev survived the executions and in 1939 he became a full member of the Politburo. When the Soviets occupied Poland in 1940, he was sent to liquidate the Polish and Ukrainian separatist movements and restore the communist party organization that had suffered in the purge.

Khrushchev also survived the 1949-1953 era when Stalin, angered and alarmed by Tito's defection from the Soviet camp and the inauguration of an independent communist Yugoslavia, began a new series of show trials. Numerous communist leaders were forced to confess to endorsing Titoism and were executed. The Soviets were subjected to a reign of terror and as time went on, Stalin himself became increasingly suspicious and paranoid. Stalin died in 1953 and within three months his henchman Khrushchev—with the aid of the top military brass—arranged for the arrest of the man he most feared: Lavrenty Beria, Stalin's secret-police chief.

In March 1958 Khrushchev became the Soviet premier. He assumed undisputed control over the Soviet Union and stirred up strife around the world. He virulently attacked capitalism. He vented his spite toward Stalin (for the fears and torments of the years of repression) by debunking the "Stalin myth" and releasing thousands of political prisoners. When Poland and Hungary revolted, Khrushchev reached an agreement with Poland, but crushed the uprising in Hungary with brute force. He built the Berlin wall and intensified the cold war.

The world will not forget Khrushchev's temper tantrums. He often rattled the Soviet missile saber. In 1960 he spoke at the United Nations and, pounding his shoe on a desk, bellowed that communism would "bury" America. He also lost his temper at a press conference after the collapse of the Paris summit.

Khrushchev is probably best remembered for the Cuban missile crisis. Thinking that John Kennedy was a pushover, Khrushchev attempted to introduce Soviet medium-range missiles into Cuba in 1962. The resulting confrontation of the Soviet missile-carrying ships with the United States Navy brought the world to the brink of war.

Khrushchev boasted that the Soviet Union would overtake the United States in agricultural and industrial production, but in the end his arbitrary policies caught up with him and he was deposed from power.

## G. Wise Words about Dishonor (29:23)

"A man's pride shall bring him low: but honour shall uphold the humble in spirit." Pride is extremely destructive. Pride transformed Lucifer into Satan. Pride brought Adam and Eve low. Pride turned Cain into a murderer and King Uzziah into a leper. Pride was the undoing of Nebuchadnezzar, Belshazzar, and Darius the Mede. Pride filled the hearts of the Pharisees and Sadducees so that they sought the chief seats in the synagogue and the places of honor at every feast. Pride has wrecked more homes, mobilized more armies, broken more friendships, and ruined more lives than any other force in the universe.

Pharaoh was so proud that he thought he was a god. He imagined himself to be the incarnation of Ra, the sun god. We can imagine his thoughts: *How dare this man Moses, this abominable shepherd, appear before me and demand that I, the pharaoh of Egypt and companion of the gods, tamely surrender my slaves to him because some unknown god named Jehovah says that I must? Who does this fellow think he is, anyway? I'll show him! Ho, guards! Double the demands on those gadflies in the ghetto in Goshen.*

Nobody understood the pharaoh's pride better than Moses. His royal foster mother had groomed him for the throne of Egypt and he knew all about the insufferable pride of its prince and the multiplicity and grossness of its gods.

When God commissioned Moses, He told him, "Against all the gods of Egypt I will execute judgment: I am the Lord" (Exodus 12:12). The various miracles of Moses were directed against the Egyptian gods as much as the Egyptian government.

Reptiles, for instance, were sacred in Egypt. Egyptians worshiped the crocodile and the pharaoh wore a symbolic serpent on his brow. So there was something particularly significant about Moses' first miracle when he turned a rod into a snake. True, the pharaoh's magicians duplicated the miracle—but Moses' snake swallowed up their snakes, and when his snake was turned back into a rod, the magicians' rods did not reappear.

The Egyptians worshiped the Nile as the source of life, so Moses turned the water of the Nile to blood. They worshiped frogs as the symbol of fecundity, so Moses multiplied the frogs and filled the Egyptians' houses with them. The plagues of lice and flies exposed the impotence of Egypt's gods; Beelzebub, the god of flies, was shown to be powerless. Cows were worshiped by the Egyptians, so another plague killed their cattle by the thousands.

The prelude to the plague of boils was ominous. Moses took ashes from a furnace and threw them toward heaven. It is likely that human sacrifices were being offered in that furnace in an attempt to propitiate the Egyptian god Typhon, "the evil one."

The plague of hail, which was accompanied by terrifying thunderstorms, was directed against two more Egyptian deities, Isis and Osiris. The plague of locusts was aimed at the god Serapis, who was supposed to protect the land from this scourge. The plague of darkness was designed to show the impotence of the sun god Ra, who was the chief god. The pharaoh was thought to be the incarnation of Ra, and the pharaoh's firstborn was in line to be the next god-manifest-in-flesh, but he was slain by the avenging angel during the final plague.

Pharaoh's pride brought him low and brought the Egyptian pantheon of make-believe gods low as well. When Jethro, Moses' father-in-law, met the emancipated people in the wilderness, he said, "Now I know that the Lord is greater than all gods: for in the thing wherein they dealt proudly he was above them" (Exodus 18:11).

Truly, "a man's pride shall bring him low: but honour shall uphold the humble in spirit." Moses could have become as proud as the pharaoh, but the Holy Spirit declares:

> By faith Moses, when he was come to years, refused to be called the son of Pharaoh's daughter; Choosing rather to suffer affliction with the people of God, than to enjoy the pleasures of sin for a season; Esteeming the reproach of Christ greater riches than the treasures in Egypt (Hebrews 11:24-26).

And has not Moses received high honor? He is known for his meekness and hence for his Christlikeness (Numbers 12:3; Matthew 11:29). The whole world remembers Moses, but who was the pharaoh he humbled? Nobody knows for sure.

### H. Wise Words about Dishonesty (29:24)

"Whoso is partner with a thief hateth his own soul: he heareth cursing, and bewrayeth it not." Light is cast upon this proverb by a statement in the Mosaic Law: "If a soul sin, and hear the voice of swearing, and is a witness, whether he hath seen or known of it; if he do not utter it, then he shall bear his iniquity" (Leviticus 5:1). In other words, it is a criminal offense to withhold information, to be a witness to a crime and not come forward and testify.

If a thief, for instance, is brought into court, those who witnessed the robbery are put under oath by the judge. From then on the witnesses are sworn to tell the truth, the whole truth, and nothing but the truth. If they withhold vital information or give false information, they become accomplices and accessories.

Years ago I drove to a town where I was scheduled to preach for a week. When I arrived on Saturday afternoon, the lady of the house where I was to stay showed me to my room. I saw no sign of her husband until later that evening. He arrived just as I was about to retire for the night. He welcomed me to his home, apologized for being so late, explained where he had been, looked embarrassed, apologized again, and said that he would be unable to attend the Sunday services. That was the last I saw of him until the end of the week.

A couple of days later the poor wife told me that her husband had locked himself in his bedroom, where he had a closet full of wine. I absented myself from the home as much as possible, preached as well as I could under the circumstances, and determined to get away quickly when my week was over. When Saturday finally came, the lady of the house was not around and as I was putting the last suitcase in the car, her husband appeared.

"I owe you an apology," he said. I shrugged it off. "Can I talk to you?" he asked. We went back into the house and sat at the kitchen table. Then he told me a story I had no reason to disbelieve, but I have never attempted to prove it. The man claimed that his father had come to the United States from Sicily. The father had been involved in organized crime and had become rich. Worse, he had inducted his son into the syndicate. My host waved a hand in the direction of his bedroom. "I have a safe full of cash in there," he said.

Recently, however, my host had become a Christian. "That has only created new problems," he said. "How can I go on doing what I am doing? On the other hand, how can I get out of the mob?" He knew too much. To quit would cost him his life. The dilemma was driving him crazy. He had to think of his wife and child. He didn't know what to do. What he actually did was to go on an occasional "bender" to try to forget his problem.

I asked, "Are you sure you're saved?"

He assured me he was.

"How do you know you are saved?" I inquired.

He gave me an intelligent confession of faith.

"If you were to die, where would you go?"

He said, "Heaven."

"You're sure of that?"

"Yes, I am."

"Very well then," I told him, "you are in the same situation Jim Vaus was in when he was saved and decided to quit running with his gangster friends. You have no option but to quit. Tell your wife the truth, give her your money, and tell her to take your daughter somewhere far away where the two of them can hide. Then turn yourself in. Tell your Mafia boss that you have become a Christian. Tell him you're through. Tell him about Christ. Tell him you're going straight and you are going to follow the Lord even to prison or to death. If they kill you to silence you, you'll go to Heaven. If you really want to get out of organized crime, that's the way."

The mob buys silence with money or with murder. That believer had no choice but to refuse any offers of money and be ready to pay with his life. He had to take his stand on the side of the Lord and the law.

## I. Wise Words about Deity (29:25-26)

Bringing the Lord back into the picture, Solomon wrote, "The fear of man bringeth a snare: but whoso putteth his trust in the Lord shall be safe" (Proverbs 29:25). When we think about *the fear of man,* we picture Simon Peter denying Christ while warming his hands at the world's fire. We also picture Moses' first flight from Egypt.

Moses was still in Egypt when he made his decision for Christ, a decision that cost him the throne of Egypt. And we cannot help wondering how he broke the news to the Egyptian princess who had been a second mother to him, who had lavished such kindness on him, and who had cherished such great ambitions for him.

After the decision was made, he went to Goshen to visit his brethren. Concern for God's people is always a good sign of genuine conversion. "We know that we have passed from death unto life," said John, "because we love the brethren" (1 John 3:14). In Goshen Moses saw an Egyptian striking a Hebrew. Moses' blood boiled and he decided to strike a blow for God. Acting in the flesh, he killed the Egyptian and buried him in the sand. Moses had become a murderer with a price on his head. Within a day he had to flee Egypt.

Moses had handed the reigning pharaoh what he had been seeking for years: an excuse to kill a dangerous rival to the throne. And the pharaoh certainly couldn't afford to let Moses gain a foothold with the Hebrew slaves. With a strong leader they could become a menace to Egypt. So Moses was in danger. The fear of man was a snare indeed. It would be forty years before Moses the murderer could safely return as Moses the missionary.

"Moses feared," said the Holy Spirit, then "Moses fled" (Exodus 2:14-15). But the second time Moses left Egypt, he left by faith. We read in Hebrews 11:27, "By faith he forsook Egypt, not fearing the wrath of the king: for he endured, as seeing him who is invisible."

When Moses returned to Egypt forty years after his first flight, he was authorized by a divine mandate and armed with might and miracle. Thus he had no cause to fear the pharaoh. In fact Moses humbled him to the dust. Led by Moses, the children of Israel and the "mixed multitude"—some three million people altogether—left Egypt. They had spoiled the Egyptians and were marching to Canaan!

Then the Lord hardened the pharaoh's heart for the last time. Aghast at the mass exodus of so many slaves, he had second thoughts. He summoned his charioteers and the crack Egyptian cavalry and moved forward to recapture his slaves and recover their spoil. The Hebrews saw the Red Sea before them and the Egyptians behind them. Exodus 14:10 says, "the children of Israel lifted up their eyes, and, behold, the Egyptians marched after them; and they were sore afraid."

But Moses was not afraid! He knew that "the fear of man bringeth a snare: but whoso putteth his trust in the Lord shall be safe." The other children of Israel saw the visible king; Moses saw the invisible King. The other Israelites were walking by sight; he was walking by faith. He said: "Fear ye not, stand still, and see the salvation of the Lord....The Lord shall fight for you" (Exodus 14:13-14). And He did!

Believers face two great snares: the fear of man and the praise of man (John 5:44; 12:43). Like Moses, we should trust the Lord and be more concerned about securing God's approval than *the favor of monarchs:* "Many seek the ruler's favour; but every man's judgment cometh from the Lord" (Proverbs 29:26).

We should not be too eager to curry the favor of those in power. All too often they are prejudiced or preoccupied, looking out for their own interests. They may be completely biased and even when kindly disposed, they can make serious mistakes.

The partial failure of the Reformation can be traced to seeking the favor of monarchs. Martin Luther and other leaders of the Protestant movement were all too ready to lean on the arms of princes. A ruler's favor was often extended—but for a price. Too frequently the Roman church was replaced by a state church, which in time became just as oppressive.

The king's favor is a very uncertain commodity. His favor today can be replaced by his frown tomorrow. A king can promise much and give little, as Wolfgang Mozart discovered. All his life he had rich sponsors, and all his life he was poor. Of all composers, Mozart was the most complete genius. He loved opera, but poured out an incredible number of works for piano, voice, orchestra, and chamber groups. In addition he was a gifted pianist, violinist, and conductor. Off and on he was forced to teach in order to add to the pittance he received for his compositions.

Mozart's genius was recognized early. His musical education began when he was three or four. Soon he started composing short minuets. He made his debut at six, playing on a harpsichord. His sister Maria Anna, also a talented pianist, participated in his first tours, arranged by their father. All his tours were triumphs—Vienna in 1762 when he was six, Paris in 1763, London in 1764, and Italy in 1769. In Vienna the Austrian emperor Francis I called him his "little magician." When Mozart slipped on the polished floor in the imperial palace, Marie Antoinette (who later became the ill-fated queen of France) helped him up. Said the boy: "You are very kind. When I grow up, I will marry you." His improvisations and compositions and his ability to sight-read astounded everyone. In Italy he was decorated by the pope.

An incident that illustrated his genius took place in Rome. On Thursday of holy week Mozart heard the Sistine chapel choir sing *Miserere* by Gregorio Allegri. This composition was jealously guarded by the authorities; there was only one copy of the score and no one was permitted to make additional copies. But after Mozart heard the elaborate work performed, he went home and wrote out the whole nine-voice score from memory! He made only one mistake, which he corrected the next day, Good Friday, when he heard the composition performed again.

In 1771 at age fifteen Mozart returned to Salzburg to become the concertmaster of the archbishop's orchestra. The next year, however, the music-loving archbishop died and Mozart lost his position. Hieronymus, the new archbishop, cared little for music.

When Mozart was twenty-one years old, he went on a tour of Germany and France. He was looking for a position equal to his genius, but he had no success. In 1781 he finally received a commission to write an opera for the Munich carnival. He had barely settled down in Munich, however, when he was summoned back to Salzburg where the archbishop had decided he wanted a tame musician. But the archbishop heaped indignities on Mozart and forced him to eat at the servants' table, so he resigned. Once again Mozart was haunted by his lifelong curse: poverty.

Then Joseph II, emperor of Austria, commissioned him to write a comic-romantic opera, *The Abduction from the Seraglio.* It was performed in Vienna in 1782 and was an immediate success. Mozart, believing that at last he was about to have some good fortune, married. But marriage added another complication to his life: his wife, Constanze Weber, always seemed to need more money than her poor husband could give her.

The emperor commissioned another opera and Mozart produced another masterpiece: *The Marriage of Figaro.* Money only dribbled in. The emperor appointed Mozart court composer, but paid him only pennies. And so the pattern was established: Mozart made the music; others made the money. Symphonies, quartets, rondos, dances, and songs poured from his pen, and all the while this stupendous genius was fighting a losing battle against debt. At last the worry began to wear him down.

About this time he received a mysterious commission to write a requiem mass and a "command" commission to write an opera for the festivities to surround the coronation in Prague of Emperor

Leopold II as king of Bohemia. Mozart finished the opera, which he called *The Clemency of Titus,* but the work evidently did not make much of an impression when it was performed and the composer's situation worsened. He became ill with typhoid and began to suffer from illusions and fantasies. It seemed to him that the requiem he was composing was for his own death.

On December 4, 1791, he gave his pupil, Franz Süssmayr, instructions for the completion of the requiem. Then Mozart went to bed and died that night. He was given a pauper's funeral. Only a few friends attended it, and a sudden storm drove them away. His body was buried in an unmarked grave.

Few people have deserved recognition more than Mozart. He left behind him some five hundred compositions, twenty-one operas, twenty masses, forty-nine symphonies, sixty other orchestral works, seventeen piano sonatas, twenty-nine piano concertos, six violin concertos, forty-five violin sonatas, fifty other pieces of chamber music, and forty songs. He accomplished much in a very short time. He began to write music when he was five and he died when he was thirty-five.

Mozart died in poverty without the favor of monarchs, "but every man's judgment cometh from the Lord." There is a higher court. What matters in life is not the goodwill of the king, but the blessing and approval of God. It remains to be seen how Mozart will fare at the last great assize. History in the meantime has been kinder to Mozart than his contemporaries were. He has taken his place, in the minds of men, with music's chief immortals.

## J. Wise Words about Détente (29:27)

"An unjust man is an abomination to the just: and he that is upright in the way is abomination to the wicked."

During the cold war we heard a lot about détente, for many people thought that the communists and the capitalists should compromise and try to get along. Today we are urged to compromise on all kinds of issues. Solomon knew perfectly well, from long experience on the throne, that sometimes détente is impossible. The question is sometimes asked, What happens when an irresistible force meets an immovable object? But there is no such situation. Something always gives way.

In Proverbs 29:27 there is no common moral ground. The opposites presented are mutually exclusive. Détente is impossible. The godly man hates the lifestyle of the wicked man. The wicked man hates the lifestyle of the godly man. The religion of Cain was incompatible with the convictions of Abel. There was no way Elijah could make friends with Ahab. Herod and John the Baptist were irreconcilable. Jesus and the Pharisees stood for absolutely opposite principles. Saul of Tarsus and Stephen had nothing in common. Détente is a dream.

When détente between the Soviet Union and the United States was being touted as a way to end the cold war, a significant cartoon appeared in an American newspaper. In the center of the cartoon stood a cow being milked by the Soviet leader. The American president was shown coming to get his share with an empty pail. The Russian leader was depicted as saying, "You can have the front end!"

We are living in a world where God and Satan are at war. There can be no compromise between good and evil, right and wrong, truth and error. Some people say that the answers to a moral dilemma are not simply black or white. But often they are.

The conflict between good and evil is illustrated in Lew Wallace's book *Ben-Hur.* Near the beginning of the story, two young men are sitting together and are deep in conversation. One is a Roman, Messala. The other is a well-born Jew, Judah Ben-Hur. Once they had been friends. But Messala had spent five years in Rome; he finished his education there and when he returned to Jerusalem, he was proud, arrogant, and sure of himself. Now he was an officer in the administration of Valerius Gratus, the fourth imperial governor of Judea.

Judea was a troublesome province for Rome to rule and a full cohort of legionnaires had been added to the existing garrison so that the Roman yoke could be tightened. The new procurator was determined to stand for no nonsense and was quite prepared to make an example of the first person to offend.

"What it is to be a Jew!" Messala jibed. "All men and things, even heaven and earth, change; but a Jew never." He continued to sneer at all things Jewish. "What is your God," he demanded, "to our Roman Jove, who lends us his eagles that we may compass the universe with our arms?"

"We had better part," said Judah later in their exchange. "I wish I had not come. I sought a friend and find a———"

"Roman," replied Messala.[11]

By the end of the conversation Judah and Messala knew that they could never be friends again. From then on, Wallace's story was all black and white, with no shades of gray.

The first climax in the book came as the entourage of Valerius Gratus with full military escort made its way into the city. The route of the parade passed the Ben-Hur mansion, where Judah and his sister Tirzah watched from the flat roof. They were leaning on a parapet of tiles as they watched and just as the governor rode beneath them, a tile broke loose and crashed to the street below. The tile struck the new procurator and Judah was aghast.

The Romans thought that Judah was an assassin, and an armed guard led by Messala rushed into the house. Judah's mother and sister were marched away into oblivion and he was condemned to the galleys to toil away at the oars for the rest of his life. Messala stood aloof from their appeals. Indeed he enriched himself greatly at their expense by seizing his share of the spoils of the wealthy house of Ben-Hur. Messala's wickedness made him behave worse and worse toward a family that had done him no wrong. There was no détente for Messala and the Ben-Hurs.

Judah was a galley slave for three years. Then in a naval battle he saved the life of noble Quintus Arrius, a rich and powerful Roman senator. Arrius adopted the young Jew, trained him, taught him the arts of war, and made him his heir. Then, in the popular movie version, Ben-Hur's benefactor died and Judah, now a ranking Roman known as the son of Arrius, returned to Judea. He was determined to find his mother and sister and take revenge on the treacherous Messala.

Judah signed up for the famous chariot race in the circus at Antioch, a race in which Messala was the general favorite. An Arab sheik provided Judah with a chariot and a team of prize Arabian horses. Judah's agent goaded Messala into accepting a wager on the outcome of the race. The bet was deliberately calculated to ruin Messala financially if he were to lose. Judah won the race. His horsemanship and skill brought him great honor, while Messala's attempts to disable Judah's chariot backfired and left Messala himself a cripple for life.

But Messala won after all, or so it seemed (at least in the movie version), for he alone knew where Judah's loved ones were imprisoned and whether or not they were still alive. In spite of all of Judah's pleading, Messala hugged the secret to himself and carried it with him to an early grave. It was not until Pontius Pilate replaced Valerius Gratus that a clue to their whereabouts was found. Messala had put Judah's mother and sister in a dark, wretched hole and walled them in. During the long years of their terrible captivity they had become lepers. The Ben-Hur women had eventually been released from prison, but only to be condemned to a leper colony.

The final climax of Wallace's book, however, still lay ahead. The two lepers heard about Jesus of Nazareth and they managed to intercept Him as He came into the city. He responded to their woeful cry, "Have mercy upon us—mercy!"[12] Jesus healed Tirzah and her mother just as Judah, who was already attracted to the new Messiah, appeared on the scene.

The terrible conflicts, so obvious at every twist and turn of the tale, had a solution after all: Jesus! In Him both good and bad people can find their final peace.

# CONCLUSION

## Proverbs 30:1–31:31

# CONCLUSION (30:1–31:31)

There has been considerable discussion about the authorship of the last two chapters of Proverbs. After reviewing all the learned arguments, I still have the inescapable feeling that Solomon is the author. The topics of Proverbs 30 and 31 are the subjects that would have interested Solomon most of all: the ways of the wild and the ways of a woman. How like Solomon to study eagles, serpents, ants, conies, locusts, spiders, lions, goats, and hounds! How like Solomon to ponder the way of a man with a maid! (A king is able to command and demand everything but love.) Above all, Solomon would have been interested in a wife whose price is beyond the price of rubies. Surely Solomon would have penned a page or two about such subjects as these.

# CHAPTER 9

Proverbs 30:1–31:31

Conclusion (30:1–31:31)

- I. The Ideal Life (30:1-33)
  - A. Personal Limitations (30:1-4)
    - 1. A Look at His Life (30:1-3)
      - a. His Prophetic Call (30:1)
      - b. His Plain Confession (30:2-3)
    - 2. A Look at His Lord (30:4)
      - a. How Inexhaustible Is His Power (30:4a)
      - b. How Inscrutable Is His Person (30:4b)
  - B. Presumptuous Liabilities (30:5-10)
    - 1. A Look at One's Bible (30:5-6)
      - a. Don't Insult God's Word (30:5-6a)
        - (1) Its Purity (30:5a)
        - (2) Its Purpose (30:5b)
        - (3) Its Perfection (30:6a)
      - b. Don't Invite God's Wrath (30:6b)
    - 2. A Look at One's Bankbook (30:7-9)
      - a. The Request (30:7-8)
      - b. The Reason (30:9)
    - 3. A Look at One's Business (30:10)
  - C. Practical Lessons (30:11-33)
    - 1. A Prophetic Observation (30:11-14)
      - a. A Defiant Generation (30:11)
      - b. A Depraved Generation (30:12)
      - c. A Disdainful Generation (30:13)
      - d. A Dangerous Generation (30:14)
    - 2. A Parabolic Observation (30:15-31)
      - a. Four Insatiable Things (30:15-17)
        - (1) The Facts (30:15-16)

(2) The Footnote (30:17)
b. Four Inscrutable Things (30:18-19)
c. Four Intolerable Things (30:20-23)
d. Four Insignificant Things (30:24-28)
e. Four Invincible Things (30:29-31)
3. A Practical Observation (30:32-33)
a. The Wisdom of Silence (30:32)
b. The Way of Strife (30:33)
II. The Ideal Wife (31:1-31)
A. The Chapter and Its Author (31:1-9)
1. The Mother of the King (31:1-2)
2. The Morals of the King (31:3-9)
a. Beware of Women (31:3)
b. Beware of Wine (31:4-7)
(1) Its Dangers (31:4-5)
(2) Its Delusions (31:6-7)
c. Beware of Words (31:8-9)
(1) Be an Advocate for Those Who Cannot Speak Up for Themselves (31:8)
(2) Be an Advocate for Those Who Cannot Stand Up for Themselves (31:9)
B. The Chapter and Its Acrostic (31:10-31)
The Model Woman:
1. How Rare She Is (31:10)
2. How Restful She Is (31:11-12)
a. Her Love Is Sure (31:11)
b. Her Loyalty Is Sure (31:12)
3. How Resourceful She Is (31:13-15)
a. How She Busies Her Hands (31:13)
b. How She Buys Her Food (31:14)
c. How She Begins Her Day (31:15)
4. How Rich She Is (31:16-19)
a. How She Invests Her Money (31:16)
b. How She Insures Her Ministry (31:17)
c. How She Increases Her Means (31:18-19)
(1) The Quality of Her Merchandise (31:18)
(2) The Quantity of Her Merchandise (31:19)
5. How Responsive She Is (31:20)

6. How Ready She Is (31:21)
7. How Respected She Is (31:22-25)
    a. Her Personal Appearance (31:22)
    b. Her Public Applause (31:23)
    c. Her Popular Approval (31:24-25)
        (1) No Trouble Selling Her Merchandise (31:24)
        (2) No Trouble Settling Her Mind (31:25)
8. How Right She Is (31:26-27)
    a. In What She Says (31:26)
    b. In What She Sees (31:27)
        (1) She Oversees Each Servant (31:27a)
        (2) She Oversees Each Second (31:27b)
9. How Rewarded She Is (31:28)
10. How Renowned She Is (31:29-31)
    a. A Superlative Woman (31:29)
    b. A Spiritual Woman (31:30)
    c. A Splendid Woman (31:31)

## I. The Ideal Life (30:1-33)

### A. Personal Limitations (30:1-4)

#### 1. A Look at His Life (30:1-3)

Probably idealizing his own life, the author of the last two chapters of Proverbs began the passage with a bevy of names: "The words of Agur the son of Jakeh, even the prophecy: the man spake unto Ithiel, even unto Ithiel and Ucal" (30:1). According to the Talmud, "Solomon was called by six names: Solomon, Jedidiah [2 Samuel 12:25], Koheleth, Son of Jakeh, Agur, and Lemuel."[1] Apparently the names were allegorical. *Agur* meant "gatherer," or "convener," or "I shall fear." *Jakeh* meant "obedient" or "pious" and may have referred to David, Solomon's father.

"Agur the son of Jakeh" shared the proverbs in chapter 30 with Ithiel and Ucal. The speculation is that Ithiel and Ucal were two of the wise man's pupils. The name Ucal occurs only here in Scripture; the name Ithiel is also found among the Benjamites listed in Nehemiah 11:7. *Ithiel* means "God is with me" and *Ucal* means "I shall be able." The suggestion is that these names were symbolic of the moral character of those who receive divine instruction.

Agur declared that what he had to say was "prophecy." We note *his prophetic call* in Proverbs 30:1. The word translated "prophecy" here is the usual Old Testament word for an oracle or a burden—usually a solemn, prophetic announcement. Isaiah used the word frequently (see Isaiah 13:1; 15:1). We can look, therefore, for an element of the prophetic, as well as the proverbial, in the Bible passage we are exploring.

After mentioning his prophetic call, the wise man drew attention to *his plain confession:* "Surely I am more brutish than any man, and have not the understanding of a man" (Proverbs 30:2). This statement could reflect Solomon's humble view of himself when he first came to the throne and felt quite unequipped to guide the destiny of God's great people Israel; he confessed to the Lord, "I am but a little child" (1 Kings 3:7). Solomon may have written the proverbs in chapter 30 when he was still young and inexperienced. He certainly recognized his limitations at that time.

Most people, if they lived in the shadow of King David, would have inferiority complexes. David was a giant no matter how we look at him. His fame as the giant-killer was sung from one end of the country to the other. (Solomon knew that he could never do what David did in the valley of Elah.) David was a charismatic leader. Bold warriors risked their lives just to get him a drink of water. He was a poet (with the Hebrew hymnbook to his credit) and a capable musician. David was a born organizer and a gifted statesman. He transformed his country from a collection of squabbling tribes into a strong unified nation that surrounding nations soon learned to leave alone.

It is no wonder that Solomon, knowing his father's great qualities and gifts, keenly felt his own limitations. When he said, "I am more brutish than any man," he was indicating that he felt inferior to an educated man, for the Hebrew word translated "man" here is *'īsh,* which means "noble man." When Solomon added, "And have not the understanding of a man," he was indicating that he lacked even the good sense of an ordinary man, for the Hebrew word translated "man" here is *'ādām,* which means "common man." Of course Solomon's view of himself changed once he had a better grasp of kingdom affairs; he became accustomed to wielding power and realized his own great gifts.

So Solomon may have confessed his limitations when he first came to the throne. Another possibility is that he wrote Proverbs 30:2 in a sudden surge of humility after God made it clear to him that his follies would lead inevitably, after his death, to the division of the kingdom. The light in him had turned to darkness, and how great had been that darkness (Matthew 6:23)! Perhaps Solomon wrote all of the closing proverbs after he came back to his senses. Perhaps he wrote them about the same time that he wrote the book of Ecclesiastes—and in the same spirit.

Still in a humble frame of mind, Solomon added, "I neither learned wisdom, nor have the knowledge of the holy" (Proverbs 30:3). This verse may be a confession that the wisdom he possessed when he was in his prime was a direct gift from God and that all his insights came from that same divine source. In other words, his wisdom was not reasoned wisdom, but revealed wisdom.

Or perhaps the words "nor have the knowledge of the holy" refer to the abysmal folly of his multiple marriages to pagan women and his consequent descent into gross idolatry. His knowledge of the holy One had been eclipsed. Maybe Solomon uttered this sad confession of his practical ignorance of personal holiness after he groped his way back to God. Perhaps he was writing later on in life after repentance had done its work in his heart. Could it be that he hid his real name because of his shame?

### 2. A Look at His Lord (30:4)

Proverbs 30:4 is one of the great Christological passages of the Old Testament. The writer penned more than his mind understood. Peter had verses like this in mind when he spoke of the prophets' "searching what, or what manner of time the Spirit of Christ which was in them did signify, when it testified beforehand the sufferings of Christ, and the glory that should follow" (1 Peter 1:11).

Turning his gaze from himself to the Lord, Solomon reminded us of *how inexhaustible is His power:* "Who hath ascended up into heaven, or descended? who hath gathered the wind in his fists? who hath bound the waters in a garment? who hath established all the ends of the earth?" Then Solomon reminded us of *how inscrutable is His person:* "What is his name, and what is his son's name, if thou canst tell?" Who? What? These questions puzzled even Solomon.

The main points of Proverbs 30:4 could be listed as follows:

- The Redeemer (30:4a-b):
  - The One who ascended into Heaven (30:4a)
  - The One who descended into Hades (30:4b)

- The Ruler (30:4c-e):
  The Ruler of the wind (30:4c)
  The Ruler of the waves (30:4d)
  The Ruler of the world (4e)
- The Revealer (30:4f-g):
  The Jehovah of the Old Testament (30:4f)
  The Jesus of the New Testament (30:4g)

The above structural analysis reveals why Solomon was unable to answer his own questions. The answers do not lie within the scope of human reasoning, no matter how astute the reasoner may be. The answers lie within the scope of divine revelation. Only God can speak on such subjects.

When the wise man of Israel raised his questions, he had little more than the Pentateuch, a few additional historic writings, and the Psalms of David to guide him. But even all thirty-nine books of the Old Testament would not have sufficed. The twenty-seven books of the New Testament would have helped, but even if he had had all sixty-six books of the Bible, he would still have felt that much more remains to be revealed. Jesus said to His disciples, "I have yet many things to say unto you, but ye cannot bear them now" (John 16:12). Not until we cross Jordan and "know even as [we are] known" will we understand all the answers to Solomon's pointed questions (1 Corinthians 13:12).

Solomon wanted to know about the Redeemer who ascended into Heaven. We know who He is and Solomon might have known too if he had paid attention to Psalm 24, the great ascension Psalm.[2] However even with those magnificent stanzas before him, he would have needed Acts 2, Ephesians 1:19-23, and Ephesians 4:8-11 to help him understand the ascension.

The One who ascended into Heaven sits there now. Having rent the temple veil (of which Solomon was so proud), He sits at the right hand of the Majesty on high. In a battle-scarred human body, He sits on the throne of God. The One who ascended has every right to be there because He is God over all, blessed forevermore. He sits in Heaven as our Great High Priest, our "advocate with the Father, Jesus Christ the righteous" (1 John 2:1).

Solomon also wanted to know about the One who descended into Hades. The wise man was probing a mystery indeed. Jonah could have given him some insight, but at the time Solomon asked his question, Jonah had not even been born. Jonah 2:2 tells us that he cried "out of the belly of hell," but he would not have understood that he was a type of Christ in His death, burial, and resurrection.

To understand the mystery fully, Solomon would have needed to hear our Lord's commentary on Jonah as recorded in Matthew 12:38-41 and to read 1 Peter 3:18-22.

When the Lord died on the cross, He commended His spirit into the hands of His Father. His body was reverently entombed and miraculously preserved from corruption, but His soul descended into Hades. Solomon did not have the benefit of Luke's Gospel, but Luke 16:19-31 helps us understand about Hades and how it was divided into two areas. It seems that after His death the Lord descended into the realm of the underworld and there proclaimed the tidings of Calvary. To those in the "place of torment" (16:28) His message was one of hopeless doom; to those in "Abraham's bosom" (16:22) His message was one of "joy unspeakable and full of glory" (1 Peter 1:8). In the New Testament some light is shed on darkness, but we will not fully understand the mystery until the rapture.

Solomon also asked about the Ruler of the wind. "Who hath gathered the wind in his fists?" the wise man demanded. We all know how capricious the wind is. Jesus said to Nicodemus, "The wind bloweth where it listeth, and thou hearest the sound thereof, but canst not tell whence it cometh, and whither it goeth" (John 3:8). We may know more about the wind and its ways today, but we certainly cannot control it. We cannot gather it as men gather the reins of a team of horses. We can fly our weather planes into the eye of a hurricane, but we cannot diminish its force or change its direction. We can describe the weather patterns that are the nurseries of tornadoes, but we cannot diminish their tantrums.

There is One however who holds the wind in His hands. When Jonah ran away to escape going to Nineveh, He summoned the stormy wind and hurled it down the sea lanes of the Mediterranean in pursuit of the disobedient prophet. That wild wind wrought His will. Jonah confessed his guilt and was thrown overboard. Then the One who had sent the wild wind gathered the screaming gale into His fists and reined it in.

Solomon wanted to know too about the Ruler of the waves. "Who hath bound the waters in a garment?" he asked. We know the answer and today we sing of that Ruler in the sailor's hymn:

> Eternal Father, strong to save,
> Whose arm hath bound the restless wave,
> Who bids the mighty ocean deep
> Its own appointed limits keep.[3]

Although Solomon had a great navy of Tarshish ships, he was essentially a landsman. The Hebrews, who relied on the Phoenicians for their ships and sailors, were never fond of the sea. As for mopping up its tides with a towel, that was just poetry! Solomon, however, might have answered his own question, had he tried, for he certainly knew about Noah. The wise man knew who broke up "the fountains of the great deep" (Genesis 7:11). Solomon knew who summoned the waves to do His will in a wicked world and afterward sent the sea back to its bed.

Solomon also wanted to know about the Ruler of the world. "Who hath established all the ends of the earth?" he asked. He knew that north of Jerusalem were Syria and Assyria and he may have had some hazy knowledge of the more distant Scythia and the lands of Mesheck, Tubal, and Magog. But beyond them, everything was a blur. Solomon knew that south of Jerusalem were Egypt, the Nile, and Sheba. The queen of Sheba had visited him. But he wondered about the source of the other Nile, the "White" Nile, that began even farther south. Solomon knew that east of Jerusalem were the Arabian desert and Babylon. Beyond that was Persia and beyond that was India. But when his thoughts reached farther east, they were swallowed up in the misty mountains and eternal snows of fabled lands. Solomon knew that west of Jerusalem was what the Hebrews called "the great sea." Hiram's sailors no doubt told him of long coastlines, barbarous peoples, and sea lanes narrowing where the sun set. Beyond that was only the sea. The sailors had turned northward to Tarshish and had traded with wild folk on a vast island. But when the sailors continued westward, day after day there was only the sea; at last they grew fearful and headed home.

But Solomon probably thought: *There must be more to the world than I know. Land and sea do not simply fade out—north, south, east, and west. Just where are the ends of the earth? Who has established them?*

Of course Solomon had the book of Job and could have read Job 26:7, which implies that the earth has no ends—that it is a sphere hung in space. And the wise man could have learned from Job 38:4-6 that the measurements of the earth are all known to God. Solomon's father could have told him that the Lord was the real answer to his question (Psalm 139:7-10).

Today we have many of the answers that Solomon sought. We have circumnavigated the globe and put a compass on "the ends of the earth." We know the diameter of our planet; we know its weight, composition, and movements in space. We know all these facts with mathematical certainty. However with all our learning we have only enlarged the field of inquiry and raised other questions and greater imponderables. Now we want to know about space and how vast *it* is. Actually we have as many unanswered questions as Solomon had. Our questions make us realize our own littleness and the Lord's immeasurable greatness, for He knows all the answers.

Finally Solomon wanted to know about the Revealer. "What is his name?" the wise man asked. In the Old Testament God revealed much about Himself by means of His names. The greatest of all His names, the name above all other names, was the name *Jehovah.* This name embraces the past, present, and future and reveals its owner to be the eternal One.

Surely Solomon had not neglected to read Psalm 23. Surely he had memorized it when he was a boy. Surely he knew that the significance of at least five of the Jehovah compound names is reflected in that short Davidic Psalm: Jehovah-Jireh, Jehovah-Shalom, Jehovah-Tsidkenu, Jehovah-Nissi, and Jehovah-Shammah. Surely he was familiar with the Jehovah-Sabaoth title used by David in Psalm 24:10.

How could Solomon have forgotten Jehovah's name? We know that he did. Otherwise he would never have gone after Ashtoreth, Milcolm, and Chemosh, to name but a few of the other gods he honored (1 Kings 11:4-8). What a doddering old fool Solomon must have become if he had to ask the name of the Creator of all time, matter, and space!

"What is his son's name, if thou canst tell?" Solomon also asked. At least he had enough wisdom left to know that God has a Son. Psalm 2 would have reminded him of that fact. Solomon can be excused for not knowing the great and glorious titles Isaiah gave to God's Son in anticipation of the incarnation (Isaiah 9:6) since Isaiah was born after Solomon died.

It was not until New Testament times that the name of God's Son was finally revealed. The angel said to Joseph, "Thou shalt call his name Jesus: for he shall save his people from their sins" (Matthew 1:21). The Jehovah of the Old Testament is the Jesus of the New Testament—and that name is the greatest and most glorious of all the names for God. We celebrate that name in many hymns; for example we sing:

Jesus! the name that charms our fears,
That bids our sorrows cease,
'Tis music in the sinner's ear,
'Tis life and health and peace.[4]

Solomon could not have known the name *Jesus,* but surely he knows it now! We can forgive him for forgetting the name *Jehovah,* for have we not often forgotten the name of Jesus? Surely if we had only remembered that name, we would not have said and done some of the things we said and did during our own backsliding.

## B. Presumptuous Liabilities (30:5-10)

### 1. A Look at One's Bible (30:5-6)

Solomon offered words of warning to all Romanists, liberals, Mormons, and cultists who tamper with the Word of God. As he spoke of its purity, purpose, and perfection, he was saying in effect, *"Don't insult God's Word."*

Referring to *its purity,* Solomon said, "Every word of God is pure" (Proverbs 30:5a). The Hebrew term translated "pure" here means "tried in a furnace" and thus describes something that has no alloy in it. Pure gold is solid gold, through and through. The Hebrew term rendered "word" here is *'imrah,* which means "saying or utterance." The Hebrew term rendered "God" here is *Eloah. 'Imrah* and *Eloah* are used only in this verse in Proverbs. When Solomon wrote Proverbs 30:5a, he may have had in mind a saying of his father David: "The words of the Lord are pure words: as silver tried in a furnace of earth, purified seven times" (Psalm 12:6).

Years ago my friend Stan Ford visited a gold mine in South Africa. Watching the refiners at work, he saw them heat the ore in a furnace, skim off the dross, and repeat the process again and again until only pure gold was left. The pure gold was then taken to the assayer, who put it in the fire. Stan asked the tour guide if this step was another part of the refining process. The guide said, "Oh, no! The gold has already been refined. The work of the assayer is not to refine the gold any further, but to prove that it is already fully refined."

We can put God's Word to the test. We can study it as a whole or study its individual parts. We can examine its books, its chapters, its verses, its words, and every jot and tittle of its letters. They are all pure gold. The original autographed documents were God-breathed—as perfect as God is perfect, as pure as God is pure. If we test the precepts, principles, and prophecies of the Word of God, they will prove to be without alloy. When we examine the histories, laws, and progressive unfolding of truth in the Bible, we find that the Book is inerrant, infallible, inspired, inimitable, and infinite. It is the Word of God.

The Bible deals firmly and frankly with sin in all its forms, but it never defiles. It exposes and condemns, but it never dwells on details; it never invites the foul mind of man to wallow in the mire. The Bible breathes a spirit of sanctity, of absolute holiness, even when dealing with the most unholy activities of fallen men and women. Its approach to human sin is not that of Hollywood.

There are no impure stories in the Bible. The Song of Solomon has been labeled as such by enemies of the Word of God, but in their attacks they are really only exposing their own impurity. No loftier book has ever been written. It is a magnificent story, portraying the chastity of the Shulamite, her fidelity to her beloved, and her unassailable integrity. In all its parts the Song of Solomon points to Christ and His church.[5]

Proverbs 30:5 continues to draw our attention to the Word of God and refers to *its purpose:* to introduce us to the One who "is a shield unto them that put their trust in [flee for refuge to] him" (30:5b). The great purpose of the Spirit of God is to use the Word of God to bring us to the Son of God, who imparts to us the salvation of God. The Bible, wise and wonderful as it is, does not save us. It directs us to One who can. It is impossible to separate the inspired Word of God from the incarnate Word of God (John 1:1,14). From Genesis 1 to Revelation 22, the whole Bible points to Him.

Having referred to the purity and purpose of the Word of God, Solomon pointed to *its perfection:* "Add thou not unto his words" (Proverbs 30:6a). God of course can add to His own words. Indeed He kept on doing so until the Old and New Testament canons were complete. Then He closed the Book firmly and finally.

Solomon's advice was not to tamper with the Word of God, "lest he reprove thee, and thou be found a liar" (Proverbs 30:6b). The wise man was saying in effect, *"Don't invite God's wrath."* The word translated "reprove" here is emphatic and means "to send a special reproof." God will not permit people to alter His Word with impunity.

Similar warnings are given elsewhere in the Bible. For example Moses wrote in his memoirs:

> Now therefore hearken, O Israel, unto the statutes and unto the judgments, which I teach you, for to do them....Ye shall not add unto the word which I command you, neither shall ye diminish ought from it, that ye may keep the commandments

> of the Lord your God which I command you (Deuteronomy 4:1-2).

Although this warning was repeated by Moses a little later (Deuteronomy 12:32), the rabbis added their traditions to the Word of God. The scribes who copied the Scriptures performed this legitimate task admirably. However, the rabbis instructed the scribes to append a host of rabbinical interpretations and rulings, which in effect replaced the Scriptures altogether.[6] The Lord Jesus roundly condemned the Jews for their traditions and thus incurred the active enmity of the rabbis, the scribes, and the Pharisees (Matthew 15:1-14; 23:1-39).

The final warning against tampering with God's Word is recorded in Revelation 22:18-19:

> If any man shall add unto these things, God shall add unto him the plagues that are written in this book: And if any man shall take away from the words of the book of this prophecy, God shall take away his part out of the book of life, and out of the holy city, and from the things which are written in this book.

When John, the last of the apostles (and therefore the last person able to write Scripture), wrote these words, the gnostics were already adding to and subtracting from the Word of God. The Roman church has since added its traditions and the ex cathedra pronouncements of its popes to the Word of God. The Mormons have added the nonsense concocted by Joseph Smith in *The Book of Mormon.* The so-called Christian Scientists have added the writings of Mary Baker Eddy. The Spiritists have added pronouncements derived from demons. The liberals, on the other hand, have specialized in deleting great portions of Scripture. And so the tampering goes on, in spite of the warnings. In the end God will settle His own accounts with those He bluntly labeled "liars."

### 2. A Look at One's Bankbook (30:7-9)

In these three verses Solomon made a request and then explained the reason for his request. We note first *the request:* "Two things have I required of thee; deny me them not before I die: Remove far from me vanity and lies: give me neither poverty nor riches; feed me with food convenient for me" (Proverbs 30:7-8). Then we note *the reason:* "Lest I be full, and deny thee, and say, Who is the Lord? or lest I be poor, and steal, and take the name of my God in vain" (30:9).

What an interesting, inspired, and instructive request! If you could make a list of all the things you would like God to do for you, what would you ask for? We would only need to analyze the majority of our own and other people's prayers to develop a typical list. Common requests would be health and healing, a better job, a more understanding employer, a marriage partner, better behaved children, a newer car, a nicer home. We could take care of most of our own requests by using the advertisement pages in big-city newspapers. It is noteworthy that the prayers in the New Testament Epistles contain almost none of the requests commonly made in church prayer meetings.

Solomon had reduced his list to two items, one dealing with the moral side of life and the other dealing with the material side of life.

Dealing with the moral side, he prayed, "Remove far from me vanity and lies." "Vanity and lies" are the two great primeval sins, the original sins of Satan. They are utterly destructive of character, life, and society. These sins are at the root of all other sins. Vanity made Lucifer aspire to the throne of God (Isaiah 14:12-17; Ezekiel 28:11-19). Among his first recorded utterances was a lie (Genesis 3:1-5). So Solomon was really praying that he would be kept from the influence of Satan. Satan appealed to Eve's vanity (he promised her she would be like God) and stuffed her ears with lies, and she sinned. Human beings have been susceptible to vanity and lies ever since.

Dealing with the material side of life, Solomon prayed, "Give me neither poverty nor riches." This prayer reflects the mature wisdom of Solomon's later years. He had come back from the paths of worldliness and wickedness he had trodden so long.

Probably Solomon never knew poverty firsthand, but he had certainly seen its effects in other people's lives. The deceitfulness of riches he knew only too well. The book of Ecclesiastes contains many of his comments about the folly of thinking that mere things can satisfy the hunger of the human heart.

The reason for Solomon's prayer was the peril of riches. The Laodicean church, which was exposed to the danger, boasted, "I am rich, and increased with goods, and have need of nothing" (Revelation 3:17). It had its money, its methods, and its "ministry" and did not see its need for Christ. It is not at all surprising that we find the Lord outside the Laodicean church (3:20).

The classic Biblical example of the peril of riches is seen in the story of the pharaoh who resisted Moses' entreaties. The pharaoh had everything that this world could offer. Moses knew all about the treasures of Egypt. They had been offered to him once, but he had renounced them (Hebrews 11:24-26). When Moses returned to Egypt he stood before the man who had eagerly picked up what he had so deliberately thrown away. Moses stood before the pharaoh as an ambassador from the throne of God, who had armed him with awesome credentials and backed him with invincible power.

In the throne room of Egypt, Moses was surrounded with evidence of wealth and splendor. The pharaohs filled their tombs with gorgeous accouterments and enormous riches, and they lived in even greater opulence. Moses looked about the pharaoh's resplendent audience-chamber—he had known the place since he was a little boy. But Moses coveted none of the treasures of Egypt, for he knew their true value. They were worthless and since they blinded people to the real world, they were also dangerous.

The pharaoh looked around him and exulted in what he saw. The opulence spoke to him of luxury, magnificence, and power. No doubt when he looked at Moses, who was dressed like a shepherd and armed with a stick, he laughed out loud. And when Moses delivered his message—"Thus saith the Lord God of Israel, Let my people go"—the pharaoh said, "Who is the Lord, that I should obey his voice to let Israel go? I know not the Lord, neither will I let Israel go" (Exodus 5:1-2). Just as Solomon said, the peril of riches is that the "full" person may deny the Lord.

The peril of rags is just as real. The poor person may steal and take the name of the Lord in vain. The rich man and the poor man both end up cursing God if they are not careful.

The unjust steward in Luke 16:1-13 was a thief. Although he was clever, he was found out and his lord sent in the auditors. The results of the audit were wholly unsatisfactory and the steward was charged with fraud. He was about to be fired, and he knew it. He was about to go from riches to rags.

Although he was frightened by the prospect of poverty, the steward was *averse to doing* anything that savored of really hard work. He said, "I cannot dig" (16:3). He was *ashamed of doing* what the beggars did. He recoiled in horror at the idea of holding out a cup as he sat at a temple gate. Never would he whine for alms! We note what he was *accustomed to doing*. He was an old hand at stealing. He did not burglarize houses or waylay people traveling from Jerusalem to Jericho. The steward was a white-collar thief, a corporate bandit who juggled accounts and manipulated people.

So, true to form, before he appeared before his lord to answer the charges, he did what he always did. He stole. The steward called in his lord's debtors and gave them enormous discounts on what they owed. He hoped that they would show their gratitude by opening their doors to him after he was fired. We are not told that he took the name of God in vain, but we can be quite sure that if the palms he so judiciously greased proved ungrateful—if the doors of the beneficiaries of his duplicity remained closed when he came calling and he was reduced to digging or begging—he would be quite capable of cursing the name of God.

### 3. A Look at One's Business (30:10)

"Accuse not a servant unto his master, lest he curse thee, and thou be found guilty." If Solomon had used today's vernacular, he would have said, "Mind your own business."

A modern proverb says, "People who live in glass houses should not throw stones." One day the tables may be turned. The person we accuse today, rightly or wrongly, may be in a position to bring countercharges against us later on. Most people have secret guilt that they would not want anyone to expose.

The classic Biblical example of tables being turned is found in the story of Joseph and Potiphar. Potiphar, a member of the pharaoh's bodyguard, purchased Joseph as a slave. Joseph soon proved his worth and before long Potiphar entrusted him with the management of his entire estate. Then Potiphar's wife entered the picture. She was a wicked woman full of lusts and wiles. When Joseph rejected her advances, she was venomous and vindictive, falsely accusing him of making improper advances. Joseph was lucky to escape with his life. Potiphar flung him into prison, where he spent years paying for a crime he never committed.

Then came his release and his spectacular promotion to the position of grand vizier. The pharaoh gave him authority to enforce emergency regulations throughout Egypt. Joseph now had both Potiphar and Potiphar's wife in his power. A lesser man would have broken up the pair and demonstrated the truth of Proverbs 30:10. Instead Joseph quietly let the matter drop. But we can imagine that Potiphar's wife especially must have trembled and walked softly for a long time.

## C. Practical Lessons (30:11-33)

### 1. A Prophetic Observation (30:11-14)

There is little doubt that these four verses, with their repetition of the phrase "There is a generation," are prophetic. Indeed

Proverbs 30 begins with an indication that the chapter embodies prophecy. Verses 11-14 in particular speak of a coming generation that will manifest terrible features.

The prophetic focus of Proverbs 30:11-14 is sharpened in the Gospels. The Lord Jesus, who said of Himself that "a greater than Solomon is here" (Matthew 12:42), made the prophecy clear. Using the expression "this generation," he referred to two different generations: the generation that would crucify Him (see Matthew 23:36); and the generation that would crown the antichrist (see Matthew 24:34). In both references a literal generation is in view: people living at a specific time and acting in a specific way. The phrase "this generation" occurs sixteen times in the Gospels; in addition phrases such as "wicked generation" and "perverse generation" occur nine times in the Gospels and Acts.

Let us consider the Lord's teaching regarding two evil generations. His public ministry, as recorded by Matthew, began with eight beatitudes and ended with eight curses (5:1-12; 23:1-39). He exposed and cursed the nation's leaders (Matthew 23) just before He gave His prophetic Olivet discourse (Matthew 24–25). In Matthew 23 He put His unerring finger on what those leaders sought, what they taught, what they wrought, and what they thought. One after another, His ominous curses sounded out like a death knell:

> Woe unto you, scribes and Pharisees, hypocrites!...Ye serpents, ye generation of vipers, how can ye escape the damnation of hell? Wherefore, behold, I send unto you prophets, and wise men, and scribes: and some of them ye shall kill and crucify; and some of them shall ye scourge in your synagogues, and persecute them from city to city (Matthew 23:13,33-34).

These words were of course fulfilled. As the Gospels tell us, the Jewish leaders rejected the ministry of the Son of God, and as the book of Acts tells us, they rejected the ministry of the Spirit of God. The Jews of the homeland and then the Jews of the diaspora turned solidly against the gospel.

There was, however, more to the curse. The Lord continued, "That upon you may come all the righteous blood shed upon the earth, from the blood of righteous Abel unto the blood of Zacharias son of Barachias, whom ye slew between the temple and the altar" (Matthew 23:35). The Jews were about to murder their Messiah, so the Lord drew their attention to two Old Testament martyrs, Abel and Zacharias. They were the first and the last martyrs of the Jewish

Bible. The Lord told the Jews in effect that the crime they were about to commit was so horrendous that if God were to take all the innocent blood shed in the entire Old Testament period and heap that blood on the heads of the Jews of His day, they would be less guilty than they already were because of the crime they were contemplating.

Then Jesus added this: "Verily I say unto you, All these things shall come upon this generation" (Matthew 23:36). He was speaking to and about his own generation. Immediately He went on to describe the impending destruction of Jerusalem. He clearly foresaw this disaster with all its attending horrors. Some of the people who were living when the Lord gave His terrible prophecy were still alive when it was fulfilled. In A.D. 70 the Romans destroyed the city and the temple and in A.D. 135, at the time of the Bar Kokhba rebellion, they banished all remaining Jews from the country and changed its name to Palestine in honor of the Philistines, the hereditary enemies of the Jews.

In Matthew's account the curses are followed by the famous Olivet discourse, which refers to a different generation and foretells end-time events in fascinating detail. In this discourse the Lord said to watch the fig tree, a symbol of the nation of Israel under the curse of God and scattered among the nations. When the fig tree puts forth its leaves, we know that summer is near (Matthew 24:32). Likewise when Israel comes back to life as a nation, we will know that a change of dispensations is coming soon. The rapture of the church, the ruin of the world, the restoration of Israel, and the return and reign of Christ are all near!

The Lord added in Matthew 24:34, "Verily I say unto you, This generation [the same expression as in 23:36 and so still indicating a literal generation] shall not pass, till all these things [begin to be] fulfilled." Obviously, in 24:34 "this generation" does not refer to the generation *to* which He was speaking, for that generation has long since passed away. "This generation" refers to the generation *of* which He was speaking, the generation that would witness the budding of the fig tree and the rebirth of the state of Israel.[7]

We do not know how long a period the end-time generation encompasses. The Lord deliberately chose a vague measure of time to discourage date-setting. In Matthew 23 the generation to which He was speaking lasted from A.D. 33 to A.D. 135.

The end-time generation of Matthew 24:34, which surely has to be our generation, is the generation that Solomon prophetically described in Proverbs 30. We can now fill in the details of the description.

Proverbs 30:11 tells us it is *a defiant generation:* "There is a generation that curseth their father, and doth not bless their mother." In other words, the end-time generation will be void of natural affection and defiant of parental authority. Ultimately they will be defiant of all authority.

*Time* magazine described the young people growing up in America today as a remorseless generation. At the time the magazine article was written, more than half of all serious crimes in America were being committed by youths aged ten to seventeen. "Many youngsters appear to be robbing and raping, maiming and murdering as casually as they go to a movie or join a pickup baseball game," the journalist said.[8] America's big-city schools have become dangerous places. In one year the FBI reported assaults on seventy thousand teachers. Gang members seem to abandon their consciences. A prospective member of one girls' gang cannot be initiated until she furnishes evidence that she has injured someone.[9] Such a generation will be ripe for the antichrist.

Proverbs 30:12 describes our generation as *a depraved generation:* "There is a generation that are pure in their own eyes, and yet is not washed from their filthiness." This generation is devoid of moral standards and contemptuous of traditional and spiritual values. We should not be surprised. In the United States the Bible has been effectively banned from the classroom for years. The ten commandments are not only ignored; they are not even countenanced in public schools. Liberal and humanistic views on sex, relative morality, criminal rights, and permissiveness are now openly taught instead of Biblical ethics and morality.

At home parents have to compete with television. Hollywood, which is notoriously anti-God, pro-sex, and pro-violence, sets the nation's behavioral norms. In most American families, television has become the dominating force in shaping the thinking and moral values of young people. By the time a typical youth reaches age eighteen, he has watched twenty-two thousand hours of dubious, dirty, and dangerous television. Far worse than the offerings of regular network and cable television channels are the pornographic offerings of movie channels. Many parents subscribe to these channels and allow their youngsters to be exposed to systematic sex, bad language, violence, and other filth.

No wonder one quarter of all fifteen-year-olds in the United States have had sexual relations, one tenth of all thirteen-year-olds have experimented with sex, and more than half of all high school students have used marijuana. The drug tide is reaching into junior high and elementary schools. In the cities adolescents—

some as young as twelve and thirteen—are joining the ranks of streetwalkers.

This generation may be pure in its own eyes, but it certainly is not washed from its filthiness. The foulest perversions are accepted by society as alternative lifestyles. People addicted to sodomy and bestiality march, chant, wave flags, and demand their rights. The church is affected too. Some denominations have capitulated entirely and have ordained practicing homosexuals and lesbians to "the ministry."

Proverbs 30:13 describes the end-time generation as *a disdainful generation:* "There is a generation, O how lofty are their eyes! and their eyelids are lifted up." This supercilious, scornful generation is marked by haughty pride.

Few people have been more utterly disdainful of the establishment, morality, common decency, and God than John Winston Lennon. A member of the music group known as "The Beatles," Lennon was a teen idol. He and his partners sold hundreds of millions of records that paved the way for the wholesale degeneration of modern society.

Lennon once boasted that he and his friends were more popular than Jesus Christ. He was admired by millions as a spokesman for nonviolence, yet according to his child's mother, he kicked the helpless infant when the baby's crying got on his nerves. One British newspaper *(Daily Express),* reviewing his life at the time of his death, said that Lennon was born angry, grew up foul-mouthed, was promiscuous, and used drugs recklessly—progressing all the way to heroin addiction.

Even so, Lennon was idolized. When he died the outpouring of grief was global. A few people even committed suicide. A candlelight celebration of his spirit was held in Los Angeles and mourners jammed the Lincoln memorial in Washington to chant his praise. A generation disdainful of God, the Lord Jesus, and the Bible, offered worship to this evil man.

Proverbs 30:14 describes our generation as *a dangerous generation:* "There is a generation, whose teeth are as swords, and their jaw teeth as knives, to devour the poor from off the earth, and the needy from among men." *Time* magazine said, "It takes a diligent search through history to discover another society that has been as vulnerable to its youthful predators."[10]

The more than 360 gangs in Los Angeles have a combined membership running into the tens of thousands. Some cities have become so dangerous that one bank actually offered cans of mace to its new depositors. On an even larger scale, our generation is plagued by syndicated violent crime and by international terrorists who will stop at nothing.

Soon the antichrist will appear. Like an international pied piper he will draw the terminal generation to himself. People will be attracted by his charisma, his power, his ability, and his absolute dedication to all sin. The evidence all seems to point in the same direction: the generation foreseen by Solomon and Christ appears to be our generation.

### 2. A Parabolic Observation (30:15-31)

#### a. Four Insatiable Things (30:15-17)

##### (1) The Facts (30:15-16)

Before Solomon gave us a fourfold picture of insatiable appetite, he mentioned a creature called the horseleach. The four insatiable things have something in common with this odious creature: they all sap away at life and demand more and more. They take everything and give nothing in return.

But what is a horseleach?[11] (The Hebrew word is *alukah.*) A particularly unlovely creature, the horseleach lurks in ponds and streams and awaits the arrival of an unwary horse. The horseleach then fastens itself on the horse's lip or nostril, crawls inside the nose or mouth, and grows rapidly, causing bleeding and obstruction.

Some scholars are not sure that "horseleach" is the best rendering of the Hebrew word. Gesenius, probably the greatest of all Hebrew scholars, suggested that *alukah* means "vampire." The Revised Version actually gives "vampire" as an alternate translation. Vampire legends were quite common in Assyria, Babylon, Palestine, and the Middle East. In the stories the vampire is a bloodsucking monster from the grave. The vampire is supposed to be the soul of a criminal, heretic, or suicide who leaves his grave at night to prey on the living by sucking their blood.

No one today puts much credence in such stories, but behind the legends is a real *alukah* lurking in the shadows. That fearful predator is Satan. He sees the human race as his legitimate prey. Like the *alukah* of Proverbs 30:15 he has two daughters: we know them as sin and death. Satan's desire is to suck every last vestige of joy, love, holiness, life, peace, and happiness out of human beings and then spit into the wound the venom of his malice, fear, misery, guilt, and shame.

Solomon showed Satan at work *where life terminates:* "Four things say not, It is enough: The grave..." (Proverbs 30:15-16). There were no graves on this lovely planet until that dread vampire flew out of the dark and dead places of the universe into Eden. He came to fasten himself on our first parents, poison them, and make them a prey to death. Satan derives great satisfaction from seeing people die. The more painful and horrifying their deaths, the more he gloats.

We see this characteristic of Satan in C. S. Lewis's classic *The Screwtape Letters.* This book contains a series of imaginary letters written by Screwtape, a senior devil, to Wormwood, a junior devil who is being instructed in the art of temptation. The subject of war comes up in one of these letters. Wormwood, it seems, was delighted because war had broken out in Europe. Screwtape accused him of being drunk and wrote, "For the first time in your career you have tasted that wine which is the reward of all our labors—the anguish and bewilderment of a human soul—and it has gone to your head."[12] The demons found war entertaining, but causing fear and suffering was not their most rewarding task. If they could make sure human beings landed in Hell, Screwtape said, their misery could be enjoyed forever.

So Satan operates where life terminates. The grave never has enough because the old vampire never has enough. "Ye shall not surely die," he said to Eve as he tried to conceal his fangs and the drool of a warped and eager appetite (Genesis 3:4).

As soon as sin entered the world, death entered. Cain murdered Abel. Then came the roll call of Genesis 5 and the endless tolling of the bell: "He died...he died..." The holocaust of the flood followed and then the overthrow of Sodom and Gomorrah. Death after death crowds the book of Genesis until its very last words are "a coffin in Egypt." Always the vampire is there, gloating over death.

Next Solomon showed Satan at work *where life originates:* "Four things say not, It is enough:...the barren womb." The spoiler lurks at the tomb and near the womb!

Solomon had observed the barren woman. He had seen the look of inconsolable disappointment over having no child. The vampire was at work, partly out of malicious spite and in Old Testament times partly out of a desire to prevent the birth of Christ. One after another, the wives of the patriarchs were barren. For a long time Sarah was barren, Rebekah was barren, and Rachel was barren. In Rachel's case the vampire made a mistake. He should have attacked Leah, for it was Leah who bore Judah! Satan made a mistake with Tamar too. He discovered too late that she was to be in the

Messianic line—he tried too late to have her murdered before that all-important boy could be born. So we see the *alukah* at work where life originates.

But Satan was unsuccessful in his attempts to prevent the birth of Christ. Christ came! He conquered, He ascended on high, and the Holy Spirit came to take His place. So now the vampire works where life originates in a different way: in the barren soul, in the barren saint, and in the barren sanctuary.

Consider first the barren soul. People are born into this world spiritually dead. However, deep down in the human soul is a place where spiritual life originates, the place to which the Holy Spirit comes and where strange stirrings and longings are born. To the human soul come a conviction of sin, an awareness of God, a revelation of His Son, a knowledge of salvation, and a realization that a new birth is needed and possible. The Holy Spirit reveals the nature of sin, the need for righteousness, and the nearness of judgment. The pleasures and pursuits of this life lose their appeal.

But whenever the barren soul first feels these stirrings of life, the vampire appears. He is there to kill and to destroy. Satan, the horseleach, comes to spoil. We learn from the parable of the sower that the birds (evil spirits) come to snatch away the seed. If that attack fails, then the thorns and thistles try to choke the seed.

Consider next the barren saint. The vampire has been foiled. New life in Christ has begun; the miracle of regeneration has taken place; a person has been born into the family of God. But when life springs up, Satan goes to work to prevent that new life from spreading to others.

When Paul was under house arrest at Rome, he had high hopes for a promising young man named Demas and mentioned him along with other "fellowlabourers" in two of his letters (Colossians 4:14; Philemon 24). Demas seems to have been well known in the church at Colossae. One of Paul's disciples, he had the makings of another Titus or Timothy or Luke. Then the vampire came. He went to work where life originates—where a passion for souls is born—and sucked the life out of Demas. Satan could not steal the spiritual life God had given to Demas, but he did steal the fruitful life God had in mind for him.

When Paul was back in prison he wrote, "Demas hath forsaken me, having loved this present world" (2 Timothy 4:10). What poison did the *alukah* use with Demas? Was it fear of persecution, an entanglement with a woman, or the offer of a well-paying pastorate in a liberal, gnostic church? One way or another, Satan rendered Demas useless.

Consider too the barren sanctuary. The church is another place where life originates; it is God's great instrument for getting things done on earth. Every local church is intended to be first a maternity ward, then a nursery, then a school, and then a base of military operations. Every local church is intended to be the birthplace of souls—a place where the lost are led to the Lord, put under His blood, brought through the water, gathered around the table in the wilderness, taken to Sinai, given bread from Heaven and water from the riven Rock, taught to slay Amalek, brought to Kadesh, and taken across Jordan to live in victory in Canaan.

Satan hates a church that is a place where life originates. So he goes to work, trying to sow discord. He sidetracks the church into programs. He puts carnal deacons on the board, worldly teachers in the Sunday school, and backslidden singers in the choir. He attacks the pastor by trying to get him involved in politics, taken up with a social cause, or entangled with someone else's wife.

So the vampire goes to work where life originates. But thank God, so does His Holy Spirit! He wants to turn that barren womb into a bearing womb. Remember, "greater is he that is in you, than he that is in the world" (1 John 4:4).

Next Solomon showed Satan at work *where life operates:* "Four things say not, It is enough…the earth that is not filled with water."

My wife and I once lived where the soil was very sandy. To get grass to grow, we had to install a watering system, a pump, and a well. In the summer when we pumped water on that soil, it would be dry again within an hour. Even though the soil was fertile enough, if it were left without water, the land would produce nothing but weeds.

Satan, who is never satisfied himself, is an expert at destroying lives that show great promise. He has a formula for sucking the life out of people: he offers the pleasures of sin and prescribes an ever-increasing dosage for an ever-diminishing return. His formula is unadvertised, but it is operating in every package of cigarettes, every bottle of beer, every act of lust, and every fix of marijuana, heroin, and cocaine. Satan's formula is behind all addiction.

Years ago I was preaching in a church where I met a lady, a registered nurse, who told me her story of addiction and urged me to tell it to everyone I met. She was raised in a Christian home, but in her teen years she became rebellious, thinking she knew it all. She joined the wrong crowd and soon she was experimenting with drugs. The vampire's formula went to work. She became hooked and her life became a living hell. She lied, cheated, stole, pushed drugs, and sold her body. She became so disgusted with herself that she attempted suicide. Still the craving grew. Satan offered her an ever-increasing craving for an ever-diminishing thrill.

Time and time again she tried to quit. Her withdrawal symptoms however were so terrible that each time she quickly went back to her drugs. Her physical condition became so bad that she could no longer keep up the pace of working two jobs in order to pay for the drugs. Her hair began to fall out and her teeth loosened in her gums. In her torment she would scream and pull out her hair. Once she took a can opener and slashed her wrists. She deteriorated to the point where she could not even spell her name or enunciate the first three letters of the alphabet. Still the lust for more and more drugs raged in her body and soul. Then she tried to drown her despair in drink and soon, on top of everything else, she was a hopeless drunkard. The vampire sucked and sucked away at her life, glutted his own lusts, and gloated over his prey.

Then she met Christ and He transformed her life. She came back from the valley of the shadow of death and the vampire went away. She became a radiant, victorious Christian. When I talked to her, she was working as a registered nurse—entrusted with the key to the drug cabinet in the hospital where she was employed. Jesus now filled her being. Her cravings had been replaced with Christ.

Satan is busy where life operates—where people live, move, and have their being. He stimulates their natural appetites and turns them into lusts. He encourages them to add new cravings. He develops lusts into dragons that maim, destroy, and kill. The vampire knows that when people die, they will take their lusts with them into a lost eternity, where those cravings will rage unquenchable forever (Luke 16:19-31; Revelation 20:10-15; 21:8; 22:11).

Finally Solomon showed Satan at work *where life perpetuates:* "Four things say not, It is enough:...the fire that saith not, It is enough." Although we shrink from the notion, the Bible clearly teaches that at death, lost people do not cease to exist. There is a Heaven to gain and a Hell to shun. The one is as real and as endless as the other. The person who dies on earth as a dope addict awakens in eternity as a dope addict. The person who dies craving the indulgence of perverted lust will awaken with the same cravings in a lost eternity.

Revelation 22:11 states the dreadful edict: "He that is unjust, let him be unjust still: and he which is filthy, let him be filthy still." Four times in this verse the word "still" rings out, undermining all hope that some change of nature will take place during the transition from this life to the next. The statement emphasizes continuity beyond the grave. In a lost eternity, lusts will burn and never be quenched. Death does not change a person's nature; only his address is changed. Death does not annihilate a person's passions; it simply fixes them so that they can never be changed. Yet there is a glorious possibility of change in this life. The Bible says, "If any man be in Christ, he is a new creature: old things are passed away; behold, all things are become new" (2 Corinthians 5:17).

When John was caught up into glory, he saw "a sea of glass" (Revelation 4:6). Nothing could be more fluctuating than the sea, but nothing could be more fixed, formed, and final than a sea of glass. Just as the sea will be a sea of glass, there will be fixed holiness for the saints in Heaven. Likewise there will be fixed hopelessness for sinners in Hell. The Bible speaks of no place (such as the purgatory envisioned by the Catholic church) where people can progress from burning to beatification. On the contrary, the last book of the Bible peals out again and again the ominous note, "for ever and ever...for ever and ever"!

"The fire [of Hell] saith not, It is enough." The fire never goes out. A thousand years from now, even ten billion years from now, eternity will have only just begun. The fuel is always there—the raging lusts of the lost—so the fire is always there. When speaking about the sins of Sodom, the Bible solemnly warns of "the vengeance of eternal fire" (Jude 7). The vengeance will be inflicted on the vampire too, for that fire was first kindled "for the devil and his angels" (Matthew 25:41).

(2) The Footnote (30:17)

The sobering thoughts of Proverbs 30:15-16 reminded Solomon of something else that he appended to these verses: "The eye that mocketh at his father, and despiseth to obey his mother, the ravens of the valley shall pick it out, and the young eagles shall eat it" (30:17). Incidentally the eye is another thing that is never satisfied (see Ecclesiastes 1:8).

The picture painted in Proverbs 30:17 is of a dying man lying where the ravens and vultures can attack. Solomon knew that these birds gather around dying animals in the wild. As soon as the animals are too weak to fight them off, the birds begin their dreadful work—and invariably they begin with the eyes.

In this proverb Solomon referred to the eye because it is the most expressive member of the body. The eye, which is spoken of as the index of the soul, is the soul's instrument for revealing scorn and rebellion.

Solomon, who had a scornful and rebellious son, feared that that son would meet an untimely death. The Bible tells us of the follies of that son, but it does not tell us how he died.

Solomon envisioned a bad end for all such sons. Apart from the intervening grace of God, a bad beginning augurs a bad end. The son who in his youth defies his parents and also despises them is heading for disaster. At the beginning of the voyage of life he throws away chart and compass, anchor and helm. When storms come, when darkness descends, when breakers thunder on the lee shore, he can only expect shipwreck.

An illustration of Proverbs 30:17 is found in Cyrus Townsend Brady's novel *Sir Henry Morgan.* The book follows the career of the ruthless buccaneer who plundered Spain's Caribbean colonies during the late seventeenth century. Operating with the unofficial support of the British government, Morgan left behind him a trail of blood, outrage, and suffering. One of his best-known acts of infamy was the capture of Panama City, Panama, a chief city of Spain's American empire. With the help of thirty-six ships and two thousand buccaneers, Morgan sacked, ravished, and plundered the city and then burned it to the ground. On the way home he deserted his colleagues and absconded with the booty. Later King Charles II knighted Morgan and made him deputy governor of Jamaica.

Against this historical background the novelist wove a colorful tale. One of his characters, Benjamin Hornigold, was a one-eyed pirate who cherished a secret grudge against his captain, Henry Morgan. Morgan had hanged Hornigold's younger brother, so while Hornigold professed loyalty to his captain, he planned his revenge. Brady ended the story with the scene of vengeance.

North of the coast of Venezuela was a barren cay, visited only by wind, tide, and birds of prey. There Morgan's enemies had chained him to spikes driven into a cliff. He had been trussed up and left to die. The tide was coming in. It lapped his feet, then crept up to his legs, his body, and finally his chin. An occasional wave swept over his head. "He could only breathe between the breaking waves," wrote Brady. Each moment promised to be his last. Then the tide receded, but he knew it would return.

Then thirst reigned—a raging, tormenting thirst. Showing up to gloat over Morgan's suffering, Hornigold drank a mug of clear, cool water in front of the wretched man. Hornigold reminded his captain of the grudge he held and was about to abandon Morgan to his fate. But before Hornigold left, he spotted something in the sky and cried, "Look up....I guess you won't have to wait for the returning tide, and the sun won't bother you long." A more suitable vengeance was at hand. Brady wrote:

> When old Hornigold had looked up he had seen a speck in the vaulted heaven. It was slowly soaring around and around in vast circles, and with each circle coming nearer and nearer to the ground. A pair of keen and powerful eyes were aloft there piercing the distance, looking, searching, in every direction, until at last their glance fell upon the figure upon the rock. The circling stopped. There was a swift rush through the air. A black feathered body passed between the buccaneer and the sun, and a mighty vulture, hideous bird of the tropics, alighted on the sands near by him.
>
> So this was the judgment of God upon this man! For a second his tortured heart stopped its beating. He stared at the unclean thing, and then he shrank back against the rock and screamed with frantic terror. The bird moved heavily back a little distance and stopped, peering at him. He could see it by turning his head. He could drive it no farther. In another moment there was another rush through the air, another, another! He screamed again. Still they came, until it seemed as if the earth and the heavens were black with the horrible birds. High in the air they had seen the first one swooping to the earth, and with unerring instinct, as was their habit, had turned and made for the point from which the first had dropped downward to the shore.
>
> They circled themselves about him. They sat upon the rock above him. They stared at him with their lustful, carrion, jeweled eyes out of their loathsome, featherless, naked heads, drawing nearer—nearer—nearer. He could do no more. His voice was gone. His strength was gone. He closed his eyes, but the sight was still before him. His bleeding, foamy lips mumbled one unavailing word:
>
> "Hornigold!"...
>
> There was a weight upon his shoulder now fierce talons sank deep into his quivering flesh. In front of his face, before a pair of lidless eyes that glowed like fire, a hellish, cruel beak struck at him. A faint, low, ghastly cry trembled through the still air.[13]

The end came at last. The author left the reader to imagine the vultures descending in a body on the weakened man, tearing out his eyes, and eating him alive. Morgan died as he had lived, a godless man full of passion, hate, and fear.

b. Four Inscrutable Things (30:18-19)

In Proverbs 30:18-19 Solomon said that four things were "too wonderful" for him. The bare facts surely did not puzzle him. He had often watched an eagle swoop down from the sky. He had often seen a serpent sun itself on a rock and then slip away into the shadows. He had often watched the great Tarshish ships, which helped to enrich his treasuries, sail into the sunset. As for the way of a man with a maid, he had written the book on it (the Song of Solomon). He was an old hand at that game. However, the deeper meaning of the four things in Proverbs 30:19 eluded him. The Holy Spirit grouped them together in Solomon's mind and moved him to write them down for us, but he frankly confessed that he saw no link.

Of course Solomon wondered—he did not have the key to understanding! He might have found it in his early days before his spiritual insights were clogged with lust, but afterward it was too late. The key is out in the open for us. The key is Christ. The four things "too wonderful" for Solomon tell us of the One who was greater than Solomon. They tell us what Christ left, how He lived, what He learned, and whom He loved.

We are reminded first of *what He left:* "There be three things which are too wonderful for me, yea, four which I know not: The way of an eagle in the air..." Just as the eagle swoops down from the blue vault of heaven, Christ left glory to come down to earth.

The eagle is born higher than other birds fly. Other birds cannot soar where the eagle soars, live where the eagle lives, or follow its tremendous lead. Solomon had watched the eagle climb into the heavens until it was a mere speck in the sky. He had watched it soar even higher until it was out of sight. The eagle inhabits such heights because it is its nature to dwell up there. It is at home in the heavens. Everything about the eagle equips it for the heights: it has five different kinds of feathers; it has bones that are lighter than its feathers; it has an eye that can see distant objects. It can spot a rabbit half a mile away. When the eagle flies so high that we cannot see it, it easily sees us. Its vision is eight times better than a man's.

Everything about the eagle speaks of Christ. From His home on high He looked down and saw us here. Leaving glory behind, He came down, down to this dark world of sin. He exchanged Heaven for earth, the celestial city for a Bethlehem barn, the acclamation of the angels for the contradiction of sinners.

Christ's home in the highest Heaven is beyond our highest thought, but the apostle John told us about his vision of the place

Christ left. John was caught up into glory and he saw that land of fadeless day. He saw the city foursquare, the rainbow-circled throne, the crystal stream, the jasper walls, the gates of pearl, and the twelve foundations ablaze with precious stones. He heard the anthems of the angels and saw the elders casting their crowns at Jesus' feet. He knew what Jesus left when He came down to that cattle shed in Bethlehem and that cross of shame in Jerusalem. That glimpse of glory was "too wonderful" for John and it is "too wonderful" for us.

We are also reminded of *how Christ lived:* "There be three things which are too wonderful for me, yea, four...the way of a serpent upon a rock." A serpent? I was puzzled too! I tried to relate Solomon's reference to a serpent to the Lord's words to Nicodemus in John 3:14: "As Moses lifted up the serpent in the wilderness, even so must the Son of man be lifted up." But that didn't help. Then it dawned on me that the *rock* symbolizes Christ.

The serpent symbolizes Satan. A serpent's activity, naturalists tell us, is influenced by the action of the sun. The normal blood temperature of a serpent is usually one degree lower than that of the air. When the air is seventy degrees Fahrenheit, the serpent slows down; at fifty degrees it is almost helpless; at forty degrees it barely shows signs of life. It is the sun that stirs the serpent into action. Thus it likes to crawl onto a large mass of stone that can retain considerable heat.

Since the fall, most people have instinctively hated serpents. We fear their fangs and their deadly poison that can cause paralysis and render their victims helpless. Serpents remind us of "that old serpent, which is the Devil" (Revelation 20:2). He bit the children of Adam's ruined race and rendered them virtually helpless. The deadly poison of sin did its work.

But then Jesus came! He was a rock and the serpent's fangs and poison were powerless against Him. There was nothing comforting to the serpent about this rock. It was as cold as ice to him. The serpent gnashed away at that rock but he made no impression on Him at all; he was wasting his time. It would be foolish for a serpent to try to sink its fangs into a rock or to inject its venom into a stone. But that is just what Satan did when he tempted Jesus in the wilderness. The Lord Jesus was impervious to temptation; He was protected by a flinty holiness that was unyielding to sin.

Three times Satan tried to get a hold on Jesus, the Rock of ages. Using the three primeval temptations he had used so successfully on Eve, Satan tempted Jesus along the lines of food, faith, and fame.

The devil suggested that Jesus satisfy His legitimate appetite in an illegitimate way; dared Jesus to put God to the test; and tried to convince Jesus to accept the crown without the cross.

Jesus did not sin because He could not sin. He was impeccable. The temptations were real, but they hit a rock. In the person and nature of Jesus there was absolutely nothing to which the old serpent could fasten his fangs. Each temptation was utterly repulsive to the Lord's absolute holiness, His total love for His Father, and His complete trust in His Father. Satan was foiled every time. Such a lesson was indeed too deep for Solomon.

Next we are reminded of *what Christ learned:* "There be three things which are too wonderful for me, yea, four...the way of a ship in the midst of the sea."

For the most part the Hebrews left seafaring to their Phoenician neighbors. The sea was an alien world to the Hebrews—a dangerous, storm-prone world in which they never felt at home. So Solomon would "know not...the way of a ship."

Just as the world of the sailor is unlike the world of the sower, the world Jesus came from is unlike our world. Our world is restless and tempestuous, surging with sin. The world of the Lord from Heaven, on the other hand, is a world of peace, harmony, love, and joy. When Jesus came here He had to learn to live in this world and how to navigate its turbulent seas. He had to find His way from the cradle to the grave without shipwreck. He had to learn "the way of a ship in the midst of the sea." He was the ship. This world was the sea.

In olden days ships were dependent on the sky and the wind. Ancient mariners looked toward heaven to know which way they should go. They looked to the sun by day and the stars by night for guidance. There were no signposts in the sea; all the signposts were in the sky. Having no compasses, no astrolabes, and no navigation charts, sailors hugged the coast whenever they could and fixed their eyes on things above.

Similarly Jesus learned to traverse the trackless sea of time with His eyes fixed on Heaven. Never for a single moment did He lose sight of His utter dependence on His Father in Heaven. He learned obedience.

In Old Testament times a ship's movements were wholly controlled by the wind. Likewise Jesus lived His whole life under the controlling influence of the Spirit of God, who is symbolized by the wind in the Bible. The Lord Himself reminded Nicodemus of this symbolism in John 3:8.

The Lord Jesus was conceived by the Holy Ghost and filled with the Holy Spirit without measure from His mother's womb. He lived in the power of the Holy Spirit, was anointed by the Spirit for His ministry, and "through the eternal Spirit offered himself without spot to God" (Hebrews 9:14). The Lord was raised by the Holy Spirit and finally He asked His Father to send the Spirit back at Pentecost to do for us what He had done for Him. In other words Jesus never made a single move apart from the moving of the Spirit of God in His life. No wonder the spiritual meaning of "the way of a ship in the midst of the sea" was beyond Solomon's grasp.

Then we are reminded of *whom Christ loved:* "There be three things which are too wonderful for me, yea, four...the way of a man with a maid." We would think that any man who collected a thousand women for his harem surely should have found no mystery in "the way of a man with a maid." But Solomon confessed that there was a mystery. And he was right, for here we have an allusion to the way of the man Christ Jesus with the chaste virgin known as the church.

To comprehend the mystery, we need to ask why Jesus left His home on high for such a world as this? Why did He whom angels worshiped—the uncreated self-existing second person of the godhead, the "altogether lovely" One, "the chiefest among ten thousand," the creator and sustainer of the universe—step out of eternity and into time to be born as a man? Why did He condescend to live life on human terms—to grow up among us and to be tempted in all the ways we are? Why, for some thirty-three years, did He live wholly dependent on His Father in Heaven and the Holy Spirit on earth? Why did He allow His life on earth to climax on a Roman cross? An old hymn provides the answer:

> Out of the ivory palaces
> Into a world of woe,
> Only His great eternal love
> Made my Savior go.[14]

Love drew Him down. Love caused Him to become the incarnate One. Love took Him every step of the way—from glory to the globe, from Galilee to Gethsemane, from Gabbatha to Golgotha, from Golgotha to the grave, and from the grave back home to glory.

> He saw me ruined by the fall,
> Yet loved me notwithstanding all;
> He saved me from my lost estate,
> His loving kindness, oh, how great![15]

Love was the way of Christ with His intended bride. Whom did He love? You and me!

Yes, Solomon, you were quite right. Some things are "too wonderful." Even with the key in our hand we can only echo your words. No doubt we'll understand better by-and-by.

c. Four Intolerable Things (30:20-23)

"For three things the earth is disquieted, and for four which it cannot bear: For a servant when he reigneth; and a fool when he is filled with meat; For an odious woman when she is married; and an handmaid that is heir to her mistress" (Proverbs 30:21-23). Note that these four things that upset the order of society and the even tenor of life on earth are introduced by a comment in verse 20 about the way of an adulterous woman, which is also intolerable.

These intolerable things, as Paul would say, "are an allegory" (Galatians 4:24). As a rule, we should avoid interpreting the Bible as allegory. But for such an odd assortment of items, an allegorical interpretation seems appropriate. Evidently in Proverbs 30 we are invited to look beyond the surface.

What do these four (or five if we count verse 20) things have in common? In each case something is obviously and radically wrong; someone is so out of place that the earth itself is affected. The key to understanding Proverbs 30:20-23 is found in Romans 8:18-22, where Paul explained that all creation groans and travails as a result of man's fall. The fall has upset everything. Everything is out of place and the result is chaos. The passage in Proverbs pictures man in his fallen state. Man—spirit, soul, and body—is lying in ruins before his Maker.

Think first of *the human spirit*. Solomon said: "The earth is disquieted...For a servant when he reigneth." Here we have the wrong man on the throne. Something has gone awry with the governing process. Although God created man to have dominion over the earth, He put his human spirit under the control and guidance of the indwelling Holy Spirit. But his human spirit, which was intended to be subservient, carried out a palace coup and seized the reins of government. The throne room of the human personality was cleared of its rightful Occupant and occupied by a usurper. The Holy Spirit was driven from His throne and "King Self" now wears the crown.

The whole planet is affected because something has gone wrong in the throne room of its Lord. We see evidence in Scripture, nature, history, and psychology. There is ruin everywhere.

Let us review what happened before the coup. When God created man He said, "Let us make man in our image, after our likeness: and let them have dominion over the fish of the sea, and over the fowl of the air, and over the cattle, and over all the earth" (Genesis 1:26). God created man a tripartite being. Man's body made him world-conscious—able to live in and relate to the physical universe. His soul made him self-conscious—able to see and recognize himself as a living, rational, emotional, volitional, responsible being. His spirit was intended to be the throne room of the Spirit of God.

Thus man was created to be inhabited by God, to be the temple of the Holy Spirit, who would grace and guide the human spirit. The human spirit was to cooperate with the Holy Spirit. Man was to make himself available to God moment by moment, situation by situation, decision by decision. The animals were made to be ruled and governed by instinct; man was made to be ruled by God.

Then the coup—the fall—took place and the Holy Spirit vacated the human spirit. The wrong power ascended the throne and man was left without the divinely appointed Ruler indwelling his life. Now the body, soul, and spirit of man are no longer subject to the Holy Spirit and as a result we live in chaos. The servant has become the sovereign. Sin reigns. Self reigns. Satan reigns. And the earth groans.

Think next of *the human soul,* which is represented by an ugly trio: "A fool when he is filled with meat;...an odious woman when she is married; and an handmaid that is heir to her mistress." In the first case, something is wrong with the mind; in the second, something is wrong with the heart; and in the third, something is wrong with the will. Since the Holy Spirit does not control the unregenerate human spirit, everything else is in disarray. Within the human personality there is a constant power struggle.

When we consider the fool full of meat, we can learn a lesson about wrong thoughts. The human intellect has been ruined by the fall. The mind has retained much of its brilliance, but is incapable of thinking properly about God—unless the Holy Spirit enlightens it. The folly of the human intellect as well as the terrible emptiness of the human spirit are advertised every time a person is deceived by and professes belief in a false religion.

The word translated "fool" in Proverbs 30:22 means "rude, ill-bred, stingy, morose." Fallen man thinks rude, mean, stingy, and morose thoughts about God. Every false creed is proof that he thinks such thoughts.

In his thinking about God, fallen man is a fool so full of meat—so satisfied with himself—that he can be taught nothing. Paul described the unrighteous this way: "Professing themselves to be wise, they became fools" (Romans 1:22). The word translated "wise" here is *sophos* and the word translated "became fools" is *mōrainō.* Our English word "sophisticated" is a derivative of *sophos,* and our English word "moron" can be traced to a Greek word akin to *mōrainō.* So, what the Holy Spirit says in Romans 1:22 could be freely rendered, "Man in sin has become a sophisticated moron in his thinking about God." Sinful men are fools from God's standpoint, although such people are often lauded by the world.

We can split the atom and put men on the moon. We can perform genetic engineering and weigh the sun. But we cannot think properly about God. Because the fall has affected the human mind, otherwise brilliant people accept such silly religious nonsense as that propagated by Mormonism and Christian Science, or they accept the foulness of Hinduism as a form of holiness. Because of the fall, people embrace atheism and teach with religious fervor the wholly unproven theories of evolution. Because the human soul is lying in ruins, men think wrong thoughts.

When we consider the odious woman who is married, we can learn a lesson about wrong emotions. Nothing stirs the emotions more than love and marriage. Normally two people marry because they have formed a deep emotional attachment to each other. But love can turn to hate, another strong emotion.

In Proverbs 30:23 we see a sad picture of a man married to the wrong woman. She was odious before he married her, but she fooled him. As soon as the glamour wore off, he discovered her true nature.

The meaning of the proverb seems obvious, but there is a deeper explanation. In the Bible marriage is a planned picture of the love relationship between Christ and His church and between the saint and the Savior. Whenever a bad woman is introduced in Scripture, she invariably symbolizes false religion. The odious woman, then, represents a false religion to which a person gives his affection and makes a deep commitment. Now his whole life is bound up in an odious relationship. All the love that he should give to Christ, he gives to a cult. He spends his strength for something utterly false. The odious woman has him in her clutches and Satan laughs. In time the person's commitment will become dreadful drudgery.

As we have thought about the human soul lying in ruins after the fall, we have learned about wrong thoughts and wrong emotions.

Now we can learn a lesson about wrong decisions as we consider the handmaid who is heir to her mistress. If this case is consistent with the other intolerable things, we will be able to find something radically wrong in this fourth disquieting situation. And we do find something very much out of place. What is wrong here is the will of the mistress.

In this part of Proverbs 30:23 we have a parable about the human will being used amiss: A wealthy woman, facing the fact of death, decides to make a will so that her wishes will be carried out after her death. She is wise to make a will, but she leaves everything to the wrong person. She exercises her will in the wrong way.

The human will, like the human intellect and the human emotions, has been ruined by the fall. We make wrong decisions. We refuse to be subject to the law of God (Romans 8:7).Because of sin's hold on us, we use our wills wrongly in countless ways. When an unregenerate person hears the gospel, even if his mind is convinced, his heart moved, his conscience awakened, and his soul stirred, his will may refuse to move. The final battle is always with the will.

So we have a fourfold picture of man in sin. But something is missing. There is reference to the human spirit and the human soul, but if the picture is to be complete, there should also be reference to *the human body.* To add this to the picture, we need to backtrack to Proverbs 30:20, which describes the adulterous woman. This verse actually begins the picture because the most evident effects of the fall are seen in what sin does to the body and the conscience.

When we consider the way of the adulterous woman, we can learn a lesson in wrong indulgence: "She eateth, and wipeth her mouth." What a picture of the body out of control or, from another perspective, in complete control. We see lustful appetite indulged without regard to precept or propriety. The woman gratifies one lust and then sits down to gratify another. There is of course nothing wrong with responding to our senses, but we are never to be sensual; we are never to gratify our appetites without regard to the laws of God and man.

Our senses of sight, touch, smell, hearing, and taste, which greatly enrich our lives, can be orchestrated into symphonies of pleasure. Pleasure itself is not wrong. In fact, as C. S. Lewis reminded us, pleasure was God's idea. The psalmist spoke rapturously of the pleasures that are at God's right hand forevermore (Psalm 16:11). What is wrong is sinful pleasure, what Paul calls "the pleasures of sin for a season" (Hebrews 11:25).

When we consider the way of the adulterous woman, we can also learn a lesson about wrong convictions, for she says, "I have done no wickedness." She has no sense of guilt. Her conscience has been stifled. It is not seared yet, because if it were she would not even mention wickedness. The fact that she is aware of right and wrong and feels called upon to justify her behavior indicates that—wicked as she is, far down the road of immorality as she is, however specious her arguments are—there is still hope.

The woman has not yet completely silenced her conscience. But the fact that she can get up from a bed of sinful indulgence and sit down to breakfast indicates that she is well on the way to total moral collapse. If she were overwhelmed with a sense of guilt, she would find the thought of food distasteful. Since she is described as "an adulterous woman," we can infer that she has surrendered her body to lust and stifled her conscience more than once.

She says to her conscience that she has done no wrong, but that of course is not true. She has wronged herself, for adultery brings its own consequences and God's sure and certain judgment (Hebrews 13:4). She has wronged her husband. She has wronged her parents and her children. She has wronged her country, for she is contributing to the breakdown of family life. She has wronged the people of God. She has wronged God Himself. Yet she says, "I have done no wickedness."

Considering Proverbs 30:20-23 as a unit, we see a graphic picture of sinful man disquieting the earth. We see the human spirit emptied of the Holy Spirit and bereft of divine government and guidance. In an incessant power struggle, man tries to usurp God's throne and run and rule his own life. We see the human soul adrift with no divine hand on the helm. His intellect is blind to real truth; his emotions run riot; his will is stubborn and determined, or weak and wayward. The human body is the instrument for sin and prone to disease, death, and decay. Man's senses are defiled or distorted and his conscience is assailed.

Then fallen man, in complete personal disarray, imposes his will on the planet where he lives. His ingenuity is great. He builds dams, moves mountains, changes the course of rivers, brings water to the wilderness, flings great highways across the land, and spans mighty gorges. Yet he creates ecological havoc in the process. No wonder all creation yearns for the day when the Second Man, the last Adam, the incarnate Son of God, the man Christ Jesus, will come back and put everything right. "We see Jesus," exclaimed the great apostle as he anticipated that day (Hebrews 2:9).

d. Four Insignificant Things (30:24-28)

Four "little" things attracted Solomon's attention. He noticed them because they are "exceeding wise"—or "wiser than the wisest," as the Septuagint can be rendered (Proverbs 30:24).

First Solomon noticed the ants. They teach us *a lesson in government:* "The ants are a people not strong, yet they prepare their meat in the summer" (Proverbs 30:25). Ants overcome their weakness as individuals by the organization and structure of their social system. They are the socialists of the insect world. Their system appeals to us at first, but a closer look at their government causes most of us to change our minds.

Although scientists have classified some fifteen thousand different species of ants, all species have one thing in common: they provide for the future. Of course they have no thought for any future beyond this life, but they are shrewd in their preparations for the future in this life. The ants' way of life works because it is not hampered by moral considerations. Their form of government is a strange mixture of bumbling confusion and astonishing efficiency. Anyone who has disturbed an anthill has seen a few minutes of frantic confusion followed by a systematic attack on the problem of repairing the damage.

The ants' social system is designed to achieve maximum utilization of available resources. All the various skills present in the ant community are harnessed so that each individual contributes something to the perpetuation of the system. If ants had a motto it would be the communist motto: To each according to his need; from each according to his ability. Among the ants the state is supreme. There are no strikes. Workers work themselves to death to "prepare their meat." Their government tolerates no dissidents. It is a government of law without repeal.

At the top of the social heap is the queen. Like all the other ants she is a prisoner of the system, although she enjoys more fringe benefits. Whole armies of ants are her attendants. Her job is to make sure that the system perpetuates itself. As long as she operates efficiently and the social structure she rules keeps growing and expanding, all is well. But if she falters in her task, she is simply removed and replaced. The fact that a queen rules the heap is not without significance, for it suggests a form of government that is at variance with God's Word.

The twentieth century has experimented with socialistic government, but the experiment has failed even when socialism has been enforced with utter ruthlessness. The failure lies in one simple fact: people are not ants.

The conies teach us *a lesson in grace:* "The conies are but a feeble folk, yet make they their houses in the rocks" (Proverbs 30:26). In the Hebrew the word translated "rocks" is singular: "They make their houses in the rock."

The coney is a rodent. It looks like a rabbit, but has no relationship to the rabbit family. The coney has a round back, no visible tail, and short sturdy legs. Its soles and nails enable it to cling to rock. Conies are essentially vegetarians, although some are said to be fond of locusts. Conies are gregarious and can often be seen having small meetings. Numbers, however, provide no protection for these feeble folk. Their one refuge from their foes is the rock, to which they have fled permanently.

The deeper significance of Proverbs 30:26 is quite evident. The coney illustrates the believer in a hostile world. Like the coneys, we have fled for refuge to the Rock. A sense of our own feebleness and vulnerability to our foes—a realization of how little strength we have in ourselves—makes us thankful for our Rock. Our Rock of course is Christ.

The locust, another illustration of the believer in the world, teaches us many remarkable lessons.

Solomon wrote, "The locusts have no king, yet go they forth all of them by bands" (Proverbs 30:27). Because locusts are a threat, man naturally hates and fears them. He would like to get rid of them but he can't, even though he employs sophisticated weapons. He has studied their weaknesses and tried to exploit those weaknesses, but he cannot eradicate them.

Likewise people in general hate believers. Unsaved people see believers as a threat and would like to eliminate them. The history of the persecution of the church reveals repeated and organized efforts to get rid of Christians. Sophisticated weapons have been used and countless millions have been killed. But more Christians are alive today than ever before. So the locusts teach us *a lesson in growth.*

A locust can go through various stages after it is born. If it has adequate living space and is not forced to be with other locusts, it remains in a solitary stage, during which it is known as a hopper. It lives and dies the way it was born, just like an ordinary grasshopper.

At times, however, a mysterious force that we do not understand affects the solitary locust and it experiences a new birth. What triggers the phenomenon nobody knows. Rain, or temperature, or humidity, or sunlight have been thought to prompt the change. But all these theories have been tested and they have proved to be inadequate explanations.

The hopper going into another stage selects a suitable twig, hangs on it upside down, breaks out of its body, pumps blood into its wings, and puts itself at the disposal of the wind. It has become a locust. Its behavior is so unlike that of the hopper that scientists took years to discover that the hopper and the locust were actually the same creature.

The spiritual application is obvious. The new birth some hoppers experience teaches us about regeneration. A person can live and die the way he was born, or a person can be born again. The factors that bring about the experience of regeneration are mysterious and often baffling. Nicodemus, the learned Hebrew doctor of the law, confessed that he was quite out of his depth when Jesus told him that he needed to be born again. When a person is regenerated, he enters a new kind of life. He puts himself at the disposal of the Holy Spirit (symbolized by the wind in John 3:8) and from then on he is a different person. The change in behavior is so complete that people have trouble identifying him as the person they used to know.

The locusts also teach us about revival. There are times when only a few isolated groups of locusts begin to congregate (they seem harmless enough then), and there are times when many groups get together. In this gregarious phase of their life cycle, the locusts swarm. They enter this stage in order to survive in a hostile environment.

When the locusts begin to swarm and ride the wind, their numbers multiply rapidly. Some swarms contain more than a million members and extend over two hundred square miles. Sometimes the locusts try short flights and sometimes they fly up to two thousand miles. Locusts can become a formidable power to be reckoned with by the world.

What a lesson for us! The locusts teach us a secret of Holy Ghost revival. When the locust changes its behavior, its numbers begin to increase. And when people of God begin to change their behavior and put themselves at the disposal of the Holy Spirit, their numbers begin to multiply in an extraordinary way and the world sits up and takes notice. The church becomes a power to be reckoned with in the world.

Then too, the locusts teach us about the rapture. The Hebrew word translated "bands" in Proverbs 30:27 is rendered *keleusmatos* in the Greek of the Septuagint. It is most instructive to note that the

Greek term *keleusma,* a word akin to *keleusmatos,* is used in the following New Testament passage, where it is translated "shout":

> The Lord himself shall descend from heaven with a shout, with the voice of the archangel, and with the trump of God: and the dead in Christ shall rise first: Then we which are alive and remain shall be caught up together with them in the clouds, to meet the Lord in the air (1 Thessalonians 4:16-17).

*Keleusma* means "a shout of command, a cry of urging on, a shout that assembles." The word could be used to describe the rhythmic shout that kept the oarsmen on a ship all rowing together.

So *keleusmatos* in Proverbs 30: 27 must indicate that the locusts all move upward to the skies at a word of command reserved for their ears alone. Similarly when we hear the *keleusma,* we will be "caught up."

Who would have imagined that the locusts could have taught us so much?

Finally the spider teaches us *a lesson in glory.* Wrote Solomon: "The spider taketh hold with her hands, and is in kings' palaces" (Proverbs 30:28).[16] How can the spider teach us a spiritual lesson when it is the villain of the insect world? The life history of a spider reads like a gruesome science-fiction fantasy. Often a female spider will murder her husband on their honeymoon and then dine on his remains. What a good start!

Spiders are the world's master murderers. The hunting spider simply jumps on its prey and consumes it on the spot. The web weaver is more crafty. Like a gargoyle it sits on its web and holds silken strands. When a carefree fly comes buzzing along, is caught by the strands, and struggles to get free, the spider feels the vibrations and can tell the distance, direction, and size of its victim. The spider walks delicately on the strands it has deliberately left unsticky and, like a practiced cowboy, immobilizes its prey by wrapping it up in silken ropes. Then the spider gets down to business. Out come the deadly fangs, which give the prisoner an injection that either kills or paralyzes. If not killed, the wretched fly waits, paralyzed and roped, for the murderer to come back. When the spider returns, it injects some chemicals that turn its victim's insides into insect soup, which it polishes off.

The spider learns its dreadful trade early in life. It is born inside a silken global nest made by its terrible mother. A baby spider that grows up faster than others in the nest soon murders his weaker siblings and eats them. When it is ready to go out on its own, it leaves behind him a shambles of baby-spider skeletons. Some species complete the story by killing and eating mother on the way out. After all, mother is getting old and weak, so why not?

We shrink with horror from such a creature and such a career, but there are people just as bad. When missionaries first went to New Hebrides, they found cannibals who were capable of equally horrible crimes. The cannibals would just as soon eat an uncle as cook a hog.

When J. G. Paton, a British missionary, applied to the British government for permission to go to New Hebrides, the officials at first refused to let him go. Then one of the lords of the admiralty spoke up on Paton's behalf. "Maybe the cannibals will eat him," he said. "That at least would give us an excuse to go and blow the islands out of the sea." Paton laughed and said he had some "gunpowder" of his own he wanted to try first.

Paton went. His wife went too and died. So depraved were the island's cannibals that Paton had to take his dog and his gun and stand guard over her grave for several days—until her body was too decomposed to tempt the appetites of the natives.

In the end the gospel proved to be "the power of God unto salvation" even for these terrible people (Romans 1:16). Many man-eating savages were saved and took their places at the Lord's table. They worshiped God and sang the praises of His Son and when their life on earth was over, He gathered them home to Heaven.

No matter how wicked we have been, we can take hold of God's offer of salvation—full, free, and forever—with the hands of faith. That is the lesson of the spider. "The spider taketh hold with her hands, and is in kings' palaces." (The expression translated "kings' palaces" is in the singular in the original.)

We cannot take hold of salvation if our hands are already full of something else. We must let go of whatever else we are trusting in, and take hold of Jesus by faith. As the old hymn says:

> Nothing in my hand I bring,
> Simply to Thy cross I cling.[17]

If we take hold of Jesus, something will happen to us that does not happen to the spider. We will be changed and made fit for the King's palace. The spider in the king's palace is an intruder, but when we arrive in the King's palace, we will be there as children of the living God.

e. Four Invincible Things (30:29-31)

Solomon linked together four more assorted creatures: "There be three things which go well, yea, four are comely in going: A lion which is strongest among beasts, and turneth not away for any; A greyhound; an he goat also; and a king, against whom there is no rising up."

We wonder what these creatures have in common: a wild animal, a domesticated animal, a clean animal, and a human being. Solomon said that they are all "comely in going"; that is, they make their way surely and certainly. We conclude that there is more in this passage than meets the eye.

The clue to the deeper meaning is found in the first and last items in the list: the lion and the king. Both point to Christ. Moreover they point to His coming again. To be consistent, the greyhound and the he-goat must do the same. Taken together, the four creatures emphasize four features of Christ's sure and certain coming again.

*He is coming like a lion, with sure and certain stealth.* Solomon said that a lion "is strongest among beasts." For good reasons we consider the lion to be the king of the beasts. He weighs up to five hundred pounds and is all iron muscle, lightning speed, and slashing strength. He can leap forty feet in a single bound and his roar can shake the forest. Although there are bigger animals, faster animals, and more crafty animals, the lion reigns. His victims have little chance of escaping, for he has eighteen claws to rip, tear, and flay, and his massive jaws are armed with large fierce teeth. When he decides to charge, he drops his head, switches his tail, growls, and then runs faster than a galloping horse.

In spite of the fact that the lion is so swift and strong, so big and heavy, he can move through tall grass so quietly that nobody can hear him coming. He arrives with sure and certain stealth. Likewise one feature of the second coming of Christ is that He will arrive when He is least expected, when the scoffers are saying, "Where is the promise of his coming?" (2 Peter 3:3-4).

When Napoleon surfaced from the crimson seas of the French revolution and began to redraw the map of Europe, people thought that he was the antichrist and the Lord's coming was at hand. When Mussolini strutted across the Italian stage and proposed to rebuild the Roman empire, people thought the same thing. When Britain received a mandate to build a national home for the Jew, when Israel became a sovereign state, and when it celebrated its first jubilee in the land, people were convinced that the Lord's coming was at hand. But He has not come yet and people are inclined to think that He is not coming at all. In fact more than half of all church members do not believe in the second coming. Millions embrace covenant theology, which denies the prophetic significance of the rebirth of the state of Israel, denies the truth of a coming millennium, and de-emphasizes the second coming of Christ.

Yet all the while, He is stealing through the tall grass of time. His flaming eyes are watching. He is preparing to spring into the air. But He knows how to bide His time. He knows exactly what He is waiting for.

A man who traveled in one of Africa's national parks told a story that illustrates exactly what the Lion of the tribe of Judah is waiting for. The traveler saw a male lion come out of the tall grass. His head hung down and he seemed to take no notice of a herd of impala grazing nearby. He simply sat down and stared at them for about fifteen minutes. He seemed to be quite unconcerned about his prey. The impala became nervous but ignored the lion.

Then from the other side of the herd came the sound of the cough of another lion. Receiving the signal, the big male twitched his ears and went into action at once. He started toward the prey, and the impala panicked. The whole herd fled, leaping and bounding away from him, and disappeared into a valley on the other side.

The traveler, who was curious, drove to the other side to see what had happened. In the valley he saw two tawny lionesses and two dead impala. The female lions were quietly waiting for the male to arrive and exercise his noble right of eating first.

What a picture of the second coming of Christ! Right now He is patiently waiting as He follows a prearranged plan. He has been sitting at the right hand of the Majesty on high for what seems to us to be a very long time and He seems to be taking no notice of what is going on down here. Wickedness is on the rise. Men are becoming more blatant in their scorn of divine authority. But although He may seem to be disinterested, He is keenly interested.

Just as the African lion was waiting for the lionesses to arrive at the other side of the herd of impala, the Lord is waiting for the church to take up its proper position on the other side of Jordan. As soon as the rapture has taken place—as soon as the church is in glory—He will go into action. And the church, His bride, will be His partner in the "short work" He intends to do on the earth (Romans 9:28). He is sitting now and the world yawns in His face. But in a moment, in the twinkling of an eye, the church will come home and His roar will sound across the world.

*Christ is also coming like a greyhound, with sure and certain speed.* Modern translators have had a wild time with the greyhound. The original word has been rendered "raven," "zebra," "war horse," "leopard," and even "cock." But the Hebrew word literally means "to be girt in the loins," a phrase that exactly suits the greyhound.

The Jews regarded the dog with particular contempt, considering it to be the epitome of the unclean animals proscribed by the law. Indeed they thought it fitting to refer to the Gentiles as "dogs."

Yet the dog has been called man's oldest friend. Long before the human race began to keep records, the dog came in from the great unknown to sit at man's fires, guard his possessions, help him hunt, and be his companion. But the Jews looked on the dog with contempt.

There is a preliminary lesson here. The Lord Jesus is man's oldest friend. Long before written records were kept, He came in from the great unknown beyond the sky to walk with Adam in paradise. In the pages of Scripture we see Him visiting Abraham in his tent, wrestling with Jacob at the Jabbok, meeting with Moses in the desert, and talking with Joshua, David, and Daniel. Finally the great yearning of His heart for the children of men reached its climax. He clothed Himself in human flesh and showed Himself to be man's truest and most faithful friend—even to the extent of dying for him. But the Jews had no use for Him. Here and there individual Jews have turned to Him, but as a people the Jews have throughout the centuries treated Him with scorn.

Solomon focused our attention especially on the greyhound, one of the oldest breeds, because it is so "comely in going." Built for speed, it is the fastest of the dogs and can attain speeds of up to nearly forty miles an hour. The symbolism of the greyhound underlines the fact that the Lord Jesus will come with sure and certain speed. His coming for the church will be like a lightning flash. One instant the church will be here; the next moment every born-again believer on earth will be gone. The day of grace will be over.

Then events on earth will be speeded up. Right now the pace is slow. Israel has slowly moved back to the land and become a sovereign state. Russia has become a notable world power. The collapase of communism nearly thrust it into economic collapse, but Russia is still armed with nuclear weapons and it has not forgotten its long-range designs on the Middle East. Europe is slowly and painfully drawing together and looking toward political confederation. Everywhere there are signs, but the pace is slow.

Once the church is removed, the speed will be accelerated. When the antichrist seizes the rebuilt temple in Jerusalem, only 1260 days will be left before the second coming of Christ (Daniel 12:7).

*Christ is also coming like a he-goat, with sure and certain steps.* The he-goat, which lives on mountain crags, easily negotiates terrain where other animals would fall. It scorns the difficulties of the way.

The Bible makes three important references to the goat: one prophetic, one pictorial, and one parabolic. The prophetic reference in the book of Daniel indicates that the Lord is coming with sure and certain steps to fulfill the prophecies of Scripture. Daniel saw a ram coming from the East and a he-goat with a great horn between its eyes coming from the West (Daniel 8:3-5). The ram represents the Persian empire, and the he-goat represents Greece and Alexander the Great. If ever there was a sure-footed conqueror, he was Alexander. In a few short years he made the ancient world his. He appeared on the stage of history and literally fulfilled the prophecies of Scripture.

The pictorial reference to the goat (in the book of Leviticus) indicates that the Lord is coming with sure and certain steps to finalize the process of salvation. Leviticus is a book of "types," a series of vivid pictures depicting God's plan of salvation. One of those striking pictures centers around the day of atonement, which in turn centered around two goats. One of these goats was slain and its blood was taken into the holy of holies and applied to the mercyseat. The other goat was called the scapegoat. Over its head were confessed the sins of the people, and it was then taken to "a land not inhabited" and left there to die alone (Leviticus 16:22).

The church has already accepted the salvation pictured by those goats. Believers have been saved by the blood of the Lord Jesus. He has carried our sins away. We have access by His blood into the holiest. But Israel as a nation persists in its rejection of this salvation. For them the process of salvation will be finalized after the great tribulation and the battle of Armageddon. Israel will "look on him whom they pierced" (John 19:37; also see Revelation 1:7). They will confess their sins and repent of their age-long rejection of Jesus.

The parabolic reference to the goat (in the Gospel of Matthew) indicates that the Lord is coming with sure and certain steps to force the purging of society after the battle of Armageddon. Because of wars, famines, pestilences, earthquakes, persecutions, and disasters, not many people will be left on earth. The remnant of Israel will have recognized Jesus as Messiah. They will have confessed their sin, and the Lord will have removed their transgression and owned them as His brethren.

The remnant of the Gentile nations will be assembled in the valley of Jehoshaphat outside Jerusalem (Joel 3:2,12). There the Lord will divide the sheep from the goats. Each person will be judged on the basis of what he did for a Jew during the great tribulation (Matthew 25:40,45). Those who refused to help a Jew will be numbered among the goats and consigned to a lost eternity. The remainder will go with the Jews into the millennial kingdom.

Finally *the Lord is coming like a King, with sure and certain strength.* Solomon referred to "a king, against whom there is no rising up." The oldest monarchy on earth today is the British monarchy, which has lasted for more than a thousand years. Until the signing of the Magna Carta at Runnymede in 1215, English kings wielded absolute power. After that, over the years the British monarchy degenerated into a constitutional monarchy, in which the monarch reigns in regal splendor but has no real power.

On June 2, 1953, Queen Elizabeth II was crowned in Westminster Abbey. But from that day to this she has never made a single legislative, executive, or judicial decision. She reigns over a kingdom, but all the elaborate ceremony and magnificent pomp are just an impressive show. All power rests with the House of Commons and the prime minister of the party in power. At the opening of Parliament she reads a speech written by the prime minister and, likely as not, advocating policies she loathes. She signs documents into law, but if she refuses to sign one, it becomes law anyway. At the whim of the prime minister she is called on to dissolve Parliament so the people can vote for a change of government if they wish. The queen has no say. Her role is one of splendor without substance.

Jesus, on the other hand, is "a king, against whom there is no rising up." God's ideal form of government is neither a democracy nor a republic. It is an absolute monarchy with all power concentrated in the hands of Jesus. King Jesus will rule the nations with a rod of iron (Psalm 2:9) and what a blessing that will be! His will will be law, and His will will be right. His will will be done on earth, as it is in Heaven. The world will say, "A greater than Solomon is here" (Matthew 12:42).

### 3. A Practical Observation (30:32-33)

Solomon concluded his series of parables with two practical observations. First he observed *the wisdom of silence:* "If thou hast done foolishly in lifting up thyself, or if thou hast thought evil, lay thine hand upon thy mouth" (Proverbs 30:32). The word translated "foolishly" here means "stupidly."

We have all done stupid things. We have all meditated with evil intent. When we have realized our foolishness, we may have used the familiar gesture Solomon mentioned. We have seen others use it too. We have heard someone make a thoughtless or inappropriate remark and then seen him clap his hand over his mouth. Solomon suggested that we cover our mouths before we speak, before we add insult to injury, before we add evil words or deeds to evil thoughts. If he were alive today he would say, "Hold your tongue."

When our children were young, on one occasion my wife and I were expecting a visit from some out-of-town relatives. The man who was coming was very big and considerably overweight. We were afraid that one of our daughters, who was noted for her free speech, would blurt out some smart remark. She invariably said the first thing that came into her head, no matter how inappropriate the thought might have been. We did not want dear old Uncle Joe to have his feelings hurt, so we did our best to prepare our precocious little girl for the visit.

We described Uncle Joe. We told our daughter that he was very big, probably the biggest man she had ever seen. We warned her not to say anything to him about his size and weight. She said she understood. As the day of the visit drew nearer, our coaching took the form of pleas and promises, explanations and threats. She said she understood.

The day of the visit arrived. There was a knock at the door. I was in the kitchen with my wife, and our little girl ran to open the door. There stood Aunt Carrie and Uncle Joe. Our daughter took one look at Uncle Joe and left the visitors standing at the door. As she came running through the house to the kitchen, we could hear her voice raised in indignant exclamation: "He's not fat! Why did you say he was fat?" My wife put her hand on her mouth. I'm sure she wished she had put a gag on our little girl's mouth. When we went to the door, the silence was charged, but the usual banalities tided us over.

Solomon also observed *the way of strife:* "Surely the churning of milk bringeth forth butter, and the wringing of the nose bringeth forth blood: so the forcing of wrath bringeth forth strife" (Proverbs 30:33).

When I was young, if a boy was caught trespassing on a neighbor's property, the neighbor would not hesitate to inflict corporal punishment on the spot. Teachers routinely flogged offending pupils in the classroom. A case had to be really serious to warrant a charge of assault and battery.

In those days a preacher of the old school stood in the open air in a rough part of town and preached the gospel to a small crowd on a street corner. He was a big man who had been a tough prizefighter before he met Christ. In the crowd was a heckler. The preacher was used to heckling and in fact he rather liked it. He had been a communist before he became a Christian and had been a heckler himself. Indeed he had gone to disrupt a tent meeting when the Holy Spirit convicted him of his need for Christ. Still, the heckler began to get on the preacher's nerves.

"There's not a word of truth in the Bible," the heckler called out. The crowd was delighted. The preacher went on preaching, ignoring the interruption.

"There's not a word of truth in the Bible," the heckler called out again, louder this time, determined to be heard. The preacher, wise in the ways of the world, went on preaching.

Adding a few choice oaths to his announcement, the heckler interrupted again. "There's not a word of truth in the Bible," he shouted.

The preacher paused. "One more word from you, mister," he said, "and I'll come down off this soapbox and deal with you."

Thus encouraged and more contentious and abusive than ever, the heckler shouted back, "There's not a word of truth in the Bible!"

The former pugilist stepped down and walked over to the heckler. "Now, mister," he said, "this is my meeting and my crowd. I give you fair warning. You say that again and I'll prove you wrong in a way you won't forget, right here on this street corner, in front of all your friends."

By now a considerable crowd had gathered. The preacher went back to his soapbox and began preaching again, and the heckler, urged on by his buddies, interrupted again. "There's not a word of truth in that there Bible," he said, adding a few more choice oaths.

The preacher got back down off his soapbox, walked over to the heckler, and opened his Bible to Proverbs 30:33. He said, "Can you read, mister?" The man belligerently agreed that he could. "Now what was that you said about this Book?" demanded the preacher. The heckler repeated his statement. The preacher said, "Read that," as he pointed to these words: "The wringing of the nose bringeth forth blood." The preacher seized the heckler by the collar and said, "I'm going to prove to you that there is at least one word of truth in the Bible—this one." Then he seized the heckler's nose with his fist, which was the size of a small ham, and wrung his nose until the blood flowed. "Now then, mister," the preacher said, "would you like me to prove any more verses for you?"

The heckler had had enough. He didn't want to have the Bible proved to him verse by verse like that! The preacher patted the fellow on the shoulder and went back to his soapbox—and to a most attentive and appreciative crowd.

Truly, "the wringing of the nose bringeth forth blood." Certain actions produce certain results as surely as night follows day. If you want a fight, just keep provoking a man until he loses his temper. That heckler would have suffered more than a bleeding nose if he had encountered that preacher when he was a communist. Before he was a Christian, the boxer would have lost his temper—and it was a fierce one. Likely as not, the heckler would have found himself in the middle of a riot and would have been taken home with some broken bones. "The forcing of wrath bringeth forth strife."

## II. The Ideal Wife (31:1-31)

### A. The Chapter and Its Author (31:1-9)

#### 1. The Mother of the King (31:1-2)

The book of Proverbs begins with the wise words of a father and ends with the wise words of a mother. "My son," said the father in Proverbs 1:8. "My son," said the mother in Proverbs 31:2. First and last, the home is the bastion of the nation. As the home is, so is the homeland. This lesson should be written in large letters over all schools, courts, halls of Congress, television studios, bookstores, and homes.

Proverbs 31:1 reads, "The words of king Lemuel, the prophecy that his mother taught him." Who was King Lemuel and who was his mother? One commentator declared that Agur and Lemuel were not Hebrews; he imagined them to be Ishmaelites. He supposed that they lived in the vicinity of Israel and therefore had some nodding acquaintance with the religion and writings of the Jews. Well, we know what kind of religion Ishmael gave the world: the religion of the Islamic fundamentalists, who have little to show of peace, purity, or true piety.

We cannot fully appreciate Proverbs 31 if we suppose it to have been written by an alien philosopher and later incorporated into the Hebrew Bible. The passage makes more sense when we accept the view of the Talmud that Agur and Lemuel were other names for Solomon.

The word translated "prophecy" in Proverbs 31:1 means "oracle" or "burden." If ever a woman had a burden for her son, it was Solomon's mother. His mother was Bath-sheba and her burden was to keep her son from repeating her mistakes. And what mistakes they were!

We know the story of David and Bath-sheba by heart. She had been the wife of Uriah the Hittite, a man of foreign ancestry and one of the most loyal of David's inner circle of mighty men. A trusted and tried soldier, Uriah was willing to die for David.

Uriah and Bath-sheba had a home near the royal palace. While Uriah was off to war, one day Bath-sheba decided to bathe on the flat roof of her house. We do not know whether she made that decision thoughtlessly or intentionally with the hope of catching David's eye. Whatever her intentions, she attracted the attention of David, who was at loose ends. Having left the battle to Joab, who was quite able to command the front line, David had remained at home with his women. Thus the trap was set by the devil. David saw Bath-sheba. The look became a lust and the desire became a decision. It was the old story of the garden of Eden all over again.

A clandestine meeting was arranged. We do not know whether Bath-sheba came to the palace because she received a royal command or because she was fascinated by David. Whatever her reason, one thing led to another and before long Bath-sheba and David were hopelessly compromised. Bath-sheba became pregnant and a major national scandal was in the making. David's enemies, of which there were not a few, would cry out against him once they heard the gossip, and the law mandated the death penalty for adultery. David knew that something had to be done.

So David sent for Uriah. Ostensibly the soldier was summoned simply as an army courier. David's true intent, of course, was to provide Uriah with an opportunity to go home to his wife so that he would think that he had fathered the child. When David's scheme didn't work, he made Uriah drunk; David hoped that under the influence of alcohol Uriah would go home, but that trick didn't work either. Finally David sent Uriah back to the front line and arranged with Joab for Uriah to be murdered. The king wrote to his general, "Set ye Uriah in the forefront of the hottest battle, and retire ye from him, that he may be smitten, and die" (2 Samuel 11:15). Once Uriah was dead, David married the widow.

A son was born to David and Bath-sheba. People were suspicious about the timing, but nobody could prove any wrongdoing. Joab had David's letter, but he was too wily a fox to make it public. Finally God sent the prophet Nathan to deal with David, and the whole wretched affair came out into the open. David was bitterly repentant, but the prophet's sentence stood: David and Beth-sheba's son would die. Moreover David would not have to seek trouble; what he had sowed he would reap in his family.

The baby died, and David and Bath-sheba were drawn closer to each other in their adversity. Another son was born to them and they named him Solomon. As they stooped fearfully over the cradle, half expecting the sword of divine vengeance to fall again, the prophet Nathan appeared—this time with a smile on his face. Second Samuel 12:24-25 tell us that David "called his name Solomon: and the Lord loved him. And he sent by the hand of Nathan the prophet; and he called his name Jedidiah [beloved of the Lord], because of the Lord."

From the beginning it was understood that Solomon was to be the heir to David's throne. Near the end of David's life, Adonijah followed in the footsteps of Absalom and made a determined attempt to foil the plan and seize the throne for himself. We can be sure that if he had succeeded, he would have made short work of Bath-sheba and Solomon. Bath-sheba, supported by Nathan, appealed to David to act at once. Adonijah's plots were thwarted (1 Kings 1:11-53) and Solomon was crowned.

No wonder Bath-sheba had a burden! She did not want Solomon to do what she and David had done. The price had been too high. The burden was so great that at first she could hardly put it into words. We can hear her saying, "What, my son? and what, the son of my womb? and what, the son of my vows?" (Proverbs 31:2) She was asking in effect, "What should I say? What can I say? What advice should I give?" Her burden was so heavy that it was hard for her to come to grips with it. The best she could do was to refer to her vows.

We can well believe that Bath-sheba had made some vows. Certainly she made some vows when she went home after that first night with David—she was guilty of adultery while her brave husband was away at war. Certainly she made some vows when she learned that she was pregnant and when she went to her husband's funeral. She made vows when she married David. Certainly she made some vows when her first child was born, when Nathan came, and when the baby was buried. Certainly she made some vows when she learned that she was pregnant again, when Solomon was born, and when Nathan came full of smiles. Surely she made vows when

Ahithophel, her grandfather, committed suicide after he tried to take revenge on David by joining Absalom.

We do not need much imagination to know what she vowed when Solomon was born. She vowed that, God helping her, she would live in the spirit of David's penitential Psalms and do all that a mother could do to bring up her son to know, love, and serve the Lord, the God of all grace.

2. The Morals of the King (31:3-9)

a. Beware of Women (31:3)

"Give not thy strength unto women, nor thy ways to that which destroyeth kings." Women had come close to destroying David. Alexander Whyte wrote:

> Polygamy is just Greek for a dunghill. David trampled down the first and the best law of nature in his palace in Jerusalem, and for his trouble he spent all his after-days in a hell upon earth. David's palace was a perfect pandemonium of suspicion, and intrigue, and jealousy, and hatred—all breaking out, now into incest and now into murder. And it was in such a household, if such a cesspool could be called a household, that Absalom, David's third son by his third living wife, was born and brought up....
>
> A little ring of jealous and scheming parasites, all hateful and hating one another, collected round each one of David's wives. And it was in one of the worst of those wicked little rings that Absalom grew up and got his education. Absalom had a sister, named Tamar, who was as beautiful as a woman as Absalom was as a man. And how her beauty became the occasion of her ruin in that horrible household the sacred historian tells us with sufficient plainness of speech. Suffice it here to say that Absalom determined, sooner or later, to wash off his sister's terrible wrongs in the blood of the wrongdoer. And, then, as the divine vengeance would have it be, that wrongdoer to one of David's fairest daughters was one of David's favorite sons.[18]

In addition to Bath-sheba, David was married to Michal, Saul's daughter; and to Abigail, Nabal's widow; and to Ahinoam of Jezreel; and to Maacah, the daughter of Talmai (king of Geshur);

and to Haggith, the mother of Adonijah; and to Abital; and to Eglah. He also had at least ten concubines. We can well believe that his home life was full of pandemonium.

There can be little doubt that Bath-sheba had David's harem in mind when she warned Solomon about women. She had known what it was like to be married to Uriah, who as far as we can tell was "the husband of one wife," the divine ideal (1 Timothy 3:2). She had known too what it was like to be added to a harem. She knew what a harem meant for the women: jealousy, intrigue, spitefulness, and resentment. And she knew what a harem meant for the king: it deteriorated his character and threatened his throne. She coveted better things for Solomon.

b. Beware of Wine (31:4-7)

Bath-sheba wanted her son to beware of wine and *its dangers.* "It is not for kings, O Lemuel," she said, "it is not for kings to drink wine; nor for princes strong drink: Lest they drink, and forget the law, and pervert the judgment of any of the afflicted" (Proverbs 31:4-5).

It is bad enough for an ordinary person to get drunk and make a fool of himself. It is even worse for a person in authority to get drunk because he is setting a bad example and because he might, while under the influence of alcohol, make a serious mistake that affects the whole country. A drunkard loses all sense of proportion and has no sense of what is right and wrong.

Unfortunately social drinking is a common practice in so-called high society. Some of the men who sit in the halls of Congress and pontificate on matters of public ethics are habitual drunkards. The fact that such men can hold on to their positions of power says something about the moral decline in our country.

Drunkenness does not seem to have been one of David's sins. He knew the law of God for the priests: "Do not drink wine nor strong drink, thou, nor thy sons with thee, when ye go into the tabernacle of the congregation, lest ye die" (Leviticus 10:9). This law was given right after Aaron's sons Nadab and Abihu "offered strange fire before the Lord" and were instantly and supernaturally slain where they stood (10:1-2). The obvious inference is that they were drunk at the time. A second inference is that the same prohibition applied, by extension, to others of the Lord's anointed: His prophets and His princes.

In actual fact, remarkably little is said in the Mosaic law about drinking to excess, although in Deuteronomy 29:6 we do read a comment on the total abstinence of Israel in the wilderness. And in Numbers 6:1-4 we read that the vow of a Nazarite required total abstinence of him as long as his vow lasted. Perhaps the cases of Noah (Genesis 9:20-27) and Lot (Genesis 19:30-38) were sufficient warning against drunkenness. Drunkenness does not seem to have been common in the early days of Israel's history, but it became a terrible vice toward the end of the monarchy.

Bath-sheba knew enough about the perils of drunkenness to make her want to warn her son against the sin. She may have had many long talks with Abigail, who had once lived with a drunken husband (1 Samuel 25:36). Abigail would have told her sad stories about her wretched life with Nabal. No doubt Bath-sheba also remembered with horror how David had made Uriah drunk so that he would lose his determination to abstain from sex while his comrades were facing danger and death at the front (2 Samuel 11:13).

Bath-sheba knew the dangers of wine and she wanted her son to beware of *its delusions.* "Give strong drink unto him that is ready to perish," she said, "and wine unto those that be of heavy hearts. Let him drink, and forget his poverty, and remember his misery no more" (Proverbs 31:6-7).

Some people see in the opening clause of verse 6 an injunction to use wine as a medicine. They say that out of deference to this statement the women of Jerusalem provided a drink of drugged wine to prisoners on their way to crucifixion. But this was the very drink that the Lord Jesus refused to accept (Matthew 27:34).

The whole tenor of Proverbs 31:6-7 is better summed up by the image of people trying to drown their problems and sorrows in drink. They look for the courage or cheer that they imagine lies at the bottom of a bottle, but all they do is add drunkenness to their other troubles. Bath-sheba was not advocating drink for Solomon or anyone else. She was simply pointing out to her son—son of a great king, heir to a throne, beloved of God—that he, of all people, did not need either the stimulus or the solace that strong drink supposedly gives.

I could not help noticing the strong emphasis on drinking in the writings of James Herriot, who authored some half dozen delightfully entertaining books about his life as a Yorkshire veterinarian. The books were an instant success and the television series based on them attracted countless fans. Herriot was able to capture the many moods and varied personalities of the people who crowded his busy and eventful life.

Drinks were often in evidence at Skeldale House, where the

Herriots lived with Jim's partner Siegfried Farnon, and the two veterinarians were frequently in and out of public houses. But one day another colleague, Granville Bennett, made Jim drink too much.

Bennett was a well-to-do specialist in small-animal surgery. The first time Herriot brought a difficult case to him, Bennett welcomed him warmly and after operating on the sick animal, treated Herriot to open-handed hospitality. Bennett took Herriot to his club where drink followed drink. The tide of beer seemed to have no effect on Bennett, but Herriot reached his limit and for him drinking became an agony. Later at Bennett's house, Herriot felt compelled to eat pickled onions and a big sandwich—and to drink neat whiskey. Driving home that night with the recuperating dog on the passenger seat, Herriot could see that she felt better than he did.[19]

But drink makes some people happy. For many the tavern takes the place of the church. They find their fellowship, meet their friends, spend their evenings, and have the world's equivalent of a good time—in a tavern. No wonder it's such a popular spot. There they become filled with the spirit—not the Holy Spirit of course, but the devil's substitute.

But the happiness found in a tavern has a dark side not seen in the beer commercials or the gin advertisements. The good feelings do not last, for real happiness does not come in bottles. Drinking often makes people do foolish things. Worse, it can lead to the slavery of addiction.

Drinking corrodes morals, it can turn people into drunkards, and it can kill. No wonder Bath-sheba urged her son to have nothing to do with strong drink—but in actual fact other vices were more tempting to Solomon.

### c. Beware of Words (31:8-9)

When a king indulges himself with women and wine, he is abusing his power. A king should use his power to *be an advocate for those who cannot speak up for themselves.* The king's mother said to her son, "Open thy mouth for the dumb in the cause of all such as are appointed to destruction" (Proverbs 31:8).

Jesus spoke up for the woman who was taken in adultery, "in the very act," as the scribes and Pharisees so maliciously added (John 8:4). The woman had nothing to say, for she had been caught red-handed. The only protest she might have raised was that her partner was not there to share her blame. Maybe the man was strong enough to throw off his pursuers. Maybe he had friends in high places. Maybe he was a son of one of the scribes. Maybe the woman wanted to protect him.

In any case the accused, like a sheep before her shearers, did not open her mouth. She was guilty of adultery. There were witnesses and the penalty of the law was implacable: death. The only reason that she had not been executed yet was that one of her judges wanted to use her as bait to trap the preacher from Nazareth into saying the wrong thing.

So the poor woman was dragged before the Prophet. The case against her was stated and the penalty of the law was rehearsed. Then the case was deferred to Jesus. Everyone waited for His answer. Would He support Moses and uphold the law or would He exonerate the woman and set aside the law? All eyes turned to Jesus—except the eyes of the poor woman who had nothing to say and nowhere to look. She stood there covered with guilt and shame.

It was as if the scribes were saying, "Open thy mouth, judge righteously," while the heart of Jesus was saying, "Plead the cause of the poor and needy" (Proverbs 31:9). Jesus knew that a king should use his power to *be an advocate for those who cannot stand up for themselves,* but for the moment He said nothing. He simply "stooped down, and with his finger wrote on the ground" (John 8:6). What he wrote on the ground is the only thing He ever wrote of which we have a record, and what He wrote has long since been blotted out. Did He perhaps write names and dates that revealed the hearts and histories of the scribes and Pharisees who stood before Him?

Thinking that they had trapped Him, they kept on pressing for a decision. He stood up, looked them in the eye, and took the side of the woman. He understood that poor, needy, hopeless soul. Jesus said to those unyielding men, "He that is without sin among you, let him first cast a stone at her" (8:7). Then, with every eye still on Him, He stooped back down and wrote more on the ground. Perhaps then they understood what He was writing. In any case, one by one they crept away, each accompanied by an accusing conscience.

When the last scribe and Pharisee had gone, Jesus stood up again and asked, "Woman, where are those thine accusers? hath no man condemned thee?" (8:10)

"No man, Lord," she said, enthroning Him (8:11).

Now Jesus opened His mouth and judged righteously: "Neither do I condemn thee: go, and sin no more."

Thus Jesus is the ultimate illustration of the advocate that

Bath-sheba tried to describe to Solomon, who in turn recorded the "prophecy" in Proverbs 31:8-9.

## B. The Chapter and Its Acrostic (31:10-31)

The rest of Proverbs 31 is an anthem to the virtuous woman. The anthem takes the form of a poem that is an acrostic. Each verse begins with one of the twenty-two letters of the Hebrew alphabet arranged in the usual order. The acrostic is a common memory device. Solomon was familiar with the device, as his father David had used it in some of his Psalms. Solomon's married life was already sadly stained and utterly contrary to his mother's sound teaching, but he hoped that others might memorize the poem and take the words to heart.

### 1. The Model Woman: How Rare She Is (31:10)

The longer Solomon played the fool when it came to women, the more the ideal woman haunted him. Proverbs 31:10-31 is, we will assume, his ode to the one woman in the world he could never have. Was he perhaps thinking of the Shulamite—the woman about whom he wrote his famous song?

How rare she was, this model woman who haunted Solomon's dreams. "Who can find a virtuous woman?" he wrote, "for her price is far above rubies" (Proverbs 31:10). The Hebrew word rendered "virtuous" here refers to much more than purity. The word means "strong in all moral qualities."

Proverbs 31:10 reminds me of Ruth. She was raised as a pagan in Moab. Then one day she met a foreigner, a young Hebrew named Mahlon. He was not a strong man, but he caught her fancy. He talked to her about another God, the true and living God. She married him and then he died, leaving her a widow almost before she was a wife.

As she passed through the deep waters of grief, Ruth learned to appreciate her mother-in-law Naomi, who was also a widow. Ruth would drink in Naomi's stories about Adam and Eve, Cain and Abel, Enoch and Noah, Abraham and Isaac, Jacob and Joseph, Moses and Joshua, Caleb and Gideon, and Barak and Deborah. The young pagan listened eagerly as Naomi talked about redemption by the blood of the Passover lamb, about the laws of Moses, about wilderness wanderings, about sacrifices, and about feast days. How different Hebrew worship was from the cruel worship of Moab!

When Naomi announced that she was going home, Ruth decided

to go with her. At the end of their journey, the poor widowed pair arrived in Bethlehem, where Ruth's goodness to Naomi, sweetness of disposition, and eagerness to know more about the God of Israel became the talk of the town.

Because it was harvest time, Naomi explained the law of the gleaner to her daughter-in-law, and Ruth set out for the field. There she met Boaz, a prince of the house of Judah. Boaz spoke kindly to her and sent her home laden with tokens of his bounty. Then Naomi taught Ruth the law of the kinsman-redeemer and, in compliance with that law, Ruth put herself at Boaz' feet. He promised to play his part and said, "All the city of my people doth know that thou art a virtuous woman" (Ruth 3:11).

Ruth is the only woman in the Old Testament who is called "a virtuous woman." Doubtless Solomon had her, or someone like her, in mind when he said that such a woman's price was "far above rubies." Solomon would have given a king's ransom for a woman like Ruth.

2. The Model Woman: How Restful She Is (31:11-12)

Solomon indicated that *her love is sure:* "The heart of her husband doth safely trust in her, so that he shall have no need of spoil" (Proverbs 31:11).

No wonder Solomon never found the ideal wife. How could he have expected to win a woman whose love was pure, passionate, and permanent, when he behaved like a cat on a tile roof? What worthy woman would want to share her husband with a thousand other women or even half a dozen other women?

I tried to figure out once, as a matter of curiosity, how a man could marry a thousand wives, let alone begin to meet all their emotional, intellectual, physical, and psychological needs. If Solomon took his first wife when he was twenty and his last when he was seventy, he had fifty years to accumulate a thousand wives. To achieve his quota he would have had to marry twenty women a year. In other words, he would have had to marry a new wife every two or three weeks—unless he married his wives in batches of half a dozen at a time. Or maybe he married them by proxy and simply put them in the line-up to wait their turn to get better acquainted. He would have had to have some kind of system.

If he did marry one wife at a time, he must have had a very busy matrimonial calendar! Getting married was practically a fulltime job. One week he got engaged, shall we say, to wife number 463. The next week he married her and they had their honeymoon. The following week he was looking around for wife number 464. One could hardly recommend such a system for finding an ideal wife. Solomon confessed quite bluntly that the system was most unsatisfactory (Ecclesiastes 7:25-28).

Solomon—with all his wealth, with all his wives, with all his wit, and with all his works—looked with envy at the shepherd-husband of the Shulamite. "The heart of her husband doth safely trust in her," he said, "so that he shall have no need of spoil." She satisfied her husband's every need. She was a woman of character and courage, as Solomon knew firsthand, and he would have given all the spoil in the world to change places with that blissfully happy young man. Solomon could not think of a single woman in his harem in whom his sensual heart could safely trust.

Continuing to write about the restful woman, Solomon indicated that *her loyalty is sure:* "She will do him good and not evil all the days of her life" (Proverbs 31:12). (The word translated "evil" here means "mischief.") How could Solomon have hoped for loyalty in a wife when he had never shown loyalty to a wife?

Many years ago I found the kind of wife Solomon coveted. Thus I am a richer man than he was, although he commanded a much higher annual income than I do. I have a wife who rules in my affections and whose dominant characteristics are honesty and loyalty.

Jean and I met and were married in the lovely city of Vancouver. At the time of our marriage I worked for a large Canadian bank with branches all across the country. Knowing that the bank frequently moved its young executives to give them exposure to different kinds of businesses, my new wife said, "I'll go anywhere in Canada—except Prince George or Prince Rupert." Both of these cities were located in the northern part of British Columbia and both were wild places in those days.

You may have already guessed that my first transfer after our wedding was to Prince George! It was indeed a rough city, the center of operations for a large number of lumber companies. In spite of what she had said earlier, Jean cheerfully and loyally moved with me. We made many friends in Prince George and we grew to like the city so well that I left the bank and became an accountant for one of the lumber companies. Three of our children were born in Prince George and we started a church there.

Then I received an invitation to join the staff of the Moody Bible Institute in Chicago. This time Jean dug in her heels. The last place she wanted to move to was Chicago. Her first reaction was something like this: "What? Leave my relatives and friends and beautiful

British Columbia to go to that huge sprawling city? No! Besides, what about the church we have started? Who will take care of it and all our babes in Christ? Besides, who would want to raise a family in Chicago?" But she moved with me! The Lord spoke to her and she came. She was loyal to the core.

And so it has been for all these many years. There have been times of testing, including those trying days when our teenage children caused anxiety and concern. But even then I always knew there was one person who was as solid as a rock, come what may: my wife. One by one our children found their way to Jesus, thanks to the prayers, integrity, goodness, and courage of their mother. Each of them knows her to be solid gold.

For many years now, I have been an itinerant preacher, traveling far and wide throughout Canada and the United States and occasionally abroad. Most of the time Jean has had to stay home. She has never complained, never given me an anxious thought, never made it difficult for me to say yet another goodbye. She is loyal, absolutely dependable, trustworthy, and true—beyond the price of rubies!

Even when home, I have had to spend an enormous amount of time studying and writing. No one except my wife knows how much. To write even one book calls for a great deal of very specialized discipline, and book after book has been sent to the publisher, put in line for publication, and come off the press. Just to craft the outlines on the Psalms took me a year. It took seven years to write my two-volume commentary on the Psalms.

Writing a book involves a series of tasks. After the structural analysis and the careful working out of alliterated outlines comes the exegesis, the verse-by-verse commentary, the search for illustrations, and the painstaking process of creating sentences, paragraphs, and chapters. After all these steps are completed, the manuscript has to be typed, then refined, retyped, and proofread. Instead of complaining about my work, my loyal wife has become my partner. She proofreads the final typing and gives me the benefit of her insights. She says, "I wouldn't say that if I were you!"

Solomon married a thousand wives, but he never married one like mine.

### 3. The Model Woman: How Resourceful She Is (31:13-15)

The ideal wife is no idler. She is not forever seeking excitement, pleasure, and change. Proverbs 31:13 tells us *how she busies her hands:* "She seeketh wool, and flax, and worketh willingly with her hands."

My wife is not only loyal. She is also resourceful. She knits, crochets, and sews. Sometimes we take long trips to distant cities and spend days traveling. All the time her hands are busy. I say, "What are you knitting now?" She says, "An afghan for old Mrs. Mierly," or "Baby shirts for African orphans," or "A sweater for Christina's birthday."

Referring to the ideal wife, Proverbs 31:14 tells us *how she buys her food:* "She is like the merchants' ships; she bringeth her food from afar."

My wife is an expert at buying food. She compares prices; she knows where the sales and bargains are; she saves promotional coupons. She makes a dollar go farther than anyone else I know, except one of my daughters who learned the tricks of the trade from her mother.

Proverbs 31:15 continues to describe the ideal wife and tells us *how she begins her day:* "She riseth also while it is yet night, and giveth meat to her household, and a portion to her maidens."

For a number of years Jean and I lived in a suburb of Chicago. To get to my desk at Moody Bible Institute by 8:00 a.m., I had to catch a commuter train by 6:30 a.m. That meant that I had to be up by 5:30 a.m. In the winter I got up in the dark and left the house in the dark. Never in all those years, unless she was sick, did Jean fail to see to it that I had a good breakfast before I left home. Even if she had been up with the children in the night, there would be bacon and eggs for breakfast.

### 4. The Model Woman: How Rich She Is (31:16-19)

Solomon indicated *how she invests her money:* "She considereth a field, and buyeth it: with the fruit of her hands she planteth a vineyard" (Proverbs 31:16). One cannot help thinking that Solomon's mind kept going back to the Shulamite. He had wanted her so badly, yet she had turned him down, firmly and irrevocably. If he hadn't played the fool with so many other women, he might have had her. He probably wished he had listened to his mother's sound advice.

Now the Shulamite was married to her shepherd. They were poor, but richer than Solomon. He could have bought her a thousand fields and stocked them with vines, figs, and olives, but she was content to make her own way in the world. She saved her husband's money and prudently spent her housekeeping allowance. She bought a field, used some of her savings to buy some tender vines, and planted a vineyard.

I have a feeling that Solomon kept himself informed about this woman. The memory of her haunted him. He wrote about her in the Song of Solomon—and he wrote about all his other ghosts in the book of Ecclesiastes.

Commenting further about the model woman, Solomon indicated *how she insures her ministry:* "She girdeth her loins with strength, and strengtheneth her arms" (Proverbs 31:17). In other words, she sees to it that she keeps healthy.

Solomon thought about the harem-bred women he kept like pet animals in a zoo. All they seemed to care about were clothes and sweetmeats. A lazy crowd, most of them soon grew fat and unattractive. All they had to do was lie around, gossip, scheme, eat, sleep, spend a passing hour with their children if they had any, and calculate their ever-decreasing chances of getting summoned to Solomon's private wing of the palace. Work? Why should they work?

The Shulamite, on the other hand, was used to hard work. She was not afraid of having her complexion spoiled by being in the sun. She was up and about, busy and energetic, into this and that, and on the run all day. She was healthy and happy, and completely unspoiled and devoted to her beloved. While the harem-types tended to be sickly and sulky, she was bursting with vigor and good spirits. The best the harem wives could manage was a sly smile, a spiteful sneer, or a lustful leer. The young Shulamite's laughter rang out across the meadow.

Heaven lay in her arms, but not for Solomon. Once in a while, I suspect, he put on old clothes and took a walk in her direction. In a kind of self-torture, he would watch the Shulamite and her shepherd, arm in arm, "roaming in the gloaming," chatting about this and that, and oblivious of him.

As Solomon concluded his comments about how rich the model woman is, he indicated *how she increases her means:* "She perceiveth that her merchandise is good: her candle goeth not out by night. She layeth her hands to the spindle, and her hands hold the distaff" (Proverbs 31:18-19).

No doubt Solomon had some of his buyers bargain with the Shulamite for her wares. They kept him informed. She was running quite a business from her house. Her spinning wheel was always at work, late into the night. If she was not spinning thread, she was carding wool. If she was not carding wool, she was weaving cloth. Her husband was a second Jacob, well known for his skill in multiplying sheep, and her wares were famous for their quality, quantity, and noble prices. Solomon's buyers were old hands at negotiating lower prices, but she knew the value of her merchandise. It was fit for a king's palace, where some of it no doubt found its way.

5. The Model Woman: How Responsive She Is (31:20)

"She stretcheth out her hand to the poor; yea, she reacheth forth her hands to the needy."

In spite of all Solomon's wise words about caring for the poor, the Bible gives no instances of Solomon actually caring for them himself. The beggars, we suspect, could lie at his gate full of sores (see Luke 16:20). We can hope he was kinder to them than the rich man was to Lazarus.

But what about his oppressive system of excessive taxation and his habit of conscripting laborers to work on his projects? It does not seem that Solomon took much more than a philosophical interest in the poor. When he died, practically the whole nation rose up to demand immediate redress of his wrongs.

But the virtuous woman he wrote about was not greedy. Shrewd and thrifty though she was, and keen as her eye was to business, her heart went out to the poor. She was a Dorcas in Israel long before there was a Dorcas in the church (Acts 9:36-42). There wasn't a poor person or needy family in all that part of the country that did not have ample reason to bless her hard-working hands.

6. The Model Woman: How Ready She Is (31:21)

"She is not afraid of the snow for her household: for all her household are clothed with scarlet." The original Hebrew wording suggests that the woman Solomon was describing provided a double change of raiment.

Snow is not at all uncommon in Israel. Two winters out of three, snow can be expected in Jerusalem. From time to time up to seventeen inches of snow can fall and it can linger in the hollows and shadows for two or three weeks. In Solomon's day warm garments were needed to brave the cold outside and inside, where usually the only heat to be had was from charcoal burning in a dish.

A cold spell in winter could be a great hardship, but not in the ideal woman's home. Her children could go out and throw snowballs or make a snowman as children do all over the world. If they got soaking wet, they could always change their clothes. If her beloved shepherd came in from the frozen hills where special measures had to be taken to protect the plants and the animals from unusual cold, he could always change his raiment. She always had a warm cloak ready for him. And there were always extra garments available for the poor and needy in special times of hardship and woe.

## 7. The Model Woman: How Respected She Is (31:22-25)

### a. Her Personal Appearance (31:22)

"She maketh herself coverings of tapestry; her clothing is silk and purple." Solomon had seen his ideal woman in the village. Not even the pharaoh's daughter, his pampered and privileged queen who was raised in the lap of luxury, was better dressed than the Shulamite. The queen might send to Egypt for her linens and to India for her silks. Her embroidered robes and imperial purple coats might come from the Phoenician emporium. But Solomon's wife—in all her glory—was not arrayed more royally than the virtuous woman who so captivated the king. She had come up in the world and her attire befitted her station. Her devoted husband liked her to dress well. She had earned the right to wear silk and purple. She was a queen in her own right.

Solomon could only sigh. When he first met the Shulamite, she was dressed in humble peasant garb. He offered to clothe her in garments laced with silver and gold (Song of Solomon 1:10-11), but she turned her back on him. Now she was more of a queen than the pharaoh's daughter would ever be. The ideal woman wore her fine clothes with an unconscious grace and a total lack of ostentatious pride.

### b. Her Public Applause (31:23)

"Her husband is known in the gates, when he sitteth among the elders of the land."

The husband Solomon was probably describing had made a name for himself. When the Shulamite and the shepherd first met on the hills where their flocks grazed, her brothers were hostile, suspicious, and threatening. Now her husband sat in the gate. As a member of the city council, he stood out from the others. His sweet wife had encouraged his strengths, helped his weaknesses, counseled him wisely, built up his confidence, molded his character, and gently smoothed his path. Now he was the most honored man in the city.

He was "known" in the places where decisions were made. Since the figure of speech used here points to a cause, we can say he was "known" because of his knowledge. His knowledge had earned him the respect of everyone at the city gate, which was the courtroom of his day. High and low, rich and poor, peasant and peer alike acknowledged him. In his own right, he was as great as Solomon.

Solomon knew her husband and knew perfectly well that whatever native talent the man had, he owed much of his present greatness to his wife. Everyone knew that applause for him was applause for her.

c. Her Popular Approval (31:24-25)

The virtuous woman has *no trouble selling her merchandise:* "She maketh fine linen, and selleth it; and delivereth girdles unto the merchant" (Proverbs 31:24).

The Shulamite's workmanship, we can imagine, was famous. Consider the girdles that bore her trademark. In the East where people wore long flowing robes, girdles were a necessity. They were used to gird up the robes during physical activity. The ordinary person wore a leather girdle, but the rich and powerful person wore a more elaborate one.

Phoenician merchants who scoured the markets of the world knew where the best workmanship was to be found. It was an open secret among them that if they wanted girdles fit for princes, Israel was the place to go. There a woman with impeccable taste made linen girdles of superb quality. No manufacturer in Egypt had better linen. Her girdles were skillfully wrought with gold, and Solomon's mines in Ophir could produce no finer gold. Her girdles were finished with silver thread, and the really exclusive ones were studded with jewels. The breastplate worn by the Hebrew high priest contained no finer jewels.

The price? Fabulous. Would she come down? Not on your life. If one merchant would not pay her price, another would. And he could be sure of profits, for her girdles could be retailed in kings' palaces.

Since the model woman is prepared for today and tomorrow, she has *no trouble settling her mind:* "Strength and honour are her clothing; and she shall rejoice in time to come" (Proverbs 31:25).

In the case of the Shulamite, success did not go to her head. Her heart was what it had been when she had resisted the blandishments of Solomon, the flattery of his court, and the hints and suggestions of his women. She wore strength and honor as a garment.

When she had been exposed to fierce temptations, she had been able to repulse them because of her strength and honor. Solomon, with all his prerogatives and power, had not dared to touch her. Her brothers had withdrawn their hostility when they heard how she had so nobly preserved her honor. As her strength had been yesterday, so it would be tomorrow. Come what may, no foe could daunt her; no fear could haunt her. She was not protected by her cleverness, success, and wealth, or by her husband's power and reputation. She was protected by her character and convictions.

## 8. The Model Woman: How Right She Is (31:26-27)

She is always right *in what she says:* "She openeth her mouth with wisdom; and in her tongue is the law of kindness" (Proverbs 31:26). The word rendered "wisdom" here is *chokmah,* the same word Solomon used the first time he mentioned wisdom in the book of Proverbs (1:2). The last mention is in 31:26. The whole book had been one long search for wisdom, and there it was staring him in the face all the time, personalized in a virtuous woman.

Solomon helped our understanding by personifying wisdom as a woman, but what was really needed was for wisdom to be incarnated in flesh and blood. Some hoped that Solomon himself might do just that. But then he married a pagan Egyptian, made her his queen, and started on a path that ended in complete folly. It would be nearly another thousand years before wisdom would be fully displayed in a man. That man was Jesus.

Proverbs 31:26 says of the model woman that "in her tongue is the law of kindness." She does not indulge in gossip, slander, or falsehoods. Even if a thought is true, if it isn't kind, she holds her tongue. She tries to say a compassionate or kind word for everyone. And being right in what she says makes her as nearly perfect as one can be in a sinful world (James 3:2).

The model woman is also always right *in what she sees:* "She looketh well to the ways of her household [she oversees each servant], and eateth not the bread of idleness [she oversees each second]" (Proverbs 31:27). In other words, she has learned the principles of good management and practices them. She keeps a tight control over employees and time. She is kind, compassionate, and considerate of others, but she is not "a soft touch." She does not reward idle behavior in others any more than she tolerates it in herself.

### 9. The Model Woman: How Rewarded She Is (31:28)

"Her children arise up, and call her blessed; her husband also, and he praiseth her." What greater reward could a woman receive?

If someone had congratulated the Shulamite's husband for a decision made in the gate, or commented on his fine new coat, or thanked him for a generous contribution to the temple fund or a magnanimous gift to help the poor, he would have said, "You'll have to thank my wife. It was all her idea."

If someone had said to one of her sons, "Congratulations on that new house you have just built. Your business must be prospering," he would have said, "You should congratulate my mother. I have been successful in business only because I've followed her advice. Besides, she gave me the property!"

If someone had said to one of her daughters, "Congratulations on your marriage," the daughter would have responded, "Joseph said he wanted to marry me because I am so much like my mom. Mom picked him out, you know. She is so wise, so loving, so kind. She never interfered, but she made sure that Joseph was the right one for me. Bless her! Now I have a husband just like my dear dad."

We can imagine Solomon's ideal woman growing old. Her husband has nothing but praise for her. Her children rise up and bless her. When she is called to her last rest, the family gather in the old home and the neighbors drop in to share their memories. The poor of the city gather at the gate and talk about what a blessing she has been to them. Unknown to everyone, the king has written down her story and the Holy Spirit will include it in His Book. Succeeding generations will read that this woman was called "blessed" and will wonder who she was. Many women will say, "I'm going to be like her." Surely one of them will be a young virgin who will live a thousand years later in a despised Galilean town called Nazareth; to her an angel will say, "Blessed art thou" (Luke 1:28).

### 10. The Model Woman: How Renowned She Is (31:29-31)

Solomon had really said all there was to say, but he simply could not stop thinking about this woman. He put down his pen and picked it up again to add a threefold benediction.

In Proverbs 31:29 Solomon indicated that the model woman is *a superlative woman:* "Many daughters have done virtuously, but thou excellest them all." In 31:30 he indicated that the model woman is *a spiritual woman:* "Favour is deceitful, and beauty is vain: but a woman that feareth the Lord, she shall be praised." In 31:31

he indicated that the model woman is *a splendid woman:* "Give her of the fruit of her hands; and let her own works praise her in the gates."

The ages have run their course since Solomon wrote his description of the model woman. He died and his kingdom was divided. He is remembered as an odd mixture of good and evil, wisdom and folly, magnificence and lust. The two kingdoms of Judah and Israel continued until the Assyrians and the Babylonians destroyed them. Under the Persians a remnant returned—poor, weak, and surrounded by foes. The Greeks came and the Romans came. The long-awaited Messiah came and was crucified. The church age came and it too will pass.

Then the Lord will return, the dead will be raised, and the books will be opened. The Judge will turn to the model woman's page and at last we will learn her name. Immortal and clothed in light, she will take her stand at the judgment seat. We can imagine that the Judge will say:

> Many daughters have done virtuously,
> but thou excellest them all.
> Favor is deceitful, and beauty is vain:
> but a woman that feareth the Lord,
> she shall be praised.
> Give her of the fruit of her hands;
> and let her own works praise her in the gates.

# NOTES

## Chapter 1

1. John Bartlett, *Familiar Quotations* (Boston: Little, Brown and Company, 1968) 279.
2. Taine, *Notes on England,* 36.
3. See Thomas B. Costain, *The Conquerors* (Garden City, NY: Doubleday, 1949) 232-245,287-288.
4. H. Rider Haggard, *Child of Storm* (London: Macdonald, 1913) 201-202.
5. Ibid., 203.
6. Ibid., 204-206.
7. Charles Dickens, *Great Expectations* (reprint, New York: Harper, 1961) 7-9,266-269,272-274.
8. London, Jack, "In a Far Country," *The Call of the Wild, The Cruise of the Dazzler, and Other Stories of Adventure* (reprint, New York: Platt & Munk, 1960) 454-455,460-464.
9. From "The Way of the Cross Leads Home" by Jessie B. Pounds.
10. Alfred Edersheim, *The Life and Times of Jesus the Messiah* (reprint, Grand Rapids: Eerdmans, 1962) 2:387.
11. G. M. Gilbert, *Nuremberg Diary* (New York: New American Library, Signet Books, 1947).
12. Frederic W. Farrar, *The Life of Christ* (New York: Cassell Petter & Galpin) 2:330-331.
13. C. S. Forester, *Mr. Midshipman Hornblower* in *Young Hornblower* (Boston: Little, Brown and Company, 1950) 23.
14. See John Phillips, *Introducing People of the Bible, Volume Three* (Neptune, NJ: Loizeaux, 1995) 61-70.
15. H. G. Wells, *Experiment in Autobiography* (New York: Macmillan, 1934) 706.
16. Wells, *Mind at the End of Its Tether* (San Francisco: Millet, 1973) 15.
17. Nan Robertson, "The Intimate Enemy," *Modern Maturity,* February-March 1992, 27.
18. Edward W. Desmond, "Out in the Open," *Time,* November 30, 1987, 80-90.
19. Boyd Gibbons, "Alcohol, the Legal Drug," *National Geographic,* February 1992, 21.
20. Joel Chandler Harris, *Uncle Remus: His Songs and Sayings* (New York: Grosset & Dunlap, 1880) 7-11.

21. Evan Thomas, "Coming In from the Cold," *Time,* February 4, 1985, 20-21.
22. Nancy R. Gibbs, "Begging: To Give or Not to Give," *Time,* September 5, 1988, 68.
23. Alexander Whyte, *Bible Characters, Ahithophel to Nehemiah* (Edinburgh: Oliphant Anderson and Ferrier, 1899) 94.
24. Dickens, *Oliver Twist* (reprint, New York: Oxford University Press, 1949) 362-363,367-369,390-391.
25. The rivalry between Spain and Portugal was so intense that Pope Alexander had drawn an arbitrary line from pole to pole on the map, the line running through a point 1,110 miles west of the Cape Verde Islands. East of that line, every non-Catholic land was to belong to Portugal; the other hemisphere was reserved for Spain. If the two nations sent their explorers in opposite directions, the pope reasoned, they could hardly find space for conflict. No one knew for sure whether the Spice Islands lay in the Portuguese hemisphere or the Spanish hemisphere. (See Charles Ford, *Death Sails With Magellan* (New York: Random House, 1917) 6-7.
26. Ibid., 181.
27. Plutarch, *The Lives of the Noble Grecians and Romans,* trans. John Dryden, rev. Arthur Hugh Clough (New York: Random House, Modern Library, n.d.) 803-805.
28. Louis Untermeyer, *Makers of the Modern World* (New York: Simon and Schuster, 1955) 321-328.
29. Dorothy L. Sayers, *Gaudy Night* (New York: Harper & Row, 1936) 392-393.
30. Arnold C. Blackman, *The Search for Tutankhamen* (New York: Mason/Charter, 1976) 75.
31. Raymonde De Gans, *Tutankhamen* (Geneva: Editions Fermi, 1978) 10.
32. Ibid., 18-19.
33. Haggard, *Finished* (London: Macdonald, 1917). Quotes are taken from pages 169-171, 188-190, and 212.
34. Sayers, *Gaudy Night,* 233-236.
35. John Greenwald, "Panic Grips the Globe," *Time,* November 2, 1987, 22-42.
36. See Merrill F. Unger, *Unger's Bible Dictionary* (Chicago: Moody Press, 1957) 412-413.

## Chapter 2

1. G. H. Pember, *Earth's Earliest Ages* (Glasgow: Pickering & Inglis, n.d.) 225-229.
2. From "Trust and Obey" by John H. Sammis.
3. See author's commentary on Ephesians 2:17 in *Exploring Ephesians* (Neptune, NJ: Loizeaux, 1993) 72.
4. G. B. Hardy, *Countdown* (Chicago: Moody, 1961).

5. Jeffery Farnol, *The Amateur Gentleman* (Boston: Little, Brown and Company, 1913) 277-281,510.
6. Agatha Christie, *Death on the Nile* (New York: Dodd, Mead and Company, 1937) 112-113.
7. Dickens, *Oliver Twist,* 268-271,399-400.
8. Samuel Shellabarger, *Captain from Castile* (Garden City, NY: Sun Dial, 1946) 43,45,107.
9. Whyte, *Bible Characters, Stephen to Timothy* (New York, Revell, n.d.) 50-51.
10. See Ed Sanders, *The Family* (New York: Avon, 1971) 79-87,267-292.
11. "The Judicial Power of the Church," *Dawn,* June 15, 1927.
12. Sayers, *Gaudy Night,* 211.
13. Farnol, *The Broad Highway* (Boston: Little, Brown and Company, 1911) 21-22,25,82-83.
14. J. B. Phillips, *The New Testament in Modern English* (New York: Macmillan, 1972) 421.
15. D. Crawford, *Thinking Black* (New York: Doran, 1912). Quotations are taken from pages v, 164, 168-169, 175-176, 208, and 229-230.
16. Hy. Pickering, comp., *Chief Men among the Brethren* (reprint, Neptune, NJ: Loizeaux, 1996) 278-279.
17. Arthur T. Pierson, *George Muller of Bristol* (Old Tappan, NJ: Revell, n.d.) 373.
18. See G. F. Vallance, *Because of the Weather* (Suffolk, England: Vallance, 1944) 13-16.
19. John Bunyan, *The Pilgrim's Progress* (Philadelphia: Henry Altemus, 1891) 202.
20. See the author's book, *Exploring the World of the Jew* (Neptune, NJ: Loizeaux, 1981) 127-128.
21. See the author's commentary in *Exploring Genesis* (Neptune, NJ: Loizeaux, 1980).
22. Edersheim, *Life and Times of Jesus* 1:630.

## Chapter 3

1. Jack London, *White Fang* (reprint, New York: Dover, 1991) 35-36,47-48.

## Chapter 4

1. Geoffrey T. Bull, *When Iron Gates Yield* (London: Hodder and Stoughton, 1955) 237.
2. Ibid., 239.
3. Harold Begbie, *Twice-born Men* (New York: Reliance Trading Company, 1909) 90-94,96,99-100.
4. Whyte, *Bible Characters, Gideon to Absalom* (Edinburgh: Oliphant Anderson and Ferrier, 1902) 183.

5. Charles Nordhoff and James Norman Hall, *Mutiny on the Bounty* (Boston: Little, Brown and Company, 1932) 376,379.
6. Begbie, *Twice-born Men*, 199-203.
7. The Century Council, 2049 Century Park East, Suite 3150, Los Angeles, CA 90067.
8. Charles Chiniquy, *Fifty Years in the Church of Rome* (reprint, London: Protestant Truth Society, 1885) 151-159.
9. Nordhoff and Hall, *Pitcairn's Island, The Bounty Trilogy* (Boston: Little, Brown and Company, 1934) 659.
10. Haggard, *The Holy Flower* (London: Macdonald, 1915) 75-76.
11. Gaius Suetonius Tranquillus, *The Twelve Caesars*, trans. Robert Graves (Harmondsworth, Middlesex, England: Penguin, 1957) 130.
12. Ibid., 143.
13. Ibid., 130.
14. Robert Louis Stevenson, *Treasure Island* (reprint, Dodd, Mead and Company, 1985) 6-9,18-20.
15. Peter Green, *Alexander the Great* (New York: Praegh, 1970) 156.
16. M. J. Phillips, S. Poucell, J. Patterson, and P. Valencia, *The Liver: An Atlas and Text of Ultrastructural Pathology* (New York: Raven, 1987).
17. Gilbert, *Nuremberg Diary*, 388-389.
18. Nordhoff and Hall, *Pitcairn's Island*, 469.
19. Ibid., 542.
20. Robert Southey, "Trafalgar" in *Great Sea Stories of All Nations* (New York: Garden City Publishing Company, 1937) 233.
21. John G. Paton, *John G. Paton: An Autobiography* (New York: Revell, 1889) 1:226-229.
22. See *U. S. News & World Report*, August 28, 1967, 38ff.
23. See Patricia Blake, "A Monster Brought to Life," *Time*, June 26, 1989, 83.

## Chapter 5

1. John Phillips, *Exploring the Psalms* (Neptune, NJ: Loizeaux, 1988) 2:428.
2. Haggard, *Nada the Lily* (London: Collins, 1892). Quotes are taken from pages 21, 184-185, and 192-193.
3. Farnol, *Amateur Gentleman*, 500,502-504.
4. Jack Schaefer, *Shane* (New York: Bantam, 1949) 108-109.
5. From the hymn "None But Christ Can Satisfy!"
6. Whyte, *Bible Characters, Ahithophel to Nehemiah*, 21-22.
7. James Hilton, *Good-bye, Mr. Chips* (Garden City, NY: International Collectors Library, 1934) 217.
8. Farnol, *The Definite Object* (Boston: Little, Brown, and Company, 1917) 43-44,47,128-129.
9. Chiniquy, *Fifty Years in the Church of Rome*, 59.
10. For the complete story of the *Titanic* and many fascinating human sidelights, see Walter Lord, *A Night to Remember* (New York: Henry

Holt, 1955). The ship's log was extracted from pages 171-172 and the quotations were taken from pages 38 and 50.
11. From "The Charge of the Light Brigade" by Alfred Tennyson.
12. Haggard, *Nada the Lily,* 248-251.
13. For a satisfactory explanation of these mysteries see A. E. Wilder Smith, *The Paradox of Pain* (Wheaton, IL: Harold Shaw, 1971).
14. Shellabarger, *Prince of Foxes* (Boston: Little, Brown and Company, 1947). Quotes are taken from pages 206-207.
15. Dickens, *Oliver Twist,* 58-60.
16. Mark Twain, *The Adventures of Tom Sawyer* (reprint, Philadelphia: Running Press, Courage Books, 1987) 12-13,21.
17. Farnol, *The Broad Highway,* 369-371.

## Chapter 6

1. Henry Drummond, *The Greatest Thing in the World* (Mount Vernon, NY: Peter Pauper, n.d.) 9-13,15-18,20,45-51.
2. Dickens, *Oliver Twist,* 192-193,127-129,131-132,134.
3. See John Phillips, *Bible Explorer's Guide* (Neptune, NJ: Loizeaux, 1987) 143-148.
4. Haggard, *The Favorite Novels of H. Rider Haggard* (reprint, New York: Blue Ribbon, 1928) 500.
5. Washington Irving, *Rip Van Winkle and Other Stories* (reprint, Garden City, NY: Nelson Doubleday, Junior Deluxe Editions, 1955) 8-13,29-30.
6. For a more complete exposition of this wonderful parallel, see the author's commentary in *Exploring Genesis,* pages 191-192.
7. From "To a Louse" by Robert Burns, *The Oxford Book of Scottish Verse,* comp. John MacQueen and Tom Scott (reprint, London: Oxford, 1966) 371-373.
8. Forester, *Captain Hornblower, The Happy Return* (London: Michael Joseph, 1939).
9. Whyte, *Bible Characters, Adam to Achan* (Edinburgh: Oliphant Anderson and Ferrier, 1898) 163.
10. Ibid., 165.
11. Walter Godfrey Bowen, *Why! The Shepherd* (San Miguel, CA: Good Shepherd Press, 1988).

## Chapter 7

1. Dickens, *Oliver Twist,* 31-32,40-41,324-325.
2. Ian Fellowes-Gordon, "John D. Rockefeller" in *100 Great Modern Lives,* ed. John Canning (New York: Beekman, 1972) 178.
3. *The Companion Bible* (Grand Rapids: Zondervan, 1964) 352.
4. See John Phillips, *Introducing People of the Bible, Volume Two* (Neptune, NJ: Loizeaux, 1993) 43.
5. Forester, *Captain Horatio Hornblower, Ship of the Line* (Boston: Little, Brown and Company, 1938) 121.

6. Alexandre Dumas, *The Count of Monte-Cristo* (reprint, New York: Grosset & Dunlap, 1946) 1289-1294.
7. See John Phillips, *Exploring Romans* (Neptune, NJ: Loizeaux, 1969).
8. Edersheim wrote in *The Bible History:* "*Twice ten times* in the course of this history does the expression *hardening* occur in connection with Pharaoh. Although in our English version only the word "harden" is used, in the Hebrew original three different terms are employed, of which one (as in Ex. vii. 3) literally means *to make hard* or *insensible,* the other (as in x. 1) *to make heavy,* that is, unimpressionable, and the third (as in xiv. 4), *to make firm* or *stiff,* so as to be immovable. Now it is remarkable, that of the twenty passages which speak of Pharaoh's hardening, exactly ten ascribe it to Pharaoh himself, and ten to God." See reprint (Grand Rapids: Eerdmans, 1956) 1:59.
9. Lot is another Biblical example of a man who thought he could have the best of both worlds.
10. The classic Biblical example of Proverbs 28:22 is the prodigal son (Luke 15).
11. Dickens, *A Christmas Carol* (reprint, New York: Weathervane, 1977). Quotations are from pages 5, 17, 114-115, 123, and 127.
12. Another Biblical example of Proverbs 28:24 is Micah, the Ephraimite (Judges 17–18).
13. Frank Spiering, *Lizzie* (New York: Random House, 1984) 202.
14. Spiering argues that the crimes were committed by Emma.
15. See John Phillips, *Exploring Revelation* (Neptune, NJ: Loizeaux, 1987).
16. Pearl S. Buck, *The Good Earth* in *House of Earth* (New York: John Day, 1931) 179.
17. Richard Behar, "A Crow Turns Stool Pigeon," *Time,* June 17, 1991, 11-18.
18. Christ's cross, no doubt, was the one meant for Barabbas.
19. Harriet Beecher Stowe, *Uncle Tom's Cabin* (reprint, Garden City, NY: International Collectors Library) 358,366,372,377,402-403,418.

## Chapter 8

1. "Brazil's Wasted Generation," *Time,* September 11, 1978, 32.
2. Ibid., 40.
3. Ian McCluskey, "Rio's Dead End Kids," *Time,* August 9, 1993, 36-37.
4. "Suffer the Little Children," *Time,* October 8, 1990, 41.
5. Ibid.
6. Nancy Gibbs, "Shameful Bequests to the Next Generation," *Time,* October 8, 1990, 43.
7. Ibid., 45.
8. Anastasia Toufexis, "Struggling for Sanity," *Time,* October 8, 1990, 47.
9. Gibbs, "Shameful Bequests to the Next Generation," 43.
10. For a complete discussion of the days of Noah, see John Phillips, *Exploring the Future* (Neptune, NJ: Loizeaux, 1992) 183-185.

11. Lew Wallace, *Ben-Hur* (reprint, New York: Heritage, 1960) 72,74.
12. Ibid., 437.

## Chapter 9

1. *The Companion Bible,* 904.
2. See John Phillips, *Exploring the Psalms* 1:180-185.
3. From "Eternal Father, Strong to Save" by William Whiting.
4. From "O for a Thousand Tongues" by Charles Wesley.
5. See John Phillips, *Exploring the Song of Solomon* (Neptune, NJ: Loizeaux, 1984).
6. The scribes and rabbis added decisions on questions of ritual (Halachot) and the new code resulting from those decisions (Mishna). They added a commentary on the Mishna (Gemara), commentaries on the Old Testament (Midrash), and ritual readings for the first evening of Passover (Haggada). Finally they added mystical interpretations (the Cabbala), which found all kinds of allegorical meanings in the Scriptures. This vast accumulation of material kept on growing. It was already cumbersome in the days of Christ. When it was finished it comprised the Talmud, a work that completely replaced the Torah in the thinking of most Jews. See John Phillips, *Exploring the World of the Jew,* 55-76.
7. See John Phillips, *Exploring the Future,* 168-203,298-313.
8. "The Youth Crime Plague," *Time,* July 11, 1977, 18.
9. "Cripplers in the War Zone," *Time,* July 11, 1977, 20.
10. "The Youthful Crime Plague," *Time,* July 11, 1977, 20.
11. Here we touch a problem in interpreting Proverbs 30:15-31. The translators disagree over the identity of some of the creatures mentioned. The multitude of competing versions makes preaching on this passage difficult. People come up to a preacher after a service and say, "But my version doesn't say 'greyhound'; it says 'cock.'" Not wanting to spend time defending this identification or that, I stay with the King James unless there is a compelling reason for using another version.
12. C. S. Lewis, *The Screwtape Letters* (New York: Macmillan, 1950) 29.
13. Cyrus Townsend Brady, *Sir Henry Morgan* (New York: Dillingham, 1903). Quotations are taken from pages 432 and 439-444.
14. From "Ivory Palaces" by Henry Barraclough.
15. From the hymn "His Loving Kindness" by Samuel Medley.
16. Some modern versions have replaced "spider" with "lizard," but "spider" is a sound rendering.
17. From "Rock of Ages" by Augustus M. Toplady.
18. Whyte, *Bible Characters, Gideon to Absalom,* 236-237.
19. James Herriot, *The Best of James Herriot* (New York: St. Martin's, 1982) 261.

# LIST OF ILLUSTRATIONS

## Proverbs 1–31